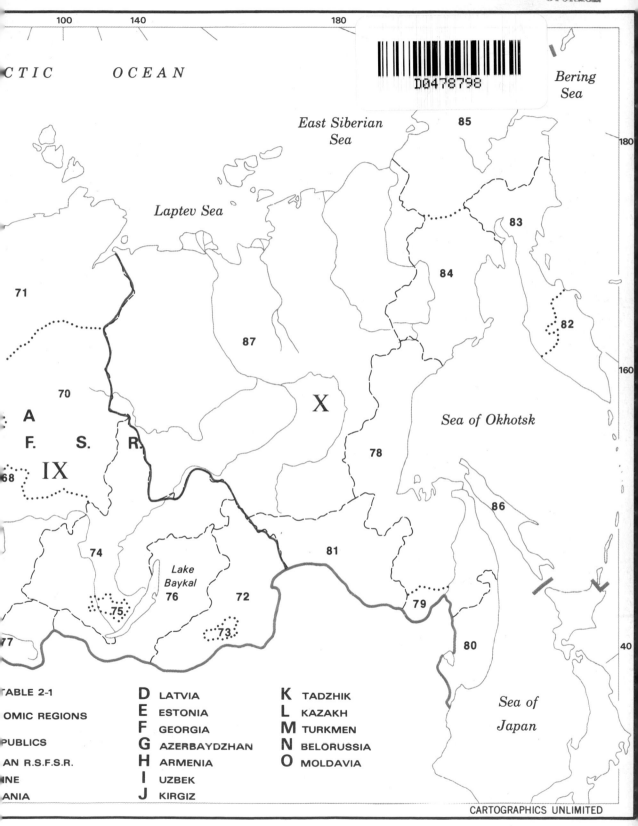

C T I C O C E A N

Bering
Sea

East Siberian
Sea

85

Laptev Sea

83

84

71

82

87

70

X

A
F. S. R.

Sea of Okhotsk

IX

78

68

86

74

81

Lake
Baykal

76   72

75

79

73

77

80

Sea of

Japan

40

TABLE 2-1

OMIC REGIONS

PUBLICS

AN R.S.F.S.R.

NE

ANIA

D LATVIA
E ESTONIA
F GEORGIA
G AZERBAYDZHAN
H ARMENIA
I UZBEK
J KIRGIZ

K TADZHIK
L KAZAKH
M TURKMEN
N BELORUSSIA
O MOLDAVIA

CARTOGRAPHICS UNLIMITED

The cover photo was taken by Professor David Kromm of Kansas State University during the 1976 meetings of the International Geographical Union in the U.S.S.R. It depicts the World War II memorial on Mamayev Hill in Volgograd (formerly Stalingrad). American geographers are in the foreground climbing the long stairway to the base of the 300-foot-high statue of "Mother Russia" pointing her sword northwestward toward Moscow.

Geography of the U.S.S.R.
TOPICAL ANALYSIS

PAUL E. LYDOLPH

Professor of Geography

University of Wisconsin—Milwaukee

Cartographers:

Don and Denise Temple

Cop a

Misty Valley Publishing

Box 323, Route 2, Elkhart Lake, Wisc.
Telephone: (414) 876-2280

Library of Congress Cataloging Data:

Lydolph, Paul E.
    Geography of the U.S.S.R.: Topical Analysis
    Catalog Card No. 78-66325

Preface

This volume which analyzes the geography of the Soviet Union topic by topic is designed as a companion volume for the author's *Geography of the U.S.S.R.*, third edition, John Wiley and Sons, 1977 which covers the country region by region. The present volume strives to illustrate geographic principles using the U.S.S.R. as the subject and to analyze spatial distributions in the Soviet Union utilizing modern geographic methods. To this end, such chapters as the ones on settlement, general economy, transformation of nature, and prospects for regional development, have been added to the more standard discussions on such topics as landforms, climate, population, agriculture, industry, transport, and trade. Thus, this book is most useful for developing generalizations about the country as a whole. For more detailed descriptions of individual places, one should refer to the regional volume.

Lengthy reading lists are provided at the ends of chapters for those who wish to pursue their enquiries further. But these are by no means the sole sources of information for the text. Many general references were utilized, the main ones of which are listed below.

Bibliographies

1. *ABSEES: Soviet and East European Abstract Series,* University of Glasgow, published from 1970 until October, 1976.

2. The American Bibliography of Slavic and East European Studies, yearly. American Association for the Advancement of Slavic Studies, Columbus, Ohio.

3. Dossick, Jesse J., "Doctoral Dissertations on Russia, the Soviet Union, and Eastern Europe Accepted by American, Canadian, and British universities, 1975–1976, *Slavic Review,* December, 1976, pp. 786–801. (This list has been published annually in the December issue of *Slavic Review* since 1964.)

4. Dossick, Jesse J., *Doctoral Research on Russia and The Soviet Union, 1960–1975: A Classified List of 3,150 American, Canadian, and British Dissertations with some Critical and Statistical Analysis,* Garland Publishing, New York, 1976, 345 pp. (Includes lists published annually in December issue of *Slavic Review* since 1964. It adds comments to these.)

5. *European Bibliography of Soviet, East European, and Slavonic Studies,* Centre for Russian and East European Studies, University of Birmingham, began annual publication in 1975.

6. Grant, S. A., *A Scholar's Guide to Resources for Soviet and Russian Studies in the Washington, D. C. Area,* George Washington University, 1977.

7. Harris, Chauncy D., *Guide to Geographical Bibliographies and Reference Works*

v

in Russian or on the Soviet Union, University of Chicago, Geography Research Paper No. 164, 1975, 478 pp.

8. Jones, David Lewis, *Books In English on the Soviet Union, 1917–73: A Bibliography,* Garland Reference Library of Social Science, Vol. 3. Garland Publishers, New York, 1975, 331 pp.

9. Lamprecht, Sandra J., *The Soviet Union and Scandinavia: A Bibliography of Theses and Dissertations in Geography,* Council of Planning Librarians, Box 229, Monticello, Illinois, 61856, 1974.

10. *Referativnyy Zhurnal* (published in the U.S.S.R. in Russian). The section on geography is one of the most complete abstract journals in the world. It lists titles and summaries of periodical articles and monographs published all over the world.

11. *Reports of The Institute of Geography of Siberia and the Far East* (in English), Academy of Sciences of the USSR, Siberian Branch, Irkutsk, 1976, 180 pp.

Atlases

1. *Atlas SSSR* (Atlas of the U.S.S.R.), Moscow, 1969, 2nd ed., 199 pp. (in Russian). The best and most recent general atlas on the U.S.S.R. Pages 6–64 are general regional maps showing great detail of landform and location. Pages 66–123 are maps of the entire country showing many aspects of the physical and economic geography of the area. Pages 124–147 are regional economic maps. The remainder of the atlas is primarily an exhaustive gazetteer of place names.

2. *Atlas razvitiya khozyaystva i kultury SSSR: 1917–1967* (Atlas on the Growth of the Economy and Culture of the U.S.S.R.: 1917–1967), Moscow, 1967, 172 pp. (in Russian). Excellent maps of all aspects of economy and culture. Map symbols are generally divided into time periods to illustrate the growth of the economy.

3. Kish, George, *Economic Atlas of the Soviet Union,* University of Michigan Press, Ann Arbor, 2nd ed., 1971, 90 pp.

4. Plummer, Thomas F., Jr., Hanne, William G., Bruner, Edward F., and Thudium, Christian C., Jr., *Landscape Atlas of the USSR,* Department of Earth, Space, and Graphic Sciences, United States Military Academy, West Point, New York, 1971, 197 pp. An excellent selection of topographic maps combined with interesting textual materials.

Encyclopedias

1. Florinsky, Michael T., ed., *Encyclopedia of Russia and the Soviet Union,* McGraw-Hill, New York, 1961, 624 pp.

2. *Kratkaya geograficheskaya entsiklopediya* (Short Geographical Encyclopedia), Moscow, 1960, 5 volumes (in Russian).

Serials

1. *Problems of Economics,* translation of Soviet journal, *Voprosy ekonomiki.* Published monthly since May, 1958. Many articles of interest to geographers.

2. *Social Sciences,* quarterly journal of USSR Academy of Sciences, published in English, French, and Spanish.

3. *Soviet Geography: Review and Translation,* published ten times per year by Scripta Publishing Company in cooperation with the American Geographical Society, edited by Theodore Shabad. An indispensable publication of translated articles from professional geographical journals in the Soviet Union. In addition Shabad compiles several pages of "News Notes" at the end of each issue. Materials from this journal have been used extensively throughout the book.

4. *Soviet Sociology,* translation of Soviet journal on sociology. Many articles of interest to geographers.

5. *Soviet Studies,* published by the University of Glasgow, Scotland. A scholarly journal with occasional articles pertinent to geography.

6. *The Annals of the Association of American Geographers.* A few articles pertaining to the Soviet Union.
7. *The Geographical Review.* A few articles pertaining to the Soviet Union.
8. *Economic Geography.* A few articles pertaining to the Soviet Union.
9. *The Geographical Journal.* A few articles pertaining to the Soviet Union.
10. *The Current Digest of the Soviet Press* (weekly since 1949) and *Current Abstracts of the Soviet Press* (monthly, except July and August, since April 1968). Translations of key news items from Soviet newspapers and magazines, published by the Joint Committee on Slavic Studies of the American Council of Learned Societies and the Social Science Research Council. Many news items of interest, especially full texts of plan goals, plan fulfillments, international agreements, and so forth. Human-interest items give pungent insight into the domestic situation.
11. *Slavic Review.* The professional journal of the American Association for the Advancement of Slavic Studies. Articles predominantly dealing with literature, political science, history, and economics.

Russian language serials of a geographical nature are:

12. *Akademiya nauk SSSR, izvestiya, seriya geograficheskaya* (Bulletin of the Academy of Sciences of the U.S.S.R., Series in Geography).
13. *Vsesoyuznoye geograficheskoye obshchestvo, izvestiya* (Bulletin of the All-Union Geographical Society).
14. *Voprosy Geografii* (Problems of Geography). A monograph series published by the University of Moscow.
15. *Leningrad Universitet, Vestnik, Seriya geologii i geografii* (Leningrad University, Bulletin, Series in Geology and Geography).
16. *Moskva Universitet, Vestnik, Seriya geografiya* (Moscow University, Bulletin, Series in Geography).

Books and Statistical Series

1. Mathieson, R. S., *The Soviet Union: An Economic Geography,* Barnes and Noble, New York, 1975, 368 pp.
2. *Narodnoye khozyaystvo* (National Economy). Annual statistical abstracts of U.S.S.R. and regions. Listed in the January issues of *Soviet Studies* beginning in 1959 (in Russian).
3. Nikitin, N. P., Prozorov, E. D., and Tutykhin, B. A., *Ekonomicheskaya geografiya SSSR, Obshchiy Obzor* (Economic Geography of the U.S.S.R., General), Prosveshcheniye, Moscow, 1973, 367 pp. *Soyuznye respubliki (krome RSFSR)* (The Union Republics without the R.S.F.S.R.), 1974, 319 pp. *RSFSR,* 1974, 351 pp.
4. Pokshishevsky, V., *Geography of the Soviet Union,* Progress Publishers, Moscow, 1974, 279 pp.
5. Saushkin, Yu. G., ed., *Ekonomicheskaya Geografiya SSSR,* Moscow University, 1971.
6. Saushkin, Yu. G., Nikolsky, I. V., and Korovitsyn, V. P., *Ekonomicheskaya geografiya SSSR, Chast II, ekonomicheskiye rayony* (Economic Geography of the USSR, Part II, Economic Regions), Izd. Moskovskogo universiteta, Moscow, 1973, 380 pp.
7. Shabad, T., *Basic Industrial Resources of the USSR,* Columbia University Press, New York, 1969, 393 pp.
8. *Sovetskiy Soyuz* (Soviet Union), 22 volumes, Izdatelstvo Mysl, Moscow, 1966–1972 (in Russian). Regional monographs covering physical landscape, history, ethnography, culture, economy, and regional subdivisions.
9. *SSSR: Administrativno-territorialnoye deleniye soyuznykh respublik,* Moscow, yearly (in Russian). A statistical compilation of all political administrative units of the country with their areas, populations, and subdivisions.
10. Tushinskiy, G. K., ed., *Fizicheskaya Geografiya SSSR,* Prosveshcheniye, Moscow, 1966. Translated by U.S. Dept. of the Army as *Physical Geography of the USSR,* J6585, 1970, 657 pp.

I wish to express my thanks to my wife, Mary, who typed all of the material several times and helped with other aspects of the work, and to Don and Denise Temple who drafted the illustrations. I also thank those who made available personal photographs, whose names are mentioned with their respective products.

The book is dedicated to our "tight little group" of geographical specialists on the Soviet Union who keep running into each other at meetings and elsewhere. Without their basic research and cooperation a book such as this would not be possible. They know who they are; their works are cited throughout. It is always a pleasure to carry on voluminous correspondence and make personal contacts with them.

PAUL E. LYDOLPH

Elkhart Lake, Wisconsin
October, 1978

Contents

Geography of the U.S.S.R.
TOPICAL ANALYSIS

The Origins and Development of the Peoples and Territory of the U.S.S.R.

The Union of Soviet Socialist Republics is the largest country on earth and the third most populous country after China and India. Its territory covers approximately one-sixth of the earth's land surface and is more than 2.3 times the size of the United States of America. Though the U.S.S.R. has existed as a political entity only since December 30, 1922, it occupies the territory put together by the Russian Tsars over half a millennium by the accretion of peripheral territories that were occupied by diverse groups of people. Tsarist Russia in turn evolved from a complex background of population movement and settlement on the East European Plain that dates back to at least the third or fourth millennium b.c. This land between Europe and Asia was ideally located to be influenced by a multitude of peoples who criss-crossed the area, some simply moving through, some settling, some dominating, some assimilating, and some whose traces have been lost forever. Thus the Soviet Union is the product of a long history of man-land relations on the same territory that have undergone successions of cultural and economic organizations. Parts of the vast territory now occupied by the U.S.S.R. evolved independently of one another and only in modern times have been thrown together under a single government. Though the Soviet system has been imposed upon everyone, racial stocks and ways of life are still imperfectly blended. To understand the present situation, one must look at the past.

HISTORY OF SETTLEMENT AND EVOLUTION OF PEOPLES

The East European Plain

Rather rich archeological evidence that is finally being unearthed indicates without a doubt that the East European Plain became the home of man about as early as other parts of the earth did. It appears that man came on the scene before the last glacial stage sometime between 400,000 and 140,000 years ago in the northern Caucasus, the Transcaucasus, and the Black Sea Steppes, as well as in scattered areas farther north. Their remains and bones of animals they ate are particularly abundant in caves in the Caucasus and in the Crimea.

By the fourth–third millennia b.c. Neolithic settlers advanced onto the southern plain from Asia Minor and the Middle East around either end of the Black Sea-Caucasus-Caspian Sea barriers, through the Balkans in the west and through Central Asia in the east. Remains of pottery relate them to early civilizations to the south in Asia Minor and the Middle East. They carried agriculture into the region from western Asia where it had begun probably during the ninth–eignth millennia b.c. Agricultural communities had appeared in the

3

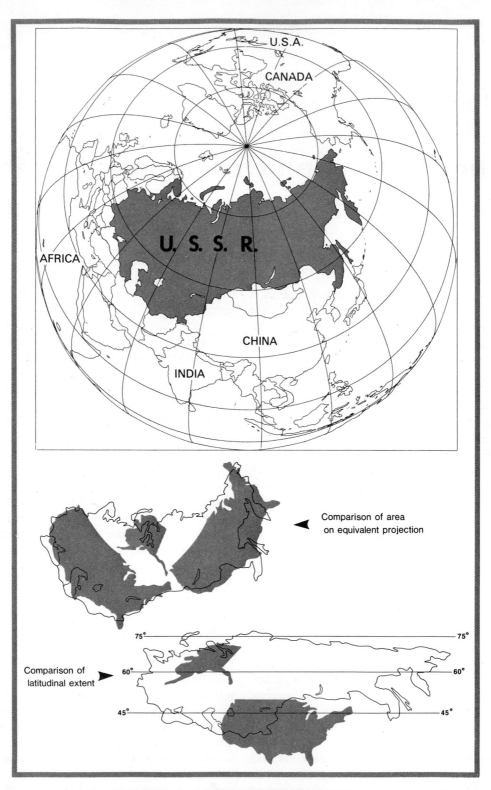

Figure 1–1   Location and size of the U.S.S.R.

southern part of Soviet Turkestan close to the Iranian border as early as the sixth–fifth millennia b.c. and in the Transcaucasus around the fifth millennium b.c. Some of the earliest communities in southwestern Ukraine date back perhaps to the fifth millennium b.c. Although settlements appear to have been most numerous in the southern steppes, particularly in the basins of the Prut, Dniester, and Southern Bug rivers in the southwestern part of the Soviet Union, they were by no means absent from other parts of the plain as far north as the Baltic Sea. The general pattern of settlement conformed primarily to agricultural potentials and favorable living conditions, climate, soils, and drainage particularly, but nodes of concentration within the general pattern related primarily to single items of critical usefulness to the aborigines. Often these were of a mineral nature, such as salt or metals used for the making of tools and weapons.[1]

The oldest remains of Indo-European peoples on the East European Plain appear to date from around 2300 b.c. Shortly thereafter food-producing agriculture and stock breeding spread throughout much of the plain except for the very northern part. The remains of Scandinavian colonies have been found deep in the area at the junction of the Kama and Volga rivers. These were probably established during the late bronze-early iron age in the second–first millennium b.c.

A Swedish expansion eastward during the early part of the first millennium b.c. occupied what is now Finland, the Baltic coast of the Baltic Republics, the Lower Oka River Valley, and the Volga Bend region around Kazan. One of the very important events of the early first millennium b.c. in eastern Europe was this development of Scandinavian trade.

This time also appears to be the beginning of the westward incursions of Siberian steppe peoples. They brought to a sedentary agricultural region in eastern Europe a highly mobile mounted nomad pastoralism. One reason for the success of these eastern warriors was the growth of a bronze industry in western Siberia

around 1000 b.c. that was based on rich deposits of copper and tin.

It is impossible to unravel the separate peoples that entered eastern Europe from Asia during this prehistoric period. The eastern incursions did not annihilate the populations already in the East European Plain. Most of the aborigines remained and mingled with the newcomers, giving rise to hybrid cultures that eventually assimilated all the older cultures. The Cimmerians were the first nomadic peoples in eastern Europe whose name has been handed down in historical records. Herodotus (fifth century b.c.) in his history reports that the Scythian nomads who dwelt in Asia crossed the River Araxes (Volga) and entered Cimmerian territory. Apparently the retreat of the Cimmerians before the Scythians took place before the tenth century b.c. Not later than the ninth or eighth century b.c. Homer remarked that the Scythians had occupied the Pontic (Black Sea) Steppe for so long that the Cimmerian occupation of the region was hard to remember. This chronology somewhat predates that of the Syrian and Greek records which mentioned the Cimmerians in Asia Minor during the eighth century b.c.

The Scythian power reached its zenith around the latter part of the seventh century b.c. when the center of the empire was in Media in western Asia. The Scythians were forced out of this region about 585 b.c. and went into the Ukraine where they dominated the region until about 200 b.c. Their culture has left the richest archeological evidence in the form of metal art objects and pottery that has filled many of the museums of Europe.

Greek commercial activity in the northern Black Sea region began no later than the ninth century b.c. The Greeks spoke of the "mare milking Scythians" and also of the "tribe of milk drinkers who used wagons for houses" who occupied the region between the Southern Bug River and the Sea of Azov as well as the Crimean Peninsula. The Greeks traded regularly with the north Pontic countries, and Greek trading posts sprang up all along the Black Sea coast. The Scythian might to the north secured the necessary peace and order for the growth of commerce after the sixth century

[1]For sketch maps of prehistoric settlements, see Sulimirski, 1970 and Mongait, 1959.

b.c., and permanent Greek colonies arose that have survived to this day. Flourishing Greek city states grew out of the Greek trading posts all the way from the Dniester River to the Sea of Azov. The strongest of these was Pantica-paeum at the site of modern day Kerch. The Greek colonists moved as far north as the Baltic along the east European waterways. They also maintained lively commercial relations with Asia Minor and the Middle East. The Greek colonies brought eastern Europe into contact with the ancient civilized world and began this period of recorded history. The Scythians bene-fited greatly from this intercourse. But about 200 b.c. the Scythians were defeated by the Sarmatians who were their kinspeople.

The origin of the Slavs is obscure. Some would place their origin in the Pripyat Marsh area, others along the northern Carpathians, and still others farther northwestward in the basins of the Vistula and Oder Rivers. Some believe that they evolved from the Scythians. At any rate, the Slavs seem to have been undergo-ing a slow concentration on the middle Dnieper region with perhaps some central settlement which was a forerunner of Kiev during the early centuries in the Christian era when the Baltic-to-Black Sea trade was developing. Perhaps they existed simultaneously alongside the Scythians and Sarmatians as sedentary agriculturalists dominated by the more mobile pastoralists. Their convergence into the Dnie-per region was perhaps hastened during the second and third centuries a.d. when the Goths from southwestern Sweden moved into the southern plain and captured most of the Greek cities along the Black Sea coast. In the Donets area about 200 a.d. the Goth movement south-eastward met up with a tribe known as the Antes which has been regarded by some authors as a Slavic tribe.

In 370 a.d. the empire of the Goths was completely destroyed by the Huns who had fled from the wrath of the Avars in north China westward through the Indo-European tribes and established themselves in the southern plain. About the middle of the sixth century the Avars crossed the lower Volga and defeated the Turkic Bulgars who had moved from the

Middle Volga-Kama River area and become established in the region between the Kuban and Don rivers.

The Khazars, who had been part of a great Turkic horde which controlled an empire during the sixth century that reached from the steppes of Central Asia to the boundaries of China, followed the Avars westward after the dismemberment of their Turkic empire. Their first center was established in the eastern part of the north Caucasian region from whence they subjugated much of the Transcaucasus and also spread northward and westward. In 720 a.d. they transferred their political center to Itil near the mouth of the Volga. Along with the Turkic Bulgars, who had resettled north of the lower Danube, they broke the Avar domi-nation of the southern plain during the seventh century.

The Bulgars and Khazars had close relations with the empire of Baghdad. Arabs used the Caspian Sea and the Volga River for access to the interior even as far north as the Baltic coast. It also was a channel for Islamic propa-ganda among the Turkic tribes, and the Bulgars embraced Mohammedanism probably sometime during the ninth or tenth centuries a.d. The Khazars, after lending an ear to Christian, Jewish, and Mohammedan mission-aries alike, generally accepted the Jewish faith from the numerous Jewish colonies that existed in the Crimea. The Khazars extended their domination into the Crimea and even into Kiev for a considerable period. They replaced the Avars as overlords of the Slavs on the Dnieper, and Kiev became the western outpost of their empire. The Slavic tribes that had formed the nucleus of the Antes Confederation had to await the arrival of the Scandinavian Rus before they were freed from the Khazars and were able to form the first extensive Russian state.

Thus, the Slavic state that evolved with its center at Kiev during the latter part of the ninth century was preceded by the Cimmer-ians, Scythians, Sarmatians, Goths, Huns, Turkic Bulgars, Avars, and Khazars. All of these conquering nomads left their marks on the Slavic tribes. The Slavs seem to have come upon the scene quietly sometime during the early part of the Christian era, but accounts of the period generally underplayed the role of the Slavs who might have been dominant in numbers but not in governmental and commercial affairs. The Slavs were very loosely organized politically and socially, generally adhering only to extended family organizations. They were interested mainly in agricultural pursuits and seem to have welcomed protection from nomadic warriors against other invaders. This probably explains why their movements were so slow and why they were so easily dominated by warlike tribes. It was the nomadic warriors who generally had the most intercourse with Greek and Baltic tradesmen, so that their role played a disproportionate part in the fragmentary accounts of the period.

Had the Islamic civilization from Khazaria and Bulgaria reached the pagan Slavic tribes, which were drawing nearer and nearer to the Volga and the lower Don, the frontiers of Europe might well have been fixed somewhere along the Carpathian Mountains. Russia was on the verge of becoming a part of the Moslem world of Asia. However this was averted by the entrance into the eastern Slavic scene by the Scandinavians and Byzantines. The Scandinavians came first and welded the eastern Slavs into a firm political block that eventually proved able to withstand the westward rush of Asiatic hordes and finally carried European civilization eastward beyond the Urals.

A lively commercial intercourse was carried on between Scandinavia and Baghdad via the Volga, but of even greater significance for the future was the Norsemen discovery of a more westerly route southward which moved up the Volkhov River to Lake Ilmen and the town of Novogorod from whence it moved over portage into the headwaters of the Dnieper and eventually to the Black Sea and Constantinopol. The upper and middle Dnieper region was a Slavic country when the Norsemen reached it, but the commercial traffic on the river was controlled by the Khazars. The Norsemen reached Kiev about 856–860 a.d., and the local Slavs (Polyane), disillusioned with the Khazars who were unable to protect them from bands of marauding nomads in the southern plains, welcomed the newcomers and willingly accepted them as overlords in place of the Khazars.

The native populations along the southern shores of the Baltic called the Scandinavian newcomers "Rus." The Estonians still call the Swedes "Rootsie." The country between Lake Ilmen, the Volkhov River, and Lake Ladoga, is apparently the "wooded and marshy island" on which some Arab writer located the original habitat of the so-called "Rus."

In 862 a.d. the Varangians (Scandinavians) under the leadership of Rurik, established a Slavic state with its center at Novgorod. The center of government was moved south to Kiev about 878–882 a.d. by Oleg, the son of Rurik, who conquered Kiev and became the founder of Kievan Rus which was the first organized Slavic state about which there is much written information.

Kievan Rus developed into a well organized, democratic, urban, commercial society over the next four centuries. Although at least 85 per cent of its people were agriculturalists, it was the 15 per cent who lived in cities and carried on trade who dominated the government and played the leading role in the history of the area. It has been estimated that at the height of its glory during the eleventh century a.d. Kievan Rus was populated by 7–8 million people who at that time were equal in number to all the Germans in Europe and 2.5 times as numerous as the English. Old church chronicles mention 300 cities which contained about 15 per cent of the total population of the state. Kiev, Novgorod, and Smolensk were the major centers and probably were as large as any city in Europe at that time. Kievan Rus embraced a territory that reached from the slopes of the Carpathians in the southwest to the Baltic in the north.

But this flourishing early start of a Slavic state was completely obliterated in 1240 a.d. by the onslaught of the Tatars under the leadership of Batu, grandson of Genghis Khan. They were a Turkic tribe of nomadic horsemen who again invaded from the east. They sacked Kiev, and the people of the area perished or fled into the surrounding forests. There is no agreement on the fate of these peoples. Little if any connection existed between the highly civilized state of Kievan Rus and the state of Muscovy that took shape during the next two centuries under the burden of the "Tatar Yoke."

The Tatars first established themselves on the lower Volga at the center of Sarai, but later they broke into three hordes centered at Kazan, Astrakhan, and the Crimea. They did not attempt to settle the land, but exacted tribute from it through intermediaries, the Slavic heads of princely city states, the most significant of which arose during this time in the middle forest zone in the headwaters of the Volga River at such places as Moscow, Tver (Kalinin), Vladimir, Ryazan, Rostov-Velikiy, and Suzdal.

The tatar horsemen, who were accustomed to the open grassy steppes, found it more difficult to move in the swamps and forests of the north and did not effectively control Novgorod, which continued to flourish as a cosmopolitan trading center with Hanseatic League connections along the Baltic. But the settlers in the area did not look upon Novgorod as an indigenous center suitable for the formation of a Slavic State as Kiev had been, for Novgorod contained western traders as well as local people who could not be relied upon in time of crisis. Nevertheless, it was from this great city that Alexander Nevsky, ruler of Vladimir, gathered his forces to defeat the Swedes on the Neva River in the north the very same year that the Tatars were sacking Kiev in the south. And it was from this center two years later that he moved northward to defeat the Livonian Knights on the ice of Lake Peipus (Chudskoye). It was then he observed that in spite of the nominal control exercised by the Tatars at this time, the real threat to the Slavs lay in the northwest, not the southeast.

The princely states in the central forest region fought many bloody intrigues among themselves while at the same time they resisted as much as possible the Tatar dominance. But by kowtowing to the Tatars they were allowed some freedom to develop on their own, and through clever and unscrupulous maneuvers a

few princes eventually consolidated the lands of many city states into a few more powerful ones. Eventually Moscow became dominant, and the Moscow prince was named the Grand Prince of all the Russias by the Tatars.

It was during the reign of Ivan III, Ivan the Great, from 1462–1505, that the State of Muscovy finally emerged supreme and took over Novgorod with all its lands to the north. It was also during his reign that Muscovy became strong enough to tackle the Tatars themselves, and a major stalemate was reached with a Tatar army on a battleground near the Ugra River south of Moscow in 1480. This data is often cited as the end of the "Tatar Yoke," because no more tribute was paid from then on, but the Tatars continued to harass the Slavic area for another century or more. Kazan was not captured until 1552 during the reign of Ivan IV, Ivan the Terrible, and as late as 1571 much of Moscow was burned to the ground by an expedition of Tatars from the Crimea.

Eventually the Tatar power was completely broken, and some individuals in the ruling classes of the Tatar Hordes intermarried with Russians. That is why the Belorussians, who consider themselves more pure Slavs than the Russians, say "scratch a Russian and you will find a Tatar." Many of the Tatars remained on the east European plain, particularly around their center of Kazan at the Great Bend of the Volga River where a Tatar Autonomous Soviet Socialist Republic still exists. Also, many of the Crimean Tatars took up farming and remained in the area until World War II when they were evacuated eastward by the Soviet government.

During the period when the Slavic princely states were fighting among themselves and resisting the Tatar Horde, various Slavic princes also were gathering armies to repulse the Swedes, the Germans, the Poles, and the Lithuanians in the north and west, and later the Ottoman Turks in the south, who had taken over the Byzantine Empire with the fall of Constantinopol in 1453. In 1410, at the battle of Tannenberg, a great pan-Slav army under a Polish-Lithuanian prince defeated the so-called Livonian Knights and thereby set the

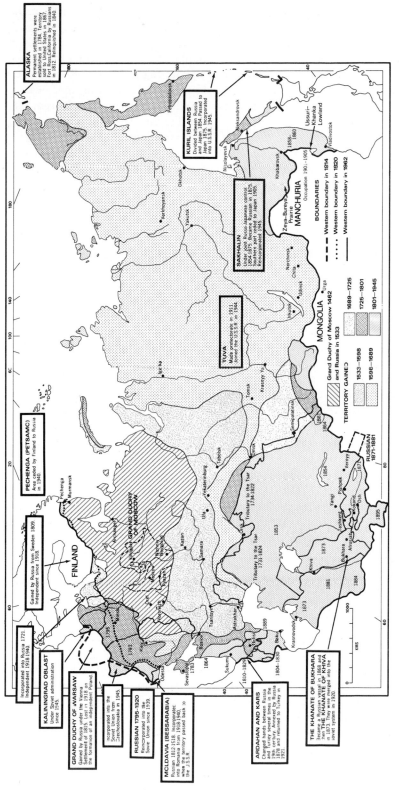

Figure 1-2 Territorial expansion of the Russian Empire and the U.S.S.R.

eastern limits of German penetration for centuries to follow.

The Slavic state, now with its center at Moscow, began to expand again over the east European plain during the fifteenth and sixteenth centuries. The mixed forest region around Moscow became populated, primarily with agriculturalists, and during the later half of the sixteen century the steppes to the south (the wild field) were gradually resettled. The forerunners of the southern movement were the so-called "Cossacks" who were renegades from the government of Ivan the Terrible in Moscow. They grouped into bands and lived a cowboy-like existence that set the stage for agricultural settlement. Though the Cossacks were scattered widely over the southern plains, they eventually became concentrated in two or three localities. So-called Don Cossacks occupied the lower Don River and established a center at Aksay only a few miles northeast of the present large city of Rostov. Other concentrations were in the Ukraine around Kiev and farther south on some islands in the rapids of the Dnieper River near the present site of Zaporozhye. It was the Cossacks in the Ukraine who during the seventeenth century rebelled against the Polish-Lithuanian state and finally established their independence of the power, bringing on the weakening of Poland. But the independence of Ukraine was short lived; in 1654 it recognized the supremacy of the Duchy of Moscow. During the same year the old city of Smolensk in the western part of European Russia was ceded to Moscow by Poland.

The advance into the rich chernozem lands of the southern steppes proceeded by spurts which established a series of ever advancing fortified lines behind which agricultural settlements were later filled in. Initially the Tula Line in the northern part of the Central Black Earth Region became famous. Here a forest belt was retained behind which the land had been cleared for agriculture. Trees were felled with their branches facing southeastward with the trunks still attached to the stumps to form what was known as an abattis to present an obstacle to the horsemen from the steppes.

Later (1650s) the Belgorod Line farther south extended all the way from the town of Belgorod northeastward through Oskol and Voronezh to Simbirsk (Ulyanovsk) on the Volga.

The flight of the Russian serfs "to the Cossacks" during this time was as much an expulsion of escaped serfs from the tyranny of the Tsarist regime in Moscow with its associated system of feudal landholdings as it was the lure of the fertile agricultural potentials to the south. During the sixteenth and seventeenth centuries the wooded steppe particularly became a continuously settled land with agriculture occupying all the usable acreage. It has been estimated that during the seventeenth and eighteenth centuries more than 3 million people migrated into the forest steppe lands as they were regained by the Russian State.[2] At least 2 million of them came from the Central Region around Moscow and perhaps as many as 700,000 from the "old" Ukrainian lands north of the Carpathian Mountains. In addition, primarily during the second half of the eighteenth century, about 500,000 people migrated into the steppe provinces farther south which were to become known as "Novorossiya" (New Russia).

Consolidation of the gains in the south under an organized government was begun by Peter I, Peter the Great, during his reign from 1698–1725. However, after a few skirmishes along the Sea of Azov with the Ottoman Turks, his attention was diverted to the north by the Swedes in the Baltic, where he first suffered a major defeat from Charles XII near the city of Narva. But in 1709 his armies recuperated to defeat Charles decisively in the Ukraine at the town of Poltava. Even though this was a major victory for the Russians, the Swedes harassed them in the Baltic throughout Peter's reign. The consolidation of the south remained undone for another half century until the ascension to the throne of Catherine II, Catherine the Great. Nevertheless, Peter's war with Sweden established a Russian foothold on the Baltic and weakened Swedish power from then on. In 1703 Peter began building St. Peters-

[2]Pokshishevskiy, 1969, p. 53.

burg on the Baltic Sea, and in 1713 he moved the national government from Moscow to his new city, where it remained until 1918. This move shifted the center of influence of the Russian government and assured a stronghold on the Baltic and a western position on the European plain.

During the reign of Catherine the Great (1762–1796) the offensive to the south was reopened and many battles were fought with and against the Austrians, the Prussians, and the Turks until by the end of her reign the entire north shore of the Black Sea was secured to Russia. The Crimea was occupied in 1783. The ancient city of Odessa, which had been captured from the Greeks by the Turks was captured by the Russians in 1774, was lost again, and was recaptured in 1789. The expansion to the northwest was completed in 1809 when Finland was acquired from Sweden, but much of this territory was lost again as a result of World War I. After the Black Sea Steppes had been wrested from the Turks, Catherine, who was of German origin, settled thousands of Germans in the newly acquired rich farm lands, as well as in the middle Volga Valley. Bukovina, west of the Dniester, which had been occupied by the Austrians in 1773, and Bessarabia, which was still in Turkish hands, both were ceded to Russia in 1812.

It was also during the reign of Catherine that the three partitions of Poland took place which led to the decision incorporated into the Paris Treaty in 1814 to put almost all the territory of Poland, including Warsaw, under the Russian throne, where it remained with varying degrees of autonomy until 1915.

The struggles with major powers to the west have continued down to the present time, and the exchanges of territories that have taken place again and again have left remnant groups of Baltic peoples, Poles, Finns, and others in the territory of what is now the western part of the Soviet Union.

Siberia and the Far East

During the latter part of the sixteenth century and the first half of the seventeenth a second wave of population was directed eastward beyond "the stone belt" as the Ural Mountains were then called. During the reign of Ivan the IV an expedition under the leadership of a Cossack named Yermak was sponsored by the fur trading family of Stroganov to open up Siberia. Russian adventurers were lured into the region in the quest of furs. The eastward movement was far less massive than the southward one, but its geographic scope was breathtaking. During the brief period, 1584–1639, Russian adventurers swept across the region from the Urals to the Pacific and secured all of Siberia for Russian control down to the present time. In 1649 Okhotsk became the first Russian settlement on the eastern coast. The movement through Siberia met with little resistance, for the area was occupied by only a few widely scattered paleoasiatic tribes who had undergone hundreds and even thousands of years of evolution in relative isolation. Most of these peoples are still identified today by nationality-based political subdivisions, but their numbers are so small and their stage of development so retarded that they exert insignificant influence on the society of present day U.S.S.R.

Since the climate of the area was so harsh, there was little inducement for settlement. Agricultural development in Siberia at this time was of minor importance, related only to the needs of the pioneers themselves and the military personnel who were transferred to Siberia to man "ostrogs" (fortress-trading posts) to exercise control over the natives who were doing the hunting and trapping of fur-bearing animals. The Russians did not stop to take up land, but continued across the continent in their race to the Pacific. In 1652 a fort was established on the Amur River on the site of the modern city of Khabarovsk. Here the Russian pioneers came into conflict with the northernmost Chinese, and in 1689 the Far Eastern territories were partitioned between the two countries by the Treaty of Nerchinsk.

Russian fur traders continued on across the Bering Straits into Alaska, where in 1784 permanent settlements were established, and they continued on down the coast of North

Figure 1–3   Relic of Bratsk Ostrog dating from 1631. Photo by Henry A. Coppock.

America until in 1812 they founded their southernmost outpost, Fort Ross, only a few miles north of present day San Francisco. Later, pressures on the central government in St. Petersburg from the Crimean War and from opposition by British fur trading companies in Canada induced the Russians in 1867 to sell Alaska to the United States and to relinquish all claims to the south along the west coast of North America.

However, in 1840–1860 Russian expansion was revived in the Far East after the weakening of the Chinese Empire and in response to the expansionist tendencies of Japan. The 1689 Treaty of Nerchinsk which had been forced on the Russians by the Chinese during one of the most organized and strongest periods in modern Chinese history, had established the boundary between the Russian and Manchu Empires along the Argun River and the Stanovoy Mountains far to the north of the present boundary. It specifically denied the Russians the right to navigate the Amur River. The Russians had never really accepted this secondary position and at the first signs of Manchu weakness around 1840 they prepared for further expansion at the expense of China. In violation of the Treaty of Nerchinsk, in 1850 they sent an expedition to explore the Amur region and to establish a Russian post at Nikolayevsk at the mouth of the Amur River. A Transbaykal army was soon organized, and military posts were established all the way to the Pacific Coast and even on Sakhalin Island. In 1858 the Treaty of Argun established a new boundary along the Amur from the mouth of the Argun to the Pacific. The territory south of the Amur and east of the Ussuri was placed under joint occupation, but two years later the Treaty of Pekin placed the entire territory east of the Ussuri under Russian control.

The first earnest Russian settlement of the Far East began in 1855 when discharged Cossacks from Transbaykalia homesteaded large parcels of land. They were later joined by Cossacks from the Urals and as far west as the Ukraine. This small stream of Cossack peasants along the overland route was joined later by many more arrivals in the Ussuri Region of Ukrainians brought in by the long sea route through the Suez and Singapore Straits. During the culmination of this sea traffic in

1883–1886 people came mainly from the north-central Ukraine and Central Black Earth Regions of European Russia where physical conditions in the wooded steppe were similar to those in the Maritime Region of the Far East.

In 1892 construction began on the Trans-Siberian Railroad and great pressure was brought to bear on China to allow the extension of the railway through northern Manchuria to Vladivostok. With the completion of the Trans-Siberian, Chinese Eastern, and Ussuri Railroads, the maritime traffic of Ukrainian peasants dwindled to nothing after 1900, and individual peasant families came in by rail to encroach on the large communal land holdings of the original Cossack villages. A new kind of settlement of more intensive agriculture finally evolved. The principal regions of cultivation became the Zeya-Bureya Prairie and the southern Ussuri-Khanka Lowland.

The Russian expansion in the Far East was halted decisively by the Russo-Japanese War of 1905 when the victorious Japanese took over the South Manchurian Railway and the southern half of Sakhalin Island. The loss of southern Sakhalin was the first diminution of Russian territory since the fifteenth century, and the year 1904 marks the greatest expanse of the territory controlled by the Tsars. The total area of the country at that time was approximately 8,550,000 square miles, about 50,000 square miles less than the present area of the Soviet Union. Of course, southern Sakhalin and the Kuril Islands were regained as a result of World War II.

The population of the Soviet Far East still reflects the earlier history of the area. Although the population on the Soviet side of the border is primarily Russian, there are some admixtures of Chinese, Koreans, and other Oriental types.

The Caucasus

The Russian advance to the Caucasus began by the founding of towns along the northern foothills of the Great Caucasus during the latter part of the reign of Catherine the Great. The movement continued across the Caucasus during the reign of Alexander I in the early part of the nineteenth century. Tbilisi, the capital of Georgia, fell to Russia in 1801. Baku, later to become the capital of the Azerbaydzhan Republic, came under Russian control in 1806, and the Black Sea coast south to Sukhumi was secured by 1810. The advance was completed in 1828 when, after the capture of Yerevan, Russia met stiff resistance from Turkey and growing British influence in Persia.

The acquisition of the Caucasian region added significant numbers of Caucasian groups of peoples with very long histories and advanced civilizations. The Georgians and Armenians had occupied their respective areas for at least 2000 years and had benefited from earlier civilizations in the area that had existed along this crossroads of intercourse between the Middle East and the European plain to the north. The Caucasians had generally evolved through the archeological ages earlier than had tribes on the northern plain and often acted as introducers of innovations to the nomadic peoples to the north. Another important group were the Turkic Azerbaydzhanis who had intimate contact with the Persian Empire for centuries. These three largest nationality groups occupied much of Transcaucasia, although there were minority groups interspersed among them. And in the Great Caucasus, particularly on their northern slopes, was a crazy-quilt pattern of nationality groups, most of them small in numbers, who represented remnants of many successions of peoples who had occupied the area over the ages. Most of these nationality groups remain to this day, isolated from one another in their individual mountain basins, little affected by the outside. Most of them have been given some political recognition by the Soviets. They will be discussed in more detail with population characteristics in Chapter 6.

Central Asia

Russian penetration of Central Asia took place during the second half of the nineteenth century primarily to subjugate nomadic tribes that periodically foraged northward into southwestern Siberia and the southeastern part of the European plain to harass Russian settlers and carry off hostages to be sold in the slave markets of Khiva or Bukhara.

The Russians had no difficulty moving across the Kazakh Steppes where there were no cities of permanently settled areas or any organized military force other than small followings at the disposal of individual tribal leaders. In the settled Khanates of the south, however, things were quite different. It was against these hotbeds of resistance that the Russians directed their efforts. Without too much difficulty the Russians captured Yangi (now Dzhambul) in 1864, Tashkent in 1865, Khodzhent (now Leninabad) in 1866, Bukhara and Samarkand in 1868, and the last remaining Khanates of Khiva in 1873 and Kokand in 1876.

Suddenly the Russians found themselves in semicontrol of this inland desert empire. Once again they had come into contact with the British influence, in India, and in 1888 boundaries were agreed upon that established Afghanistan as a buffer country between Russia and India. Some of the Moslem colonies, such as Bukhara and Khiva, remained nominally independent under the Russian regime until 1920, when finally the Bolsheviks won the civil wars in the area and established Soviet rule.

The nineteenth century Russian acquisition of what is now the Kazakh Republic and the four republics of Soviet Central Asia brought into the Empire very ancient civilizations whose histories of riverine settlements and irrigation agriculture dated back to at least 2000–3000 b.c. Before the coming of the Russians the region had been subjected to many invasions and conquests, the principal ones being the Arabs in the seventh and eighth centuries a.d. and the Mongols in the thirteenth century.

The only part of the region about which any coherent information was available before the Arab conquest was Sogd which lay between the Oxus (Amu-Darya) and Jakhartes (Syr-Darya) rivers in the region that later became known to western historians as Transoxania. The people of Sogd were of Iranian origin, but they formed only a small part of the vast nomadic Turkic Empire that stretched from the Urals to Mongolia and southward to the high mountains of Central Asia. The valleys and oases were apparently fairly densely populated and were ruled over by princelings living in castles. Persian culture had a greater influence on the settled areas than did Islam. None of the early conquerers colonized the region to any extent, and none except the Moslem Arabs and Persians exercised any profound cultural influences. The original population of Turkestan, as well as probably much of the steppe region to the north, was of the same Iranian stock as the Persians, and the attachment of Transoxania to the Persian Empire until the end of the tenth century resulted in the introduction of the Iranian cultural influences that are still apparent today in large towns. But from the sixth century a.d., the successive Turkic invasions from the east ended in the complete Turkification of the nomadic elements. This situation hardly changed during the Mongol invasions since these were not carried out by hordes of Mongols but mainly by Turkic tribes recruited by Mongolian officers. The ravaging of the cities of Turkestan during the thirteenth century was mainly done by peoples from the Kazakh Steppe to the north, which resulted in the further encroachment of Turkic influence on the settled areas.

Some of the Kazakhs submitted to Russian rule in 1730 in order to get protection from the Kalmyk or Oyrat invasion coming out of Sinkiang. This was the last wave of nomadic invasions out of Central Asia, and the Kalmyks finally settled in the semidesert region just to the west of the Volga delta.

Before the Soviet regime the distinction of the peoples of Central Asia was not between nationalities or even between Turkic and Iranian elements, but between nomads and sedentary peoples. The nomads were exclusively Turkic, but the sedentary peoples included both Iranian and Turkic elements. The settled peoples regarded themselves as Moslems and regarded the nomads as being beyond the pale of Islam. All people thought of themselves as members of tribes or clans rather than as nationalities. The settled peoples were known to the Russians as "Sarts," although there was some confusion that this had a racial connotation. It was the Soviet regime that identified nations, which, although in some cases largely arbitrary and artificial to begin with, have acquired certain realities with time.

The Soviet Period

The ultimate result of defeat in World War I, followed by revolutions, civil wars, and intervention by the Allies, was the loss of Finland, Estonia, Latvia, Lithuania, and Poland, which became independent countries, and Bessarabia and northern Bukovina in the southwest to Rumania. Various national areas such as Ukraine, the Transcaucasian areas of Georgia, Armenia, and Azerbaydzhan, and some of the areas in Central Asia east of the Caspian declared their independence and set up their own governments. So-called white republics were established within Russia by such military monarchs as Denikin in the northern Caucasus and Kolchak in Siberia. But such resistance forces failed to integrate their efforts and one by one they were crushed by the Red Army as Lenin appealed to the non-Russian nationalities by proclaiming national self determination. The result was that essentially all of these areas were brought within the boundaries of the newly constituted Soviet Union by 1923.

All the territories lost as a result of World War I, except for Finland and part of the Polish area, were regained at the end of World War II, and some territory that never had been under the Russian Empire also was acquired at this time. Poland was partitioned again in 1939 between Germany and the Soviet Union, but this was negated by Germany's attack on the U.S.S.R. After the war, all of eastern Poland became part of Belorussia or the Ukraine within the Soviet Union, while the country of Poland was shifted westward. The Baltic states of Estonia, Latvia, and Lithuania were regained by the Soviet Union during the early part of the war. Bessarabia was later regained and Bukovina newly gained from Rumania to be incorporated partly into the new republic of Moldavia and partly into western Ukraine. Small pieces of territory were taken over from Finland, particularly the Pechenga area in the far north, which contains important nickel and copper deposits, and the Karelian Isthmus in the south next to Leningrad. Two areas in the west that were taken after World War II which had never been under Russian control were the Ruthenian area of Czechoslovakia, which became Transcarpathian Ukraine, and the northern half of east Prussia, which became Kaliningrad Oblast. In the Far East, southern Sakhalin and the Kuril Islands were regained from Japan. Also, in 1944, Tuva joined the Soviet Union, after the establishment of a protectorate that dated back to 1911. By 1946 the area of the Soviet Union had become 8,606,300 square miles, which compares to 3,615,210 square miles in the United States of America.

Reading List

1. Allen, William Edward David, *A History of the Georgian People from the Beginning down to the Russian Conquest in the Nineteenth Century,* Barnes and Noble, New York, 1971, 429 pp.
2. Armstrong, Terrence, ed., *Yermak's Campaign in Siberia,* The Hakluyt Society, London, 1975, 315 pp.
3. *Atlas Obrazovaniie i razvitiie Soyuza SSR* (Atlas of the Formation and Development of the U.S.S.R.), Moscow, 1972, 116 pp.
4. Chevigny, Hector, *Russian America; the Great Alaskan Venture, 1741–1867,* Viking Press, New York, 1965, 274 pp.
5. Chew, Allen F., *An Atlas of Russian History,* Yale University Press, New Haven, 1967, 113 pp.
6. Dvornik, Francis, *The Slavs, Their Early History and Civilization,* American Academy of Arts and Sciences, Boston, 1959, 394 pp.
7. Gibson, James R., *Feeding the Russian Fur Trade: Provisionment of the Okhotsk Seaboard and the Kamchatka Peninsula, 1639–1856.* University of Wisconsin Press, Madison, 1969, 337 pp.

8. ———, Imperial Russia in Frontier America: The Changing Geography of Supply of Russian America, 1784–1867, Oxford University Press, New York, 1976, 256 pp.

9. Gilbert, Martin, *Russian History Atlas,* Macmillan, New York, 1972, 146 maps and 34 pp.

10. Glaskow, W. G., *History of the Cossacks,* Robert Speller & Sons, New York, 1972, 163 pp.

11. Harrison, John A., *The Founding of the Russian Empire in Asia and America,* University of Miami Press, Coral Gables, 1971, 156 pp.

12. *Istoricheskaya geografiya Rossii, XII nachalo XX b.* (Historical geography of Russia from the twelfth to the beginning of the twentieth century), Nauka, Moscow, 1975, 345 pp.

13. Lantzeff, George V., and Pierce, Richard A., *Eastward to Empire: Exploration and Conquest on the Russian Open Frontier, to 1750,* McGill-Queen's University Press, Montreal and London, 1973, 276 pp.

14. Mongait, A. L., *Archeology in the USSR,* Foreign Languages Publishing House, Moscow, 1959, 429 pp.

15. Morris, A. S., "The Medieval Emergence of the Volga-Oka Region," *Annals of the Association of American Geographers,* December 1971, pp. 697–710.

16. Parker, W. H., *An Historical Geography of Russia,* Aldine, Chicago, 1969, 416 pp.

17. Pokshishevsky, V. V., "Migration of U.S.S.R. Population Described," in *Translations on U.S.S.R. Resources,* No. 52, JPRS 49279, 19 November 1969, pp 51–66.

18. Riasanovsky, Nicholas V., *A History of Russia,* Third Edition, Oxford University Press, New York, 1977, 762 pp.

19. Sulimirski, Tadeusz, *Prehistoric Russia,* Humanities Press, New York, 1970, 449 pp.

20. Ulam, Adam B., *A History of Soviet Russia,* Praeger, New York, 1976, 312 pp.

Territorial Organization

POLITICAL ADMINISTRATIVE REGIONS

The Union of Soviet Socialist Republics came into being on December 30, 1922 after the chaos of civil war had subsided and the Bolsheviks had established nominal control over most of what had been the Russian Empire. The newly constituted country consisted of four Soviet Socialist Republics: The Russian Soviet Federated Socialist Republic, the Ukrainian Soviet Socialist Republic, the Belorussian Soviet Socialist Republic, and the Transcaucasian Soviet Federated Socialist Republic. Within these four republics there were some subdivisions created to give recognition to lesser nationality groups. In addition there were minor civil divisions which were subdivided for administrative convenience.

According to Marxian doctrine the political subdivisions were to reflect the economy of the areas, but Lenin's government felt it imperative to give overt recognition to nationalities. The old Russian Empire, which had often been called a prison of nations, had been beset by seething nationalism just below the surface for a long time, and the Bolsheviks at the time of the Revolution in 1917 had capitalized on this by promising national self determination as one of the four main planks in their platform. In addition, a great deal of tradition was attached to the old "gubernia" that had been set up by Peter the Great and Catherine the Great during the eighteenth century. This was particularly true in European Russia where the administrative seats of these gubernia had grown well beyond the size of other cities and had become accustomed to dominating the political, economic, and social life in their respective surrounding areas. Therefore, the Soviets retained most of these areas much as they had been, but now called them oblasts.

In the next few years more nationality groups were given political recognition and many political administrative regions were upgraded to succeedingly higher levels. By 1936 things had changed so much that a new constitution was adopted to fit reality more closely. This is often referred to as the Stalin Constitution. It recognized 11 Soviet Socialist Republics and a variety of subdivisions at various administrative levels. With the acquisition of the Baltic Republics at the onset of World War II, each of these was accorded the status of Soviet Socialist Republic, as was Moldavia which was acquired a little later from Rumania. And during the war the Soviets constituted the Karelian area north of Leningrad as the Karelo-Finnish Soviet Socialist Republic, apparently hoping that this would somehow pacify the Finns across the border, even though the Karelian area did not satisfy the constitutional requirements for a republic (at least one million people, the majority of

Table 2–1   Territory and Population by Political Units and Economic Regions, January 1, 1976

Administrative Units. Numbers Correspond to Map Inside Front Cover	Territory 1000 km.²	Population 1000	Population Change 1970–1976 Per Cent	Per Cent Urban	Change in Per Cent Urban 1970–1976	Rural Population Change 1970–1976 Per Cent	Persons Per km.²
U.S.S.R.	22,402	255,524	+5.7	61	+5	− 6.4	11.5
R.S.F.S.R.	17,075	134,650	+3.5	68	+6	−13.4	7.9
I. Northwest	1,662	12,905	+6.1			−13.3	7.8
1. Archangel Oblast	587	1,448	+3.3	72	+6	−15.4	2.5
2. Nenets A. Okrug	177	41	+5.1	60	+5	−5.6	.2
3. Leningrad City		4,372	+10.7	100	0	0	
4. Leningrad Oblast	86	1,510	+5.2	63	+2	−1.8	68.5
5. Murmansk Oblast	145	930	+16.4	89	0	+14.3	6.4
6. Novgorod Oblast	55	719	−.42	62	+9	−19.3	13.0
7. Pskov Oblast	55	852	−2.7	52	+9	−18.0	15.4
8. Vologda Oblast	146	1,286	−.77	56	+8	−17.5	8.8
9. Karelian A.S.S.R.	172	735	+2.9	76	+7	−19.7	4.3
10. Komi A.S.S.R.	416	1,053	+9.1	69	+7	−11.7	2.5
II. Central	486	28,376	+2.6			−17.8	58.4
11. Bryansk Oblast	35	1,518	−4.0	57	+10	−20.7	43.5
12. Ivanovo Oblast	24	1,320	−1.3	80	+5	−18.9	55.2
13. Kalinin Oblast	84	1,682	−2.1	64	+7	−19.5	20.0
14. Kaluga Oblast	30	990	−.50	60	+8	−16.7	33.1
15. Kostroma Oblast	60	802	−7.9	63	+10	−26.1	13.4
16. Moscow City		7,734	+9.5	100	0	0	
17. Moscow Oblast	47	6,112	+5.9	73	+4	−7.5	294.6
18. Orel Oblast	25	885	−4.9	52	+13	−25.1	35.8
19. Ryazan Oblast	40	1,363	−3.5	56	+9	−20.3	34.4
20. Smolensk Oblast	50	1,089	−1.5	58	+10	−21.1	21.9
21. Tula Oblast	26	1,924	−1.5	78	+7	−22.8	74.9
22. Vladimir Oblast	29	1,552	+2.6	73	+5	−14.7	53.5
23. Yaroslavl Oblast	36	1,405	+.36	77	+7	−21.5	38.6
III. Volgo-Vyatka	263	8,275	−.87			−17.2	31.5
24. Gorky Oblast	75	3,658	−.68	71	+6	−19.9	48.9
25. Kirov Oblast	121	1,662	−3.7	63	+8	−21.1	13.8
26. Chuvash A.S.S.R.	18	1,271	+3.8	44	+8	−8.8	69.4
27. Mari A.S.S.R.	23	699	+2.0	53	+12	−18.3	30.1
28. Mordvinian A.S.S.R.	26	985	−4.4	44	+8	−16.4	37.6
IV. Central Chernozem	167	7,761	−2.9			+18.5	46.5
29. Belgorod Oblast	27	1,264	+.24	48	+13	−20.1	46.6
30. Kursk Oblast	30	1,403	−4.8	45	+12	−22.5	47.1
31. Lipetsk Oblast	24	1,206	−1.5	53	+9	−16.9	50.0
32. Tambov Oblast	34	1,404	−7.1	47	+8	−19.8	40.9
33. Voronezh Oblast	52	2,484	−1.7	53	+7	−14.8	47.4
V. Volga	680	19,078	+3.8			−14.3	28.1
34. Astrakhan Oblast	44	910	+4.8	68	+7	−14.6	20.6
35. Kuybyshev Oblast	54	3,043	+10.6	78	+6	−13.1	56.8
36. Penza Oblast	43	1,493	−2.8	52	+8	−16.1	34.6
37. Saratov Oblast	100	2,522	+2.8	71	+6	−16.0	25.2
38. Ulyanovsk Oblast	37	1,234	+.73	61	+9	−18.5	33.1
39. Volgograd Oblast	114	2,434	+4.7	71	+5	−12.2	21.3
40. Bashkir A.S.S.R.	144	3,833	+.37	56	+8	−14.1	26.7
41. Kalmyk A.S.S.R.	76	276	+3.0	41	+7	−6.8	3.6
42. Tatar A.S.S.R.	68	3,333	+6.5	61	+9	−13.8	49.0
VI. North Caucasus	356	15,099	+5.7			−3.6	42.4
43. Krasnodar Kray	84	4,692	+4.0	51	+4	−3.2	56.1
44. Adyge A. Oblast	8	400	+3.6	46	+6	−7.7	52.7
45. Stavropol Kray	81	2,436	+5.6	49	+7	−6.0	30.2
46. Karachay-Cherkess A.O.	14	355	+2.9	42	+9	−11.2	25.1
47. Rostov Oblast	101	4,023	+5.0	68	+5	−8.6	39.9
48. Checken-Ingush A.S.S.R.	19	1,142	+7.2	44	+2	+3.7	59.2
49. Dagestan A.S.S.R.	50	1,560	+9.2	38	+3	+3.9	31.0
50. Kabardino-Balkar A.S.S.R.	13	654	+11.0	57	+9	−9.7	52.3
51. North Osetian A.S.S.R.	8	592	+7.0	68	+4	−3.6	74.0

Administrative Units. Numbers Correspond to Map Inside Front Cover	Territory 1000 km.²	Population 1000	Population Change 1970–1976 Per Cent	Per Cent Urban	Change in Per Cent Urban 1970–1976	Rural Population Change 1970–1976 Per Cent	Persons Per km.²
VII. Urals	681	15,385	+1.3			−16.6	22.6
52. Chelyabinsk Oblast	88	3,382	+2.8	82	+4	−14.3	38.5
53. Kurgan Oblast	71	1,061	−2.2	51	+8	−15.5	14.9
54. Orenburg Oblast	124	2,073	+1.1	60	+7	−14.0	16.7
55. Perm Oblast	161	2,989	−1.2	73	+6	−19.2	18.6
56. Komi-Permyak A. Okrug	33	182	−14.1	23	+4	−18.0	5.5
57. Sverdlovsk Oblast	195	4,417	+2.3	85	+4	−19.8	22.7
58. Udmurt A.S.S.R.	42	1,463	+3.2	65	+8	−16.0	34.8
VIII. Western Siberia	2,428	12,503	+3.2			−13.4	5.1
59. Altay Kray	262	2,643	−1.0	53	+7	−13.0	10.1
60. Gorno Altay A. Oblast	93	169	+.6	28	+4	−6.2	1.8
61. Kemerovo Oblast	96	2,932	+.48	86	+4	−19.1	30.7
62. Novosibirsk Oblast	178	2,559	+2.2	71	+6	−14.8	14.4
63. Omsk Oblast	140	1,898	+4.1	64	+9	−15.2	13.6
64. Tomsk Oblast	317	835	+6.2	67	+8	−13.4	2.6
65. Tyumen Oblast	1,435	1,636	+16.3	59	+10	−6.1	1.1
66. Khanti-Mansi A. Okrug	523	425	+56.3	74	+11	+11.9	.8
67. Yamal-Nenets A. Okrug	750	126	+57.5	56	+13	+19.6	.2
IX. Eastern Siberia	4,124	7,904	+5.9			−11.0	1.9
68. Krasnoyarsk Kray	2,402	3,079	+4.0	68	+6	−13.3	1.3
69. Khakass A. Oblast	62	474	+6.3	67	+7	−12.8	7.7
70. Evenki A. Okrug	768	14	+7.7	35	+7	0	.02
71. Taymyr A. Okrug	862	43	+13.2	64	+2	+7.1	.05
72. Chita Oblast	432	1,215	+6.1	63	+6	−6.8	2.8
73. Aga Buryat A. Okrug	19	68	+3.0	29	+8	−5.8	3.6
74. Irkutsk Oblast	768	2,492	+7.7	77	+5	−10.6	3.2
75. Ust-Orda Buryat A. Okrug	22	134	−8.2	20	+3	−10.7	6.0
76. Buryat A.S.S.R.	351	865	+6.5	56	+11	−14.7	2.5
77. Tuva A.S.S.R.	171	253	+9.5	41	+3	+3.5	1.5
X. Far East	6,216	6,579	+13.8			−1.6	1.1
78. Khabarovsk Kray	825	1,514	+12.5	80	+2	+2.3	1.8
79. Jewish A. Oblast	36	190	+9.8	69	0	+9.3	5.3
80. Maritime Kray	166	1,933	+12.3	76	+3	−2.4	11.6
81. Amur Oblast	364	901	+13.6	66	+4	+.66	2.5
82. Kamchatka Oblast	472	357	+24.4	83	+7	−11.8	.8
83. Koryak A. Okrug	302	34	+9.7	40	+6	0	.1
84. Magadan Oblast	1,199	433	+23.0	78	+3	+7.9	.4
85. Chukchi A. Okrug	738	125	+23.8	74	+5	+3.2	.2
86. Sakhalin Oblast	87	662	+7.5	83	+5	−15.0	7.6
87. Yakutsk A.S.S.R.	3,103	779	+17.3	63	+7	−13.8	.3
Ukraine S.S.R.							
XI. Donets-Dnieper	222	20,829	+3.8			−10.9	93.8
88. Dnepropetrovsk Oblast	32	3,570	+6.8	80	+4	−10.2	111.9
89. Donetsk Oblast	27	5,141	+5.0	89	+2	−8.1	194.0
90. Kharkov Oblast	31	2,976	+5.3	74	+5	−10.2	94.8
91. Kirovograd Oblast	25	1,261	+.08	50	+6	−10.3	51.2
92. Poltava Oblast	29	1,733	+1.6	48	+8	−12.6	60.2
93. Sumy Oblast	24	1,435	−4.7	49	+5	−13.8	60.3
94. Voroshilovgrad Oblast	27	2,819	+2.5	85	+2	−10.0	105.6
95. Zaporozhye Oblast	27	1,894	+6.7	71	+5	−9.9	69.6
XII. Southwest	271	21,313	+3.0			−7.5	78.6
96. Cherkassy Oblast	21	1,554	+1.2	43	+6	−9.0	74.4
97. Chernigov Oblast	32	1,515	−2.9	42	+7	−13.9	47.5
98. Chernovsty Oblast	8	880	+4.1	36	+1	+12.7	108.6
99. Ivano-Frankovsk Oblast	14	1,311	+4.9	35	+4	−1.0	94.4
100. Khmelnitsky Oblast	21	1,577	−2.4	33	+6	−11.0	76.6
101. Kiev City }	29	2,013	+23.3	100	0	0 }	134.5
102. Kiev Oblast }		1,875	+2.1	43	+7	−9.1 }	
103. Lvov Oblast	22	2,517	+3.7	52	+5	−4.9	115.5
104. Rovno Oblast	20	1,095	+4.5	33	+5	−3.2	54.5
105. Ternopol Oblast	14	1,173	+1.7	28	+5	−4.9	85.0
106. Transcarpathia Oblast	13	1,134	+7.3	35	+5	−.40	88.6
107. Vinnitsa Oblast	27	2,073	−2.8	32	+7	−11.6	78.2
108. Volyn Oblast	20	1,011	+3.7	37	+5	−4.5	50.0
109. Zhitomir Oblast	30	1,585	−2.5	42	+7	−12.9	53.0

Table 2-1   (Continued)

Administrative Units. Numbers Correspond to Map Inside Front Cover	Territory 1000 km.²	Population 1000	Population Change 1970–1976 Per Cent	Per Cent Urban	Change in Per Cent Urban 1970–1976	Rural Population Change 1970–1976 Per Cent	Persons Per km.²
XIII. South	114	6,933	+8.6			−4.0	60.8
110. Crimea Oblast	27	2,062	+13.7	67	+4	+3.1	76.4
111. Kherson Oblast	29	1,113	+8.0	59	+5	−4.6	39.1
112. Nikolayev Oblast	25	1,215	+5.8	60	+7	−9.8	49.4
113. Odessa Oblast	33	2,543	+6.4	61	+5	−5.2	76.4
XIV. Baltic	189	8,035	+6.0			−7.0	42.5
114. Lithuanian S.S.R.	65	3,315	+5.9	57	+7	−9.3	50.8
115. Vilna City		447	+20.2	100	0	0	
116. Lativa S.S.R.	64	2,497	+5.6	66	+4	−4.6	39.2
117. Riga City		806	+10.1	100	0	0	
118. Estonia S.S.R.	45	1,438	+6.0	68	+3	−4.0	31.9
119. Tallinn City		408	+12.4	100	0	0	
120. Kaliningrad Oblast	15	785	+7.2	77	+4	−7.2	52.0
XV. Transcaucasus	187	13,477	+9.6			+3.5	72.1
121. Georgia S.S.R.	70	4,954	+5.7	51	+3	0	71.1
122. Tbilisi City		1,030	+15.9	100	0	0	
123. Abkhaz A.S.S.R.	9	500	+2.7	48	+4	−3.7	58.1
124. Adzhar A.S.S.R.	3	343	+10.6	46	+2	+7.5	114.3
125. South Osetian A. Oblast	4	103	+3.0	40	+3	−3.2	26.3
126. Azerbaydzhan S.S.R.	87	5,689	+11.3	52	+2	+7.7	65.7
127. Baku City		1,406	+11.1	100	0	0	
128. Nakhichevan A.S.S.R.	6	227	+12.4	25	+1	+1.1	41.2
129. Nagorno-Karabakh A. Oblast	4	156	+4.7	41	+3	−1.1	35.4
130. Armenia S.S.R.	30	2,834	+13.7	64	+5	+1.7	95.1
131. Yerevan City		928	+21.0	100	0	0	
XVI. Central Asia	1,277	23,514	+17.8			+14.4	18.4
132. Uzbek S.S.R.	447	14,079	+17.7	39	+3	+13.1	31.5
133. Andizhan Oblast	4	1,259	+18.8	28	+4	+12.8	299.9
134. Bukhara Oblast	143	1,149	+23.0	34	+3	+18.1	8.0
*135. Dzhizak Oblast	20	426		19			21.0
136. Fergana Oblast	7	1,593	+19.8	35	+2	+16.9	224.0
137. Kashka Darya Oblast	28	972	+21.2	20	+3	+16.0	34.2
138. Khorezm Oblast	5	666	+20.2	19	0	+19.5	148.0
139. Namangan Oblast	8	1,024	+20.9	34	+5	+12.3	129.6
140. Samarkand Oblast	25	1,610	+9.5	30	+3	+4.8	65.7
141. Surkhan Darya Oblast	21	801	+21.0	18	+2	+18.0	38.5
*142. Syr Darya Oblast	5	416	−43.6	30	+7	−48.2	78.5
143. Tashkent City }	.16	1,643	+18.6	100	0	0 }	214.0
144. Tashkent Oblast }		1,695	+14.5	43	+3	+9.0 }	
145. Kara Kalpak A.S.S.R.	166	825	+17.5	38	+2	+12.1	5.0
146. Kirgiz S.S.R.	199	3,368	+14.8	39	+2	+12.0	17.0
147. Frunze City		498	+15.5	100	0	0	
*148. Issyk Kul Oblast	44	349		31			8.0
*149. Naryn Oblast	50	214		17			4.3
150. Osh Oblast	74	1,463	+18.7	31	0	+17.8	19.8
151. Tadzhik S.S.R.	143	3,486	+20.2	37	0	+19.9	24.4
152. Dushanbe City		448	+19.8	100	0	0	
153. Kulyab Oblast	13	446		25			34.6
154. Leninabad Oblast	26	1,116		38			42.8
155. Gorno-Badakhshan A. Oblast	64	116	+18.4	13	0	+17.4	1.8
156. Turkmen S.S.R.	488	2,581	+19.6	49	+1	+18.2	5.3
157. Ashkhabad City }	95	297	+17.4	100	0	0 }	6.9
*158. Ashkhabad Oblast }		360		32		}	
*159. Chardzhou Oblast	94	553		46			5.9
*160. Krasnovodsk Oblast	139	297		82			2.1
*161. Mary Oblast	87	588		33			6.8
*162. Tashauz Oblast	74	488		31			6.6

Administrative Units. Numbers Correspond to Map Inside Front Cover	Territory 1000 km.²	Population 1000	Population Change 1970–1976 Per Cent	Per Cent Urban	Change in Per Cent Urban 1970–1976	Rural Population Change 1970–1976 Per Cent	Persons Per km.²
XVII. 163. <u>Kazakh S.S.R.</u>	2,719	14,377	+11.6				5.3
164. Aktyubinsk Oblast	299	609	+10.7	47	+2	+7.6	2.0
165. Alma Ata City ⎫		851	+16.6	100	0	0 ⎫	
166. Alma Ata Oblast ⎭	105	820	+15.0	20	+2	+12.9 ⎭	16.0
167. Chimkent Oblast	116	1,474	+30.7	40	−1	+33.7	12.7
168. Dzhambul Oblast	145	905	+13.8	45	+5	+5.3	6.3
*169. Dzhezkazgan Oblast	313	462		80			1.5
170. East Kazakhstan Oblast	97	864	+2.1	60	+3	−5.0	8.9
*171. Guryev Oblast	112	371	−25.7	62	−4	−15.4	3.3
*172. Karaganda Oblast	85	1,251	−19.4	86	+5	−39.2	14.6
173. Kokchetav Oblast	78	611	+3.6	34	+4	−1.2	7.8
*174. Kustanay Oblast	115	934	−5.2	46	+7	−16.6	8.2
175. Kzyl Orda Oblast	228	542	+10.2	60	+5	−2.7	2.4
*176. Mangyshlak Oblast	167	239		90			1.4
177. North Kazakhstan Oblast	44	558	+.18	42	+4	−6.7	12.6
178. Pavlodar Oblast	128	778	+11.6	55	+6	−2.0	6.1
179. Semipalatinsk Oblast	180	760	+6.7	49	+5	−1.0	4.2
180. Taldy Kurgan Oblast	119	671	+1.0	41	+2	+6.4	5.7
*181. Tselinograd Oblast	125	812	−7.8	57	+7	−20.2	6.5
*182. Turgay Oblast	112	262		32			2.3
183. Uralsk Oblast	151	563	+9.7	36	+5	+1.1	3.7
XVIII. 184. <u>Belorussia S.S.R.</u>	207	9,371	+4.1			−11.6	45.3
185. Brest Oblast	32	1,334	+3.0	42	+7	−9.0	41.3
186. Gomel Oblast	40	1,563	+1.9	49	+9	−13.5	38.7
187. Grodno Oblast	25	1,126	+.45	40	+7	−9.7	45.0
188. Minsk City ⎫		1,189	+29.8	100	0	0 ⎫	
189. Minsk Oblast ⎭	41	1,525	−.97	32	+5	−8.8 ⎭	66.5
190. Mogilev Oblast	29	1,244	+1.4	52	+9	−16.2	42.9
191. Vitebsk Oblast	40	1,390	+1.5	54	+9	−14.3	34.7
XIX. 192. <u>Moldavian S.S.R.</u>	34	3,850	+7.8	37	+5	−.98	114.3
193. Kishinev City		471	+32.3	100	0	0	

Source: *Narkhoz SSSR*, 1969, pp. 13–18 and 1975, pp. 16–21.
*Created or changed during 1970–1976.
Underlined names are the nineteen official Soviet economic regions for planning and statistical reporting.
The author is grateful to Julie Mintz for compiling this table.

which must be of the titular nationality group). After this maneuver had failed to serve its purpose, in 1956, simply by inserting a sentence in the newspaper, the Soviets abolished the Karelo-Finnish Republic and downgraded it to the status of A.S.S.R. within the Russian Republic.

Since 1956 the political subdivision of the country has remained fairly stable, although there have been a multitude of minute changes going on constantly. But the fifteen S.S.R.s have remained as they were since 1956 and are listed in Table 2–1 with their present subdivisions, grouped according to economic regions. (Also, see map inside front cover) The new constitution adopted on October 7, 1977 left the current administrative units intact even though the Russians have migrated into national areas and diluted the national populations so much over the years that hardly any of the A.S.S.R.s satisfy the titular majority requirements of the present constitution and two of the S.S.R.s no longer do. (Tables 6–8 and 6–9)

The Kazakh S.S.R. is the most obvious discrepancy. Russians outnumber Kazakhs in the entire republic, and the far flung territory of the republic contains two distinctly different populated areas, the north and the south, which are separated by a wide expanse of practically uninhabited desert. The northern tier of oblasts is primarily Russian, Ukrainian, and German agricultural settlers whose economic and social situations are much more similar to adjacent parts of Western Siberia than they are to the rest of the Kazakh Republic. The southern tier of oblasts is a mixture of rural natives carrying on irrigation agriculture and Russian cities which are similar to the oasis settlements in the Central Asian Republics adjacent to them. The Kazakh Republic had no tradition prior to the Bolshevik takeover, and is a mental construct of the Soviet Regime. It has never been a good geographical region. It appeared for a while during the 1950s when the Virgin Lands in Northern Kazakhstan were being opened up that the stage was being set for splitting off this part of the Republic and perhaps joining it with the West Siberian Region in the Russian Republic. A new political entity, Tselinnyy Kray (Virgin Lands Kray), was constituted as a super region to encompass five existing oblasts in the virgin lands of northern Kazakhstan. But later other krays were formed in the Kazakh Republic that made less sense, and then finally all the krays were abolished and the republic reverted back again to simply an oblast subdivision.

Now, in 1976 the Soviet Union adopted a geographic code, similar to that developed by the Bureau of Census in the United States in 1973, to designate existing political entities by ten-digit code numbers. Two volumes containing more than 1000 pages have been published to be circulated throughout the country so that people can refer to the Soviet Union's 2000 cities, 3700 urban workers settlements, and 41,000 rural places that are seats of rural Soviets by number to facilitate mailing and so forth.[1] All this elaborate computerization and codification of the political subdivisions of the country would seem to indicate that no significant changes are anticipated in the foreseeable future. Thus, it appears that tradition and local

vested interest have won out in the long run over Marxian ideology and the political administrative units will be more enduring than economic situations.

At the beginning of 1976 the Soviet Union was subdivided as is shown in Table 1. Fifteen Soviet Socialist Republics (S.S.R.s, Union Republics) represent fifteen of the most populous and culturally advanced groups of peoples in the U.S.S.R. Administratively they correspond somewhat to the 50 states of the United States.

Actually, according to the constitution of the U.S.S.R., the Union Republics have wider latitudes of jurisdiction than do the states of the United States. The constitution of the U.S.S.R. is really a confederate one, reserving the rights of the individual member republics to coin money, enter into foreign agreements, and secede from the Union at any time. In practice, little attention is paid to the constitution in the Soviet Union, and the individual republics have little latitude of operation outside the surveillance of Moscow. The Russian Republic is much bigger and much more populous than any of the other republics, and it definitely is the "first among equals." The provisions of the constitution are adhered to only when it is expedient to do so. A good illustration of this is the fact that three seats are occupied in the United Nations by the Soviet Union; one for the U.S.S.R., one for the Ukrainian Republic, and one for the Belorussian Republic, with the contention that these republics really are independent countries.

The union republics, except for some of the smaller ones, are divided into oblasts, krays, and autonomous soviet socialist republics (A.S.S.R.), all of which are on a commensurate level of jurisdiction, and all of which are directly responsible to their respective union republics. The oblast is purely an administrative subdivision that contains no significant nationality group other than the titular nationality of the union republic within which it is located. The A.S.S.R. administratively serves the same function as the oblast, but its boundaries have been drawn to give political recognition to an important minority nationality group. A kray is a kind of combination of the

[1]*Obshchesoyuznyy klassifikator. Sistema oboznacheniy obyektov administrativno-territorialnogo deleniya Soyuza SSR i soyuznykh respublik a takzhe naselennykh punktov* (All-Union Classifier. System of designations for administrative-territorial entities of the U.S.S.R. and its Union Republics as well as for populated places), Statistika, Moscow, 1976. Volume 1 (606 pages) covers the R.S.F.S.R., and Volume 2 (470 pages) the 14 other union republics.

Table 2–2   Numbers of Political Subdivisions by Union Republics as of January 1, 1976

	A.S.S.R.	Autonomous Oblast	Autonomous Okrug	Krays and Oblasts	Rayons	City Rayons	Cities Total	Cities: Those Directly Under the Jurisdiction of Republics, Krays, Oblasts, or Okrugs	Urban-Type Settlements	Rural Soviets
U.S.S.R.	20	8	10	126[1]	3118	567	2029	904	3757	41175
R.S.F.S.R.	16	5	10	55[1]	1783	342	994	539	1998	22681
Ukraine				25	477	115	394	124	892	8561
Belorussia				6	117	16	96	33	109	1514
Uzbek	1			11	134	9	76	44	86	960
Kazakh				19	210	29	82	49	183	2125
Georgia	2	1			66	8	51	13	60	924
Azerbaydzhan	1	1			61	10	60	11	125	1043
Lithuania					44	7	92	9	21	600
Moldavia					34	3	21	9	36	710
Latvia					26	6	56	7	36	507
Kirgiz				3	34	4	17	15	32	360
Tadzhik		1		2	41	4	18	12	47	289
Armenia					36	7	24	21	33	468
Turkmen				5	40	3	15	12	73	227
Estonia					15	4	33	6	26	206

[1]Includes 6 krays.
Source: Narkhoz SSSR, 1975, p. 44.

other two. Its boundaries have been laid out rather arbitrarily, primarily for administrative facility, but it contains within it lesser political subdivisions that are based on nationality groups — autonomous oblasts (A.O.) or autonomous okrugs or both. Theoretically any administrative unit can contain within it nationality-based political units on any of the lower echelons. For instance, several oblasts encompass autonomous okrugs. But an oblast cannot contain an autonomous oblast. An administrative unit containing an autonomous oblast would become a kray. In a sense, then, the kray is a higher unit than is the oblast, but they are both directly responsible to a union republic. (Fig. 2–1)

Oblasts, krays, and A.S.S.R.s are all divided into "rayons." The rayons are composed of village soviets in rural areas and a number of lesser units in urban areas, the lowest of which is the "settlement of urban type." Urban type settlements and small cities are under the jurisdiction of their respective rayons, but when an urban center reaches a certain size, usually 50,000 population, but less if it has a special economic significance, it may be moved from the rayon control and placed under the jurisdiction of the A.S.S.R., oblast, kray, autonomous oblast, or autonomous okrug in which it is situated. A number of major cities are placed under the direct control of union republics. These include republic capitals and, in the

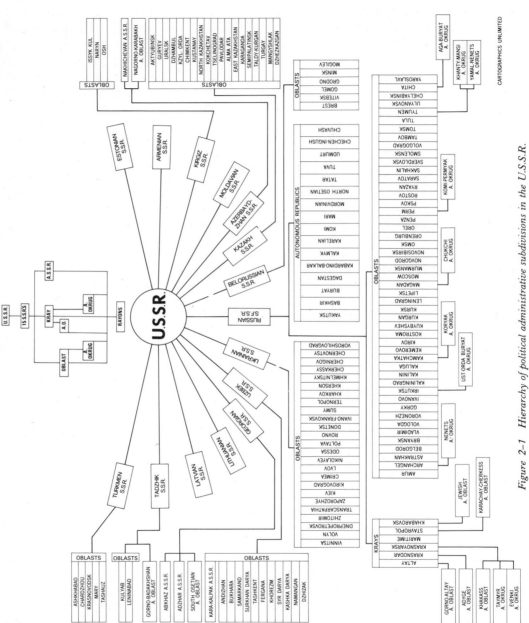

Figure 2–1   Hierarchy of political administrative subdivisions in the U.S.S.R.

R.S.F.S.R., some other centers with populations exceeding 300,000. Such cities themselves are divided into urban rayons.

A nationality group is given political recognition in one of the following four administrative units ranked in decreasing order of importance: (1) S.S.R., (2) A.S.S.R., (3) A.O., and (4) Autonomous Okrug. The autonomous okrug is usually assigned to large remote areas of sparse population such as areas in northern Siberia occupied by seminomadic reindeer herders. In cultural development these areas might be likened to Indian reservations in the United States. However, the autonomous okrugs in the Soviet Union do have some representation in the national government. There are many small nationality groups in the U.S.S.R. that have no political identities because of their limited numbers. There are also some larger and more significant groups, particularly the Germans and Poles, who have no regional identities because their people are scattered.

The political administrative organization of the U.S.S.R. is complex. It embodies elements of administrative convenience, nationality recognition, and traditionalism. It also contains some inconsistencies. Tuva came into the Soviet Union in 1944 and was made an autonomous oblast directly responsible to the Russian Republic (R.S.F.S.R.). Since then it has been elevated to the status of A.S.S.R. Primorskiy (Maritime) Kray in the Far East has no nationality-based political unit within it. It once included oblasts and was therefore called a kray. The oblasts were later abolished, but the kray designation remained. For a few years in the early 1960s, several krays were established in Kazakhstan, each of which contained several oblasts but no nationality-based subdivisions. Now these krays have been abolished.

Each nationality-based political unit has representation in the House of Nationalities in the legislative branch of the national government as follows: each S.S.R., 32 representatives; each A.S.S.R., 11; each A.O., 5; and each autonomous okrug, 1. In the House of the Union, on the other hand, one representative is chosen for every 300,000 people. Thus the U.S.S.R. has a bicameral legislature with a House of Nationalities corresponding roughly to the United States Senate and a House of the Union corresponding to the United States House of Representatives. There the analogy ends, however, for the two houses in the U.S.S.R. always meet in joint session as the Supreme Soviet and act only as a rubber stamp body to approve legislation initiated by the Central Committee of the Communist Party. The executive and judicial branches of the government grow out of the Supreme Soviet and are dependent on it. A Council of Ministers, stemming from the economic administrative setup, is the real political administrative body, and since many of its members also hold high-ranking positions in the Communist Party, it does an efficient job of carrying out party directives.

ECONOMIC ADMINISTRATIVE REGIONS

It is obvious that the political administrative regions in the Soviet Union have not corresponded very closely to economic conditions, because there have been simultaneous uses made of systems of economic regions ever since the GOELRO (State Commission for the Electrification of Russia) plan formulated in 1920. Shortly thereafter the State Planning Committee (GOSPLAN) was established, and one of its stated functions was to divide the country into economic regions for planning purposes. In 1921 GOSPLAN put forth such a regionalization which divided the U.S.S.R. into 21 major economic regions. This was laid out to facilitate the achievement of two major considerations: (1) a geographical division of labor within the country that would result in each economic region acquiring a specialization in one or more of the main branches of the economy, and (2) the creation of a diverse, largely self-sufficient economy within each region.

This apparent conflict of goals for homogeneity on the one hand and heterogeneity on the other has created a lasting source for debate about regionalization schemes for the Soviet Union and the investment of capital therein. The balance between regional specialization and regional self-sufficiency has teeter-tottered through time as the national and international scenes have varied. Standing as a counterbalance to the entire regionalization hierarchy has been the planning and management of the economy by vertically centralized sectors through ministries located in Moscow. This was particularly true during the Stalin era and has been true again since 1965.

Therefore, even though a two-tiered system of 13 major economic regions for planning purposes and a subordinate set of more numerous, smaller management regions for industry and agriculture existed with a minimum of change from 1940 to 1957, the major economic regions had no planning or administrative bodies of their own and were in actuality nothing more than statistical reporting regions for the use of GOSPLAN. The subordinate economic-administrative regions controlled only agriculture and industries of local importance, while the industries of national importance were managed from the center through the various ministries.

In 1957 Khrushchev initiated a major break in the previous system. Most of the ministries were abolished and 105 soviets of the national economy (sovnarkhozy) were established to plan, budget, and manage all forms of economic activity within their respective regions. A few sectors of the economy such as the construction of large hydroelectric plants or management of railroads remained under centralized control, but the 105 sovnarkhoz regions became the primary controlling units, although a framework of major economic regions was retained to oversee and coordinate the work of the sovnarkhozy, apparently to assure the integration, diversification, and development of each of the larger subdivisions of the U.S.S.R. However, the larger units did not function very well, and the sovnarkhozy quickly usurped most of the power and developed regional autarkies as inflexible and detrimental to the general economy as the ministerial ones had been.

In 90 out of 105 cases the sovnarkhozy areal

units coincided with preexisting political administrative divisions at various levels, and for a time it looked as though there was going to be a rapid convergence of political and economic administrative regions. But the rapid development of regional autarky and consequent inefficiencies induced in the production process prompted the Soviet leadership to initiate more changes, and in 1961–1963 the 105 sovnarkhoz regions were consolidated into 47 larger units while the 13 major economic regions were increased to 19 (18 + Moldavia, which doesn't belong to any region!) and for the first time provided with their own organizing bodies. These were the councils for the coordination of planning, whose functions were to coordinate the plans of the various sovnarkhozy within their regions and to plan the integrated economic development of each major region as a whole. However, these councils for coordination and planning were still purely advisory and could only submit recommendations to the sovnarkhozy on the one hand and to the U.S.S.R. and republican GOSPLANS on the other, which either adopted them or rejected them at will. The 47 sovnarkhoz regions became referred to as industrial management regions (IMR), and the 19 major economic regions were MER.

The system of control became extremely complex, and there was much functional overlap between such bodies as the GOSPLANS of the U.S.S.R. and its constituent republics, the planning commissions for the major economic regions, the industrial management councils for the industrial management regions, executive committees at the level of the economic administrative areas, and the managements of individual farms, factories, and other enterprises. In addition, in late 1962 there had been created U.S.S.R. state production committees for various country-wide industries which had extraterritorial jurisdiction within the various regions. And certain very specialized regions were put in control of similar industries in neighboring regions. For instance, the Middle Volga IMR, which was very specialized in oil and petrochemicals, was given jurisdiction over the oil industry in adjacent Perm and Orenburg oblasts of the western and southern Urals IMRs respectively. In like manner, the iron and steel plants of the Bashkir A.S.S.R., which lay within the Central Volga IMR, were operated by the south Urals industrial management council.

One of the problems of all regionalization schemes for the planning and management of the economy has been the principle of ethnic autonomy. Political administrative regions based on ethnic groups are not to be divided and placed in different economic regions in juxtaposition with other areas. A nationality-based political unit can be combined in its entirety with other political units in a given economic region, or a nationality based political unit can be subdivided into several different economic regions, but a part of a nationality-based political unit cannot be included with other areas in a given economic region and other parts of that same nationality-based political unit placed in other economic regions. As time has gone on, the Soviets have tried to play down this principle of ethnic autonomy, and at present they are talking about a Soviet nationality rather than all the individual nationalities of the Soviet Union, but they still have to pay a good deal of lip service to the various national groups.

During the early 1960s the term "territorial production complex" (TPC) came into popular discussion. This was conceived as a functioning territorial unit that would be identified first of all according to a specialized activity in a region, but which also would have to have auxillary industries to supply certain necessities to the specialized industries, and also industries such as production of building materials and consumer goods that were necessary to any region to make it an economic whole. Thus the territorial production complex should have a diversified economy but one in which most of the production is "organically interrelated and mutually conditioned." (Incidentally, such a diversified or rounded economy would also provide full employment, the achievement of which has become quite a problem in many developing areas where one major heavy industry, such as mining or forestry or a construction project, has enticed men into an area but has left the rest of the members of the family without jobs in such things as light industries to which they were accustomed.)

About the time it appeared that some sort of all-purpose regional subdivision of the U.S.S.R. was about to emerge, in 1965 the new regime after the demise of Khrushchev quickly swung into action to reverse the trends of the previous eight years and reestablish a strong centralized control of industry. In October 1965 the Supreme Soviet adopted a law that established 28 ministries, some all-union and some union-republic. The powers of the U.S.S.R. GOSPLAN were expanded, and regional economic councils at all levels were abolished. Now the only territorial units remaining with any economic functions are the union republics, and even at this level the branch management principle is paramount. The 19 major economic regions have been retained pretty much as they were established in 1961, except for some shifting of political subdivisions from one region to another, but these again have become only statistical reporting regions, with perhaps some planning functions, although they have no planning bodies of their own. GOSPLAN to a certain extent uses these regions to provide a framework for planning future development capital. (See map inside front cover)

It appears that some sort of compromise between branch and territorial systems of industrial management is still in the offing, since neither on its own has so far proved completely satisfactory, but at present the branch line of management holds the upper hand. This will be covered in more detail in Chapter 16 in a discussion of prospects for regional development.

Reading List

1. Bone, Robert M., "Regional Planning and Economic Regionalization in the Soviet Union," *Land Economics,* August 1967, pp. 347–354.
2. Dewdney, John C., *Patterns and Problems of Regionalization in the U.S.S.R.,* Research Papers

Series No. 8, Department of Geography, University of Durham, 1967, 42 pp.

3. Lonsdale, R. E., "The Soviet Concept of the Territorial-Production Complex," *Slavic Review,* September 1965, pp. 466–478.

4. Lydolph, Paul E., "The Soviet Reorganization of Industry," *American Slavic and East European Review,* October 1958, pp. 293–301.

5. Melezin, Abraham, "Soviet Regionalization: An Attempt at the Delineation of Socio-economic Integrated Regions," *Geographical Review,* October 1968, pp. 593–621.

6. Mieczkowski, Z., "The 1962-63 Reforms in Soviet Economic Regionalization," *Slavic Review,* September 1965, pp. 479–496.

7. ———, "The Major Economic Regions of the U.S.S.R. in the Khrushchev Era," *Canadian Geographer,* September 1965, pp. 19–30.

8. ———, "The Economic Regionalization of the Soviet Union in the Lenin and Stalin Periods," *The Canadian Slavonic Papers,* 1966, pp. 89–124.

9. ———, "The Economic Administrative Regions in the U.S.S.R.," *Tijdschrift voor Econ. en Soc. Geografie,* July–August 1967, pp. 209–219.

3

Geological Structure and Land Form[1]

The huge land mass of the Soviet Union contains a wide variety of geological structures and surface forms that have evolved separately during different geological epochs. Segments of land formed by a succession of orogenic processes have at the present time coalesced into a rather compact land mass which very simply consists of the most extensive plain on earth in the western half of the country fringed by a modern orogenic belt of mountains and seas on the south that spreads eastward to include the entire width of the Asian landmass along the margins of the Pacific. (See fold map at end of book) Different segments of the earth's crust in the Soviet Union have participated in four basic geosynclinal sequences that have initially undergone prolonged subsidence and accumulation of great thicknesses of sediments, and then been subjected to extreme lateral pressures, metamorphoses, and upfoldings generally associated with magmatic intrusions and extrusive volcanic activity. In the older geosynclinal areas this has been followed by peneplanation and sometimes subsequent block faulting and broad warping.

The oldest structures within the boundaries

of the Soviet Union are the Russian Platform in the west and the Siberian Platform in the east. (Fig. 3–1) These two areas underwent the so-called Caledonian orogeny during the lower Paleozoic, since which time they have been peneplaned and moved vertically a few hundred meters up and down out of the sea accumulating veneers of horizontal strata of sedimentary materials on top of basement complexes of extreme alteration and intermingling of igneous and metamorphic materials. For the last half billion years or more these two parts of the earth's crust have acted as stable blocks that have resisted orogenic movements against whose fringes weaker materials in younger geosynclinal troughs have been crushed up into mountain ranges or downwarped farther into mountain foredeeps. Such are the Uralian geosyncline that developed through much of the Paleozoic era and finally resulted in the elongated Ural Mountains on the eastern side of the Russian Platform and the Angaran geosyncline that formed at about the same time in the area that is now northeastern Kazakhstan, the Altay Mountain area of Western Siberia, and the southern fringes of Eastern Siberia extending northeastward east of Lake Baykal. Orogenic movements culminated in these regions during the middle Carboniferous-Permian geological periods that was known as the Hercynian orogeny.

A broad area of the more continental parts of

[1]For more detailed information on individual parts of the Soviet Union, see appropriate sections of Lydolph, Paul E., *Geography of the U.S.S.R.,* third edition, Wiley, New York, 1977.

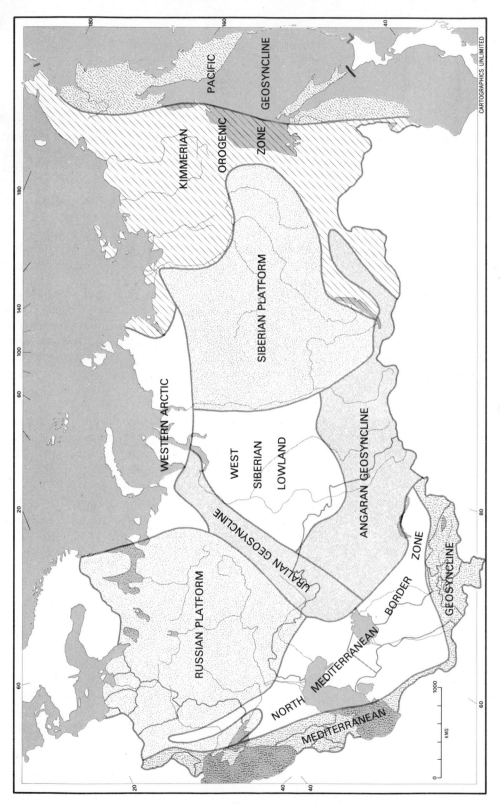

Figure 3-1   Geological structure of the U.S.S.R. Modified from Nalivkin, 1960, p. 152.

the Soviet Far East along the eastern edge of the Siberian Platform underwent a geosynclinal process a little later and reached its mountain building culmination in the Kimmerian orogeny during the Triassic-Jurassic-lower Cretaceous periods of the Mesozoic era. The fourth and youngest geosynclinal process which is now undergoing extreme orogenic movement includes two widely separated regions, one extending eastward from the Mediterranean to the Black Sea-Caucasus-Caspian Sea-Central Asian Mountains, and the other extending along the Pacific border lands. This is known as the Alpine orogeny which began in the upper Cretaceous period and is still continuing.

In between these most easily identified geosynclinal regions lie intermediate areas of complex structures which have undergone processes related to the geosynclinal actions on either side. For instance, the broad expanse of the West Siberian Lowland between the Urals and the Siberian Platform has been formed by both marine and continental sedimentation to depths of 3000–6000 meters in a gigantic depression that was downwarped primarily during the late Paleozoic-early Mesozoic periods.

The merged surface expressions of these geosynclinal regions and their intermediate areas result today in a number of gross regions such as the East European Plain, the Urals, the West Siberian Lowland, the Central Siberian Upland, the Caucasus, Central Asia, and the high mountains along the southern and eastern fringes of the country. Each of these topographic regions will be taken up in turn and related to the aforementioned orogenic movements.

THE EAST EUROPEAN PLAIN

The East European Plain is underlain by a Precambrian basement complex of metamorphic and igneous rocks over which a veneer of several hundred meters thickness of Paleozoic and Mesozoic marine sediments have been laid in nearly horizontal fashion as the area has been depressed and uplifted as a single block in and out of the sea.

The Basement Complex

The surface of the Precambrian basement overall describes a basin which is more deeply covered by sedimentary layers in the center than on the edges. In the vicinity of Moscow the sedimentary mantle is more than 1200 meters thick while north of Leningrad the sedimentary cover pinches out entirely, and the basement complex becomes the surface rock throughout Karelia and the Kola Peninsula. Also in the south, the basement complex rises toward the surface in the Ukrainian crystalline massif southwest of the Dnieper River and in fact is exposed at the surface in some of the deeper river valleys, especially that of the Dnieper where the river ceases flowing southeast along the strike of the structure and makes a right turn toward the southwest, cutting through the crystalline structure and flowing down the gentle slope of the sediments on the surface of the Black Sea Steppes.

Although the gross feature of the surface of the basement complex is that of a basin, there are many irregularities, some of them of great magnitude. (Fig. 3-2) Chief among these is the broad Voronezh Dome underlying the southern portion of the present Central Chernozem Region and adjacent parts of Ukraine, where the basement rises to within 400 meters of the surface, and the adjacent Dnieper-Donetsk trough on its southwest which describes a deep, narrow downfolded and faulted Precambrian trench that runs from the Donets Basin in the eastern Ukraine northwestward to the southeastern edge of the Belorussian Rise. In places within this trough the Carboniferous layers reach thicknesses of 10,000–12,000 meters. They consist primarily of shaly limestones containing thick seams of coal, the Shebelinka gas field south of Kharkov, the Priluki oil fields east of Kiev, and the Rechitsa oil fields in southeastern Belorussia.

Other major discrepancies in the basement complex are the Moscow Basin centered on the

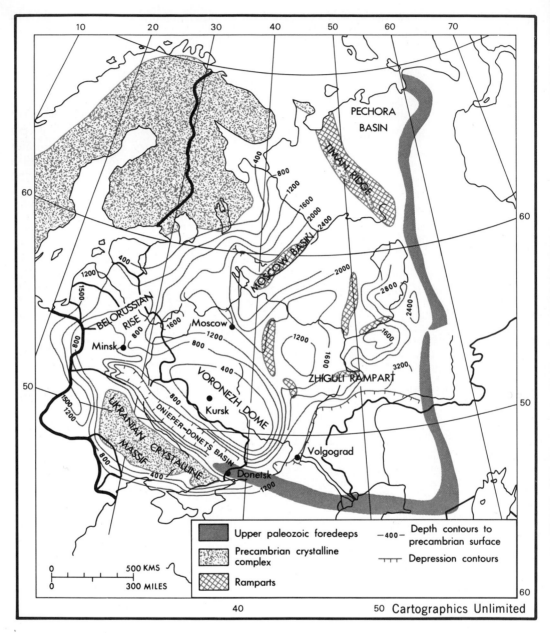

Figure 3–2   Surface configuration of Precambrian basement complex of Russian Platform. Depth contours in meters below ground surface. After Shlygin, p. 50.

Sukhona River Valley northeast of the city of Moscow, where the sediments are more than 2400 meters thick, and further northeast the Timan Ridge which runs northwestward from the middle Urals to the Arctic Coast and across the northern end of the Kanin Peninsula. The warped sedimentary layers overlying both of these features also contain significant quantities of mineral fuels. The Moscow Coal Basin has been producing low grade brown coal for many years primarily along the southwestern edge of the Moscow Basin where it comes into contact with the Voronezh Dome.

The Krivoy Rog and Kursk iron ore deposits

are found in Precambrian quartzites associated with the Voronezh Dome and the Ukrainian Crystalline Massif, as is the Nikopol manganese deposit. In the Kola Peninsula and Karelia the crystalline mass contains apatite, nickel, copper, and small iron deposits.

Many other lesser deviations occur on the basement surface which in some cases are expressed at the surface of the sedimentary rocks and in some cases are metalliferously significant. The largest of these consist of a series of subsurface ridges that lie in the vicinity of the middle and lower Volga generally producing prominent rises in surface topographic features. The most conspicuous of these is the Zhiguli Ridge, an east-west flexure that cuts across the general north-south strike of the features in this area and forces the large horseshoe bend of the Volga River at Kuybyshev. This, and other subsurface features that have surface expressions, will be discussed in the next section.

Around the edges of the Russian Platform a downwarped foredeep parallels the western edge of the Urals all the way from the Arctic to the Caspian Lowland and then swings westward into the Donets Basin. Devonian, Carboniferous, and Permian sediments contain the Pechora Coal Basin in the north, the Perm, Tatar, and Bashkir oil fields in the center, the Emba oil fields in the southeast, and the Donets Coal Basin in the west. This foredeep is picked up again along the southwestern border of the Platform in the northeastern foothills of the Carpathians where mineral fuels, salts, and sulfur are found. All mineral deposits will be discussed in detail in Chapter 11.

Surface Rock Structure and Topography

The sedimentary veneer has filled in the basins and troughs of the basement complex and produced a surface that is essentially level throughout the East European Plain. However, the minor vertical movements that have lifted this broad plain in and out of the sea have caused some horizontal warping, and occasionally the subsurface structure also is expressed topographically. Although warpings of the sedimentary strata have been incomparably broader than they have high, dip slopes of rocks commonly being much less than one degree, this has been enough to influence stream erosion processes which through the years have produced a cuestaform plain. Thus, the plain is far from featureless. In some areas it is deeply eroded and quite hilly, and along its southern and northern margins there are actually small mountains.

One of the main upwarps forms the so-called Central Russian Uplands which extend north-northwest — south-southeast across the middle of the plain from the Valday area northwest of Moscow to the southern portion of the Central Chernozem Region bordering on the eastern Ukraine. Elevations rise to 343 meters above sea level in the northern portion of the upland and diminish to less than 275 meters in the southern end. The upland generally stands 100 meters or more above the lowlands on either side. (Refer to fold map at end of book)

To the east of the upland a major downwarp with much less eroded surface stretches from the Volga Valley in the north across the Oka River and into the drainage basin of the Don River in the south. This plain is generally known as the Oka-Don Lowland or the Tambov Plain after the city of Tambov which sits in the center of it. The land rises again to the east into the Volga Heights which stretch along the west side of the Volga River all the way from the bend at Kazan to Volgograd in the south. The upland dips below a saddle occupied by the Volga-Don Canal and then rises a little again in the so-called Yergeny Upland in the western part of the Kalmyk A.S.S.R.

The Volga River in its erosional process has adjusted to the strike of the rock in this area and worn its way laterally down the dip slope of the rock toward the west, thereby keeping a steep escarpment on the right bank of the river and planing off a low, flat region on the left bank known as the Trans Volga Meadows. The Volga Heights reach 329 meters above sea level just to the west of the city of Saratov.

Farther north, the transverse block of the Zhiguli reaches heights of 375 meters above sea level and 335 meters above the water level of the Volga at this point. Hence the local relief here is more than 1000 feet, a truly imposing topographic feature that resembles low mountains.

The Zhiguli are the most imposing feature on the entire East European Plain other than the fringing mountains on the south, in the Crimea and the Carpathians, and the Khibiny in the far north on the Kola Peninsula. This block of dense limestone has been formed by a flexure in the earth's crust that dips 20–40° along the northern limb and only 3–5° on the south. The northern limb is terminated by a fault line that presents an imposing scarp on the north side of the ridge overlooking the river to the north. The Volga River has been forced to make a large horseshoe bend, known as the Samara Bend for the small Samara River that comes in from the southeast at this point, until finally the Volga breaks through the structure in what is known as the Zhiguli Gate with high ground on both the west and the east. Since the Zhiguli are composed primarily of limestone, a great deal of karst topography has been developed from underground solution of the limestone. Therefore slopes are much steeper than normal surface stream eroded slopes, and the valley bottoms generally are not occupied by streams, having been formed by sinking in from underneath.

East of the Trans Volga Meadows the land rises again toward the Ural Mountains in a broad swell that stretches from the upper Kama River area in the north where it is known as the "Uvaly" or "hummocks" southward through the central portion known as the Ufa Plateau in the Bashkir A.S.S.R. and on southward to the vicinity of the Ural River where it is known as the Obschchiy Syrt, or "upland erosion surface." The highest and most topographically rugged portion of this mountain foreland is the Ufa Plateau in the center where the Ufa, Belaya, and tributary streams have cut canyon-like valleys into horizontal strata which cap flat topped interfluves in mesa and butte formations. The highest

elevation, 418 meters, is reached southwest of the city of Ufa. Considerable karst topography is scattered about this area. The broad gentle flexures of the rock strata in the foreland have formed excellent traps for oil in the Bashkir and Tatar Republics and surrounding areas which since World War II have been the primary oil producing regions in the country. Because of the gentleness of the warping and the constant pitch of the rocks the contour flooding technique of oil extraction is ideally suited to this region.

Farther north, the Timan Ridge, which has already been mentioned as a subsurface feature, forms a broad arch running northwestward from the central Urals to the Arctic coast and on through the northern end of the Kanin Peninsula. Elevations reach 471 meters above sea level. This upwarp separates the drainage basin of the Pechora River to the northeast from those of the Mezen and Northern Dvina Rivers to the southwest. It forms a conspicuously hilly upland in an otherwise very flat region, and provides the flexures in the sedimentary rocks that form traps for petroleum and natural gas.

In the far southwestern part of the country, a broad upwarp is oriented more west-east than north-south. This is known as the Volyn-Podolian Upland in its broadest section in the western Ukraine and the Donets Ridge in its narrow eastward extension after its interruption in the Dnieper Valley. In the west heights reach 471 meters above sea level just east of the city of Lvov, while the Donets Ridge rises to 367 meters. Both areas have been deeply dissected by streams and in places are very hilly.

These upwarps in many cases are fringed by cuestas that have been eroded down the dip slopes of rocks by streams working on layers of different resistances. Many major streams have adjusted to the strike of the rocks so that they maintain high banks on one side and low, flat banks on the other. This is true of practically all the southward flowing rivers such as segments of the Dnieper, Northern Donets, Don, and Volga. Some of the more prominent cuesta escarpments are the Glint in the north-

Figure 3-3   Juncture of Dnieper and Desna Rivers from high western bluff at Kiev. Photo by Irving Cutler.

west, a thick limestone cliff running along the southern shore of the Gulf of Finland and extending inland south of Leningrad and the southern ends of Lakes Ladogda and Onega, the Klin-Dmitrov Ridge running west-east about 75 kilometers north of Moscow, the various escarpments facing the western banks of the middle Volga and middle Dnieper Rivers, and the Belgorod chalk scarp in the southern part of the Central Chernozem Region. The scarps in the north tend to be highly eroded and obscured by thick mantles of weathered materials so that the surface expressions are often nothing more than zones of hilly land, but in the drier south the cuesta escarpments stand up more as rock cliffs and become very prominent features on the landscape.

At the base of each cuesta escarpment is an inner lowland which is usually a broad flattish area that frequently contains major river courses, lakes, and swamps. Chief among these is the inner lowland along the contact zone between the crystalline shield in Karelia and the sedimentary plain to the south. This lowland at the base of the Glint escarpment is partially occupied by such bodies of water as the Gulf of Finland, Lake Ladoga, Lake Onega, and the western and eastern arms of the White Sea. This so-called "great lakes" area of the Soviet Union was scooped clean, deepened, and transformed by subsequent glacial action much as was the Great Lakes region of North America along the contact zone between the Canadian Shield to the north and the sedimentary plain to the south. Another major inner lowland is occupied by the west-east portion of the Volga River at the base of the Klin-Dmitrov Ridge north of Moscow.

Glaciation

Also, in the north the bedrock features are often buried deeply beneath glacial till which tends to control the surface topography more than the rock structure does. The East Euro-

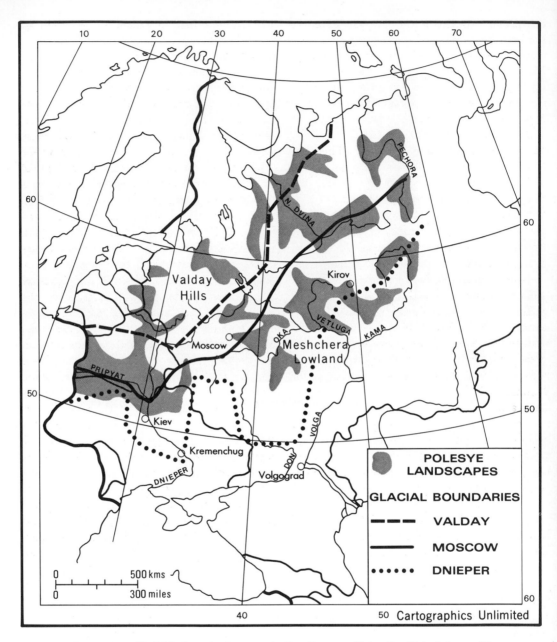

Figure 3–4   Glacial limits and polesyes on the East European Plain. After Shcherbakov, p. 27.

pean Plain was strongly affected by four continental ice sheets that advanced southeastward from the Scandinavian Shield. In order of occurrence, they were the Oka, Dnieper, Moscow, and Valday stages. The Dnieper ice sheet expanded farthest south and obscured the effects of the Oka glaciation before it. One lobe extended down the Dnieper Lowland approximately to the city of Kremenchug and another lobe extended down the Don Lowland to within 150 kilometers of Volgograd. (Fig. 3–4) In between the two lobes the Central Russian Upland retarded the ice movement.

The Moscow stage extended southward to

the present course of the Pripyat River in southern Belorussia and then swung northeastward just southeast of the present city of Moscow and onward to the Pechora River Basin and the northern part of Western Siberia. At one standstill during its retreat, the Moscow stage deposited a prominent moraine approximately through the cities of Warsaw, Minsk, Smolensk, and Moscow. This has provided a somewhat higher irregular stretch of land leading from eastern Europe into the heart of the Russian Plain which affords better drainage than either the land to the north or the south for a major highway and railroad leading from Warsaw to Moscow. It has also provided a route of invasion for armies from the west such as Napoleon's and Hitler's.

The Valday stage was the most limited in extent. In the west it extended southward to about the northern border of Belorussia and then swung abruptly northeastward across the present site of the Rybinsk Reservoir and on to the Arctic Coast to the east of the Kanin Peninsula. Along certain stretches of this boundary a prominent terminal moraine was left, particularly where the ice edge crossed the Valday limestone escarpment at an acute angle in the headwater regions of the Volga River. The morainal material buried the escarpment in this region and produced an upland of irregularly dumped glacial materials interspersed with large numbers of lakes and swamps in an interfluve area that has become the drainage divide between the Volga, Dnieper, Western Dvina, and the Lovat-Ilmen-Volkhov drainage systems. This is the famous Valday Hills area that figured so prominently in the portage of boats and supplies between the Baltic and the Black Sea when the river routes of this area were the only means of transport.

In the center of ice accumulation on the Scandinavian Shield the primary erosion process was one of scouring and plucking away the loose material leaving a hard bedrock surface with thousands of intervening lakes and short, clear streams with many rapids picking their way across the hard rock landscape. The shield consists of Precambrian schists, gneisses, and granites that in places are overlain by quartzites, sandstones, and shales. Everywhere the crystalline massif has been cut by tectonic fractures trending generally west-northwest — east-southeast. In places there is also a set of fractures running south-southwest — east-northeast. Thus the region consists of blocks, some of which have been elevated and others depressed with respect to each other. The depressed zones are occupied by hundreds of interconnecting lakes that are elongated in a northwest-southeast direction as are the deep embayments of the White Sea, the Onega and Dvina Gulfs in the south and Kandalaksha Bay in the north. Some of the tectonic movements were accompanied by volcanic activity which formed massive laccoliths, the highest of which are the Khibiny Mountains in the central Kola Peninsula which rise to a maximum elevation of 1191 meters above sea level. However, much of the Kola Peninsula and Karelia are rough rolling peneplanes with elevations 400–500 meters above sea level. Karelia contains more than 50,000 lakes which occupy nine percent of the total territory.

The material that was scoured off the Scandinavian Shield was moved southward and deposited by the ice in a variety of glacial forms on the sedimentary plain. The glacial forms resulting from the most recent Valday stage are still intact and dominate the landscape on the northwestern part of the plain. The surface forms of the Moscow stage have been modified somewhat by subsequent stream action, but the remains of this stage are still quite evident in the form of morainal materials and large, flat, ill-drained lowlands which represent the beds of proglacial lakes that were formed temporarily when the ice blocked the normal course of rivers. Chief among these are the Pripyat Marshes in southern Belorussia and northwestern Ukraine, the Meshchera Lowland in southeastern Moscow Oblast, and the Volga-Vetluga Lowland southwest of Kirov. These and many other polesye-type landscapes are shown on Figure 3–4. They are flat, sandy, ill-drained lowlands occupied by forests, swamps, and marshes.

Glacial materials deposited by the Dnieper

Figure 3-5   The lake-studded, ice-scoured plain of Karelia. Photo by Irene Milass.

stage and the older Oka stage beneath it, have been reworked by streams so that the forms no longer exist, but the materials are still identifiable, particularly the outwash materials in river valleys. In general this portion of the plain, and the unglaciated portion to the south, are much better drained than the areas occupied by the Valday and Moscow stages, the glaciofluvial effects of which extended well beyond the margins of the ice in such areas as the polesye landscapes just mentioned.

In the far northeastern part of the plain, in the basins of the Pechora and Northern Dvina rivers, a post-glacial invasion of the Arctic Ocean occurred immediately after the melting of the ice before the isostatically depressed land had time to spring back. In this way much of the form of glacial materials was destroyed by wave action for a short time in shallow water.

URALS

During much of the Precambrian and Paleo-

zoic periods the Urals region acted as a continually subsiding geosyncline that accumulated enormously thick sedimentary and effusive deposits. The Hercynian orogeny during the Upper Paleozoic transformed this area into a young folded mountain chain which subsequently was reduced essentially to a peneplane by the Middle Triassic period. At the end of the Triassic, block movements created a new mountain system in which Upper Triassic and Jurassic coal bearing strata were deposited in wide intermontane valleys. The Urals were again peneplaned during the Upper Jurassic and Miocene periods. During Pliocene times longitudinal fractures with resultant block elevations created the present mountains.

In the north the Urals rise abruptly from a coastal plain 40 kilometers inland from the Kara Sea to a height of 1363 meters in Konstantinov Kamen. From there southward to about latitude 62°N they extend as one continuously high and narrow ridge, a barren rocky region well above the tree line which has been heavily glaciated. Local mountain glaciers still exist in some of the more protected valleys. On either side this ridge drops off abruptly to extremely flat plains that have been washed by the waters of the Arctic Ocean in post Pleistocene times. The range reaches its highest elevation, 1894 meters, at Narodnaya Gora (Peoples Mountain) at 65°N latitude. South of there the Urals split into two or more ranges which lower and become discontinuous in the mid section of the region. Here the mountains slope gradually toward the foreland on the west already mentioned with the east European plain and toward the east to the West Siberian Lowland. Farther south, the ranges rise again to a maximum elevation of 1640 meters at Yamantau. South of the Russian-Kazakh border the mountains trail out into a broad, eroded, semiarid upland known as the Mugodzhar Mountains whose highest elevations are around 400 meters.

The present Ural Mountains are not very impressive topographically. But economically they are extremely important for their great variety of minerals: oil, gas, coal, and salts in the sedimentary western foreland and metallic ores and gemstones plus more coal and such things as asbestos on the igneous, metamorphic, and sedimentary east side. The mining and processing of these ores will be discussed later with their respective industries.

Novaya Zemlya might be considered an extension of the northern Urals, although the North Siberian Lowland paralleling the Arctic coast forms a complete break in the geological structures. At times during the Pleistocene the island acted as a center for glacial accumulation. Therefore it is scoured and deeply scarred by fiords, one of which cuts the island in two at Matochkin Shar. Much of the north island is still under a glacial cap. The highest elevation is reached in this area where a nunatak juts through the ice to an elevation of 1547 meters.

WEST SIBERIAN LOWLAND

The West Siberian Lowland is one of the largest, flattest plains on earth. Marine and continental sediments have accumulated to depths of 4000–6000 meters above a Paleozoic floor that slopes consistently downward toward the center to form a large basin. Much of the time from the Jurassic period onward this area has been inundated by the sea either from the north or from the southwest through the Turgay Strait at a time when the Middle East was occupied by the eastern extension of the Mediterranean geosyncline. Many of the sediments deposited by these marine transgressions have been found to be oil and gas bearing.

The present surface of the lowland is essentially flat with an almost imperceptible slope toward the center which makes drainage very difficult. A discontinuous series of low rises runs from west to east across the basin at about the 63rd parallel and divides the lowland into two parts, a northern basin and a southern basin. Much of the lowland is drained by the Ob River and its major tributary, the Irtysh, as well as many other tributaries and the shorter Taz River in the north, all of which have carved enormously wide, shallow valleys through the lowland with extensive development of cutoff meanders and natural levees. Oxbow lakes and other forms of lakes, some of them of thermokarst origin, abound among the swamps. During spring the southern headwaters of the streams thaw out before the downstream portions do in the north, and huge ice jams cause widespread flooding.

During the Pleistocene the lowland was affected by all but the earliest glacial stage. The Samara and Taz, corresponding to the Dnieper and Moscow stages on the European plain, covered the northern portion of the basin with continuous ice sheets as far south as the 60th parallel, but the Zyryan stage, corresponding to the Valday stage, affected the lowland only along the fringes of mountain glaciers centered in the northern Urals on the west and the Putorana Mountains on the Siberian Platform to the east. Although the glacial ice did not advance as far southward as the present steppes of southern Siberia, the steppe region was greatly affected by glaciofluvial activity. Huge lakes formed in broad, shallow basins of blocked stream valleys, the largest of which are represented today by the three main steppe regions in southwestern Siberia, the Ishim Steppe in the west, through which the Ishim River flows northward to the Irtysh, the Baraba Steppe in the center between the Irtysh and Ob Rivers, and the Kulunda Steppe southeast of the Baraba Steppe. These old lake beds are flat as floors and are the best farming areas in Western Siberia.

Ponded water in the river valleys during the Pleistocene eventually filled up the basins and overflowed the divides toward the southwest toward the Turgay Straits leading to the Aral Sea. Striking evidence of this remains today in the form of broad, shallow glacial spillways that cross the Kulunda Steppe and portions of the Ob Plateau and Baraba Steppe in a northeast-southwest direction. Many of these broad rills are now occupied by portions of streams or lakes, some permanent, some temporary, all elongated northeast-southwest.

As was the case to the west of the Urals, the northern section of the West Siberian Lowland was inundated by the Arctic immediately after the glacial meltbacks, so that much glacial evidence has been erased from that portion of the plain. Rising sea level since the Pleistocene has flooded the estuaries of the Ob, Taz, and other streams and formed deep embayments in the Arctic coast which separate the region into three huge peninsulas, the Yamal on the west, the Taz in the center, and the Gydan on the east.

North of about 62° latitude much of the West Siberian Plain is underlain by permafrost, permanently frozen subsoil. *Pereletoks,* patches of short-term frozen subsoil after a series of cold winters, continue southward all the way into the steppes along the Trans Siberian Railroad. (Fig. 3-6) Since permafrost conditions are much more pronounced farther east, typical forms and consequences will be discussed in the next section.

THE SIBERIAN PLATFORM

The Siberian Platform is another stable block of the earth's crust similar to the Russian Platform. It occupies much of the area between the Yenisey and Lena Rivers and in the southeast extends beyond the Lena and its major tributaries the Vitim and Aldan Rivers. (Fig. 3-1) In the south it merges with younger geosynclinal zones as it does also in the north where it is terminated by the extensive North Siberian Lowland that stretches east-west along the Arctic and separates the Central Siberian Uplands from the Byrranga Mountains on the Taymyr Peninsula. However, for simplicity of discussion, the Taymyr Peninsula will be discussed along with the Central Siberian Upland.

Everywhere the Siberian Platform is underlain by a complex of Precambrian rocks. These outcrop in places to form massifs such as the Anabar in the north-central portion of the upland, the Olenek in the northeast, the Aldan-Vitim in the southeast, and the Turukhansk in the west-central portion of the upland. But in most places the Precambrian is covered deeply by nearly horizontally bedded Paleozoic and Mesozoic deposits intruded in places by enormous flows of Triassic traps (volcanic basalts). There are widespread deposits of Permian, Jurassic, and Lower Cretaceous coal beds, by far the most extensive in the country, and perhaps in the world. The Tunguskan and Lena coal fields will be discussed with the other coal fields of the country under energy in Chapter 10.

Most of the Central Siberian Upland is a good example of a peneplane, a rolling upland with elevations generally 500-700 meters above sea level. River valleys are well incised, particularly the major right bank tributaries of the Yenisey, the Angara, the Stony Tunguska, and the Lower Tunguska, as are the headwaters of the Lena River and its tributaries the Vilyuy in the west and the Vitim, Olekma, and Aldan Rivers in the southeast. Locally the upland rises into low mountains, the highest of which are the Putorana in the northwest where a maximum elevation of 1701 meters is reached. Other promontories include the Yenisey Ridge in the southwest along the right bank of the Yenisey River which rises to 1104 meters.

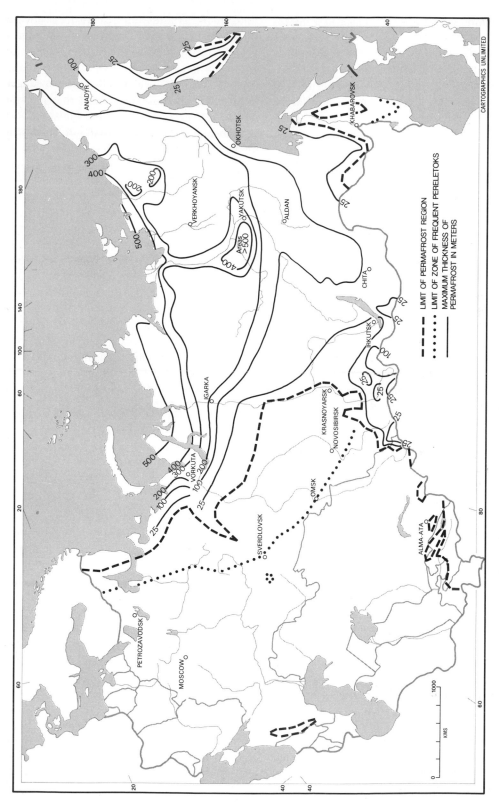

Figure 3–6   Distribution and thickness of permafrost. After Bondarev, p. 29.

The Putorana Mountains consist of a combination of volcanic and sedimentary rocks that have not subsided as much as surrounding areas in recent geological movements. On the west and north the upland drops off abruptly to the Yenisey and North Siberian Lowlands. During the Pleistocene valley glaciers cut deep U-shaped valleys in the western and northern edges of the Putorana which are now occupied by spectacular finger lakes blocked by terminal moraines in the lower valleys. Similar conditions exist in the Byrranga Range across the North Siberian Lowland to the north, where some small contemporary glaciers still exist in the higher eastern portions that reach elevations of 1146 meters.

Continental glaciation at its greatest extent covered the Central Siberian Upland southward to a line extending from the mouth of the Stony Tunguska River northeastward to the delta of the Lena. However, glacial topography is not very prominent here. In places extensive karst topography exists on limestone structures, particularly in the interfluves between the upper portions of the Lower Tunguska River and the upper portions of the Vilyuy. In this area Kimberlite pipes intruded in limestone and dolomite bedrock yield large quantities of diamonds. Many other areas of the upland are mineralized with the mineral fuels, iron ore, nickel, copper, and so forth, which will be discussed in Chapter 11 with the metalliferous industries.

Almost all the surface of the Siberian Platform is underlain by permafrost, some of it very thick. Along the Arctic coast and in the lower Vilyuy Valley west of Yakutsk thicknesses of more than 500 meters are found. (Fig. 3–6) Throughout much of the upland the permafrost reaches thicknesses of 200–300 meters. This diminishes southward to only 25–50 meters in the middle Angara region and disappears along the upper Yenisey near Krasnoyarsk, although scattered areas of short-term permafrost can be found far to the southwest of that. A permafrost research station has been established in the city of Yakutsk which has become the primary center for permafrost research in the world. In the vicinity of Yakutsk the so called "active layer" of top soil which thaws out most summers is only about 1.5 meters thick. In the city itself, where the ground is shaded much of the time by buildings, the active layer is only about one-half meter thick. Because of uneven thawing, the permafrost presents many problems to the construction of buildings, roads, hydroelectric installations, and so forth. Taliks, thawed layers underneath the permafrost which are remnants of warmer years, are under great hydrostatic pressure and may burst with explosive force when intersected by construction machines. Meltwater trickling into the cracks in the soil during summer refreezes upon contact with the permafrost below and causes ice wedging. Pingos often form in drained lake beds where advancing fronts of groundwater freeze and expand to cause blisters on the surface which may heave 8–10 centimeters per year and eventually reach heights of several meters. A crater usually forms in the center due to partial thawing of the ice core. (Fig. 3–7)

MOUNTAINS, PLATEAUS, AND BASINS IN THE SOUTH AND EAST

Mediterranean Geosyncline

Carpathian Mountains

The westernmost mountains in the Soviet Union are the Carpathians, the mid section of which was acquired by the Soviet Union from eastern Czechoslovakia after World War II. They consist of a system of ranges running northwest-southeast with elevations primarily between 500 and 1500 meters. The highest peak within the Soviet Union has an elevation of 2061 meters above sea level. Higher portions of the ranges are generally composed of crystalline rocks which weather into rather sharp ridges, but where weaker sediments exist round summits are more common. Frequent cuesta formations ring the foothills. These are usually capped by limestone or conglomerates and underlain by shales. In the small segment of the Hungarian Plain that the Soviet Union owns on the southwest side of the Carpathians,

Figure 3–7   Pingo in drained lake bed near Yakutsk. Photo by Sam Outcalt.

Figure 3–8   Thermokarst development after clearing forest along road from Yakutsk to Magadan. Photo by Sam Outcalt.

Figure 3-9   Permafrost Institute with mammoth statue, Yakutsk. Photo by Sam Outcalt.

extinct volcanic eruptions have produced conical hills that stand 700 meters or so above the
lowland.

The Carpathian ranges are being eaten into
by the headwater streams of the Dniester and
Prut Rivers on the northeast and the Tisza
River on the south, which is tributary to the
Danube. During the Pleistocene, continental
ice moved southward into the foothills of the
Carpathians and met mountain glaciers coming
down the northern slopes. In the later stages of
the Pleistocene, isolated mountain glaciers existed in the valleys which carved the mountains
into typical mountain glacial features such as
U-shaped valleys, cirques, and tarn lakes.
Thus, the mountains have more of an alpine
look than one might expect from their elevations.

Crimean Mountains

The Crimean Mountains are primarily a
fault block system that has lifted upward along
a major fault zone that cuts across the northern
part of the Black Sea in line with the Caucasus Mountains to the southeast. The steep fault
scarp faces southeastward toward the Black
Sea and the northern slope is much more
gradual. Stream erosion has divided the mountains into three main ranges conforming to
cuestas capped by thick limestones and inter-
bedded with weak shales. The highest range
occurs in the most southerly portion where a
maximum elevation of 1545 meters is reached.
The summit of this range consists of a series of
plateau-like uplands that are known locally by
the Tatar word, "yayla."

Much of the precipitation that falls in the
mountains falls in winter as snow which is
blown into depressions where it remains into
early summer and provides sources of meltwater which seeps slowly through the limestone
and forms hundreds of caves and general karst
topography. The underground solution of the

Figure 3–10 New apartment building in Yakutsk built on pillars to prevent melting of permafrost by heat from building. Photo by Sam Outcalt.

limestone, combined with frequent earthquakes, causes many landslides and avalanches which are attested to by the rumpled surface of the foothills between the limestone cliffs and the sea.

Caucasus

The Crimean Mountains lower eastward across the Kerch Peninsula to no more than a few mud volcanoes and fumaroles, which continue across the Kerch Strait onto the Taman Peninsula that eventually rises into much higher, much more rugged mountains, the Caucasus. The Caucasus consist primarily of two mountain systems, the Great Caucasus on the north and the Lesser Caucasus on the south. Between is a broad synclinal lowland that runs the full length of the isthmus between the Black and Caspian Seas. The Great Caucasus is by far the higher mountain system, which itself consists of several ranges. The overall structure of the system is a great asymmetrical fold that slopes gently on the north to the North Caucasian Foreland but plunges steeply on the south to the synclinal lowland. The primary drainage divide is the so-called Main Range, which is paralleled on the north by the Front Range, which is less continuous but contains the highest peaks in the entire system. These are dead volcanic cones that sit atop the rest of the structure. The highest, Mount Elbrus, reaches an elevation of 5642 meters. North of the Front Range lie three giant cuestas eroded into massive limestones and sandstones which themselves are of mountainous proportions. The dip slopes of the cuestas are pock-marked by considerable karst topography, as are the main ridges of the Caucasus themselves, particularly in the low northwestern portion. Hundreds of caves honeycomb the hills along the coast of the Black Sea.

The higher parts of the Caucasus exhibit

extreme mountain glacial features. During the ice age the lower boundary of perpetual snow in the humid western part of the mountains lay at about 2000 meters. The high central portions of the Main Range and Front Range are cut by U-shaped valleys with hanging tributaries which experience many landslides and avalanches. The higher peaks are all snow capped at the present time, and glacial tongues extend down some of the valleys to elevations as low as 2000 meters.

The northern slope of the Great Caucasus and the northern cuestas have been cut into separate segments by the Kuban, Terek, Sulak, and lesser streams flowing down the north slopes to the Black and Caspian Seas. East of the Daryal Gorge of the Terek River, the climate becomes quite dry, even in the higher mountains, and the topography becomes almost a badlands in the eastern part of the north slope in the republic of Dagestan just west of the Caspian Sea. The Sulak River in this region has cut a canyon to a depth of 1500 meters.

The synclinal lowland to the south of the Great Caucasus has been divided into two parts, the Colchis Lowland in the west and the Kura Lowland in the east, by the low Surami Range which runs south-southwest — north-northeast across the grain of the Caucasus to produce a drainage divide in the synclinal lowland in eastern Georgia. This transverse arch rises to about 1000 meters above sea level and is continued on the north slope of the Great Caucasus in the form of the Stavropol Plateau which descends toward the north through a dryish plain to the structural sag occupied by the Manych Depression, an old glacial spillway from the Caspian to the Sea of Azov.

The Kura River is the longest in the Trans-caucasus. It heads in eastern Turkey and winds its way through the Surami Range past Tbilisi in eastern Georgia and then traverses the entire Kura Lowland to the Caspian. The eastern section of the lowland is exceedingly flat and semiarid. It represents an old arm of the Caspian when the water level was much higher during the Pleistocene. In the west, at the

eastern end of the Black Sea, the Colchis Lowland is less extensive and the rivers flowing into it are much shorter, but the climate is the most humid of the Soviet Union and such streams as the Rioni and Inguri flowing down the southwestern slopes of the Great Caucasus carry great amounts of water and sediment which has filled in the Colchis Lowland behind sand bars that have been built by the waves completely across the mouths of the streams. The aggraded lowland is very marshy and filled with numerous abandoned channels, oxbow lakes, and meander scars.

To the south of the synclinal lowland the Lesser Caucasus consist of eight discontinuous ranges which generally lie at elevations of 1500–2500 meters, but reach as high as 3373 meters just north of Lake Sevan. In many places the alignment of the individual ranges is obscured by enormous quantities of volcanic materials that have poured out of elongated fissures and filled up all the intervening valleys and in some cases covered many of the ranges themselves. This volcanic region, which extends into northeastern Turkey and northern Iran, is known as the Armenian Plateau. The plateau surface generally lies between 2500–3500 meters, but individual cones tower above the general level of the plateau. The highest peak in Soviet Armenia is Mount Aragats, northwest of Yerevan, with an elevation of 4090 meters. The highest peak in the entire Armenian Plateau is across the border in Turkey about 65 kilometers south of Yerevan where Mount Ararat reaches an elevation of 5156 meters.

The major stream on the Armenian Plateau is the Araks River, which flows eastward along the international border and joins the Kura River shortly before it enters the Caspian. A short tributary of the Araks, the Razdan River, drains Lake Sevan from the north through the city of Yerevan. Lake Sevan sits at an elevation of 1900 meters above sea level and has a surface area of about 1400 square kilometers. It is thus one of the largest high lakes in the world. The Razdan, in its course of less than 100 kilometers, descends about 1000 meters to the Araks River south of Yerevan.

Figure 3-11   Mt. Ararat from Yerevan.

The upwarp of the Great Caucasus descends in elevation eastward but continues through the Apsheron Peninsula jutting 85 kilometers into the Caspian Sea and under the sea as an underwater ridge eastward to the Turkmenian shore where the upwarp emerges again in a series of small mountain ranges known as the Balkhans. This anticlinal ridge that stretches from Baku in the west to east of Krasnovodsk on the east shore of the Caspian has been one of the longest producing oil regions in the Soviet Union. Oil has also been exploited on the north slopes of the Great Caucasus in the vicinity of Groznyy and Krasnodar. These and other mineral deposits will be discussed in Chapters 10 and 11.

Central Asia and Southern Kazakhstan

The Central Asian segment of the Mediterranean geosyncline is characterized by two structural troughs with intervening and surrounding uplands, all of which are fringed on the south by high rugged mountains that increase in elevation eastward toward the Pamir knot on the border of China, Pakistan, and Afghanistan. In the west is the Caspian trough occupied by the Caspian Sea and its northward extension, the North Caspian Lowland, which at an earlier time was part of the sea bed. The North Caspian Lowland is a featureless plain that slopes gradually southward into the sea. Between the Ural and Emba

Figure 3–12   Mountain village in Azerbaydzhan. Photo by Irving Cutler.

Rivers in the northeastern part of the lowland, low domes mark the existence of buried salt plugs which have remained intact as the sediments have subsided around them. These form the domed structures that are the basis for the Emba oil fields in this region. They also form the basis for a number of autoprecipitating salt lakes located on their surfaces, such as Lake Baskunchak east of the lower Volga which is one of the main salt sources for the Soviet Union.

The lowland ends abruptly southward along the Caspian coast in the Mangyshlak Peninsula where it abuts against a horst structure known as the Karatau that reaches elevations of 556 meters. This merges on the east with the Ustyurt Plateau, a broad, flattish, dry upland fringed by fault zones on all sides that occupies the space between the Caspian and Aral seas. To the southwest the Krasnovodsk Plateau is another upfaulted block that plunges abruptly to the Caspian on the west and the Kara-Bogaz-Gol on the north, the large eastern embayment of the Caspian Sea. South of the Krasnovodsk Plateau a narrow coastal plain fringes the eastern shore of the Caspian southward to the Iranian border. A system of dry stream channels borders the southeastern edge of the Ustyurt and Krasnovodsk Plateaus winding through salt encrusted dry lake beds. This is the so-called "Uzboy System" that not too many hundreds of years ago drained the Aral Sea southwestward to the Caspian.

In the center of the Central Asian region lies the Turanian Lowland which extends south-southwest — north-northeast through Central Asia and central Kazakhstan and adjoins the Siberian Lowland farther north. The mid section of the Turanian Lowland is occupied by the Aral Sea, the fourth largest lake in the world, with a surface area of about 64,000 square kilometers. It is a shallow sea and contains thousands of islands, from which the word "Aral" comes. Since the Aral Sea drained into the Caspian a short time ago, it has not accumulated much salt. Its average salt content is only about 1 per cent, as compared to 14 per cent in the southeastern part of the Caspian. Precipitation in the Aral Sea area totals less

than 100 millimeters (4 inches) per year. If it were not for the surface inflow of the two large rivers, the Amu Darya and the Syr Darya, flowing northward out of the high southern mountains, as well as subsurface seepage of artesian water, the Aral Sea would soon dry up. As it is, the continually expanding use of irrigation water from the two streams has caused the Aral Sea level to drop precipitously during the last 30 years.

To the south of the Aral Sea lies the Kara Kum, the most extensive sand desert in Central Asia. About 90 per cent of the area is covered by elongated ridges of relatively fixed sand topped by smaller shifting barchan dunes. Only the southern and northern fringes of this sand desert have alluvial soils that are fit for agriculture. North of the Aral Sea the Turanian Lowland continues as the Turgay Trough.

Between the Amu Darya and Syr Darya lies the Kyzyl Kum which is higher, rockier, and more devoid of sand than the Kara Kum to the southwest. Farther northeast more sand deserts are represented by the Muyun Kum, along the northeastern side of which flows the Chu River, and the broad sandy desert south of Lake Balkhash which is traversed by the Ili, Karatal, Aksu, and Lepsy Rivers flowing northwestward out of the Tien Shan Mountains toward Lke Balkhash. Lake Balkhash is the third large interior drainage basin in Central Asia, along with the Caspian and Aral Seas. It lies at a higher elevation than either of the other two and is rapidly being filled in by alluvial fans being built by the streams flowing in from the south. In fact it has already been severed in several places. Lakes Sasykkol and Alakol, as well as Lake Ebi-Nur in China are remnants of the previous, much longer lake. A distributary of the Ili River has now built a sand spit almost across the mid section of the present lake.

The high, rugged mountains in the south start in the west with the Kopet Dag along the Iranian border. This is a fault block range with an abrupt scarp facing northeastward across the Kara Kum. Stream erosion has stripped the sedimentary layers down the dip slope to the southwest and exposed spectacular overhanging cliffs on the northeast. Although the Kopet Dag reach elevations of 2246 meters on the Soviet side of the border, the area is so dry that even in their highest elevations the mountains are practically devoid of vegetation.

With a slight break along the Iranian-Afghanistan border, the mountains rise again into the high Hindu Kush which lie entirely within northern Afghanistan. But streams flowing out their northern flanks enter the deserts of Soviet Central Asia and bring some irrigation water to small oases such as the city of Tedzhen on the Tedzhen River and the city of Mary (old Merv) on the Murgab River. On the border of northeastern Afghanistan, Pakistan, and the Soviet Union, the Hindu Kush merge into the high Pamir Knot out of which radiate several mountain ranges in various directions. In the Soviet Union the Pamir-Alay Ranges extend westward throughout much of the Tadzhik Republic and into the southeastern portion of the Uzbek Republic. In the northeastern part of Tadzhikistan these contain the first and third highest peaks in the Soviet Union, Mount Communism in the Academy of Sciences Range at an elevation of 7495 meters, and Mount Lenin in the Trans-Alay Range at an elevation of 7134 meters. These and other high peaks in the area are heavily glaciated by contemporary mountain glaciers, the largest of which is Fedchenko Glacier, one of the most extensive mountain glaciers on earth.

The western half of the Pamir-Alay Ranges are deeply dissected by the headwaters of the Amu Darya, particularly the Pyandzh, which for a long distance forms the international boundary with Afghanistan, and the Vakhsh and other smaller streams that flow southwestward across a rolling upland in southwestern Tadzhikistan which is the main agricultural region of the republic. In the northwestern part of Tadzhikistan, three subparallel ranges extend in an east-west direction. From south to north these are the Gissar, Zeravshan, and Turkestan Ranges. Between the Zeravshan and Turkestan Ranges, the Zeravshan River flows westward out of Tadzhikistan into the deserts of southeastern Uzbekistan where it waters the famous old oases at Samarkand and Bukhara. The Zeravshan River ends in a stagnant pool of water known as Karakul shortly before reaching the Amu Darya.

North of the Alay and Zeravshan Rivers the mountains continue in a broad series of essentially east-west oriented ranges interspersed here and there by broad intermontane basins. These continue northward along the Chinese border as far as the depression east of Lake Balkhash. Collectively they are known as the Tien Shan, a Chinese term meaning heavenly mountains. Individual ranges are given individual names. In many areas the Tien Shans exceed 6000 meters in elevation. They reach their highest point, 7439 meters, at Mt. Pobeda (Victory), the second highest peak in the Soviet Union, on the Kirgiz-Chinese border.

The most important intermontane basin in the Tien Shans is the Fergana Basin which contains such important old irrigation agricultural civilizations as the Khanate of Kokand. Such settlements are located primarily in the mid sections of alluvial fans, particularly around the southern fringe of the basin where short streams flowing down the north slopes of the Alay Range have built large alluvial fans across the floor of the Fergana Basin and formed an asymmetrical valley floor with the lowest section running close to the northern foothills. The Syr Darya flows east-west the full length of the basin along this northern trough after receiving its main headwater stream, the Naryn, from the mountains to the east.

The Syr Darya breaks through the narrow western neck of the basin onto the Golodnaya (Hungry) Steppe, an utterly flat, fertile, dry lake bed that has been transformed almost entirely into irrigated cotton fields. From there the Syr Darya turns northwestward to flow through the northeastern edge of the Kyzyl Kum in southern Kazakhstan to the Aral Sea. Many smaller streams flow northward out of the Tien Shans into the deserts of southern Kazakhstan where they end in the sand or in Lake Balkhash. Chief among these are the Chu, the Ili, and the Talas. These and other smaller streams form the basis for much irrigation agriculture along the loess foothills of the

Figure 3–13   Southwestern part of Fergana Basin. Sokh River and other streams building alluvial fans at base of southern glacial-capped Alay Mountains. Syr Darya flowing southwestward through northwest quadrant of picture. Landsat imagery.

northern slopes of the Tien Shans. More details will be given on this irrigation agriculture in the discussion of agriculture in Chapter 9.

Another major intermontane basin in the Tien Shans is occupied almost entirely by Issyk-Kul (Hot Lake) which gets its name from the fact that subterranian volcanic activity produces hot springs that keep the lake warm. After a major break in the mountain chains where the Ili River flows westward out of China into the Soviet Union, the mountains rise again into the Dzungarian Alatau, at the eastern end of which lies the down faulted graben of the Dzungarian Gate so famous in caravan travel from western China to Central Asia.

Several small mountain ranges extend northwestward from the main mass of the Tien Shans into the deserts of southern Kazakhstan. Chief among these are the Karatau, a somber gray fault block range that reaches an elevation of 2176 meters, and the Chu-Ili Range which runs northwestward between the Chu and Ili Rivers to the western end of Lake Balkhash. The Karatau will be mentioned in Chapter 11 in conjunction with rich phosphate ore deposits.

Along the northern foothills of most of the mountain ranges extending all the way from the Chinese border in the east to southern Turkestan in the west is a discontinuous belt of thick loess deposits that have been blown out of the desert sands to the north into the foothills by the prevailing northerly winds. This is one of the most extensive and thickest loess belts in the world. It provides the excellent soils for the irrigated oases of the region and the building materials for the native adobe huts and walls that serve as fences.

THE ANGARA GEOSYNCLINE

The Angara Geosyncline, which underwent mountain building processes during the Hercynian orogeny of the Upper Paleozoic era stretches from the southern Urals across northeastern Kazakhstan and the mountainous regions of the southeastern part of Western Siberia to the very southern part of Eastern Siberia extending around the southern end of Lake Baykal into Transbaykalia. (Fig. 3–1) In northeastern Kazakhstan this encompasses the so-called "Kazakh Hillocky Country" which since the end of the Paleozoic has been eroded down to a rough rolling upland surmounted occasionally by conical shaped summits that reach elevations of more than 1000 meters. The maximum elevation of 1565 meters lies southeast of Karaganda. The Kazakh Hillocky Country merges eastward with the Altay and southward with the Betpak-Dala, a featureless dry upland plain west of Lake Balkhash. The Nura River rises in the northeastern edge of the Kazakh Hillocky Country and flows westward through Karaganda to its terminus in Lake Tengiz, which lies in a structural depression in the west-central portion of the upland. The Ishim River rises in this upland basin and flows westward and northward to the Irtysh

and eventually to the Ob. Erosion of the original mountains in the Kazakh Hillocky Country down to the bare stumps that remain today has exposed a variety of rocks of differing ages which contain a wealth of minerals, such as coal, copper, and iron. These will be discussed in Chapters 10 and 11.

The high mountains continue northeast of the Dzungarian Gate. First is the Tarbagatay Range, a horst reaching elevations of 2992 meters between the downdropped graben of the Dzungarian Gate to the southwest and the graben occupied by Lake Zaysan to the northeast. In this graben the upper Irtysh River flows westward out of China and then northwestward across northeastern Kazakhstan to join the Ob much farther north in the West Siberian Lowland. To the northeast of the upper Irtysh lies the mountain mass of the Altay ranges, the main portion of which lie in Mongolia and China. They extend northwestward into southwestern Siberia where they reach an elevation of 4506 meters along the Siberian-Kazakh border. The higher peaks in this area are occupied by perpetual snowfields and glaciers which feed the headwaters of the Ob River, the Biya and the Katun. Two lower prongs, the Salair Ridge and the Kuznetsk Alatau, extend northwestward from the main mass on either side of the Tom River, another tributary of the Ob, to form the coal-rich Kuznetsk Basin, which will be discussed at length with energy and metallurgical industries in Chapters 10 and 11.

East of the Kuznetsk Alatau broad basins are rimmed by folded and fault block mountains. The Western Sayans run southwest-northeast across the upper Yenisey Valley and separate the Tuva Basin to the south from the Minusinsk Basin to the north. At their eastern extremity the Western Sayans intersect the mid section of the Eastern Sayans which are oriented northwest-southeast along the divide between tributaries flowing westward to the upper Yenisey and those flowing northward and eastward into the Angara River. The Minusinsk Basin is a triangular-shaped lowland between the Kuznetsk Alatau on the west which reaches elevations of 1820 meters, the

Figure 3–14   Amur River near Khabarovsk. Photo by Toni Crane.

Western Sayans in the south which rise as high as 2930 meters, and the Eastern Sayans in the northeast which reach 3492 meters. Farther up the Yenisey, the Tuva Basin is bordered by the Western Sayans on the north and west and the Tanu-Ola mountains in the south along the Mongolian border.

The Eastern Sayans terminate on the southeast with the Irkut River, beyond which the mountains related to the Angara Geosyncline lie primarily in northern Mongolia. However, they swing northeastward again east of Lake Baykal in a narrow zone of mountains with elevations generally less than 1600 meters. The main range is the Yablonovyy Mountains which run southwest-northeast and form the divide between the right-bank tributaries of the Selenga River in the west, which flows through the basin around Ulan-Ude into Lake Baykal, from the headwaters of the Shilka on the east which joins with the Argun to form the Amur.

PACIFIC GEOSYNCLINE

Kimmerian Zone

The Kimmerian orogeny of the Mesozoic era affected a huge area of the more continental parts of the Soviet Far East all the way from the Arctic to the southern border of the country. Much of this region today consists of mountain ranges of intermediate heights with broad intervening basins. The most settled and agriculturally significant of these basins is the Amur-Zeya plain surrounding the Zeya River which flows southward into the Amur, the Jewish Autonomous Oblast drained by the small Bira and Bidzhan Rivers southward to the Amur, and the Ussuri-Khanka Lowland drained by the Ussuri River northward along the Chinese border to the Amur at Khabarovsk. Although most of these southern basins are subhumid to semiarid climatically, because of permafrost which underlies much of the area even along the southern border, much land is ill drained, frequently with standing water, particularly after the melting period in spring or during the rainy season in middle and late summer. Thus, agriculture in these basins has to contend with both drought and poor drainage.

In the north, east of the Lena River the Verkhoyansk, Chersky, and Moma Ranges, reaching heights of 2300–3200 meters, separate the valleys of the Yana, Indigirka, and Kolyma Rivers flowing northward to the Arctic across the broad North Siberian Lowland. Although these mountains are not extremely high, in this high latitude they lie mostly above the tree line so that they are primarily covered by tundra vegetation.

The southwestern prong of the Kimmerian Zone includes the rift valley system in which sits Lake Baykal. This is sometimes considered to be the southern edge of the Siberian Platform. Although rocks are quite old throughout much of this region, tectonic movements have been very active right up to the present. The basin which contains Lake Baykal took shape primarily during the Tertiary period about 25 million years ago. Lake Baykal has many unique features. It is the deepest lake in the world, 1620 meters (more than 1 mile), and contains the greatest volume of any fresh water lake in the world. It is credited with one-sixth of all the fresh water on earth, nearly as much as all five of the North American Great Lakes combined. The surface of the Lake lies at 455 meters above sea level. The lake is surrounded almost everywhere by precipitous mountains that in the northern and southern ends reach elevations above 2000 meters. Many small streams flow into the lake, but only the Angara flows out. The large volume and constancy of flow provided by the lake imparts tremendous hydroelectric potential to the Angara River and the Yenisey farther downstream.

formed during the Upper Cretaceous, Tertiary, and recent times in an extremely unstable zone of the earth's crust which experiences frequent severe earthquakes and volcanic activity. In the northeast the huge Kamchatka Peninsula is ribbed by a central mountain range reaching elevations of as much as 3621 meters, east of which lies a discontinuous belt of currently active volcanoes, the highest of which is Mt. Klyuchevskaya at an elevation of 4750 meters. Between the central range and the eastern volcanic belt lies an interior lowland drained by the Kamchatka River. The volcanic belt continues southwestward as an underwater ridge with many individual volcanic cones rising above the water level to form the Kuril Island chain leading southwestward to Hokkaido Island in northern Japan.

In the west, paralleling the mainland across the narrow Tatar Strait, lies the island of Sakhalin which consists primarily of two parallel mountain chains with a central valley in between that broadens northward to include the entire width of the island. The highest elevation on Sakhalin is 1609 meters. On the mainland between the coast and the Ussuri-Amur Lowland lies the Sikhota-Alin mountain system with heights up to 2077 meters. The Sikhota-Alin are tightly folded mountain ranges that have been partially peneplaned into a ridge-and-valley topography. During the Quaternary the narrow eastern fringe of the area was affected by outpourings of lava that produced lava-plateau-relief deeply dissected by steep, short streams plunging eastward into the sea. In the east the Sikhota-Alin hugs the Pacific Coast and provides few embayments for port facilities, but in the south the individual ranges trail into the water with large intervening embayments that provide the natural ports occupied by Vladivostok, Nakhodka, and Vostochnyy (Wrangel).

Alpine Zone

The continental margins, peninsulas, and islands along the Pacific coast have been

Reading List

1. Bondarev, P. D., "A General Engineering — Geocryological Survey of the Permafrost Re-

gions of the U.S.S.R. and Methods of Construction in Permafrost Areas," *Problems of the North*, No. 3, 1959, pp. 23–47.

2. Domanitskiy, A. P., Dubrovina, R. G., and Isayeva, A. I., *Reki i ozera Sovetskogo Soyuza* (Rivers and lakes of the Soviet Union), Gidrometeoizdat, Leningrad, 1971, 104 pp.

3. Lazko, E. M., *Regionalnaya geologiya SSSR* (Regional Geology of the U.S.S.R.) Nedra, Moscow, 1975, 2nd ed., Vols. I and II, 332 and 464 pp.

4. Markov, K. K., and Popov. A. J., eds., *Lednikovyy period na territorii evropeyskoy chasti SSSR i Sibiri* (The ice age in European U.S.S.R. and Siberia), Moscow, 1959, 560 pp.

5. Nalivkin, D. V., *Geology of the U.S.S.R*, Oliver & Boyd, Edinburgh, 1973, 855 pp. (Translation by Nicholas Rast of *Geologiya SSSR*, 1962).

6. ———, ———, *The Geology of the U.S.S.R: A Short Outline*, Pergamon, New York, 1960, 170

pp. plus colored geological map of U.S.S.R. at scale of 1:7,500,000.

7. Shcherbakov, Yu. A., "Factors of Swamp Formation in the Polesies of the Russian Plain," *Soviet Geography: Review and Translation*, May 1963, pp. 26–29.

8. Shlygin, E. D., *Kratkiy kurs geologii SSSR* (A short course on the geology of the U.S.S.R.), gosgeoltekhizdat, Moscow, 1959, 271 pp.

9. Suslov, S. P., *Physical geography of Asiatic Russia*, Freeman, San Francisco, 1961, 594 pp.

10. Tushinskiy, G. K., ed., *Physical Geography of the U.S.S.R.*, Translated by Headquarters, Department of the Army, Office of the Assistant Chief of Staff for Intelligence, Washington, 1970, 657 pp. (Translation No. J-6585).

11. Tushinskiy, G. K., and Davydova, M. I., *Fizicheskaya Geografiya SSSR* (Physical Geography of the U.S.S.R.), Moscow, 1976.

4

Climate

The climatic stage in the Soviet Union is set primarily by high latitude and extreme continentality. At its extremities, the country stretches latitudinally for almost 5000 kilometers from 35°8′N at the southern border of Central Asia to 77°45′N at Cape Chelyuskin on the Arctic Coast of Eastern Siberia. Arctic islands carry Soviet territory farther north to 81°50′ in Franz Josef Land. West-east the country extends for almost 10,000 kilometers from 19°38′E in Kaliningrad Oblast to 169°2′W at Ratmanov (Big Diomede) Island in the Bering Straits. At this high latitude, such a distance spans eleven time zones. When a new day dawns in the Soviet Far East, it is still evening in the Soviet west. Much of the country lies north of the 50th parallel, and therefore compares more to Canada than to the United States. The only other land mass on earth that resembles Eurasia climatically is North America, and the similarity between the two is not very close because of different arrangements of land and water, mountain systems, and atmospheric patterns.

Much of the territory of the Soviet Union receives little influence from the sea. High mountains along most of the southern periphery, and additional land to the south in southern Asia, the Arabian Peninsula, and Africa, isolate the Soviet Union from warm moist southerly flows of air such as those that so profoundly influence the eastern half of North America. The southern mountains expand eastward to cover much of the width of the Soviet Far East in an intersecting labyrinth of basins and mountains of intermediate height. These, combined with the generally westerly air flow over the region, rule out much influence from the Pacific except in the shore areas themselves. The Arctic, which is frozen right up to the coast during winter all the way from the Bering Straits westward to the eastern part of the Kola Peninsula, acts much as a snow-covered land mass. The surface air over the Arctic ice does derive some heat from the unfrozen water underneath which keeps the surface air over the Arctic 15–20°C warmer than over the snow-covered land surface to the south, but this temperature differential of the surface air induces land winds that blow across the coast from south to north during much of the winter which further diminishes influences of the sea on the land. During summer, the Arctic exerts greater influence in the coastal areas, but the Arctic air modifies rapidly as it penetrates inland over the warming land mass, and its influence along the coast is largely negative since it further cools the area which lacks heat anyway because of high latitude.

About the only extensive maritime influence on the Soviet Union comes from the Atlantic in the west, and this is far removed from much of the Soviet Union. Atlantic maritime air must cross the entirety of Europe before reaching the

U.S.S.R. Nevertheless, because of the prevailing westerly winds the influences of the Atlantic are carried far eastward well into Siberia and Central Asia, especially during summer. Except in the Soviet Far East, much of the precipitation that falls in the Soviet Union is derived initially from the Atlantic and its bordering seas.

ATMOSPHERIC CIRCULATION

During winter sea level equivalent isobars show a large atmospheric high pressure cell centered over northwestern Mongolia dominating much of the land mass of the Soviet Union. This is the famous Siberian High. However, as can be seen in Fig. 4–1, the high is not centered in Siberia nor does it cover all of Siberia. A great concavity exists in Western Siberia on its northwestern side where the eastern end of the Icelandic Low juts over the continent much of the time and spreads along the Arctic Coast as far east as the Lena River delta. A northeastern extension of the high, often with a separated cell of high pressure, occupies much of what the Soviets consider the Soviet Far East and produces a strong contrast along the northwestern shore of the Sea of Okhotsk with the western extension of the Aleutian Low in the North Pacific. A less pronounced westerly protrusion forms a so-called "great axis" across northern Kazakhstan, the lower Volga Region, and the central Ukraine.[1] This generally separates easterly or northeasterly surface winds in the Black Sea Steppes from the southwesterly winds over much of the rest of European U.S.S.R.

Since the high is not centered in Siberia, does not cover the northwestern half of Siberia, and much of it lies outside of Siberia in the Soviet Far East and adjacent regions, it is obvious that the terminology, "Siberian High," is a misnomer. The Soviets never call it this, they usually refer to it as the "Asiatic Maximum."

It appears that the high is primarily thermally induced since it is a very shallow feature. Even as low as the 850 millibar level (1300–1500 meters above sea level) it no longer exists. (Fig. 4–2) Since in many places in southern and eastern Siberia the land surface rises above this level, it is obvious that the high does not exist as a single integrated entity but rather as separate pools of cold air in individual intermontane basins. The sea level high is thus a mental construct derived by extrapolating down to sea level pressure and temperature conditions found at isolated recording stations, all located in intermontane basins, using standard formulas that do not apply to the abnormal atmospheric conditions found in the basins, particularly the extremely cold temperatures and strong temperature inversions.

The pressure trough on the 850 millibar map that extends southeastward across Siberia from the eastern end of the Icelandic Low around Novaya Zemlya to the western end of the Aleutian Low in the Sea of Okhotsk intensifies aloft until at the 500 millibar (5100–5550 meter) level it forms one of the two most intense standing waves in the upper atmosphere of the Northern Hemisphere, matched only by the one over eastern North America. (Fig. 4–3) The western limb of this trough feeds cold Arctic air southeastward into the core area of the Asiatic High to help maintain it, along with surface radiational cooling over a snow-covered surface.

In spite of strong surface temperature inversions that form in the basins in early winter, radiational cooling continues at the surface until a balance is reached between the transfer of heat upward from the snow-covered surface and the transfer of heat downward from the warmer air in the inversion layer. This balance generally is not effected until the surface temperature has lowered to about −50 to −70°C since the snow, in spite of the fact that it is much colder than the air in the inversion layer above, is a more efficient radiator of heat than the atmosphere, radiating heat across the entire spectrum of wave lengths while the air radiates only at selected wave lengths according to the gases in the atmosphere. Temperature

---

[1]The term "great axis" was coined by the famous Russian climatologist, A. I. Voyeykov, around the turn of the century.

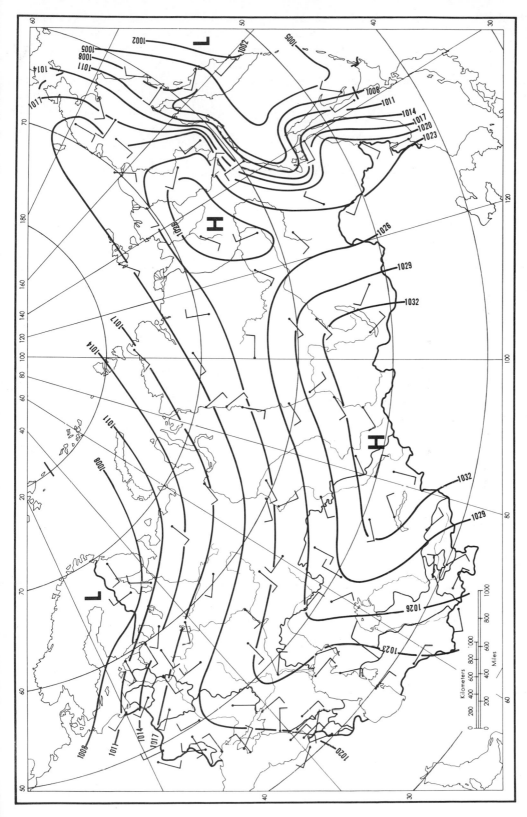

Figure 4–1   Mean sea level pressure and winds, January. After Lydolph, Climates of the Soviet Union, p. 9.

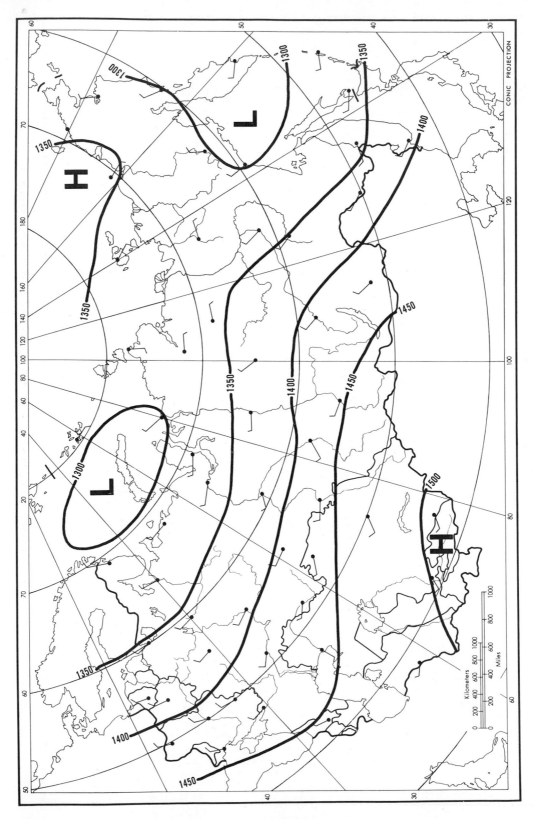

Figure 4–2   Mean heights at 850 mb., January, in meters. After Lydolph, Climates of the Soviet Union, p. 9.

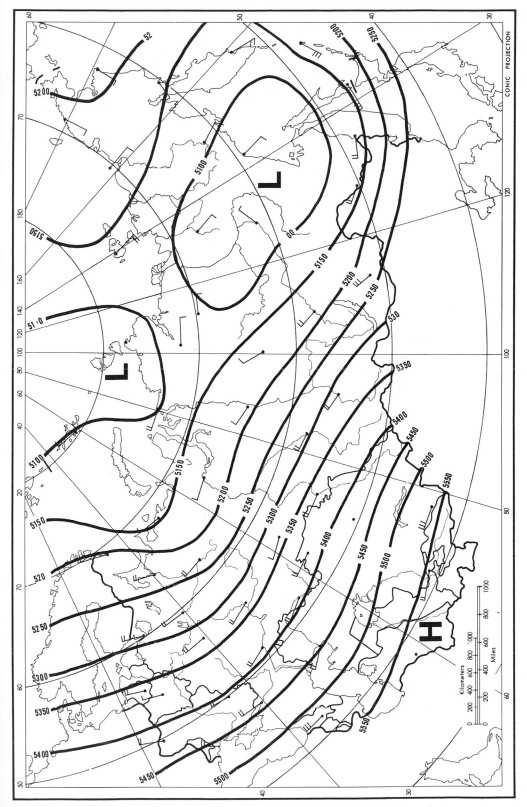

Figure 4–3   Mean heights at 500 mb., January, in meters. After Lydolph, Climates of the Soviet Union, p. 10.

inversions frequently extend upward to 2–3 kilometers, and temperatures as cold as surface temperatures are not reached again until heights of seven or eight kilometers. (Fig. 4–4) Although the core of the Asiatic Maximum usually is located in northwestern Mongolia, the strongest temperature inversions are generally found in the northeastern part of the Soviet Far East extending into the Chukchi Peninsula. This is probably due to a surface divergence of air outward from this region during winter toward the Arctic Coast to the north and the Sea of Okhotsk to the south, both of which have warmer surface air temperatures than the intervening land mass in spite of being frozen over at this time of year. Thus, in this region radiational cooling effects at the surface are enhanced by adiabatic heating from subsidence aloft.

The strong temperature inversions in the intermontane basins of the eastern part of the U.S.S.R. during winter profoundly affect weather conditions. The extreme stability of the thick inversion layer holds moisture and pollutants close to the earth's surface and insulates the surface from weak traveling fronts that occasionally cross the area during winter. These frequently remain as fronts aloft, skimming across the tops of cold surface pools of air in intermontane basins. (Fig. 4–5) Under such conditions, the floors of the basins do not experience frontal passages as such, but only high cloudiness and an occasional light fall of dry, powdery snow.

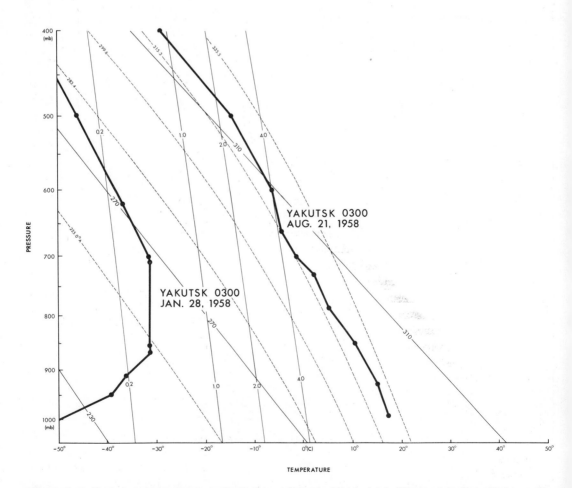

Figure 4–4   Typical vertical temperature distributions at Yakutsk. After Lydolph, Climate of the Soviet Union, *p. 97.*

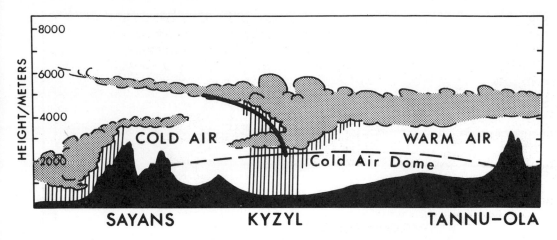

Figure 4–5   Upper cold front riding across cold air dome in Tannu-Tuva Basin. After Lydolph, Climates of the Soviet Union, *p. 94.*

Atmospheric circulation and associated weather in the European part of the country and much of Western Siberia stands in great contrast to that just described in the interior parts of Eastern Siberia and the Soviet Far East. During winter rapid successions of cyclonic storms follow tracks that extend from the eastern portions of the Icelandic Low in the North Atlantic either eastward along the northern coast of Scandinavia through the Barents and Kara Seas into the Ob Gulf region or northeastward up the Baltic and across the northern part of European Russia into the Ob Gulf. Also at this time of year the Mediterranean acts as a region of intense cyclogenesis which sends storms northeastward through the Black Sea and Caucasus regions across the southern part of the Russian Plain and Western Siberia, again into the Ob Gulf region where they join up with storms following the northerly routes. Thus, much of European U.S.S.R. and Western Siberia, and particularly the Ob Gulf, experiences frequent storminess and extreme cloudiness during winter. Although the air masses involved in these storms are all cool and stable, thus holding little potential for large amounts of precipitation, gray overcast skies with featureless stratus clouds and light snow flurries are typical. In fact, this type of weather is so common during winter that the Russians have a special name for it, "pasmurno," which can only be translated as "dull, dreary weather." Moscow during December averages 23 days with overcast skies.

During late winter and early spring cyclonic storms frequently form along a segment of the Polar Front in the Middle East and move into Soviet Central Asia where they usually die against the high mountains of that area. These bring 300–500 millimeters (12–20 inches) of rain to the mountain foothills and as much as 1000 millimeters (40 inches) of precipitation to higher elevations in the mountains, mostly in the form of snow.

The Arctic and Pacific coasts during winter are characterized by high winds that stand in stark contrast to the calm, clear, consistently cold conditions of the interior. (Fig. 4–6) These winds that blow from land to sea are induced by the air temperature differences across the coasts already described. Although temperatures in the coastal regions are typically 15–20°C warmer than they are in the interior, wind chill factors reach their minimum in the coastal areas. Dikson Island along the northeastern shore of the Yenisey Gulf has registered wind chills as low as −152°C. (Fig. 4–7) Even as far south as Sovctskaya Gavan on the Pacific Coast of the Sea of Japan wind chills as low as −115°C have been reached.

During spring a complete changeover in

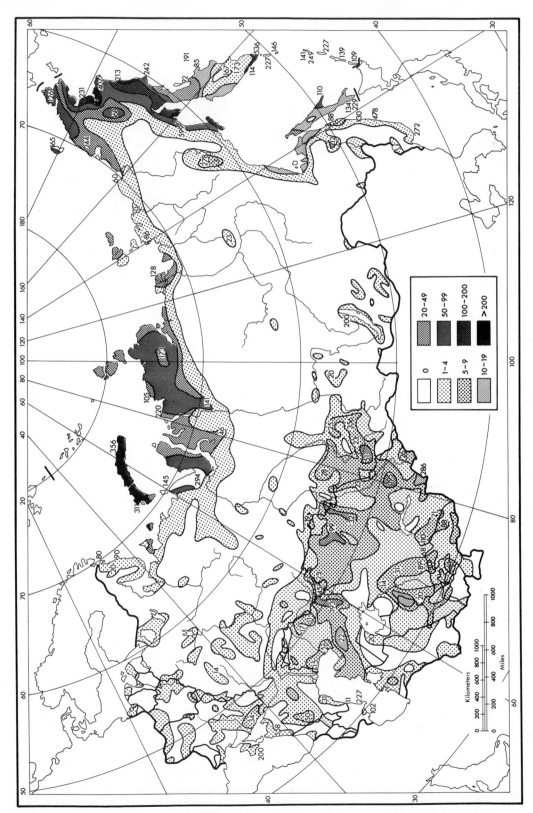

*Figure 4–6   Number of days with wind speeds exceeding 20 meters/sec. (44.6 miles/hr.) during the period 1956–1965.
After Lydolph, Climates of the U.S.S.R., p. 347.*

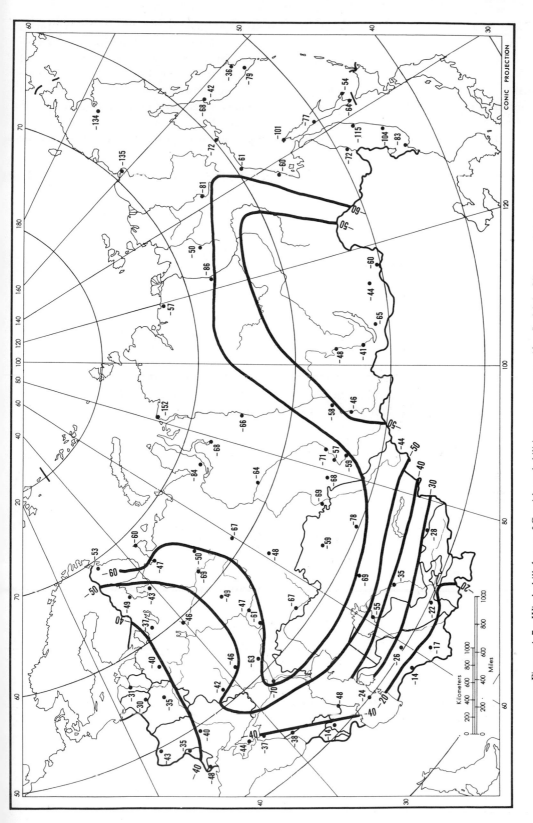

Figure 4-7 Wind chill factors, °C, with probabilities once per year. After Lydolph, Climates of the Soviet Union, p. 258.

pressure patterns takes place as the Asiatic High weakens and finally disappears and the eastern end of the Azores High juts across southern European U.S.S.R. into central Kazakhstan. By July a broad, diffuse low has expanded northward from a center in the Middle East to include much of the Soviet Union. (Fig. 4–8) The upper air flow becomes essentially zonal. (Fig. 4–9) With this type of surface pressure pattern and upper air flow it is easier for outside air, particularly from the west, to penetrate the continent than it is during winter. Atlantic air penetrates to the Lena River and beyond. Stiff sea breezes set up along the Arctic Coast as air over the sea, held near the freezing point by melting ice floes, moves inland to displace warmer, lighter air over the continent. As the invading Arctic air is warmed in its southward path over the land, surface convective activity sets off numerous instability showers in northern Siberia and the Soviet Far East. In the Amur region cyclonic storms developing along the Mongolian segment of the Polar Front, which becomes established in this region at this time of year, move east-northeastward toward the Sea of Okhotsk and, rotating counterclockwise, pull in some Pacific air at the surface in their northeastern quadrants.

Despite reduced cyclonic activity during summer, the greater penetration of maritime air and convective activity at this time of year bring maximum rainfall to most parts of the Soviet Union, except for Central Asia, parts of the Caucasus, and the southeastern coast of Crimea.

Local Winds

Since the southern perimeter of the country is occupied by high, rugged mountains, local winds abound. The most notable are caused by topographic effects on certain patterns of general atmospheric circulation, but there are also many mountain and valley breezes induced by thermal effects. In the Caucasus perhaps the best known wind is the Novoros-

siysk bora which is a cold wind that funnels through Markhotskiy Pass in the western Great Caucasus to descend on the port of Novorossiysk on the Black Sea coast. These winds are most common in November and December when they may whip up waves on the Black Sea to deposit glaze ice on all the roads and moorings along the coast. They frequently reach speeds of more than 60 miles per hour and sometimes separate gusts reach as much as 150 miles per hour. Temperatures in Novorossiysk during the bora commonly fall to −15 or −20°C. Bora are also experienced around the eastern end of the Great Caucasus along the Caspian Sea coast.

Even more significant to the agriculture of the Caucasus are the foehns, warm descending winds that frequent many mountain slopes. Foehns may also cause extreme avalanche hazards during winter and spring, bringing on snow melt too quickly. The most famous foehns in the Transcaucasus are those that descend the western slopes of the low Surami Range during winter and blow into the city of Kutaisi, the commercial center of the Colchis Lowland in western Georgia. This region experiences foehns more than 100 days per year. Maximum speeds reach about 75 miles per hour once per year. Temperatures have been known to rise in December to 17.5°C while relative humidities have fallen to 8 percent. Such conditions over the period of a day or more may cause much damage to fruit crops and induce the trees to drop their leaves.

Central Asia is a windy place as most dry regions are. The great amount of convective activity due to surface heating mixes higher velocity winds downward from aloft and enhances the surface wind speeds particularly during the daytime. As a result there is usually a turbid haze in the air. With particularly strong winds dust may be raised to 3000 meters or more into the air and remain there for days before settling out. The prevailingly northerly winds that sweep across the Central Asian deserts over the millions of years have sifted the finer particles of dust from the surface materials and carried them southward to lodge

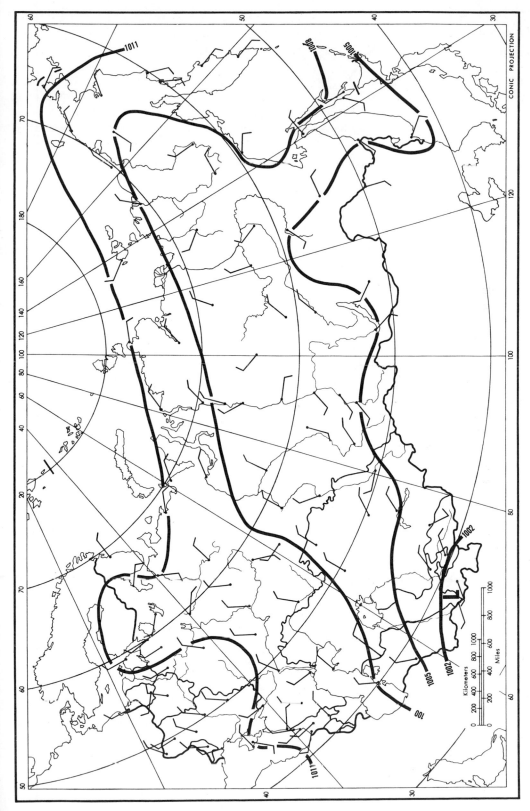

Figure 4–8   Mean sea level pressure and winds, July. After Lydolph, Climates of the Soviet Union, p. 14.

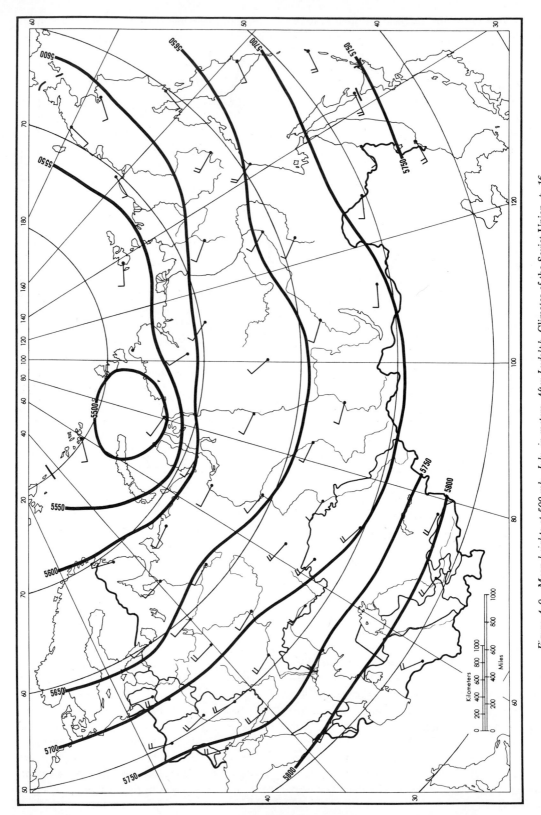

Figure 4–9 *Mean heights at 500 mb., July, in meters. After Lydolph, Climates of the Soviet Union, p. 16.*

against the mountain foothills as thick deposits of wind blown soil known as loess. Along the mountain fringes identifiable winds occur at mouths of canyons and mountain passes.

The best known foehn in the area is the one that blows from either direction through the Dzungarian Gate on the Soviet-Chinese border east of Lake Balkhash between Lake Alakol on the northwest and Lake Ebi-Nur on the southeast in China. The Dzungarian Gate is only 10 kilometers wide at its narrowest near Lake Zhalanaskhol. The town of Zhalanaskhol has strong winds 100 days per year with maximum velocities of 70 meters per second (150 miles per hour). The winds that blow from the southeast are the best known since they create intense, broadscale foehn conditions on the Soviet side of the border which keeps this area open to grazing during the winter. After temperatures have been 20–30°C below zero, thaws occur and the snow dissipates. These winds are generally known as the "Ibe" because they blow out of the Lake Ebi-Nur region. However, local inhabitants in the Alakolskoy Valley call them the "evgey."

Another well known foehn in Central Asia is the so-called "Ursatevskiy." This is an east wind that blows with great force through the narrow western throat of the Fergana Basin onto the flat plain of the Hungry Steppe to the west. It takes its name from the railroad junction of Ursatevskaya which is situated in the southeastern portion of the Hungry Steppe. Foehn winds also blow from the northeast down the Chirchik River Valley into the city of Tashkent. All the trees in the valley lean toward the southwest. Many other foehns, as well as bora winds, abound in the mountains.

Local winds are famous around Lake Baykal in the southern part of Eastern Siberia. The strongest are generally bora winds that blow down the narrow steep river valleys in the early winter when a strong pressure gradient is set up between the lake and surrounding regions before the lake freezes over. The best known of these is the "Sarma," which blows from west to east down the Sarma River Valley in the central portion of the western shore of the lake. The Sarma blows 113 days per year

with speeds up to 40 meters per second (more than 80 miles per hour).

Sukhovey

A special type of atmospheric phenomenon is the well known Russian Sukhovey. This occurs throughout the dry southern plains, including the deserts of Central Asia, but is best known in the eastern Ukraine and lower Volga region where it has the greatest effect on agricultural crops. It is not so much a wind as a desiccating condition due to a combination of air flow, high temperature, and low relative humidity. But it may be accompanied by fairly strong winds. When it occurs it has a devastating effect on vegetation, frequently significantly reducing yields of crops after only a short period of occurrence. Most sukhovey conditions are formed in place in the southern plains primarily in air that originates in the Arctic and moves southward to stagnate over the southern plains. This air starts out with cool temperatures, high relative humidities, and low absolute humidities. As it moves south it picks up heat and the temperature increases, so the relative humidity drops rapidly. Since the air has little absolute humidity in it, insolation is great, and by the time the air reaches the southern plains it has reached temperatures of 30°C or more and relative humidities of 10 per cent or less.

THERMAL CONDITIONS

Temperatures in the Soviet Union reflect the high latitude and the high degree of continentality. They are generally cool and experience great seasonal fluctuations. Because of the influence of the Atlantic in the western portions of the country, temperatures are usually at least normal or above for the latitude, but the latitude is comparable to Canada, not the United States. Moscow, for instance, corresponds latitudinally with Churchill on the western shore of Hudson Bay. Therefore, temperatures on the East European Plain are cool compared to such areas as the American corn belt, especially during summer. Kiev in the Ukraine, which the Russians think of as a balmy place climatically, corresponds in latitude to Winnipeg, Canada and has summer temperatures comparable to those in Bismarck, North Dakota and winter temperatures comparable to Omaha, Nebraska. Thus, while individual days during summer can get quite warm in Kiev, the average is relatively cool. July averages 19.3°C in Kiev, as compared to 22.3°C in Bismarck, North Dakota. The maximum temperature ever recorded in Kiev is 39°C, while in Bismarck it is 43°C. During January, with a mean temperature of −5.9°C, Kiev averages about the same as Omaha with −5.4°C, but its absolute minimum temperature is −33°C while Omaha is only −29°C. Thus, while European U.S.S.R. on the average gains heat from the Atlantic during winter, it is subject to Arctic intrusions from the north that are more severe than anything in the corn belt of North America.

In the northeastern part of the country, which has much greater continentality, seasonal extremes are much greater. During January the region averages more than 20°C below normal for the latitude, and during July 4–8°C above. (See insets in Figs. 4–10 and 4—11) This area has the greatest temperature ranges on earth. (Fig 4–12) The Verkhoyansk-Oymyakon area has a 103–104°C absolute temperature range, which is certainly the greatest on earth. Although temperatures during winter are colder in the Antarctic, there are no summers there to provide the large annual range. The lowest temperature ever recorded outside the Antarctic is −71°C at Oymyakon. This compares to −88°C at Vostok in Antarctica. However, Oymyakon is at an elevation of 740 meters, while Vostok is at 3420 meters. Verkhoyansk has a minimum temperature of −68°C and sits at an elevation of only 137 meters. Therefore, one can say that Verkhoyansk is the coldest spot on earth at low elevation. On the other hand, Verkhoyansk has experienced termperatures as high as 35°C in July, while Vostok has never experienced temperatures higher than −21°C.

It can be seen in Fig. 4–10 that during January isotherms form a set of semi-concentric lines around an eccentric center in the northeastern part of the Soviet Union, while in Fig. 4–11 July isotherms show a more latitudinal pattern. This is another consequence of high latitude. At these latitudes there is little daylight during winter anywhere, the angle of the sun during the day is very low above the horizon, and the high albedo of the snow cover reflects much of the meager sunlight that is received. Thus, the effects of insolation are minimal throughout the country during the winter, so there is no reason to expect much latitudinal difference in heat received. Therefore, the influence of advection from the sea is much more important than insolation during winter. During summer, it is just the opposite. Days are very long and the albedo over the forests, grasslands, and agricultural crops is relatively low. Therefore insolation effects are paramount. Only along the immediate border of the Pacific, with its monsoonal influx of air during summer, does the advection of sea air take precedence. It is very important along the Arctic coast, too, but here the land-sea effects coincide in direction with the latitudinal effects, serving only to enhance them rather than distort their pattern.

The far easterly location of minimum temperatures during winter shown on Fig. 4–10 and 4–13 is largely due to the lack of mountains in the west to block the marine flow of air from the Atlantic. Thus, there is considerable marine influence during the winter from the Atlantic as far east as central Siberia. This stands in contrast to the North American situation where north-south oriented mountains in the western part of the continent block the marine influence from the Pacific and allow the coldest temperatures in North America to be more centrally located in the middle of the continent. The extremely cold temperatures of the Soviet Far East are also enhanced by the mountain topography in that region, which causes air stagnation in intermontane basins with resultant extreme surface temperature inversions and abnormally low surface temperatures. Since most data recording stations are situated on basin floors, one gets the impression that this region has uniformly extremely cold

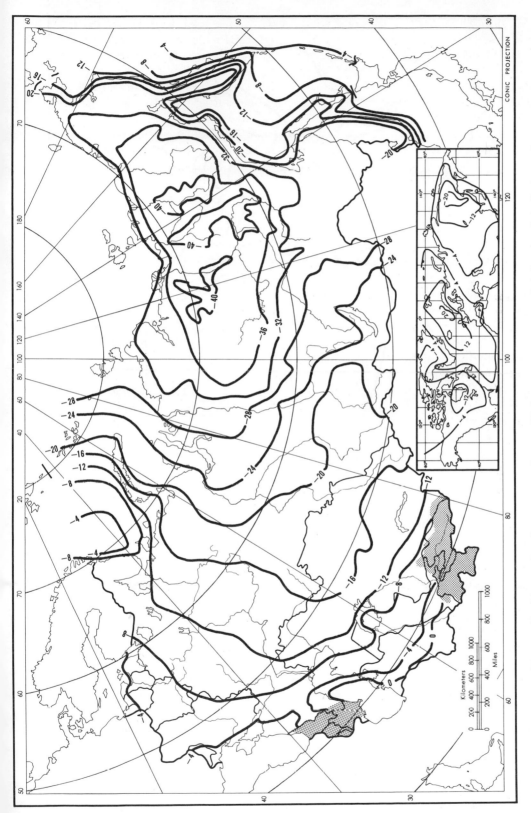

Figure 4–10 Mean surface air temperature, January, °C. Inset: mean temperature deviations from latitudinal normals, January. After Lydolph, Climates of the Soviet Union, p. 248.

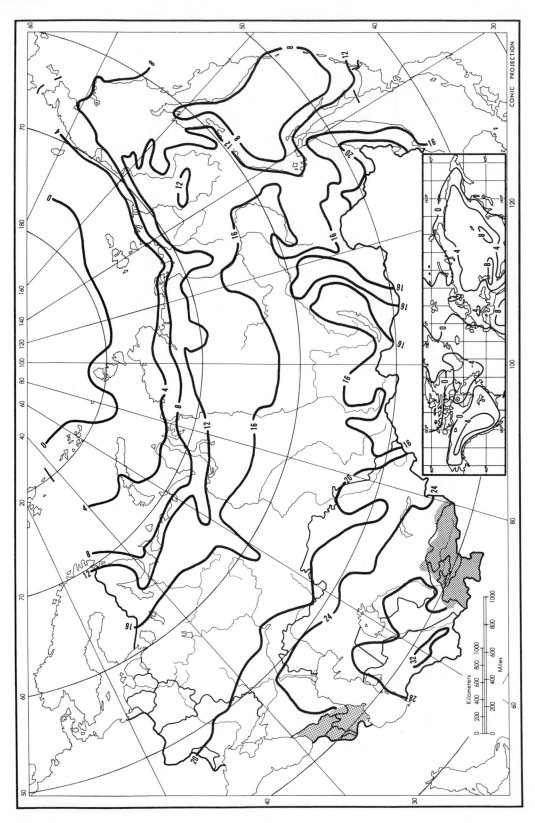

Figure 4-11 Mean surface air temperature, July, °C. Inset: temperature anomalies, July. After Lydolph, Climates of the Soviet Union, p. 252.

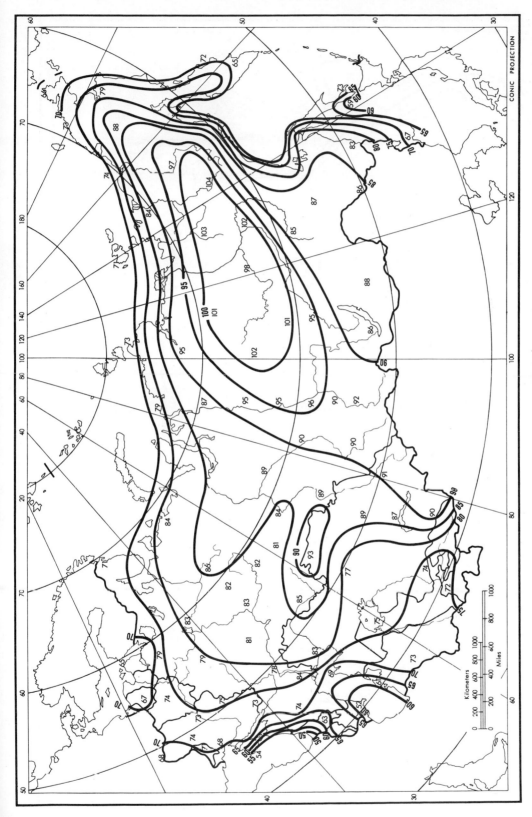

Figure 4–12   Absolute temperature range, °C. After Lydolph, Climates of the Soviet Union, p. 255.

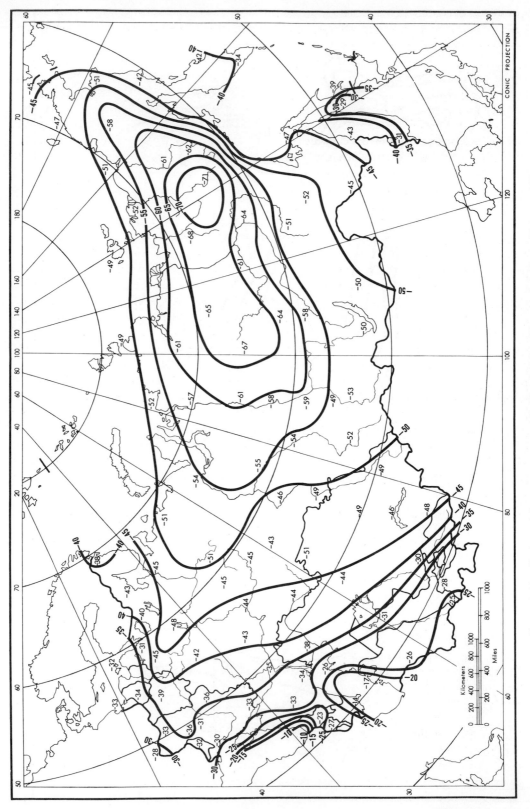

Figure 4–13   *Absolute minimum temperature,* °C. After Lydolph, Climates of the Soviet Union, *p. 256.*

temperatures. However, if one had data from mountain slopes situated within the temperature inversion layers, one could see that there are areas of considerably warmer temperatures scattered about the region.

The mountain-basin topography in the Far East also emphasizes diurnal ranges of temperature during summer. Oymyakon has a mean diurnal range during July of 23°C, which is even greater than the deserts of Central Asia where the maximum range at Termez is only 19°C. These ranges are much greater than anything in European U.S.S.R. where ranges are on the order of 11–15°C.

Although absolute minimum temperatures show a core area in the northeastern part of the country with eccentrically concentric arrangements of temperatures around it, wind chill factors are much colder along the Arctic and Pacific coasts, as was discussed earlier and shown in Fig. 4–7. Wind speeds under the inversion layers in intermontane basins during winter are practically nil. From December through February the average wind speed at Oymyakon is only 0.3 meters per second (less than 0.7 miles per hour). Under such cold, stable conditions, even the breath of animals or the by-product water vapor from combustion of fossil fuels is enough to saturate the air. Condensed and frozen water particles may hang in the air without visible motion through much of the winter, accumulating day after day to form a pale of haze and fog over any inhabited area or reindeer grazing land. If one is lost in this frozen wilderness, one has only to look for a low hanging cloud of human pollution to spot a settlement.

Some of the saturation in the lower air may take place naturally as higher water vapor pressure in the warm air of the temperature inversion induces a continual movement of moisture downward into the cold air underneath even though the cold air may already be saturated. The downward moving moisture crystallizes into tiny ice particles in the frigid air below. During the long, still, and starry winter nights the downward motion of these ice crystals makes a faint rustling sound which the Yakuts refer to as the "whisper of the stars."

Another consequence of high latitude is an asymmetrical annual regime of temperature. Winter is by far the longest season, and usually temperatures average about the same for three or four months during which they fluctuate up and down somewhat with individual weather events, thus leading to the term "coreless winter" which is often applied to these areas. Summer on the other hand is short with peaked temperatures in the middle which reach quite high values for a very short period of time. Transitional seasons are exceedingly short, the temperature rising very rapidly in spring and falling rapidly in autumn. Especially spring is practically nonexistent. The additional heat gained through insolation as the equinox is approached is used primarily in the form of latent heat to melt the snow, thaw the ground, and evaporate the meltwater. By the time all this has been accomplished, the season is approaching the maximum insolation period of the summer solstice. Suddenly, when the ground has dried and no more latent heat is needed, surface air temperatures shoot up to their maximum values in mid July. The decline of temperature in the fall is more gradual, since there is no snow cover to be dealt with. In fact, as the ground begins to freeze in late fall, the latent heat of fusion that is given off retards a little the decline in surface air temperatures.

Threshold Temperatures and Significant Events

Many economic activities respond critically to certain levels of temperature. This is particularly true in agriculture. Undoubtedly the most critical temperature is the freezing point of water, which determines the growing season for many types of plants and the beginning of freezing and thawing of streams and other water bodies that are being used for navigation, hydropower production, and fishing. On the average on the East European Plain, the frost free period begins about the fourth week in April in the Black Sea Steppes and North Caucasus and lags northward to about the third week in May around Moscow and the end of May farther north where agriculture essentially ceases. (Fig. 4–14) In Central Asia the last killing frost is normally experienced around the second week in March in the far southern part of the country and lags northward to around the first of April near Tashkent, the fourth week in May in northern Kazakhstan, and the first week in June in the agricultural belt of southwestern Siberia. In the Far East, it occurs about May first around Vladivostok, and the second or third week of May in the Jewish Autonomous Oblast and the Zeya-Bureya Lowland.

The first killing frost in fall on the average occurs about the last week in October in the Black Sea Steppes, the third week in September around Moscow and the first week in September along the northern fringes of agriculture in European U.S.S.R. In Central Asia it occurs about the first of November in the far south, the second week in September in northern Kazakhstan, and the first week in September in southwestern Siberia. (Fig. 4–15) Thus, the average length of the frost free period in open plains sites ranges from about 210 days in the Crimea to about 130 days around Moscow to less than 75 days in the Komi A.S.S.R. in northeast European Russia. In Central Asia the frost free period ranges from 225 days in the south to 120 days in northern Kazakhstan and about 100 days in southwestern Siberia. (Fig. 4–16) The longest growing seasons in the country are in the Transcaucasus where portions of the region have 270 days or more.

There is no area in the Soviet Union that has a year-round growing season. Even in the Transcaucasus hard frosts occur every year. And at the high latitudes at which much of the Soviet Union lies large fluctuations occur between years. The growing season in the mildest region of western Georgia can be as short as 180 days. On the European Plain the minimum length of growing season ranges from about 150 days in the southern Crimea to less than 90 days near Moscow and less than 30 days on the Arctic coast. The frost free period can be as short as 180 days on the southern boundary of Central Asia, and 75 days in southwestern Siberia. Only the southern steppes and the western borderlands of the U.S.S.R., including much of Belorussia and the Baltic Republics, can be sure of no frosts in July and August. Although they occur only rarely, frosts have occurred during mid summer throughout much of the populated areas of the country. In the vicinity of Moscow, frosts can be expected to occur during July and August 10–30 per cent of the years, depending upon topographic sites. Standard weather records are misleading with respect to frost hazards, because they are generally taken in large cities which have profound effects on minimum temperatures, but phenological records collected in the countryside clearly show the effects of summer frosts.

Streams and other water bodies do not freeze and thaw immediately when the temperature crosses 0°C, for they have much heat stored in them which must be exchanged before the water can change state. The lower Volga freezes about the third week in December while the upper Volga freezes in late November. The headwaters of the Ob freeze around the third week in November, but near the mouth it is frozen about the first of November. The lower Amur River of the Far East freezes about the third week in November. The breakup of the ice normally takes place about the first week of April on the lower Volga and the second week of April on the upper Volga. On the Ob it occurs about the third week of May in the headwaters and the first of June near the mouth. The lower Amur breaks up during the first or second weeks of May. Thus, the lower Volga is frozen about 120 days per year while the upper Volga is frozen about 140 days. The upper Ob is frozen about 160 days per year, and the lower Ob about 220. The lower Amur is frozen about 180 days per year. Since the northward flowing streams in Siberia and portions of the European north thaw in their headstream portions before they do in their downstream portions, extensive spring floods occur when ice jams on the lower rivers will not allow passage of meltwaters coming from upstream.

Throughout much of Siberia, the Far East,

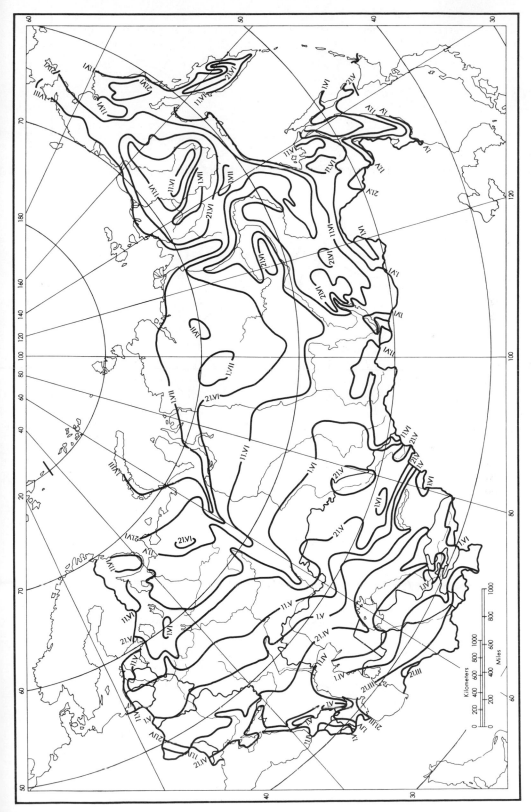

Figure 4–14   Mean date of beginning of frost-free period on open plain sites. After Lydolph, Climates of the Soviet Union, p. 261.

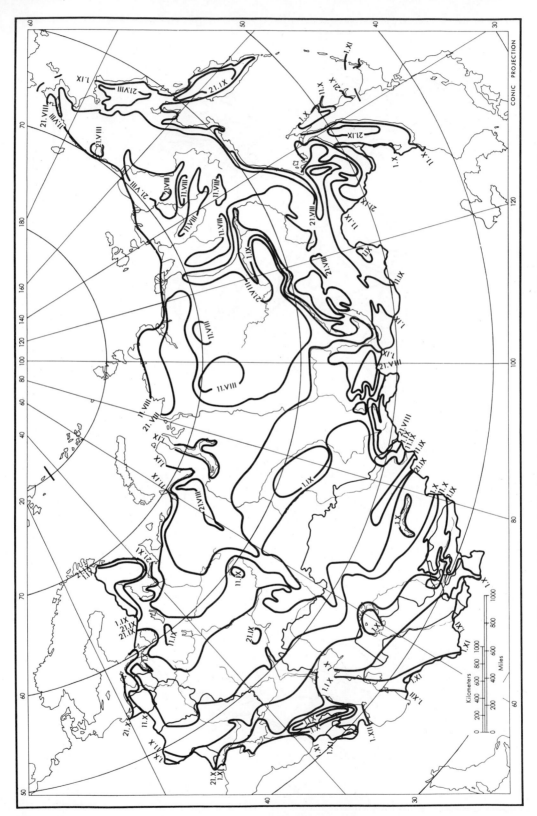

Figure 4–15   Mean date of end of frost-free period on open plain sites. After Lydolph, Climates of the Soviet Union, p. 262.

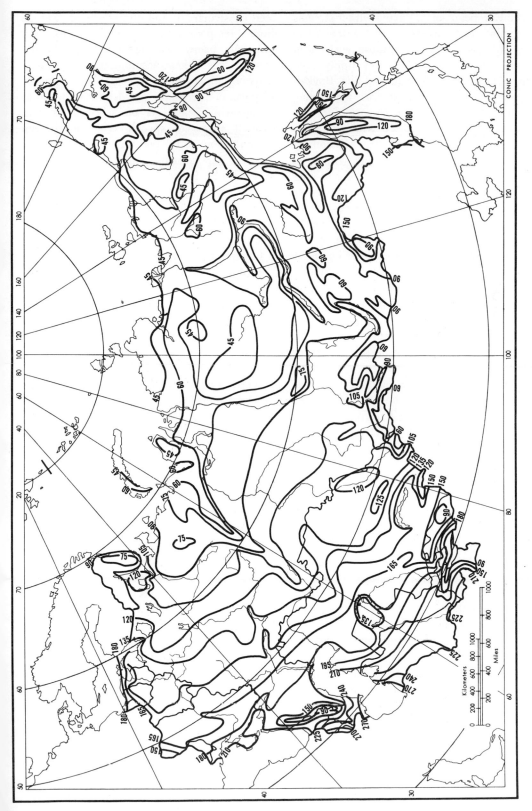

Figure 4-16 *Average length of frost-free period on open plain sites. After Lydolph, Climates of the Soviet Union,* p. 262.

and the European north, during winter streams and shallow lakes freeze to the bottom. The larger streams, particularly those with steep gradients and consistent sources of supply, such as the Angara flowing out of Lake Baykal, continue to flow under the ice crust which may be 2–3 meters thick. The Angara does not freeze at all for several miles downstream from its outlet from the lake, and other portions of streams may be kept open during winter on downstream sides of dams by the fluctuating level of the water due to different uses of hydropower at different hours of the day.

The ground freezes to depths of 2–3 meters throughout much of the inhabited parts of Siberia. At Bratsk, water pipes must be laid 4 meters below the surface. In much of Siberia and the Far East, the subsoil is permanently frozen. (Fig. 3–6) Even along the southern border of Eastern Siberia most of the territory is underlain by permafrost with thicknesses of as much as 60 meters. The northern third of Eastern Siberia has permafrost everywhere with thicknesses of more than 250 meters. During the short summers only the first meter or so of topsoil thaws out. The frozen subsoil does not allow percolation of meltwaters downward so that during the thawing season the surface of much of the area is waterlogged. If one wants to travel in the north, one usually waits until winter when it is frozen and can be negotiated by dog sled or reindeer sleigh, which often use the frozen streams as roads. During the summer the area is a morass, and the intruder is beset by swarms of mosquitoes, gnats, and other noxious insects. The builders of the Bratsk Dam tell of swarms of black gnats which caused them to wear head nets at all times during the summer season.

In addition to the freezing point of water, other threshold temperatures become important in certain instances. Soviet agroclimatologists have attached much significance to the 10°C level. They have determined that many domesticated crops lie dormant below this temperature and begin to grow only when the temperature rises above that point. Thus, the 10°C temperature level is considered to be the threshold of plant growth. Many maps have been constructed to indicate when the average diurnal temperature rises above 10°C in spring and falls below that level in fall. During summer logs of heat accumulation in terms of sums of temperatures above 10°C are kept for all parts of the country to determine whether the growing season is on schedule or not. Growth stages of specific crops have been related to sum-of-temperatures values. The use of these for classification purposes will be illustrated by Fig. 4–23 a little later.

THE MOISTURE ELEMENT

Precipitation over most of the Soviet Union is only light to modest. This again reflects the high latitude of the country with attendant cool air temperatures and low capacities to hold moisture as well as the high continentality of much of the area which precludes the intrusion of maritime tropical air masses over much of the territory. Most of the country receives between 400 and 800 millimeters of water equivalent per year.[2] (Fig. 4–17) Mountain slopes exposed to moisture-bearing winds, particularly in the southern parts of the country, as well as the Colchis and Lenkoran Lowlands in the Transcaucasus, receive considerably more than this, and large areas in Central Asia, Kazakhstan, the eastern plains of the North Caucasus and Transcaucasus regions, and some of the northeastern extremities of the country receive well under 400 millimeters per year. Sections of Central Asia receive less than 100 millimeters per year. Scattered parts of the Kara-Kum Desert and the basin of Lake Karakul near Bukhara receive only about 30 millimeters per year.

The greatest amount of precipitation at a low-altitude recording station occurs at Batumi in the southern foothills of the Colchis Lowland on the eastern shore of the Black Sea where the yearly average is 2504 millimeters (100 inches). The greatest amount recorded anywhere is at Achishko, a mountain station on

[2]One millimeter equals approximately 0.04 inches.

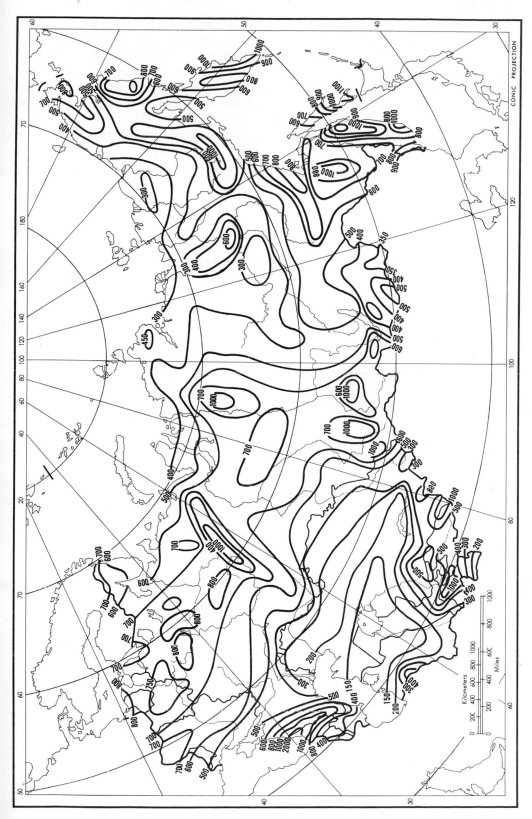

Figure 4–17   *Mean annual precipitation, in millimeters. After Lydolph, Climates of the Soviet Union, p. 296.*

the southern slopes of the western segment of the Great Caucasus, which at an elevation of 1880 meters receives an average annual precipitation of 2617 millimeters (105 inches).

Across the plain of European U.S.S.R. the greatest decrease in precipitation takes place in a southeasterly direction from the Baltic Sea to the Caspian and on into Central Asia. Since the potential evapotranspiration increases southeastward, the area gets dry very quickly in this direction. According to a so-called "hydrothermic coefficient" in wide use in the Soviet Union, during the critical growth months, May–July, the available moisture supply varies from 1.8 in Latvia to less than 0.2 throughout most of Central Asia. (Fig. 4–18) That is, most of Central Asia has less than 0.2 of the moisture that it needs during this period, and the Baltic area has 0.8 more than it needs. The 1.0 line, which signifies the correct moisture balance, runs through central Ukraine, the central Chernozem Ragion, middle Volga, southern Urals, and southwestern Siberia. Of course, this is based on a long-term average, and during any particular growing season moisture supply may vary greatly. Since the high latitudes generally experience greater year-to-year variations in weather conditions than lower latitudes do, the Soviet Union suffers great annual variations. Moderate to severe droughts may occasionally be experienced as far north as Moscow, and adequate moisture supplies are occasionally found in the lower Volga region.

It can be seen in Fig. 4–18 that most of Siberia and the Far East has an adequate moisture supply. However, some of the more densely settled intermontane basins along the southern fringe of Siberia and the Far East experience moisture deficits, as do some of the lowlands much farther north in the Yakutsk region. East of there the precipitation varies greatly from place to place according to topographic situation, but it generally increases as the Pacific is approached. The Pacific slopes of Maritime Kray, Sakhalin Island, and Kamchatka Peninsula, with 800–1000 millimeters of precipitation per year, high relative humidity, and great amounts of cloud and fog, are very moist, as are the Kuril Islands which have a completely marine controlled climate.

The general precipitation gradient across the Eurasian plain is broken occasionally by low mountain groups. The Urals, though they rarely rise above 1500–2000 meters, present an elongated obstruction oriented almost perpendicular to much of the air flow across the Eurasian plain and increase precipitation as much as 200–400 millimeters annually above that which is received on the surrounding plain. The southwestern slopes of the mountains generally are the wettest because of the southwest-northeast movement of most of the cyclonic storms that pass through the area. The Putorana Mountains, which rise to heights of about 2000 meters east of the Yenisey River in north-central Siberia, have a similar effect. In the southern part of the European plain the Carpathian Mountains in places receive more than 1500 millimeters of precipitation annually, and the crest of the Crimean Mountains receive as much as 1100 millimeters.

Precipitation varies drastically according to elevation and exposure to moisture-bearing winds in all the high mountains along the southern fringes of the country. The maximum in the western part of the Caucasus has already been mentioned. The eastern Great Caucasus generally exhibit quite dry aspects in spite of their continuing high elevations. In Central Asia the Tien Shans and Pamir-Alay ranges receive more than 1000 millimeters per year on some of the westward-facing slopes at intermediate altitudes. But in the high eastern portions of the Pamirs, summits generally are above most storms, and as little as 75 millimeters per year may fall in some portions of eastern Tadzhikistan, where the climate has a very dry aspect in spite of the fact that temperatures are always quite cold and evaporation rates are low. Much of the precipitation that falls in the Central Asian mountains falls during winter in the form of snow, which is very important to irrigation usage on the plains to the northwest. If the winter precipitation fell as rain it would run off immediately and probably cause more harm than good, but as it is the snow remains in the mountains through the winter and the

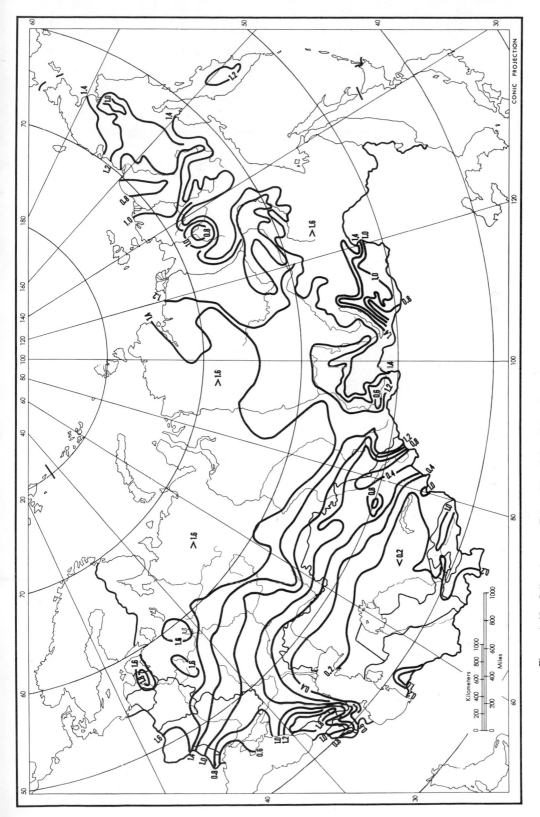

Figure 4-18 Soil moisture coefficient, May–July. <0.3 = desert; 0.3–0.6 = semidesert; 0.6–0.8 = steppe; 0.8–1.0 = forest steppe; >1.0 = forest and tundra. After Lydolph, Climates of the Soviet Union, p. 338.

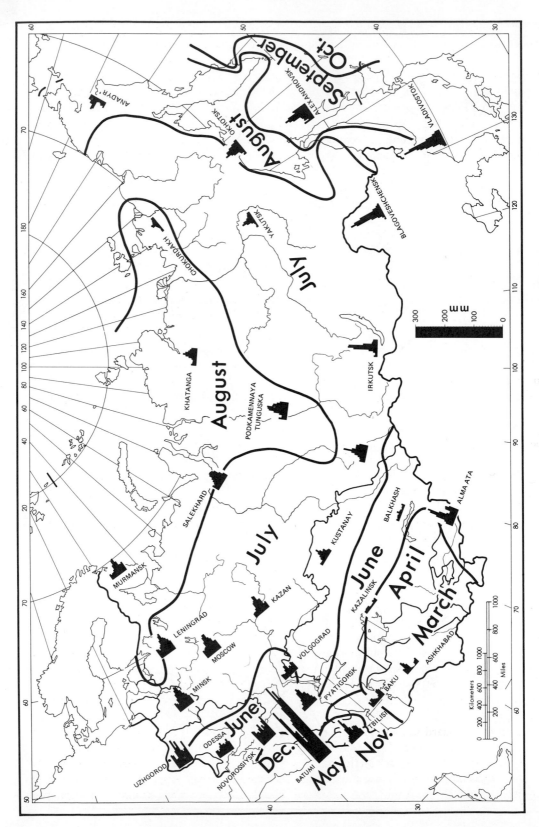

Figure 4–19   Annual regimes of precipitation and months of maxima. After Lydolph, Climates of the Soviet Union, p. 299.

greatest meltwater runoff occurs in mid summer when it is most needed by irrigated crops.

Most of the Soviet Union experiences great seasonality in precipitation amounts. (Fig. 4–19) Over most of the country the warm season has much greater precipitation than the cold season does. Such a regime is common to continental interiors where summer shower activity produces more rainfall than winter cyclonic storms do. In the Soviet Union this tendency is reinforced by the seasonal reversal of pressure patterns, with the Asiatic High in winter and the thermal low in summer. It also reflects the contrast in moisture-holding capacity of the air during the two seasons.

In the broad central section of the plain extending across European U.S.S.R. and northeastward through Siberia and the interior portions of the Far East, precipitation maxima occur quite regularly in July and there is a fairly symmetrical arrangement of precipitation amounts around mid summer, although usually precipitation is skewed a bit toward autumn rather than spring. Minima in this region usually occur in later winter. As one proceeds northward from this central zone, precipitation maxima lag into August, and southward they advance into June. This lag in the summer precipitation maxima with latitude is common of continental interiors and is related to the gradual northward shift of the Polar Front during the summer as well as the northward progression of convective activity as the heating of the land surface sweeps northward during summer, the rise in surface air temperatures occurring later with higher latitudes as the latent heat used by thawing and evaporation lags later into summer. Thus, northern areas not only suffer from short growing seasons, but the harvest season is often the wettest time of the year. The August maximum dips far southward in Western Siberia and in the northwestern part of European U.S.S.R., which is a great hazard to harvesting in those areas that have limited periods for harvesting anyway because of temperature conditions.

In the continental portion of the Soviet Far East, particularly in the south, the summer maximum is more pronounced than anywhere else in the country. The second half of summer receives considerably more precipitation than the first half, which reflects the monsoonal nature of the climate in this region. During summer a Mongolian segment of the Polar Front develops which spawns cyclonic storms that move east-northeastward to the Sea of Okhotsk. The warm sectors of these storms pull in warm, humid, conditionally unstable air from the southwest off the Chinese land mass which, rising up the slopes of warm fronts, produces widespread precipitation and severe thunderstorms. Underneath the warm fronts in the northeastern quadrants of storms, easterly circulations pull in cooler, more stable Pacific air which produces prolonged light rainfall, drizzle, and fog on the seaward slopes of coastal mountains such as the Sikhota Alin. As one proceeds seaward the summer maximum lags later and later into autumn, and the regime becomes more complicated. The seaward fringe of the Soviet Far East from Kamchatka southward receives significant amounts of precipitation in autumn from typhoons which at this time of year follow a route northeastward from Japan. They do not come close enough to the Soviet Union to produce wind damage, but they do cause perturbations in the air flow that produce prolonged precipitation over wide areas.

The southern extremities of the country have much different precipitation regimes. Here the summers are dominated by the eastern extension of the Azores High which produces generally clear, hot weather. The rainfall comes primarily with cyclonic storms that develop during winter in the Mediterranean and Middle East and move east-northeastward into the Black Sea-Caucasian-Caspian-Central Asian regions. On the southeast coast of the Crimea and the northeastern coast of the Black Sea in the Transcaucasus maximum precipitation usually falls in December–January. Farther east, the precipitation maximum lags into March in Central Asia and April in southern Kazakhstan. There is an abrupt changeover from April to June in middle Kazakhstan as the primary precipitation control shifts from winter cyclonic storms in the south to summer thundershowers in the north.

The Caucasian region exhibits the greatest complexities in precipitation amounts and regimes of any part of the Soviet Union. A mid winter maximum of precipitation holds true only along the northeastern coast of the Black Sea where Novorossiysk receives a primary maximum in December. However the rest of the year is almost as wet, and it is obvious that summer thundershowers are about as important as winter cyclonic storms. As one proceeds southeastward down the coast to Batumi, the maximum shifts to September. The only consistency in the rainfall regime along the Black Sea coast is the May minimum, which seems to be the low point in both cyclonic storms at the end of winter and thunderstorms at the beginning of summer. At this time the sea water has reached its lowest temperature, so convective activity is diminished. However, as one proceeds eastward into the Transcaucasus, much of the area receives a May maximum of precipitation, which is associated primarily with thunderstorms. As one approaches the Caspian coast the maximum shifts to October–November. North of the Great Caucasus the maximum in most places occurs in June.

There is essentially no correspondence between amounts of rainfall and frequencies of rain and cloud cover. In many cases frequencies of precipitation seem to be geographically and seasonally distributed almost opposite to amounts of precipitation. During the summer half year, the Arctic fringe of the country extending inland 700 kilometers or more in Eastern Siberia experiences some type of precipitation over a total duration of 700–1000 hours. This duration of precipitation decreases steadily southward to less than 150 hours in Central Asia. Much of the wooded steppe and steppe regions of southern European U.S.S.R. receive precipitation for 150–500 hours.

The most intense precipitation generally falls in the southern part of the country. Figure 4–20 shows that parts of the Transcaucasus and the Transcarpathian area in western Ukraine receive more than 100 hours of thun-

derstorms per year. As many as 5 days per year, thunderstorms in the Transcaucasus are associated with hail. This is so damaging to costly crops, such as grapes and other fruit, that a hail supression research station has been established in the Caucasus.

Clouds

On the average during the year the cloudiest part of the country is the northwest extending inland from the Barents Sea. During January much of the European Plain southeastward to the Central Chernozem Region averages more than eight-tenths sky cover. In July this diminishes to between six and seven tenths. The region with the least yearly average cloudiness is Central Asia with five-tenths coverage. This increases to about seven-tenths in January and decreases to two-four tenths in July. The southern part of the Soviet Far East shows the greatest seasonality in cloudiness. It receives its greatest amounts during summer with buildup of cyclonic storms along the Mongolian Front and the monsoon influx of Pacific air. In January the very southern part of this region has only about four-tenths sky cover, while in July it has eight-tenths.

Fog

Fog occurs most frequently in the northern, eastern, and western peripheries of the country. Along the Arctic coast fog occurs 70–90 days per year. Along the shores of the Sea of Okhotsk and the Sea of Japan it occurs from 50–70 days per year. The very southern tip of Kamchatka receives 115 days per year, and the northern end of Sakhalin Island, 85 days. In the west, parts of Belorussia and surrounding regions receive at least 70 days of fog per year, and on the Stavropol Plateau north of the Great Caucasus a small area receives more than 90 days per year.

The coastal areas receive most of their fog in summer when the sea is much cooler than the land and strong sea breezes set up by tempera-

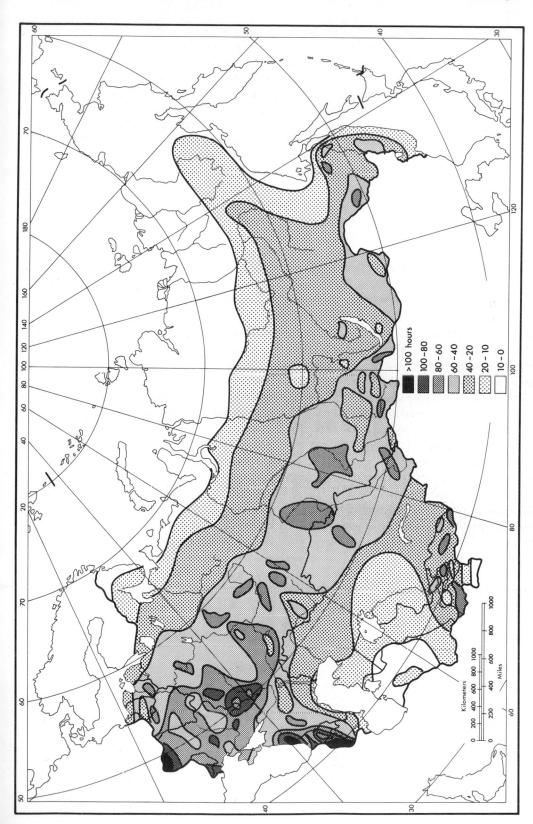

Figure 4–20   Mean annual duration of thunderstorms, in hours. After Lydolph, Climates of the Soviet Union, p. 319.

ture differences carry advection fog inland from the sea. Interior areas on the other hand usually receive their fog in winter. Throughout the colder parts of the country much of this fog is of an Arctic steam nature arising from rivers and lakes in early winter before they freeze over. Irkutsk almost always experiences some fog during winter rising from the unfrozen portion of the Angara which does not freeze immediately downstream from Lake Baykal. Hence, Irkutsk shows 103 days per year with fog, all during the winter. Since most of the recording stations in the sparsely settled eastern parts of the country are in cities in river valleys, the recorded data give an inflated idea of the frequency of fog in this region. On the interfluves between streams fog would not occur nearly as frequently.

The fog occurring on the eastern slope of the Stavropol Plateau in the North Caucasus is primarily upslope fog during winter when there is a steady easterly flow of air around the southern edge of the "great axis" that extends westward from the Asiatic High. Cold, moist air moves up the gradual eastern slope of the plateau underneath a temperature inversion and frequently forms dense fog. As the air descends the western slope it warms and the fog dissipates. Condensation on the eastern slope often takes place at temperatures below freezing, so the fog is frequently associated with rime ice. A similar situation exists over the Donets Ridge in eastern Ukraine where 70–100 days per year experience fog, and glaze and rime ice are common occurrences. Certain slopes of the Ural mountains also register high amounts of glaze and rime ice. In places there rime ice may accumulate on transmission lines to thicknesses of more than 100 millimeters (4 inches).

Snow

Since the Soviet Union is a high latitude country, throughout much of its territory significant portions of its precipitation falls as snow. Greatest amounts are received in some of the mountain regions. On some of the south-

western slopes of the western extension of the Great Caucasus more than 300 centimeters are received from winter cyclonic storms moving in from the Black Sea. Much of the plain of European U.S.S.R. except the very southern portion receives between 150 and 300 centimeters of snow per year. This diminishes east of the Volga to about 50 centimeters in central Yakutia. Much of the Far East, except the coastal margins, receives only very light snowfall, considerably less than 50 centimeters. As the Pacific is approached, this picks up rapidly. The seaward slopes of the Sikhota Alin receive more than 100 centimeters and the eastern half of Kamchatka more than 150. On some exposed mountain slopes totals would be much higher than that. The deserts of Central Asia generally receive 50–150 centimeters.

However, it is not the receipt of snow so much as the amount on the ground that is important to such things as wintering crops or transportation. Since throughout much of the country there are few thaws during winter, much of the snow that falls accumulates on the ground. During the ten days of winter with maximum snow cover, the depth averages about 20 centimeters along the western border of Belorussia and Ukraine and increases eastward to more than 50 centimeters in Moscow and 80 centimeters on the western slopes of the Urals. (Fig. 4–21) It diminishes in the Ob Basin to less than 50 centimeters but increases again to more than 80 centimeters on the western rise of the Central Siberian Upland east of the middle Yenisey Valley. Much of the Far East has a modest snow cover, which increases greatly along seaward margins. On Kamchatka more than 100 centimeters may be found on some mountain slopes. In the southern part of the Far East along the Amur Valley is found some of the sparsest snow cover in the country, less than 20 centimeters. Here the ground may be laid bare to deep frosts during much of winter, which causes severe winter kill of crops. Throughout most of Central Asia and the Transcaucasus, as well as the Black Sea Steppes and North Caucasian regions, much of the winter is without snowcover. Some of the heaviest snow cover in the country is found in

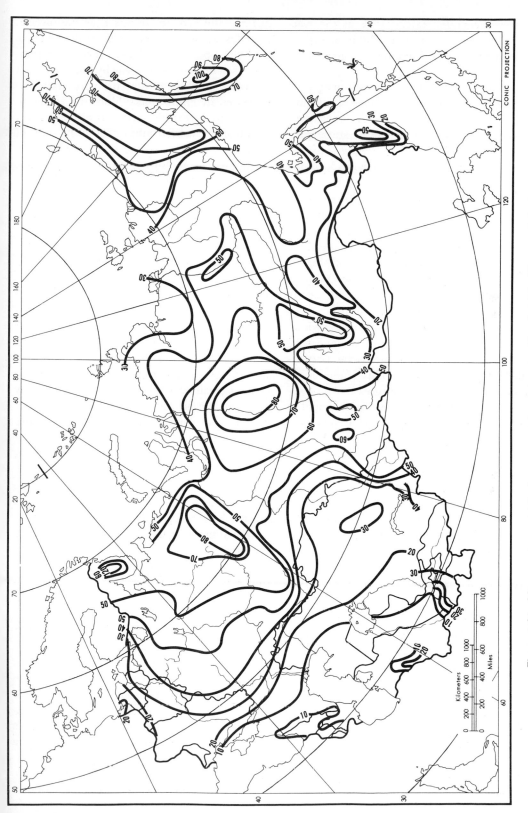

Figure 4-21 Mean maximum depth of snow cover, in centimeters. After Lydolph, Climates of the Soviet Union, p. 325.

localized mountain regions, such as the Khibiny in the Kola Peninsula, where more than 120 centimeters may accumulate on exposed slopes.

The snow cover is very important to agriculture since wintering crops, such as winter wheat, rye, and alfalfa, need to be insulated from the extreme fluctuations of surface air temperatures that occur over much of the Soviet Union during winter. About 30 centimeters of snow is an ideal insulating layer. If it is thinner, the ground experiences deep freezing and frequent fluctuation of temperature; if it gets too thick, crops tend to rot from lack of ventilation. Since much of the agriculture of the Soviet Union is located in the south-central zones of European U.S.S.R. and Western Siberia where average snow cover amounts to about 10–40 centimeters, the prospect of a correct amount of snow cover during the winter is very questionable. Therefore, the Soviets usually sustain extensive winter kill in portions of the country every year. This is one of the primary problems of agriculture.

For best protection, the snow cover should be established before extremely cold weather sets in. Usually a consistent snow cover becomes established throughout Siberia and the Far East between October 1 and November 1, but this lags through European U.S.S.R. in a south-westerly direction to about December 1 in the Central Chernozem Region and January 1 in the Black Sea Steppes. The snow cover usually melts in spring about February 1 in the Black Sea Steppes, April 1 in the Central Black Earth Region and May 1–June 1 throughout much of Siberia and the Far East as well as higher elevations in southern parts of the country. The central Russian plain generally has from 120–160 days with snow cover. (Fig. 4–22)

CLIMATIC DISTRIBUTION

Figure 4–23 depicts the climatic regions of the Soviet Union devised by two well-known Soviet climatologists on the basis of a thermal index (the radiation balance at the earth's surface) and a moisture index, or the inverse, an index of aridity (calculated by dividing the radiation balance at the earth's surface expressed in calories per year by the latent heat of evaporation times the yearly precipitation expressed in millimeters). Since the radiation balance at the earth's surface is ordinarily not available, it has been substituted for by sums of temperatures above 10°C during the season when the average diurnal temperature remains above 10°C, which has been found to be correlated linearly with the annual radiation balance at the earth's surface. Thus, moisture and temperature conditions are shown as the two primary parameters determining the major climatic zones of the country, and winter conditions (January average temperature and average depth of snow cover during the ten days when the snow cover is deepest) are used as secondary parameters to subdivide the major zones. This classification scheme has resulted in a map that seems to fit the distributuion of such things as soils and natural vegetation, and hence agricultural potentials, better than any other scheme previously devised.[3]

As can be seen in Figure 4–23, the moisture categories describe a zonal pattern in the Soviet Union with the most humid conditions along the Arctic and progressively drier conditions southward, except for some mountainous areas such as the Caucasus. Sums of temperatures during the growing season also tend to show a zonal pattern, but winter temperatures deviate significantly from a latitudinal distribution. A significant boundary based on winter temperature runs southward from the White Sea and then swings southeastward into Central Asia. This separates a region on the west with moderately mild winters, January averages between 0 and −13°C, from a region to the east which has a January average ranging from −13 to −32°C. This distinguishes an area in the west which is primarily marine controlled from the east which is primarily continentally controlled. It is interesting that Moscow is to the west of this line in a region having a

[3]For a more detailed explanation of the climatic scheme see Lydolph, *Climates of the Soviet Union*, pp. 357–362.

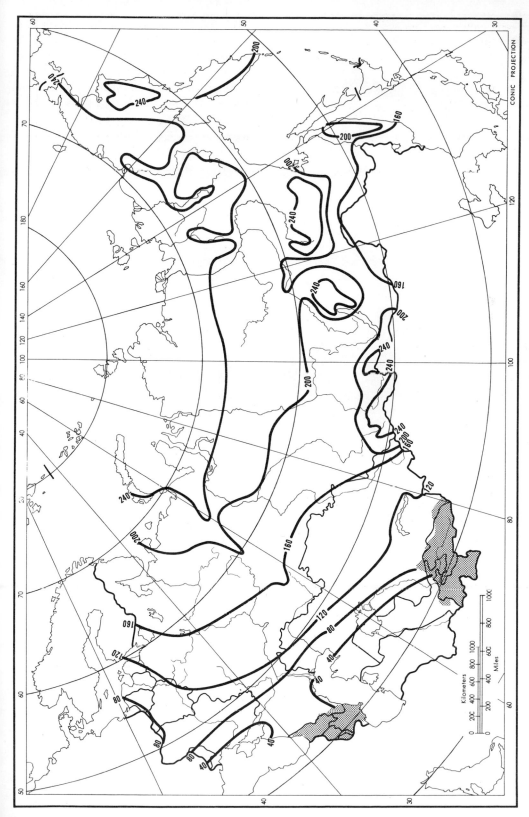

Figure 4–22   Mean annual number of days with snow cover. After Lydolph, Climates of the Soviet Union, p. 326.

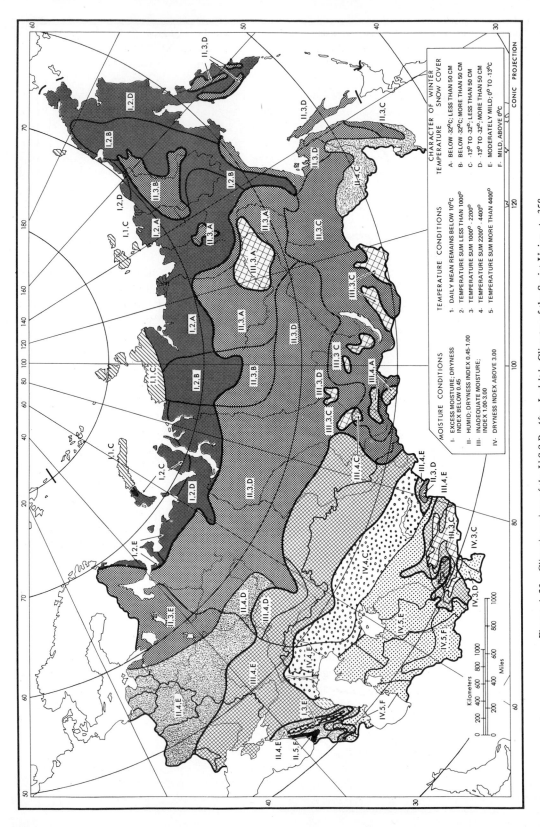

Figure 4–23 Climatic regions of the U.S.S.R. After Lydolph, Climates of the Soviet Union, p. 358.

MOISTURE CONDITIONS

I – EXCESS MOISTURE; DRYNESS INDEX BELOW 0.45
II – HUMID; DRYNESS INDEX 0.45-1.00
III – INADEQUATE MOISTURE; INDEX 1.00-3.00
IV – DRYNESS INDEX ABOVE 3.00

TEMPERATURE CONDITIONS

1 – DAILY MEAN REMAINS BELOW 10°C
2 – TEMPERATURE SUM LESS THAN 1000°
3 – TEMPERATURE SUM 1000° - 2200°
4 – TEMPERATURE SUM 2200° - 4400°
5 – TEMPERATURE SUM MORE THAN 4400°

CHARACTER OF WINTER
TEMPERATURE   SNOW COVER

A – BELOW -32°C; LESS THAN 50 CM
B – BELOW -32°C; MORE THAN 50 CM
C – -13° TO -32°; LESS THAN 50 CM
D – -13° TO -32°; MORE THAN 50 CM
E – MODERATELY MILD; 0° TO -13°C
F – MILD, ABOVE 0°C

CONIC PROJECTION

moderately mild winter. Although to most non-Russians Moscow seems quite cold during winter, with a January average of −10°C and an absolute minimum temperature of −42°C, for its high latitude, 55°45′N, it is anomalously warm because of the marine influence from the west. During summer, on the other hand, this western portion of the plain is cooled by the marine influence. Sums of temperatures during the growing season are higher at similar latitudes in the east.

Along the Arctic fringe precipitation in most cases is quite light, no more than 250 millimeters per year, if that, but temperatures are so cool year-round that evaporation rates are low, and when the surface of the soil thaws out during the short summer the region is generally waterlogged. Thus, Category I is classified as a zone having excessive moisture. Immediately along the coast and on islands offshore daily mean temperatures usually do not rise above 10°C. Since this is the threshold temperature for tree growth, most of the vegetation in this area is tundra. In the west, around the fringes of the Barents Sea, which remains open during winter, the zone is moderately mild, but farther east it becomes extremely cold in Eastern Siberia and the Far East where the zone expands far southward because of higher elevations.

Category II, 3, which covers the broad north-central portion of the country and expands eastward to include much of Eastern Siberia, is a region of humid conditions with temperature sums between 1000° and 2200°C. These temperatures are conducive to the growing of coniferous and small leaved trees. In general it is too cool for agriculture, although small regions of cultivation are found in sheltered areas where probably the climate locally does not fit the categories shown. Category II, 4, with humid conditions and temperature sums between 2200° and 4400°C corresponds closely to the zone of mixed forests in west-central European U.S.S.R. Generally this region does not suffer from drought, and with its greater heat resources it is adaptable to a considerable variety of crops. A similar region with colder winters occupies much of the Amur

Basin and the Ussuri-Khanka Lowland in the Far East. Category III generally outlines steppe country with somewhat inadequate moisture supplies. Although it suffers from drought, it has the best soils in the country and thus contains some of the best agriculture, particularly grain growing. Category IV covers the deserts of Kazakhstan, Central Asia, and the eastern part of the Transcaucasus. Although it suffers from lack of water, it has the greatest heat resources in the country, and therefore irrigation agriculture has been developed as widely as possible.

The Caucasus present a mixture of climatic types ranging from excessively wet, cool conditions along the crest of the Great Caucasus to humid, very warm conditions in the Colchis Lowland at the eastern end of the Black Sea, to dry, hot, conditions in the Kura and Araks River valleys to the east and south. The most distinctive feature of the climate of the Transcaucasus at low elevations is the mild winter which everywhere averages above freezing (subcategory F). Except for some sheltered spots in the very southern part of Central Asia and along the southeastern coast of the Crimea, such mild winters do not exist anywhere else in the U.S.S.R. And the Transcaucasian lowlands are protected more from occasional intrusions of cold northerly air than these other localities are. It is the relative freedom from hard frosts that imparts the special agricultural character to portions of the Transcaucasus where crops such as citrus and tea are grown.

It is significant that across the Eurasian plain moisture and thermal zones run essentially parallel to one another with their gradients pointed in opposite directions. It gets colder toward the north and drier toward the south. This is quite a different arrangement from that in eastern North America where the thermal gradient is directed northward and the moisture gradient is directed westward. Thus, the moisture and thermal zones in eastern North America are essentially perpendicular to one another. The explanation for this difference between the two areas lies primarily in the different shapes of the continents and different orientations of their major mountains.

The result is that the Soviet Union finds fewer combinations of heat and moisture than is the case in eastern North America. Whereas eastern North America contains combinations of hot and humid, hot and dry, cold and humid, cold and dry, and gradations in between, the Soviet Union has only gradations of hot and dry and cold and humid. And because of the generally high latitude, the warmer places in the Soviet Union usually do not have very long, warm growing seasons, except for small areas in the Transcaucasus and Central Asia. On the European plain even the best farming regions of the Ukraine and North Caucasus are constrained by their limited heat resources.

Reading List

1. Borisov, A. A., *Climates of the USSR,* Aldine, Chicago, 1965, 255 pp.
2. ———, *Klimaty SSSR, v proshlom, nastoyash-chem, i budyshchem* (Climates of the U.S.S.R., past, present, and future), Izd. Leningrad Universitet, Leningrad, 1975, 432 pp.
3. ———, *Paleoklimatologiya SSSR* (Paleoclimatology of the U.S.S.R.), Kaliningrad University, Kaliningrad, 1974, 304 pp.
4. Huning, James Robert, *A Visualization of Seasonal and Annual Precipitation Variability in the Soviet Union,* PhD Dissertation, California, Riverside, 1976.
5. Lydolph, Paul E., *Climates of the USSR, World Survey of Climatology,* Vol. 7, Elsevier, Amsterdam, 1977, 443 pp.
6. ———, "The Russian Sukhovey," *Annals of the Association of American Geographers,* September 1964, pp. 291–309.
7. ———, "Some Characteristics of the Climate of the USSR with a Direct Bearing on Human Activity," *Soviet Geography: Review and Translation,* March 1977, pp. 145–163.
8. Rauner, Yu. L., "The Periodicity of Droughts in the Grain-Growing Areas of the USSR," *Soviet Geography: Review and Translation,* November 1977, pp. 625–646.

5

Natural Vegetation, Soils, and Potentials for Agriculture

The gross features of the geographical distribution of natural vegetation and soils correspond closely to those of heat and moisture conditions illustrated in Figure 4–23. The zone designated as tundra on Figure 5–1 corresponds to the zone on Figure 4–23 which has temperature sums of less than 1000°C during the period when the average diurnal temperature remains above 10°C. The taiga zone corresponds to the zone having temperature sums between 1000 and 2200°C and a dryness index from 0.45 to 1.00. The mixed forest corresponds to temperature sums between 2200 and 4400° and a dryness index of 0.45–1.00. The steppe corresponds to temperature sums of 2200–4400°C and a moisture index of 1.00–3.00. In between the steppe and the mixed forest lies a zone of forest-steppe which is a transition between the two and straddles the heat and moisture boundary between II, 4, and III, 4, in Figure 4–23. The semidesert in north-central Kazakhstan corresponds to a dryness index of more than 3.00 and temperature sums of 2200–4400°C, while the desert zone in southern Kazakhstan and Central Asia has a dryness index of more than 3.00 and temperature sums greater than 4400°C.

In mountainous areas, of course, a variety of heat and moisture balances corresponding to rapid changes in exposure to the sun and moisture-bearing winds produces complicated distributions of vegetation and soil types that are too detailed to be shown on a small scale map. Some irregularities in the zonal pattern are shown in Figures 4–23 and 5–1 where fairly homogeneous conditions exist over large enough areas. This is the case in such places as the intermontane basins of southern Siberia where the dryness index rises above 1.0, as opposed to a dryness index of less than 1.0 in surrounding uplands. The basins generally were vegetated originally by grasses while the uplands are forested. These differences in moisture and natural vegetation have also induced differences in soil development. The same is true in the Lena-Aldan-Vilyuy Lowland in the vicinity of Yakutsk where the dryness index is right around 1.0. The area is spotted with clumps of taiga forest interspersed with steppe-like grasses and other low plants.

Converse to the steppe basins in Siberia, the Donets Ridge in eastern Ukraine rises just high enough to lift the area out of a general region of steppe and transform it into forest-steppe. The same is true of the mountains in the southern Crimean Peninsula and the loess foothills of the Central Asian mountains which receive more than 350 millimeters of precipitation each year. But these areas are too small to show on the map.

In the sheltered lowlands of the Transcaucasus temperature sums during the growing season generally exceed 4400°C and winters average above freezing. However, moisture

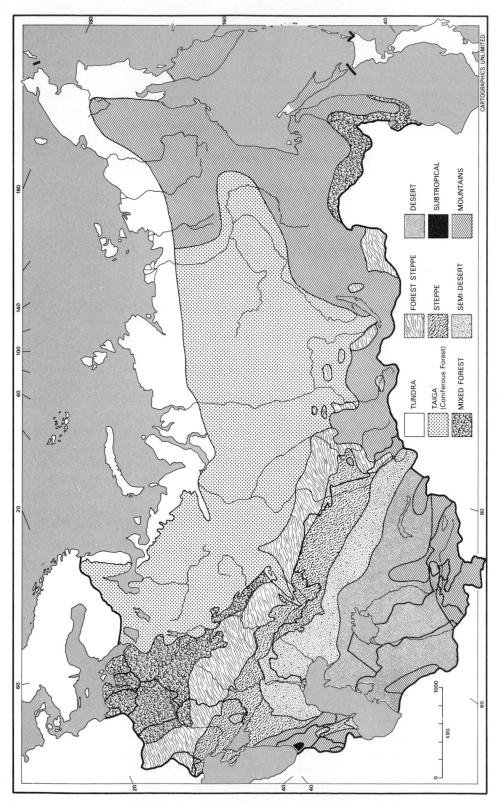

Figure 5–1 Vegetation zones of the U.S.S.R. Modified from Berg, p. 352.

conditions grade from humid in the west to very dry in the east, so the vegetation in the wet Colchis Lowland in the west is of a subtropical forest type, while the dry eastern part of the Kura Lowland is semidesert.

ZONAL DESCRIPTIONS

Tundra

"Tundra" is a Finnish term meaning treeless, marshy plain. Although originally it was primarily a term to describe vegetation, it has become commonly used around the world also for climatic and soil descriptions. A tundra type of climate is usually considered to be one which has no month averaging above 10°C (50°F) which is considered to be the limit of tree growth. As was seen in Figure 4–23, a narrow strip along the Arctic coast of the Taymyr Peninsula and the Arctic islands offshore never have any days averaging above 10°C. During summer strong sea breezes set up along the coast between the cold water offshore and the heated interior. Since ice floes remain in the water even near the shore, sea surface temperatures always hover near the freezing point. The low temperature plus the consistently strong winds make this shore area very raw indeed. Inland, individual days do average above 10°C, but no entire month averages above that.

To the Laplanders in the Kola Peninsula and adjacent Scandinavia, the word "tundra" means "bald mountain top." Alpine tundra covers much of the Khibiny low mountains in the central Kola Peninsula and extends far southward on the mountains of the Soviet Far East east of the Lena River. There is a great interfingering of tundra and taiga types in the Soviet Far East all the way to the southern border of the country, tundra extending southward on the mountains and taiga northward in the valleys. The same is true in the northern Urals, Kamchatka, Sakhalin Island, and the Kuril Island chain. Even at low elevations, the northern plain of Sakhalin and the northern islands of the Kuril chain are rendered treeless by the consistently cool, stiff winds that blow off the Sea of Okhotsk and the Pacific.

Tundra soils are notoriously infertile. The great amount of water in the topsoil when it is thawed has leached much of the mineral constituents from the soil, and the meager growth of vegetation has produced little humus. Permafrost underneath the active layer hinders percolation so that during the short summer the topsoil everywhere is waterlogged. This region holds little promise for agriculture other than sparse pasture for reindeer herding.

Taiga

Taiga is a term used by the Turkic Yakuts and Buryats in Siberia to refer to the vast forests of Siberia. It has become used throughout the world to designate the northern coniferous forests. However, these forests in many places have a rich admixture of small leaved trees such as birch, poplar, aspen, and willow, particularly along the southern margins, or, as in the case of willow, in poorly drained areas. In the Soviet Union taiga vegetation covers much of the region extending from the western border with Finland through the northern 40 per cent of the European part of the country and expanding in Siberia to cover much of the width of the country in Eastern Siberia except for tundra in the north and alpine tundra and steppe basins in the south. It covers the intermediate slopes of the southern mountains, being limited by drought in the lower levels and by cold in the upper levels, so that the basin floors are generally covered with steppe grasses and the mountain tops by alpine tundra. In the Far East, where much of the country is mountainous, most of the lower and intermediate slopes are forested. In the Verkhoyansk and Cherskiy ranges of the northeast forests generally do not extend above 200 meters above sea level, but along the Stanovoy range in the south larch taiga with admixtures of pine on southern exposures may extend upward to 1000 meters, above which a thin forest finally grades into a stunted growth of Japanese stone pine, birch, and alder above 1650–1700 meters. The summits above 2200 meters are alpine tundra.

Different species of trees dominate in different parts of the taiga. Throughout much of Karelia and the southern half of the Kola Peninsula various pines are the predominant species with admixtures of fir, birch, and other trees. The plain through Archangel Oblast and the Komi A.S.S.R., as well as the western slopes of the Urals in Perm Oblast have a predominance of fir, although pines are still common, and in some regions birch predominates. Southern edges of the taiga in European U.S.S.R., as well as in Western Siberia, are dominated by birch. Much of the lowland of Western Siberia is dominated by various species of pine that in most cases are somewhat different from the pines in the European part of the country. South of the juncture of the Irtysh and Ob Rivers, birch becomes the dominant species, and it predominates along much of the contact zone between the West Siberian Lowland and the Central Siberian Upland along the Yenisey River throughout the taiga zone. East of this strip, throughout the Central Siberian Uplands and most of the lower mountain slopes throughout the Far East southward to the Amur River, larch, a deciduous coniferous tree, dominates. It is well adapted to the permafrost conditions that exist throughout much of this region because it has a shallow root system that can spread out and sustain the plant in the thin active layer of soil during the summer.

Throughout the taiga zone, much land is devoid of trees, primarily because of poor drainage. Here marsh grasses and bushes take over. This is particularly true throughout the West Siberian Lowland and the various polesye of northeast European U.S.S.R. The taiga commonly is characterized by rather sparse stands of timber, the individual trees of which are usually no more than 30 centimeters in diameter. Only in the better areas of the Onega and Northern Dvina valleys in northwestern European Russia, the Kama River region on the western slopes of the Urals, portions of Tomsk Oblast and the western slopes of the Altay in Western Siberia, and parts of Irkutsk Oblast in Eastern Siberia have dense stands of fairly large trees.

The taiga is generally bordered on the north and on the intermediate slopes of the Far Eastern mountains by a zone of forest tundra with widely scattered spindly coniferous trees that grades into completely treeless tundra to the north and at higher elevations. On the southern fringe of the taiga mixed forest regions exist in European U.S.S.R. and the lower elevations of the southern and more maritime parts of the Soviet Far East. Throughout much of Siberia this zone is absent, the taiga grading directly into the steppes through a narrow fringe of forest-steppe occupied primarily by steppe grasses interspersed with birch and other small leaved trees.

Throughout the taiga zone the soils are podzolic in character, a Russian term coined from the contraction of words meaning "ashy gray underneath." Tannic acid derived from partially decomposed needles that cover the ground underneath the coniferous trees has made the water a strong solvent which has leached out not only most of the plant minerals but also most of the iron and aluminum, leaving only silica (quartz), a sterile colorless material, to form the topsoil. In addition, the needles decompose very slowly and add essentially no humus to the soil.

The typical mature profile of a podzol is 8–10 centimeters of partially decomposed needles on top underlain by a grayish-white A horizon perhaps 20–30 centimeters thick which grades below into a gray-brown B horizon that at a depth of approximately one-half meter below the surface may culminate in a dark brown hardpan consisting of cemented iron oxides that have been leached down from above. This hardpan layer is fairly impervious to water and further impedes percolation of surface waters downward during the thawing season, which, along with the permafrost, turns the surface into a morass of standing water and waterlogged soils.

Hence, infertile and waterlogged soils combine with cool summers to rule out agriculture for much of the region except for reindeer herding or scattered plots of cultivation in sheltered basins and river valleys in the south where alluvial soils offer greater fertility. But even in those southern fringes crops are limited to hay, hardy small grains, and potatoes that largely support a livestock economy. Flax may be adapted as a cash crop within the taiga zone. The Lena Lowland around Yakutsk has become famous for its northern agriculture. Here strains of wheat and rye have been developed that will ripen within 60 days of planting. However, the operation is marginal at best.

Mixed Forest

In the west and eastern parts of the country the taiga grades into a belt of mixed forest which is predominantly coniferous evergreen in the north and broadlead deciduous in the south. This zone covers much of the width of the country in the west where it stretches from the Baltic coast southward to the western Ukraine at about the latitude of Kiev. It narrows rapidly eastward to pinch out almost entirely between the taiga of the north and the forest-steppe of the south in the vicinity of Gorky, after which it broadens a little again and a narrow strip continues eastward to the Urals. East of the Urals it is largely absent until Amur Oblast, after which it continues eastward, interspersed with steppe basins and taiga covered mountains, to the Pacific.

On the European Plain, pines usually dominate in the ill drained sandy areas such as the polesye of southern Belorussia and northwestern Ukraine, but on the better drained areas broadleaf trees such as oak, beech, and hornbeam take over. In the Far East a rich mixture of fir, silver fir, pines, birch, oak, and other broadleafed trees native to the Far Fast grow on the slopes of the Sikhota Alin in Maritime Kray and the lower elevations of Sakhalin Island, Kamchatka, and the southern Kurils.

Throughout the European Plain, and to some extent in the Far East as well, large areas have been put into cultivation in the mixed forest zone. In Moscow Oblast, for instance, forests still occupy about one-third of the territory. Much of the rest is in cultivation. Although the gray-brown forest soils are podzolic in character, they are not as infertile as the soils in the taiga to the north, and under proper farming methods and heavy fertilization they can be kept very productive. This region has the advantage of slight drought hazard as compared to the better soils in the steppes to the south. It is adapted best to mixed farming based on livestock supported by hay crops, small grains, potatoes, and flax as a cash crop.

Forest-Steppe

The forest-steppe, a transition zone between the forest on the north and the steppe on the south, occupies a belt about 250–500 kilometers wide running from west-southwest to east-northeast across the European plain from the western Ukraine and northern Moldavia to the Bashkir Republic on the western slope of the Urals. It continues in the basins of the south-central Urals and then picks up again as a continuous zone about 200 kilometers wide across the southern part of Western Siberia. It ends abruptly against the Altay Mountains in the southeastern part of Western Siberia and extends southward along their lower western slopes through the Kulunda Steppe of Altay Kray. East of there the forest-steppe is limited to intermontane basins such as that running along the Trans Siberian Railroad from Krasnoyarsk to Irkutsk and the Ulan Ude, Chita, and other basins in the southern part of Eastern Siberia and the Far East. The forest-steppe zone is the northern part of the famous "black earth belt" of the Soviet Union. An original grass vegetation interspersed only here and there by clumps of trees, often in river valleys, has been conducive to the development of a very black topsoil rich in humus. Since the zone straddles the humid-dry boundary, the soil contains about the right balance of minerals also. This type of soil has become known around the world as "chernozem," a contraction of two Russian words meaning "black soil." In places where trees have taken over, the soil has been a little leached and is known as degraded chernozem.

The chernozems are the best soils in the world, and the wooded-steppe zone has about the best combination of moisture and heat resources in the Soviet Union outside a few local areas such as the Colchis Lowland in western Georgia. Although the zone is subject to drought, it is not as prone as the steppes and deserts to the south, and it has much better heat resources than the forest zones of the north. Thus, while it does not have the maximum amount of heat in the Soviet Union nor the maximum amount of moisture, it has the best combination of the two. This with the excellent soils makes this the potentially best agricultural region in the country, adapted to a wide variety of crops, many of which are raised on a cash basis such as sugar beets, and wheat, and a variety of other grains.

Most of the original vegetation has been plowed up and the land put into cultivation except on the steeper slopes of streams and gullies. On the Podolian Upland of the western Ukraine the topography is fairly rough and erosion has been a tremendous problem. This is true also in parts of the Central Chernozem Region in the Russian Republic north of the Ukraine. Drought and erosion are the two biggest problems of the area. Much of the erosion has been accomplished by streams, but also wind erosion is significant, since the soil is fine grained and easy to blow. Much of the area has an admixture of loess in the top soil because of the constant shifting of dust by the wind. Some of this has been derived locally and some has been blown in from the east and south, particularly during winter when fairly strong easterly winds prevail along the southern edge of the western protrusion of the Asiatic High. Much of the forest-steppe zone has been densely populated by rural inhabitants for many centuries, and they have depleted many of the forest stands along the steeper stream banks in their constant search for firewood for their huts during winter. This has greatly aggravated the erosion problem. Some reforestation has been sponsored by the Soviets to combat water erosion, and shelter belts have been planted to combat wind erosion.

Steppe

South of the wooded-steppe lie the open steppes of the southern plains that are virtually treeless. These cover the southeastern half of Ukraine including the Crimean Peninsula, except for the mountains, and extend east-northeastward across the Volga and southern Urals into the very southern edge of Western Siberia and the northern part of Kazakhstan. Southeast of the Sea of Azov the steppes also cover the western half of the North Caucasian Foreland. In the steppe zone drought is a constant companion, which has ruled out much tree growth and allowed for an original vegetation of short steppe grasses which have led to high humus content in the soil and a good balance of plant minerals. Although the soils are not as high in humus, and therefore not as dark colored, as the chernozems in the wooded steppe zones to the north, these soils are still exceedingly fertile and with adequate moisture can be some of the most productive soils in the world. Soil color grades from almost black along the northern fringes of the steppe through dark brown and chestnut color in the middle to light brown and yellow-brown in the drier south.

Like the chernozems, steppe soils are well drained, well structured, and easy to cultivate. Heat resources in this zone are greater than anything to the north, but the moisture supply becomes less and less the farther south one goes. Therefore, crop combinations are somewhat more limited in the steppe zone than in the wooded-steppe zone. The steppe zone is well suited to the raising of wheat and sunflowers. Corn has been introduced rather heavily since the mid 1950s although it finds neither optimum moisture nor optimum heat supplies here. The steppe zone is even more susceptible to wind erosion than is the wooded-steppe to the north, and generally contains thicker deposits of loess. Dust swept out of the Ukraine by southeasterly winds during winter has been detected as far north as Scandinavia. Almost all the land in the steppe zone has been brought under cultivation.

Semidesert

A semidesert region rings the northern end of the Caspian as far north as Volgograd and

Saratov and continues east-northeastward across north-central Kazakhstan. This zone suffers from constant moisture deficits and is virtually useless for cultivation without irrigation. In the past it has been primarily a region of nomadic herding. The soils here are high in mineral content but low in humus. With proper irrigation they can be made quite productive for certain crops.

Desert

The southern half of Kazakhstan and all but the mountains of Central Asia lies in desert conditions. The soils are high in minerals, but contain practically no organic matter. Where the mineral content is not so high that the soil becomes alkaline or saline, many crops can be grown under irrigation. The natural vegetation is sparse, consisting of various kinds of brush and saxaul trees, a small gnarled tree that is unique to the Central Asia area. It can exist on practically no water and survive in almost pure sand. It reaches heights of 6–7 meters, although most of it is considerably shorter than that. Large areas of the desert floor are not vegetated at all. Wind erosion has been extreme in this region, sorting the finer particles out of the topsoil and blowing them away as dust toward the southern mountains. Large areas of the desert consist of shifting sand dunes which can hardly be utilized for anything. Since the prevailing winds in this region throughout the year are from the north, most of the wind-blown dust has become lodged against the foothills of the southern mountains where some of the most extensive and thickest loess deposits in the world now exist. These loess deposits, plus river alluvium in the lower portions of streams, form about the only cultivatable soil throughout the desert region. It is these areas that have been irrigated where possible and now support a thriving agriculture of cotton, alfalfa, and a wide variety of fruits and vegetables.

High mountains of Central Asia have vertical zonations of climate, vegetation, and soils. Desert conditions extend upward to about 1200–1500 meters, although on the loess foothills at this elevation steppe grasses prevail, and sage brush may cover the rockier heads of alluvial fans. From about 1200 meters to about 2300 meters, depending upon the exposure of the slopes, mountain broadleaf forests are the dominant vegetation. Above 2300 meters coniferous forests prevail up to about 3000 meters, above which subalpine meadow-steppes and alpine tundras are found. Above 5000 meters little vegetation exists since it is very cold and little precipitation is derived from cloud systems that are generally below this level. Many of the higher summits are covered with perpetual snowfields and glaciers.

Subtropics

Two small areas in the Transcaucasus are classified as subtropical in climate, vegetation, and soils. These are the Colchis Lowland in western Georgia at the east end of the Black Sea and the much smaller Lenkoran Lowland in the southeast part of Azerbaydzhan wedged between the Talysh Mountains on the west and the Caspian Sea on the east. These are the only two regions in the Soviet Union that have mild enough winters for the growing of such things as tea and citrus fruits. And even here strong frosts do occur occasionally. Though these subtropical areas are important to the Soviet Union for their unique potential to produce crops exotic to the rest of the country, the regions are so limited in area that they fall far short of supplying the subtropical crops needed by the rest of the country.

Reading List

1. Berg, L. S., *Natural Regions of the USSR,* Macmillan, New York, 1950, 436 pp.
2. Gerasimov, I. P., Armand, D. L., and Yefron, K. M., eds., *Natural Resources of the Soviet Union: Their Use and Renewal.* English edition edited by W. A. Douglas Jackson. W. H. Freeman, San Francisco, 1971, 349 pp.
3. Gerasimov, I. P., Rikhter, G. D., and Chikishev, A. G., eds., *Prirodnye usloviya i estestvennye resursy SSSR* (Natural conditions and natural

resources of the U.S.S.R.), Nauka, Moscow, 1963–1972, 15 volumes.

4. Jackson, W. A. Douglas, *Soviet Resource Management and the Environment,* American Association for the Advancement of Slavic Studies, Columbus, Ohio, 1976, 232 pp.

5. Milkov, F. N., *Prirodnye zony SSSR* (Natural Zones of the U.S.S.R.), 2nd ed., Mysl, Moscow, 1977, 293 pp.

6. *Soil-Geographical Zoning of the USSR,* I.P.S.T., Daniel Davey and Company, New York, 1963, 480 pp.

6

Population

INTRODUCTION

The population of a country is its greatest asset and its greatest liability. Almost everything that is done within a country is done to maintain its populace, and how a country's resources are put to use depends upon the energies, attitudes, and education of its people. The distribution of population within a given country is a spatial expression, cumulative over time of the linkage between man and land in the process of ecomonic activity and provides a measure of two of the most important influences on the continuing location of productive forces — manpower and market. A country's standing in the world depends primarily upon its population numbers and characteristics, and the distribution of economic activity within a country is influenced to a large extent by the distribution of the population. How this population distribution developed over time is closely related to the history of the country itself, the expansion of territory and the development of its economy.

As can be deduced from Chapter 1, the population of the Soviet Union is a polyglot of widely varying groups of people who were brought into the Russian Empire individually by the constant acquisition of territory along the periphery of the country. These peoples have long histories of occupance of the same pieces of land which have intrajected traditions and attitudes so deeply ingrained that even the monolithic Soviet system has not been able to alter them very rapidly. The people who presently find themselves within the confines of the Soviet Union have undergone far different experiences than peoples in the United States. Whereas the Unites States in the beginning was essentially empty land where immigrants, from whatever origin, underwent common experiences that were conducive to amalgamation and the eventual molding of a new American person, the Soviet population has remained largely a combination of diverse groups still living in their ancient homelands, rather than a meld of homogeneous Soviet citizens.

This diversity lends color to the Soviet population, but it also presents many problems to the Soviet leadership. Varying groups of peoples in discrete regions of the country find themselves at different stages of cultural and economic development and do not adjust equally well to the socialist policies of the Soviet government which are striving rapidly to industrialize the country and equalize conditions in all its parts. Many of the non-Slavic groups, particularly in Central Asia, do not adapt well to regular hours of factory work. Therefore, the Soviet government has found it necessary to induce resettlement of Slavs into many areas of the country in order to provide needed industrial labor force. This has brought on a rapid evolution of social mores and ways of life in all parts of the country. Thus, the present is a time of population movement and rapid transition. This renders any current population study difficult and partially meaningless since it might be caught in the stride of a changing trend.

SOVIET POPULATION STUDIES

The Soviets inherited a poor background of population studies, and did not deem such studies particularly relevant or rewarding until the last couple of decades. As long as there was plenty of excess population on farms to be drawn into urban factories the Soviet regime, preoccupied by a multitude of pressing problems, did not see the need to be very concerned about population itself. But since the late 1950s it has become increasingly obvious that population is no longer a free good that exists in inexhaustible supply ready to be moved about at will to suit the needs of the economy. The rural population in many parts of the country has been drained of its best elements, and the maldistribution of manpower with respect to regional needs has caused some serious concern among top planners in the country. It has induced some sweeping reforms calculated to make more efficient use of the population and has prompted the creation of several agencies specifically to study population problems.[1]

Such concerns and measures have brought about a real renaissance in the study of population in the country. A number of economists, sociologists, and geographers have concentrated their efforts along such lines of research. As a result, there is now a good body of authoritative literature by Soviet authors regarding the population of the Soviet Union and the socioeconomic problems that are posed. These studies have been based on solid statistics

[1]Foremost agencies doing studies on population are: (1) Institute of Ethnography, Academy of Sciences of the U.S.S.R.; (2) Demographic Laboratory of the Scientific Research Institute, Central Statistical Administration; (3) Laboratory for the study of Population Problems, Moscow State University; and (4) the Scientific Research Economics Institute, U.S.S.R. Gosplan.

provided by the 1970 and 1959 censuses, as well as by birth and death registrations and police records of departures and arrivals of individuals in all parts of the country. Although such records are not complete, at least they have provided insights into areas that previously were completely devoid of data.

Before World War II the Soviets took censuses and reported their results in 1939 and 1926. Data from these censuses give some bases for comparison with the 1959 and 1970 census results and afford assessments of progress throughout the Soviet period. Prior to the Soviet period the Russian Empire took a census in 1897. This was the first official enumeration of the population of the entire Russian Empire. Before that counts had been made only of adult male populations living in the "gubernias" of the European plain. This was done in order to enumerate households for tax purposes. These so-called, "revisia" were taken in 1857, 1850, 1833, 1815, 1811, 1795, 1782, 1762, 1744, and 1719. Populations for the Russian Empire for these dates must be estimated from the resultant figures on adult male population in the European part of the country. Understandably considerable error may be involved. For the period prior to 1719 there are no data to work with at all, although some estimates have been made of population numbers and types of society at critical points in history, such as the height of Kievan Rus.

HISTORY OF POPULATION DEVELOPMENT

The Eighteenth and Nineteenth Centuries

The expansion outward from Muscovy that took place so rapidly during the fifteenth and sixteenth centuries under the two Ivans, continued during the seventeenth–nineteenth centuries as did the consolidation of control by the tsarist government. By the end of Peter the Great's reign in 1725 almost all the East European Plain, except for the Turkish-held steppes along the north coast of the Black Sea, was under the secure control of Tsarist Russia.

When Peter's government organized the first revisia in 1719 to enumerate households for tax purposes 7,788,927 male adults were counted in the provinces of European Russia. The first official estimate of population of the Russian Empire was given as 17,900,000 in 1724. (Table 6–1) At this time the population in the old settled regions around Moscow northwest-ward toward St. Petersburg was characterized by a high birth rate, a high death rate, and a moderate population growth which was sufficient to sustain the streams of migration going southward and eastward.

During the span of the ten revisia, 1719–1857, the male population in European Russia grew from 7,788,927 to 29,633,126 for a total

Table 6–1   Vital Statistics, Russia and the U.S.S.R., 1724–1977

Year	Source	Population (1000) Pre-1939 Boundaries	Population (1000) Post-1939 Boundaries	Per Cent Urban	Per Cent Rural	Per Cent Male	Per Cent Female	Rates/1000 Births	Rates/1000 Deaths	Rates/1000 Natural Increase	Life Expectancy, Years Male	Life Expectancy, Years Female	Life Expectancy, Years Total
1724	1	17,900											
1801	2	37,540						43.7	27.1	16.6			
1810	2	40,667						40.0	26.5	13.5			
1820	2	48,647						42.7	27.5	15.2			
1830	2	56,127						45.6	33.6	12.0			
1840	2	62,460						49.7	39.4	10.3			
1850	2	68,513		5.5	94.5			52.4	39.4	13.0			
1860	2	74,120		11.3	88.7			51.9	38.7	13.2			
1870	2	84,521		12.3	87.7			49.1	35.5	13.6			
1880	2	97,705		12.9	87.1			48.7	34.2	14.5			
1890	2	117,788		12.7	87.3			49.0	36.2	12.8			
1897	2 (3)	125,640	(124,600)	12.4	87.6	(49.0)	(51.0)	49.4	32.4	17.0	(31)	(33)	(32)
1900	2	131,710		12.8	87.2			47.7	31.0	16.7			
1910	2	153,768		14.3	85.7			45.2	29.0	16.2			
1913	2 (3)	161,723		14.6	85.4	(49.7)	(50.3)	(47.0)	(30.2)	(16.8)			33[4]
1914	3 (2)		159,200	18.0	82.0			(41.0)	(25.3)	(15.7)			
1917	2	169,230		16.9	83.1								
1920	2	137,093		16.7	83.3			29.1	38.1	−9.0			
1923	2	133,467		16.1	83.9			40.5	21.5	19.0			
1926	2 (3)	147,028		17.9	82.1	(48.3)	(51.7)	(44.0)	(20.3)	(23.7)	41.0	45.1	44[4]
1930	2	157,700		19.9	80.1			39.2	20.4	18.8			
1939	2 (3)	170,467		32.9	67.1	(47.9)	(52.1)	(36.5)	(17.3)	(19.2)			47[4]
1940	3		194,100	33	67	47.9	52.1	31.2	18.0	13.2			
1950	3		178,500	39	61	43.9	56.1	26.7	9.7	17.0			
1959	3		208,827	48	52	45.0	55.0	25.0	7.6	17.4			
1970	3		241,720	56	44	46.1	53.9	17.4	8.2	9.2	65	74	70
1977	5		257,900	62	38	46.5	53.5	18.5	9.5	9.0	64 [a]	74 [a]	70 [a]

Sources: (1) Lorimer, Frank, *The Population of the Soviet Union: History and Prospects,* League of Nations, Geneva, 1946.
(2) Eason, Warren W., *Soviet Manpower: The Population and Labor Force of the USSR,* University Microfilms, Ann Arbor, 1959.
(3) *Narodnoye khozyaystvo SSSR v 1970g.,* Statistika, Moscow, 1971.
(4) Osipov, G. V., ed., *Town, Country, and People,* Studies in Soviet Society, Volume 2, Tavistock Publications, London, 1969.
(5) *The USSR in Figures for 1976,* Statistika, Moscow, 1977, pp. 7 and 22.
[a] 1971–1972, from *Narkhoz SSSR,* 1975, p. 161.
Note: Census dates are underlined.

growth of 280 per cent. Over the 138-year period the population in Novorossiya (the southern steppes) increased at an annual average rate of 2.6 per cent. In the lower Volga region it averaged 2.43 per cent, in the southern Urals 1.87 per cent, in Siberia 1.25 per cent, in the central Urals 1.15 per cent, and in the central Volga Valley 0.82 per cent. By 1860 the population of the entire Russian Empire had risen to more than 74,000,000.

During the nineteenth century the economic system based on fuedal landholdings gradually changed to a capitalistic system with a growing importance of industrialization. The emancipation of the serfs in 1861 left many peasants landless and free to move. This initiated an upsurge of migration into the cities and into the newly acquired territories of the Caucasus and Central Asia. The bulk of the migrating peasants were looking for new agricultural lands, but many, in their disappointments, turned to urban occupations, and the new coal and metallurgical industries in the Donets Basin and Krivoy Rog region of the eastern Ukraine became a particular center of attraction. During this time 12–13 million people migrated southward. The central chernozem provinces which earlier had been recipients of immigrants from the central provinces immediately to the north, now became major contributors to the southward stream of migrants into the steppe. During this time Siberia, north Kazakhstan, and the Far East absorbed 4.5–5.0 million migrants.

The establishment of industries by Russian and foreign capital fostered the movement of Russians, Ukrainians, and Belorussians into all parts of the empire to supply a labor force for the factories which were unable to draw significantly from indigenous non-Slavic groups. Throughout Siberia and the Far East where the native population was sparse the Russians soon became dominant in numbers. In the more densely settled regions of the Caucasus and Central Asia the Slavs formed only minority groups, but in many of the cities of these regions they soon became more numerous than the natives themselves, and the Russian way of life became the accepted mode.

The 1897 Census

The first all-Russian census, taken in 1897, showed approximately 125 million people in the empire. These were concentrated in the European part of the country west of the Volga River.[2] The population was most dense in the highly urbanized area around Moscow where Moscow Province averaged between 60 and 80 persons per square kilometer. The density was equally great in parts of the western Ukraine. Much of the rest of the European part of the country averaged between 25 and 60 persons per square kilometer. Generally densities were greater in the forest-steppe than in either the forests to the north or the steppes to the south. Belorussia with its poor drainage conditions stood out as an area of lesser density, while St. Petersburg Province, because of the capital city, stood out as a region of higher density than its surroundings. But in spite of the large city of St. Petersburg, the hinterland was so sparsely settled that the entire province averaged only 45–60 persons per square kilometer.

By 1897 the ecumene of the country had pretty well taken shape. A tapering wedge of higher density population extended from the western border of the country eastward across the Urals into southwestern Siberia where it butted up against the Altay Mountains, beyond which it continued in scattered intermontane basins all the way to the Pacific. The middle and southern Urals averaged between 5 and 15 persons per square kilometer, and much of Western Siberia and what is now Kazakhstan averaged between 1 and 5 persons per square kilometer. Much of the rest of Siberia and the Far East, as well as the northern part of European Russia averaged less than 1 person per square kilometer. Two significant outliers of population were the Caucasus and Central Asia. Parts of Georgia and Armenia in the Transcaucasus had from 25 to 35 persons per square kilometer, and the more densely settled

---

[2]For an 1897 population density map, see Lorimer, pp. 14–15.

provinces of Central Asia averaged between 5 and 15 persons per square kilometer. Of course, in the southern dry regions the population distribution was very uneven. In some of the irrigated oases population densities over restricted areas probably were considerably greater than they were in European Russia, while large intervening areas were practically devoid of population. This distribution of population very closely conformed to the agricultural potentials of the land. The wedge across the central portion of the country occupied the natural zones of the mixed forest, wooded steppe, and steppe in the west and the wooded steppe and steppe in the east.

This distribution of population which fits so closely the agricultural potentials of the land has been maintained essentially the same to the present time. The growth of population since 1897 and the urbanization and industrialization that have taken place primarily during the Soviet period have generally increased population densities throughout the settled portions of the country and have produced intensified nodes of urban population in regions that have spawned large cities for one reason or another, but the basic pattern of population distribution has not changed significantly during the last 80 years.

The census of 1897 recorded numbers of people who had moved into and out of individual areas. Those regions that were receiving the greatest influx of population immediately prior to 1897 were the Far East and most of Siberia, particularly Tomsk Province which, at that time contained the Kuznetsk Coal Basin. In many of these provinces more than 30 per cent of the resident population had moved in from other regions of the Russian Empire. The only other area that had such high inmigration was the Kuban territory of the northern Caucasus whose rich farming potentialities, very similar to those in the better parts of the Ukraine, were attracting Cossack and Ukrainian farmers. Much of the European part of the country was experiencing heavy outmigration. This was particularly true of the central provinces, as well as of some provinces in the west and northwest, where more than 12 per cent of

the population had moved to other regions of the empire.

An interesting feature in the eastern regions, already observable at that time, was the high degree of outmigration as well as inmigration, which signified the unrest of the peoples of those regions and their transitory nature. This was particularly true in Sakhalin Province. The high mobility of the eastern populations is still one of the characteristic features of these regions, which plagues economic planners with high labor turnover.

In 1897 the urbanization process was already underway. Urban inmigration was quite high throughout much of the country, and was particularly high in the Far East and certain provinces of Central Asia and Kazakhstan. The pattern of rural inmigration was significantly different.[3] The Far East still appeared as an area of high inmigration for rural population as well as urban, but there was no rural inmigration to speak of in the southern regions, other than in Kuban district in the North Caucasus. Rural inmigration was rather heavy in Western Siberia, particularly in Tomsk Province, and a significant rural inmigration was going on throughout much of Eastern Siberia. Most of the European part of the country was losing population to migration processes. The final stages of a southerly migration from the wooded steppe into the drier steppes along the northern coasts of the Black and Azov Seas and east-northeastward through the south-central Volga-Urals region was still slightly discernable on the 1897 map.

Summary of Migration, 1500–1900

The results of migration processes during the entire period from the sixteenth century to the beginning of the twentieth century are shown in Figure 6–1. It can be seen that during these four centuries the mixed forest zone of the European part of the country served as a reservoir of natural population growth that

[3]For maps showing migration just prior to 1897, see Leasure and Lewis, 1968, pp. 379 and 384.

supplied population to new regions as the Russian Empire expanded. The wooded steppe zone to the southeast, as well as the coniferous forest zone to the northeast, first received an influx of population from the originally settled mixed forest zone, and then joined the mixed forest zone as a reservoir of population that was sending people to other parts of the expanding empire. The Volga-Vyatka region in the southern coniferous forest zone in the basins of the Volga and Vyatka Rivers still stands out conspicuously as one of the regions of highest outflow of population.

Much of the steppe zone in southern European Russia, southern Siberia, and northern Kazakhstan received inmigrants during this long period as Russian control continually extended the frontier southeastward into the drier steppes where the rich soils enticed agricultural settlers. Particularly in the eighteenth and nineteenth centuries, the steppe regions experienced a rapid transition from an economy of nomadic and seminomadic herding to one that was predominantly based on sedentary agriculture. This was especially true in the more humid parts of the steppe where moisture conditions were usually sufficient for grain growth. In the drier steppe and semideserts nomadic herding continued to be dominant well into the Soviet period. In the old settled civilizations of the Transcaucasus, and the oases of Central Asia no significant influx or outflow of population occurred during the sixteenth–nineteenth centuries.

The initial wave of Russians that overran Siberia left little imprint on the land, since there were too few Cossacks to do more than exercise nominal control over the region and exact tribute from the natives in the form of furs. The mode of settlement at this time was the erection of far flung strings of "ostrogs," fortresses which also served the purpose of fur collection points. More intensive agricultural colonization of this region began in the second half of the nineteenth century, preceded slightly by a gold rush beginning in 1840 that brought a flurry of prospectors to the Yenisey region and south-central portions of the area on either side of Lake Baykal.

1897–1926

Between the 1897 census and the 1926 census so much chaos occurred in the Russian area that it is impossible to follow the trends of population growth and distribution through the intervening period. Undoubtedly there were many ups and downs of birth rates, death rates, and migrational processes that are obscured by any statistical means that might be computed for the 29-year period. Also significant exchanges of territory took place. As a result of World War I and the Revolution, as enumerated in Chapter 1, the Soviets lost Finland, the Baltic Republics, and Poland. The 1926 census counted a little more than 147 million persons in the newly formed Soviet Union. The average birth rate was a little lower than it had been in 1897, and the death rate was considerably lower, so that the natural increase was significantly higher than in 1897. Life expectancy had increased from 32 years in 1897 to 44 years in 1926. (Table 6-1) But the chaos of World War I and the ensuing revolutions and civil strife had taken their toll, and the 1926 population contained a constricted number of children in the 5–9 age group and significantly more women than men in ages above 15.

The war, revolutions, and civil strife arrested the processes of urbanization and industrialization that were beginning to make headway before World War I. The per cent of population classified as urban dwellers rose from 12.4 in 1897 to 18.0 in 1914, but then fell back during the period 1914–1922. It began to rise again during the period of the New Economic Policy in the 1920s, but by the census of 1926 it still was no higher than it had been in 1914. (Table 6-1) The portion of the labor force in agriculture actually rose from 57.6 per cent of the total in 1897 to 65.1 per cent in 1926. Industry had occupied 13.4 per cent of the labor force in 1897, and in 1926 it occupied only 12.1 per cent.

Migration patterns remained somewhat the same during the period 1897–1926 as they had been prior to 1897. The central part of the European Plain from the western border to the Ural Mountains continued to lose population

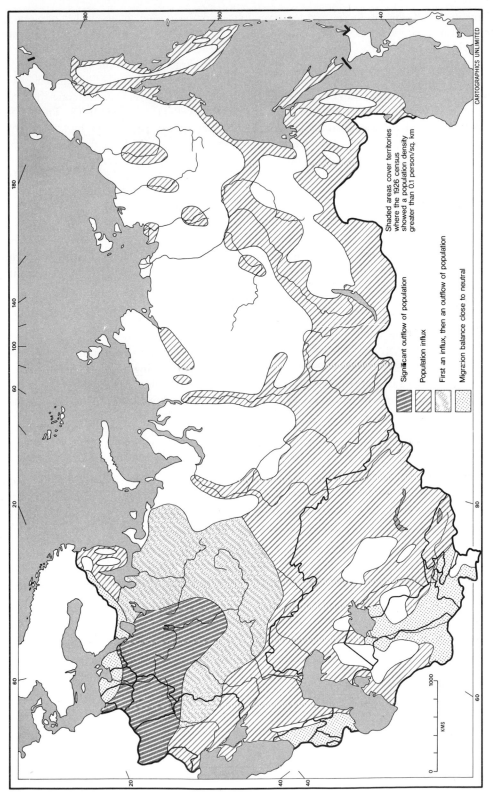

Shaded areas cover territories
where the 1926 census
showed a population density
greater than 0.1 person/sq. km

Significant outflow of population

Population influx

First an influx, then an outflow of population

Migration balance close to neutral

CARTOGRAPHICS UNLIMITED

KMS

Figure 6–1   Results of migration processes, 1500–1900. After Pokshishevsky, 1969, p. 55.

to migration, and the southern and eastern regions continued to gain. But in the latter part of the period a shift began to take place in the relative importance of the two migration streams. The eastern regions were now becoming the regions of primary inmigration, particularly in the chernozem belt along the Trans Siberian Railroad all the way from the Urals to the Pacific. In some oblasts of this zone more than 45 per cent of the total population had moved in from elsewhere prior to 1926.[4] Scattered areas of heavy inmigration also existed in the European part of the country where rapid urbanization and mining activities were being developed.

Outmigration continued to be high in some of the areas of high inmigration, particularly in parts of Eastern Siberia and the Far East. This again signified the transient nature of the population in many of the eastern regions. A great deal of intraregional movement was taking place, particularly in the northern parts of Eastern Siberia and the Far East where extractive industries ran their course over short periods of time and workers moved on to new short-run opportunities.

The population density map for 1926 reveals a general increase in densities throughout the occupied territory of the country. Rural population densities of more than 70 people per square kilometer occupied the central Ukraine west of the Dnieper River, and rural densities between 50 and 70 persons per square kilometer continued the high density zone eastward and northeastward into the Central Black Earth Region of Russia. The population was predominantly rural throughout the country except in Moscow and Leningrad Oblasts.[5]

1926-1939

During the 1926–1939 period the birth and death rates continued to drop as urbanization increased rapidly, and the natural increase of the population remained fairly constant

through the period at about 1.9 per cent per year. The life expectancy continued to creep slowly upward, but had not yet taken a rapid upward surge. In 1939 the total population of the Soviet Union was estimated to be 170,467,000, of which almost one-third were urban dwellers. (Table 6–1) The age-sex structure of the population had not changed greatly since 1926, although there were more irregularities in numbers among the younger age groups. The constricted group of children who had been born during the difficult years 1917–1921 had risen up the age ladder and now produced a constriction of offspring in ages 15–24. A second constriction appeared in the age group 5–9, which probably stemmed from the civil unrest and famine brought on by collectivization of agriculture in the early 1930s. The 0–4 age group was somewhat constricted, probably as the result of changing social attitudes toward the family as an institution, the rapid industrialization and urbanization that was taking place, and the disruption of families produced by the Stalin purges that were being carried out after 1936. No doubt there was also some ripple effect of the constricted group of cohorts in the 20–24 age group who were now the principal childbearing parents.

The population distribution continued much as it had been, with population densities increasing throughout the settled areas and rapid growth of clusters of cities in the Central Region around Moscow, in the Donets Coal Basin of the eastern Ukraine, and in many individual cities along the Trans Siberian Railroad in southern Siberia and the Far East.[6]

The industrialization drive got under way in the Soviet Union with the initiation of the five-year plans in 1928. This induced a rapid influx of people into the cities and brought about for the first time absolute decreases in rural population over large portions of the western half of the country.[7] This process has continued down to the present time, and the rural population of the country has continued

[4]Leasure and Lewis, 1967, pp. 484–485.
[5]Lorimer, pp. 66–67.

[6]Lorimer, pp. 146–147.
[7]Lorimer, pp. 158–159.

to decrease in practically all regions except Central Asia and parts of the Caucasus. During the period 1926–1939 the total population underwent an absolute decrease in a crescent-shaped area fringing the western and southern sides of the Central Region as well as throughout Kazakhstan.[8] This distribution of population decrease has shifted subsequent to 1939.

Between the 1926 and 1939 censuses it appears that more than four million persons migrated to Siberia, the Far East, and Kazakhstan. This was approximately equivalent to one-fifth of the natural population increase in the country during the period. It appears that during this time an equilibrium was reached between population and resources in the south, so that the movement southward essentially ceased.[9]

1939–1959

The intercensal period 1939–1959, of course, was a very abnormal period because of World War II. Shortly after the 1939 census was taken, about 20 million people were added to the Soviet Union by the annexation of the Baltic Republics and parts of Finland, Poland, and Rumania. Later during the war Tanu Tuva became a part of the Soviet Union, and at the end of the war the Soviet Union acquired the eastern end of Czechoslovakia and the southern half of Sakhalin Island and the Kuril Island chain.

The war produced chaos in the most heavily populated parts of European U.S.S.R. and caused great losses of life, particularly of young men of military age and of infants. In addition, the disruption of war resulted in great birth deficits as families were not being formed and children were not being born. Nobody knows exactly what the war losses were, but it has been estimated that as many as 25–30 million excess deaths might have occurred because of war related causes and as many as 15 million births might not have been realized because of

the war. It appears that only about one-third as many children were born in the Soviet Union during 1943–1944 as during 1939–1940. The results of the war are shown in Figure 6–2 as a great constriction in numbers of people centered on age 16 and a preponderance of women above age 30. The cities suffered the most during the war and recuperated most slowly afterward. Although births increased significantly in the cities after the war, they did not compare favorably with births in the countryside. Thus, in 1959 there were many more children in the rural population than in the urban. (Fig. 6–3)

Regardless of the war, birth and death rates declined continually throughout the 1939–1959 period as industrialization and urbanization took place. The natural growth rate remained steady around 17 per 1000 after a sharp drop during the war. (Table 6–1) In 1959 for the total population the birth rate was 25.0 per thousand, the death rate was 7.6 per thousand, and the natural increase was 17.4 per thousand.

Although the process of urbanization was badly disrupted by the war in the devastated parts of European U.S.S.R., it continued unabated in the eastern regions and resumed at a rapid pace in the west after the war. By 1948 most of the war-ravaged cities had regained at least the stature they had held before the war, and development took place rapidly during the next decade, so that by the 1959 census 48 per cent of the total population were classified as urban.

In addition to the losses in the total population, the war brought about almost overnight an eastward movement of people that the Soviet government had been trying rather unsuccessfully to effect since the beginning of the industrialization drive in 1928. According to railroad statistics, between June, 1941 and February, 1942 10.4 million people were evacuated eastward. A second wave later in 1942 raised the total of evacuees to about 20 million by October, 1942. Although this was planned to be a temporary shift, many of the people stayed in the Urals, Western Siberia, Kazakhstan, and Central Asia.

[8]Lorimer, pp. 162 163.
[9]Pokshishevsky, 1969, p. 53.

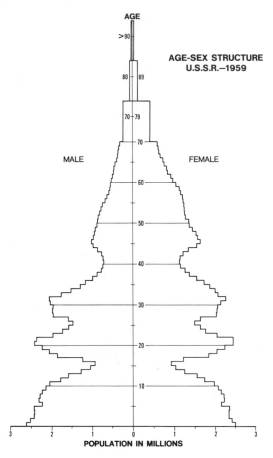

Figure 6-2   Age-sex distribution of the U.S.S.R. popula-
tion, 1959. Data from Baldwin, 1973, p. 15 and Itogi
vsesoyuznoy perepisi naseleniya 1970 goda, *tom II, pp.*
14-15.

The war also brought about mass movements of certain nationality groups who were
considered to be security risks. These included
such groups as the Crimean Tatars, the Volga
Germans, and the Kalmyks, Chechen, Ingush,
Balkars, and Karachay in the North Caucasian
region. Although Khrushchev declared a general amnesty to most of these peoples in 1956,
their numbers swelled the eastern regions until
then, and many of them still remain there. This
is particularly true of the Volga Germans and
Crimean Tatars whose political entities were
not reconstituted in the late 1950s as were
those of the peoples in the North Caucasus.

At the end of the war mass exchanges of
people took place in border areas where territories had been exchanged. About 1,800,000
Poles and Jews were expatriated to Poland and
500,000 Ukrainians, Belorussians, and Lithuanians were moved into the Soviet Union. In
general, incoming peoples have been scattered
eastward through the Soviet Union, and the
empty areas left in the west by expatriation
have been filled by Russians or Russified
peoples from the local nationalities who have
spent some time in the interior of the U.S.S.R.
The 1,500,000 Germans who found themselves
in Kaliningrad Oblast after the northern half
of what had been East Prussia was transferred
to the Soviet Union were largely expatriated
and 600,000 Russians were moved in. In the
Far East, 370,000 Japanese were resettled

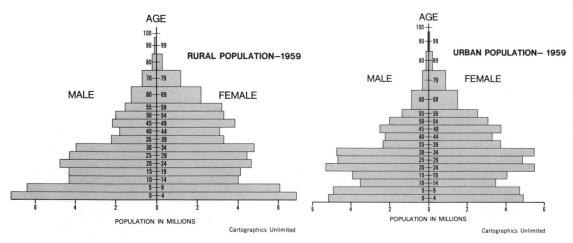

Figure 6-3   Age-sex distributions of the rural and urban populations of the U.S.S.R., 1959. Data from Itogi vsesoyuznoy
perepisi naseleniya 1970 goda, *tom II, pp. 14-15.*

from southern Sakhalin and the Kuril Islands. Certain "border purifications" have taken place along the Chinese frontier since the late 1930s.

The net effect on population distribution during the 1939–1959 period was to add about 18 million people to the regions east of the Urals. The other 20 million gained during the period was accounted for by the addition of new territories in the west. Thus, the twenty-year period that included World War II resulted in only an 18 million increase in population if the 20 million new people in the west are discounted. And all of the 18 million population increase occurred in the eastern regions. While the entire Soviet population increased 7.7 per cent, the population of the Urals increased 32 per cent, Western Siberia 24 per cent, Eastern Siberia 34 per cent, the Far East 70 per cent, Kazakhstan 53 per cent, and Central Asis 30 per cent. During the twenty-year span, the share of the east in the total population of the country rose from 29 per cent to 35 per cent.

During the 1939–1959 period the population of "old Russia" remained almost exactly the same. In fact, it lost about 7 million people between 1940 and 1955, but natural increase made this up during the 1955–1959 period. During the 1940–1955 period, much of the East European Plain lost population except for the Central Region, Latvia, and Estonia. The area completely surrounding the Central Region suffered a loss of more than 10 per cent its population due to intense outmigration and war destruction. It is interesting that this outmigration occurred in areas that were not occupied by the Germans during World War II as well as in areas that were.

During the years 1955–1959, a total population increment in the U.S.S.R. approximately equal to that which occurred during the years 1940–1955 was far more evenly distributed across the country. During this period natural growth was the dominant factor in each region. Only the Valday area northwest of the Central Region and western Belorussia showed declines in population. Migrations continued into the sub-Arctic, Middle Volga, Kazakh, and Cen-

tral Asia industrial areas, but flows to Eastern Siberia and the Far East were no longer evident. These years saw a temporary revival of rural inmigration in Western Siberia and northern Kazakhstan to implement the famous Virgin Lands Program there. It was also at this time that Khrushchev's amnesty decree took effect and nationality groups began to be repatriated to the North Caucasian area.

POPULATION CHARACTERISTICS AND TRENDS SINCE 1959

Since the 1959 census, another census was taken in 1970, the results of which over a period of four years were tabulated in considerable detail in seven published volumes. This has provided the basis for a large number of studies analyzing population characteristics and changes during the 1959–1970 intercensal period. Among other things the census data allow the analysis of age-sex structures of population throughout the entire country and its political subdivisions, nationality makeup, educational levels, occupational breakdowns, regional growth, and migration.

The Soviets now say that they are going to take another census in January, 1979. Until then, data since the 1970 census are limited to those included in annual statistical handbooks, which allow for analyses of vital statistics for the Soviet Union as a whole and in some cases for individual union republics and, more rarely, for major economic regions. They also allow for regional analyses of overall population growth at the oblast level and such things as specific birth rates and death rates for the country as a whole. But they do not provide information on such things as age-sex structures, nationality composition, or migration. A special statistical handbook was published in 1975 that covered many aspects of population during the one year, 1973, which allows for some comparison of regional growths and migrational trends with earlier periods that were reported by the 1970 census.[10] Therefore,

[10]*Naselenie SSSR 1973.*

the following discussion will mix data that sometimes are as recent as 1977, at other times date from 1973, and more often must hark back to the 1970 census results.

Vital Statistics

On January 1, 1977, the Soviet Union had a total population of 257,900,000 people, which made it the third most populous nation on earth after China and India. The crude birth rate was 18.5 per thousand and the death rate was 9.5 per thousand, so the natural increase was 9.0 per thousand. 46.5 per cent of the total population were men and 53.5 per cent were women. 62 per cent of the population were urban dwellers and 38 percent were rural. (Table 6–1) Life expectancy has not been reported since 1972. At that time it was 64 years for men and 74 years for women, the widest spread between men and women anywhere in the world.

The age-sex structure of the Soviet population at the time of the 1970 census was still very abnormal. (Fig. 6–4) There were constrictions of numbers in the age group centering on 51, which represented birth deficits during the tumultuous years at the beginning of the Bolshevik Regime; centering on 36, which probably related to the havoc and famine that accompanied the collectivization of agriculture in the early 1930s; and centering on 26 which represented the birth deficits during World War II. In addition, in ages above 42 females outnumbered males; the descrepancy between the sexes becoming greater the older the age. By age 65 women outnumbered men more than 2 to 1. This sex descrepancy was due to the fact that more men than women lost their lives during times of strife and that under normal circumstances women live longer than men do.

These abnormalities have progressed up the age ladder since 1970, of course, but they are producing ripple effects in younger age groups that will be evident for generations to come. For example, the reduction of numbers below the age of nine in 1970 was due primarily to

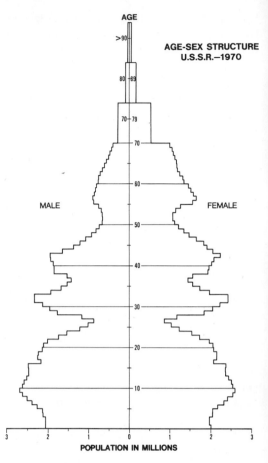

Figure 6–4   Age-sex distribution of the U.S.S.R. population, 1970. Data from Baldwin, 1973, p. 16 and Itogi vsesoyuznoy perepisi naseleniya 1970 goda, tom II, pp. 12–13.

the coming of age of the "thin generation," the surviving babies of World War II, who were becoming the primary parents of the newborn. Since 1970 the base of the pyramid has broadened again as greater numbers of parents born during the 1950s baby boom have been producing more offspring.

Not all the reduction of births during the 1960s was due to the thin generation. Age-specific birth data published during that time revealed a declining fertility in almost all ages of women. This reflected a growing antinatalist attitude among Soviet women which stemmed from various causes. Most important no doubt were the shortage of housing and the high percentage of working women, but other more subtle psychological factors were also at work. The aggregate results of industrialization and urbanization during the Soviet period have been decreasing both birth rates and death rates as has been common to all societies undergoing these processes.

In spite of generally pronatalist intentions, the Soviet government has been faced with ideological tenets and economic realities that have resulted in governmental policies and individual actions that in most cases have had anti-natalist results. Half-hearted governmental attempts to compensate women for having children have been counterbalanced by the ideological premise that parents have the right to decide whether or not a child should be born. This has led to free and legal abortions during much of the Soviet period and wide dissemination of contraceptives and birth control information. In addition, the rapidly expanding economy and shortage of adult men in the population have induced women to work to an unusual degree. Generally low basic wages have also induced families to provide the opportunity for the wife to work. Presently women make up 51 per cent of the total labor force in the country. More than two-thirds of all women beyond the age of 16 are economically active. In 25 per cent of the families of the Soviet Union the wife earns more than the husband and is thereby considered to be the head of the household.

Before the Bolshevik Revolution, birth and death rates were both high and the natural increase was moderate. Birth rates declined drastically during the 1930s as the industrialization drive got under way accompanied by large rural-urban migration. At the same time the death rate dropped some with improved health standards, and the natural increase dropped rapidly. During World War II the birth rate plunged, no one knows how much. After the war birth rates and death rates decreased at about the same rate until around 1960 so the natural increase remained essentially constant from 1950 to 1960. However, after 1960 there was a renewed drop in the birth rate, and the death rate leveled off and

began to increase as the population became older. (Fig. 6-5) At present the U.S.S.R. is faced with low birth rates, low death rates, low increases, and an aging population.

The death rate reached a minimum of 6.9 per thousand in 1964. Since then it has been rising consistently as the population has aged. By 1976 it had risen to 9.5 per thousand. One might expect eventually it will rise to about 14 per thousand if the age structure becomes similar to that in stable population areas such as Scandinavia. The rise in the death rate in recent years cannot be explained entirely by the aging population, since the death rate has risen recently in practically every age group except ages 5-19. (Table 6-2) One of the most unexplainable things has been a significant rise in the death rate of infants under the age of 1 year. Infant mortality reached a minimum of 22.9 per thousand in 1971, but rose consistently to 27.9 per thousand in 1974, the latest reporting date. Although some of this apparent increase might be due to more complete reporting of births and deaths of infants in places like Central Asia, it cannot all be attributed to that, since infant mortality increases have been reported also in such places as the Baltic region which has had complete reporting for many years. These recent rises in infant mortality and age-specific death rates have gone unexplained, as has a drop by one year in the life expectancy of men, from 65 years in 1970 to 64 years in 1972. Perhaps the fact that life expectancies have not been estimated since 1972 and infant mortality rates have not been reported since 1974 signifies some problem that the Soviets are unable to reveal until they have a solution in hand.

The birth rate bottomed out at 17.0 per thousand in 1969, after which it has risen steadily. In 1976 it was reported at 18.4 per thousand. Natural increase also reached a minimum in 1969 with 8.9 per thousand. After that it rose somewhat, but fell again to 8.9 per thousand in 1973. It rose to 9.3 per thousand in 1974, then fell to 8.8 per thousand in 1975, and rose to 8.9 per thousand in 1976. Some of this year-to-year bouncing about may be due to errors in yearly population estimates. At any

Table 6–2   Number of Deaths per 1000 People by Age Categories, U.S.S.R., 1896–1976

Age	1896–1897	1938–1939	1958–1959	1965–1966	1970–1971	1974–1975	1975–1976
All Population	32.4	17.4	7.4	7.3	8.2	9.0	9.4
0–4	133.0	75.8	11.9	6.9	6.7	8.2	8.7
5–9	12.9	5.5	1.1	0.8	0.7	0.7	0.7
10–14	5.4	2.6	0.8	0.6	0.5	0.5	0.5
15–19	5.8	3.4	1.3	1.0	1.0	1.0	1.0
20–24	7.6	4.4	1.8	1.6	1.6	1.7	1.7
25–29	8.2	4.7	2.2	2.0	2.2	2.1	2.1
30–34	8.7	5.4	2.6	2.6	2.8	3.0	3.0
35–39	10.3	6.8	3.1	3.2	3.8	3.7	3.8
40–44	11.8	8.1	4.0	3.9	4.7	5.2	5.3
45–49	15.7	10.2	5.4	5.1	6.0	6.7	6.9
50–54	18.5	13.8	7.9	7.9	8.7	9.0	9.3
55–59	29.5	17.1	11.2	11.1	11.8	13.0	13.4
60–64	34.5	24.5	17.1	17.2	17.9	18.3	18.9
65–69	61.6	35.1	25.2	25.5	26.9	27.4	28.0
>70	89.0	78.9	63.8	65.8	74.9	73.3	75.0

Source: Narkhoz SSSR, 1922–1972, p. 43, *Narkhoz SSSR,* 1975, p. 43, and *Narkhoz SSSR za 60 let,* p. 73.

rate, it appears that the natural increase has stablized at around 9 per thousand.

Soviet Concern About Fertility

Most Soviet leaders consider an actively growing population to be a good thing and agree that stimulation of the presently low birth rate is desirable. Such attitudes probably reflect traumatic experiences of the past rather than rational thoughts about the inevitable consequences for the future. The first 30 years of the Soviet period were filled with so many catastrophies that the average annual growth rate of the population was reduced to less than half that of the United States. Only during the 1950s and early part of the 1960s has the U.S.S.R. experienced rapid population growth. The Soviets have become so conditioned by these events that they automatically view with alarm any drop in the growth rate. Their fears range all the way from such vague ideas as the future prestige of the Soviet Union depends

upon its maintaining its relative standing in world population to such specific problems as manning new industries in an ever expanding economy.

The latter concern now probably takes precedence in most people's minds, since the Soviet Union has already been forced to face up to a number of manpower problems. The Soviets have tacitly conceded that certain unused elements of their present population cannot be considered as reservoirs of manpower eligible for recruitment into industrialized labor. Many of the non-Slavic nationalities, particularly those in Central Asia, have not been adaptable to regular hours of factory work. In addition, most of the people remaining on farms even in the Slavic areas of the country, predominantly uneducated, untrained, older women, are unadaptable to such employment. Thus the expansion of the labor force in the future will have to depend almost entirely on the induction of boys and girls into the labor force at age 16. The increment of youths into

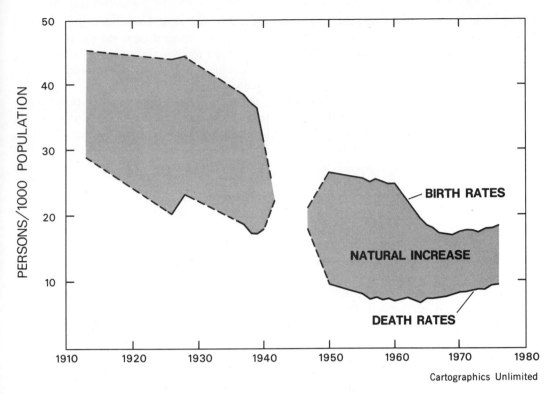

Figure 6-5   Birth and death rates per 1000 people, U.S.S.R., 1913–1976. Data from Narkhoz SSSR, *1922–1972, p. 40* and Narkhoz SSSR za 60 let, *p. 69. All data are for present boundaries of the U.S.S.R.*

the labor force is now on the rise as the increased cohorts of the 1950s become the parents of the seventies. But this will peak in 1980, and after that it will drop rapidly. And at least half of this increment during 1970–2000 will come from the Central Asian nationality groups. Add to this a general maldistribution of labor with respect to labor needs in various regions of the country, and one can see looming a manpower crisis of major proportions.

Thus, the Soviet government would like to stimulate births. However, so far it has been rather ineffectual in doing so. A number of demographers in various disciplines have tried to analyze why and to offer some solutions. It appears that one of the main drawbacks has been the fact that state subsidies to families begin only with the birth of the fourth child, and therefore do not affect most families outside Central Asia and parts of the Caucasus. It has been argued by many that what really

needs to be stimulated are births of second and third children in Slavic and Baltic areas where most couples stop with only one child, or even none. The same people argue that it is wrong to keep encouraging very large families in Central Asia and elsewhere where mothers are not normally part of the working force anyway. Such practices tend to accelerate the relative decline of the Slavic groups in the total population, a trend which many leading Soviets view with some alarm. It has been advocated that those most economically active members of the population be stimulated to have more children by providing realistic subsidies for first, second, and third children, by discontinuing subsidies for fourth children and beyond, by paying subsidies as percentages of base wages of the mothers involved, and by granting much longer maternity leaves to working women. It is thought that among other things such provisions might stimulate young people to marry earlier. Throughout much of the Russian Republic the average age for newly married couples has been in the upper twenties. This is considered by many to be one of the prime deterrents to higher birth rates.

A number of demographers and medical personnel, concerned with high abortion rates and their effects on the health of potential mothers, have called for more effective contraceptives. They have pointed out that in 1974 there were around 10 million abortions in the Soviet Union as compared to only 4.5 million births. This amounted to 180 abortions per 1000 women in the most productive ages, 15–44. This was five times higher than the rate of the second leading nation, Japan, and ten times higher than the United States. According to Soviet law, any woman over the age of 18 is entitled to abortion on demand. By and large, Soviet women are using abortions in lieu of contraceptives. Stalin outlawed abortions in 1936, but in 1955 Khrushchev legalized them again, partially in response to the great number of illegal abortions that were thriving.

At present, a woman in the Soviet Union gets three days' unpaid leave from work for an abortion. If she earns less than 60 rubles per month her abortion is free. If she earns more than that she pays five rubles. In order to avoid assembly lines at hospitals, many more affluent women get out-of-hospital abortions from skilled physicians at about 30–50 rubles each. Demographers argue that an abortion reduces the likelihood of a woman having a child for many months to come. If a young married woman delays having a family for several years by having four or five abortions, it may well be that she will not be able to have any more children when she is ready to have them. Therefore, it is argued, if abortions can be reduced by the use of better contraceptives, this might in the long run stimulate births.

During recent years the Soviet government has enacted some legislation that has gone part way in responding to such suggestions. Women are now given 112 days maternity leave with full pay and their jobs are kept open for them for a year. If a woman has twins or triplets her maternity leave with pay is extended to 126 days. Women who have born five or more children and reared them to the age of at least 8 are entitled to pensions at age 50 after having worked for only 15 years. Thus, child raising is equated with socialist work.

Such measures, coupled with propaganda, seem to have stimulated births during recent years, particularly among younger women. Female fertility rates in ages 15–24 increased consistently from 1963 to 1975, and in age group 25–29 from 1969 to 1975. However, 1976 showed a slight decline in age group 20–24 and a significant decline in age group 25–29. On the other hand, some older ages experienced small increases. (Table 6–3) Increases in younger age groups have been offsetting declines in older age groups, so that the overall fertility of women ages 15–49 has been rising slowly since 1970. The most dramatic percentage increase in fertility has been in first births for females ages 15–19. This increased 48 per cent from 1963–1964 to 1973–1974. Of greater significance in the long run, however, will be the increased incidence of second and third births among women of prime reproductive ages. It appears that young women are now having more children in their families.

Population Projections

Future population trends anywhere are notoriously hard to predict, but taking into account the present age-sex structure and current fertility trends, it can be predicted that the crude growth rate of the Soviet population will increase a little from the current level of 9 per thousand to around 10 per thousand in the 1980s, but after 1990 it will drop rapidly to around 6 per thousand by the year 2000. The preworking age group, 0–15 years, has declined from 32.2 per cent of total population in 1950 to 30.7 per cent in 1970 and will continue to decline until the 1980s. It will rise a little in the 1990s, but then drop again to 25.2 per cent by the year 2000. The working age group, 16–54 for women and 16–59 for men, has decreased from 57.4 per cent of total population in 1950 to 54.2 per cent in 1970. It

*Table 6–3   Female Fertility Rates   (Births/1000 Women by Age Category),
1938–1976*

Year	15–49 Years (General Fertility Rate)	15–19 Years	20–24 Years	25–29 Years	30–34 Years	35–39 Years	40–44 Years	45–49 Years
1938–1939	139.5	32.8	214.4	230.6	183.5	131.7	68.1	19.0
1954–1955	86.2	15.6	146.9	172.9	127.6	74.4	35.4	7.1
1960–1961	90.6	35.2	164.8	160.7	110.0	60.7	23.5	4.8
1961–1962	87.2	29.6	162.8	155.8	105.2	56.4	22.7	3.8
1962–1963	83.2	24.1	162.1	151.4	101.3	54.2	22.3	3.7
1963–1964	78.4	22.7	162.6	145.6	97.6	52.0	21.4	3.9
1964–1965	73.5	23.7	157.6	138.9	95.5	50.9	20.3	4.2
1965–1966	70.8	25.5	159.6	136.0	97.0	50.6	19.1	4.4
1966–1967	68.5	26.9	158.6	132.7	97.0	49.2	17.7	4.0
1967–1968	66.3	27.7	158.0	129.7	94.7	47.9	16.9	3.8
1969–1970	65.7	30.4	163.9	128.7	88.1	48.5	15.3	2.9
1970–1971	66.9	32.0	170.2	132.1	87.1	49.6	14.9	2.4
1971–1972	67.2	32.4	173.9	137.1	84.3	49.4	14.6	2.0
1972–1973	66.4	32.4	172.3	135.9	81.8	48.0	14.3	1.9
1973–1974	66.8	33.3	173.4	134.8	79.3	45.5	14.4	1.7
1974–1975	67.8	34.3	176.8	133.5	77.9	42.7	14.4	1.8
1975–1976	68.5	35.0	176.7	131.5	78.0	40.2	14.6	1.8

Sources: Leedy, "Demographic Trends in the USSR," p. 439, and various issues of *Narkhoz SSSR.*

is now on the rise and will reach a peak of 58.3 per cent in 1980. But after that it will drop rapidly to 55.4 per cent in 1990 and remain at essentially that level until the year 2000. Pensioners have increased from 10.4 per cent in 1950 to 15.1 per cent in 1970, and will continue to rise steadily to 19.2 per cent by 2000. By the year 2000 the discrepancy in numbers between males and females will have worked its way up the age ladder essentially beyond the working age. Although a large discrepancy will remain in the pensioner group, this will be due primarily to the different life spans of the two sexes. Already by 1977 the two sexes were essentially equal in numbers up to the age of 49.

Variations in Vital Statistics

Average birth rates, death rates, and natural increase rates are not too meaningful at present in the Soviet Union because they are merely averages of wide variations. The Soviet population is far from homogeneous. Different backgrounds and different ways of life result in wide variances in age-sex population structures, birth rates, and natural growth rates. (Table 6–4) Such structures vary with nationality and region and between city and country within regions. The greatest differences exist among nationality groups. The Baltic and Slavic groups have much lower birth rates and natural increases than do the Central Asians and Transcaucasians. The two extreme cases at the present time at the union republic level are the Latvians and the Tadzhiks. In 1976 the Latvian Republic had a birth rate of 13.8 per thousand, a death rate of 12.1 per thousand, and a natural increase of 1.7 per thousand. In contrast, the Tadzhik Republic had a birth rate of 38.2 per thousand, a death rate of 8.5 per thousand, and a natural increase of 29.7 per

Table 6–4 Births, Deaths, and Natural Increases per 1000 Population, by Republics and Economic Regions, 1965–1976

Region	1965			1970			1976		
	Births	Deaths	Increase	Births	Deaths	Increase	Births	Deaths	Increase
U.S.S.R.	18.4	7.3	11.1	17.4	8.2	9.2	18.4	9.5	8.9
R.S.F.S.R.	15.7	7.6	8.1	14.6	8.7	5.9	15.9	10.0	5.9
Northwest	14.4	7.8	6.6	13.5	9.0	4.5	14.8	9.2	5.6
Central	12.6	8.3	4.3	12.4	9.5	2.9	13.1	10.0	3.1
Volga-Vyatka	15.8	8.0	7.8	14.3	9.5	4.8	14.6	9.8	4.8
Central Chernozem	14.1	8.4	5.7	12.6	9.5	3.1	12.8	10.5	2.3
Volga	17.7	7.6	10.1	15.1	8.2	6.9	15.6	8.8	6.8
North Caucasus	18.0	7.4	10.6	16.3	8.3	8.0	16.7	9.0	7.7
Ural	16.2	7.2	9,0	15.3	8.5	6.8	16.9	9.1	7.8
Western Siberia	16.3	6.9	9.4	15.2	8.1	7.1	17.5	8.5	9.0
Eastern Siberia	18.4	6.7	11.7	17.5	7.7	9.8	19.2	8.1	11.1
Far East	17.9	6.2	11.7	17.8	7.2	10.6	18.6	7.3	11.3
Ukraine S.S.R.	15.3	7.6	7.7	15.2	8.9	6.3	15.2	10.2	5.0
Baltic Region									
Lithuania S.S.R.	18.1	7.9	10.2	17.6	8.9	8.7	15.7	9.6	6.1
Latvia S.S.R.	13.8	10.0	3.8	14.5	11.2	3.3	13.8	12.1	1.7
Estonia S.S.R.	14.6	10.5	4.1	15.8	11.1	4.7	15.1	12.0	3.1
Transcaucasus									
Georgia S.S.R.	21.2	7.0	14.2	19.2	7.3	11.9	18.2	7.8	10.4
Azerbaydzhan S.S.R.	36.6	6.4	30.2	29.2	6.7	22.5	25.7	6.6	19.1
Armenia S.S.R.	28.6	5.7	22.9	22.1	5.1	17.0	22.7	5.5	17.2
Central Asia									
Uzbek S.S.R.	34.7	5.9	28.8	33.6	5.5	28.1	35.3	7.1	28.2
Kirgiz S.S.R.	31.4	6.5	24.9	30.5	7.4	23.1	31.3	8.2	23.1
Tadzhik S.S.R.	36.8	6.6	30.2	34.8	6.4	28.4	38.2	8.5	29.7
Turkmen S.S.R.	37.2	7.0	30.2	35.2	6.6	28.6	34.7	7.7	27.0
Kazakh S.S.R.	26.9	5.9	21.0	23.4	6.0	17.4	24.3	7.2	17.1
Belorussia S.S.R.	17.9	6.8	11.1	16.2	7.6	8.6	15.7	8.8	6.9
Moldavia S.S.R.	20.4	6.2	14.2	19.4	7.4	12.0	20.6	9.0	11.6

Sources: Narkhoz SSSR za 60 let, pp. 72–73, and Malinin and Ushakov, pp. 22 and 28.
Note: Data for economic regions within the R.S.F.S.R. are for 1965, 1970, and 1974.

thousand. Hence, the natural increase of the Tadzhik Republic was 17.5 times that of the Latvian Republic. This, coupled with the fact that the Latvian Republic has suffered much more from recent wars and civil strife than the Tadzhik Republic has, results in tremendous differences in the age-sex distributions of the two populations. (Fig. 6–6)

The large Russian Republic, which contains more than half the total population of the Soviet Union, and which within itself contains many non-Russian nationality groups, shows an age-sex distribution somewhere between these two extremes. But within this huge territory there are regional differences even within the Russian nationality group. The eastern regions of the Russian Republic still tend to have considerably higher birth rates and natural increases than do the older settled areas in the west. Although these differences were decreasing during the 1960s, it appears that they have increased again in the early 1970s.

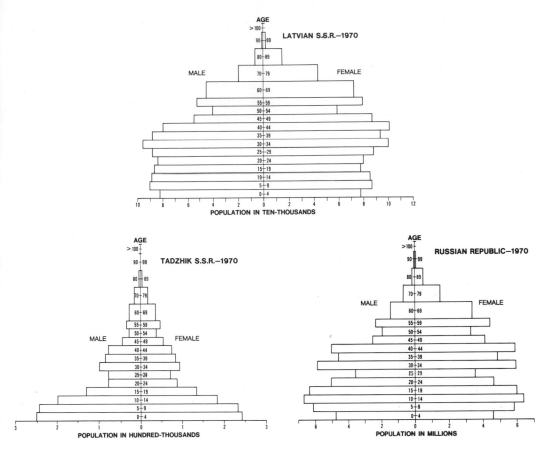

Figure 6-6   Age-sex distributions for the Latvian, Tadzhik, and Russian Republics, 1970. Data from Itogi vsesoyuznoy perepisi naseleniya 1970 goda, *tom II, pp. 16–17, 52–53, and 60–61.*

These regional differences are due mainly to migrational tendencies and rural-urban ratios. Since the eastern regions are primarily regions of inmigration, while the western regions are primarily regions of outmigration, the eastern regions generally have much higher portions of their total populations represented by young adults who are the ones who do most of the migrating. These potentially fertile young people leave areas of outmigration and enter areas of inmigration. In 1974 Eastern Siberia had the highest birth rate in the Russian Republic, 19.2 per thousand, and the Far East was second with 18.6 per thousand. However, since inmigration has been more active in the Far East than in Eastern Siberia, the death rate in the Far East was significantly lower because of the younger age structure of the total population. The death rate in the Far East was only 7.3 per thousand, while in Eastern Siberia it was 8.1 per thousand. Therefore, the Far East had the highest natural increase of any region in the R.S.F.S.R., 11.3 per thousand, as compared to Eastern Siberia with 11.1 per thousand. These figures contrast with the Central Chernozem Region south of Moscow which had the lowest birth rate, 12.8 per thousand, highest death rate, 10.5 per thousand, and lowest natural increase, 2.3 per thousand, of any region in the Russian Republic.

Death rates do not vary as much among regions as birth rates do. The Soviets have done an admirable job of reducing age-specific death rates everywhere by improved sanitation and health care. Among the republics, in 1976

Latvia had the highest death rate, 12.1 per thousand, and Armenia the lowest death rate, 5.5 per thousand. These differences are due primarily to the different age structures of the populations. Armenia, with a much higher birth rate than Latvia, has many more young people in its population, and hence a lower death rate. Regional variations in natural increase, then, are primarily the result of regional differences in birth rates and age-sex structures, which in turn are due partially to differences in birth rates, and to a certain extent to regional differences in the effects of past catastrophies such as World War II.

As has been pointed out earlier, in recent years the age-specific death rates seem to be increasing slightly. This, coupled with aging populations, has produced absolute increases in the crude death rate in every republic since 1970. This has produced a decrease in the natural growth rate in all republics except the Tadzhik and Belorussian Republics, which have increased, and the Russian Republic which has stayed the same. The decline in the natural increase has been especially rapid in Azerbaydzhan, which seems now to be undergoing a rapid decline in the birth rate, as Georgia did previously. It is becoming difficult to generalize about entire regions anymore. Growth rates in Georgia are beginning to look more like those in the Russian Republic, while Kazakhstan adjacent to Central Asia is begin-

ning to look more like Azerbaydzhan and Armenia in the Transcaucasus. Although the four Central Asian Republics as a whole still exhibit high birth rates, relatively low death rates, and high rates of natural increase, there are differences from republic to republic, and they have been varying differently over time during the last decade. During 1965–1976, the Tadzhik Republic experienced first declines in both the birth and death rates and then recoveries to the highest levels ever, with a corresponding decline in natural increase and then recovery to a level somewhat lower than 1965. The Uzbek Republic experienced a decline and recovery in the birth rate and a slight decline and then rapid increase in the death rate which resulted in a continual decline in the natural increase. The Kirgiz and Turkmen Republics also experienced continual declines in the natural increase.

The 1970 census data revealed large differences in the age-sex structures of the country between rural populations and urban populations. (Fig. 6–7) The pyramid for the rural population dramatically reveals the outmigration from rural areas of young people in the 20–29 age groups. In regions where migration has been heavy, either in or out, the differences in numbers of the 20–29 age groups between cities and villages have become so great that birth rates have become somewhat higher in the cities than in the countrysides. This is

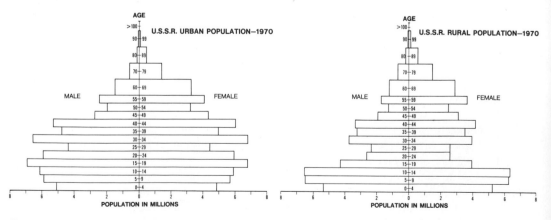

Figure 6–7   Age-sex distributions of the urban and rural populations of the U.S.S.R., 1970. Data from Itogi vsesoyuznoy perepisi naseleniya 1970 goda, *tom II, pp. 14–15.*

particularly true in some parts of the Baltic Republics. Of course, these differences are greater among minor civil divisions in the country than they are between large economic regions or union republics.

An interesting contrast in the numbers of urban and rural people by age categories is presented by population pyramids for Kirov Oblast in the Volga-Vyatka Region, which is a region of low birth rates and heavy outmigration that has been undergoing moderate urbanization, and in Gorno-Badakhshan A.O. in the high mountains of the Tadzhik Republic of Central Asia, which is a region of very high birth rates, low mobility, and slight urbanization. (Fig. 6–8) During the eleven-year intercensal period, 1959–1970, Kirov Oblast changed from a predominantly rural population to a predominantly urban one. Heavy outmigration left the 20–29 age group very small, particularly in the rural areas. As a consequence of this and other factors, birth rates dropped rapidly, so the 0–9 age group is quite small. Old people, 70 years of age and beyond, make up a significant portion of the population. In the Gorno-Badakhshan A.O.,

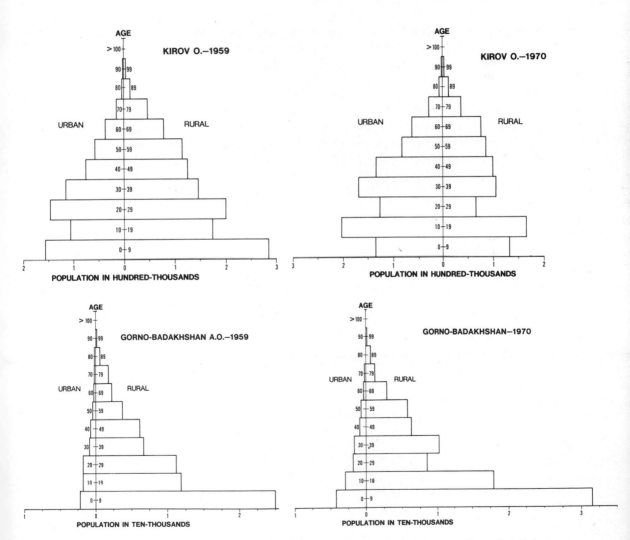

Figure 6–8   Urban-rural distributions by age categories of the populations in Kirov Oblast and Gorno-Badakhshan Autonomous Oblast, 1959 and 1970. Data from Itogi vsesoyuznoy perepisi naseleniya 1970 goda, tom II, pp. 109 and 244.

on the other hand, there has been little change in urbanization during the intercensal period. The population remains predominantly rural, and there are very high birth rates which give rise to an exceedingly large number of children and relatively few old people. Some outmigration has left the 20–29 age groups somewhat constricted, particularly in the rural areas.

As was mentioned before, the greatest differences in vital statistics correspond to differences in nationality. However, these differences are probably conditioned more by stage of socio-economic development than by differences in inherent characteristics such as religious beliefs and mores, which are rapidly disappearing under the Soviet Regime. It is apparent that each nationality group in turn as it has been drawn into the main stream of Soviet life has undergone a rapid decline in births. The Baltic and Slavic peoples are leading the pack in this decline, but the process is evident in different stages in all parts of the country, except for Tadzhikistan. The Georgians in the Transcau-

casus have already evolved most of the way to a low birth rate. It is the remaining peoples of the Caucasus and particularly the peoples of Central Asia who are maintaining the average birth rate of the U.S.S.R. even at the modest rate that it now stands. As the Caucasians and Central Asians are drawn more and more into the socio-economic mainstream, their birth rates undoubtedly will drop rapidly, and this will allow the average birth rate to continue to decline.

In 1973–1974 female fertility rates ranged from 53.4 per thousand women between the ages of 15–49 in Latvia to 170.6 per thousand in Tadzhikistan. (Table 6–5) The Baltic Republics, Russia, Belorussia, and the Ukraine all were between 53.4 and 60.9. The Russian Republic had the second lowest fertility. All of Central Asia was high, with the Kirgiz S.S.R. lowest, and the Transcaucasus were intermediate with Azerbaydzhan by far the highest.

Taking into account the present age-sex structure of the population and fertility trends,

Table 6–5   Female Fertility (Number of Births per 1000 Females 15 to 49 Years of Age) in the U.S.S.R., by Republic, 1958 to 1974

Republic	1958–1959	1965–1966	1969–1970	1972–1973	1973–1974
U.S.S.R.	88.7	70.8	65.7	66.4	66.8
Baltic Republics					
Estonia	59.9	55.3	59.3	58.5	57.9
Latvia	59.2	51.9	53.5	53.8	53.4
Lithuania	82.8	68.6	67.2	63.1	60.9
R.S.F.S.R.	82.9	59.0	53.4	54.9	55.3
Belorussia	91.0	67.1	61.3	59.7	58.9
Ukraine	70.7	57.1	55.2	56.2	55.7
Moldavia	111.7	79.2	71.6	75.6	75.1
Transcaucasian Republics					
Georgia	85.0	78.2	73.3	69.0	69.4
Armenia	159.2	122.4	92.9	87.3	84.7
Azerbaydzhan	163.3	165.8	134.6	111.4	108.0
Kazakhstan	143.0	107.9	96.1	93.6	94.1
Central Asia					
Uzbekistan	158.8	165.3	158.5	156.0	156.8
Turkmenia	161.6	176.6	165.6	159.3	158.6
Kirgizia	140.1	137.2	134.7	132.9	131.6
Tadzhikistan	123.5	166.2	166.4	168.0	170.6

Source: Feshbach and Rapawy, 1976, p. 124.

Feshbach and Rapawy predict that by 1980 the overall birth rate of the Soviet Union will have risen to 19.2 per thousand, the death rate will be around 9.3 per thousand, and the natural increase will be 9.9 per thousand. (Table 6–6) By 1990 the birth rate will have fallen to 17.3 per thousand, the death rate will have risen to 9.8 per thousand, and the natural increase will have fallen to 7.5 per thousand. By the year 2000, the birth rate will have fallen to 16.0 per thousand, the death rate will have risen to 10.2 per thousand, and the natural increase will have fallen to 5.8 per thousand. It is projected that natural increases will remain highest in Central Asia, intermediate in Kazakhstan and the Transcaucasus, and low in the rest of the country. By the year 2000 natural increases will range from 29.1 per thousand in Central Asia to 14.2 per thousand in Transcaucasia, 1.7 per thousand in the Baltic Republics, and only 0.1 per thousand in the R.S.F.S.R. It is significant that the Russian and Ukrainian Republics project the lowest growth rates of all, even lower than the Baltic Republics.

Nationalities

The 1970 census, which allowed individuals to classify themselves into any ethnic or linguistic denomination, resulted in a list of more than 800 ethnic denominations corresponding to 122 major nationalities and over 300 linguistic and dialectical denominations corresponding to 114 languages. Not all of these were recorded in the final census results, but population figures were still given for 104 individual nationality groups, and 151,942 people were lumped together in "other nationalities." (Table 6–7)

Those whose languages belong to the Indo-European family are by far the most numerous, comprising over 84 per cent of the entire population. This family includes the Slavs of which the Russians themselves made up 53.4 per cent of the total U.S.S.R. population in 1970. The Ukrainians made up 16.9 per cent, and the Belorussians made up 3.7 per cent. The Slavs came into being in the European part of the U.S.S.R., but since then have moved into almost every region of the country. (Fig. 6–9) The Russians and Belorussians have been the most mobile of all the nationality groups and have been the primary migrants who have moved into all cities of the country to man new industries. Most cities, no matter in what parts of the country they are located, have become populated predominantly by Russians. Another Slavic nationality that numbers more than one

Table 6–6   Projected Births, Deaths, and Natural Increases, 1980–2000, per Thousand Population

Region	1980			1990			2000		
	Births	Deaths	Natural Increase	Births	Deaths	Natural Increase	Births	Deaths	Natural Increase
U.S.S.R.	19.2	9.3	9.9	17.3	9.8	7.5	16.0	10.2	5.8
Baltic Republics	15.7	11.0	4.7	14.5	11.2	3.4	13.5	11.8	1.7
R.S.F.S.R.	16.7	10.2	6.5	13.7	11.3	2.4	12.4	12.3	0.1
Belorussia	18.2	8.7	9.5	16.1	9.2	6.9	14.0	10.1	4.0
Ukraine	16.0	10.3	5.6	13.8	11.2	2.6	12.8	12.0	0.8
Moldavia	22.1	8.3	13.9	19.2	8.7	10.5	17.5	9.2	8.3
Transcaucasus	25.0	6.9	18.1	24.3	6.8	17.6	21.1	6.8	14.2
Kazakhstan	26.0	6.7	19.3	24.4	6.8	17.6	21.7	7.0	14.7
Central Asia	36.5	6.2	30.3	36.8	5.5	31.3	34.0	5.0	29.1

Source: Feshbach and Rapawy, 1976, p. 123.

Table 6–7   Nationalities in the U.S.S.R.

Nationality Group	1970 Population (1000)	Per Cent Change 1970/ 1959	Per Cent Speaking National Language as Native Language	Per Cent Speaking Second U.S.S.R. Language Fluently	
				Russian	Other
Total U.S.S.R.	241,720	15.8	93.9	17.3	4.2
Indo-European	198,109	12.5			
Slavs	180,371	12.0			
Russian	129,015	13.1	99.8	0.1	3.0
Ukrainian	40,753	9.4	85.7	36.3	6.0
Belorussian	9,052	14.4	80.6	49.0	7.3
Pole *a*	1,168	−15.4	32.5	37.0	12.7
Bulgarian	351	8.3	73.1	58.8	7.9
Czech	21	−16.0	42.9	35.6	21.4
Slovak	12	−20.0	52.0	39.3	31.3
Romanian	2,817	21.4			
Moldavian	2,698	21.9	95.0	36.1	3.6
Rumanian	119	12.3	63.9	28.5	16.3
Lett-Lithuanian	4,095	9.9			
Lithuanian	2,665	14.6	97.9	35.9	1.9
Latvian	1,430	2.1	95.2	45.2	2.4
Armenian	3,559	27.7	91,4	30.1	6.0
Jew *b*	2,151	−5.2	17.7	16.3	28.8
German	1,846	14.0	66.8	59.6	1.1
Iranian	2,762	45.1			
Tadzhik	2,136	52.9	98.5	15.4	12.0
Osetian	448	18.2	88.6	58.6	10.7
Kurd	89	50.8	87.6	19.9	36.2
Iranian	28	33.3	36.9	33.9	12.7
Tat	17	54.5	72.6	57.7	15.3
Afghan	4	125.5	70.7	26.7	31.9
Greek	337	9.1	39.3	35.4	14.5
Indian	177				
Gypsy	175	32.6	70.8	53.0	16.4
Peoples of India and Pakistan	2	424.2	87.7	47.8	2.2
Albanian	4	−16.3	56.7	47.4	7.0
French	2	143.8	75.1	19.6	17.7
Caucasian	5,667	29.2			
Kartvel	3,245	20.5	98.4	21.3	1.0
Georgian	3,245	20.5	98.4	21.3	1.0
Adygo-Abkhaz	528	32.3			
Kabardian	280	37.3	98.0	71.4	0.8
Adygey	100	25.0	96.5	67.9	1.4
Abkhaz	83	27.7	95.9	59.2	2.8
Cherkes	40	33.3	92.0	70.0	2.5

Nationality Group	1970 Population (1000)	Per Cent Change 1970/ 1959	Per Cent Speaking National Language as Native Language	Per Cent Speaking Second U.S.S.R. Language Fluently	
				Russian	Other
Abaza	25	25.0	96.1	69.5	6.1
Hakh	771	46.9			
Chechen	613	46.3	98.7	66.7	1.0
Ingush	158	49.1	97.4	71.2	0.9
Dagestan	1,124	46.0	96.5	41.7	8.9
Avar	396	46.7	97.2	37.8	5.7
Lezgin	324	45.3	93.9	31.6	22.3
Dargin	231	46.2	98.4	43.0	2.8
Lak	86	34.4	95.6	56.0	3.5
Tabasaran	55	57.1	98.9	31.9	10.2
Rutul	12	79.1	98.9	30.7	18.8
Tsakhur	11	57.1	96.5	12.2	43.5
Agul	9	31.3	99.4	39.8	9.6
Semito-Khamit	24	9.1	64.5	46.2	14.7
Semit	24	9.1	64.5	46.2	14.7
Assyrian	24	9.1	64.5	46.2	14.7
Ural	4,510	4.8			
Finn	4,281	4.5			
Mordvinian	1,263	−1.7	77.8	65.7	8.1
Estonian	1,007	1.8	95.5	29.0	2.0
Udmurt	704	12.6	82.6	63.3	6.9
Mari	599	18.8	91.2	62.4	6.2
Komi	322	12.2	82.7	63.1	5.4
Komi-Permyak	153	6.3	85.8	68.5	4.6
Karelian	146	−12.6	63.0	59.1	15.1
Finn	85	−8.6	51.0	47.0	8.5
Vep	8	−50.0	34.3	32.8	16.4
Saam	2	5.6	56.2	52.9	9.3
Ugor	194.7	7.9			
Hungarian	166	7.1	96.6	25.8	9.8
Khanty	21	10.5	68.9	48.1	7.3
Mansi	8	20.3	52.4	38.6	5.4
Samodi	34	24.3			
Nenets	29	26.1	83.4	55.1	3.3
Selkup	4	13.2	51.1	40.8	8.6
Nganasan	1	25.0	75.4	40.0	15.7
Altay	32,788	39.2			
Turk	32,284	39.4			
Uzbek	9,195	52.9	98.6	14.5	3.3
Tatar	5,931	19.4	89.2	62.5	5.3
Kazakh	5,299	46.3	98.0	41.8	1.8

Table 6–7   (*Continued*)

Nationality Group	1970 Population (1000)	Per Cent Change 1970/ 1959	Per Cent Speaking National Language as Native Language	Per Cent Speaking Second U.S.S.R. Language Fluently	
				Russian	Other
Azerbaydzhanian	4,380	49.0	98.2	16.6	2.5
Chuvash	1,694	15.2	86.9	58.4	5.5
Turkmen	1,525	52.2	98.9	15.4	1.3
Kirgiz	1,452	49.8	98.8	19.1	3.3
Bashkir	1,240	25.4	66.2	53.3	2.6
Yakut	296	27.0	96.3	41.7	1.1
Karakalpak	236	36.4	96.6	10.4	3.6
Uygur	173	82.1	88.5	35.6	9.5
Gagauz	157	26.6	93.6	63.3	8.6
Kumyk	189	40.0	98.4	57.4	1.2
Nogay	52	33.3	89.8	68.5	1.1
Dolgan	5	25.6	89.8	61.9	3.2
Tuvinian	139	39.0	98.7	38.9	0.4
Karachai	113	39.5	98.1	67.6	1.2
Turk	79	125.7	92.3	22.4	—
Khakass	67	17.5	83.7	65.5	3.4
Balkar	60	42.9	97.2	71.5	2.5
Altay	56	24.4	87.2	54.9	3.2
Shor	16	6.7	73.5	59.8	5.9
Mongol	452	25.9			
Buryat	315	24.5	92.6	66.7	2.7
Kalmyk	137	29.2	91.7	81.1	1.5
Tungus-Manchurian	52	12.3			
Evenki	25	0.0	51.3	54.9	7.5
Even	12	33.3	56.0	46.4	17.6
Nanay	10	25.0	69.1	58.0	9.4
Ulchi	2	14.3	60.8	56.8	7.0
Udege	1	7.1	55.1	46.0	10.1
Orochi	1	37.5	48.6	44.4	6.6
Paleoasiatic	28	18.3			
Chukchi	14	16.7	82.6	58.7	4.8
Koryak	7	19.0	81.1	64.3	5.5
Nivkhi	4	18.9	49.5	43.8	5.6
Itelmen	1.3	18.2	35.7	32.5	4.3
Yukagir	1	50.0	46.8	29.1	32.8
Eskimo-Aleut					
Eskimo	1	17.0	60.0	50.5	3.4
Aleut	.4	4.8	21.8	18.8	1.8
Ket	1	20.0	74.9	59.1	2.0
Korean	358	13.7	68.6	50.3	1.7

Nationality Group	1970 Population (1000)	Per Cent Change 1970/ 1959	Per Cent Speaking National Language as Native Language	Per Cent Speaking Second U.S.S.R. Language Fluently	
				Russian	Other
Chinese	39	77.3	94.3	48.0	5.7
Dungan	39	77.3	94.3	48.0	5.7
Other Nationalities *c*	152	36.8	81.3	33.9	19.0

Source: *Itogi vsesoyuznoy perepisi naseleniya 1970 goda,* tom IV, pp. 9–11.

a Many Poles considered their native language to be Russian, Ukrainian, or Belorussian.

b In 1970 78.2 per cent of the Jews stated Russian as their native language. Most of these did not speak a second language.

c In addition to the groups listed above, the census listed seven other small groups by name.

million people is the Poles, who also are scattered widely in the country.

Other nationalities of the Indo-European family who number more than one million people each are the Moldavians in the southwest next to Rumania, the Lithuanians and Latvians in the Baltic Region, the Armenians in the Transcaucasus, the Tadzhiks in Center Asia, and Jews and Germans who are scattered.

The Altaic family, which comprises more than 11 per cent of the total population, includes the numerous Turkic groups who also have become widespread. They include such important nationalities as the Azerbaydzhanis and Karachay in the Caucasus; the Chuvash, Tatars, and Bashkirs in the Middle Volga Basin; the Kazakhs, Uzbeks, Turkmen, Kirgiz, and Karakalpak in Central Asia; and the Yakuts in Eastern Siberia.

The Uralic family, which comprises more than 2 per cent of the total population, includes the Finnish groups such as the Mordvinians, Udmurt, and Mari in the middle Volga valley; the Estonians and Karelians in the northwest; and the Komi in the northeastern part of European U.S.S.R. The other large family, the

Caucasians, are found in the Caucasus region and include such populous groups as the Georgians and Chechens.

The broad expanses of Siberia and the Far East originally were peopled by very sparsely settled groups of Paleoasiatic, Uralic, and Oriental peoples, but these peoples have become far outnumbered by inmigrating Russians, and now comprise only insignificant groups in the region.

When the Bolsheviks took over in 1917 they recognized the political advantage of appealing to the many nationality groups by guaranteeing them the right to national self determination. And although this has not been allowed to proceed to its ultimate consequence, secession from the Union, wherever significant concentrations of nationality groups exist the Soviet regime has made an effort to award some political recognition. (Fig. 6–10)

Some populous nationalities are so scattered that they have not been accorded political regions. Outstanding are the Germans and Poles. Before World War II there was a Volga-German Autonomous Republic centered on the middle Volga River near Saratov, but it was abrogated during the war and the inhabi-

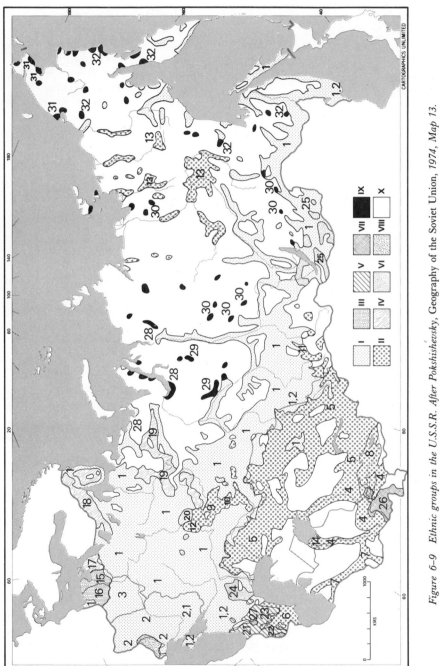

Figure 6–9 Ethnic groups in the U.S.S.R. After Pokshishevsky, Geography of the Soviet Union, 1974, Map 13.
I–Slavonic group; II–Turkic group; III–Lettish-Lithuanian group; IV–Finnish group; V–Caucasians; VI–Mongolian group; VII–Iranian group; VIII–Moldavians; IX–nationalities of the North; X–sparsely inhabited territories.
1–Russians; 2–Ukrainians; 3–Byelorussians; 4–Uzbeks; 5–Kazakhs; 6–Azerbaydzhanians; 7–Turkmens; 8–Kirgizes; 9–Tatars; 10–Bashkirs; 11–Khakassians; 12–Chuvash; 13–Yakuts; 14–Karakalpaks; 15–Latvians; 16–Lithuanians; 17–Estonians; 18–Karelians; 19–Komi; 20–Maris; 21–Georgians; 22–Armenians; 23–Chechens, Kabardinians, Ingushes, Cherkessians, peoples of Dagestan; 24–Kalmyks; 25–Buryats; 26–Tadzhiks; 27–Osetians; 28–Nentsi; 29–Khanti and Mansi; 30–Evenks; 31–Chukchi; 32–other national minorities of the North.

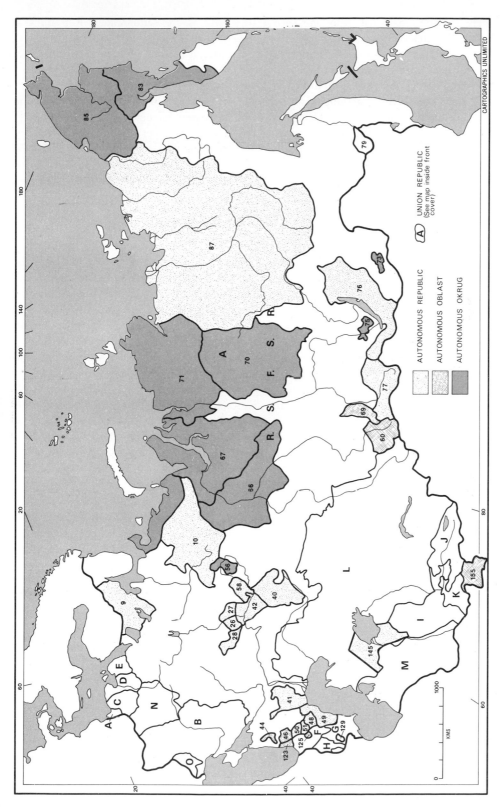

Figure 6–10   Nationality-based political units. Numbers correspond to those in Table 2–1.

tants were moved eastward into northern Kazakhstan, Western Siberia, and Central Asia. There had also been a concentration of German farmers in the Black Sea Steppes before World War II, and some of them too were moved eastward. Many accompanied the retreating German army back to Germany during the latter part of the war. The Poles are scattered through the western regions, particularly in some of the territory acquired as a result of World War II in what is now western Ukraine and Belorussia.

Another important group that is scattered throughout much of the country, primarily in the cities, are the Jews. They are particularly numerous in some of the larger cities in the west, such as Kiev, Moscow, and Leningrad. There is a Jewish Autonomous Oblast that was established in the Far East in 1934, but not many Jews have moved to it and most of the people there are Russian.

As has already been discussed, vital statistics vary widely from one nationality group to another. This, of course, continually alters relative numbers among the groups. Since in general the Central Asians and the Caucasians have much higher rates of natural increase than do the Slavs and Baltic peoples, the former groups are increasing at the expense of the latter. During the 1959–1970 intercensal period peoples in the Slavic groups declined from 77.1 per cent of the total population to 74.6 per cent, while the peoples of the Turkic groups increased from 11.1 per cent to 13.4 per cent of the total population. Russians, who had constituted 54.7 per cent of the Soviet population in 1959 constituted only 53.4 per cent in 1970. The Ukrainians decreased from 17.8 per cent to 16.9 per cent.

Among the major nationality groups, the ones who gained the most during the 1959–1970 period were the Uzbeks and Tadzhiks who were increased by 52.9 per cent during the eleven-year period. During the same period the Russians gained only 13.1 per cent, and the Ukrainians only 9.4 per cent. Among the union republic titular groups, the Estonians gained the least, only 1.9 per cent. Some actual decreases in numbers have occurred in nation-

ality groups in Autonomous Republics and Autonomous Oblasts and among groups who are scattered without political identities. (Table 6–7) Most populous among these were the Jews who decreased 5.2 per cent, the Poles who decreased 15.4 per cent, the Mordvinians who decreased 1.7 per cent, the Karelians who decreased 12.6 per cent, the Finns who decreased 8.2 per cent, the Czechs who decreased 16 per cent, and the Slovaks who decreased 20 per cent.

Russification

These decreases were due primarily to assimilations, although in some instances there were emigrations and repatriations to other countries. There is an inevitable process of Russification that accompanies the industrialization and urbanization of the country. Russian has become the *lingua franca* of the factories and the cities. In order to get ahead young men of all nationalities must learn the Russian language and act as Russians do. The nationality groups that are most susceptible to Russification and assimilation are those who are closest in their nationality characteristics to the Russians, such as the Belorussians and Ukrainians, and those who are scattered throughout the country.

The Jews, probably more than any other group, are becoming Russified in a society which has scattered them among other peoples and repressed their national institutions. Only 17.7 per cent of the Jews who reported themselves as Jews in the 1970 census reported Yiddish as their native language. 78.2 per cent of them reported their native tongue as Russian. And there were probably other persons who had reported themselves as Jews in previous censuses who switched to Russian or some neighboring nationality, such as Ukrainian or Belorussian, in the 1970 census.

Language is a good indicator of degree of assimilation. The next step after the switch to the Russian language is often a changeover in the nationality itself. And since people are recorded in censuses simply as they say they are, there are significant numbers of changeovers. Changeovers occur particularly frequently between generations, since a young person of mixed parentage when his internal passport is issued at the age of 16 has the choice of declaring himself a member of the nationality of either of his parents.

Groups that have the highest percentage of persons who have shifted to another language also show a high percentage who speak some second language fluently. (Table 6–7) Both these indices are lowest among the major nationality groups who constitute the union republics. They are higher among the peoples who constitute the autonomous republics and autonomous oblasts and highest among the peoples who are dispersed geographically and more liable to assimilation. In 1970, in addition to almost 100 per cent of the Russians who claimed Russian as their native language, 13 million non-Russians named Russian as their mother tongue. An additional 41.9 million indicated Russian as the second language that they spoke fluently. Thus 54.9 million, or approximately half of the non-Russian population of the U.S.S.R., are in perfect command of Russian. 76 per cent of the total Soviet population speak Russian well.

Certain constituents of the Soviet population frequently change their nationality identities for one reason or another. It is apparent that in the 1959 census part of the population of the western regions of the Belorussian and Ukrainian republics, who spoke the Belorussian or Ukrainian languages but who had formerly professed the Greek Orthodox religion, ranked themselves with the Poles, but in the 1970 census they considered themselves to be Belorussians and Ukrainians. This reflects the continuing eradication of religious beliefs of the people who were acquired with these western territories during World War II. Also considerable switchings back and forth take place in the small nationalities of the north and the Far East where nationality feelings are largely lacking. How the individuals are grouped depends to a great extent upon the way questions are asked by the census takers.

Some of the smaller non-Russian nationality groups constantly are being assimilated either by Russians or by neighboring groups. The number of nationalities recorded in the censuses has decreased from about 200 in 1926 to 108 in 1959 and 104 in 1970. This is not very surprising since many of the less culturally developed peoples, particularly in the Asian part of the country felt no nationality ties before the Soviet Regime identified their nationalities for them. Prior to the Bolshevik takeover such peoples felt allegiance only to extended families or clans and did not consider themselves as parts of larger nationality groups. Thus, in some instances nationality has been a rather artificial thing and official recognition of such has meant little to those involved. On the other hand such peoples as the Ukrainians, Balts, and Caucasians have fierce nationalistic feelings and are determined to maintain their identities in the face of inmigrating Russians, intermarriage, and the growing use of the Russian language. Of the larger groups of peoples, the Belorussians, who numbered over 9 million in the 1970 census, are the most in danger of disappearing as a separate entity. Their lands have often been split, as they still are today, between the Russians, the Poles, and the Lithuanians, and the mere fact that the Soviet Union has created a Belorussian Soviet Socialist Republic does not completely remedy the lack of cohesion among this group.

Migration among regions is a potent factor in changing nationality mixes within regions. Since it is the Slavic groups, and the Russians particularly, who are most apt to migrate, most of the nationality groups are becoming diluted with Russians. This has caused many anachronisms among the political units of the country that allegedly are established on nationality principles. The Kazakh S.S.R., for instance, in 1970 had only 32.7 per cent of its population made up by the titular group, while Russians made up 42.4 per cent of the population of the republic. (Table 6–8) In the Kirgiz Republic the titular group, with 43.8 per cent of the total population, remained a plurality but not a majority.

Hence, neither of these republics any longer satisfies the constitutional requirements for a republic. Hardly any of the Autonomous Soviet

Table 6–8   Nationality Composition of the U.S.S.R. by Republics, 1970, in Per Cent

Nationality

S.S.R.	Russian	Ukrainian	Belorussian	Uzbek	Kazakh	Georgian	Azerbaydzhani	Lithuanian	Moldavian	Latvian	Kirgiz	Tadzhik	Armenian	Turkmen	Estonian	Tatar	Jew	Other
U.S.S.R.	53.4	16.9	3.7	3.8	2.2	1.3	1.8	1.1	1.1	0.6	0.6	0.9	1.5	0.6	0.4	2.4	0.9	6.8
R.S.F.S.R.	82.8	2.6	0.7	—	0.4	0.1	0.1	—	0.1	—	—	—	0.2	—	—	3.7	0.6	8.7
Ukraine	19.4	74.9	0.8	—	—	—	—	—	0.6	—	—	—	—	—	—	—	1.6	2.7
Belorussia	10.4	2.1	81.0	—	—	—	—	—	—	—	—	—	—	—	—	—	1.6	4.9
Uzbek	12.5	0.9	—	65.5	4.0	—	—	—	—	—	0.9	3.8	—	0.6	—	4.9	0.9	6.9
Kazakh	42.4	7.2	1.5	1.7	32.6	—	—	—	—	—	—	—	—	—	—	2.2	—	12.4
Georgia	8.5	1.1	—	—	—	66.8	4.6	—	—	—	—	—	9.7	—	—	—	1.2	8.1
Azerbaydzhan	10.0	—	—	—	—	—	73.8	—	—	—	—	—	9,4	—	—	—	—	6.8
Lithuania	8.6	0.8	1.5	—	—	—	—	80.1	—	—	—	—	—	—	—	—	0.8	8.2
Moldavia	11.6	14.2	—	—	—	—	—	—	64.6	—	—	—	—	—	—	—	2.7	6.9
Latvia	29.8	2.3	4.0	—	—	—	—	1.7	—	56.8	—	—	—	—	—	—	1.6	3.8
Kirgiz	29.2	4.1	—	11.3	0.8	—	—	—	—	—	43.8	0.7	—	—	—	2.4	—	7.7
Tadzhik	11.9	1.1	—	23.0	0.3	—	—	—	—	—	1.2	56.2	—	—	—	2.4	0.5	3.0
Armenia	2.7	—	—	—	—	—	5.9	—	—	—	—	—	88.6	—	—	—	—	2.8
Turkmen	14.5	1.6	—	8.3	3.2	—	—	—	—	—	—	—	1.1	65.6	—	1.7	—	4.0
Estonia	24.7	2.1	1.4	—	—	—	—	—	—	—	—	—	—	—	68.2	—	0.4	3.2

Source: Boyarskogo, pp. 90–91.

Socialist Republics satisfy constitutional requirements anymore. (Table 6-9) Russians now predominate in almost all of them. Nevertheless, as pointed out in Chapter 2, it appears that these political entities have gained a permanency that transcends nationality considerations. In 1976 the Soviet Union adopted a geographic code that codified existing political administrative units, and in 1977 a new constitution was adopted that changed nothing, even though this was the prime opportunity to effect sweeping changes.

Education

The Soviets have transformed the education of the population of their country. They have established compulsory secondary education (through grade ten) and provided all sorts of opportunities for continuing education for adults. As late as 1920 only 44 per cent of the population in the age group 9-49 were literate. Today 99.7 per cent of this group are literate. In 1920 there were great discrepancies between men and women, between urban and rural places, and between different regions of the country. 57.6 per cent of the men were literate whereas only 32.3 per cent of the women were. 73.5 per cent of the urban dwellers were literate while only 37.8 per cent of the rural dwellers were. The highest literacy was found in the Ukraine where 51.9 per cent of the people could read and write, and the lowest was found in what is now the Tadzhik Republic where only 3.1 per cent could read and write. Among some of the indigenous populations of Middle Asia and northern Siberia illiteracy was almost universal. Some peoples had no written language at all. By 1959 most of these differences had been erased, and by 1970 the differences amounted to only fractions of one per cent. The 1970 census recorded only about 440,000 illiterate people, mainly persons who had been prevented from going to school because of poor health.

In 1975-1976 almost 93 million people were taking some sort of schooling. This amounted to 36 per cent of the entire population. All Soviet children enter primary school (grades 1 to 3) at age 7 and are now required to continue through the incomplete secondary education program (grades 4 to 8) and the complete secondary program (grades 9 and 10). In 1972 more than 86 per cent of the eight-year graduates continued their education either in general secondary schools, specialized secondary schools, or vocational-technical programs. About 20 per cent of the high school graduates were admitted to higher educational institutions.

The level of educational attainment still varies considerably from group to group and from region to region. In 1970 throughout the entire population 483 persons out of every 1000 above the age of 10 had completed at least eight years of educational training. This ratio ranged from a high of 554 per thousand in Georgia to a low of 382 per thousand in Lithuania. The range was even greater among some of the minor political subdivisions. This is especially true in some of the sparsely populated outlying areas where inmigrants of young well trained Russians form significant portions of total populations. For instance, in 1970 in the Chukotsk Autonomous Okrug in the Far East, where a new mining boom has been taking place, 703 out of every 1000 people aged 10 or above had finished at least eight years of schooling. On the other hand, in the Komi-Permyak N.O. in the western Urals only 339 per thousand had done so.

Among the major nationalities Jews are by far the most highly educated. (Table 6-10) Next are the Georgians, Armenians, and Russians. Jews also have by far the highest percentage of their young people in higher educational institutions. (Table 6-11) They are followed by Buryats, Osetians, Circassians, Georgians, Balkars, and Adyge. Russians are well down the list. It is apparent that some of the smaller groups are much over represented in the institutions of higher education.

Of the 483 people per thousand of the U.S.S.R. population who had completed at least eight years of schooling in 1970, 241 had completed only eight years of schooling, 187 had completed a secondary education, 13 had

Table 6–9   Nationality Composition of the A.S.S.R.s in the R.S.F.S.R., 1970, in Per Cent

A.S.S.R.	Nationality																	
	Bashkir	Buryat	Dagestani	Kabardino and Balkar	Kalmyk	Karelian	Komi	Mari	Mordvinian	Osetian	Tatar	Tuvinian	Udmurt	Chechen and Ingush	Chuvash	Yakut	Russian	Other
Bashkir	23.4	—	—	—	—	—	—	2.9	1.1	—	24.7	—	0.7	—	3.3	—	40.5	3.4
Buryat	—	22.0	—	—	—	—	—	—	—	—	1.2	—	—	—	—	—	73.5	3.3
Dagestan	—	—	74.3	—	—	—	—	—	—	0.1	—	—	—	2.8	—	—	14.7	8.1
Kabardino-Balkar	—	—	0.4	53.7	—	—	—	—	—	1.6	0.5	—	—	—	—	—	37.2	6.6
Kalmyk	—	—	2.5	—	41.1	—	—	—	—	—	0.5	—	—	1.8	—	—	45.8	8.3
Karelia	—	—	—	—	—	11.8	—	—	0.2	—	0.4	—	—	—	0.3	—	68.1	19.2
Komi	—	—	—	—	—	—	28.6	—	0.3	—	1.2	—	0.2	—	0.7	—	53.1	15.9
Mari	—	—	—	—	—	—	—	43.7	0.3	—	5.9	—	0.4	—	1.3	—	46.9	1.5
Mordvinian	—	—	—	—	—	—	—	—	35.4	—	4.4	—	—	—	—	—	58.9	1.3
N. Osetian	—	—	1.4	0.4	—	—	—	—	—	48.7	0.3	—	—	3.6	—	—	36.6	9.0
Tatar	0.1	—	—	—	—	—	—	—	1.0	—	49.1	—	0.8	—	4.9	—	42.4	1.2
Tuva	—	—	—	—	—	—	—	—	—	—	0.4	58.6	—	—	—	—	38.3	2.7
Udmurt	0.1	—	—	—	—	—	—	0.6	—	—	6.1	—	34.2	—	0.2	—	57.1	1.7
Chechen-Ingush	—	—	1.8	—	—	—	—	—	—	0.2	0.5	—	—	58.5	—	—	34.5	4.5
Chuvash	—	—	—	—	—	—	—	0.2	1.7	—	3.0	—	—	—	70.0	—	24.5	0.6
Yakut	—	0.3	—	—	—	—	—	—	0.3	—	1.2	—	—	—	—	43.0	47.3	7.9

Source: Boyarskogo, pp. 92–93.

taken some college work, and 42 had graduated from a four- or five-year college course. The greatest portion of the most highly educated people live in the cities. In 1970, 62 out of every 1000 persons in cities had completed a college education, while only 14 per thousand in the rural areas had done so. Among the total population who have completed college training, men still considerably outnumber women, but it has been reported that among current graduates women slightly outnumber men. In 1969–1970 women made up 48 per cent of all students in higher education and 54 per cent of students in paraprofessional secondary education institutions. They constituted well over half of the students in education, the arts and motion pictures; economics and law; and health, physical culture, and sports. (Table 6–12)

Table 6–10   Per Cent of Population Aged Ten and Over Having at Least Eight Years of Education, by Major Nationalities, 1970

Nationality	Per Cent
Jews	80.0
Georgians	57.8
Armenians	51.8
Russians	50.8
Latvians	48.8
Ukrainians	47.6
Estonians	46.2
Tatars	45.0
Belorussians	43.8
Turkmens	43.0
Azerbaydzhanis	42.4
Uzbeks	41.2
Kirgiz	40.0
Tadzhiks	39.0
Kazakhs	39.0
Lithuanians	35.3
Moldavians	33.8

Source: Lewis, Rowland, and Clem, 1976, p. 340.

Table 6–11   Students in Higher Educational Institutions per 1000 Population Aged 16–24, by Nationality, 1970

Nationality	1970
Jews	512.4
Buryats	259.8
Osetians	225.1
Circassians	224.8
Georgians	211.6
Balkars	208.3
Adyge	203.6
Kalmyks	190.2
Karachay	184.8
Armenians	179.4
Abkhaz	174.3
Azerbaydzhanis	166.6
Karakalpaks	166.6
Yakuts	161.2
Kabardinians	155.9
Estonians	157.5
Kirgiz	158.0
Lithuanians	147.1
Russians	146.1
Kazakhs	143.1
Peoples of Dagestan	139.0
Altays	137.8
Latvians	136.9
Uzbeks	134.4
Khakas	124.9
Turkmens	122.4
Ukrainians	115.1
Tadzhiks	111.1
Karelians	109.5
Belorussians	109.3
Tatars	105.5
Bashkirs	102.0
Ingush	98.8
Udmurts	85.7
Tuvinians	85.5
Moldavians	85.2
Chuvash	80.7
Komi	80.6
Mordvinians	79.2
Mari	66.5
Chechens	61.4

Source: Lewis, Rowland, Clem, 1976, p. 341.

Table 6–12   Women as Per Cent of Students in Higher and Paraprofessional Secondary Educational Institutions

	1927–1928	1960–1961	1969–1970
Women as per cent of students in higher education	28	43	48
Including in institutions:			
For industry and construction, transport and communications	13	30	37
For agriculture	17	27	29
For economics and law	21	49	60
For health, physical culture, and sports	52	56	55
For education, the arts, and motion pictures	49	63	66
Women as per cent of students in paraprofessional secondary educational institutions	38	47	54
Including in institutions:			
For industry and construction, transport and communications	9	33	41
For agriculture	15	38	37
For economics and law	36	75	83
For health, physical culture, and sports	89	84	87
For education, the arts and motion pictures	53	76	81

Source: "Women in the USSR: Statistical Data," *Soviet Sociology,* Summer, 1972, p. 74.

Occupation

The universal training of the people coupled with urbanization and industrialization have transformed the structure of the labor force of the Soviet Union. Whereas in 1913 mining, manufacturing, and construction occupied only 9 per cent of the labor force, in 1974 they occupied 35 per cent. (Table 8–5) Farming and forestry, which had occupied 75 per cent of the labor force in 1913, occupied only 30 per cent in 1974. Although this is still a high percentage for a developed country, it is a remarkable change. It is interesting that in the farming category more labor is expended on private plots than on all state farms and almost as much as on all collective farms. This will be

elaborated on in the chapter on agriculture. The service sector has shown the highest gain, from one per cent in 1913 to 16.8 per cent in 1974, but services still account for only about half the portion of labor in the U.S.S.R. that they do in the U.S.A.

Role of Women

The role of women in the labor force has been growing constantly through much of the Soviet period. Initially, this growth was no doubt in response to the large deficits of males in the working age groups. But as time has gone on and the male deficits have risen up the age ladder, the percentage of women in the labor force has continued high, so it now appears that working women have become a way of life in the Soviet Union which has transcended its original stimulation. By 1970 the share of women in the labor force had risen to 51 per cent, and it has remained at that level since. (Table 6–13) This is more than double the percentage in 1924 when women comprised only 24 per cent of the labor force. They make up almost half the labor force in the two primary production sectors of the economy, industry and agriculture, and they make up more than three fourths of the labor force in trade. They are particularly prevalent in certain professions. In 1975 they accounted for 65 per cent of all the administrators in the country and 84 per cent of the medical doctors.

Table 6–13   Women as Per Cent of All Workers and Employees, by Branch of Economy, 1975

Total	51
Industry	49
Agriculture	44 [a]
Transport	24
Communications	68
Construction	28
Trade	76
Services	53
Health	84
Education	73
Culture	71
Arts	47
Science	50
Credit and Finance	82
Administration	65

Source: Narkhoz SSSR, 1975, p. 543.
[a] Does not include work on private plots.

They are even more preponderant in some of the so-called "auxillary enterprises" which lie outside socialized labor and which therefore have no official statistics, such as the intensive working of private plots of land which are allotted to families on farms and in some industrial settlements. In those places they account for as much as 90 per cent of the labor performed in raising garden produce and live-stock. As might be expected working women vary by region and nationality. They make up the greatest percentage of the work force in Estonia, Latvia, the R.S.F.S.R., Belorussia, Ukraine, Lithuania, and Moldavia, and are least in the Tadzhik, Turkmen, and Uzbek republics.

Regional Distribution of Population Growth

The 1970 census revealed a regional pattern of population growth during 1959–1970 that was considerably different from that during the intercensal period 1939–1959 or the intercensal period 1926–1939. Whereas the eastern regions grew disproportionately rapidly during the previous periods, particularly during World War II and its immediate aftermath, this was not the case during 1959–1970. While the entire Soviet population increased 16 per cent, the Urals increased only 7 per cent, Western Siberia 8 per cent, and Eastern Siberia 15 per cent. Certain sections of the eastern regions still grew rapidly percentagewise, but these were generally sparsely settled areas, and the rapid percentage growth did not involve large numbers of people.

The three regions that experienced the greatest percentage increases in the entire country were Guryev Oblast (which at that time included the Mangyshlak Peninsula) along the northeastern coast of the Caspian Sea, the Khanti-Mansi Autonomous Okrug in the West Siberian Lowland, and the Chukotsk Autonomous Okrug in the far northeastern corner of the country. (Fig. 6–11) But most portions of these territories had population densities of less than one person per square kilometer. Their rapid percentage increases during the last intercensal period were due to newly initiated mining activities that brought some boom towns into these sparsely settled regions. In Guryev Oblast it was the Mangysh-lak oil, in the Khanti-Mansi Autonomous Okrug the newly opened West Siberian oil fields, and in the Chukotsk Autonomous Okrug gold, tin, tungsten, and mercury.

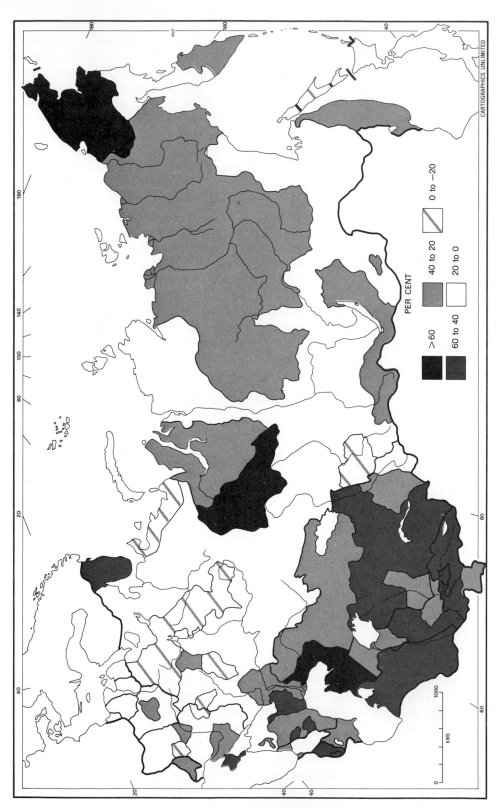

Figure 6–11 Percentage population changes by oblast, kray, and ASSR, 1959–1970. After Lydolph and Pease, p. 247.

To a lesser degree the same reasoning applies to most of the rest of the regions of Siberia, the Far East, and Kazakhstan where percentage gains between 40 and 60 per cent were registered during the period. Relatively high percentage gains are explained more by low population bases than by large influxes of people. Generally it was the less settled and less urbanized parts of the eastern regions that increased most percentagewise. The more heavily urbanized and industrialized areas in southern Siberia and the adjacent Urals experienced some of the lowest population gains. In some areas there were actual losses of population during the period. In most cases these were the very areas that had shown some of the highest growth rates during the 1939–1959 period. In general the growth that took place in the eastern regions during 1959–1970 was due to natural increase. Net migration from most of the regions was negative.

Large sections of central European Russia continued to lose population, as they had in previous periods, but the people that were moving out of these regions during 1959–1970 were generally going south into a zone extending from the southern Ukraine, especially Crimea Oblast, eastward through parts of the north Caucasus into Central Asia. This was a major change in the direction of migration away from these areas, which during the previous half century had been mainly eastward.

Since 1959 was a breakpoint between two intercensal periods of relatively long lengths, it appeared that a drastic change in distributional trends of growth took place in 1959. However, maps of growth rates plotted for individual years during 1959–1970 indicate that the reversal in regional trends must have taken place somewhat prior to 1959 and that the reduction of growth rates in the eastern regions was an intensifying process during the 1959–1970 period. Unfortunately, reliable yearly data are not available prior to 1959, so one cannot pinpoint the date when most of Siberia stopped growing faster than other regions of the country. But a comparison of Figure 6–11 with Figure 6–12 well illustrates a continued spread of territories in the European part of the country, Western Siberia, and northern Kazakhstan that experienced population decreases during the period. The areas of population loss are much more extensive on the 1968–1969 map than on the map of the entire period, 1959–1970.

It also becomes evident that one can no longer talk about population changes by gross regions. Certainly one cannot compare simply easten versus western regions. There are areas of population growth and areas of population loss in both the east and west, and this is true even within political entities for which statistics are compiled. Unfortunately, in most cases the regional refinements of statistics are not good enough to depict intraregional differences.

Any cartographic representation of population changes by regions entails distortions in visual impressions because of the great differences in sizes of regions and differences in their population densities. Thus, a relatively high percentage growth rate in huge, sparsely populated Yakutsk A.S.S.R. and adjacent regions gives a visual impression on a map of large population gains in Eastern Siberia and the Far East. In order to reduce this erroneous impression a map has been plotted showing absolute increases in people per area, in other words population growth density. (Fig. 6–13) Using this index, practically all of Siberia and the Far East are smoothed into an area that shows the lowest population increase of the entire country. The three areas of highest percentage growth rates are now submerged in extensive areas of mimimum growth densities. On the other hand, many smaller regions of higher population densities that showed only moderate percentage growth rates now show up as areas having extremely high growth densities. Such are the highly urbanized and industrialized oblasts of Moscow, Kiev, and Donetsk, as well as such heavily populated, relatively small territories as Crimea, Moldavia, and Armenia. In Central Asia the small, densely populated oblasts of Khorezm and Fergana are lifted out of a general region of relatively high percentage growth rates and are now shown to have the highest category of growth density. At the same time, some of the

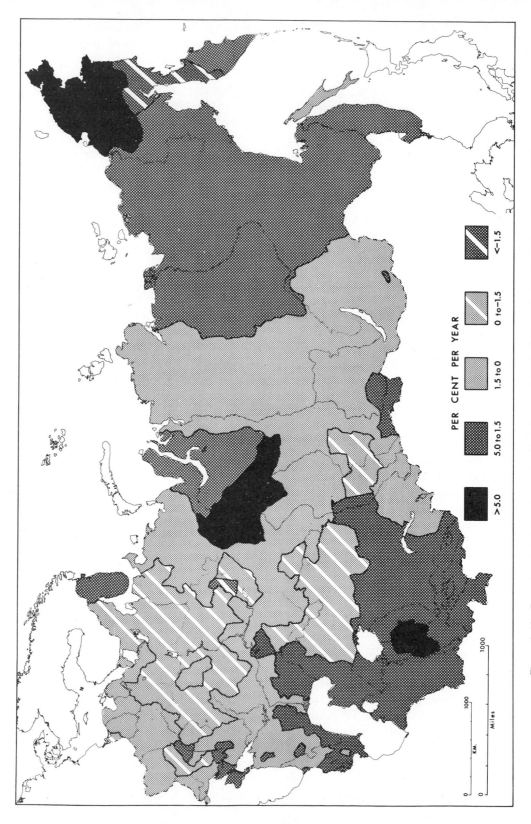

Figure 6–12   Percentage population changes by oblast, kray, and ASSR, 1968–1969. After Lydolph and Pease, p. 248.

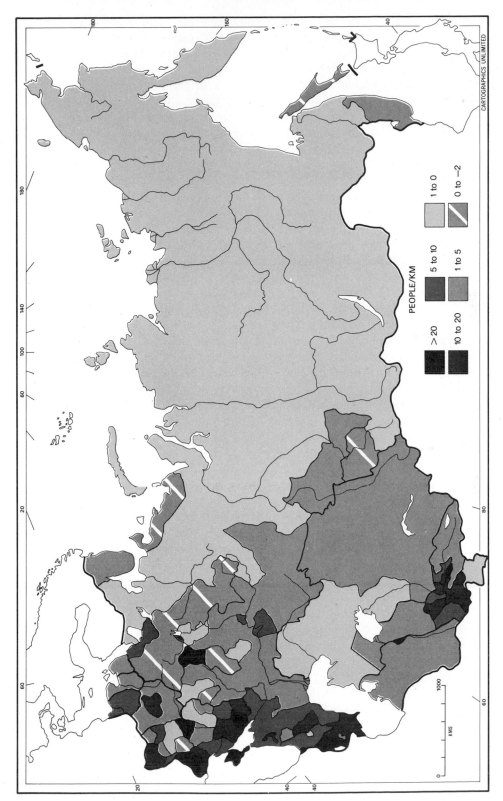

Figure 6–13 Population growth densities by oblast, kray, and ASSR, 1959–1970. After Lydolph and Pease, p. 250.

larger adjacent oblasts, which had higher percentage growth rates than Khorezm and Fergana, now appear to have near minimum growth densities. It can now be seen that in terms of absolute numbers the highest growths by far during 1959–1970 were in the southern portions of the country, particularly in a discontinuous belt extending eastward from western Ukraine across Moldavia and south-eastern Ukraine, the north Caucasus and the Transcaucasus, into portions of Central Asia.

Though no data comparable to the results of the 1970 census are available for population changes since that time, the annual statistical handbooks have included population estimates by oblast and comparable political units which have allowed Figure 6–14 to be compiled. From this map it is evident that some patterns of growth have been continued since the 1959–1970 period and some have changed. All of the Far East seems to be experiencing renewed growth, including Kamchatka and Sakhalin Island, which during certain years of the 1959–1970 period showed absolute decreases in population. Eastern Siberia continues to show intermediate growth rates, and in Western Siberia the oil-and-gas-rich areas of Tyumen Oblast continue to show very high percentage growth rates, while more heavily populated southern parts of Western Siberia and the Urals show very low growth rates. Within this area, Kurgan Oblast, Altay Kray, and Perm Oblast show absolute decreases in population. However, the northern oblasts of Kazakhstan, which showed the beginnings of absolute population declines in the late 1960s, now show moderate gains. Guryev Oblast and its newly spawned Mangyshlak Oblast continue to show high gains in the expanding oil regions northeast of the Caspian Sea. Central Asia uniformly shows high growth rates due to continuing high birth rates and natural increases in the area.

In European Russia and adjacent parts of the north central Ukraine the large central area that displayed population losses throughout the 1959–1970 period continues to lose population, but there has been some minor shifts in the distribution. Whereas previously largest losses

had been experienced in portions of the Volgo-Vyatka Region, the two oblasts of most extreme losses are now Kostroma in the northeastern part of the Central Region and Tambov in the eastern part of the Central Black Earth Region. Large sections of the Northwest Economic Region, specifically the Karelian A.S.S.R. and Archangel Oblast, which had shown absolute losses in 1968–1969, now show slight gains. Areas around Moscow, smack in the center of the loss region, continue to show moderate gains, as do Leningrad Oblast and the adjacent Baltic Republics. On the other hand, Belorussia, which showed consistently moderate gains during the 1959–1970 period now has a large central core showing population losses. In the south, Moldavia, the South Economic Region, and parts of the Donets-Dnieper Region continue to show moderate gains, and the Crimea continues to show high gains.

During 1970–1976, while the population of the entire U.S.S.R. increased 5.7 per cent, the Tadzhik Republic increased 20.2 per cent, the Turkmen Republic 19.6 per cent, the Uzbek Republic 17.7 per cent, and the Kirgiz Republic 14.8 per cent. The Kazakh Republic increased 11.6 per cent, and in Transcaucasia Armenia increased 13.7 per cent and Azerbaydzhan 11.3 per cent. The other republics increased at much slower rates. In the Russian Republic, the Far East Economic Region increased 13.8 per cent, Eastern Siberia increased 5.9 per cent, Western Siberia increased only 3.2 per cent, and the Urals increased only 1.3 per cent. Thus, Western Siberia and the Urals are still increasing less rapidly than even the Russian Republic average, let alone the U.S.S.R. average. The Volgo-Vyatka and Central Chernozem Regions lost population absolutely, with the Central Chernozem Region losing the largest percentage.

The rural population continues to decrease in almost all parts of the country except the high birth areas of Central Asia, Azerbaydzhan, parts of south-central Kazakhstan, and some developing areas such as the northeastern part of the country and Murmansk Oblast in

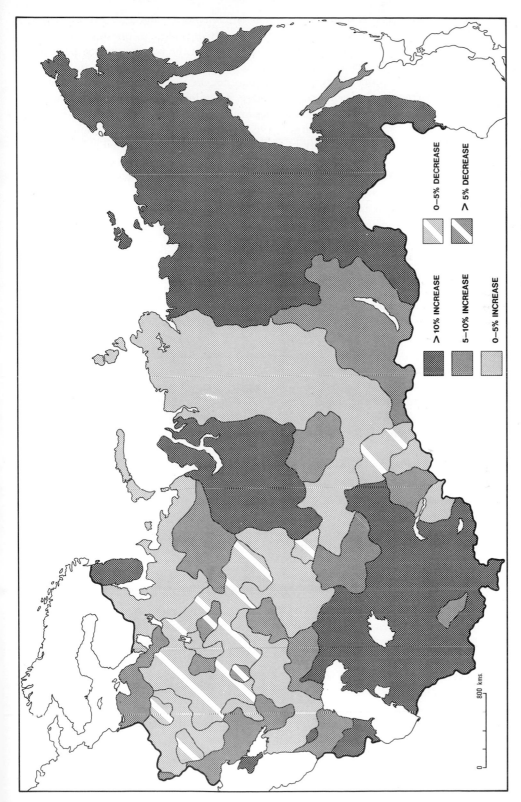

Figure 6–14 Percentage population changes by oblast, kray, and ASSR, 1970–1976. Compiled by Julie Mintz from data in Narkhoz SSSR, 1969, pp. 13–18 and 1975, pp. 16–21.

> 10% INCREASE

5–10% INCREASE

0–5% INCREASE

0–5% DECREASE

> 5% DECREASE

800 kms.

0

the far northwest. (Fig. 6–15) Large rural population decreases are being experienced throughout much of Eastern and Western Siberia, the Urals, and European Russia, as well as the north-central Ukraine. Very large losses are being incurred in the more rural parts of the Central Chernozem, Central, and Volgo-Vyatka Regions. Everywhere a large rural-urban migration is going on. It is only in those areas with exceedingly high birth rates in rural areas that natural increase can supply rural-urban migration and still show large rural population growth. This is limited now almost entirely to Central Asia and adjacent parts of Kazakhstan. The Transcaucasus are rapidly becoming more like European U.S.S.R. The Azerbaydzhan Republic still shows a relatively high rural population growth, but Armenia now shows a very low growth, and Georgia shows just about a balance between natural increases in rural areas and net migrations out of rural areas.

The pattern of population growth that has been discussed in the previous section is due to a combination of natural increase, migration, and urbanization. It is difficult to ascertain these components, since most Soviet statistical handbooks do not include direct information on migration or urbanization and break down natural increase rates only by union republic at best. Such a regional breakdown is practically worthless, since the Russian Republic is so huge compared to the rest of the republics. There have been occasional monographs that have broken down natural increase rates by the nineteen economic regions, and these have helped some. Among other things, they have allowed migration to be computed by region as a residual difference between actual growth and natural increase. However, one is on pretty shaky ground treating migration only as a residual if one realizes that the natural increase data might not be very accurate.

Migration

The 1970 census was the first census to make an attempt to gain some direct informa-

tion on short-term migration processes in the country. It included a question that asked whether or not the respondent had been living in the same place for more than two years. If he had not, he was asked where he had lived before. Therefore, some crude migration statistics are available from the census for the years 1968–1969. However, as was pointed out by Grandstaff and later by Shabad, the census migration data for these two years do not seem to correspond very well with migration data worked out indirectly for the total intercensal period, 1959–1970.[11] Therefore, although some analysis will be given of these 1968–1969 data, they must be viewed with caution.

In 1975 a separate statistical handbook on population was published for the year 1973 which included detailed migration statistics, but only into and out of urban places and only at the union republic and major economic region level, rather than the oblast level that had been the case for the 1968–1969 data.[12]

Migration trends have been analyzed for the 1959–1970 intercensal period and for the years 1968–1969 by Shabad.[13] Although some discrepancies came to light between the two periods, indicating some inadequacies in the data, the following generalizations were made. During 1959–1970, the three Baltic Republics, the Northwest, Center, and Volga regions of European Russia, and the Donets-Dnieper Region of the eastern Ukraine were characterised by net inmigration and rural depopulation. Low rates of natural increase in these regions made net inmigration the principal source of population growth during this period. In many places the rural population became so depleted of its youthful members that the natural increase became lower in the rural areas than in the urban areas of the regions.

The four Central Asian Republics, Kazakhstan, Moldavia, the Southern Region of Ukraine, the North Caucasus, Armenia, and the Far East Economic Regions experienced net inmigration coupled with rural population

[11] Grandstaff, 1974 and Shabad, 1977, pp. 184–186.
[12] *Naselenie SSSR, 1973.*
[13] Shabad, 1977, pp. 173–196.

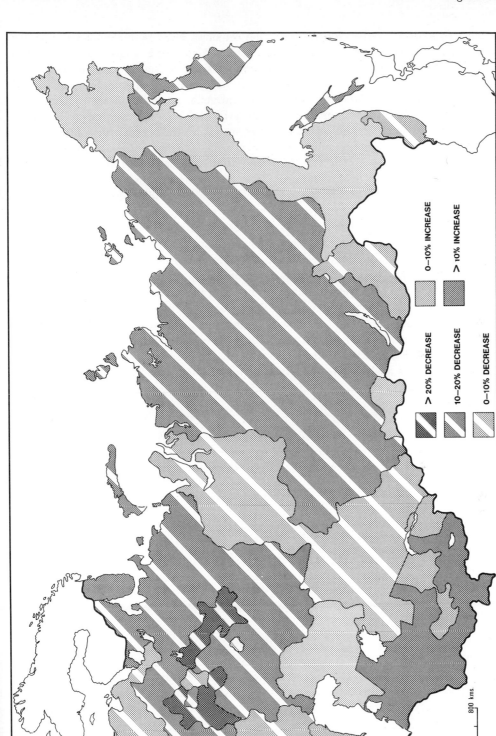

Figure 6-15   Rural population change by oblast, kray, and ASSR, 1970–1976. Compiled by Julie Mintz from data in Narkhoz SSSR, 1969 and 1975.

increase. Eastern Siberia, Western Siberia, the Urals, the Volgo-Vyatka, the Central Chernozem Region, Belorussia, and the Southwest Economic Region in the Ukraine all experienced net outmigration with rural depopulation. Georgia and Azerbaydzhan in the Transcaucasus had the distinction of being the only regions that experienced net outmigration with rural population increases.

Analysis of the 1968–1969 data indicated some shifts in interregional migration streams toward the end of the 1959–1970 intercensal period. According to the data of those two years there was a net inmigration into the Russian Republic as a whole and net outmigrations from Central Asia and Kazakhstan. The Belorussian migratory pattern seems to have changed from net outmigration to a virtual balance. The apparent reversals in flow between Central Asia and Kazakhstan on the one hand and the R.S.F.S.R. on the other has been questioned by some analysts who suspect the responses given by individuals to the 1970 census takers might have been biased in attempts by individuals to conceal the fact that they had recently moved from Russia to Central Asia, a migration which is frowned upon by the central government because of surplus labor already in Central Asia. However, the data might indicate a real reversal in migration streams between these republics. The change in Belorussia probably relates to the growing need for industrial labor within Belorussia which has been distinguished by the highest industrial growth rate among the 15 Soviet Republics since the middle 1960s.

Migration streams involving the most people during 1968–1969 are shown in Table 6–14. The Central and Northwest Economic Regions in European Russia obviously attracted much inmigration. Nine streams of migration from other regions entered central Russia and only two left. Four streams entered the Northwest Region and none left. The attraction of the two

Table 6–14   Major Net Migration Streams, 1968–1969, in Thousands

From: To:	R.S.F.S.R.								Ukraine			Tr	Ka	CA
	Ce	VV	CC	Vo	NC	Ur	WS	ES	Uk	DD	SW			
R.S.F.S.R.														
Northwest	24	11							22		20		13	
Center		14	30	13	22	12			37		33	11	14	38
Volga		11	12		13									15
North Caucasus						26	19					15	15	
Urals		10												
West Siberia						14								
East Siberia						10	15							
Far East	10				11		12	13	15	10	7		11	
Ukraine		19				26	18					10	18	18
Donets-Dnieper		16				17	9				21		12	
South						9	6			11	35		6	
Belorussia													9	
Kazakhstan						23								35

Source: Shabad, 1977, p. 187.
Note: With a few exceptions, regions generating and receiving large net migration streams in excess of more than 10,000 are shown.
Ce=Center, VV=Volgo-Vyatka, CC=Central Chernozem, Vo=Volga, NC=North Caucasus, Ur=Urals, WS=Western Siberia, ES=Eastern Siberia, Uk=Ukraine total, DD=Donets-Dnieper, SW=Southwest, Tr=Transcaucasus, Ka=Kazakhstan, CA=Central Asia.

regions is primarily explained by the presence of the two major urban agglomerations of the country, Moscow and Leningrad. Moscow recorded a net inmigration of 116,000 people during the two-year period, 1968–1969. 202,000 people entered and 86,000 people left. Two-thirds of the arrivals originated outside central Russia.

The two principal regions of European Russia that generated outmigration were Volgo-Vyatka and Central Chernozem. These have been losing population through net migration for many years, and the ultimate result has been a drastic rural depopulation. The Volgo-Vyatka Region sent people primarily to the Northwest, Center, and Volga, while the Central Chernozem Region sent them to Central Russia and southward to the Ukraine, especially to the industrial Donets-Dnieper Region.

The Volga Region had a positive migration balance. It serves as a transit area on east-west migration routes between European Russia and the eastern regions. Since much migration is step-by-step between adjacent regions, migration intensity in the Volga Region is quite high. Often people moving eastward settle temporarily in the Volga Region and then later move on eastward into the Urals and Siberia.

The North Caucasus is the only economic region in European Russia that gained both urban and rural population through migration. 42 per cent of all the migrants into the North Caucasus went to rural destinations. Many of these people were returnees from the Urals, Western Siberia, and Northern Kazakhstan. This stream is also frowned upon by the central government, since people are leaving labor deficit areas and settling in labor surplus areas. Many of them cannot find jobs in the North Caucasus and therefore must eke out livelihoods on private plots of land in the rural areas.

The outmigration of both rural and urban migrants has been a distinguishing feature of the Urals Economic Region since the late 1950s. The Urals experienced the largest net outflow of any of the ten economic regions of

the R.S.F.S.R. during 1968–1969. A net of 110,000 people left the Urals region during these two years. The Urals had a net outmigration balance with all Soviet regions except the Volgo-Vyatka Region which was supplying eastward migration streams that were temporarily settling in the Urals before they moved on to Siberia and the Far East. West Siberia has experienced a similar migration although not quite as drastic as the Urals. Its net outmigration during 1968–1969 was second only to that of the Urals. Eastern Siberia, on the other hand, changed from net outmigration during much of the intercensal period to net inmigration during the last two years of that period.

The Far East has exhibited consistent net inmigration with streams originating from many parts of the Soviet Union, including such net inmigration areas as Central Russia and the North Caucasus. This net flow to the Far East has been fostered by government sponsored migration programs and monetary incentives.

In the Ukraine, the industrialized Donets-Dnieper region and the climatically attractive South along the Black Sea coast, including the Crimea, were net inmigration areas, while the densely populated and under-industrialized Southwest Region generated the largest net outmigration of any of the Soviet regions, 123,000 during 1968–1969.

In Kazakhstan it appears that the settling of the Virgin Lands has been completed. The net inflow of migration which had been characteristic since the mid 1950s has now reversed, and 1968–1969 showed a net outflow, primarily to European Russia.

Mobility

Interregional migration streams are not the total picture of population movement in the Soviet Union. There is a great deal of intraregional movement and even movement within single settlements. All this causes economic disruption and consternation to Soviet planners. These intraregional moves frequently involve more people than the interregional moves do, since people tend to move short distances. Frequency of moves between points diminishes exponentially with distance. Since any move, whether it is short or long, usually involves changes in job, housing, and interpersonal relations, mobility of the population is an important factor in economic development.

In the past the development of the national economy was limited by equipment, but now it is limited by people. There are labor deficits in most large cities of the country and in many parts of the country there are labor deficits on the farms also. The farm population ultimately absorbs the loss, because of the large rural-urban migration in all regions. Youth tend to spurn agricultural work. In surveys taken to ascertain reasons for rural-urban migration, the most common reason that emerged was the aversion to agricultural work. In occupational preference surveys young people commonly list agricultural employment lowest, along with certain service jobs. It appears that rural youth are moving more to get away from agricultural work than to get away from rural living conditions. It has been estimated that of the needed manpower on collective farms, only 70 per cent is available in Western Siberia, 71 per cent in Kazakhstan, 76 per cent in the Northwest, 80 per cent in Estonia, and 83 per cent in Eastern Siberia. On the other hand, the Kirgiz Republic has 122 per cent of what it needs, Ukraine and Moldavia have 128 per cent, Belorussia 142 per cent, and Georgia 199 per cent. And still people leave places where there are manpower shortages and move to labor surplus areas. Present migration streams seem to be exacerbating regional labor imbalances rather than solving them. People seem to be moving primarily to the "sun belt" in search of better climate.

In the cities workers tend to shun menial jobs such as sales clerks, checkers, and piece work on mass production lines in factories. It has been reported that lack of workers accounts for more than 40 per cent of full shift down time in the machine building industry and more than half the time lost in the textile industry. Industrial labor shortages exist even in Central Asia with its large surplus of rural labor. The natives do not adapt well to factory work, and often Russians and other outsiders have to be brought in to man the new factories that are being built in the area.

It appears that the Soviet population has become increasingly mobile with time. One of the great problems of the labor force is its transitory nature in many regions of the country, particularly in the eastern regions where stability is so much needed. It has been reported that in 1970 31 per cent of all the workers in the country changed jobs. 67 per cent of these people changed jobs of their own volition without government planning or sanction. On the average a worker loses two months' work during a move. It has been estimated that during 1970 100 million man days were lost because of job changes.[14]

Although everyone beyond the age of 16 is supposed to have an internal passport and a work record book and is supposed to register at points of departure and arrival, not to mention get permission to leave one job and look for another, it would seem that the government could keep track of everyone. But in practice the authorities have winked at these rules, and people are moving about pretty much at will. They have fallen into the habit of leaving one job and showing up looking for a job and residence in another place. It has been reported that in recent years 90 per cent of all new hirings by industrial enterprises have been done "at the gate." In labor deficit areas plant managers are so eager to hire anyone that they tend to aid people to consummate their illegal moves and do not question them when they say they have lost their documents and ask for new ones.

Industrial plant managers are so eager to get workers that they offer fringe benefits that entice workers to move about from one job to another. This practice has become so pernicious that some Soviet economists have recommended that, in order to eliminate competition among factories, indivisible funds marked for housing, hospitals, kindergartens, and so forth now being dispensed by individual ministries

[14] Kupriyenko, 1972, p. 62.

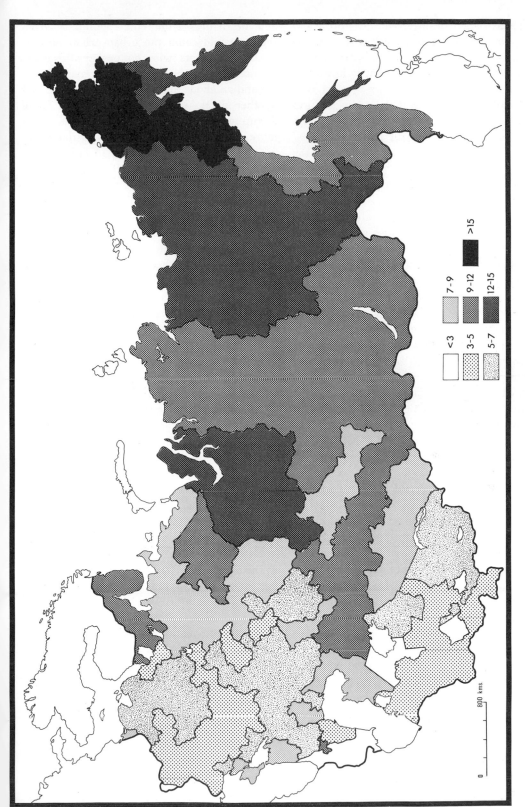

Figure 6-16 *Annual average population mobility, 1968-1969. Total arrivals and departures as percents of total populations of oblasts, krays, and ASSRs. Compiled by Richard Johnson from data in Itogi vsesoyuznoy perepisi naseleniya 1970 goda, tom VII, pp. 158-162.*

<3

3-5

5-7

7-9

9-12

12-15

>15

800 kms.

and enterprises be transferred to city Soviets so that plant managers no longer will have the option of offering such things as better housing to skilled workers that they want to lure away from other enterprises.

A map of population mobility by political divisions of the country has been compiled from the 1970 census data for the two years 1968–1969. (Fig. 6–16) This shows percent of the total population of each region that were involved in arrivals or departures during the period. Although this counts intraregional moves twice, it is not too unrealistic, since a move by one person will cause disruptions at both his point of departure and his point of arrival. And it is primarily the disruptions to the economy that lend significance to his move.

It is clear that the highest mobility exists in the eastern and northern parts of the country, especially the developing parts of those areas where labor generally is in short supply and stability is so much needed. Highest of all political unites is Magadan Oblast in the far northeastern part of the country where recent exploitation of gold, tin, tungsten, and mercury has induced the movement of considerable numbers of miners and support personnel into, out of, and within a region of sparse population. Almost 20 per cent of the population in this area move annually. Lowest mobility is found in the western and southern parts of the country, especially in much of Central Asia, the Transcaucasus, and Transcarpathian Ukraine. Only 1.5–3 percent of the population move annually in most of these areas where large labor surpluses could well support active outmigration.

Naselenie S.S.S.R., 1973 provides migration data into and out of urban areas for union republics and major economic regions. (Table 6–15) These data include rural-urban, urban-rural, and urban-urban movements, both intraregional and interregional. They do not include rural-rural movements which seem to be considerable, but such movements would not affect the industrial labor force to any extent. A simple addition of numbers of arrivals to cities

and departures from cities within a given region would count the urban-urban intraregional movements twice, but perhaps this is not too unreal since the transfer of a person from a job and an abode in one city to another job and another abode in another city would cause disruption in urban areas at both ends of the move. And it is these urban disruptions in which we are interested here in order to get some measure of economic effect on industrial activity. The most important data that are missing are moves within the same city, which must be quite high. Since these missing elements tend to cancel each other to a certain extent, the total of urban arrivals and departures probably is not too bad an index to estimate general population mobility within urban areas. At least, it allows for a relative comparison among regions.

As can be seen in Table 6–15, in 1973 more than 7 per cent of the total population of the U.S.S.R. was involved in urban arrivals and departures. The eastern regions from the Urals to the Pacific tended to have very high mobility. The Far East Economic Region had the highest mobility of all, more than 14 per cent of the total population. The Donets-Dnieper region in the Eastern Ukraine also had high mobility, as did the Northwest Economic Region. Estonia, Latvia, the Volga Region, and the North Caucasus were above average. Lowest were the Transcaucasian, Central Asian, and Moldavian Republics. These data do not reveal high levels of rural outmigration from regions such as the Southwest. Therefore, the data are good for assessing population mobility disturbances in urban areas but not in assessing general mobility levels involving rural departures. Again, perhaps this is not too detrimental, since rural movement out of a region does not particularly affect the cities of that region, only the cities in the regions into which the people are moving.

RURAL-URBAN COMPOSITION

One of the most outstanding characteristics of the Soviet period has been rapid urbaniza-

Table 6–15   Population Mobility, by Republic and Economic Region, 1973

	Arrivals to Urban Areas	Departures From Urban Areas	Sum of Arrivals and Departures	Moves as Per Cent of Total Population
U.S.S.R.	9,925,092	8,017,512	17,942,604	7.15
R.S.F.S.R.	6,128,575	4,966,298	11,094,873	8.35
Northwest	649,991	511,794	1,161,785	9.21
Center	1,023,026	772,785	1,735,811	6.38
Volgo-Vyatka	314,129	256,681	570,810	6.90
Central Chernozem	252,351	188,433	440,784	5.63
Volga	844,536	645,302	1,489,838	7.90
North Caucasus	583,195	490,025	1,073,220	7.20
Urals	786,993	700,631	1,487,624	9.77
Western Siberia	661,498	557,317	1,218,815	9.92
Eastern Siberia	484,459	408,713	893,172	11.55
Far East	485,258	397,630	882,888	14.01
Ukraine S.S.R.	1,807,509	1,482,366	3,289,875	6.78
Donets-Dnieper	940,822	823,367	1,764,789	11.70
Southwest	578,268	434,416	1,012,684	4.79
South	288,419	223,983	512,402	7.60
Baltic				
Lithuania S.S.R.	118,204	86,484	204,688	6.27
Latvia S.S.R.	98,402	77,233	175,635	7.16
Estonia S.S.R.	62,238	52,052	114,290	8.06
Transcaucasus				
Georgia S.S.R.	64,394	54,318	118,712	2.43
Azerbaydzhan S.S.R.	98,481	90,051	188,532	3.42
Armenia S.S.R.	47,411	23,614	70,025	2.57
Central Asia				
Uzbek S.S.R.	242,050	182,704	424,754	3.19
Kirgiz S.S.R.	93,799	81,624	175,423	5.45
Tadzhik S.S.R.	66,165	56,549	122,714	3.74
Turkmen S.S.R.	64,542	54,763	119,305	4.91
Kazakh S.S.R.	573,722	479,572	1,053,294	7.56
Belorussian S.S.R.	354,493	248,272	602,765	6.50
Moldavian S.S.R.	105,107	81,612	186,719	4.96

Source: Computed from *Naselenie S.S.S.R., 1973,* pp. 188–189 and 194–197. The author is grateful to Richard Johnson for the computations.

tion. The portion of the population classified as urban has jumped from 18 per cent in 1926 to 62 per cent in 1976. (Table 6–1) The process is still going on at an unabated pace. In fact, the absolute growth rate of urban population has increased through time. Relatively the percentage of the population that is classified as urban is growing at a fairly constant rate of almost 1 percentage point per year. This, in spite of government efforts during recent years to slow urban growth, limit the size of cities, and retain some of the more able young people on farms.

The portion of urban population growth due to rural-urban migration has been increasing absolutely even though some rural areas in the European part of the country have become depleted of surplus labor. The average annual net rural-urban migration during the period

1961–1965 was 1.4 million persons, during the period 1966–1970 it was 1.7 million persons, and during 1970–1975 it was 2.0 million persons. Rural-urban migration is still the biggest component of urban growth in the entire country, although this varies by region. Conversions of rural villages to urban settlements have also consistently added about 350,000–450,000 persons per year to the urban population. Natural increase within cities is rising rapidly as the total population in cities grows. In many areas of the western part of the country natural increase in cities now is higher than it is in the countrysides which have been depleted of their youthful elements by migration.

The rural-urban migration involves considerably more mobility than the net figures indicate. During 1970–1975, approximately 4 million people moved annually from rural areas into cities, but there was a return flow to rural areas of about 2 million persons per year. Therefore, while the net rural-urban migration was 2 million persons per year, it involved about 6 million moves per year.

The Soviet government is particularly eager to restrict movement into larger cities. Official policy regards overgrown cities as blots on the landscape. But these efforts seem to be failing dismally. (Table 6–16) Throughout the Soviet period, total population in larger cities has been growing at the expense of smaller cities. The per cent of total population living in cities of more than one-half million population each almost doubled from 15.6 per cent in 1926 to 29.1 per cent in 1975. During the 1970–1975 period the largest gains, both absolute and percentage, occurred in cities of more than 500,000 size. Absolute gains decreased steadily with decreasing size of city. Population in all cities of less than 50,000 each lost relatively, and in small cities with less than 3000 each the population declined absolutely. The two largest cities in the country, Moscow and Leningrad, continued to grow faster than the population of the entire country. Much of this growth involved inmigrants even though these two cities are supposed to be closed to inmigration.

Areas immediately surrounding large cities are gaining population very rapidly. Most large cities have a surplus of jobs and a shortage of housing. Migrants often move from rural areas to small or medium sized cities surrounding major cities rather than into the major cities themselves. Gaining residence permission presents no problem in an area outside a major city while it can be practically impossible inside the city. People living in the suburban zone of Moscow now constitute 10–12 per cent of Moscow City's labor force. Thus there is a huge commuter movement going on.

Unlike most commuters in the United States

Table 6–16   Urban Population, by Settlement-Size Category, 1926–1975

Settlement Size, Thousands	Number of Inhabitants, in Millions (% Distribution in Parentheses)				
	1926	1939	1959	1970	1975
<3	1.2 (4.6)	0.9 (1.5)	1.6 (1.6)	2.1 (1.5)	2.0 (1.3)
3–5	1.3 (4.9)	2.1 (3.5)	3.6 (3.6)	4.1 (3.0)	4.1 (2.7)
5–10	2.7 (10.3)	5.3 (8.8)	9.2 (9.2)	10.0 (7.4)	10.7 (7.0)
10–20	3.5 (13.3)	6.9 (11.4)	11.2 (11.2)	12.7 (9.3)	13.7 (8.9)
20–50	4.0 (15.2)	9.7 (16.0)	14.8 (14.8)	18.5 (13.6)	19.5 (12.7)
50–100	4.1 (15.6)	7.0 (11.6)	11.0 (11.0)	13.0 (9.6)	15.4 (10.1)
100–500	5.4 (20.5)	15.7 (26.0)	24.4 (24.4)	38.3 (28.2)	43.1 (28.2)
>500	4.1 (15.6)	12.8 (21.2)	24.2 (24.2)	37.3 (27.4)	44.6 (29.1)
Total	26.3 (100)	60.4 (100)	100.0 (100)	136.0 (100)	153.1 (100)

Sources: Narkhoz S.S.S.R., 1970, p. 46 and 1974, p. 32.

who are largely white collar workers that have moved from central cities to suburbs as they have become economically affluent, commuters in the Soviet Union overwhelmingly consist of unskilled workers who have come to urban agglomerations to find jobs but have not been able to locate housing very near their work. They have settled in surrounding towns, and commuting has become a substitute for migration and a deferred urbanization. The commuters fulfill not only quantitative needs in the labor deficit areas of large cities but also qualitative ones, taking up jobs that city dwellers shun. 70–80 per cent of the commuter movements are accomplished by public transport, typically bus for trips up to 25 kilometers in length and trains for longer journeys. Shorter movements are by foot.

All this commuting entails large expenditures of time and energy which result in worker weariness as well as great strains on heavily subsidized public transportation networks. A study in Kiev in 1970 showed that nearly 70 per cent of the workers in Kiev spent more than 1 hour each way per day traveling to work. Yet, it appears that for many commuters a preferred life style has evolved which combines an urban job with a semi-rural residence, and many of these commuters would not be willing to migrate into the cities where they work. Thus it appears that there will be continued high rates of commuting, not only for work, but also for cultural service trips. The present practice of the Soviets to establish large new apartment complexes in skyscrapers scattered widely among rural areas surrounding large cities is building in the necessity for continued mass commuting. Even in completely new areas, such as Bratsk in Eastern Siberia, the settlement has been dispersed in eight separate nodes, and people must be bussed 10–20 kilometers between nodes to work. This will be discussed further in the next chapter under the context of settlement.

PRESENT DISTRIBUTION OF POPULATION

The population of the U.S.S.R. remains very unevenly distributed across the territory of the country. (Fig. 6–17) The bulk of the population still lives in a wedge which has its broad base along the western border of the country and tapers eastward across the mid section of European U.S.S.R. and southern Siberia. Two important outliers are the nodal settlements in the Caucasus and Central Asia. The pattern still reflects primarily the widely varying differences in agricultural potentials of the

Table 6–17 People and Territory of the U.S.S.R. According to Population Density Categories

People/ Sq. Km.	1000 Square Kilometers	1000 People	Per Cents of Total	
			People	Area
<1.0	6,210.0	2,736	1.1	27.9
1.1–5.0	9,063.2	20,685	8.7	40.7
5.1–10.0	1,558.5	10,219	4.3	7.0
10.1–25.0	2,470.2	39,465	16.5	11.1
25.1–50.0	1,757.6	65,987	27.6	7.9
50.1–75.0	778.4	45,667	19.1	3.5
75.1–100.0	174.5	14,271	6.0	0.8
100.1–150.0	163.4	17,642	7.4	0.7
>150	100.5	22,233	9.3	0.4
Total	22,276.3	238,905	100.0	100.0

Source: Valentey and Sorokina, eds., *Naselenie trudovye resursy S.S.S.R.,* p. 141.

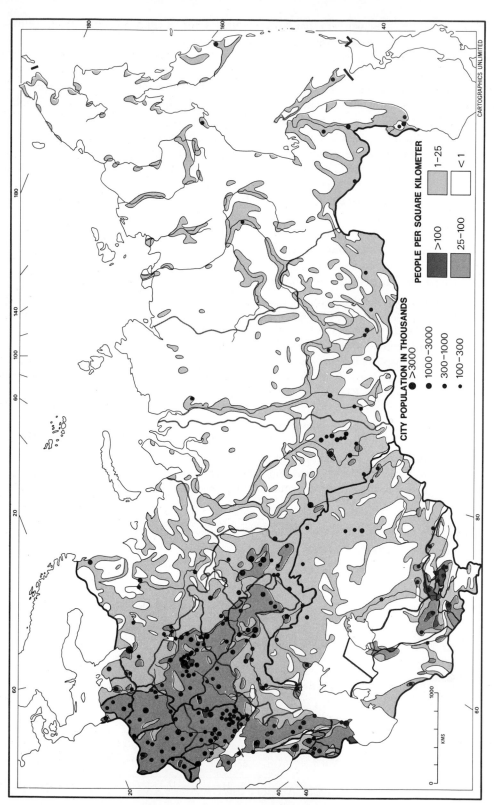

Figure 6-17 Current population distribution.

land. Huge sections of the northeast are too cold for crop growth, and large sections of the south are too dry. In these regions there are only scattered settlements based on mining or some other exploitative activity, such as forestry in the north.

Population densities of individual political units vary from as little as 0.02 persons per square kilometer in the Evenki Autonomous Okrug in central Siberia to 294.6 persons per square kilometer in heavily urbanized Moscow Oblast and 299.9 persons per square kilometer in densely rural populated, irrigated Andizhan Oblast in the Fergana Basin of Central Asia. 27.9 per cent of the country has less than 1 person per square kilometer, and 68.6 per cent has a population density of less than 5 persons per square kilometer. (Table 6–17) Less than 2 per cent of the territory of the entire country has a population density of more than 75 people per square kilometer. The bulk of the population, 63.2 per cent, lives in areas with population densities between 10 and 75 people per square kilometer. 9.3 per cent of the total population lives on 0.4 per cent of the land which has population densities of more than 150 persons per square kilometer.

Reading List

1. Allworth, Edward, ed., *The Nationality Question in Soviet Central Asia,* Praeger, New York, 1973, 236 pp.

2. ———, *Soviet Nationality Problems,* Columbia University Press, New York, 1971, 296 pp.

3. Baldwin, Godfrey, *Projections of the Population of the USSR and Eight Subdivisions, by Age and Sex: 1973 to 2000,* U.S. Department of Commerce, International Population Reports, Series P-91, No. 24, Washington, D.C., 1975, 36 pp.

4. Ball, Blaine, and Demko, George J., "Internal Migration in the Soviet Union," *Economic Geography,* April 1978, pp. 95–114.

5. Brook, S. I., "Population of the USSR: Changes in its Demographic, Social, and Ethnic Structure," *Geoforum,* 9, 1972, pp. 7–22.

6. Carey, D. W., "Developments in Soviet Education," *Soviet Economic Prospects for the Seventies,* Joint Economic Committee, Congress of

the United States, Washington, 1973, pp. 594–636.

7. Chinn, Jeffrey, "The Soviet Urban Labor Deficit; The Role of Commuters and Pensioners," American Association for the Advancement of Slavic Studies paper, St. Louis, 1976, 17 pp.

8. Clem, Ralph S., ed., *The Soviet West: Interplay Between Nationality and Social Organization,* Praeger, New York, 1975, 161 pp.

9. Davidovich, V. G., "On the Mobility of Population in the National System of Cities, Towns, and Villages of the USSR," *Soviet Geography: Review and Translation,* September 1973, pp. 413–449.

10. Dima, Nicholas, *Rural Population Change in the Soviet Union and its Implications: 1959–1970,* PhD Dissertation, Columbia University, 1976, 309 pp.

11. Dubnow, S. M., *History of the Jews in Russia and Poland: From the Earliest Times Until the Present Day,* 3 vols., KTAV Publishing House, New York, 1975.

12. Dunn, Stephen P. and Ethel, eds., *Introduction to Soviet Ethnography,* Highgate Road Social Science Research Station, Berkeley, 1974, 708 pp.

13. Eason, Warren W., "Demographic Problems: Fertility," in *Soviet Economy in a New Perspective,* Joint Economic Committee, Congress of the United States, Washington, 1976, pp. 155–161.

14. Feshbach, Murray, and Rapawy, Stephen, "Soviet Population and Manpower Trends and Policies," *Soviet Economy in a New Perspective,* Joint Economic Committee, Congress of the United States, Washington, 1976, pp. 113–154.

15. Grandstaff, Peter J., "A Note on Preliminary 1970 USSR Census Results Concerning Migration," *ACES Bulletin,* Fall, 1974, pp. 33-39.

16. ———, "Recent Soviet Experience and Western Laws of Population Migration," *International Migration Review,* winter, 1975, pp. 479–497.

17. Guthier, Steven L., "The Belorussians: National Identification and Assimilation, 1897–1970," *Soviet Studies,* January 1977, pp. 37–61 and April 1977, pp. 270–283.

18. Harris, Chauncy D., "Urbanization and Population Growth in the Soviet Union, 1959–1970." *Geographical Review,* January 1971, pp. 102–124.

19. Heer, David M., "Recent Developments in

Soviet Population Policy," *Studies in Family Planning,* November 1972, pp. 257–278.

20. *Itogi vsesoyuznoy perepisi naseleniya 1959 goda* (Results of the all-union population census of 1959), Gosstatizdat, Moscow, 1962–1963, 16 vols.

21. *Itogi vsesoyuznoy perepisi naseleniya 1970 goda* (Results of the all-union population census of 1970), Statistika, Moscow, 1972–1973, 7 vols.

22. Kabuzan, V. M., *Izmeneniya v razmeshchenii naseleniya Rossii v XVIII-pervoy polovine XIX v.* (Changes in the distribution of population in Russia in the eighteenth and first half of the nineteenth century), Nauka, Moscow, 1971, 189 pp.

23. Katz, Zev, Rogers, Rosemarie, and Harned, Frederic, eds., *Handbook of Major Soviet Nationalities,* Free Press and Collier Macmillan, New York and London, 1975, 481 pp.

24. Khorev, B., "Migration mobility of the population of the USSR," *Problems of Economics,* April 1977, pp. 71–86.

25. Khorev, B. S., and Moiseyenko, V. M., eds., *Migratsionnaya podvizhnost naseleniya v SSSR* (Migratory mobility of population in the U.S.S.R.), Statistika, Moscow, 1974, 159 pp.

26. Kosinski, Leszek A., ed., *Demographic Developments in Eastern Europe,* Praeger, N.Y., 1977, 343 pp.

27. Kosven, M. O., Lavrov, L. I., Nersesov, G. A., and Khashaev, Kh. O., eds., *Narody Kavkaza* (Peoples of the Caucasus), Institut etnografii, Adademiya Nauk SSSR, Moscow, Vol I, 1960, 611 pp.

28. Kozlov, V. I., "Ethnic Processes in the USSR," *Geoforum,* 9, 1972, pp. 47–53.

29. Kupriyenko, L., "Influence of the Standard of Living on the Movement of Labor Resources," *Problems of Economics,* September 1972, pp. 61–77.

30. Leasure, J. William, and Lewis, Robert A., "Internal Migration in Russia in the Late Nineteenth Century," *Slavic Review,* September 1968, pp. 375–394.

31. ———, "Internal Migration in the USSR: 1897–1926," *Demography,* Vol. 4, No. 2, 1967, pp. 479–496.

32. Leedy, F. A., "Demographic Trends in the USSR," *Soviet Economic Prospects for the Seventies,* Joint Economic Committee, Congress of the United States, Washington, 1973, pp. 428–484.

33. Levin, M. G., and Potapov, L. P., eds., *The*

Peoples of Siberia, The University of Chicago Press, Chicago, 1964, 948 pp.

34. Lewis, Robert A., and Leasure, J. William, "Regional Population Changes in Russia and the USSR since 1851," *Slavic Review,* December 1966, pp. 663–668.

35. Lewis, Robert A., Rowland, Richard H., and Clem, Ralph S., *Nationality and Population Change in Russia and the USSR: An Evaluation of Census Data, 1897–1970,* Praeger, New York, 1976, 494 pp.

36. Lorimer, Frank, *The Population of the Soviet Union: History and Prospects,* League of Nations, Geneva, 1946, 289 pp.

37. Lydolph, Paul E., "Manpower Problems in the USSR," *Tijdschrift voor econ. en soc. geografie,* Sept./Oct. 1972, pp. 331–344.

38. Lydolph, Paul E., Johnson, Richard, Mintz, Julie, and Mills, Margaret E., "Recent Population Trends in the USSR," *Soviet Geography: Review and Translation,* October 1978.

39. Lydolph, Paul E., and Pease, Steven, "Changing Distributions of Population and Economic Activities in the USSR," *Tijdschrift voor econ. en soc. geografie,* July/August 1972, pp. 244–261.

40. Malinin, E. D., and Ushakov, A. K., *Naselenie Sibiri* (Population of Siberia), Statistika, Moscow, 1976, 166 pp.

41. Miller, Wright, *Who are the Russians?: A History of the Russian People,* Taplinger, New York, 1973, 240 pp.

42. *Naseleniye SSSR 1973 goda* (Population of the U.S.S.R. in 1973), Statistika, Moscow, 1975, 204 pp.

43. Perevedentsev, V. I., "Contemporary Migration in the USSR," *Soviet Geography: Review and Translation,* April 1969, pp. 192–208.

44. ———, "The Influence of Ethnic Factors on the Territorial Redistribution of Population," *Soviet Geography: Review and Translation,* October 1965, pp. 40–50.

45. ———, *Migratsiya naseleniya i trudovye problemy Sibiri,* Nauk, Novosibirsk, 1966. Translated as "Population Movement and Labor Supply in Siberia," and serialized in *Soviet Sociology,* various issues, 1969–1972.

46. Pokshishevsky, V. V., "Migration of USSR Population Described," *Translations on USSR Resources,* No. 52, JPRS 49279, 19 November 1969, pp. 51–66.

47. ———, "Urbanization in the USSR," *Geoforum,* 9, 1972, pp. 23–32.

48. Powell, David E., "Labor Turnover in the Soviet Union," *Slavic Review,* June, 1977, pp. 268–286.

49. ———, "The Rural Exodus," *Problems of Communism,* November–December 1974, pp. 1-13.

50. Rachewiltz, Igor de., *Index to the Secret History of the Mongols,* Uralic and Altaic Series, Vol. 121, Indiana University, Bloomington, 1972, 347 pp.

51. Rapawy, Stephen, *Estimates and Projections of the Labor Force and Civilian Employment in the USSR: 1950 to 1990,* U.S. Department of Commerce, Bureau of Economic Analysis, Foreign Economic Report No. 10, September 1976, 76 pp.

52. Sallnow, John, "The Population of Siberia and the Soviet Far East (1965–1976)," *Soviet Geography: Review and Translation,* November 1977, pp. 689–698.

53. Semenov-Tian-Shansky, B., "Russia: Territory and Population: A Perspective on the 1926 Census," *Geographical Review,* 1928, pp. 616–640.

54. Shabad, Theodore, "News Notes," *Soviet Geography: Review and Translation,* September 1975, pp. 466–472.

55. ———, "Soviet Migration Patterns Based on 1970 Census Data," in Kosinski, Leszek A., ed., *Demographic Developments in Eastern Europe,* Praeger, New York, 1977, pp. 173–196.

56. Silver, Brian David, *Ethnic Identity Change Among Soviet Nationalities: A Statistical Analysis,* PhD Dissertation, University of Wisconsin, 1972.

57. Simmonds, George W., ed., *Nationalism in the USSR and Eastern Europe in the Era of Brezhnev and Kosygin,* University of Detroit Press, 1977, 534 pp.

58. Slater, Paul B., "A Hierarchical Regionalization of RSFSR Administrative Units Using 1966–69 Migration Data," *Soviet Geography: Review and Translation,* September 1975, pp. 453–465.

59. Stuart, Robert C., "Aspects of Rural-Urban Migration in the USSR," *ACES Bulletin,* Winter 1976, pp. 35–48.

60. Stuart, Robert C., and Gregory, Paul R., "A Model of Soviet Rural-Urban Migration," *Economic Development and Cultural Change,* October 1977, pp. 81–92.

61. Taagepera, R., "National Differences Within Soviet Demographic Trends," *Soviet Studies,* April 1969, pp. 478–489.

62. Vorobyev, V. V., "The Population Dynamics of East Siberia and Problems of Prediction," *Soviet Geography: Review and Translation,* November 1975, pp. 584–593.

63. *Vsesoyuznaya perepis' naseleniya 1926 goda* (The all-union population census of 1926), izdanie tsentralnogo statisticheskogo upravleniya SSSR, Moscow, 1929, 66 vols.

64. Vucinich, Wayne S., ed., *Russia and Asia: Essays on the Influence of Russia on the Asian Peoples,* Hoover Institute Press, Stanford, 1972, 521 pp.

65. Wädekin, Karl-Eugen, "Internal Migration and the Flight from the Land in the USSR, 1939–1959," *Soviet Studies,* October 1966, pp. 131–152.

66. ———, "Manpower in Soviet Agriculture — Some Post-Khrushchev Developments and Problems," *Soviet Studies,* No. 3, 1969, pp. 281–305.

67. Wheeler, Geoffrey, *The Peoples of Soviet Center Asia: A Background Book,* Bodley Head, London, 1966, 126 pp.

68. Zaslavskiy, T. I., ed., *Migratsiya Selskogo naseleniya* (Migration of rural population), Mysl, Moscow, 1970.

7

Settlement: Site, Size, Form, and Function

RURAL SETTLEMENTS

Early Slav settlements in the forest were characterized by slash-and-burn agriculture which shifted position every few years as soils became depleted and new areas were cleared. This evolved into a *perelog* (infield-outfield) system of permanent settlements with small fields nearby which were manured and cultivated every year surrounded by shifting fields. Except in the Baltic Republics where dispersed settlement has been the rule, Slavic rural settlements characteristically have been nucleated. This stemmed from a number of factors:

Defense   From the beginning the sedentary Slav agriculturalists were cast into a struggle for survival against marauding nomads. This intensified in the southeast after the Tatar takeover in the thirteenth century and continued into at least the middle of the eighteenth century in the southern steppes. Therefore farmers banded together for common defense in villages rather than dividing their forces in individual homesteads. As towns developed later, they too, first and foremost, were designed for defense. The Russian word for city, *"gorod,"* originally meant fortress or citadel. *Gorodishchi,* temporary refuges, were often placed strategically throughout the countryside to serve as strongholds in time of danger. Although originally these were not permanently settled, they often became the nuclei for permanent settlements later.

Colonization   Many villages were platted, either by the state, aristocratic landowners, or the church which owned much land in old Russia. Such a process generally meant great regularity in settlement patterns and forms. This was particularly born out by Belorussian villages after the land reform instituted in 1557.

Serfdom.   Serfdom came to the east European plain later than it did in the West and remained much longer, until 1861. This provided for greater ease of control by an authoritarian centralized government.

Communication   The broad expanses of the plains, severity of the natural environment, and undeveloped nature of so much of the territory pitted man against nature and isolation and fostered the desire for ready communication with neighbors in self sufficient communities.

Communal Landholdings   The long persistence of medieval agricultural systems, especially the three-field system with common cultivation and periodic reallocation of strips of land, necessitated the agglomeration of peasants into communities. Peasants did not own plots of land, but rather shared community fields. The mir (commune) became the responsible body for parcelling out land to individual households, paying taxes to the state, conscripting individuals for the armed forces, and so forth. About the only exception to nucleated settlements were manorial farmsteads and isolated huts of prospectors, forest workers, transportation workers, and millers.

In 1552 the three-field system was introduced to Lithuania. This had spread early across western Europe where it was gradual and unrecorded. Only in Lithuania was it sudden and recorded. This "voloka reform" was accomplished in about 12 years in Lithuania, which at that time included much of what is now western U.S.S.R., but it dragged into the seventeenth century in Russia. A *voloka,* peasant strip of land, was delineated in each of three fields where it was cultivated collectively. Each voloka included eleven *morgi* which was equal to about 1.8 acres of land. Land was exchanged between noblemen and the crown in order to lay out these large strips of arable in a rectangular pattern, although in such places as the Polesye this was impossible because of the pattern of drainage. Old villages were uprooted and cabins were relocated along a straight line on a single street along the border of the middle field with threshing barns and other farm buildings located in a straight line across the street from the izbas (single-dwelling log cabins). Thus, a reordering of the entire rural landscape took place at this time, which among other things led to the great numbers of line villages stretching for long distances along single streets that have become the most common form of rural village throughout most of European Russia.

Crops in the three fields were rotated annually between winter grains (usually winter rye in the north), spring grains (oats, barley, buckwheat, peas, and so forth), and fallow. The fallow was usually pastured and thereby manured each third year. The peasants did not own their strips of land but rented them from the crown, the church, or private landholders. In the north they usually paid their rent by working on the manorial arable. The common practice was two days work per week for the landowner in return for the use of the peasant holding. Such an arrangement was known as "barshchina." In effect this introduced serfdom to the area. Prior to this, peasants could buy and sell land, but after 1558 they were denied the right to shift from one estate to another.

In some cases peasants rented their holdings for money, which was known as the "obrok" system. In other instances, services were performed by such people as priests, smiths, carpenters, and so forth in return for the use of peasant holdings. In some cases holdings were assigned in exchange for military service in times of need, an arrangement that could only work where extended families were common so that other members of the family could take over the farming duties when the head of the household was away at war. A bailiff managed the estate, sold the excess produce, and collected taxes for the state.

During the sixteenth century new villages were continually being hewn out of the forests, and each village constantly increased its arable land at the expense of the forest. A tax moratorium of up to eight years was usually given to landholders for clearing forests, and this sometimes became the main incentive.

Later, in the nineteenth century, when the process of settlement had been accomplished in European Russia, the pressure of population on available arable and pasture land increased until the Russians began to consider the possibility of draining swamp areas which covered about 10 per cent of the surface in this area. In 1873 the Ministry of State Property established the so-called "Western Expedition for the Drainage of Swamps" whose task it was to reclaim the vast swamps of Polesye in the basin of the Pripyat River. Concurrently the "Northern Expedition" was established in St. Petersburg. The activities of the Western Expedition eventually spread to Meshchera southeast of Moscow, while the Northern Expedition extended its work into Vologda and Yaroslavl governments in the northeast and some parts of the Baltic provinces in the northwest. Within

25 years the Western Expedition built approximately 5000 kilometers of canals and improved the drainage on nearly 25,000 square kilometers in the Polesye and reclaimed another 480 square kilometers in the Meshchera region of central Russia.

Most of the reclaimed land became hay or pasture land, although some was put under cultivation. Later in the nineteenth and beginning of the twentieth century, up to Wold War I, about 3200 kilometers of canals were constructed in the swamps of the Baraba Steppe in southwestern Siberia where 3500 square kilometers of land were drained and made available for new settlers. Drainage efforts have continued unabated during the Soviet Period, as has an expansion of ancient irrigation systems in Central Asia and the eastern Transcaucasus. These transformations of the landscape will be elaborated more fully in Chapter 9.

The three-field system continued down to collectivization in the late 1920s and early 1930s in many parts of the country. Although an emancipation proclamation was issued in 1861 to free the serfs, it had little immediate impact on settlement since much of the land that was taken away from landholders was turned over to villages for communal administration and cultivation. The Stolypin land reforms of 1905–1906 affected the settlement pattern much more, since it led to what one might call the Russian enclosure movement. The reforms allowed a community where the majority were in favor to parcel out community lands, or individuals could opt out of the commune and require a separate allocation of land. Peasants could sell thier shares of land to richer peasants, and many of them did, particularly tradesmen who were primarily engaged in nonagricultural pursuits. Many peasants when they acquired their own plots of land transferred their houses to them as separate farmsteads, which became known as *khutors.*

In many cases, village lands were parcelled in such a way that each landholder could have his house on his individual plot and still remain within the nucleated village, but in addition many thousands of isolated *khutors* were set

up. By 1916 approximately 2.5 million householders, about one-fourth of the total, had separated from village communes. The process was most intense in the west bank Ukraine where more then 48 per cent of the landholders with more than 50 per cent of the land separated out. The portion was high also farther south in so-called "New Russia" and in Belorussia farther north. The process dwindled northward, as only 16 per cent separated out in the central region and about 7 per cent in the areas along the northern limits of agriculture. In Belorussia many new *khutors* were set up on land reclaimed from the swamps by the Western Expedition. In the Baltic Republics the process of breakup of village continued much longer, including the period of independence between the two world wars. In Lithuania during 1919–1938 more than 6500 villages were broken up, and in Latvia more than 4500. The single dwelling farmstead became the dominant form of settlement in the Baltic Republics.

During the Soviet Period a concerted effort has been made to renucleate rural settlements and amalgamate them into larger, more compact settlements where it is economically feasible to provide communal utility services such as running water and sewage disposal. There has been much talk about the creation of *"agrogorods,"* agricultural cities composed of multistoried blocks of apartment buildings to replace villages of single family cabins. However, the lack of investment capital and construction materials has shelved this program indefinitely except on a few of the more progressive or newer farms. As long as supplies are short, they will be used for the construction of productive farm facilities rather than residential houses. Thus, most farmers still live in their old log cabin *izbas* in the forested northern part of the country and their adobe *khatas* in the treeless steppes of the south. (Figs. 7–1 and 7–2) About the only modernization has been the substitution of sheet metal roofs for older thatched roofs, although in the southern part of the country there are still many thatched roofs. Many farm families perfer to live in single family dwellings than to be

Figure 7–1   Log cabin izba in the forest zone near Lake Baykal, Eastern Siberia.

Figure 7–2   Adobe huts in the old part of Tashkent. Photo by Toni Crane.

Figure 7–3   The village waterworks. Listvyanka near Lake Baykal, Eastern Siberia.

herded into apartment blocks, and many new cabins are being constructed exactly the same as the old. In light of the impossibility of state provision of new rural housing, the government has encouraged individual house-building by extending loans and allowing farms to make available to villagers sections of forests for log cutting, and so forth. Generally several farm families cooperate in the building of each others homes, and crews of semiskilled laborers hire themselves out to perform portions of the work that require specific skills.

The Soviets would still like to consolidate small villages into fewer larger ones in order to provide such services as schools, hospitals, adequate roads, and so forth. In order to do this, Soviets consider that they need settlements of at least 1000–2000 population. However, it has been pointed out that in sparsely populated areas such as Novgorod and Pskov Oblasts in northwest European Russia in order to have villages of such size they would be so few in number that farmers would be far removed

from their fields, so travel to and from work would become excessive. Therefore, the Soviets presently are faced with the dilemma of creating culturally and economically viable villages and at the same time overcoming the distance factor of moving farmers and machinery to fields. One solution might be the establishment of auxiliary settlements in outlying portions of farms where workers can stay temporarily while working the land in that particular part of the farm. This has already been done on some of the large steppe farms of the south and particularly in the southern deserts and mountain foothills where transhumance of livestock takes place on a grand scale. Since an average farm now includes several villages within its boundaries, some division of labor might be worked out within the farm whereby villagers could work that portion of the farm within their immediate vicinities. A new central settlement might be constructed to provide major services for people living everywhere on the farm, and the original villages could act in auxiliary capacities to the central settlement. However, until farms become affluent enough to divert funds to build new central settlements, this type of arrangement is largely wishful thinking.

The 1970 census revealed that rural villages still range in size all the way from single households to more than 20,000 inhabitants. Small settlements are by far the most numerous, but they do not contain the bulk of the rural population. 292,600 settlements with less than 100 inhabitants each accounted for 62.3 per cent of total settlements in the rural parts of the country but only 7.1 per cent of the rural population. (Table 7-1) Middle sized villages between 101 and 1000 inhabitants each contained almost half the rural population, and almost 44 per cent of the population lived in villages of more than 1000 inhabitants each. Large settlements over 1000 inhabitants in size gained considerably in total population since 1959 when they contained only 36.9 per cent of the rural population. The per cent of total population declined in both middle size and small settlements during the 1959-1970 intercensal period.

As large settlements grow and accumulate industrial functions they are constantly upgraded to urban-type settlements, which will be discussed a little later. Thus, there is an ongoing process of elimination of single households and very small villages, growth of middle sized villages into large villages, and official change of designation from rural villages to urban-type settlements. Many single dwellings and small villages have been eliminated by dismantling old log izbas and bodily moving them to central settlements where they are set up exactly as they were before.

Regional Variation

The size, density, form, and site locations of settlements vary fairly consistently from north to south in the country. In the far north settlements are sparse and small, often only scattered huts strung along river terraces especially at confluences of streams. The siting often relates to the river traffic that existed at the time of establishment. In places with large numbers of glacial lakes such as Karelia small settlements are often lined up along lake shores. Since villages are small, there are usually large numbers of villages within the jurisdiction of one collective farm. For instance, in the Komi A.S.S.R. a collective farm may include as many as 55 different settlements. In recent years, in the far north somewhat larger permanent bases have been established for former nomadic reindeer herders. Nowadays only the herders move with the animals; their families remain in the permanent settlements. Chains of supplementary temporary settlements or individual cabins have been set up for the nomadic herders. The same is true for fishing and hunting collectives. Forestry villages typically own scattered barracks which

Table 7-1   Rural Settlements, 1970

Size of Settlement (Inhabitants)	Number	Per Cent of Total	Population	Per Cent of Total Rural Population
<100	292,600	62.3	7,500,000	7.1
101-1,000	153,200	32.7	51,900,000	49.1
>1,000	23,500	5.0	46,300,000	43.8
Total	469,300	100.0	105,700,000	100.0

Source: Kovalev, 1972, p. 38.

can be occupied temporarily while particular tracts of forest are being exploited. Only the central villages have permanently located sawmills.

In the southern taiga and northern fringe of the mixed forest, villages are a little larger and form a much denser network. Most of the villages occupy the better drained sites on morainic hills in this ill-drained region of recent glaciation. (See Minsk area, Fig. 7–4) The individual villages are still only hamlets, and in the Baltic area there are many individual households. The villages get still larger and the network of villages becomes denser in the southern part of the mixed forest zone, but even here individual villages rarely exceed 200 inhabitants.

In the forest-steppe and northern part of the steppe zones is found one of the densest networks of settlements, many of them quite large, often over 1000 inhabitants each. The most common form is very long street villages strung out along both sides of streams for many kilometers, sometimes for the entire lengths of short steppe streams. In this dryish region the villages cling to the waterways for water supply as well as for transport in the days before the development of railroads. Also, in the valleys cottages are afforded some protection from the steppe winds. The linear pattern of villages laid out on first terraces of river valleys is nicely shown by the Voronezh map in Figure 7–4. In addition to this kind of village form, a rambling pattern along sides of valleys and ravines is common in the right bank Ukraine. (Vinnitsa map) These villages have more of a clustered shape, often around a square or mainstreet from which branch out secondary streets and alleys. There is an absence of any orderly system. Villages often occupy the sunny sides of slopes. Also in the wooded-steppe and northern steppe zones begins the occurrence of large villages laid out in strictly rectangular pattern, which was the beginning of the settlement forms produced during the reoccupation of the steppes in the seventeenth century, usually spearheaded by large Cossack settlements called *stanitsas*. These are found in more classic form farther south.

In the Black Sea Steppes and Kuban region of the North Caucasus villages are usually very large, commonly with more than 1000 inhabitants. In the North Caucasus they often have more than 5000 inhabitants and sometimes as many as 20,000. The original Cossack settlements show strict rectangular street patterns or very long villages up to 12 kilometers in length broken by large squares which represent the original Cossack parade grounds. (Krasnodar map) One reason for the highly nucleated concentration of settlement in the south was the limited water supply, either along rivers or around wells. Wells were deep and costly and encouraged high concentration of population.

In the extreme south the dry steppe and semi-desert regions contain much sparser networks of villages, although individual villages are still fairly large. There are many more recently established settlements in this region which originally was occupied by nomadic herdsmen who had no permanent settlements to begin with. These newer permanent settlements are accompanied by distant summer and winter camps on pastures often as much as 200 kilometers away from parent villages. If there is any arable land it is near the main settlement, often with supplemental irrigation. Farther south in the irrigated oases of Central Asia where great amounts of manual labor are used on small areas of land population density, and hence settlement density, is very high. Settlements are typically located in the middle or lower portions of alluvial fans and along canals. Large new settlements, frequently laid out in rectangular form, are found in newly irrigated areas such as the Golodnaya Steppe southwest of Tashkent.

In the southern mountains of the Caucasus and Central Asia settlements are of varied sizes and form. In the main valleys of the Caucasus villages are usually quite large, reflecting the original need for defense in numbers. But higher up the valleys in the mountains there are scattered chains of small villages or even hamlets. In the Dagestan region there are many dispersed individual homesteads. Transhumance of animals in these southern moun-

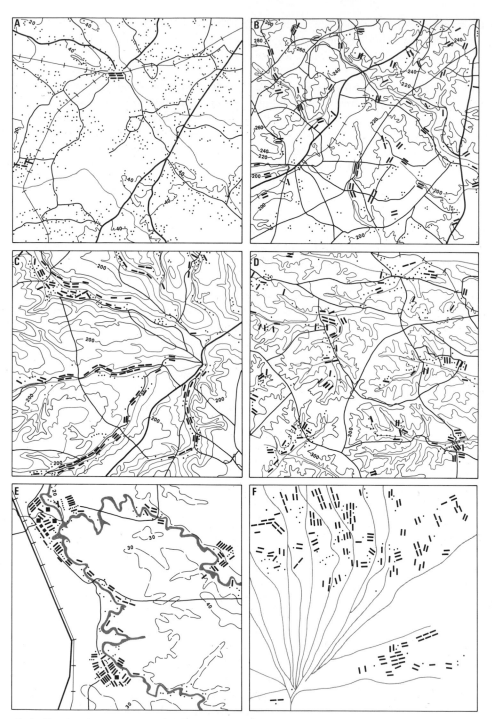

Figure 7–4   Rural settlement patterns. (A) Scattered individual farmsteads southwest of Tallin, Estonia. (B) Small line villages along roads on interfluves southwest of Minsk, Belorussia. (C) Large line villages stretching along both sides of entire lengths of small streams in the forest-steppe northwest of Voronezh, Central Chernozem Region. (D) Large, densely spaced, clustered villages in stream valleys northeast of Vinnitsa, Right Bank Ukraine. (E) Large rectangular stanitsas *north of Krasnodar, Kuban District, North Caucasus. (F) Villages along distributary channels and irrigation canals on mid slope of alluvial fan, Fergana Basin, Central Asia. Adapted from Plummer, et. al.,* Landscape Atlas of the U.S.S.R.

tains has led to sets of related villages with permanent villages located at lower elevations and summer huts in the high mountain pastures. There may also be isolated huts on winter pastures in remote areas of the deserts of Central Asia.

The gradation of village size is shown nicely by the two maps in Figure 7–5. It can be seen that small villages of less than 100 inhabitants each contain more than 40 per cent of the rural population in the northern fringes of the mixed forest zone and southern fringes of the taiga zone in the northwestern part of the country extending eastward from the Baltic States. Such villages contain less than 2 per cent of the population in much of southwestern Ukraine, the North Caucasus, the eastern portion of the Transcaucasus, much of Central Asia and adjacent southern Kazakhstan, and the settled southern portions of Siberia and the Far East. Large villages of more than 1000 people each account for more than 70 per cent of the rural population in southwestern Ukraine, the North Caucasus, Armenia, and southeastern Kazakhstan. They contain less than 10 per cent of the rural population in the Baltic Republics and adjacent parts of the Russian Republic. In 1970 there were 2913 rural settlements with more than 3000 population each. These were most numerous in the western half of the North Caucasus where about 490 such settlements existed. This region was followed by the Southwest Economic Region in the western Ukraine which contained about 350 such settlements. Moldavia contained at least 200 such settlements and, considering its small area, probably had the densest network of large settlements anywhere in the U.S.S.R.

URBAN SETTLEMENTS

Towns began on the East European Plain much as rural settlements did, first as walled sanctuaries and second as centers of trade and services. Often the beginning of a town would be a fortified enclosure on a hill containing a prince's castle and perhaps a cathedral surrounded by a wall and a moat. This was the so-called *detinets* or *vyshgorod,* the upper city, which became known as the *kremlin*. At the foot of the kremlin typically developed a *posad* settled by artisans, craftsmen, and tradesmen. The central feature was usually the open-air market. Later churches and other communal buildings developed. Often the posad also became walled. Craftsmen such as tinkers, potters, coopers, carpenters, shoemakers, and so forth often formed *ryads* or rows of shops of the same speciality. Most of these tradesmen were also engaged in agriculture, which in some instances was the major portion of their income. Most cottages had large kitchen gardens attached, some as large as 0.5–1 hectare in size, right in the middle of towns. Thus, there was a melding of urban and rural life.

Around the vyshgorod and posad often were fortified monastaries, also walled enclosures, some of which were precursors of towns and some of which were established later to act as first lines of defense against invaders. For instance, Moscow was ringed by fortified monastaries, most of which still stand, now mainly inside the Garden Ring on the south side of the city. Novodevichy Convent guarded the southwestern approaches to Moscow where a common route of invasion crossed the Moscow River. (Fig. 7–6)

From the very beginning towns were much under the control of centralized authorities with little autonomy of their own. They were founded either by the state, the church, or aristocratic land owners (*boyars*) who looked upon them as sources of revenue and services. Towns were granted according to their charters trading monopolies over their hinterlands and rights to hold as many as 3 market days per week and 1–4 fairs per year. Many towns were founded by noblemen on their land in order to gain tax deferments which were granted by the Tsarist government in order to establish towns along defensive perimeters. The landowners considered the towns to be part of their patrimony from which services and income could be derived and which could be passed on as part of the family inheritance. While landowners often encouraged trade and urban construction in

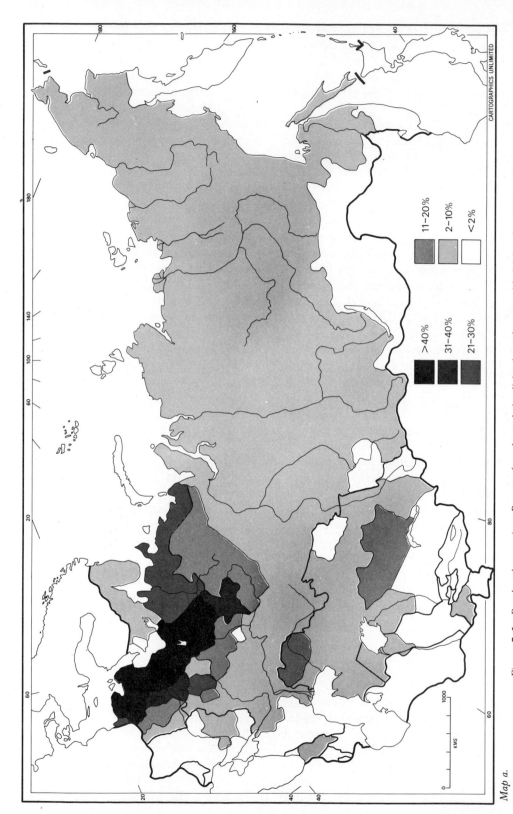

Figure 7-5   Rural settlement sizes. Percent of rural population living in settlements with (a) less than 100 inhabitants and (b) more than 1000 inhabitants. After Kovalev, Geoforum, 9/72, pp. 42–43.

Map a.

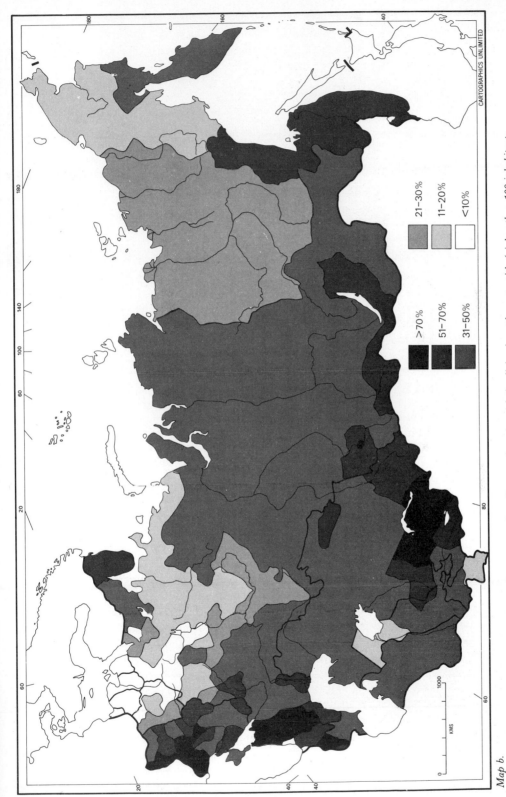

Figure 7-5   *Rural settlement sizes. Percent of rural population living in settlements with (a) less than 100 inhabitants and (b) more than 1000 inhabitants. After Kovalev, Geoforum, 9/72, pp. 42–43.*

Map b.

>70%	21–30%
51–70%	11–20%
31–50%	<10%

CARTOGRAPHICS UNLIMITED

Figure 7–6 Novodevichy Convent. Photo by Toni Crane.

order to enhance revenue, they retained control over the political and military apparatus of the towns. As towns grew, *voyvoda*, military governors, were appointed by the state to administer the towns, and locally elected officials were subordinated to them. Such administrative arrangements stymied civic development and kept the towns in a state of overgrown rural villages, simply nodes of state power in the countryside which directed and controlled defense and trade. This led many foreign observers to question whether Russia had any cities at all.

The emancipation of the serfs in 1861 began an urban transformation that continued down to World War I. The average annual increase in urban population between 1867 and 1913 was 2.3 per cent, as compared to only 1.5 per cent between 1811 and 1867. Rural-urban migration was the dominant cause for the urban growth during this period. The reason for much of this migration was job opportunity in the personal services sector which included domestic service and day labor. Particularly for

women, primary motives for migrating were opportunities for jobs in domestic service and marriage. Although industrialization became a major force for urbanization toward the end of the nineteenth century, as late as the first Russian census in 1897 it was revealed that many factories had been established in rural areas, that 60 per cent of the industrial work force of the Russian Empire resided in rural areas, and that in some regions such as the Urals and the Volga-Vyatka Region, as many as 80 per cent of the industrial work force were considered to be rural. Some of the most rapidly growing cities during this period were located in the south in the Black Sea littoral, and these were related primarily to trade. Such were the grain exporting ports of Novorossiysk, Nikolayev, and Odessa.

During the period of chaos beginning with World War I and continuing through two revolutions and civil war, the cities throughout much of the country experienced massive losses of population as people returned to the countryside to find food and a better way of life.

After things had quieted down people began to return to the cities during the NEP period, 1921–1928, and the ensuing five year plans set the stage for a second urban transformation that was unmatched previously anywhere in the world.

Beginning in the late 1920s and continuing through the 1930s the Soviet leadership initiated the five-year plans to set out on a course of rapid industrialization, and everything else was subordinated to this goal. Throughout this and the rest of the Soviet period urbanization took place primarily in response to the establishment of industries. During the period 1926–1939 the urban population increased at an annual average rate of 6.5 per cent.

During this time social planners and architects did much philosophizing about the creation of a new Soviet man partially through the design of cities and buildings. Several schools of thought emerged. The so-called "garden city" ideal was revived from its origins in the latter part of the Tsarist period, the proponents of which now saw the opportunity to develop because now all land was publicly owned and Marxian tenets provided for a degree of local self government never before realized. Garden city deurbanists called for a scattering of industry among idyllic cottages in the countryside. There was envisioned a complete merger of city and country with cities being "smashed into 10,000 pieces and scattered across the countryside." On the other hand, urbanists called for equally bizarre development. The ultimate of house planning consisted of a highrise structure with the ground floor, roof, and one intermediate floor devoted to recreation and dining and the other floors consisting of identical glass enclosed spaces with no interior partitions except for planting boxes and carpeting which allowed 5.5 square meters per worker furnished only with a bed.

However, all these philosophical ideals were smashed head-on in a collision with the stark realities of extreme shortage of housing and investment capital. Stalin derisively labeled the garden city plan "kulak democracy" to signify his contempt of any degree of local self government. On the other hand, the house communes never became popular among the people, who complained of loss of privacy and individuality, separation from their children, monotony of design, and distasteful food in communal dining halls.

The five-year plans included no comprehensive urban theory. The Stalin period became known as the period of monumental classical construction consisting of repetitious superblocks of low-rise apartment buildings, generally five stories without elevators, built around central areas for schools, playgrounds, and shops. Most of the 1000 new towns were simply designed around a public square or a series of squares which were expansive enough to accommodate organized demonstrations, parades, and mass meetings. It appeared that the Soviet inability to construct workable elevators dictated more architectural policy at this time than any other single factor. Hence, the low, squat skylines of most Russian cities. However, such monstrosities as the seven "wedding cake" structures of Moscow pierce the skyline to heights of 20–30 stories. (Fig. 7–7)

After World War II the low population density and monotony of the superblocks led planners to create the concept of "microrayon," a neighborhood unit disigned to accommodate 6000–10,000 residents with schools and shopping facilities located nearby. However, this did not result in the expected sense of community either. Research indicated that friendships were formed because of age, occupation, and educational similarities, but seldom because of residential proximity. The microrayon is still a developing concept, but more and more cities are going to 9- and 16-story buildings in order to limit urban sprawl and reduce the unit costs of construction. Since the newer buildings are generally being built on the peripheries of cities, sometimes even as separate bedroom settlements in open country outside cities, the skylines of cities are taking on dish shapes with the lower structures in the middle and higher structures around the edges.

Throughout the Soviet period much of the construction of housing and other urban build-

Figure 7–7   A "wedding cake" pierces the otherwise squat skyline of Moscow. Photo by Toni Crane.

ings has been by individual ministries working through their industrial enterprises, which are more than just places of work. The industrial enterprise sets aside some of its income as indivisible funds which are to be used to provide medical, educational, recreational, and other services to its workers. In other words, it is a small world unto itself. Most factories have tried to create housing for their workers next to the factory gate and are responsible for water supply, sewage systems, heating plants, clubs, shops, and so forth. These things have tended to develop as a contained unit without regard for the overall development of the city. Services to homes have been subordinated to services to the industrial plant. For instance, in the metallurgical center of Magnitogorsk in the southern Urals, the metallurgical combine routinely cuts off electricity to homes whenever the production in the plant requires extra output. Generally local representatives of industrial ministries have wielded much more clout than representatives of local governments, so that most cities have grown like topsy without any

overall planning at all. As far as city services are concerned, there have been many instances of individual industrial enterprises failing to cooperate with each other in city-wide efforts such as snow removal, power line construction, and so forth. Machines sit idle rather than work on "foreign" industrial territory.

World War II destroyed 1700 cities including the housing for perhaps as many as 25 million people and damaged much other property. This set the Soviets back in their efforts to provide adequate housing and caused them to double their efforts to build housing and other structures after the war. Between 1956 and 1966 about half of the entire Soviet population moved into new apartments or improved their housing situation. In order to amass such a crash program in housing construction, the simplest and cheapest possible methods had to be used. During the Khrushchev period the utilization of prefabricated reinforced concrete slabs came to the forefront. These sections 2–3 meters square were swung into place by giant cranes, bolted together, and left unfinished either inside or out. In this way great quantities of housing could be provided in short time, but at the complete sacrifice of quality and subsequent maintenance and repair.

As was pointed out in Chapter 6, in spite of changing government policies, cities are continuing to grow at an unabated pace. Although most of them are growing at a reduced percentage rate because of higher base populations, the absolute growths are as great as ever, and the rural-urban migration in absolute terms has again increased during recent years. The Soviet Union has become a country of great cities. In 1976 it contained 41 cities with more than 500,000 population each, more than any other country in the world. (Table 7–2) The development of so many large cities has brought on what some analysts interpret as a third shift in urban transformation that has abandoned the philosophical goals of social development of the 1930s and turned more to simple management of bigness. Much more attention is now being paid to urban problems and the development of an urban theory in the Soviet Union, but planning has turned from idealism to technocratic planning to meet practical problems.

During the Soviet Period there has been a fairly consistent growth in numbers of urban settlements of all size categories. (Table 7–3) As intermediate sized cities have grown into large cities, small cities have grown into intermediate cities, urban-type settlements have grown into small cities, and a constant supply of new urban-type settlements has been created from rural villages or from scratch. The Soviets use two official designations for urban settlements, "urban type settlements" and "cities." Definitions of these terms are set at republic level and vary from one republic to another. The lower limit for city designation varies from 5000 to 12,000 population and from two-thirds to three-fourths of the population employed outside agriculture. Urban-type settlements usually require more than 3000 population plus a predominantly nonagricultural work force.

The Soviets are quick to point out that the urbanization process is reflected not only in the numbers and sizes of urban settlements but also in the restructuring of occupation, amenities, and ways of life in the countryside, all of which are part of the urbanization process. Between 1959 and 1970 57 new urban-type settlements were created each year on the average and 23 urban-type settlements were promoted to cities. Usually the prerequisite for the reclassification of a rural place into an urban-type settlement is the establishment of a large industrial enterprise nearby. Since government policy during the last two decades or more has been to pour more industrial investment capital into the small and medium sized cities of the country, particularly the western portions of the country, many settlements have seen their status upgraded in recent years.

Geographical Distribution of City Growth

A basic policy to develop the eastern portions of the country caused rapid city growth in those portions of the country until sometime during the late 1950s. The growth of cities between the two censuses, 1939 and 1959, revealed that every city from the Volga eastward to the Pacific, with the exceptions of Astrakhan and Dzhambul, experienced average annual growth rates greater than 3 per cent. Particularly high growths were experienced in clusters of mining towns, as in the Kuznetsk Basin of Western Siberia and the Urals, and similarly high growth rates were registered by many regional centers. Some cities in European Russia also grew more than 3 per cent annually, but the bulk of the cities in the western part of the country grew less rapidly. Six cities in the western part of the country, including Leningrad, experienced absolute declines due to wartime destruction.

The 1970 census revealed a much different distribution of growth during the 1959–1970 period. Almost every city in western European Russia, Belorussia, western Ukraine, and the Baltic Republics grew at an annual rate of more than 3 per cent. There were also unusually high gains in the North Caucasus, the Transcaucasus, and Central Asia, as well as some of the smaller and intermediate sized

Table 7–2   Population of Cities With More Than 500,000 Inhabitants in 1976, in Order of Size, and Per Cent Increase, 1959–1970 and 1970–1976

	1976	% Increase 1959–1970	% Increase 1970–1976
1. Moscow	7,734,000	17	9.3
2. Leningrad	4,372,000	19	9.7
3. Kiev	2,013,000	47	23.3
4. Tashkent	1,643,000	49	18.6
5. Baku	1,406,000	30	11.1
6. Kharkov	1,385,000	28	13.2
7. Gorky	1,305,000	24	11.5
8. Novosibirsk	1,286,000	31	10.8
9. Minsk	1,189,000	80	29.7
10. Kuybyshev	1,186,000	30	13.5
11. Sverdlovsk	1,171,000	32	14.2
12. Tbilisi	1,030,000	27	15.9
13. Odessa	1,023,000	34	14.7
14. Omsk	1,002,000	41	22.0
15. Chelyabinsk	989,000	27	13.0
16. Dnepropetrovsk	976,000	31	13.2
17. Donetsk	967,000	24	10.0
18. Kazan	958,000	30	10.2
19. Perm	957,000	35	12.6
20. Yerevan	928,000	55	21.0
21. Ufa	923,000	41	19.7
22. Volgograd	918,000	38	12.2
23. Rostov-on-Don	907,000	32	15.0
24. Alma-Ata	851,000	60	16.6
25. Saratov	848,000	31	12.0
26. Riga	806,000	26	10.1
27. Voronezh	764,000	48	15.8
28. Zaporozhye	760,000	46	15.5
29. Krasnoyarsk	758,000	57	17.0
30. Krivoy Rog	634,000	43	10.6
31. Lvov	629,000	35	13.7
32. Yaroslavl	577,000	27	11.6
33. Karaganda	570,000	36	9.0
34. Krasnodar	543,000	48	17.0
35. Novokuznetsk	530,000	31	6.2
36. Vladivostok	526,000	52	19.3
37. Izhevsk	522,000	48	23.7
38. Irkutsk	519,000	23	15.1
39. Barnaul	514,000	45	17.1
40. Khabarovsk	513,000	35	17.7
41. Tula	506,000	32	9.5

Source: Narkhoz SSSR, 1975, pp. 22–31.

Table 7–3   Numbers of Urban Settlements by Size Category

Settlement Size (000's)	1939	1959	1970	1975
Total	2762	4619	5505	5752
<3	467	843	1118	1110
3–5	530	904	1028	1050
5–10	761	1296	1430	1514
10–20	501	798	919	984
20–50	316	474	600	632
50–100	98	156	189	222
100–500	78	123	188	201
>500	11	25	33	39

Source: Narkhoz SSSR, 1974, p. 32

cities in the southern Urals, Western Siberia, Eastern Siberia, the Far East, and northern Kazakhstan. But the bulk of the cities in Siberia and the Far East, particularly the larger cities, grew at slower rates. A few cities of more than 100,000 population experienced absolute declines. These were a cluster of four intermediate sized coal mining cities in the Kuznetsk Basin, the coal mining center of Kopeysk next to Chelyabinsk in the eastern Urals, and Novoshakhtinsk in the Rostov Oblast section of the Donets Coal Basin. These declines signified the relative decline of coal in the fuel balance of the country.

The difference between the growth rates of the two periods showed that city growth increased during the latter period in practically all the European part of the country except for major clusters around Moscow and Donetsk. At the same time there were almost universal declines of growth in the Urals and overwhelming declines in Western Siberia. Every single city in the Kuznetsk Basin experienced declines in growth, as did the larger cities in Western Siberia, such as Novosibirsk and Omsk. There were also notable declines in growth along the Volga. In central Asia most of the cities showed increases in growth rates. There were generally increases in Eastern

Siberia and the Far East also, although Irkutsk and Komsomolsk showed declines. The most significant changes between the 1939–1959 period and the 1959–1970 period were the widespread declines of city growth in the Urals and Western Siberia and the increase in city growth in the European part of the country except for the clusters around Moscow and Donetsk.

It is clear that a spurt in growth took place primarily in less developed areas and less developed cities within the European part of the country, the Caucasus, and Central Asia. The growth rate declines of city clusters in the Kuznetsk Basin, the Urals, around Moscow, and around Donetsk indicated the tendency for dispersal of industrial development and urbanization and the decline of coal as a preferred fuel. They also indicated a trend away from concentration on heavy industry to increased emphasis of diversified lighter industries. Such conclusions are corroborated by data on growth rates of total urban population by economic region, which include population in cities of less than 100,000 in size. The region having the highest urban population growth during the 1959–1970 period was Moldavia (76 per cent), which in 1959 was only 22 per cent urbanized, the least urbanized area in the country. Other regions in order of high urban growth rates were Armenia, Tadzhikistan, Kazakhstan, Uzbekistan, Kirgizia, Belorussia, the Central Black Earth Region, Lithuania, southern and southwestern Ukraine, the Volga Region, and the North Caucasus, most of which were well below the national average in urbanization. The Urals, Siberia, and the Far East, on the other hand, all of which were more highly urbanized in 1959 than was the U.S.S.R. as a whole, showed universally low urban growth rates during 1959–1970. The highly industrialized Urals showed the lowest urban growth rate of any region in the entire country.

The geographical distribution of the city growth shown in Figure 7–8 for the period 1970–1977 essentially continues the pattern established during the period 1959–1970. The more undeveloped parts of western U.S.S.R.,

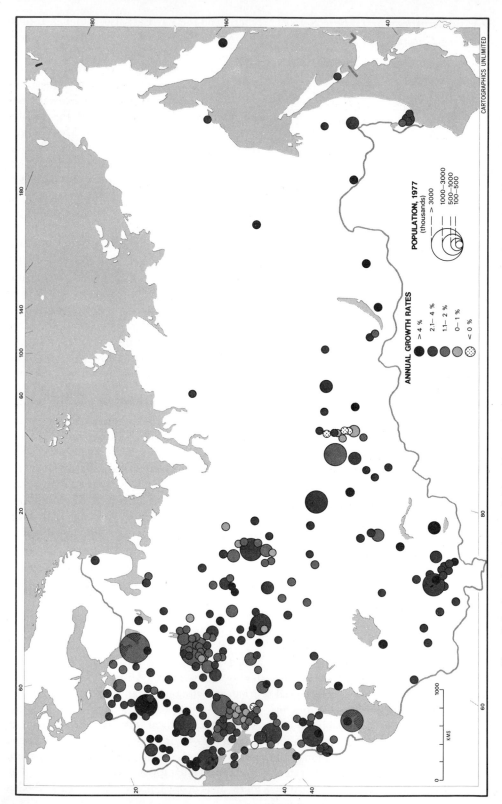

Figure 7–8   Annual growth rates of cities with more than '100,000 inhabitants, 1970–1977. Compiled by Margaret E. Mills and William Stanley from data in Narkhoz SSSR za 60 let, pp. 59–69.

particularly Belorussia and the western Ukraine, underwent rapid city growth, especially in smaller cities. Minsk has been the fastest growing "million" city in the country for most of the post World War II period. (Table 7-2) In addition, fast growing small and intermediate sized cities are scattered throughout portions of the Volga Region and the southern and eastern parts of the country. Long established urbanized areas such as the Central, Donets-Dnieper, Northwest, Baltic, Urals, and West Siberian Economic Regions, generally experienced slower city growths.

The growth rate of most cities has decreased in recent years. Almost all cities with populations greater than 100,000 grew more slowly during 1970-1977 than during 1959-1970. Changes of growth rates seem to be related more to stages of development than to geographical location. Those cities experiencing large declines in growth rates are the ones that underwent major industrial or administrative development and consequent spurts in population growth during the 1960s, but which have tapered off since. They are scattered about the country and include various primary functions such as electrical and chemical complexes at places like Almetyevsk, Sterlitamak, Salavat, Novokuybyshevsk, Cheboksary, and Balakovo in the Volga Region, Bratsk and Usolye-Sibirskoye in Eastern Siberia, and Nevinnomyssk and Sumgait in the Caucasus; and metallurgical centers at Cherepovets in the northwest Region, Kremenchug in the Ukraine, Temirtau in Kazakhstan, and Achinsk in Eastern Siberia. The iron mining center of Rudnyy in northern Kazakhstan experienced the largest decline of any city. Other cities that experienced significant declines in growth included various regional centers, such as Frunze, the capital of the Kirgiz Republic, which had been one of the fastest growing large cities in the country during 1959-1970, and the Black Sea resort city of Sochi.

The few cities that showed significant increases in growth rates between 1959-1970 and 1970-1977 were those that received special attention for development investment during recent years. There is a tendency for some geographical concentration of these in previously underdeveloped western areas such as the Southwest Economic Region in the Ukraine and adjacent Belorussia. But rapid increases in growth have also occurred in a few outlying centers that have experienced new growth recently, such as Norilsk in the far north of Eastern Siberia, and Yakutsk, Blagoveshchensk, and Yuzhno-Sakhalinsk in the Far East. Table 7-4 lists alphabetically the 1976 population and percent change from 1970 to 1976 for all cities of more than 50,000 population.

Figure 7-9 shows level of urbanization by region along with cities of more than 300,000 inhabitants in 1970. It can be seen that high percentages of total population classified as urban exist in both densely populated, highly industrialized areas such as Moscow Oblast in the Central Region, Donetsk Oblast in the eastern Ukraine, and Kemerovo Oblast in the Kuznetsk Basin, and in sparsely populated areas where rural population is low and a few large cities based on mining or some other exploitative activity contain most of the population of the area. Such are Murmansk Oblast in the Northwest and Karaganda Oblast in central Kazakhstan. Relatively high urbanization prevails throughout the sparsely settled northern portions of the country all the way from the western border to the Pacific coast, except for a few areas where little development has taken place. Particularly low values of urbanization exist in some of the oases of Central Asia and heavily rural parts of western Ukraine, Central Black Earth Region, and the Caucasus.

City Functions

Overwhelmingly the larger cities of the Soviet Union are of a diversified administrative nature or industrial. Other functions, such as transport, education, resorts, and naval bases, are also important in many cities, but seldom constitute the dominant function. In most cases, the larger cities of the Soviet Union have

Table 7–4 Alphabetical Listing of Cities With Populations Greater Than 50,000, as of January 1, 1976, and Per Cent Change, 1970–1976

	1976 Population 1000	% Change 1970–1976		1976 Population 1000	% Change 1970–1976
Abakan	120	33.3	Berezniki	172	17.8
Achinsk	114	17.5	Birobidzhan	65	16.1
Aktyubinsk	179	19.3	Biysk	209	12.4
Alapayevsk	52	0	Blagoveshchensk	171	33.6
Aleksandriya	78	13.0	Bobruysk	185	34.1
Aleksandrov	57	14.0	Bor	62	12.7
Aleksin	65	6.6	Borisoglebsk	69	7.8
Alma-Ata	851	16.6	Borisov	102	21.4
Almalyk	95	17.3	Borovichi	58	5.5
Almetyevsk	102	17.2	Bratsk	195	25.8
Andizhan	220	17.0	Brest	162	32.8
Angarsk	231	13.8	Bryanka	68	−4.2
Angren	99	30.3	Bryansk	375	17.9
Antratsit	59	7.3	Bugulma	81	12.5
Anzhero-Sudzhensk	104	−1.9	Buguruslan	53	8.2
Apatity	56	21.7	Bukhara	144	28.6
Archangel	383	11.7	Buzuluk	75	11.9
Armavir	158	9.0	Chapayevsk	87	1.2
Arsenyev	58	23.4	Chardzhou	110	14.6
Artem	69	13.1	Chaykovskiy	63	31.3
Artemovsk	91	11.0	Cheboksary	278	28.7
Arzamas	85	26.9	Chelyabinsk	989	13.0
Asbest	80	5.3	Cheremkhovo	88	−11.1
Ashkhabad	297	17.4	Cherepovets	238	26.6
Astrakhan	458	11.7	Cherkassy	221	40.0
Azov	73	23.7	Cherkessk	82	22.4
Baku	1406	11.1	Chernigov	225	41.5
Balakovo	135	31.1	Chernogorsk	69	15.0
Balashikha	106	15.2	Chernovsty	209	11.8
Balashov	90	8.4	Chervonograd	52	18.2
Balkhash	78	2.6	Chimkent	296	19.8
Baranovichi	123	21.8	Chirchik	128	19.6
Barnaul	514	17.1	Chistopol	66	10.0
Bataysk	100	17.6	Chita	290	20.3
Batumi	117	15.8	Chusovoy	58	0
Bekabad	61	5.2	Daugavpils	112	12.0
Belaya Tserkov	137	25.7	Derbent	66	15.8
Belgorod	219	45.0	Dimitrovgrad	97	19.7
Belogorsk	64	12.3	Dmitrov	57	9.6
Beloretsk	72	7.5	Dneprodzerzhinsk	248	9.3
Belovo	111	2.8	Dnepropetrovsk	976	13.2
Beltsy	121	19.8	Dolgoprudny	63	18.9
Bendery	97	34.7	Donetsk	976	10.0
Berdichev	80	12.7	Drogobych	66	17.9
Berdsk	63	18.9	Druzhkovka	60	13.2
Berdyansk	117	63.0	Dubna	50	13.6

	1976 Population 1000	% Change 1970–1976		1976 Population 1000	% Change 1970–1976
Dushanbe	448	19.8	Kamensk-Shakhtinskiy	75	10.3
Dzerzhinsk	245	10.9	Kamensk-Uralskiy	185	9.5
Dzhalal-Abad	53	20.5	Kamyshin	108	11.3
Dzhambul	246	31.6	Kansk	97	2.1
Dzhezkazgan	82	32.3	Karaganda	570	9.0
Ekibastuz	54	22.7	Karshi	91	28.2
Elektrostal	134	8.9	Kaunas	352	15.4
Elista	62	24.0	Kazan	958	10.2
Engels	159	22.3	Kemerovo	446	15.8
Feodosiya	75	15.4	Kentau	60	9.1
Fergana	132	18.9	Kerch	152	18.8
Frunze	498	15.5	Khabarovsk	513	17.7
Gatchina	73	15.9	Kharkov	1385	13.2
Georgi-Dezh	52	6.1	Khartsyzsk	59	15.7
Georgiyevsk	50	13.6	Khasavyurt	64	18.5
Glazov	79	16.2	Kherson	315	20.7
Gomel	349	28.3	Khimki	103	18.4
Gori	54	12.5	Khmelnitskiy	161	42.5
Gorkiy	1305	11.5	Kiev	2013	23.3
Gorlovka	342	2.1	Kimry	59	11.3
Grodno	176	33.3	Kineshma	100	4.2
Groznyy	381	11.7	Kirov	376	12.9
Gubkin	67	24.1	Kirovabad	211	11.1
Gukovo	70	7.7	Kirovakan	130	21.5
Guryev	131	14.9	Kirovograd	224	18.5
Gus-Khrustalnyy	69	6.1	Kirovo-Chepetsk	62	21.6
Inta	51	.02	Kiselevsk	125	−1.6
Irbit	52	6.1	Kishinev	471	32.3
Irkutsk	519	15.1	Kislovodsk	97	7.8
Ishim	62	10.7	Klaipeda	169	20.7
Ishimbay	57	5.6	Klimovsk	52	20.9
Iskitim	57	26.7	Klin	88	8.6
Ivano-Frankovsk	139	32.4	Klintsy	66	13.8
Ivanovo	458	9.0	Kohtla-Jarve	71	4.4
Izhevsk	522	23.7	Kokand	152	14.3
Izmail	78	11.4	Kokchetav	97	19.8
Izyum	58	11.5	Kolomna	144	5.9
Kadiyevka	141	2.9	Kolomyya	50	22.0
Kalinin	395	14.5	Kolpino	102	45.7
Kaliningrad (Kaliningrad O.)	345	16.2	Kommunarsk	129	4.9
			Komsomolsk	246	12.8
Kaliningrad (Moscow O.)	119	12.3	Konotop	76	11.8
			Konstantinovka	111	5.7
Kaluga	255	20.9	Kopeysk	157	0.6
Kalush	55	34.1	Kopkino	67	5.6
Kamenets-Podolskiy	77	35.1	Korosten	61	8.9

Table 7–4   (Continued)

	1976 Population 1000	% Change 1970–1976		1976 Population 1000	% Change 1970–1976
Kostroma	247	10.8	Makhachkala	231	24.2
Kotlas	62	10.7	Margilan	113	18.9
Kovrov	138	12.2	Mary	70	12.9
Kramatorsk	167	11.3	Maykop	127	15.5
Krasnoarmeysk	59	7.3	Melitopol	155	13.1
Krasnodar	543	17.0	Mezhdurechensk	89	8.5
Krasnogorsk	71	12.7	Miass	145	10.7
Krasnokamsk	57	3.6	Michurinsk	101	7.4
Krasnoturinsk	59	0	Mikhailovka	57	14.0
Krasnovodsk	54	10.2	Mineralnyye Vody	62	12.7
Krasnoyarsk	758	17.0	Mingechaur	52	20.9
Krasnyy Luch	105	1.9	Minsk	1189	29.7
Kremenchug	202	21.7	Mogilev	264	30.7
Krivoy Rog	634	10.6	Molodechno	64	28.0
Kropotkin	73	7.4	Moscow	7734	9.3
Kstovo	55	14.6	Mozyr	69	40.8
Kumertau	52	18.2	Mukachevo	69	21.0
Kungur	82	10.8	Murmansk	369	19.4
Kurgan	297	21.7	Murom	111	12.1
Kursk	363	27.8	Mytishchi	133	11.8
Kustanay	151	21.8	Naberezhnyye Chelny	225	492.1
Kutaisi	177	9.9	Nakhodka	127	22.1
Kuybyshev	1186	13.5	Nalchik	195	33.6
Kuznetsk	94	11.9	Namangan	217	24.0
Kyzyl	57	9.6	Naro-Fominsk	54	10.2
Kzyl-Orda	143	17.2	Narva	71	22.4
Labinsk	57	14.0	Navoi	85	39.3
Leninabad	121	17.5	Nebit-Dag	65	16.1
Leninakan	188	13.9	Neftekamsk	62	34.8
Leningrad	4372	9.7	Nevinnomyssk	100	17.6
Leninogorsk			Nezhin	68	21.4
(E. Kaz. O.)	69	−4.2	Nikolayev	436	20.4
Leninogorsk			Nikopol	143	14.4
(Tatar A.S.S.R.)	51	8.5	Nizhnekamsk	112	128.6
Leninsk-Kuznetskiy	131	2.3	Nizhnevartovsk	63	293.8
Lida	55	14.6	Nizhniy Tagil	396	4.8
Liepaya	103	10.8	Noginsk	111	6.7
Lipetsk	363	25.6	Norilsk	168	24.4
Lisichansk	123	4.2	Novgorod	172	34.4
Lutsk	128	36.2	Novoaltaysk	52	6.1
Lvov	629	13.7	Novocheboksarsk	69	76.9
Lysva	75	2.7	Novocherkassk	183	13.0
Lyubertsy	154	10.8	Novokuybyshevsk	113	8.7
Magadan	112	21.7	Novokuznetsk	530	6.2
Magnitogorsk	393	8.0	Novomoskovsk		
Makeyevka	437	1.9	(Dnepropetrovsk O.)	68	11.5

	1976 Population 1000	% Change 1970–1976		1976 Population 1000	% Change 1970–1976
Novomoskovsk			Pushkino	62	29.2
(Tula O.)	146	9.0	Pyatigorsk	103	10.8
Novopolotsk	62	55.0	Ramenskoye	72	18.0
Novorossiysk	150	12.8	Rechitsa	59	22.9
Novoshakhtinsk	101	−1.0	Reutov	58	16.0
Novosibirsk	1286	10.8	Revda	61	3.4
Novotroitsk	95	14.5	Riga	806	10.1
Nukus	96	29.7	Rizhev	68	11.5
Obninsk	66	34.7	Romny	51	6.3
Odessa	1023	14.7	Roslavl	55	12.2
Odintsovo	78	16.4	Rostov-on-Don	907	15.0
Oktyabrskiy	86	11.7	Rovenki	62	1.6
Omsk	1002	22.0	Rovno	162	39.7
Ordzhonikidze	276	16.9	Rubezhnoye	67	15.5
Orekhovo-Zuyevo	128	6.7	Rubtsovsk	171	17.9
Orel	282	21.6	Rudnyy	108	12.5
Orenburg	435	26.4	Rustavi	127	30.0
Orsha	114	12.9	Ryazan	432	23.4
Orsk	243	8.0	Rybinsk	236	8.3
Osh	155	29.2	Rzhev	68	10.3
Osinniki	60	−3.2	Safonovo	53	15.2
Panevezhis	94	28.8	Salavat	130	14.0
Pavlodar	247	32.1	Salsk	57	14.0
Pavlograd	97	21.2	Samarkand	304	13.9
Pavlovo	68	7.9	Saran	54	10.2
Pavlovskiy Posad	69	4.5	Saransk	241	26.2
Penza	436	16.6	Sarapul	848	12.0
Perm	957	12.6	Saratov	107	10.3
Pervomaysk	73	23.7	Semipalatinsk	277	17.4
Pervouralsk	125	6.8	Serov	100	−1.0
Petrodvorets	64	6.7	Serpukhov	131	5.6
Petropavlovsk	196	13.3	Sevastopol	290	21.3
Petropavlovsk-			Severodonetsk	109	21.1
Kamchatskiy	202	31.2	Severodvinsk	180	24.1
Petrozavodsk	216	17.4	Shadrinsk	81	11.0
Pinsk	84	35.5	Shakhtersk	72	10.8
Podolsk	191	13.0	Shakhtinsk	51	27.5
Polevskoy	62	6.9	Shakhty	222	8.3
Polotsk	75	17.2	Shchekino	71	16.4
Poltava	270	22.7	Shchelkovo	89	14.1
Poti	54	17.4	Shevchenko	104	76.3
Priluki	66	15.8	Shostka	64	0
Prokopyevsk	267	−2.6	Shuya	72	4.3
Przhevalsk	50	19.0	Shyaulyay	112	20.4
Pskov	155	22.0	Simferopol	286	14.9
Pushkin	86	8.9	Slavyansk	137	10.5

Table 7–4   (Continued)

	1976 Population 1000	% Change 1970–1976		1976 Population 1000	% Change 1970–1976
Slavyansk-on-Kuban	56	7.7	Tselinograd	217	20.6
Smela	60	9.1	Tuapse	61	19.6
Smolensk	258	22.3	Tula	506	9.5
Snezhnoye	64	0	Tulun	51	4.1
Sochi	251	12.0	Turkestan	60	11.1
Soligorsk	54	42.1	Tyumen	335	24.5
Solikamsk	95	6.7	Ufa	923	19.7
Solntsevo	51	24.4	Ukhta	78	23.8
Spaask-Dalniy	52	15.6	Ulan-Ude	302	18.9
Staryy Oskol	80	53.8	Ulyanovsk	436	24.2
Stavropol	239	20.7	Uman	79	25.4
Sterlitamak	210	13.5	Uralsk	157	17.2
Stryy	56	16.7	Urgench	91	19.7
Stupino	64	8.5	Usolye-Sibirskoye	100	14.9
Sukhumi	118	15.7	Ussuriysk	145	13.3
Sumgait	168	35.5	Ust-Kamenogorsk	262	13.9
Sumy	199	25.2	Uzhgorod	77	18.5
Surgut	67	97.1	Uzlovaya	64	3.2
Sverdlovsk			Velikiye Luki	101	18.8
(Sverdlovsk O.)	1171	14.2	Verkhnyaya Salda	51	13.3
Sverdlovsk			Vichura	52	−1.9
(Voroshilovgrad O.)	71	4.4	Vilnyus	447	20.2
Svetlogorsk	56	40.0	Vinnitsa	288	35.8
Svobodnyy	70	11.1	Vitebsk	279	20.8
Syktyvkar	157	25.6	Vladimir	278	18.8
Syzran	185	6.9	Vladivostok	526	19.3
Taganrog	282	11.0	Volgograd	918	12.2
Taldy-Kurgan	82	34.4	Vologda	219	23.0
Tallinn	408	12.4	Volsk	72	4.3
Tambov	262	13.9	Volzhsk	53	23.3
Tartu	99	10.0	Volzhskiy	195	37.3
Tashauz	81	28.6	Vorkuta	96	6.7
Tashkent	1643	18.6	Voronezh	764	15.8
Tbilisi	1030	15.9	Voroshilovgrad	439	14.6
Temirtau	200	20.5	Voskresensk	73	9.0
Termez	55	22.2	Votkinsk	86	16.2
Ternopol	127	49.4	Vyazma	50	13.6
Tikhoretsk	63	5.0	Vyborg	71	9.2
Tikhvin	52	52.9	Vyshniy Volochek	75	1.4
Tiraspol	137	30.5	Yakutsk	143	32.4
Tobolsk	51	4.1	Yalta	76	22.6
Toglyatti	463	84.5	Yangiyul	60	9.1
Tokmak	54	28.6	Yaroslavl	577	11.6
Tomsk	413	22.2	Yefremov	53	10.4
Torez	96	3.2	Yegoryevsk	71	6.0
Troitsk	92	8.2	Yelets	112	10.9

	1976 Population 1000	% Change 1970–1976		1976 Population 1000	% Change 1970–1976
Yelgava	64	16.4	Zelenodolsk	86	11.7
Yenakiyevo	114	−.6	Zelenograd	121	36.0
Yerevan	928	21.0	Zhdanov	467	12.0
Yessentuki	73	12.3	Zheleznodorozhnyy	59	21.0
Yevpatoriya	92	16.5	Zheleznogorsk	57	83.9
Yeysk	71	10.9	Zheltyye Vody	51	27.5
Yoshkar-Ola	210	26.5	Zhitomir	229	42.2
Yurga	73	17.7	Zhukovskiy	85	14.9
Yurmala	59	9.3	Zima	50	19.0
Yuzhno-Sakhalinsk	131	23.6	Zlatoust	195	8.3
Zagorsk	100	8.7	Zyryanovsk	54	−3.6
Zaporozhye	760	15.5			

Source: Narkhoz SSSR, 1975, pp. 22–31.
The author is grateful to Julie Mintz for compiling this table.

higher percentages of their work force engaged in industrial pursuits than is true in most cities of the world, and there are low percentages in various types of trade. Nearly 90 per cent of the Soviet cities with populations of more than 50,000 are either diversified administrative centers or industrial cities, about equally divided. The predominance of these two types reflect the command economy of the Soviet Union directed by the party and government aparatus with the result that the political administrative structure operated through the urban hierarchy plays a key role in directing and coordinating the entire economic life of the country. It also reflects the strong party and government interest in the industrial sector of the economy, especially in the production of material goods in mines, forests, and factories.

The thirty largest cities of the Soviet Union are all diversified administrative centers. These and smaller administrative centers represent central places that tend to be rather evenly spaced over the ecumene of the Soviet Union to perform complex functions in a broad spectrum of economic activities as well as nonmaterial activities such as administration, finance, education, science, health, and cultural activities in their legally determined tributary areas in their respective political administrative regions. In almost all cases these administrative cities are the largest cities in their respective political administrative regions, in most cases conspicuously large compared to the rest of the cities in their regions.

In contrast to the widely spaced pattern of administrative cities, industrial cities show clustering or specific localization on certain resources. The strictly manufacturing cities are concentrated in the Central Region, the Volga, the Donets-Dnieper Region, the North Caucasus, and the Urals. In most cases machinery production is the primary manufacturing function, although textiles, chemicals, metallurgy, and so forth are also important. However, these types of manufacturing may have even larger enterprises in the administrative centers which are generally larger cities than the strictly industrial cities are. Those industrial cities which include mining are concentrated in coal basins such as the Donbas in the eastern Ukraine, the Kuzbas in Western Siberia, and the Urals. There are few large cities in the Soviet Union that are devoted primarily to mining alone. Most of the mining cities are of a

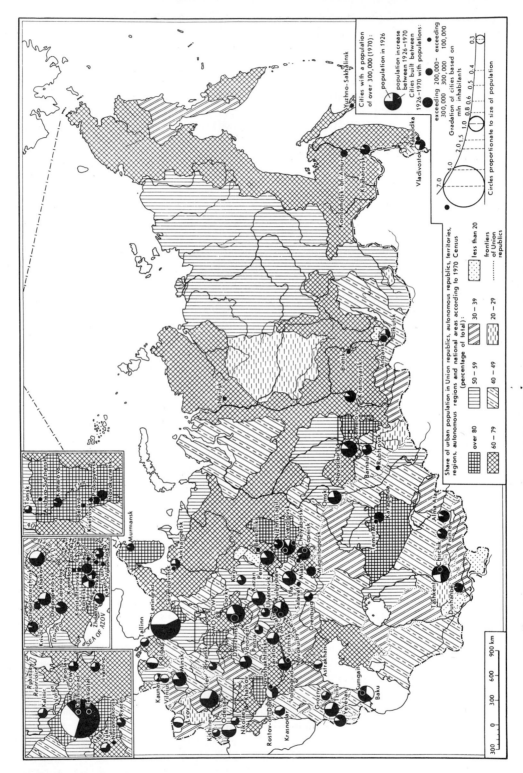

Figure 7-9   Urban population as percent of total population, and city sizes and growths, 1926–1970, of cities with 1970 populations greater than 300,000. After Pokshishevsky, Geoforum, 9/72, p. 30.

smaller size; only ten have populations exceeding 50,000. This is true also of other types of centers such as transport centers, resorts, and centers for education and research. These functions are usually combined with more predominant functions in larger cities, and only some of the smaller cities can be classified strictly as transportation centers and so forth.

Urban Hierarchies

As cities have developed in the Soviet Union they have fallen into a pattern of interrelationships that link them together in a hierarchical system. (Fig. 7-10) Because of the chain-of-command nature of governmental control in the Soviet Union, the urban system there operationally is more hierarchical than it is in most countries. Moscow occupies the center of this system, and all the other republic capitals are directly subordinated to it, as are all cities exceeding one million in population. Nearly all other cities down to the size of 100,000 inhabi-

tants, except for a few outlying centers such as Murmansk and Archangel in the north, fall into nine urban regions, as shown in Figure 7-10.

The Central Region is focused on Moscow. The West and Baltic area focuses on Leningrad, by far the largest city in the region, but also contains the capital cities of the three Baltic Republics and Belorussia which are subordinated directly to Moscow through political administrative channels. A southwestern region focuses on Kiev, and the eastern and southern Ukraine focuses on Kharkov with lower level linkages among cities of the Donets-Dnieper industrial region and some direct links to Moscow. The Volga Region focuses to a certain extent on Kuybyshev with interlinkages among adjacent cities in the elongated region. Most of the cities in the Urals focus on Sverdlovsk. The West Siberian Region focuses on Novosibirsk, including the cities of the Kuznetsk Basin even though Novosibirsk lies to the west of the basin. The Caucasus are somewhat bimodal, focusing on both Baku and

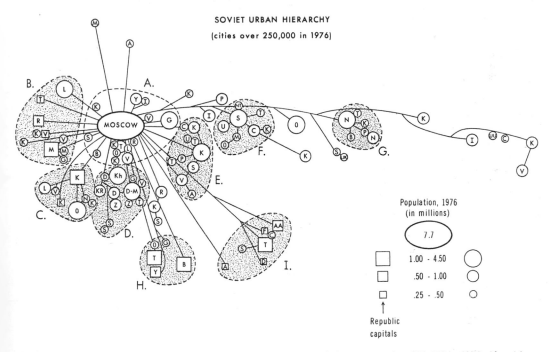

Figure 7-10   Urban hierarchy in the U.S.S.R. among cities with populations greater than 250,000 in 1976. After Adams, Soviet Geography: Review and Translation, May, 1977, p. 314.

Tbilisi. In Central Asia Tashkent is the obvious focal center.

In spite of the fact that the Soviet urban system is very structured in a hierarchical sense, the huge size of the country with large empty spaces separating nodes of population, and the diverse ethnicity of the country with its nationality-based political units, tends to disperse countrywide functions and corresponding population growth among a number of separate centers. In a study of rank-size relationships among Soviet cities, Harris has demonstrated that Moscow is not as dominant in the Soviet Union as is London in England, Paris in France, New York in the United States, or Tokyo in Japan. While London contains about 22 per cent of the population of England, Paris about 17 per cent of the population of France, Tokyo-Yokohama about 15 per cent of the population of Japan, and New York about 8 per cent of the population of the United States, Moscow contains less than 4 per cent of the population of the Soviet Union. According to rank-size relationships, if Moscow truly served urban functions for the entire Soviet Union, its population would be about twice as large as it is. Perhaps some of this evident lack of growth may be due to government policy to limit the size of big cities, but this is probably a minor consideration.

City Forms

Though the characteristics of site, such as river banks and lake shores, have dictated individual variations in city pattern, three basic forms have evolved over the years which generally reflect the functions of the settlements at the times of their foundation. Most of the old historical cities which originated as kremlins for defense have a circular-radial street pattern. Moscow exemplifies this in its most developed form. (Fig. 7–11) The city is roughly circular with streets and railways radiating outward in all directions from the center crossing circular boulevards and railways in an ever widening pattern. The Kremlin in the center was erected originally in 1147 as a high construction of walls along the bank of the Moscow River that contained all the important buildings at that time. As the city grew walls were constructed around successive peripheries of the expanding city to defend it from marauding nomads from the southeast. The present kremlin wall of weathered red brick dates back to the fifteenth century. (Fig. 7–12) Early in the sixteenth century a so-called "white wall" was constructed around the boundaries of the city at that time, and later in the sixteenth century another rampart of wood and earth, the so-called "earthen wall," or "garden wall," was built to defend against Tatar attacks. In 1943 when a ten-year plan to revamp the city of Moscow was launched, all the old walls except the Kremlin wall were pulled down and the areas they occupied were used for the construction of wide circular boulevards. About one-half mile from the Kremlin, Boulevard Ring occupies what was once the site of the white wall, and about a mile from the Kremlin is the twelve-lane Sadovaya, or Garden Ring, which occupies the site of the garden wall. The expansive squares formed where the radiating streets cross the circular streets are still known by the names of gates, reminders that these streets previously passed through gates in the walled city.

Farther from the center of the city a railway encircles Moscow and eliminates train traffic from the heart of the city. Several train stations are located along the circular railway at the ends of eleven trunk railways that come in from various parts of the country. Train traffic terminates at these stations, and connections with the central part of the city are made by subways, which now constitute a well-developed system of branching lines diametrically crossing under the city and intersecting with a line that encircles the inner city. A second circular subway line is planned for the future as the radial lines extend farther and farther into new green-belt apartment complexes. A dual belt highway 109 kilometers long has been completed around the newly expanded city limits to shunt future traffic away from the center of the city. Beyond this a green belt approximately ten kilometers wide has been

Figure 7–11 The annular-radial pattern of Moscow.

preserved from further agricultural and industrial development. Primarily wooded with pine
and birch trees, this belt contains residential
suburbs and dachas, or summer homes, of

people living in Moscow. More than one
million people live within the confines of the
green belt.

Cities that evolved during the reoccupation

Figure 7–12   View of the Kremlin across the Moscow River. Photo by Irene Milass.

of the southern steppes during the seventeenth century, which often originated as Cossack settlements under a military type of organizational control, are generally rectangular in pattern arranged around a monumental central square or series of squares that were large enough to accommodate mass meetings and parades. A good example of this is Kharkov in the northeastern Ukraine which arose during the middle of the seventeenth century. However, even here the railroad pattern, which was developed during the later part of the nineteenth century, radiates outward from the center of the city to cities in the distance in all directions.

Many of the newly developed or newly expanded Soviet cities also are laid out on rectangular patterns around central squares. However, another city pattern has continued into the Soviet period that evolved during the garden city concept in the late nineteenth and early twentieth centuries. This is a sort of linear city which is laid out with alternating strips of land use. An agricultural strip is bordered by a residential strip bordered by a green strip and then an industrial strip along which a main transport artery is laid out. This arrangement serves the function of bringing the city and country together and protects the residential strip from the industrial strip and transport artery by a green strip in between.

Whatever the pattern of the city, during the Soviet period the use of dachas has become widespread as city dwellers have become more affluent and desire relief from apartment living within the confines of the city. There is essentially no suburban sprawl of single family homes in the Soviet Union as is so common in North America, and the only way that city dwellers can get a taste of country living is to acquire a part-time residence or dacha in green belts surrounding cities. These are usually simply built cottages without central utilities that would not be suitable for year-round living. Many people own their dachas, but many rent from other people.

In addition to dachas, and in many cases as successions to them, many cities have developed large areas subdivided into tiny garden plots each with a small shed to serve as temporary quarters and storage for tools. This has provided both recreation and purposeful use of leisure time for many city dwellers. As cities expand, the dacha communities keep moving farther and farther into the country, and their sites are often taken over by such garden subdivisions. These suburban gardens have added significantly to the agricultural production of the country, and will be discussed again in Chapter 9.

Reading List

1. Adams, Russell B., "The Soviet Metropolitan Hierarchy: Regionalization and Comparison with the United States," *Soviet Geography: Review and Translation,* May 1977, pp. 313–329.
2. Barr, B., Lindsay, I., and Reinett, E., "Patterns of Urban Spacing in the USSR: Analysis of Order Neighbor Statistics in Two-Dimensional Space," *Journal of Regional Science,* No. 2, 1971, pp. 211–224.
3. Berton, Kathleen, *Moscow: An Architectural History,* Studio Vista Publishers, London, 1977, 256 pp.
4. Bater, James H., *St. Petersburg: Industrialization and Change,* Studies in Urban History 4, McGill-Queen's University Press, Montreal, 1976, 474 pp.
5. Chinn, Jeffrey Bernard, *The Socio-Demographic Consequences of Urbanization in the Soviet Union,* PhD Dissertation, University of Wisconsin-Madison, 1975, 374 pp.
6. "Commuting to Work in the USSR," Special issue, *Soviet Geography: Review and Translation,* June 1978.
7. Cybriwsky, Roman A., "The Pre-Soviet Village in Ukraine," *Association of Pacific Coast Geographers, Yearbook,* 1972, pp. 119–136.
8. Davidovich, V. G., "On the Patterns and Tendencies of Urban Settlement in the USSR," *Soviet Geography: Review and Translation,* January 1966, pp. 3–31.
9. DiMaio, Alfred J., Jr., *Soviet Urban Housing: Problems and Policies,* Praeger, New York, 1974, 250 pp.
10. Fedor, Thomas S., *Patterns of Urban Growth in the Russian Empire During the Nineteenth Century,* University of Chicago, Department of Geography, Research Paper No. 163, 1975, 245 pp.
11. Filvarov, G. I., "Measuring the Social Quality of the Structure of a Settlement System," *Soviet Geography: Review and Translation,* April 1978, pp. 252–265.
12. French, R. A., "Field Patterns and the Three-Field System — the Case of Sixteenth Century Lithuania," *Institute of British Geographers, Transactions, No. 48,* December 1969, pp. 121–134.
13. ———, "The Making of the Russian Landscape," *Advancement of Science,* May 1963, pp. 44–56.
14. Fuchs, Roland J., and Demko, George J., "Commuting and Urbanization in the Socialist Countries of Europe," *ACES Bulletin,* Spring 1977, pp. 21–38.
15. Glushkova, V. G., and Shepelev, N. P., "Problems in the Spatial Management of Weekend Recreation Outside Large Cities (with particular reference to Moscow)," *Soviet Geography: Review and Translation,* February 1977, pp. 100–107.
16. Gohstand, Robert, "Moscow: Aspects of Urban Morphology," Map Supplement No. 20, *Annals of the Association of American Geographers,* March 1976.
17. Gustafson, Glen C., and Huzinec, George A., "Distance as an Explanatory Factor in Urban Growth Rates: A Test for Moscow Oblast," *Soviet Geography: Review and Translation,* May 1978, pp. 311–324.
18. Hamilton, F. E. Ian, *The Moscow City Region,* Oxford University Press, 1976, 48 pp.
19. ———, "Muscovites Move Away From the Centre," *The Geographical Magazine,* March 1973, pp. 451–459.
20. Hamm, Michael F., ed., *The City in Russian History,* The University Press of Kentucky, Lexington, 1976, 350 pp.
21. ———, "The Modern Russian City: An Historiographical Analysis," *Journal of Urban History,* November 1977, pp. 39–76.
22. Harris, Chauncy D., *Cities of the Soviet Union,* Rand McNally, Chicago, 1970, 484 pp.
23. ———, "City and Region in the Soviet Union," in Beckinsale, R. P., and Houston, J. M., *Urbanization and its Problems,* Basil Blackwell, Oxford, 1968, pp. 277–296.
24. ———, "Population of Cities of the Soviet Union, 1897, 1926, 1939, 1959, and 1967:

Tables, Maps, and Gazetteer," *Soviet Geography: Review and Translation,* May 1970, 138 pp.

25. ———, "Urbanization and Population Growth in the Soviet Union, 1959–1970," *The Geographical Review,* January 1971, pp. 102–124.

26. Hooson, David J. M., "The Growth of Cities in Pre-Soviet Russia," in Beckinsale, R. P. and Houston, J. M., eds., *Urbanization and its Problems,* Basil Blackwell, Oxford, 1968, pp. 254–276.

27. Houston, Cecil James, *The Spatial Components and Consequences of Contemporary Urban Population Growth in the Central European USSR,* PhD Dissertation, University of Toronto, 1975.

28. Huzinec, George A.. "The Impact of Industrial Decision-making upon the Soviet Urban Hierarchy," *Urban Studies,* June 1978, pp. 139–148.

29. Jackson, W. A. Douglas, "Soviet Society in Flux: Urban Expansion," *Problems of Communism,* November-December 1974, pp. 14–24.

30. Jensen, Robert G., "Urban Environments in the United States and the Soviet Union: Some Contrasts and Comparisons," *Urbanization and Counterurbanization,* 2, pp. 31–42.

31. Khorev, B. S., "A Study of the Functional Structure of Urban Places of the USSR," *Soviet Geography: Review and Translation,* January 1966, pp. 31–51.

32. ———, *Problemy gorodov* (Problems of Cities), Mysl', Moscow 2nd ed., 1975, 428 pp.

33. Kochetkov, A. V., and Listengurt, F. M., "A Strategy for the Distribution of Settlement in the USSR: Aims, Problems, and Solutions," *Soviet Geography: Review and Translation,* November 1977, pp. 660–675.

34. Konstantinov, O. A., ed., *Geografiya naseleniya v SSSR: osnovnye problemy* (The Geography of Population in the U.S.S.R.: Principal Problems), Akademiya Nauk, Moscow, 1964, 278 pp.

35. ———, "New Cities in the System of Urban Settlement of the USSR," *Izvestiya Vsesoyuznogo Geograficheskogo Obshchestva,* 1975, No. 1, pp. 22–28.

36. ———, "Types of Urbanization in the USSR," *Soviet Geography: Review and Tranlation,* December 1977, pp. 715–728.

37. Kovalev, S. A., "Regional Peculiarities in the Dynamcis of Rural Settlement in the USSR

(1959–70)," *Soviet Geography: Review and Translation,* January 1974, pp. 1–12.

38. ———, "Tranformation of Rural Settlements in the Soviet Union," *Geoforum,* 9, 1972, pp. 33–35.

39. Lappo, G. M., "Problems in the Evolution of Urban Agglomerations," *Soviet Geography: Review and Translation,* November 1974, pp. 531–542.

40. ———, "Trends in the Evolution of Settlement Patterns in the Moscow Region," *Soviet Geography: Review and Tranlation,* January 1973, pp. 13–24.

41. Lappo, G., Chikishev, A., and Bekker, A., *Moscow: Capital of the Soviet Union; a Short Geographical Survey,* Progress Puonshers, Moscow, 1976, 153 pp.

42. Lewis, Robert A., and Rowland, Richard H., "Urbanization in Russia and the USSR: 1897–1966," *Annals of the Association of American Geographers,* December 1969, pp. 776–796.

43. Listengurt, F. M., "Criteria for Delineating Large Urban Agglomerations in the USSR," *Soviet Geography: Review and Translation,* November 1975, pp. 559–568.

44. Lola, A. M., and Savina, T. M., "Regularities and Prospects of Transformation of Rural Places in the Nonchernozem Zone of the RSFSR," *Izvestia Akademii Nauk SSSR, seriya geograficheskaya,* 1978, No. 1, pp. 77–89.

45. Lydolph, Paul E., "A Visit to Bratsk," *Soviet Geography: Review and Tranlation,* November 1977, pp. 681–689.

46. Morris, A. S., "The Medieval Emergence of the Volga-Oka Region," *Annals of the Association of American Geographers,* December 1971, pp. 697–710.

47. Osipov, G. V., ed., *Studies in Soviet Society,* Vol. 2, *Town, Country, and People,* Tavistock Publications, London, 1969, 260 pp.

48. Paperskaya-Serdobova, M. A., "Stages of Formation of the Urban Network in Central Russia," *Soviet Geography: Review and Translation,* March 1974, pp. 142–155.

49. Parkins, Maurice, *City Planning in Soviet Russia,* University of Chicago Press, 1953, 257 pp.

50. Pokshishevsky, V. V., "Urbanization in the USSR," *Geoforum,* 9, 1972, pp. 23–32.

51. Polskiy, S. A., *Demograficheskiye Problemy Razvitiya Minska* (Demographic Problems in the Growth of Minsk), Minsk, 1976.

52. Rowland, Richard H., *Urban In-Migration in*

Late Nineteenth Century Russia, PhD Dissertation, Columbia University, 1971.

53. Rozman, Gilbert, *Urban Networks in Russia, 1750–1800, and Premodern Periodization,* Princeton University Press, Princeton, 1976, 337 pp.

54. Shaw, Denis J. B., "The Nature of the Russian City," Review article, *Journal of Historical Geography,* 1977, No. 3, pp. 267–270.

55. ———, "Planning Leningrad," *The Geographical Review,* April 1978, pp. 183–201.

56. ———, "Urbanism and Economic Development in a Pre-industrial Context: the Case of Southern Russia," *Journal of Historical Geography,* April 1977, pp. 107–122.

57. Thiede, Robert L., *Town and Function in Tsarist Russia: A Geographical Analysis of Trade and Industry in Towns of New Russia, 1860–1910,* PhD Dissertation, University of Vashington, 1971.

59. ———, "Urbanization and Industrialization in Pre-Revolutionary Russia," *The Professional Geographer,* February 1973, pp. 16–21.

59. Tikhomirov, M., *The Towns of Ancient Rus,* Foreign Languages Publishing House, Moscow, 1959, 502 pp.

60. Valentey, D. I., Pokshishevskiy, V. V., and Khorev, B. S., eds., *Problemy urbanizatsii v SSSR* (Problems of Urbanization in the U.S.S.R.), Moscow University, 1971, 114 pp.

61. Vedenin, Yu A., Filippovich, L. S., Panchuk, S. I., and Yudina, Ye G., "Cottage Settlements and Garden Cooperatives in the Moscow Area," *Soviet Geography: Review and Translation,* May 1977, pp. 329–339.

62. *Voprosy Geografii,* No. 96, 1974, (Urbanization of the World), has four articles on the Soviet Union.

8

General Economy

NATIONAL INCOME

The Soviet economy is second largest in the world. Although its national income is a poor second to that of the United States, it is well above that of the third leading nation, Japan. (Table 8–1) In many items it is the leading producer in the world. (Table 8–2) Its national income per capita however is not so impressive, lagging behind not only the United States but also most of the countries of Europe, Canada, Australia, and Japan. (Table 8–3) In terms of world power, then, the Soviet Union ranks second, according to its total production, but in terms of standard of living it still ranks fairly low, even below some of its satellite countries of Eastern Europe. The standard of living of the Soviet people is lower even than the per capita national income might suggest, because so much is spent on defense or is plowed back into the economy in the form of capital investment. Consumer welfare thus has received a considerably smaller portion of the national income in the Soviet Union than in most other countries of the world.

The various components of the Soviet gross national product make up considerably different portions than they do in most of the other developed countries of the world. This is particularly true in comparison with the United States which has so much of its gross national product represented by services. In

Table 8–1 National Incomes of the U.S.S.R. and Leading Capitalist Countries, 1975 [a]

Country	Billion Dollars
U.S.A.	849
U.S.S.R.	503
Japan	242
West Germany	196
France	139
Great Britain	92
Italy	80
Canada	61

Source: Narkhoz SSSR, 1975, p. 123.
[a] National Income as defined by the Soviets is limited to material production and does not include services and government expenditures.

comparison with the other developed countries, the U.S.S.R. is still very heavy on agriculture, and it is somewhat heavy on construction and transportation, since it is building so rapidly and the country is so large that things have to be hauled long distances. Its commerce and service sectors are relatively small. (Table 8–4) Employment shows a distribution similar to production. (Table 8–5)

Because the Soviet gross national product does not include such a high portion of services, it has much more muscle in it than the gross

Table 8–2   Production of Selected Items, U.S.S.R. and Other Leading Industrial Countries, 1975

Product	Unit	World	U.S.S.R.	U.S.A.	Japan	West Germany	United Kingdom	France	Italy
Electricity	Billion KwH	6439	1039 (2)	2001	476	302	272	179	146
Oil, Including Gas Condensates	Million Tons	2646	491 (1)	413	0.6	5.7	1.2	1.0	1.0
Natural Gas [b]	Billion Cubic Meters	n.a.	270 (2)	560	2.7	21	35	10	14
Coal (Hard)	Million Tons	2368	485 (2)	568	19	97	129	24	—
Lignite	Million Tons	863	160 (1)	18	—	123	—	3	1
Iron Ore (Iron Content)	Million Tons	500	127 (1)	49	0.3	1.1	1.1	15	0.3
Pig Iron	Millions Tons	489	103 (1)	75	89	30	12	18	12
Steel	Million Tons	643	141 (1)	106	102	40	20	22	22
Aluminum	Thousand Tons	12000	1500 (2)	4373	1439	713	485	490	341
Mineral Fertilizers	Million Tons	n.a.	90.2 (1)	82.8	16.1	18.9	6.5	22.4	8.1
Sulfuric Acid (100% H_2SO_4)	Million Tons	100	18.6 (2)	29.4	6.0	4.2	3.2	3.8	3.0
Caustic Soda (100% NaOH)	Million Tons	24.9	2.4 (4)	8.4	2.9	2.5	n.a.	1.1	1.0
Soda Ash (100% Na_2CO_3)	Million Tons	17.7	4.7 (1)	2.5	1.1	1.2	n.a.	0.8	n.a.
Chemical Fibers	Thousand Tons	n.a.	955 (3)	3000	1300	800	600	300	400
Diesel & Electric Locomotives	Each	n.a.	1770 (1)	1442 [a]	325 [a]	422 [a]	252 [a]	227 [a]	93 [a]
Motor Vehicles	Thousands	n.a.							
Passenger Cars		25210	1201 (7)	6717	4568	2905	1268	2951	1349
Commercial Vehicles		8000	765 (3)	2270	2380	286	381	347	110
Tractors, Large	Thousands	n.a.	550 (1)	270 [a]	207 [a]	116 [a]	120 [a]	57 [a]	116 [a]
Grain Combines	Thousands	n.a.	97.5 (2)	28.6 [a]	117 [a]	18.9 [a]	6.0 [a]	7.6	2.0 [c]
Roundwood	Million Cubic Meters	2421	386 (1)	296	37	26	3	29	7
Sawnwood	Million Cubic Meters	393	115 (1)	75	38	9.0	1.8	8.3	1.8
Cement	Million Tons	690	122 (1)	62	66	34	17	30	34
Cotton Fabrics	Million Square Meters	n.a.	6600 (1)	4000	1900	900	400	900	900
Woolen Fabrics	Million Square Meters	n.a.	740 (1)	100	320	100	180	170	250
Silk Fabrics (Including Synthetics)	Million Square Meters	n.a.	1508 (3)	6500	3000	420	420	370	280 [a]
Leather Footwear	Million Pairs	n.a.	698 (1)	400	n.a.	120	180	220	280 [a]
Granulated Sugar	Thousand Tons	81691	8200 (1)	5680	459	2571	725	2712	1429
Fish and Sea Products	Thousand Tons	69700	9876 (2)	2799	10509	442	980	806	406
Meat	Thousand Tons	94757	13440 (2)	16690	1392	3664	2301	3524	1799
Milk	Thousand Tons	n.a.	90800 (1)	52300	4800 [a]	21600 [a]	14100 [a]	30800 [a]	10800 [a]
Butter	Thousand Tons	n.a.	1320 (1)	445	42	521	47	555	63
Flour, Wheat	Thousand Tons	123,500	41968 (1)	10029	3996	2375	3887	3361 [a]	7268

Sources: The USSR in Figures for 1975, Statistika, Moscow, 1976, pp. 56–61 and *United Nations Statistical Yearbook*, 1976.
[a] 1974.
[b] At temperature of 0°C and pressure of 760 millimeters.
[c] 1973.
Numbers in parentheses after U.S.S.R. figures indicate rank in world. n.a. = not available.
— = negligible.

Table 8–3 Per Capita National Income, U.S.S.R. and Leading Capitalist Countries, in Dollars

Country	Year	Dollars
U.S.A.	1975	5660
W. Germany	1975	4480
Denmark	1973	4160
Canada	1973	4120
Sweden	1972	3985
France	1973	3760
Belgium	1973	3670
Netherlands	1973	3615
Switzerland	1971	3360
Japan	1973	3020
Norway	1972	2655
Australia	1971	2640
U.S.S.R.	1975	2507

Source: Narkhoz SSSR, 1975, p. 123. U.S.S.R. figure computed from data given for the U.S.S.R. and the U.S.A. in Block, 1976, p. 246.

Table 8–4 Gross National Product by Sector of Origin, U.S.S.R. and U.S.A., 1970, in Per Cent of Total

Sector	U.S.S.R.	U.S.A.
Industry	28.7	29.9
Construction	8.8	4.8
Agriculture	20.4	3.2
Transportation	7.8	3.9
Communications	0.8	2.3
Trade	6.1	17.0
Services	23.9	39.0
Unallocated	3.6	0.0
Total	100.0	100.0

Source: U.S.S.R. data computed from Greenslade, 1976, p. 284. U.S.A. data computed from *Statistical Abstract of the United States*, 1975, p. 382.
[1] Includes forestry and fishing.

national products of most of the other developed countries. In other words, a greater share of the gross national product consists of material production. And since so much of this material production is either directly related to military preparedness or is reinvested in the

Table 8–5 Civilian Employment by Branch of the Economy, U.S.S.R., 1974, and U.S.A., 1975, in Per Cents of Total

	U.S.S.R.	U.S.A.
Agriculture, Forestry, and Fisheries	30.1	4.1
State Farms	8.6	
Collective Farms	11.7	
Private Plots	9.5	
Forestry	0.4	
Non Agricultural	69.9	95.9
Mining and Manufacturing	26.7	23.6
Construction	8.3	5.9
Transport and Communications	8.4	6.6
Trade	7.0	20.6
Services	16.8	33.5
Government Administration	1.7	5.6
Other	1.0	0.1

Sources: Data for the U.S.S.R. computed from Rapawy, 1976, pp. 51, 53, and 55; Data for the U.S.A. computed from *Statistical Abstract of the United States*, 1976, p. 356.

economy to build up heavy industry, which further increases the capabilities of production for industrial and military uses, it is estimated that the military capability of the Soviet economy is roughly equal to that of the United States.

Historical Perspective

Gross national product of the fledgling United States overtook that of Tsarist Russia around 1860 when both countries had about the same total GNP. However, since Russia had 2.5 times as many people as the United States did at that time, the per capita gross national product in the United States was 2.5 times that of Russia. (Table 8–6) The United States continued to forge ahead, and by 1913 at the eve of the First World War, the GNP of Russia equalled only 39 per cent that of the United States, and the per capita GNP was only 24 per cent that of the United States.

Table 8–6   Long-Term Comparison of Russian/Soviet and United States GNP

	GNP in Toto (Billion 1975 Dollars)				GNP per Capita (in 1975 Dollars)			
	Russia or U.S.S.R.	United States	Difference	Soviet-United States Ratio (Per Cent)	Russia or U.S.S.R.	United States	Difference	Soviet-United States Ratio (Per Cent)
1860	25–26	25–26	0	100	350	860	510	40
1913	95	243	148	39	600	2500	1900	24
1928	95	353	248	27	629	2931	2302	21
1940	176	420	244	42	904	3182	2278	28
1948	174	599	425	29	993	4085	3092	24
1950	218	657	439	33	1213	4315	3102	28
1955	295	810	515	36	1506	4884	3378	31
1956	323	825	502	39	1616	4886	3270	33
1957	329	837	508	39	1619	4867	3248	33
1958	364	827	463	44	1762	4731	2969	37
1959	379	880	501	43	1802	4952	3150	36
1960	394	902	508	44	1833	4993	3155	37
1961	417	919	502	45	1913	5007	3094	38
1962	433	980	547	44	1954	5255	3301	37
1963	442	1019	577	43	1966	5388	3422	36
1964	476	1075	599	44	2088	5602	3514	37
1965	504	1143	639	44	2182	5882	3700	37
1966	539	1218	679	44	2307	6193	3886	37
1967	563	1249	686	45	2384	6286	3901	38
1968	598	1307	709	46	2510	6513	4003	38
1969	612	1342	730	46	2546	6623	4077	38
1970	661	1337	676	49	2722	6523	3801	42
1971	683	1381	648	49	2785	6667	3882	42
1972	695	1466	771	47	2810	7018	4208	40
1973	747	1553	806	48	2993	7379	4386	41
1974	771	1519	748	51	3058	7168	4110	43
1975	786	1489	693	53	3088	6972	3884	44

Source: Block, 1976, p. 246.

World War I, revolutions, and ensuing civil wars wreaked havoc with the Russian economy. During the period 1917–1921, which is commonly known as "War Communism," the Soviets ran the country as a command economy to meet one dire emergency after another as best they could, with the main objective of keeping themselves in power. Labor and materials were moved about by consignment, and little attention was paid to money values and bookkeeping. After the Soviets had consolidated their political power, in 1921 Lenin launched the New Economic Policy (NEP) conceived to rehabilitate the economy of the devastated country. By 1928 the Soviet gross national product had regained roughly the 1913 level of the Russian Empire. But by this time the American gross national product had increased to the point where the Soviet GNP was only 27 per cent that of the U.S.A.

The Soviet GNP grew rapidly during the 1930s with the launching of the five-year plans and the determination rapidly to industrialize the country at the expense of human welfare.

By 1940 the Soviet GNP was 42 per cent that of the United States. But the growth was interrupted again by war, and not until 1948 did the Soviet Union regain its 1940 GNP. By then the United States had grown to the point where the Soviet GNP was only 29 per cent that of the U.S.A.

Since 1948 the Soviet GNP has been growing steadily as no more catastrophies have taken place in the country. However, during the 1950s and most of the 1960s the gross national product of the United States grew at even greater absolute rates than that of the Soviet Union, so although the Soviet GNP was gaining percentagewise on that of the U.S.A., it was still losing relatively in absolute value. Whereas the difference between the two GNPs in 1950 had been 439 billion dollars, in 1969 it was 730 billion dollars. The difference in per capita GNP during this time increased from 3102 dollars in 1950 to 4077 dollars in 1969. (Table 8-6)

During the 1970s the Soviet GNP has continued to increase constantly albeit at successively slower rates, while the GNP of the U.S.A. has fluctuated up and down with the world economy. During the period 1969–1971 the Soviet GNP gained absolutely on that of the United States. However, the gap widened again in 1972 and 1973. In 1974 and 1975 the Soviet GNP gained on that of the United States again, so that the difference between the two in 1975 was only slightly greater than it had been in 1967.

Present Growth Rates

It must be realized in comparing the gross national products of the U.S.S.R. and the U.S.A. that that of the U.S.A. is delicately balanced between supply and demand. The market for most kinds of goods in the United States has been essentially saturated for a considerable length of time, and the growth of the GNP represents only the ability to expand the market, not the ability to produce. On the other hand, in most cases the market for goods in the Soviet Union has not yet been satiated,

and the growth of the GNP represents the growth of the capacity to produce. In the past the Soviets have experienced rather consistently high growth rates because they were simply producing as much as possible, the only limitations being set by supplies of raw materials and intermediate products to feed the economic machine. But more recently, particularly during the 1970s, their economy in many sectors has begun to reach the mature stage where they have to pay more attention to supply and demand. And the growth rate has dropped accordingly. During 1971–1975, the average annual growth rate of the GNP in the Soviet Union was only 3.7 per cent, as opposed to the planned growth of 5.8 per cent and an acutal growth during the 1966–1970 period of 5.5 per cent. (Table 8-7) Of course part of this decrease was due to a disastrous period for agriculture during 1971–1975, but at the same time industrial output grew at a decreasing rate also, and was well below the planned value. (Table 8-8)

The tenth five-year plan, 1976–1980, stresses the need for quality and labor efficiency rather than rapid growth of the economy. It points out that attention must be paid to the infrastructure of the economy, particularly adequate transport (primarily road building) and storage (warehouses and so forth). Also an increasing portion of the economy must be allotted to environmental protection. The Soviets are beginning to become aware of the finiteness of their industrial labor supply, water, energy, usable land, and so forth. It is generally acknowledged that under present technological conditions there is little agricultural land to be opened up anymore, and any increase in agricultural production must be effected through increased yields on presently cultivated land. In this regard also it has become evident that the farms must retain some of their better trained youth in order to realize greater agricultural yields through correct applications of fertilizers, pesticides, herbicides, land melioration, and mechanization. The necessity to retain quality labor on the farms has brought the Soviets to the realization that they no longer have an inexhaustible reservoir

Table 8–7   Average Annual Rates of Growth, Per Cent

	Achievement					Plan	
	1951–1955	1956–1960	1961–1965	1966–1970	1971–1975	1971–1975	1976–1980
GNP	6.0	5.8	5.0	5.5	3.7	5.8	5.0
Investment				6.3	5.5		
Consumption				5.1	3.8	5.0	4.0
Agricultural Production	4.1	4.1	2.4	4.5	−0.6	3.5	5.5
Industry Production	11.3	8.7	7.0	6.8	6.0	8.0	6.5
Inputs	7.4	5.3	6.4	5.5	4.5		
Labor	4.2	1.1	2.9	3.1	1.5		
Captial	12.0	11.3	11.2	8.7	8.7		
Productivity	3.6	3.2	0.6	1.3	1.5		
Labor	6.9	7.6	4.0	3.6	4.5		
Capital	−0.6	−2.3	−3.8	−1.8	−2.4		

Sources: Greenslade, 1976, pp. 272 and 279; *Soviet Economic Plans for 1976-80*, p. 3; and *Soviet Economic Problems and Prospects*, p. 2.

of rural labor to draw into the cities for industrial uses. Those few areas of the country where excess labor still exists on farms, such as much of Central Asia and parts of the Caucasus, do not represent pools of labor available for other parts of the country, since these people are unskilled and unadaptable to work other than the menial tasks that they are already performing in their own rural areas. Therefore, much of the growth in industrial production in the future must be achieved by improvements in labor efficiency.

Water, which in the past has been looked upon pretty much as an inexhaustible resource, much as labor had been, is now becoming a scarce item. The Soviets are beginning to realize that this is as precious a commodity as many of their minerals. Therefore, much attention is now being paid to water quality and water conservation. All this requires capital investment. Much attention is now being paid to the possibilities of diverting large portions of northern rivers from flowing uselessly into the Arctic to flow usefully southward into the Steppe and desert regions of European U.S.S.R., Kazakhstan, and Central Asia. Such projects will be huge undertakings that will tie

up large amounts of capital over prolonged periods of time before any benefits can be gained.

In the past the continued growth of the gross national product has been stimulated primarily by increasing capital investments. At the same time the return on investments has generally been decreasing. (Table 8–7) The Soviets realize that this trend has to be reversed, and consequently they are attempting to pull back on capital investments, particularly in industry. To reduce investments during the tenth five-year plan they have committed themselves to completing half-done projects and expanding existing facilities rather than starting new projects. This, of course, is a one-shot gain, and in the future they will have to figure out some other way to maintain economic growth while limiting capital investment.

There is considerable reason for doubting that investment can be limited. During the 1971–1975 period, the share of GNP allocated to investment grew from 27 per cent to 29 per cent. Once the Soviets have used up their slack by completing projects long underway and expanding and modernizing existing facilities, large outlays of investments will be necessary

Table 8–8   Average Annual Rates of Growth of GNP by Sector of Origin Excluding Weapons (Factor Cost), in Per Cent

	1951–1955	1956–1960	1961–1965	1966–1970	1971–1975
Gross National Product	5.8	5.8	4.9	5.3	3.7
Industry	10.3	8.9	6.6	6.2	5.9
Ferrous Metals	11.3	7.8	7.5	5.5	4.2
Nonferrous Metals	12.9 (3)	6.8	7.7	8.2 (3)	5.0
Coal	8.4	6.0	2.8	2.0	2.3
Oil and Gas	11.6	15.4 (1)	9.9 (3)	7.8	7.1 (4)
Electric Power	13.1 (2)	11.4 (3–4)	11.5 (2)	7.9	7.0
Civilian Machinery	9.9	11.4 (3–4)	7.9	6.9	8.9 (1–2)
Chemicals	11.1	9.6	11.6 (1)	8.7 (2)	8.9 (1–2)
Forest Products	7.2	6.1	3.0	3.5	3.7
Paper and Paper Products	9.9	6.5	7.8	7.2	5.1
Construction Materials	14.7 (1)	13.9 (2)	5.2	5.4	5.1
Light Industry	11.2	7.0	2.4	8.0 (4)	2.6
Food Industry	9.6	6.9	7.0	4.7	3.7
Construction	11.0	10.4	4.5	5.8	5.6
Agriculture	4.1	4.1	2.4	4.2	−2.0
Transportation	12.2 (4)	10.9	8.7 (4)	6.7	6.3
Communications	8.1	7.0	7.1	8.9 (1)	7.2 (3)
Trade	10.4	8.5	4.9	6.5	5.0
Services:	2.4	2.2	4.7	4.2	3.6

Source: Greenslade, 1976, p. 272.
Numbers in parentheses indicate ranks.

to start new long-term projects, particularly if they go ahead with grandiose plans to reverse the flows of water in various river basins. Agriculture is absorbing more and more investment since the mid 1960s when it was changed from the exploited sector of the economy to one of the favored sectors. During the present five-year plan it is to receive more than one-fourth of total investment in the economy. The continued improvement of agriculture is necessary not only to feed people better but, from an economic standpoint, to provide more consumer goods to absorb excess wages, to neutralize consumers politically through satisfaction of their demands, and to combat the accumulation of unusable cash and consequent black market situations.

The two very poor harvests in 1972 and 1975 necessitated the import of large amounts of grain, and this, combined with record imports of foreign equipment and technology, created large hard currency deficits for the Soviets every year during the ninth five-year plan. Part of their negative trade balance was alleviated by rapidly rising prices in their two main export commodities, oil and gold, but they still find themselves trying to dig out of an international financial hole incurred during the ninth five-year plan. The Soviets apparently have decided that the key to increased productivity, and hence to continued growth of the economy with limited capital investment, is significantly improved technology. And the way to achieve this is to import technology from the West. This then faces them with the additional problem of how to promote a better balance between imports and exports during the coming years. Considerations of this will be taken up in Chapter 17 on foreign trade.

An average annual growth rate of 3.7 per cent for the Soviet gross national product during 1971–1975 looks pretty good set in world context. During that period the United States GNP grew only 0.6 per cent per year, that of West Germany 1.6 per cent, and Italy 2.1 per cent.[1]

Different sectors of the economy have grown at widely varying rates in the Soviet Union because the Soviets, controlling the economy from the center and not responding directly to market, have set arbitrary priorities. Industry has been favored over agriculture, and heavy industry, the means of production, has been favored over light industry, consumer goods. Over the long run machine construction has been the leading growth sector in industry and is projected to remain in one of the two top positions. (Table 8–9) In the mid 1970s machine building and metalworking contrib-

uted almost 28 per cent of the gross product of industry and used 40 per cent of the industrial labor. (Tables 8–10 and 8–11) The rapid expansion of the chemical industries since the mid 1950s has propelled the growth of this sector onto a par with machinery, although it still constitutes only 7 per cent of gross industrial production and 5 per cent of industrial labor. By contrast consumer goods industries generally have grown only one-third to one-half as fast as machinery and chemicals.

Whereas most industries have shown a fairly consistent growth through the years, agriculture has fluctuated up and down drastically year by year with weather conditions. Because of the two disastrous years, 1972 and 1975, during the ninth five-year plan agricultural production actually dropped absolutely by an average annual rate of 0.6 per cent as compared to the eighth five-year plan. (Table 8–7) More analyses of individual sectors and their growth rates will be elaborated in the chapters on agriculture and industry.

Table 8–9   *Production Ratios by Sectors of Industry, 1913–1975*

	1940 / 1913	1965 / 1940	1970 / 1965	1975 / 1970	1975 / 1913
All Industry	7.7	7.9	1.50	1.43	131
Electricity		12 (4)	1.54 (3)	1.41 (4)	
Fuel	6.5	4.8	1.32	1.33	54.7
Heavy Metallurgy	5.8	7	1.32	1.28	68
Chemicals	17.5 (2)	15 (3)	1.78 (1)	1.65 (2)	772 (2)
Machine Construction and Metalworking	29.7 (1)	16 (2)	1.74 (2)	1.73 (1)	1449 (1)
Wood Industries		3.7	1.31	1.29	
Construction Materials		18 (1)	1.50 (4)	1.42 (3)	
Textiles	4.7	3.0	1.42	1.26	28
Food	3.8	3.2	1.33	1.29	20.8

Source: Narkhoz SSSR, 1975, pp. 194–197.
Numbers in parentheses indicate ranks.

[1] According to C.I.A., *Soviet Economic Plans for 1976-80: A First Look*, August 1976, p. 3.

Table 8–10   Gross Product by Branch of Industry, Per Cent of Total

Branch	1965	1970	1975
Electric Power	2.8	2.9	2.8
Fuels	7.0	6.2	5.7
Chemicals and Petrochemicals	5.0	6.0	6.9
Machine Building & Metal Working	19.9	23.0	27.8
Timber, Woodworking and Paper	5.9	5.2	4.6
Construction Materials	4.1	4.1	4.1
Light Industry (Textiles, etc.)	17.0	17.0	14.9
Food Industry	24.1	21.2	19.0
Other	14.2	14.4	14.2

Source: Narkhoz SSSR, 1975, p. 197.

Table 8–11   Employment in the U.S.S.R. by Branch of Industry, 1974, in Millions of Man-Hours

Total	60,671
Machine Building and Metal Working	24,397
Light Industry (Textiles, etc.)	9,138
Food Industry	5,658
Timber, Woodworking, and Paper	5,082
Construction Materials	3,893
Chemical and Petrochemical	3,000
Ferrous Metallurgy	2,469
Coal	1,727
Non-Ferrous Metallurgy	1,364
Electric Power	1,244
Oil and Gas	489
Other	2,210

Source: Rapawy, 1976, p. 47.

THE SECOND ECONOMY

The foregoing discussion of the general economy of the U.S.S.R. is incomplete because it does not include the so-called "second economy," which in some cases is substantial. This is the economy that is carried on by individuals either legally or surreptitiously. Such transactions yield no statistics to be included in social-ist production. The CIA estimated in 1968 that 10 per cent of the Soviet gross national product originated in the legal private sector. This was down from 22 per cent in 1950. At present, the legal private sector probably accounts for a little less than 10 per cent of the Soviet gross national product.

It was estimated in 1968 that the legal private sector consisted of 76 per cent agricultural produce, 22 per cent housing construction, and 2 per cent services. The large amount in agriculture is represented primarily by production, consumption, and marketing of produce grown on private agricultural plots. It was estimated that in 1968 such activity accounted for 31 per cent of the value added in Soviet agricultural production and marketing. Much of the new housing, particularly in rural areas, is built by individuals or groups of individuals who help each other acquire materials and construct their own dwellings. It was estimated that in 1968 such activity accounted for 32 per cent of the value added in housing completions. In addition, there is a good deal of trafficking in private services by professional and skilled tradesmen in such fields as medicine, plumbing, carpentry, and so forth. In 1968 it was estimated that individual arrangements for such services amounted to 5 per cent of the value added in all services of the country. The legal private sector produces almost nothing besides consumer goods, including new residential construction and household services. Since household consumption in 1968 claimed about half the gross national product, the contribution of private value added to household consumption must have been at least 15 per cent, and in household food consumption perhaps as much as 25 per cent.

In addition to the legal private sector, there is widespread development of extralegal procedures and exchanges, without which the socialized economy would probably come to a grinding halt. The supply problem is so bad in the Soviet Union that plant managers and farm chairmen will do most anything to make sure they have the supplies on hand when they need them in order to meet the production quotas the state has set for them. It is common practice for industrial plants and farms to retain "procurers," individuals in the know who can get what you need when you need it, to assure a proper flow of supplies to your operation. These private operators are given cash or other pay for each job they do, and some of them do very well. This is all strictly illegal, but unless it is too blatant authorities usually do not crack down because they realize it is a necessary adjunct to the socialist production process.

Soviet production statistics are frequently understated, particularly in such industries as food and light consumer goods, where diversion of goods into illegal market channels is relatively simple, the State never given full accounting of materials a factory produces. On a more individual basis, there is much petty profiteering by sales clerks in state stores who receive substantial tips from preferred customers who buy goods in scarce supply that have been laid away for them under the counters.

The 1977 Soviet constitution contains some open-ended wording that may be interpreted to indicate a trend toward more private initiative in the economy. It provides for lawful "individual labor activity" based exclusively on the individual labor of citizens and members of their families in the areas of crafts and trades, agricultural service to the public, and "other forms of labor activity." Thus, it appears that the Soviet leadership recognizes the need for some such activity to accomplish substantial amounts of goods and services that are not being provided adequately by the socialist sector of the economy. They seem to be providing for a broader legalization of activities that have been common extralegal practices for many years. This might eventually provide the basis for better statistical reporting of such economic activity.[2]

REGIONAL DISTRIBUTION OF THE ECONOMY

History of Development

Like population, economic production is very unevenly distributed across the Soviet Union. This is because of widely varying resource bases as well as historical factors. The initial economy in what is now the Soviet area was agricultural and therefore its distribution was closely related to climate and soil characteristics. This set the pattern for population distribution which was concentrated in the so-called "fertile triangle" between the taiga and tundra to the north and the dry steppes and deserts to the south. This triangle of tolerable agricultural land had its broad base on the western border of the country where it stretched all the way between the Baltic and Black Seas and tapered eastward across the south-central Urals into southwestern Siberia. Within this triangle settlement developed first in the European area and then later in the Urals and Western Siberia. Thus by the time industrialization began, primarily during the reign of Peter the Great in the first quarter of the eighteenth century, the population distribution pattern was largely set with a densely populated core in the central portion of the Russian plain in eastern Europe. Since the first industries were largely labor intensive industries such as food and textiles they naturally were located in heavily populated areas where the people served both the needs for labor and market. Raw materials were of secondary importance. Much of the manufacturing began as cottage industries in which unemployed household members, particularly women, would be supplied raw materials by a jobber who would travel from door to door and then come back later to pick up the finished products. As time went on, workers became concentrated in factory buildings to reduce the local transport of goods.

Thus, the distribution of early industries corresponded closely to the distribution of population, which in turn corresponded closely to the agricultural potentials of the land. The light industries involved depended primarily on imported raw materials, either from other regions of the empire or from other countries.

[2] For a succinct, up-to-date account of the second economy, see Grossman, Gregory, "The 'Second Economy' of the USSR," *Problems of Communism*, Volume 26, No. 5, Sept.–Oct. 1977, pp. 25–40.

Linen textiles, of course, had a local flax base, as did the woolen industry to a certain extent. But cotton textiles largely depended on raw cotton supplies from such places as the United States, Egypt, and India. Bakeries and other food industries depended on the "bread basket" of the Central Chernozem Region and the Ukraine to the south for their grain and animal products.

As the metallurgical industries developed, largely during the second half of the eighteenth century during the reign of Catherine the Great, many of the heavy industries became resource oriented, but still within the populated triangle. The central Urals became the treasure house for mining. Many metallurgical plants were established near the sources of raw materials in the Urals by large estate owners in the old settled areas of European Russia, heavily subsidized by the Tsarist government which was encouraging them to man the factories of the Urals with excess serfs from the overpopulated and impoverished rural areas of central European Russia. Thus the wealth of the varied mineral resources in the Urals stimulated an early eastward movement across the Volga into the Urals region that was sustained unabated from about 1760 until around 1880 when the eastern Ukraine began to develop in earnest. During this period the Urals became the first major iron supplier of Russia, and around 1800 was actually the largest pig iron producer in the world, surpassing England and exporting pig iron to her. But as technology for iron making changed from the use of charcoal as a fuel to coke as a fuel, the last two decades of the nineteenth century brought about a shift in emphasis from the establishment of new iron and steel plants from the coal poor Urals to the coal rich eastern Ukraine where huge deposits of iron ore and manganese had also been discovered. Thus, the incipient industrial revolution that began in Russia during the 1880s and continued into the early part of the twentieth century under the able direction of finance minister Witte was accompanied by a geographical shift in the main core of heavy industry to the eastern Ukraine with its burgeoning new industries while the Urals went into a period of relative stagnation, although they did share some in the rapid industrialization of this period, particularly in the machine building industries. However, the center of machinery production became the old Central Industrial Region around Moscow which still is the most heavily populated part of the country and the primary center of textiles and other light industries. In addition, St. Petersburg had developed into the largest city in the country because of its role as capital after 1713, and in spite of a lack of resources in its immediate hinterland, it became the largest single center of machine building and diversified industries in the country. However, St. Petersburg was a single city sitting in the swamps of the Neva River semi-isolated from the rest of the populated ecumene of Russia, and the production of this single city could not match the total production of the somewhat smaller city of Moscow with its numerous intermediate-sized satellite cities around it.

By the time of the Bolshevik Revolution, then, the industry of the Russian Empire was concentrated in three major nodes plus the city of Petrograd (the name St. Petersburg had been abandoned during World War I as being too Germanic). In order of value added by manufacture and numbers of people employed, these main nodes were the Central Industrial Region around Moscow, the Donets-Dnieper area in the Eastern Ukraine, and the Urals. The industries of the Central Industrial Region and Petrograd were labor, market, and capital oriented industries that turned out a wide variety of finished goods, while the industries of the eastern Ukraine and the Urals were primarily metallurgical industries based on mineral resources. Most of the rest of the industry of the Empire was scattered about European Russia, mainly in the provincial capitals.

This concentration of industry and population in the European part of the country did not correspond with the new Soviet doctrine that all parts of the country should be developed. The almost total devastation of much of the Tsarist industry by World War I, two revolutions, and the civil war afforded the

Soviets the opportunity to start pretty much from scratch and develop the economy in the geographical pattern that they wanted. But the population and industrial expertise were concentrated in the west, and when Lenin turned much of the responsibility for industrial rehabilitation back to previous owners and plant managers with the initiation of his so-called "New Economic Policy" (NEP) in 1920, the industrial pattern was reestablished much as it had been.

By 1928 the economy of the Soviet Union had regained essentially the overall level of production of the Russian Empire in 1913, and the Soviets considered the time ripe for the country to embark more directly on the road to communism. Much discussion had taken place among the top echelons of party and government during the latter years of NEP regarding the direction that economic development should take. It was finally decided that: (1) the country should rapidly industrialize, largely at the expense of agriculture and consumer welfare, (2) economic activity should be distributed as evenly as possible throughout the entire territory, (3) development should be located so to stimulate backward nationalities, (4) production should take place close to raw materials and markets in order to minimize transport, and (5) specialized types of production should be promoted in regions that possess uniquely favorable conditions for such development: either natural resources, transport facilities, accumulations of fixed capital, skilled labor, or historic precedence.

To implement these principles, the famous five-year plans were initiated in 1928, conceived to establish complete central control, along with the collectivization of agriculture which was devised as a means for the government to control the distribution of much of the agricultural produce in order to feed the people streaming into the cities to man new industries, to accumulate capital to pay for industrialization, and provide exports to pay for needed imports. Although the equalization of living conditions between the countryside and the city was also a basic tenet of Marxian doctrine, Soviets paid only lip service to it at this time

and did not seriously consider this as one of their basic goals. It was obvious that someone was going to have to underwrite financially the industrialization drive, and the only available source was the large peasantry. They were going to have to provide both the manpower and the accumulation of capital necessary for the growth of cities and industries, as well as feed these cities and provide a surplus for export to pay for the imports which were going to be necessary because the Russians had dropped so far behind technologically that they were going to have to import considerable amounts of prototype equipment and industrial knowhow. Although the Soviets have always had a basic desire to be self sufficient, they wanted to take the opportunity while they were rapidly expanding their industrial plant to modernize, and the only way they could do this was through adaptation from the most developed capitalistic countries. Fortunately for the Soviets, the Western world at this time was plunged into the depths of an economic depression, so that most capitalist corporations were eager to sell expertise and equipment wherever they could at relatively low prices.

During the early 1930s it soon became evident that the drive for rapid industrialization of the overall economy of the U.S.S.R. was going to be the overriding principle and that all other desires would be subordinated to it. Also, because capital was scarce, it would have to be invested so that maximum returns would be realized. It immediately became evident that one could not expand the entire economy most rapidly by dispersing it into undeveloped areas. Points 2 and 4, of course, had been mutually exclusive from the outset, for all parts of the country could not be developed while transport was being minimized by building industrial plants next to raw materials and/or markets. Although the geographical dispersal principle found some support in a vaguely expressed, emotionally-based drive toward the east, it immediately became evident that if the eastern regions were to be built up, the industries of the west would first have to be strengthened because they were going to have to supply the production materials for the east.

The eastward drive was abetted by strategic considerations, since the Soviets realized that they had time and again been exposed to invasion from the west. And as Hitlerite Germany emerged during the 1930s it became quite evident to the Soviet leadership that they were soon going to have to gird for war. The most outstanding regional expression of these strategic considerations was the establishment in the early 1930s of the "Urals-Kuznetsk Combine," which, in addition to establishing the largest iron and steel plant in the country in the southern Urals, established the Kuznetsk Basin among the prongs of the Altay Mountains in southwestern Siberia as a fourth node of industrialization in the country, albeit a poor fourth compared to the leading three.

The German attack in June 1941 forced an eastward movement that the Soviet government had been unable to accomplish previously. Movable parts of industrial plants and equipment in the European part of the country were loaded onto trains and flatcars and moved bodily to the Urals and beyond. The Urals eventually produced 40 per cent of all the war industrial materials. Between 1940 and 1943 the industrial production of Western Siberia increased 3.4 times. By 1945 the Urals and the Kuznetsk Basin were producing 75 per cent of the country's pig iron, steel, and rolled steel products.

Although these hastily relocated industries remained in the eastern regions after the war, the overall importance of the industrial production in the eastern regions settled back down very quickly with the end of the war. The rehabilitation of the heavy industries in the eastern Ukraine began even before the war was over and were largely restored by 1948. By 1960 the share of the eastern regions in the iron and steel industry had decreased to 43 per cent of the country's total. However, this was still considerably higher than it had been in 1940 before the war when it accounted for only about 30 per cent of the country's iron and steel products. Although there has been a slow relative decline in the eastern regions since 1960, the Urals, Western Siberia, and Kazakhstan in 1976 still accounted for 39.6 per cent of

the pig iron of the country, and these regions plus Uzbekistan accounted for 43.4 per cent of the steel production. Thus, it might be said that up to now the war has effected about a 10–12 per cent relative increase in the share of the eastern regions in heavy metallurgical industries. However, new iron and steel plants now under construction and on the drawing boards, as well as most of the expansion in older plants, are currently in the European part of the country, so it appears that in the near future the eastern regions will suffer another relative decline in basic industries.

During the last fifteen years the trend in industrial location has been primarily a filling-in process in small and medium sized cities in previously undeveloped areas of the European part of the country. The Volga Valley in particular has industrialized and urbanized rapidly because of its position between the Central and Ural industrial nodes and its sudden exploitation of energy resources.

As can be seen in Table 8–12, the value of industrial production of the U.S.S.R. is still overwhelmingly concentrated in the European part of the country. The country's most productive single economic region, the Center, turns out more than 20 per cent of the country's total. The Ukraine as a whole, which contains three of the country's nineteen economic regions, turns out almost 19 per cent of the country's industrial production. The Urals, Northwest, and Volga regions each produce about 7–9 per cent of the total. In terms of per capita production, the old established areas in the Volgo-Vyatka, Center, Northwest, and Urals regions remain outstanding.

The European part of the country also has most of the agricultural production. (Table 9–7) Among individual economic regions, the Southwest, Center, and Donets-Dnieper regions lead in total production. But some of the smaller regions outrank them in per capita production. The old farming areas in the Central Chernozem Region and Moldavia are in the lead, as might be expected from their rich natural endowments and long established agriculture. But they are followed closely by

Table 8–12 Total and Per Capita Industrial Production (Value Added) by Economic Region, 1975

Region	Total Billion Rubles	Per Capita Rubles
U.S.S.R.	135.34	530
R.S.F.S.R.	90.69	674
Northwest	10.48	812
Center	27.42	966
Volgo-Vyatka	8.03	970
Central Chernozem	3.20	412
Volga	9.27	486
North Caucasus	5.56	368
Urals	11.57	752
Western Siberia	7.84	627
Eastern Siberia	3.90	493
Far East	3.42	520
Ukraine S.S.R.	25.33	516
Donets-Dnieper	12.23	587
Southwest	10.08	473
South	3.02	436
Baltic	5.55	691
Transcaucasus	3.25	241
Central Asia	3.65	155
Kazakh	3.15	220
Belorussia	5.88	627
Moldavia	—	—

Sources: Computed from Telepko, p. 82 and *Narkhoz SSSR,* 1975, pp. 16–21 and 199.

the Baltic and Belorussian regions which are not so richly endowed. In fact within the Baltic Region, Lithuania and Estonia outstripped all other areas in per capita value of agricultural products. Of course some of this can be explained by regional price differences paid by the state for agricultural produce which generally favor the northern areas. But scientific knowhow and practical expertise are part of the reason also. By farming more intensively and concentrating on livestock production, the Balts have compensated for limited natural endowment with personal initiative and skilled work. Of course, relative positions of regions with regard to agricultural production vary considerably from year to year because of regional differences in weather conditions. 1975 was an exceedingly hot, dry summer in many of the better agricultural areas of the Soviet Union.

Over the years there has been some tendency toward regional parity in industrial production as disproportionate capital investments have been poured into some of the less developed areas. The most highly productive areas such as the Center, Ukraine, and Northwest regions have not shown the percentage growth rates that some of the lesser developed areas have. (Table 8–13) Between 1940 and 1950 parts of the Baltic and Volga-West Siberian regions gained at the most rapid rate. Most of the growth in the Volga, Urals, and West Siberian Regions came during the early part of the period during World War II when they were the recipients of many relocated industries from the west. Estonia and Latvia showed rapid rates of gain immediately after the war when the base level of industrial production in this devastated region was low. Industrial production continued to grow rapidly in most of the Baltic Region during the 1950s and 1960s, and Belorussia and Moldavia were added to this rapidly expanding group. At the same time there was a tendency to pour more capital investments into Central Asia and parts of the Transcaucasus. In fact during the 1960s the Kirgiz Republic showed the highest percentage growth rate in the entire country. During 1970–1975 capital investments in the Baltic Region were curtailed somewhat and shifted toward some of the lesser developed parts of European Russia as well as parts of Central Asia and Eastern Siberia. Belorussia and Moldavia became the leading growth regions during that period. During the entire period, 1940–1975, the three Baltic Republics along with Moldavia and the Volga Region have shown the largest percentage gains. Of course, Moldavia is still relatively unindustrialized, and therefore its high percentage growth does not mean much in terms of absolute production. To a lesser degree this also applies to Belorussia.

Table 8–13   Industrial Production Ratios by Union Republics and Economic Regions of the U.S.S.R., 1940–1975, in Per Cent

	$\frac{1950}{1940}$	$\frac{1960}{1950}$	$\frac{1970}{1960}$	$\frac{1975}{1970}$	$\frac{1975}{1940}$
U.S.S.R.	173	303	227	142	1700
R.S.F.S.R.	175	282	215	136	1500
Northwest	129	286	194	136	980
Central	150	265	187	135	1000
Volgo-Vyatka	221	279	231	150	2100
Central Chernozem	112	390 (3)	247	145	1600
Volga	259 (5)	348	256	152	3500 (5)
North Caucasus	116	303	228	138	1100
Ural	284 (4)	264	217	144	2300
Western Siberia	323 (2)	283	227	148	3100
Eastern Siberia	196	301	256	153 (3–5)	2300
Far East	166	242	237	137	1300
Ukraine S.S.R.	115	317	228	146	1200
Donets-Dnieper	110	302	211	137	960
Southwest	135	343	257	150	1800
South	104	356	256	137	1300
Baltic Region	281	397	264	145	4200
Lithuania S.S.R.	191	539 (1)	303 (2)	148	4600 (1)
Latvia S.S.R.	303 (3)	363 (5)	248	137	3700 (4)
Estonia S.S.R.	342 (1)	336	242	139	3900 (2–3)
Transcaucasus	154	239	219	148	1200
Georgia S.S.R.	156	248	216	143	1200
Azerbaydzhan S.S.R.	139	204	195	151	830
Armenia S.S.R.	249	316	271 (5)	148	3100
Central Asia	177	243	219	149	1400
Uzbek S.S.R.	183	230	204	153 (3–5)	1300
Kirgiz S.S.R.	215	288	308 (1)	153 (3–5)	2900
Tadzhik S.S.R.	151	285	231	141	1400
Turkmen S.S.R.	143	235	201	147	1000
Kazakh S.S.R.	232	316	255	142	2700
Belorussia S.S.R.	115	370 (4)	294 (3)	162 (1)	2100
Moldavia S.S.R.	206	436 (2)	278 (4)	156 (2)	3900 (2–3)

Sources: Mazanova, M. B., *"Territorialnye proportsii narodnogo khozyaystva SSSR,* Nauka, Moscow, 1974, p. 114; *Narodnoe khozyaystvo SSSR 1922–1972,* p. 135; and *Narodnoe khozyaystvo SSSR v 1975g.,* p. 199.
Underlined names are the nineteen official Soviet economic regions for planning and statistical reporting. Numbers in parentheses indicate ranks of leading regions.

Regional Levels of Economic Development

An attempt has been made to measure the level of economic development for each region of the U.S.S.R.[3] The level of economic develop-

ment of a region has been defined as a combination of the economic potential that has been created in an area and the level of productivity that has been reached. The economic potential in turn is a combination of the means of production (plant and equipment) and people engaged in production. Therefore, Figure 8–1

[3] Kantsebovskaya and Runova.

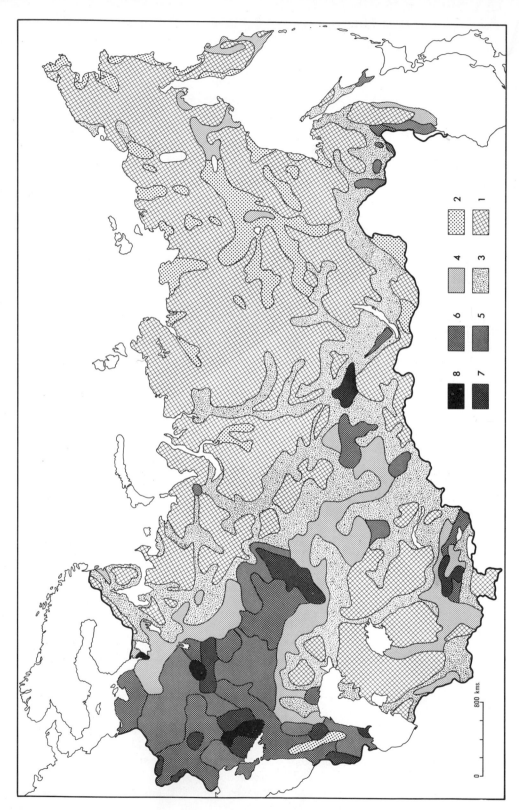

Figure 8–1   Levels of economic development, on an eight-interval scale with no absolute values assigned, from 1 (low) to 8 (high). After Kantsebovskaya and Runova, 1974, p. 570.

has been derived from a combination of the three parameters: value of plant and equipment, value of gross output, and number of population, all per unit area. Giving all parameters equal weight, the level of development of each oblast in the country was calculated and these values were grouped into eight categories, ranging from 1 (low) to 8 (high), with no absolute values given. Figure 8–1 clearly shows the high level of development in the industrial regions of the Center, the Donets-Dnieper, and Urals regions, as well as such outliers as Leningrad and Baku. It also reveals the high level of development in densely populated agricultural areas such as the Fergana Valley of Central Asia.

The most highly industrialized regions in the country, in terms of per capita industrial employment and fixed capital assets, are the Donets-Dnieper Region of the Eastern Ukraine, the Northwest, and the Urals. (Fig. 8–2) The large, sparsely settled Northwestern Region has little potential for agriculture, and therefore most of its economy is based on mining and manufacturing. The Central Region, with the greatest amount of overall industrial production and the highest per capita industrial production in the country also has an important agricultural economy and its industries are labor and market oriented and somewhat undercapitalized. (Table 8–14) The Donets-Dnieper and Urals Regions with their heavy metallurgy and associated chemical and machine building industries require more fixed capital and less labor than do the diversified industries of the Central Region. Fixed capital per capita is highest in some of the outlying regions of the country. Greatest of all is the Far East, which is capitalized 1.66 times as much as the Central Region is. This is followed by Eastern and Western Siberia and the Northwest.

During 1970–1975, the largest percentage increases in capital investments occurred in Central Asia, Western Siberia, Kazakhstan, Belorussia, and the Far East. Wide regional discrepancies between capital investment and production will be discussed in Chapter 16.

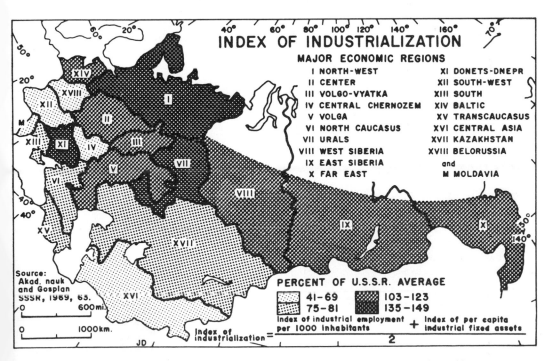

Figure 8–2   Index of industrialization, by economic regions. After Dienes, 1972, p. 439.

Table 8–14   Fixed Industrial Capital, by Region, 1975

Region	Total Billion Rubles	Per Capita Rubles	Per Cent Increase 1970–1975
U.S.S.R.	723.81	2833	135
R.S.F.S.R.	447.31	3322	133
Northwest	50.94	3947	122
Center	88.02	3102	127
Volgo-Vyatka	19.87	2401	127
Central Chernozem	17.88	2304	145
Volga	66.36	3478	120
North Caucasus	35.55	2354	134
Urals	49.03	3187	137
Western Siberia	49.77	3981	157
Eastern Siberia	36.04	4560	122
Far East	33.85	5145	147
Ukraine	119.31	2431	108
Donets-Dnieper	68.11	3270	88
Southwest	33.61	1577	144
South	17.59	2537	142
Baltic Region	21.97	2734	135
Transcaucasus	26.39	1958	110
Central Asia	39.73	1690	177
Kazakh S.S.R.	47.42	3308	155
Belorussian S.S.R.	21.68	2314	153
Moldavian S.S.R.	n.a.	n.a.	n.a.

Source: Computed from Dienes, 1972, p. 440 and *Narkhoz SSSR, Narkhoz RSFSR,* and *Narkhoz UkSSR,* 1975.

Reading List

1. Blackwell, William L., ed., *Russian Economic Development from Peter the Great to Stalin,* New Viewpoints, New York, 1974, 460 pp.
2. Block, Herbert, "Soviet Economic Power Growth — Achievements Under Handicaps," in *Soviet Economy in a New Perspective,* Joint Economic Committee, Congress of the United States, Washington, 1976, pp. 243–268.
3. Bornstein, Morris, and Fusfeld, Daniel R., eds., *The Soviet Economy: A Book of Readings,* 4th ed., Richard D. Irwin, Homewood, Illinois, 1974, 543 pp.
4. Bronson, David W., "Soviet Manpower Prospects for the 1970s," in *Prospects for Soviet Economic Growth in the 1970s,* Second Revised Edition, NATO, Directorate of Economic Affairs, Brussels, 1975, pp. 73–84.
5. Dienes, Leslie, "Investment Priorities in Soviet Regions," *Annals of the Association of American Geographers,* September 1972, pp. 437–454.
6. *The Economic Performance of the Soviet Union and Eastern Europe in 1976,* Harvard Faculty Club, Cambridge, February 7, 1977, 21 pp.
7. Greenslade, Rush V., "The Real Gross National Product of the USSR, 1950–1975," *Soviet Economy in a New Perspective,* Joint Economic Committee, Congress of the United States, Washington, 1976, pp. 269–300.
8. Gregory, Paul E., and Stuart, Robert C., *Soviet Economic Structure and Performance,* Harper and Row, New York, 1974, 478 pp.
9. Grossman, Gregory, "The Second Economy of the USSR," *Problems of Communism,* September–October 1977, pp. 25–40.
10. *Guidelines for the Development of the National Economy of the USSR for 1976–1980,* Draft prepared by the CPSU Central Committee for the 25th Congress, Moscow, 1976, 111 pp.
11. Harvey, Mose L., and Kohler, Foy D., eds., *Soviet World Outlook,* A monthly report on the view from the Kremlin on issues critical to U.S. interests. Center for advanced international studies, University of Miami. April 15, 1976 issue contains economic reports on 25th Party Congress.
12. Höhmann, Hans-Hermann, Kaser, Michael, and Thalheim, Karl C., eds., *The New Economic Systems of Eastern Europe,* University of California Press, Berkeley and Los Angeles, 1975, 585 pp.
13. Hunter, Holland, ed., *The Future of the Soviet Economy: 1978–1985,* Westview Press, Boulder, 1978, 175 pp.
14. Kantsebovskaya, I. V., and Runova, T. G., "Problems in the Methodology of measuring and mapping the Level of Economic Development of the USSR," *Soviet Geography: Review and Translation,* November 1974, pp. 566–572.
15. Nove, Alec, *The Soviet Economic System,* Allen and Unwin, Inc., 1977, 408 pp.
16. *RRC Newsletter,* Russian Research Center, Harvard University, biweekly. Initiated in 1977.
17. *Soviet Economic Problems and Prospects,* Joint

Economic Committee, Congress of the United States, Washington, August 8, 1977, 30 pp.

18. *Soviet Economic Prospects for the Seventies,* Joint Economic Committee, Congress of the United States, Washington, 1973, 776 pp.

19. *Soviet Economy in a New Perspective,* Joint Economic Committee, Congress of the United States, Washington, 1976, 821 pp.

20. Telepko, L. N., *Urovni ekonomicheskogo razvitiya rayonov SSSR* (Levels of Economic Development in the Regions of the USSR), Ekonomika, Moscow, 1971, 207 pp.

9

Agriculture

The Soviet Union has the second largest agricultural economy in the world. By Western estimates the value of total agricultural output of the Soviet Union at the present time is approximately 85 per cent that of the United States. The U.S.S.R. annually produces more than one-fourth of the world's wheat and oats, almost one-fourth of the world's barley, more than one-third of the world's rye, about 85 per cent of the world's buckwheat, almost one-third of the world's potatoes and sugar beets, more than half the world's sunflower seeds, about one-fifth the world's cotton, and about 70 per cent of the world's flax fiber. In all these crops the U.S.S.R. ranks first. It also ranks first in the production of milk and butter. But it still lags badly in the production of meat and poultry products, as well as fresh fruits and vegetables. On a per capita basis the U.S.S.R. currently produces only about two-thirds as much meat as the United States, and much of it is of poorer quality.

The agricultural program of the Soviet Union since the beginning of Khrushchev's regime in 1954 has been oriented around the goal to rectify the livestock products situation. Although much progress has been made since then, much still remains to be done. The main drawback to the livestock economy is the lack of an adequate feed base such as that in the United States which is based heavily on the high carbohydrate grain, corn, and the high protein soybean. While the United States produces about half the world's corn and two-thirds of its soybeans, the U.S.S.R. produces only small amounts of either. The main reason for the difference is the natural environment, which in some of the major agricultural regions of the United States is ideally suited for the growing of corn and soybeans while in the Soviet Union there is hardly any area that is so endowed. Corn particularly, which requires a long, hot, moist growing season, does not find ideal growing conditions anywhere and is grown only under extremely marginal moisture and heat supplies in the southern parts of the country. Although soybeans are more adaptable than corn to the droughty conditions of the main grain growing areas of the Soviet Union, so far the crop has not been introduced widely.

Thus, although the Soviet Union, and Russia before it, has long been outstanding in the total production of small grains, potatoes, and flax, which are well adapted to short cool growing seasons, and sunflowers, which are adapted to droughty conditions in the south, it conspicuously lacks the environmental resources to produce large quantities of bulky feedstuffs such as corn and soybeans. Therefore the livestock economy is being developed against handicaps. Although great strides made during the last quarter century have added more livestock products and a variety of other things to the Soviet diet, in the mid 1970s it still consisted of approximately 50 per cent grain and potato products, 23 per cent meat, fish, fats, and oils, and 27 per cent other things, while the U.S. diet consisted of only 24 per cent grain and potato products, 38 per cent meat, fish, fats, and oils, and 38 per cent a variety of other things.[1] Although the Soviets can boast that they have raised their caloric intake to approximately the level of the United States, there is still a great difference in the makeup of the two diets. In 1974 the per capita meat consumption in the U.S.S.R. was 108 pounds, while in the United States it was 251 pounds, in West Germany 174, in Czechoslovakia 173, in Hungary 146, and in Poland 137. In per capita meat consumption, then, the Soviet Union lags well behind the North American and European areas, including most of the countries of Eastern Europe.

It is a well known fact that Soviet agriculture works against the environmental hazards of high latitude and extreme continentality. As has been pointed out before, much of the territory lies north of the U.S.-Canadian border. Thus much of the territory is too cold for agriculture. Also high latitude imparts large annual swings in climatic elements due to accentuated changes from year to year in the standing waves of the upper atmosphere. The presence of high mountains along much of the southern periphery of the country, as well as more land to the south, induces drought in the warmer southern parts of the country. Since thermal and moisture zones run essentially parallel to one another, few combinations of heat and moisture exist. In the north it is cool and moist, often water-logged, and in the south it is warmer but dry, with large areas of desert in Kazakhstan and Central Asia. Even in the south, the growing season is generally limited by lack of heat, except for portions of Central Asia and the Transcaucasus. Even in those areas, hard frosts occur, so that growing of crops such as citrus is hazardous even there.

As a result of climate and soil conditions, only about 27 per cent of the territory of the

Soviet Union is considered to be agricultural land, and only about 10 per cent is arable. Almost three-fourths of the territory consists of forests, swamps, deserts, and mountains, which are largely beyond the use of agriculture. Thus, although the U.S.S.R. contains about 2.4 times the territory of the United States it normally sows only about 1.6 times as much area to crops as the United States does. And in most cases this cultivated acreage yields less heavily than it does in the United States. Therefore, the crop-growing capacities of the two countries are similar.

The Soviet Union is subject to larger annual variations in crop production than the United States is. Since so many of its crops are located in less than ideal growing conditions, on the margins of heat and moisture requirements, small deviations from normal weather can produce large variations in crop yields. While a 50 per cent deviation from normal growing-season precipitation in the United States might make the difference between poor and good crops, in the Soviet Union it might lead to variations ranging from disastrous to excellent, depending on the direction of deviation.

The natural environment is only one of the drawbacks of Soviet agriculture. The system of land management, in large unwieldy units, and lack of proper incentives have led to inefficiency and apathy in production, and the traditional lack of material inputs, such as fertilizers and machinery, has not allowed maximum realization of yields, either per area or per person. The Soviets have been trying to improve this, and during 1950–1975 they increased total agricultural output about 140 per cent while the U.S.A. was increasing only 50 per cent. But the increase in the Soviet Union was due as much to increased inputs as it was to improvement in factor productivity, while the increase in the United States was due almost entirely to increase in factor productivity. During 1950–1975 Soviet agricultural inputs increased about 60–70 per cent while U.S.A. inputs remained essentially constant.

Agriculture still occupies more than one-fourth the labor force of the Soviet Union while in the United States it now occupies less than 4

[1] Diamond, Figure 9.

per cent. The output per farm worker in the United States is about ten times as much as in the U.S.S.R. During the 1970–1973 period the U.S.S.R. required 1.8 man-hours to produce 1 centner of grain on collective farms and 1.2 man-hours on state farms. The United States required only 0.3 man-hours to produce a centner of grain. This was a considerable improvement in the ratio between the two countries over the 1960–1963 period when it took 5.9 man-hours on U.S.S.R. collective farms and 2.1 man-hours on U.S.S.R. state farms while it took only 0.4 man-hours on U.S.A. farms. Cotton shows an even greater discrepancy. In 1970–1973, 36.5 man-hours were required to produce a centner of cotton on U.S.S.R. collective farms, 29.0 man-hours on U.S.S.R. state farms, and only 3.6 man-hours on U.S.A. farms. The largest discrepancy between the two countries in labor productivity is in the livestock industry. In 1970–1973, 63.5 man-hours were required to produce a centner of beef on U.S.S.R. collective farms, 45.8 man-hours on U.S.S.R. state farms, and 3.7 man-hours on U.S.A. farms. These figures were down from 1960–1963 when it required 110.2 man-hours per centner of beef on U.S.S.R. collective farms, 64.5 on state farms, and 6.2 on U.S.A. farms.

Thus, while the U.S.S.R. is a great agricultural country, with the second highest overall output in the world and first rank in many individual crops, it suffers from a number of chronic problems. And its agriculture is characterized by an organizational scheme, settlement pattern, and production process that differs from most other countries in the world. Each of these characteristics will be taken up in turn.

ORGANIZATION

When the Bolsheviks took over the Tsarist government they set out to eliminate private landholding and organize farm labor in a way that was similar to industrial labor. This, in spite of their promise of "land to the peasants," which was one of the three main planks

initially in their political platform to appeal to large segments of the population. Throughout the NEP period, from 1921 to 1928, some desultory collectivization of farms took place, but the primary emphasis was on the rehabilitation of the economy, and quasiprivate enterprises were allowed which fostered the development of a "kulak" class of relatively wealthy individual farmers. But in late 1928 and 1929 a rapid collectivization was essentially forced on farmers as the government desperately tried to get its hands on enough farm produce to feed the burgeoning cities that were being flooded by rural immigrants into newly established industrial areas. The government also needed to manipulate prices of farm produce, which was the main consumer item that could be used to generate profits for the government to finance its industrialization drive. Also, foodstuffs were about the only products available for export to pay for imports of machinery and expertise that were needed for industrialization. Therefore, within the course of about two years, almost all the land in the Soviet Union was brought under the jurisdiction of either collective farms or state farms.

Kolkhoz and Sovkhoz

The Bolsheviks would have liked to establish state farms everywhere so that the government could own the operations and hire workers as wage earners, thereby controlling all the harvest. But in the better farming areas peasant attachments to the land through many generations had become so strong that the Bolsheviks envisioned an agrarian revolt if the state took over outright. Therefore, the collective farm (kolkhoz=collective economy) was conceived as a sort of halfway house that for the time being would achieve the control of farm produce that the government needed without completely alienating the peasants. State farms (sovkhoz=Soviet economy) initially were limited primarily to outlying areas where peasant traditions were not so strongly developed.

In the early 1930s, even on the collectives,

peasants often strongly opposed the new order and frequently slaughtered their livestock rather than turn them over to the newly formed collectives. Open revolt flared up in many places, particularly in the Ukraine, and a massive famine developed in the winter of 1933 as a result of the chaos. Things would probably have been even worse had the Russian peasantry had a strong tradition for land ownership. However, even after the 1861 emancipation of the serfs in Tsarist Russia, most peasants did not own the land they tilled. The "mir" or commune acted as the responsible entity. Therefore, the collective farm did not represent such a large departure from the past.

The collective farm has become more than a place of work. It encompasses all of life. The farm management sets aside indivisible funds each year which are used for social welfare of the farm membership. The farm has its own school, its own medical clinic, recreational hall, small store, and so forth. Many of the farm members spend most of their lives on the farm, seldom leaving it. A large farm may contain several villages where the people live and three or four centers for agricultural buildings corresponding to specific uses, such as dairying in one area, truck gardening in another, wine making in another, and so forth.

Private Plot

Another concession to the peasants was made right from the start in the form of private plots. The Soviets prefer to refer to them as personal plots since no land ownership is involved. The state owns the land in any case, on collectives as well as on state farms. But collective farmers have the perpetual right to the use of the land as long as they continue to farm it. The right to private plots was granted to collective farmers to placate some of their psychological needs for continued attachment to specific parcels of land. But over time these plots have evolved into a necessary adjunct to socialist agriculture. They have afforded the state freedom of concern for the sustenance of the peasants and have provided the means for peasants to con-

vert inedible farm produce, such as hay and coarse grains, that they have received from the collectivized sector of the farm as payment for work performed on the collective fields. The plots have provided work, and hence a financial worth in the family structure, for members of the household who do not have regular jobs in the socialized sector of the economy. This is particularly true of mothers of large families who could not possibly leave their children to take a job away from their immediate home. It is also true of many elderly people, particularly grandmothers, who often are parts of extended families in rural areas. If they did not have the wherewithall to contribute their share of income to the family through work in their own gardens, they would be nothing but burdens on the rest of the family members. In some labor surplus areas, such as the North Caucasus, private plots have become a vehicle whereby returning evacuees of World War II could be accommodated in their home regions after the land they were forced to abandon had been taken up by others.

Although the private plot originally was envisioned only as a means for personal provision of foodstuffs, it has turned out to be also a major source of cash income for individual farm families. Although the plots have never been very large, they have produced out of proportion to their sizes, because of the great amount of effort put into them. Therefore, during the growing season there is usually a surplus of vegetables, fruit, and livestock products that can be sold either in the collective farm markets of neighboring cities or to state or cooperative marketing organizations. Until the mid 1950s, cash incomes from surplus products on private plots were about the only cash incomes that many collective farmers realized from their efforts, since the state requisitioned most of the produce from the collectivized sector of agriculture.

The private plots have varied in size through time and from one region to another in the country. And the right to the use of private plots has been extended beyond collective farms to state farmers and even factory and office workers in outlying parts of cities where open land is available for subdivision into small "victory gardens." At present the size of individual plots for collective farmers is limited to one-half hectare (about 1.2 acres) and plots for state farmers and city workers are considerably smaller. Since the size of the plot usually includes the ground under which the house is sitting, as well as whatever outbuildings may exist for livestock and tools, the acutal area available for cultivation is rather small. However, with intensive hand cultivation a great many things can be produced on this size plot.

Before the Khrushchev era the aggregate territory in private plots totaled as much as six per cent of the cultivated land in the country. This was reduced to about half during the Khrushchev regime when many individuals were induced to donate their livestock to their respective collective farms. It was envisioned that soon the private plots would be phased out entirely as the production from the socialized sector of agriculture improved so rapidly that collective farmers would find it unnecessary and undesirable to work their private plots. However, the socialized production did not expand as rapidly as anticipated, and the private plot has remained very much alive. It is estimated that there are now about 50 million of them.

The present regime has taken a slightly positive attitude toward the plots as it has encouraged collective farms to make available pasture and fodder to their individual farm families to feed to their livestock on their private plots. And, as mentioned before, during recent years the use of private plots has been extended widely to city dwellers. It was reported in *Soviet Life,* March, 1978, that as of September 1, 1976, the private plots of collective and state farmers totaled 4.1 million hectares and the small holdings of factory and office workers totaled 3.9 million hectares, which in total amounted to more than 4 per cent of the farm land in the country. On this 4 per cent of agricultural land, it was reported by *Soviet News,* on 6 December 1977, that in 1975 personal plots accounted for 27 per cent of gross agricultural output of the country.

This is a considerably higher percentage than has been reported in recent years by official statistics which generally place the share of agricultural production of private plots at around 10–11 per cent. However, official statistical compilations generally are based on marketed goods and tend to ignore the great amount of garden and livestock products consumed by farmers themselves. This, of course, is a hard item to quantify, and may be considerably larger than even the 27 per cent figure indicates.

Since the subsidiary farm operation, as the Soviets call it, involves little land and much labor, it is natural that farm households grow high value products on their limited acreage. Thus, the private plot operation is organized around livestock products and certain high-yielding, high-value vegetables and fruits. Whereas little grain and no industrial crops, such as cotton or sugar beets, are grown on private plots, the plots produce 62 per cent of the country's potatoes, 27 per cent of the meat, 30 per cent of the milk, and 37 per cent of the eggs. (Table 9–1) Private plots supply the bulk of fresh meat through the mechanism of kolkhoz markets in neighboring towns where the meat can be slaughtered and sold the same day before it spoils. State stores find it virtually impossible to handle fresh meat products since

Table 9–1   Share of Private Plots in Production and Marketable Agricultural Produce, 1976, in Per Cents

	Total Production	Marketable Produce
Potatoes	62	42
Vegetables	27	10
Meat	31	16
Milk	30	6
Eggs	37	7
Wool	20	19
Grain	1	0
Cotton	0	0
Sugar Beets	0	0

Source: Soviet Life, March 1978, p. 55.

the transportation and refrigeration systems of the country are so poorly developed. The same is true of most of the fresh fruits and vegetables. State stores deal mainly in canned commodities.

Although private plots are limited individually to one cow and two calves and one sow and litter of pigs, in aggregate the plots own a very large portion of the livestock of the country. The ownership of milk cows on January 1, 1977 was reported to be 15,537,000 on collective farms, 12,784,000 on state farms, and 13,300,000 on private plots. The private plots accounted for more than three-fourths of all the goats in the country. They also accounted for a large share of the poultry, since private ownership of poultry is not limited. (Table 9–2)

MTS

Another institution that appeared on the agricultural scene with collectivization was the machine tractor station (MTS) which was a state owned and operated entity that provided heavy machine work and technological expertise to collective farms. A typical machine tractor station consisted of a crew of tractor drivers, implement operators, mechanics, agronomists, and zootechnicians who did the field work, serviced the machinery, and advised on problems of agronomy and animal husbandry for several collective farms. The collective farms were entirely dependent on the machine tractor stations because they had little machinery of their own and few trained personnel. In the early days, the crews of the machine tractor stations also included some political agitators who represented the arm of the government in the rural areas.

The machine tractor stations gradually outlived their usefulness as political arms in the countryside, and economically they became stumbling blocks to further expansion of production because their roles often conflicted with collective farm managements. Therefore, in 1958 the machine tractor stations were phased out and machinery was made available for sale to collective farms. Although repair and technical stations retained some of the functions of the machine tractor stations, over time the usefulness of these entities has decreased also as collective farms have developed their own mechanics and other trained personnel.

Amalgamation and Conversion

From the outset the collective farm and private plot were looked upon as temporary measures that were necessary gradually to condition the peasantry to complete state takeover of the agricultural operation. Through time there has been a continual process of amalgamation of smaller collective farms into fewer, larger farms and conversion of collectives to state farms. The abolishment of

Table 9–2   Livestock Numbers in the Socialized and Private Sectors of Agriculture as of January 1, 1977, in Thousand Head

	Cattle	Milk Cows	Hogs	Sheep	Goats
Collective Farms and Interfarm Complexes	47,827	15,537	28,475	50,380	477
State Farms and Other State Enterprises	39,706	13,062	22,812	64,959	776
Private Plots	22,813	13,388	11,768	24,495	4,286
Total	110,346	41,987	63,055	139,834	5,539

Source: USSR Agricultural Situation: Review of 1977 and Outlook for 1978, p. 35.

the machine tractor station in 1958 and the availability of machinery for purchase by collective farms led to a sudden mass conversion of many collectives to state farms. The poorer collective farms were unable to raise the money necessary to purchase the machinery that they needed and were induced to convert to state farms rather than to go hopelessly into debt to the state for purchase of machinery.

As a consequence of amalgamation and conversion, the number of collective farms dwindled from 235,500 in 1940 to 121,400 in 1950, 44,000 in 1960 and 36,300 in 1965. With the announcement of a new farm program in 1965, the new Brezhnev-Kosygin regime announced a moratorium on further conversions of collective farms to state farms, but statistics in Soviet yearbooks show that the process is still going on, although at a slower pace. Between 1975 and 1976 the number of collective farms decreased from 28,500 to 27,300 and the number of state farms increased from 18,100 to 19,600. Since state farms average considerably larger in area than collective farms, they now control more agricultural land than collective farms do. (Table 9–3) On the first of November, 1976, collective farms were reported to contain a total of 270,700,000 hectares of agricultural land, of which 105 million were arable. State farms controlled 772,000,900 hectares of land, of which 118,100,000 were arable. However, collective farms still involve considerably more people than state farms do.

Now that collectives have their own machinery and technical personnel and the kolkhozniki are guaranteed monthly wages and pensions, there is little difference remaining between the two farm systems except the form of management. Both systems now operate much on a cash basis, collective farmers are becoming more affluent, and more and more people living on the farms are finding part-time or even full-time jobs for cash wages in nearby towns. Farms are beginning to realize that they are becoming housing areas for nonfarm members who commute to work daily, often using farm-supplied trucks to do so. This is usually the younger generation of extended family households who do not move away from home immediately upon reaching adulthood but who disdain farm work. Farms thus find themselves providing housing and other services for people who have no connection with the farms' work.

THE AGRICULTURAL PROGRAM

Government policy toward agriculture can be divided into three phases that match the three regimes that have existed since the 1920s, although the Brezhnev-Kosygin program has been pretty much an extension of the Khrushchev program, differing more in degree than in kind. The real break in agricultural policy came with the death of Stalin in 1953.

The Stalin Program

Stalin's policy had continued that of Tsarist Russia which viewed agriculture as an exploitable part of the economy to provide revenue and personnel for urban-industrial development and export commodities. From 1929 to 1953 collective farms were burdened with impossible government norms that required a variety of different kinds of deliveries of farm produce to the state at prices that often did not cover costs of production. The kolkhozniki

Table 9–3   Average Sizes of Collective and State Farms, 1976

	Collective	State
Agricultural Land, Hectares	6600	18,100
Arable Land, Hectares	3700	5,900
Area Sown, Hectares	3600	5,700
Number of Households	486	n.a.
Tractors	39	57
Cattle	1715	1,890
Milk Cows	566	652
Swine	957	1,002
Sheep and Goats	1837	3,284

Source: Narkhoz SSSR za 60 let, pp. 270–271.

(collective farmers) received income only once a year at the end of the harvest season, often in kind, as leftover portions of crops were divided among them according to numbers of days each had worked. Generally there was little crop left to be divided, and the kolkhozniki were almost entirely dependent upon income from their private plots to eke out an existence. Farm production did not improve over the entire period, because of lack of proper investments, and in fact per capita consumption of meat and other farm products generally declined.

The Khrushchev Program

In 1953, Khrushchev, a Ukrainian, who was more knowledgeable about agriculture than Stalin was and who was much more interested in improving its situation, swung into action a multifaceted agricultural program that was conceived to show immediate rapid gains in agricultural production that would help to consolidate his political power.

Improvement of Livestock

The program was built around the central desire to increase substantially and improve the livestock products part of the diet of the Soviet people. In order to accomplish this, an adequate feed base had to be established. Khrushchev, who had visited Iowa, was impressed with the yields of grain and green matter that could be derived from corn. Although the Soviet Union does not contain any region that is ideally suited to the growth of corn, it was perceived that even under less than ideal conditions corn could produce more fodder for livestock than most other crops.

Introduction of Corn

Therefore, the Soviet government set out to reorder the crop complex in European U.S.S.R. by establishing corn as a major crop. In short order during the mid 1950s the Soviets planted about 26,000,000 hectares of corn. Since corn requires as much heat and moisture

as possible and good soils, it took over some of the better wheat areas of the Ukraine and North Caucasus regions.

The Virgin Lands

Not wanting to suffer a decline in wheat production, the Khrushchev government initiated the famous Virgin Lands program in northern Kazakhstan and adjacent regions. In this semiarid region vegetated only by grasses, the land could be plowed, sown, and harvested in one year. From 1954 to 1958 over 40 million hectares (100 million acres) of new land (more than the arable land of France, West Germany, and the United Kingdom combined) were brought under cultivation, primarily for wheat growing. By 1961, additional scattered areas, some as far south as the mountain foothills of Central Asia and as far east as Maritime Kray, expanded the new lands to 47,000,000 hectares, equal to 30 per cent of total cultivated land in the U.S.S.R. in 1953. Although much of this new territory was quite dry, with annual precipitation between eight and sixteen inches, and therefore average yields could be expected to be low, total production of wheat was maintained, and in fact increased, by the cultivation of such large areas.

The new lands also helped to stabilize some of the wide yearly fluctuations in grain production, since they were removed from the old wheat lands of southern European U.S.S.R. by distance equal to about one-half wave length of the standing waves of the upper atmosphere which meant that under normal circumstances they could expect weather essentially opposite that in the old wheat growing areas. In other words, when drought occurs in the Ukraine, northern Kazakhstan can normally expect above average precipitation. It was this complementary nature of the weather of the two grain areas that tipped the balance in favor of going ahead with the Virgin Lands program. During the quarter century that the Virgin Lands have been under production, this theory has been borne out quite well. Particularly in 1972, when the European part of the country experienced the worst drought it has ever had, the Virgin Lands produced their best crop. Only in 1975 have the two areas experienced some drought simultaneously, causing a drastic decline for that one year in total grain production of the country.

Although many problems have arisen with regard to wheat growing in the Virgin Lands, and yields have tended to be somewhat lower than had been hoped for, the Virgin Lands project cannot be judged separately but must be evaluated as an integral part of the overall agricultural program which was a necessary adjunct to the introduction of corn as a fodder base for livestock in European Russia. Under these considerations it would have to be concluded that the Virgin Lands program has been a success. True, in the initial stages, both wheat planting in the Virgin Lands and corn planting in southern European U.S.S.R. were overextended. Since then sowings have shrunken somewhat in area, yields have improved, and the agriculture in most areas has been diversified somewhat by the rotation of other crops into the complex and the establishment of livestock industries. The villages of northern Kazakhstan today have a much more permanent look to them than the initial tent cities of the Komsomol (young communist league) who pioneered the area in the mid 1950s.

Other Reforms

In addition to the physical addition of crops and land, the Khrushchev program introduced economic reforms conceived to provide more physical inputs to agriculture and to improve the lot of the peasants to give them more incentive to work for higher yields. A crash program to provide greatly increased quantities of mineral fertilizers to agriculture was attached to a general program of expansion of the chemical industries of the country, and the machine building industries were exhorted to provide many more tractors and farm implements to the farming effort. The machine tractor stations eventually were abolished, which not only gave collective farms control over their own machinery, but also eliminated the first order payment that collective farms

had to make to the state for work and services rendered by the machine tractor stations. Other state procurements were consolidated into one main sale and prices were raised significantly so that most farms began to make profits which in part filtered down to individual collective farmers. Some land amelioration, primarily irrigation and drainage, was undertaken.

Consequences

Very favorable weather in 1958 produced a bumper crop that allowed agricultural production that year to register a value 50 per cent higher than it had been in 1953 when Khrushchev's program began. This caused Khrushchev to become so ebullient that he decided agriculture had taken off on its own and he could afford to draw back on certain inputs, such as continued price rises for agricultural commodities and state investments in the chemical industry. He bagan to divert investment funds from the agricultural budget to the chemical industries on the basis that the chemical industries were providing the mineral fertilizers for agriculture. These measures led to a leveling off of agricultural growth, and the drought year of 1963 plunged crop production. Thus, it was agriculture, which during the first four years of his regime brought Khrushchev so much favorable attention, that eventually contributed to his downfall.

Brezhnev-Kosygin Program

Soon after the demise of Khrushchev, the new Brezhnev-Kosygin regime in March 1965 announced a new program for agriculture that essentially picked up the pieces where Khrushchev had failed and applied the same measures more effectively. Prices paid for crops were raised again to levels that allowed most farms to make profits. Guaranteed wages were instituted for collective farmers and monthly payments in cash and kind instead of once-per-year payments primarily in kind. Many farm debts to the state for purchases of machinery and fertilizers were liquidated and more credit was made available to farms for further purchases. The fertilizer industry was greatly expanded as was the farm implement industry. More and more of the total state budget was allotted to agricultural investment. In 1977 it was reported that 27 per cent of the total investment capital of the country was earmarked for agriculture. In view of the fact that agriculture was only providing about 20 per cent of the gross national product of the country, it is obvious that agriculture is now receiving more than its share of investment money.

Prices for agricultural produce rose 75 per cent between 1959 and 1974 while those for industrial goods increased only 10 per cent. At the official exchange rate, in 1974 the average state procurement cost per hundred-weight of cattle was $99.00 and per hundred-weight of swine $92.00. These were nearly three times the average prices paid to U.S. farmers in 1974. Since state retail prices have remained essentially constant in the Soviet Union, it is obvious that the Soviet government is sustaining one of the highest subsidies to agriculture anywhere in the world.

The 1965 decree removed restrictions over private subsidiary plots, numbers of private livestock were increased, and feed from the collective sector was made available to private livestock holders. In 1966 another decree established pensions for collective farmers. Land amelioration, particularly irrigation and drainage, have been stepped up, and much more electricity has been made available to farms. Since 1953 almost all peasant households have been electrified.

The Nonchernozem Zone

One of the main thrusts of the current long-term plan which began in 1976 is the revamping of agriculture and peasant life in the so-called "Nonchernozem Zone of European Russia." This region which extends throughout northern European Russia from the chernozem zone to the Arctic is a cool, humid region that ususally does not suffer from drought. It holds considerable potential for

improved production with land melioration and heavy use of mineral fertilizers which can be more effective here than in the dry south where under drought conditions they might actually be harmful to crops. The southern half of this region is an old settled part of Russia which presently contains almost a quarter of the population of the country and 29 per cent of its urban dwellers. Hence it affords the opportunity of high prices for produce supplied to large urban markets.

Land reclamation is to be carried out on a large scale, which will consist primarily of the drainage of many areas, bulldozing of copses and old fence lines, and the consolidation of small fields into large plots adaptable to mechanized farming. In addition, the living conditions of the people are to be improved considerably through the construction of roads, consolidation of small villages into larger ones that can afford schools, medical facilities, and recreational amenities, and the construction of new housing which will include centralized utilities.

It is hoped that among other things the improvement of agriculture in this humid area will further stabilize annual swings in production for the country as a whole. In the past the Soviet Union has been typified by extreme variations in crop production because so much of the cultivated land lies in marginal climatic belts where relatively small variations in moisture or heat supply or wintering conditions can cause large variations in crop yields. The nonchernozem zone with its more abundant moisture supply and better winter snow cover does not respond so critically to year-to-year changes in weather.[2]

Other Measures

Two processes that have been going on with increasing intensity in recent years have been the establishment of specialized, urban-oriented state farms in the vicinity of most metropolitan areas of the country and the

[2] For a detailed analysis of the program for the nonchernozem zone, see Lydolph, "The Agricultural Potential for the Nonchernozem Zone."

establishment of interfarm cooperatives to carry out land melioration schemes, construction projects, and marketing operations that are beyond the scope of individual collective farms. Many interfarm agencies have set up food processing plants so that farms can control their production all the way to the market. This has improved the efficiency and quality of food production and provided extra work for collective farmers and their families who are not fully employed by the collective farm operation.

The urban-oriented state farms are generally specialized in one aspect of the livestock industry, such as dairying, hog raising, or poultry and egg producing. Such establishments operate at tremendous scales of hundreds of thousands of animals per year. They have newly constructed farm buildings adapted to their specialized operation, with mechanized feeding facilities, and so forth. Such farms are greatly improving the quantity and quality of livestock products in the Soviet diet, but they are making larger and larger demands on the feed base, particularly on grains, which further increases the need for importation of feedstuffs that cannot be produced domestically.

GROWTH OF AGRICULTURAL INPUTS AND OUTPUTS

The major physical inputs to agriculture are land melioration, fertilizers, equipment, buildings, and roads. The main forms of melioration are irrigation and drainage. As can be seen in Table 9–4, irrigation and drainage of land has been taking place at a rapid pace. Although it is difficult to ascertain net increases, particularly in irrigation, where significant acreages constantly are going out of use because of secondary salinization, according to the statistical yearbooks from the Soviet Union the areas added to irrigated and drained land have been very impressive and increasing through time. During the 1971–1975 plan period, 920,000 hectares of additional land were irrigated each year and 882,000 hectares were drained.

Irrigation

In 1976 a total of 15,078,700 hectares of land were being irrigated, as contrasted with 8,318,000 in 1950. This was about three-fourths as much as in the United States. 11,891,900 hectares of this irrigated land were under cultivation, 1,069,800 hectares were in orchards, vineyards, and other types of perennial crops, and the rest was in natural meadows used for haying and pastures.

The 11,891,900 hectares of irrigated land under cultivation represented only about 5.5 per cent of all the sown area in the country, but it contributed more than 20 per cent of the agricultural output of the country. Of this,

Table 9–4   Improvements of Cropland, Annual Averages

	1966–1970	1971–1975	1976–1980 Plan
Addition of Irrigated Land (Hectares)	360,000	920,000	930,000
Addition of Drained Land (Hectares)	782,000	882,000	940,000
Area Limed (Hectares)	4,500,000	6,000,000	8–10 million
Mineral Fertilizer Deliveries to Agriculture (Million Tons of Standard Units)	37.0	61.3	93.4

Source: Carey, p. 587.

3,026,900 hectares were in grain, 3,268,500 hectares in technical crops, and 4,642,400 in fodder crops. Whereas most of the irrigation used to be applied only to technical crops, now much is applied to grain and fodder crops as well. Also, there is a gradual shift to sprinkler irrigation which is more efficient than flooding or furrow irrigation.

All cotton and rice are irrigated, and an increasing amount of vegetables and fruits. Grain crops occupy a significant percentage of total irrigated area, but other than rice production irrigated land accounts for only about 5.2 per cent of total grain acreage. Likewise, fodder crops cover a sizeable portion of irrigated area, but this amounts to only about 5.7 per cent of the fodder lands of the country. About 3.4 per cent of all irrigated lands are found in private plots, a percentage which is commensurate with the percentage of total cultivated area occupied by private plots.

As can be seen in Figure 9–1, most of the irrigated land is in Central Asia and adjacent southern Kazakhstan, the eastern Transcaucasus, the North Caucasus, and the southern Ukraine. Secondary areas are scattered through much of the steppe zone of European U.S.S.R. and the southern Urals, northeastern Kazakhstan, and parts of southern Siberia and the Far East, as well as around Yakutsk in the middle Lena River Valley. Traditionally the Uzbek Republic of Central Asia has had the bulk of irrigated land and adjacent republics in Central Asia and Kazakhstan, as well as Azerbaydzhan in the eastern Transcaucasus have been next in importance. But recently the Russian Republic has shot into the lead, as the North Caucasus and the lower Volga Region have come under intensive irrigation, and other irrigation projects of lesser importance have been scattered widely throughout the drier parts of the republic. Also, in recent years the Ukrainian Republic has become prominent. A major share of investment for irrigation during the current five-year plan, 1976–1980, is for improvement of facilities in the dry grain areas of the middle and lower Volga Valley, North Caucasus, southern Ukraine, and Kazakhstan. A major attempt will be made to acclimatize

soybeans under irrigation to parts of the southern Ukraine, Kazakhstan, and Central Asia. Plans are to expand significantly the irrigation of vegetables and potatoes on truck farms around large cities.

Major Irrigation Projects

The Kara-Kum Canal   The Kara-Kum Canal, different phases of which have been under construction since 1953, is the largest single irrigation project in the country. By 1976 the canal stretched 850 kilometers westward from Kerki on the upper Amu Darya to about 45 kilometers northwest of Ashkhabad. It is supposed to be extended to the Caspian coast at Krasnovodsk by 1985, and a branch is to run southward to the Atrek River on the border with Iran. At that time the total length of the canal will be about 1500 kilometers. The canal has an average width of about 100 meters and a depth of 5 meters with a drawing capacity of about 400 cubic meters per second (12.6 cubic kilometers per year). It augments the water supply of the old Merv Oasis around the present city of Mary on the Murgab River and the Tedzhen Oasis on the Tedzhen River, as well as the smaller irrigated district around Ashkhabad, all in the southern part of the Turkmen Republic. In 1975 this system irrigated about 500,000 hectares of land. It is planned that by 1980 water withdrawal into this system from the Amu Darya will reach about 700 cubic meters per second, and there will be further expansions in the future. Ultimately it is planned to withdraw about 70 per cent of the Amu Darya's average annual flow into this system, which at that time would be enough to irrigate about 1.5 million hectares of land.

The Fergana Valley   The Fergana Valley has been the most important irrigated cotton region of the U.S.S.R. Ancient Moslem centers carried on irrigation here deriving water from small streams forming alluvial fans at the base of the mountains, particularly along the southern fringes of the valley. The Soviets have greatly expanded the irrigation in this region,

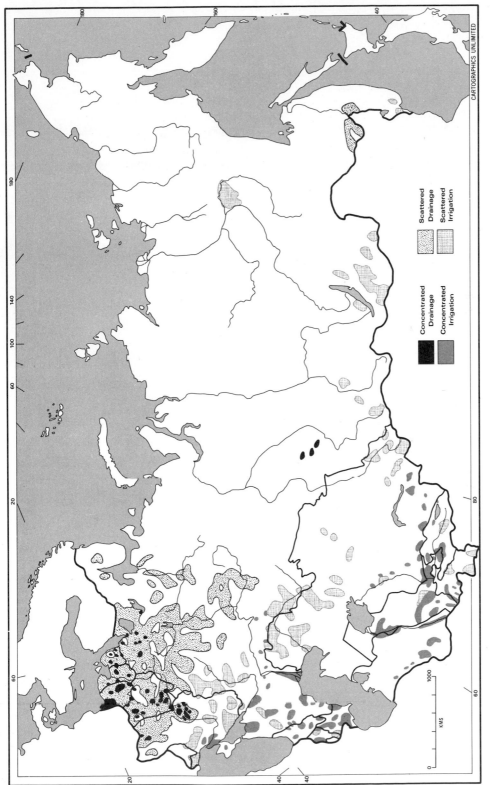

Figure 9–1   Areas of irrigation and drainage. Adapted from C.I.A., U.S.S.R. Agriculture Atlas, p. 22.

Figure 9–2 Irrigation ditch and vineyard, Rostov Oblast. Photo by Irving Cutler.

beginning with the construction of the Great Fergana Canal in the 1930s and continuing with the North Fergana Canal, the Central Fergana (Andizhan) Canal, and the Great Namangan Canal which is now being completed. Approximately one million hectares are now under irrigation in the Fergana Valley.

Khiva The Khiva region near the mouth of the Amu Darya is another area of important ancient irrigation which has been enhanced in recent years by new construction projects.

The Zeravshan Valley The Zeravshan Valley, containing the famous old cities of Samarkand and Bukhara, was one of the main valleys developed for irrigation agriculture before the Soviet period. The Soviets have greatly expanded the irrigated land in this region, and in recent years have added to the water of the Zeravshan River by building a major canal from the Amu Darya just above

Chardzhou to the Zeravshan near Bukhara. On the other hand, another recently built canal system is taking some of the Zeravshan water southward to the Karshi Steppe to augment the water of the small Kashka Darya.

The Karshi Steppe The Karshi Steppe irrigation system has been under construction since 1964. It is based on the limited water resources of the Kashka Darya augmented by water from the Amu Darya and the Zeravshan. Its primary source is now the Amu Darya where it draws off about 200 cubic meters per second from a point opposite the headworks of the Kara Kum Canal. The irrigated area in this region is now around 160,000 hectares. Apparently it can be extended to nearly one million hectares if enough water is found.

The Golodnaya Steppe The Golodnaya (Hungry) Steppe is an ancient lake bed south of Tashkent and west of the Fergana Valley which has undergone a major expansion of irrigated cotton growing since the completion of the Farkhad Dam on the Syr Darya in 1948. Water for this project was augmented in 1957 by the Kayrak-Kum Project that formed a reservoir on the Syr Darya in the western approaches to the Fergana Basin which has become known as the Tadzhik Sea. Then in 1964 a large reservoir was created by the Chardara Dam on the Syr Darya downstream from the Hungry Steppe. Apparently 500,000 or more hectares are now under irrigation in the Steppe, and ultimately there may be nearly one million hectares.

Other Irrigation Projects in Central Asia and Kazakhstan Many other significant areas of irrigated agriculture exist in Central Asia and adjacent southern Kazakhstan. These include such areas as the plateau country in southwestern Tadzhik Republic along the Vakhsh River and other headwaters of the Amu Darya, the Chu River Valley on the northern slopes of the Tyan Shans around the city of Frunze, the Taldy-Kurgan area in southeastern Kazakhstan, the lower Syr Darya region in south-central Kazakhstan, and many other minor areas too numerous to mention.[3]

Transcaucasus A great deal of land is irrigated in the dry Kura Lowland of the eastern Transcaucasus, particularly associated with the Mingechaur Reservoir which was constructed on the middle Kura River during 1950–1955. The Araks River Valley on the border of Turkey and Iran, on a much smaller scale, has irrigation agriculture similar to the Kura Valley. This narrow belt of agriculture expands northwestward into the basin around Yerevan, the capital of the Armenian Republic. Other minor irrigation systems lie along smaller streams in eastern Georgia.[4]

The North Caucasus The North Caucasus Economic Region has undergone intense irrigation development since World War II.

Major zones have been created along the lower Don River in association with the Tsimlyansk Dam completed in 1952, and along the Kuban, Sulak, and Terek Rivers flowing down the north slopes of the Great Caucasus Mountains westward to the Sea of Azov and eastward to the Caspian. About 1.5 million hectares of land was under irrigation in this region during the mid 1970s.[5]

Ukraine Irrigation in the southern Ukraine has grown from about 150,000 hectares in 1950 to about 1,500,000 hectares by the mid 1970s. Most of this expansion has been associated with the Kakhovka Reservoir on the lower Dnieper River. The North Crimean Canal which was completed in 1975 carries water 400 kilometers southeastward across the Perekop Isthmus onto the Crimean Peninsula and eastward all the way to the city of Kerch. This canal averages 50–80 meters in width, 1.7–5.8 meters in depth, and has a carrying capacity of 380 cubic meters per second. When fully utilized it can irrigate 660,000 hectares of land. Another system carrying Kakhovka water is the so called Kakhovka system whose main canal runs eastward from the reservoir 125 kilometers to the Azov Sea. The system is designed to withdraw 550 cubic meters per second and irrigate 800,000 hectares of land. Another irrigation system that is planned for the lower Dnieper will have a capacity of 365,000 hectares of irrigated land.[6]

The Volga Valley During the last two decades irrigation has been expanding in the zone east of the middle and lower Volga River from Kuybyshev southward to the Caspian. The irrigated area increased from around 174,000 hectares in 1965 to 900,000 in 1975. It is planned that this will be expanded to 1,900,000 hectares by 1980. Much of the irrigation is being applied to spring wheat fields. Three major canals have been designated to supply this area. The Saratov Canal, begun in

[3] For a more detailed account of the irrigated districts of Central Asia, see Lydolph, Paul E., *Geography of the USSR,* third edition, Wiley, 1977, pp. 312–320.
[4] For more details, see Lydolph, *ibid.,* pp. 272–276.

[5] For a map showing the irrigated districts of the North Caucasus, see Lydolph, *ibid.,* p. 246.
[6] For a map of the irrigation districts in the Ukraine, see Lydolph, *ibid.,* p. 102.

Figure 9–3   Water Buffalo in pond west of Baku, Azerbaydzhan. They are still used as draft animals in this part of the Transcaucasus. Photo by Irving Cutler.

1972, and completed in 1974, leaves the Saratov Reservoir slightly above the city of Balakovo and archs southeastward for 130 kilometers in the center of Saratov Oblast. This irrigates about 140,000 hectares of land. Farther north the Kuybyshev Canal takes off from the central portion of the Saratov Reservoir and ultimately will stretch 470 kilometers to the east, irrigating 200,000 hectares of land. By 1975, about 50 kilometers of the canal had been constructed.

A much larger project involves the Volga-Ural Canal on which construction started in 1975. It is to run 474 kilometers eastward to the Ural River and will provide a source of water for feeder canals running southward down the gentle slope of the North Caspian Lowland. The project is being constructed in three stages, with the first stage scheduled to irrigate about 120,000 hectares of land. It is

thought that eventually about two million hectares of land can be irrigated in this lowland if enough water is supplied to the Volga by diversion projects from the northern part of European Russia.[7]

Drainage

In 1976 the U.S.S.R. had 14,413,100 hectares of land under drainage. Of this, 5,581,800 hectares were cultivated, 4,640,300 hectares were in natural meadows and pastures, 46,300 hectares in orchards and other perennial crops, and 143,900 in private plots.

[7] For an excellent, up-to-date summary of current irrigation developments, see Philip P. Micklin, "Irrigation Development in the USSR During the Tenth Five Year Plan (1976–1980)," *Soviet Geography: Review and Translation,* January 1978, pp. 1–24.

Figure 9–4   Kolkhoz market in Khiva, Central Asia. Photo by Edward Furstenberg.

The sown area under drainage represented about 2.5 per cent of the total sown area of the country. Of the drained area being cultivated, about half was in grains and half in fodder crops. Small amounts were in technical crops, potatoes, vegetables, and melons.

Drainage is concentrated in the northwestern part of the country, particularly Kaliningrad Oblast, the Baltic Republics, and Belorussia, as well as adjacent parts of the R.S.F.S.R. and Ukraine. (Fig. 9–1) Minor areas occur in the southern part of the Soviet Far East, particularly in the Jewish Autonomous Oblast and around Khabarovsk.

Mineral Fertilizers

The expansion of mineral fertilizer production has been taking place at a very rapid rate. (Table 9–4) During the 1966–1970 five-year plan, an annual average of 37 million tons of mineral fertilizers were delivered to agriculture. During the 1971–1975 plan, this almost doubled to an annual average of 61.3 million tons. The plan for 1976–1980 calls for 93.4 million tons annual average. In 1977, 77 million tons of mineral fertilizer were delivered to agriculture. The plan for 1980 is 115 million tons, excluding feed additives. In the mid 1970s the Soviet Union was consuming about one-sixth of the world's supply of mineral fertilizers. Its average application rate per cultivated hectare was approximately the same as that of the United States and about twice as much as the world average. However, it was still less than half as much as applications in the developed countries of Western Europe.

Applications, of course, vary with crop and with region. During 1977 on the average the Soviet Union applied 469 kilograms per hectare to sugar beets, 395 kilograms per hectare to cotton, 274 kilograms to potatoes, 135 kilograms to grain corn, and 48 kilograms to other grains. Essentially all sugar beet and cotton land was fertilized in 1977, 94 per cent of the potato land, 89 per cent of the corn land, and 52 per cent of the other grains. Of course, many of the small grains, particularly wheat, are grown in the drier southern portions of the country which do not need so much mineral fertilizers. In fact, in some instances the application of fertilizer might be counterproductive. The cotton grown in this dry region is, of course, all irrigated, so large applications of fertilizer are needed. Grain crops receive much more fertilizer in the cool humid northwestern parts of the country than in the drier south. Mineral fertilizer applications to small grains vary from 230 kilograms of nutrients per hectare in Belorussia to only 7 kilograms in Kazakhstan.

Liming of agricultural soils in the more humid northern parts of the country is also being done on an extensive scale. During 1971–1975 an average of 6 million hectares was limed annually. (Table 9–4) The 1976–1980 plan calls for an annual average of 8–10 million hectares. Much of this program is part of the program to upgrade the nonchernozem zone of European Russia and signifies the intentions to expand greatly the area in legumes, primarily clover and alfalfa, to increase the availability of high protein feed for livestock. (The Soviets are also attempting to increase their high protein feed by acclimating soybeans in the southern Ukraine and Central Asia, as was mentioned earlier.)

Herbicides and Pesticides

The Soviet Union is still very lacking in herbicides and pesticides. After discussing large-scale land melioration projects, fertilizers, machinery, and the like, agronomists will usually come down to the fact that at the present time the greatest problem in agriculture is weeds. The Soviets are trying to overcome these deficits, and are importing significant quantities of herbicides and pesticides. Domestic production is planned to be 615,000

tons in 1980, which is up from 456,000 in 1976.

Machinery

Mechanization still remains low in spite of the fact the Soviet Union now produces more tractors and some other kinds of farm implements than any other country in the world. As of 1974, the Soviet Union still had only about half as many farm tractors as the United States and less than half as many farm trucks. One of the problems entailed in building up the machinery park is the high scrapping rate in the Soviet Union caused by poor quality production and lack of spare parts. Every year the Soviets scrap 12 to 13 per cent of their tractor fleet, suggesting that the average life expectancy for a Soviet tractor is about 8 years. Since 1975 the agricultural sector has been receiving more than 350,000 new tractors annually, but around 300,000 tractors are discarded each year. This scrapping rate has not decreased with time. (Table 9–5)

The Soviets have estimated that at any time one-fourth of the farm machinery is under repair and that 20 per cent of the usable equipment stands idle during harvest for "technical" reasons. The chronic deficit of spare parts has led to larger than necessary machine fleets on farms to ensure that adequate numbers will be in working order and to the cannibalization of machinery in order to get needed parts for identical machines. Selkhoztekhnika (Agricultural Equipment and Supply Organization) performs only about 18 per cent of all repair work for collective and state farms. The remainder of the repair is done by poorly equipped, poorly trained mechanics on the farms themselves. Government policy has exacerbated the situation by subsidizing purchase of new machines and leveling surcharges on spare parts, so that it turns out a farm can optimize its expenditures better by buying new machinery than by repairing old.

Poor roads in rural areas have led to higher scrapping rates also, especially among trucks. During the spring thaw the mud roads in the

Table 9–5 Inventories, Deliveries, and Scrapping Rates of Tractors, Farm Trucks, and Grain Combines, 1966–1977, in Thousands

	Tractors			Farm Trucks		Grain Combines		
	Inven-tories	Deliv-eries	Scrapping Rate	Inven-tories	Deliv-eries	Inven-tories	Deliv-eries	Scrapping Rate
1966–1970 ave.	1748	293	12.6%	1061	144	558	94	13.8%
1971–1975 ave.	2120	333	12.3%	1230	220	650	90	12.3%
1976	2336	369	13.0%	1396	269	680	98	12.1%
1977	2402	364	12.8%	1442	265	685	101	14.1%

Source: USSR Agricultural Situation: Review of 1977 and Outlook for 1978, pp. 24–25.

rural areas are generally impassable to trucks and can be negotiated only by tractors. Tractors and trailers perform much of the work on farms in the Soviet Union that would be done by pickup trucks in the United States.

Roads

Presently there is a long-range program for providing every village with at least one hard-surfaced connection to a main road network, but this is far from being realized. The responsibility for the construction of farm roads lies with farm managements. Since farms are mainly concerned with meeting production quotas, they cannot be expected to spend any more than the bare minimum of expense and time on roads. Consequently, although roads leading to large farms are usually adequate, road systems within farms are barely passable. Russian specialists have estimated that two-thirds of agricultural labor time is spent on transport. More than half of total agricultural investment is in transport. Thus, it is obvious that the biggest single drag on the expansion of marketable farm produce is the transport system.

Buildings

Another major problem is storage space. Large quantities of grain and other produce are lost each harvest season because of lack of adequate storage. The same is true of mineral fertilizers. One can frequently see piles of wheat on the ground or on the drier highways exposed to the elements waiting to be shipped to consuming areas. Since late summer and fall is the rainiest part of the year in much of the Soviet Union, the grain often starts to sprout and is therefore spoiled. One can also see stretches of mineral fertilizers exposed to the elements piled along railroad sidings waiting for shipment to farms where it can be spread on the fields. Under such conditions the minerals in the fertilizers often congeal into a hard rock consistency which can only be broken apart by blasting. Then it is very difficult to spread on the fields with any kind of mechanized equipment. Major outlays of investment capital are now being made for the construction of grain elevators and general warehousing for fertilizers and other farm produce, but the Soviets have a long way to go.

Results

As a result of the above measures, according to Soviet statistics the value of agricultural output, in constant prices of 1973 rubles, increased from 51 billion rubles in 1953 to 117.4 billion rubles in 1976, which was somewhat lower than the peak year of 1973 with 122 billion rubles. Although it is difficult to test the validity of such agglomerated figures, it cannot be denied that during the last quarter century the Soviet leadership has been generously supporting agriculture and in return agriculture has responded spectacularly. Although crop production has fluctuated annually with the weather, there has been a constant rapid increase in the running mean. This is well illustrated by Figure 9-5 which shows total grain production by year.

All the improvement in crop production since 1960 has been due to increased yields on essentially constant acreage. And almost all the increase in total farm output has been in the socialized sector. The private sector has remained fairly constant, fluctuating some year-by-year. Collective farmers are receiving more income each year, and if one includes their personal foodstuffs and cash incomes from their private plots as well as incomes from part-time work off the farm it is probable that now collective farmers are making wages commensurate with state farmers or even industrial workers. This might lead eventually

to the reduction of the role of the private plot. It is already evident that many young people on farms disdain working private plots and perfer to buy their food in state stores or kolkhoz markets.

CROP AND LIVESTOCK PRODUCTION AND DISTRIBUTION

General

The Soviet Union has been sowing about 218,000,000 hectares of land in recent years which is a little over 10 per cent of the total territory of the country and about 50 per cent more than the sown land in the United States. Grain takes up more than half of this, 128 million hectares, of which wheat takes up about 60 million and barley about 34 million. (Table 9-6) By far the greater area is occupied by spring wheat and barley. Other important crops are oats, rye, corn, millet, buckwheat, and rice, in order of acreage occupied. Fodder crops occupied over 66 million hectares, of which 25 million were in perennial hay crops, 16.6 million in annual hay crops, 18.1 million in corn for silage and green fodder, and 1.9 million in root crops used for livestock feed, primarily potatoes and sugar beets. 14.6 million hectares were in so-called technical crops, of which 4.5 million were in sunflowers, 3.7 million in sugar beets, 3 million in cotton, and 1.2 million in flax for fiber. Potatoes occupied 7.1 million hectares, vegetables 1.6, and 11.7 million hectares were in clean fallow.

The small grains, especially wheat, have been the mainstay of Soviet agriculture and Russian agriculture before the Soviet Period. As has been pointed out before, these crops are more adapted to the limited climatic resources that the Soviet Union affords than are such heavily growing crops as corn or soybeans. Most of the crop land in the Soviet Union is wedged into the central belt of the country between the cold north and the dry south. (Fig. 9-6) And, if anything, the crops are pushed beyond normal limits into the dry lands of the

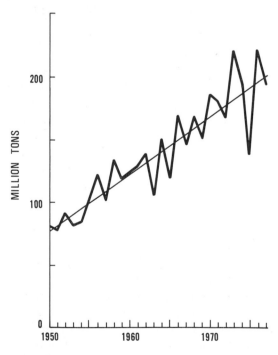

Figure 9-5 Annual fluctuations and running mean growth in grain production. Data from various issues of Narkhoz SSSR.

Table 9–6 Areas Sown to Individual Crops, 1976, in Millions of Hectares

Total Sown Areas	217.9
Grain Crops	127.8
Winter Grains	27.5
Wheat	17.3
Rye	9.0
Barley	1.2
Spring Grains	100.3
Wheat	42.2
Grain Corn	3.3
Barley	33.1
Oats	11.3
Millet	3.0
Buckwheat	1.4
Rice	0.5
Pulses	5.2
Technical Crops	14.6
Cotton	2.95
Sugar Beets	3.75
Flax	1.21
Hemp	0.14
Oil Seeds	5.91
Sunflowers	4.53
Potatoes, Vegetables, and Melons	9.2
Potatoes	7.1
Vegetables	1.6
Fodder Crops	66.3
Perennial Hay	25.1
Annual Hay	16.6
Corn for Silage and Green Chop	18.1
Root Crops and Pumpkins	1.9
Clean Fallow	11.7

Source: Narkhoz SSSR za 60 let, p. 301.

south in a search for warmer growing seasons. In many cases crops are not growing under optimal conditions because optimal conditions simply do not exist. They are grown either where they can thrive best under the limited climate and soil resources available or they have been pushed into marginal areas by higher priority crops.

As a general rule, in determining geographical distributions of crops, Soviet leaders go through the following thought sequence: (1)

Since the Soviets desire to be as self sufficient as possible in all crops, those crops with limited environmental tolerances are given priority in areas where they can grow. A good example of such crops are cotton in the irrigated oases of Central Asia and Azerbaydzhan and tea and citrus fruits in mild, humid western Georgia. Since these are the only areas where these crops can grow, these crops take precedence even though they might not yield the highest returns. Other crops have been moved out of these areas in order to make room for these specialty crops. (2) If there is not such a specialty crop to take precedence, the choice will be given to the highest yielding crop. A good example of this is the introduction of corn in the southeastern Ukraine and North Caucasus traditional winter wheat growing areas. Although these regions are ideally suited for winter wheat and not very well suited for corn, because corn will produce much more green matter per hectare to support the livestock industry it has taken precedence and wheat has been pushed eastward into northern Kazakhstan and southwestern Siberia, areas that yield much less than the Ukraine and North Caucasus. However, spring wheat can survive in the new lands of northern Kazakhstan, and by planting extensive areas the total production of wheat can be maintained even though yields decrease. (3) If neither a specialty crop nor a high yielding crop takes precedence, then the area is usually sown to the crop best adapted to it. Examples of this are winter wheat in remaining areas of the Ukraine and North Caucasus; sugar beets in the north-central Ukraine and Central Chernozem region; and oats, rye, flax, alfalfa, and clover in the cool, humid regions of central and northwestern European U.S.S.R.

Sometimes a crop is grown in a given region because it is an important part of the crop rotation scheme. A good example of this is alfalfa in the irrigated cotton growing areas of the south. Alfalfa is an ideal rotation crop for irrigated cotton since it is somewhat salt tolerant and uses up some of the salts that tend to accumulate in the soil after prolonged irrigation. It is also a legume which fixes atmospher-

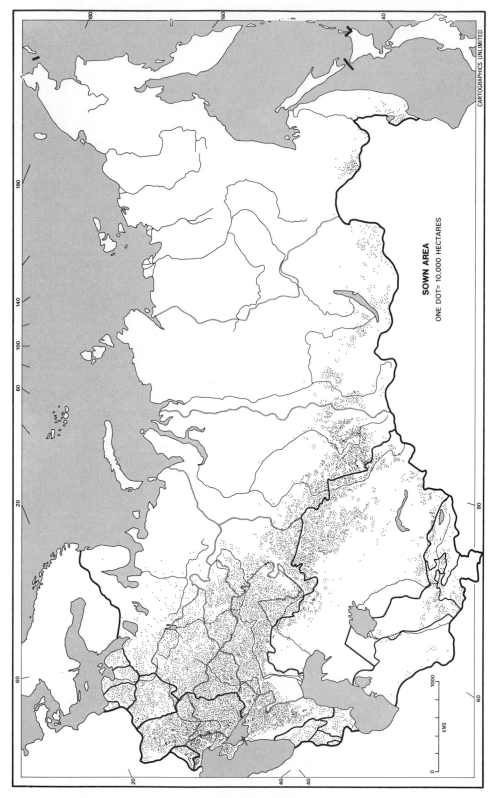

SOWN AREA

ONE DOT= 10,000 HECTARES

CARTOGRAPHICS UNLIMITED

Figure 9-6   Distribution of sown area in U.S.S.R. From Atlas Razvitiya Khozyaystva i Kultury, pp. 62–63.

ic nitrogen in the soil. Therefore, irrigated cotton areas are also usually livestock producing areas since they have the large alfalfa fodder base. Another good example of a necessary rotation crop is oats. Oats is usually used as the cover crop for the establishment of clover and alfalfa. These two legumes do not establish themselves well in open sunlight and therefore are planted simultaneously with oats which becomes much taller than the legumes the first year. The oats are harvested the first year, and the hay crops are harvested for a number of years thereafter as long as they are not crowded out by weeds. In most cases, it is the legume fodder crops that are most desired in the cool, humid regions of the north for livestock feed base, and the main purpose for the planting of oats there is to establish the legumes. Of course, oats themselves are a good feed grain, being higher in protein than most of the other grains.

In some cases the Soviets have structured regional price differentials in such a way that they induce the planting of certain crops in areas that are not very well suited for them. For instance, in the mid 1960s they restructured wheat prices in order to induce more wheat growing in the nonchernozem zone of European U.S.S.R. Resultant regional price differentials ranged from 67 rubles per ton in the Kuban District of the North Caucasus which is one of the best wheat growing areas in the country to 130 rubles per ton in the northern half of the European part of the country where wheat does not grow very well. This was done to try to equalize profits in the two areas so that the northern regions would be competitive in wheat growing. It entailed a huge subsidization of agriculture in the northern part of European U.S.S.R. and a consequent outlay of investment for the Soviet government. But, it did induce more wheat growing in the cool, humid north which has a more consistent annual production because it is seldom affected by drought.

Livestock distributions generally fit the crop distributions, with the greatest numbers of livestock raised in the better cropping areas. However, livestock products account for more of the agricultural economy in some of the poorer crop areas in the northern half of European U.S.S.R. Where cash crops cannot be grown so well, the cropping pattern turns to a supportive role for livestock. Such crops are hay of various sorts, oats, and some other small grains, as well as some root crops. Considerable quantities of feedstuffs, particularly grains, are shipped into these areas to support the livestock economies.

Since the northern half of European U.S.S.R. contains so many of the large metropolitan areas of the country which provide ready markets for all sorts of livestock products, fruits, and vegetables, the region is well able to support this high-cost, high-priced type of agriculture. This factor, together with the regional price differentials, places the value of agricultural produce in some of the more densely populated regions of the nonchernozem zone on par with that of some of the better physically endowed regions of the south. In Table 9–7 it can be seen that the Center compares favorably in total agricultural output to such areas as the Donets-Dnieper, Southwest, and North Caucasus Economic Regions. And the Baltic Republics and Belorussia compare favorably with the better farming regions of the country as far as per capita and per hectare outputs go. In fact, Lithuania and Estonia, with their cool, humid climates, acidic soils, and poor drainage, have the highest per capita outputs in the country, and Belorussia is only a step behind Moldavia, which is much better naturally endowed for agriculture. In terms of output per hectare, Moldavia stands well above the rest, and the Southwest Economic Region which contains some of the best farming areas of the Ukraine is second. But Lithuania and Estonia are next in line.

Grain

The U.S.S.R. plants far more land to grain than any other country in the world. However, since Soviet yields average considerably lower than U.S. yields, total production in the U.S.S.R. is usually about equal to that in the

Table 9–7 Agricultural Production by Union Republic and Economic Region (Total, Per Capita, and Per Hectare of Agricultural Land and Per Cent of Total Value Accounted for by Livestock Products), 1975

Region	Total Million Rubles	Per Cent Livestock	Per Capita Rubles	Per Hectare Rubles
U.S.S.R.	89,215	53.8	349	162
R.S.F.S.R.	42,755	59.0	318	193
Northwest	2,422	65.8	188	312
Center	7,659	54.1	270	333
Volgo-Vyatka	2,946	57.3	356	274
Central Chernozem	4,194	56.6	540	310
Volga	6,444	64.9	338	135
North Caucasus	6,762	51.9	448	267
Urals	3,533	70.1	230	127
Western Siberia	4,732	59.2	378	132
Eastern Siberia	2,368	61.3	300	104
Far East	1,393	55.6	212	209
Ukraine S.S.R.	20,359	52.1	415	482
Donets-Dnieper	7,215	55.5	346	419
Southwest	9,497	51.8	446	571
South	3,647	46.2	526	432
Baltic Region	4,272	66.4	532	499
Lithuania	2,007	63.9	605	563
Latvia	1,163	68.2	466	432
Estonia	800	67.5	556	532
Kaliningrad Oblast	302	72.5	385	373
Transcaucasus	3,083	35.0	229	365
Georgia	1,372	30.7	277	448
Azerbaydzhan	1,187	34.6	209	294
Armenia	524	46.9	185	391
Central Asia	6,962	29.6	296	99
Uzbek	4,083	24.7	290	160
Kirgiz	1,054	51.4	313	106
Tadzhik	962	27.4	276	234
Turkmen	863	28.7	334	28
Kazakh S.S.R.	5,066	62.7	353	27
Belorussian S.S.R.	4,969	53.0	530	508
Moldavian S.S.R.	2,051	31.0	533	775

Source: Narkhoz SSSR, 1975, pp. 16–21 and 336–337. Underlined names denote major economic regions.

United States. However, the types of grain in the two countries are quite different. Whereas the Soviet Union concentrates on food grains, particularly wheat, the United States concen- trates on feed grains, particularly corn. In 1974 the Soviet Union produced 89,900,000 metric tons of food grains while the United States produced only 43,500,000, but the United

States produced 133,900,000 tons of feed grains while the Soviet Union produced only 72,600,000.

The Soviets have been making steady gains in grain yields over the last 20 years, due to improved inputs mentioned earlier, so that now under comparable environmental conditions they are about on par with yields in the United States. However, so much of the Soviet grain is in less well endowed climatic areas that overall yields are still rather low. Spring wheat, for instance, which is largely grown in the very dry areas of northern Kazakhstan and surrounding regions, still yields only about half as much as in the United States. The corn that is produced for grain in the Soviet Union yields only about half as much as in the United States. It is questionable how much more yields can be increased in these cases, since the moisture and heat supplies of the growing seasons are limited.

Since the U.S.S.R. is short on feed grains, it has been importing considerable quantities of grain in recent years. Major suppliers have been the United States, Canada, Australia, Argentina, Brazil, Hungary, and France, with the U.S.A. standing well ahead of any other country, generally supplying more than half of total grain imports. (Table 17–3) Until the Soviet Union made the decision greatly to improve livestock products of the country, Russia was always known as a major wheat exporter. But now with the greater demand for feed grains, which includes some wheat, the Soviet Union seems to have turned into a perpetual grain importer. This began with the bad crop in 1963 and continued sporadically through the 1960s and early 1970s. The very bad crop year of 1972 forced the Soviets again to become a large importer of grains, which among other things triggered off an explosion in wheat prices in the domestic markets of the United States. This episode led to a U.S.A.-U.S.S.R. agreement aimed at stabilizing wheat purchases and wheat prices which specified that the Soviet Union would continue to buy between six and eight million tons of grain from the United States each year for a five-year period, with possible extensions in the future.

These six to eight million tons are to be split approximately equally between wheat and corn.[8] Further sales are possible, but only with the approval of the United States government.

Table 9–8 shows that, except for 1974–1975, the Soviet Union has been a major grain importer since the early 1970s. The two years of heaviest imports followed the very bad drought summers of 1972 and 1975. The mediocre harvest of 1977 has also been followed by heavy grain imports, heavier than anyone had anticipated, which seems to imply that in the future grain imports will be tied as much to demands in the Soviet Union for increased livestock products as they are current weather conditions. It thus appears that the Soviet Union is destined to continue to be a major grain importer as the livestock industry expands rapidly. The Soviet Union also has continuing commitments to export grain, particularly to other socialist countries. (Table 17–3)

Table 9–8 shows that net food grain utilization in the Soviet Union has remained very constant at around 45 million metric tons per year while feed grain usage has increased and is now about 2.5 times as much as the food grain consumption. Since food grain production in the Soviet Union has been running about twice as much as food grain consumption, it is obvious that the Soviets are never critically in need of wheat for human consumption. Rather, a poor grain crop is felt eventually in the overall supply of livestock products. This is often a delayed effect since after a poor harvest excess slaughtering of livestock because of shortage of feedstuffs might temporarily increase the supply of meat in stores. But a year or two later when feedstuffs become more adequate and herds are being rebuilt, slaughtering is curtailed, and then the pinch is felt in the meat market.

Thus, while the Soviets want to maintain a constant feed supply so as to avoid distress slaughtering and assure consistent supplies of livestock products, a poor grain crop does not

---

[8] Actually, during 1971–1972 — 1975–1976, annual average net imports of wheat amounted to 3.7 million tons while those of feed grains amounted to 6.3 million tons.

Table 9–8   Total Supply and Estimated Utilization of Grain,
U.S.S.R., 1964/1965–1977/1978, in Millions of Metric Tons

Year Beginning July 1	Production	Net Trade	Availability	Utilization						
				Total	Seed	Industrial	Food	Dockage and Waste	Feed	Stock Change
1964/1965	152	− 1	151	131	22	3	45	17	44	+20
1965/1966	121	+ 4	125	139	24	3	44	12	56	−14
1966/1967	171	− 1	170	144	24	3	44	14	59	+26
1967/1968	148	− 4	144	147	24	3	44	12	64	− 3
1968/1969	170	− 6	164	161	25	3	44	17	72	+ 3
1969/1970	162	− 6	156	177	23	3	45	23	83	−21
1970/1971	187	− 7	180	187	25	3	45	22	92	− 7
1971/1972	181	+ 1	182	180	26	3	45	13	93	+ 2
1972/1973	168	+21	189	187	26	3	45	15	98	+ 2
1973/1974	223	+ 5	228	213	27	3	45	33	105	+15
1974/1975	196	0	196	205	27	3	45	23	107	− 9
1975/1976	140	+26	166	179	28	3	45	14	89	−13
1976/1977	224	+ 7	231	215	27	3	45	32	108	+16
1977/1978	196	+17	213	220	27	3	45	30	115	− 7

Source: USSR Agricultural Situation, p. 3.
—, Minus indicates net exports or draw-down of stocks.

cast the country into a panic situation where they are willing to do anything to get their hands on imported grain. Therefore a poor grain crop does not place the Soviet Union in a politically vulnerable position whereby economic sanctions imposed by a grain exporting country can bring about desired political results.

It can be seen in Table 9–8 that unusually large amounts of grain are lost to "dockage and waste." Part of this stems from the stringent conditions under which the harvest is usually conducted and part is due to poor transportation and storage facilities in the Soviet Union. With short, cool growing seasons and early autumns throughout much of the agricultural area of the Soviet Union and a tendency in most of the country for maximum precipitation to occur in late summer and early fall, the harvest process is usually squeezed into a limited time period which often has cloudy, rainy weather. Lack of adequate equipment and personnel often delays the harvest, and

lack of adequate storage space sometimes allows the grain to spoil even after it is harvested. It is not uncommon to see large quantities of wheat piled on the ground exposed to the elements because there is no inside storage available.

The newly harvested grain usually contains large amounts of pieces of weeds and other extraneous materials. As has been mentioned, grain fields are often weedy because of lack of herbicides. Also green matter may be picked up in the process of two-stage harvesting. Since in most grain growing areas the harvest season is too short to allow the grain to ripen on the stock enough to be combined, the grain is usually cut and allowed to cure on the ground in windrows after which it is picked up and threshed by a combine. During the curing period, grass and weeds, or sown legumes, begin to grow up through the cut grain.

The introduction of a long growing crop such as corn into the crop rotation sequence in traditional winter wheat growing areas of southern European U.S.S.R. also compounds the harvesting problem, since it is desirable to leave the corn in the field as long as possible to let it get as ripe as possible. But if this is to be followed by winter wheat the next year, it delays the planting of winter wheat in the fall until so late that the wheat does not get very well established before hard freezes come on, which may cause excessive amounts of winter kill. In some instances this becomes so severe that the ground sown to wheat in the fall has to be plowed up the next spring and put in some spring-sown crop because not enough of the winter wheat has survived to make it worthwhle to keep. In some cases the harvest of corn has dragged on so late in the fall that winter wheat is not planted at all. Planting is delayed until the following spring when spring wheat is planted. Since spring wheat generally yields less and has lower quality than winter wheat, this reduces the wheat yields in the area.

In order to make the harvesting more efficient, the Soviets are actually flying tractors, combines, and harvesting crews from early harvest areas such as the Ukraine to later harvest areas such as northern Kazakhstan and Western Siberia in order to make maximum use of limited equipment and personnel with a minimum loss of time. This is a costly operation, but deemed necessary given the shortages that exist. As time goes on and more and more grain elevators and other storage facilities are built and farm roads are improved, perhaps some of these harvesting losses should be alleviated.

Wheat

As mentioned before, the Soviet Union is by far the largest wheat producer in the world, normally producing more than one-fourth of the world's wheat and two times as much as the second largest producer, the United States. Wheat is the biggest crop in the Soviet Union. It normally occupies about half the grain area and accounts for half the grain production. It usually occupies between one-fourth and one-third of all cultivated land in the U.S.S.R. Over

the 1971–1975 period the area in wheat averaged 61,487,000 hectares annually. Of this 43,025,000 hectares were in spring wheat and 18,443,000 were in winter wheat. On the average the spring wheat yielded 1.1 metric tons per hectare, while the winter wheat yielded 2.26 metric tons per hectare. Thus, the production of the two was similar, 47,345,000 metric tons of spring wheat and 41,590,000 metric tons of winter wheat. During the last few years there has been some reduction in the area of spring wheat and an increase in the area of winter wheat, with a consequent increase in the production of winter wheat at the expense of spring wheat. In 1977 winter wheat production totalled 51,945,000 tons and spring wheat totalled 40,097,000.

Most of the wheat sowing is in the wooded steppe and steppe zones extending from the western Ukraine and Moldavia eastward across the middle Volga Region, the southern Urals, and into northern Kazakhstan and adjacent parts of Western Siberia. There is a major extension southeastward from the Ukraine into the North Caucasus region and scattered sowings throughout the Transcaucasus, the loessial foothills of Central Asia, the steppe basins of Eastern Siberia and the Far East, and the nonchernozem zone of European U.S.S.R. (Fig. 9–7)

Among the 19 economic statistical reporting regions, Kazakhstan has by far the greatest wheat acreage, 95 per cent of which is spring wheat. Winter temperatures are too severe and the snow cover too thin for winter wheat to survive in much of this area. Farther north, the Urals, West Siberia, East Siberia, and Far East Economic Regions grow only spring wheat. The Volga Region has the second largest wheat sowing, 87 per cent of which is spring wheat and 13 per cent winter wheat. There is a mixture of spring and winter wheat throughout much of the Volga Region, the Volga-Vyatka Region, the Central Region, and the Central Chernozem Region. Southwest of those areas almost all the wheat is winter wheat, although there is a little spring wheat grown in most economic regions. The largest sowing of winter wheat by far is in the North

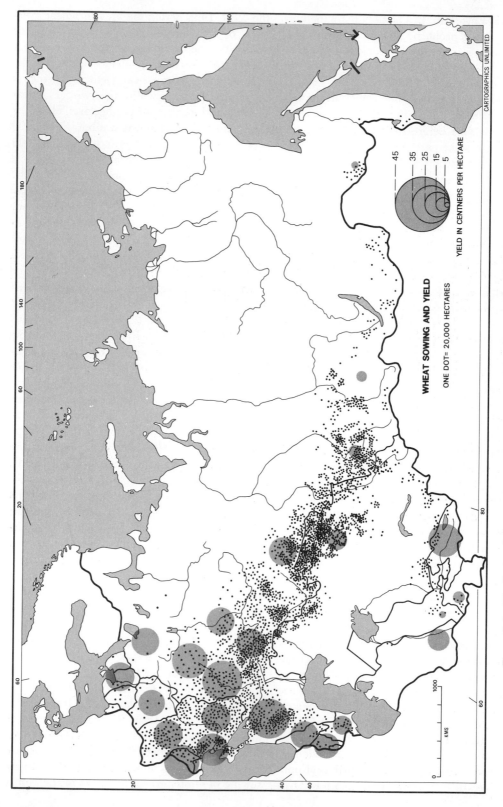

Figure 9–7   Distribution of wheat sowing and yield. Compiled from U.S.S.R. Grain Statistics, p. 40 and data in Narkhoz SSSR, RSFSR, and UkSSR, 1975.

Figure 9–8   Wheat stubble in the foothills of the Kura Lowland west of Baku, Transcaucasus. Photo by Irving Cutler.

Caucasus where 98 per cent of the wheat is winter wheat. This is followed by the Donets-Dnieper Region which also has 98 per cent winter wheat and the South Economic Region which has almost completely winter wheat.

Much of the wheat acreage now extends from the Volga region eastward. However, yields are much higher in the southwest part of the country. Moldavia averages around 3.5 metric tons per hectare, the Donets-Dnieper Region around 3.2 and the South about 3.0. In Kazakhstan yields average only about one metric ton per hectare. Consequently, the Ukraine as a whole produces more wheat than Kazakhstan. However, since the Ukraine is divided into three economic reporting regions, all of which are much smaller in area than Kazakhstan, no one region produces nearly as much wheat as Kazakhstan. On the average Kazakhstan produces more wheat than any other of the economic regions, although the Volga Region is a close second. In 1974, a rather poor year for the eastern regions, the Volga Region produced a little more wheat than Kazakhstan. However in 1972 when European U.S.S.R. was experiencing one of its most severe droughts, Kazakhstan produced its largest crop, which was almost three times as much as the Volga Region. Thus, the theory was borne out that the new lands in northern Kazakhstan should experience their wettest weather when the older wheat lands of European U.S.S.R. were experiencing their driest. A strong third in wheat production is the North Caucasus Region. Then comes the Donets-Dnieper, West Siberian, Urals, and Southwest Economic Regions.

Barley

Barley is the second most important grain raised in the Soviet Union. It accounts for about one-fourth the total grain production in the Soviet Union, and the Soviet Union accounts for about one-fourth the world's barley production. Barley accounts for more than half the U.S.S.R. feed grain production. It yields more than any other feed grain except corn, and since corn is not well adapted to the Soviet Union, the livestock industry depends upon barley for the fattening process. Consequently, more acreage is being devoted to barley all the time. During the last decade barley production has approximately doubled.

Kazakhstan contains the most extensive sowings of barley, with the Volga a strong second and the Central Chernozem and North Caucasian regions poor third and fourth. However, Kazakhstan has low yields, only about 1 metric ton per hectare on the average, while the Volga Region averages about 1.6 tons per hectare and the Southwest Economic Region and adjacent Moldavia have the highest yields with about 2.7 tons per hectare. In total production, the Volga Region generally ranks first, the Central Chernozem Region second, the North Caucasus third, and the Donets-Dnieper Region fourth. However, barley is adapted to most of the agricultural regions in the country, and is therefore widely cultivated. It is usually sown as a spring grain, and is often sown in areas where winter grains have been lost to winter kill. It is thus used as a backup crop for wheat, and often reaches its greatest acreages after a hard winter.[9]

Oats

Oats is the third largest grain crop in the Soviet Union, and the Soviet Union produces more than one-fourth of the world's supply. Oats have already been cited for their value as a cover crop for the establishment of legumes in the rotation scheme of the cool, humid part of European U.S.S.R. and their high protein value as an animal feed. During the Khrushchev years the area sown to oats dwindled from 14,811,000 hectares in 1955 to only 5,734,000 in 1964. Since then the area has

[9] Barley and oats sowings and yields have not been reported by economic regions in recent years. Therefore, it is not possible to construct maps comparable to those for wheat, corn, and some other crops.

been expanding consistently, until in 1977 it amounted to 13,026,000 hectares. In the meantime, yields have been increasing, with annual fluctuations because of weather, so that now production is larger than it ever was. In 1977 the total production of oats in the Soviet Union amounted to 18,379,000 metric tons, which was about 50 per cent more than it had been the first half of the 1950s before the Khrushchev reduction in acreage took place.

Although oats can be grown in most agricultural regions of the U.S.S.R., they are concentrated in the cool, humid northern areas where they are well adapted to the climatic conditions and acidic soils. The most extensive sowing of oats takes place in Western Siberia, the Central Region, the Urals, and the Volga Region. Since yields are somewhat higher in the west, the Central Region is first in total production, Western Siberia second, the Urals third, and the Volga fourth. The smaller Volga-Vyatka Region is fifth and the Central Chernozem Region sixth. Highest yields of all are found in the Central Chernozem Region and the Baltic Republics.

Rye

Rye occupies fourth place in grain production in the Soviet Union. Although production has declined significantly since the early 1950s, the Soviet Union still accounts for about a third of the world's rye production. The area sown to rye is now less than one-third of what it was in the peak year of 1951. However production has not dropped that badly, since yields have improved considerably. The decline can probably be attributed to the increasing preference for wheat bread in the country. There is very little pure rye bread anymore. Most of the rye bread now is a mixture of rye and wheat flour.

Rye is adaptable to the cool, moist, acidic soil regions of the northern agricultural regions of the Soviet Union, and also winter-sown rye withstands early summer drought in the Volga region better than do spring sown crops. The Volga Region normally has the greatest acreage and largest production of any economic region in the country. It is followed by the Volga-Vyatka Region, the Central Region, the Urals, and Belorussia. Rye is also an important crop in the Baltic Republics, the Southwest Economic Region, and the Central Chernozem Region. Yields are highest in the South and Moldavia, but little is grown there, preference being given to higher yielding crops. (Fig. 9–9)

Corn

Corn for ripe grain is a minor crop in the Soviet Union because of limited climatic conditions. It requires a long, hot, moist growing season which is ideally realized only in the western portion of Georgia. There and in Moldavia it is a traditional crop, being used for human consumption as well as livestock feed. But during the late 1950s and early 1960s it was introduced widely into the Ukraine and North Caucasus. These are the best regions the Soviet Union has to offer for corn growing, but they are on the dry side, and the growing season is not that long and hot either. Many years corn does not ripen even in these areas. Much more corn is grown for silage and green fodder than for ripe grain. Only one-fifth or less of the corn planted is harvested as grain. Grain corn accounts for only about six per cent of total Soviet grain output. In recent years the grain corn acreage has been reduced to less than half what it was during the peak year, 1961. Yields have improved a little over time, but total production has never again equalled the 1961 level. Consequently, with the expanding livestock industry, corn is a major item of import, mainly from the United States, Argentina, and Brazil.

The Donets-Dnieper region has by far the largest area sown to grain corn and is the largest producer. (Fig. 9–10) Next are the Southwest, South, Moldavia, and North Caucasus Regions. Corn is also an important crop in the hot, humid Colchis Lowland of western Georgia and in the southern portions of the Central Chernozem Region. Some corn is now being grown in the irrigated oases of Central Asia.

Rice

The Soviet Union grows little of the world's rice. But rice has been a basic food in parts of Central Asia, the Transcaucasus, and the Soviet Far East for a long time, and the Soviets have put on a drive during the last couple of decades to become self sufficient. Rice production has been expanded, particularly in Central Asia where the Fergana Basin, Tashkent area, and Khiva area have been traditional rice growing regions. To those have been added the long stretch of rice fields along the lower Syr Darya in south-central Kazakhstan. But the big expansion in recent times has been in the North Caucasus, primarily the delta of the Kuban River next to the Sea of Azov, and in the newly irrigated lands of the southern part of the Ukraine between the Kakhovka Reservoir and the Crimea. The largest rice growing area in the country today is the Kuban Delta in the North Caucasus, followed by the lower Syr Darya in southern Kazakhstan, the Fergana Basin-Tashkent region in Central Asia, and the southern Ukraine. Lesser areas exist in the irrigated strip on the lower Volga-Akhtuba floodplain and in the Khanka Lake region of Maritime Kray in the Soviet Far East. In 1975 the Soviet Union planted 500,000 hectares to rice and produced about 2,000,000 metric tons.

Millet

Millet is a traditional food crop in parts of Russia, used in types of gruel and bread. It is a small round grain that forms in large heads on top of the plant. The plant is fairly resistent to drought and has a relatively short growing season, so it is ideally suited to the spring wheat belt of the Volga, Urals steppes, and North Caucasus. It does not produce very heavily, and its sowing has been diminishing through the years. Between 1955 and 1975 millet acreage diminished from 7,783,000 hectares to 2,774,000.

Buckwheat

Buckwheat is another food grain that has

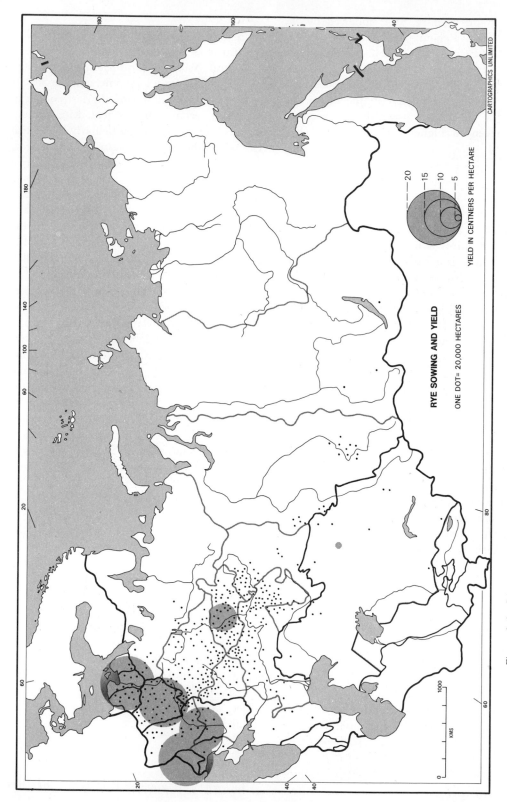

Figure 9–9 Distribution of rye sowing and yield. Compiled by Gennady Shmidov from data in Narkhoz SSSR, RSFSR, and UkSSR, 1975.

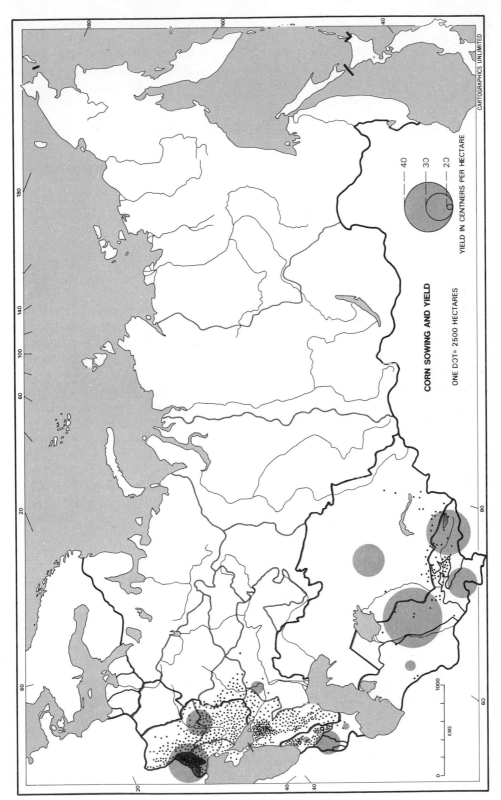

CARTOGRAPHICS UNLIMITED

CORN SOWING AND YIELD

ONE DOT = 2500 HECTARES

YIELD IN CENTNERS PER HECTARE

40
30
20

Figure 9–10   Distribution of corn sowing and yield. Source same as Figure 9–9.

been grown for many years in small amounts, primarily in the cool, moist region of north-western European U.S.S.R. It is particularly favored as a food in Belorussia where it is made into the well known kasha (porridge). The sowing of buckwheat has also diminished through time, from 2,761,000 hectares in 1955 to 1,459,000 hectares in 1975.

Non Grain Food and Beverage Crops
Sugar Beets

The Soviet Union produces about one-third of the world's sugar beets. Sugar beets are the only source of domestic sugar in the Soviet Union. The area sown to sugar beets has increased slowly through time as the crop has been dispersed from the traditional zone in central and western Ukraine and adjacent Central Black Earth Region to such areas as the Kuban in the North Caucasus, the irrigated oases in the Chu River Valley and Taldy-Kurgan areas of the Kirgiz and southern Kazakh Republics, Belorussia and the Baltic Republics, and portions of the southern basins of Siberia and the Soviet Far East, particularly Altay Kray in Western Siberia and the Khanka Lowland in Maritime Kray in the Far East. Yields have improved with additions of fertilizers and better cultivation, so that total production of sugar beets has grown steadily from an annual average of 25,600,000 tons during the period 1956–1960 to 76,000,000 metric tons during the period 1971–1975. 1976 was a particularly good year for sugar beets, and production rose to 99,900,000 tons. It fell back slightly in 1977 to 93,291,000.

In spite of these gains in production, the Soviets have not been able to keep up with their demand for sugar and have imported increasingly larger amounts of Cuban raw cane sugar. The desire to expand sugar beet plantings have been restricted by the four-to-six-year field rotation pattern necessary to reduce the plant's susceptibility to pest and disease problems. The largest producing areas in the Soviet Union currently are the Southwest Economic Region, which accounts for more than 40 per cent of the

crop, and the Donets-Dnieper Region, Central Chernozem Region, and the Kuban district of the North Caucasus. Highest yields are realized in irrigated oases in southern Kazakhstan and adjacent Kirgiz Republic. (Fig. 9–11)

Sunflowers and Other Oil Crops

Sunflower seed is the source of almost half the domestic production of vegetable oil in the U.S.S.R., and in addition the seeds are roasted and eaten much as peanuts in many other countries of the world. The Soviet Union normally produces about 55 per cent of the world's sunflower seed. Recently, sunflower seed oil has been the third most valuable Soviet agricultural export. A residue oil seed cake is used for livestock feed. The area sown to sunflowers and production of sunflower seeds has declined a little during the past decade, but the vegetable oil derived from the seeds has increased a little as improved varieties have been developed.

Sunflowers are drought resistant and well suited to the southern steppes of European U.S.S.R. The largest producing areas by far are the Donets-Dnieper region and the North Caucasus. Other important areas are the South, the Volga Region, the Central Chernozem Region, and the Southwest. Some are grown in the southern Urals, northern Kazakhstan, and southwestern Siberia. The highest yields are realized in the Donets-Dnieper Region. (Fig. 9–12)

Other than sunflower seeds, vegetable oil is derived from cotton seed, linseed, soybeans, caster beans, and mustard, and a little from peanuts, hemp, and tung. Of these, by far the most important has been cotton seed, followed by linseed. However, there is now an effort to expand soybean production, primarily under irrigation in the Ukraine, North Caucasus, Kazakhstan and Central Asia. At the present time most of the soybeans that are raised in the country are in the Zeya-Bureya Lowland in the Soviet Far East. In 1976 soybean oil production took a quantum leap forward from 22,000 metric tons in 1975 to 323,000 metric tons in 1976. The previous best year was 1973

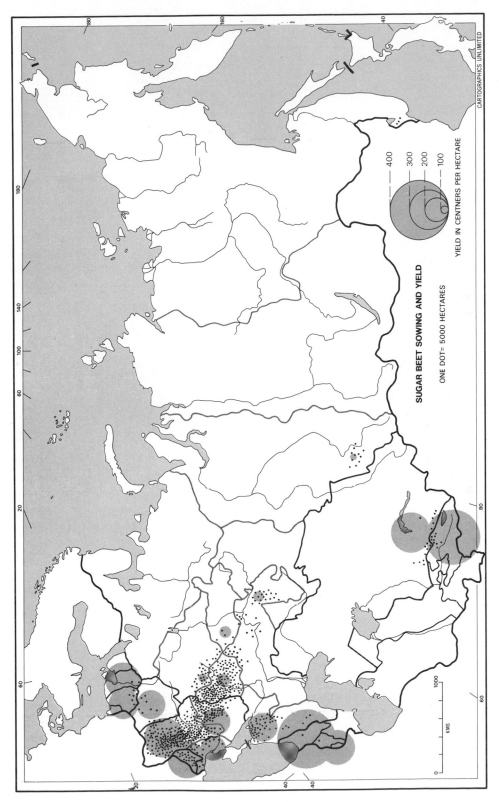

SUGAR BEET SOWING AND YIELD

ONE DOT= 5000 HECTARES

YIELD IN CENTNERS PER HECTARE

Figure 9–11   Distribution of sugar beet sowing cnd yield. Source same as Figure 9–9.

CARTOGRAPHICS UNLIMITED

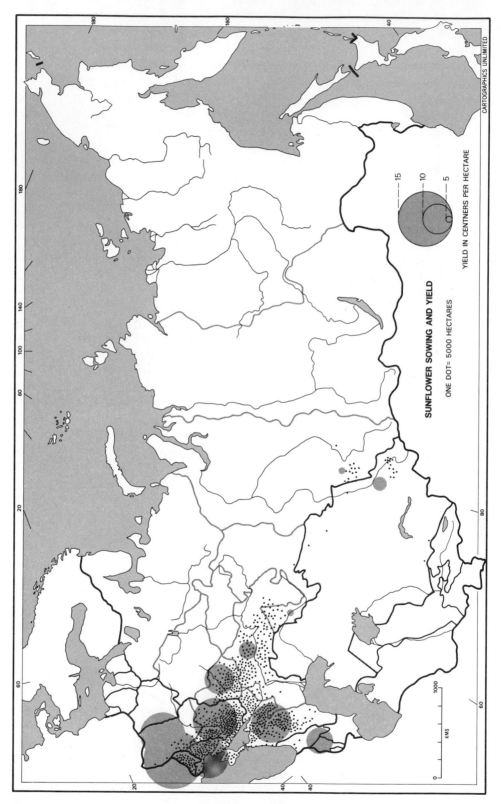

SUNFLOWER SOWING AND YIELD

ONE DOT= 5000 HECTARES

YIELD IN CENTNERS PER HECTARE

Figure 9–12   Distribution of sunflower sowing and yield. Source same as Figure 9–9.

with 169,000 tons. Cotton seed oil reached a peak production of 737,000 tons in 1975. Linseed oil has been declining over the years as less flax has been grown for its seed. The distribution of cotton and flax will be covered under fiber crops.

Potatoes

Russia long ago embraced the potato as a heavily bearing crop that was ideally suited to cool, humid climate and acidic soil regions of the north-central part of the country. The Russians often refer to the potato as the "second bread." Potatoes have become the second most important food crop after grain, and are also used for animal feed and as a raw material for industrial products. The Soviet Union normally produces about 80–90 million tons of potatoes per year, which is about one-third of the world's production. A peak of 108 million tons were harvested during the weather-favorable year, 1973, when potatoes made up 23 per cent of the total value of Soviet crop production.

Over 60 per cent of the potatoes normally are grown in private plots. Hence, potato growing is distributed throughout most agricultural areas of the country. But it is concentrated in the central portion of European U.S.S.R. The Central Region around Moscow has more area planted to potatoes than any other economic region in the country. This central potato growing area extends into surrounding regions including the entirety of the Ukraine, Belorussia, and the Baltic States. Highest yields are attained in Estonia, Lithuania, Belorussia, the Central Economic Region, the Volga-Vyatka Region, and Latvia, in that order. The average yield per hectare in Estonia during 1971–1975 was 16.4 metric tons, a yield incomparably greater than can be achieved with any grain. The Central Economic Region, whose area is considerably larger than any of the Baltic Republics, normally is the largest producer of potatoes in the country. However, the year-to-year production of potatoes fluctuates widely in all regions with weather conditions.

Vegetables

On the average, vegetables yield even more highly than potatoes, and generally have a higher value. But environmental limitations in the Soviet Union and eating habits eliminate such vegetables as sweet corn, beans, and lettuce from the crop complex. The primary vegetables in the Soviet Union are beets, cabbages, carrots, cucumbers, onions, and tomatoes. Russians have always had insatiable appetites for fresh cucumbers and tomatoes, and in order to serve those desires huge hothouse complexes have been established in many settlements all the way to the Arctic.

More and more vegetables are being grown under irrigation in specialized state farms established outside large metropolitan areas. However, vegetables still occupy only about 1,600,000 hectares of land each year, as compared to about 8,000,000 for potatoes. Therefore, the total production of all vegetables other than potatoes is only about one-fourth that of potatoes alone. Yields vary greatly with crop and from region to region. Average yields of all vegetables are generally highest in the Northwest and Central Economic Regions of European Russia and adjacent Estonia in the cool, humid part of the country, in Armenia in the Transcaucasus, and in some of the irrigated oases of Central Asia.

Fruit

The Soviets have been trying to expand and improve their fruit production, but the environment sets definite limitations. Most fruit is grown in southern areas, such as Moldavia, the Ukraine, the North Caucasus, the Transcaucasus, and Central Asia, although some hardy apples and pears can be found in northern agricultural regions as well. However, the varieties are such that the fruit is often small and not very high quality. Fruit trees, especially apples, are often planted in elongated belts along highways to augment shelter belts and thus serve the dual purpose of windbreaks and fruit production. This is particularly true in the southern steppes. Fruit trees are also grown

Figure 9–13   Vineyards in the foothills of the middle Kura Lowland. Photo by Irving Cutler.

in profusion along many boulevards in cities and in recreational parks, where they provide fruit as well as shade.

Grapes are one of the main fruit crops, and these also are limited to southern portions of the country. Moldavia has by far the densest planting of vineyards, the total area of which accounts for almost one-fourth that of the entire country. The Ukraine has almost as much, but scattered over much more territory and limited to warmer parts of the Republic, primarily the South Economic Region, including the Crimean Peninsula, and the small area in Transcarpathia. Azerbaydzhan and Georgia in the Transcaucasus are next in importance, followed by the North Caucasus, where during recent years a considerable expansion of vineyards has taken place under irrigation. The republics in Central Asia do not grow so many grapes, but some of the irrigated oases there raise some of the best table grapes in the country. Over the years the area in vineyards has expanded slowly and yields have increased

sharply, so that total production has improved significantly. During the decade of the 1960s grape production approximately doubled.

Citrus trees are limited to the foothills around the Colchis Lowland and Black Sea shoreline in western Georgia and a very small area in the Lenkoran Lowland in southeastern Azerbaydzhan bordering the Caspian Sea. Even in these areas, winter frosts are too severe for the growing of grapefruit and many varieties of oranges. Thus, the types grown are limited to local varieties of oranges, tangerines, and lemons, and many years these fail because of frosts. The industry is not very well organized to market fruits in the northern part of the country, and much of the citrus that is found in the markets of cities such as Moscow are imported from places such as Morocco.

Tea

Tea is the national drink of the Soviet Union. Traditionally in Russia the afternoon tea has been as ceremonious as it has been in England. Also, the non-Russian nationalities in Central Asia and the Transcaucasus have traditionally drunk tea. Although tea cultivation was introduced into Russia in the mid 1800s, it was not until the 1930s that it was expanded substantially. There was another major expansion during the 1950s, but it appears that since 1970 it has leveled off at about 76,000 hectares. This seems to indicate that the area suitable for tea growing has been exhausted. Tea growing is limited primarily to western Georgia and the adjacent part of Krasnodar Kray extending northward along the Black Sea Coast. About 10 per cent of the tea is planted in the Lenkoran Lowland of Azerbaydzhan. Tea thus competes with citrus and tung trees for the same areas. Tea yields most highly in Adzharia, the southwestern part of Georgia, but it is crowded out of this region by citrus which has even more stringent temperature requirements than tea. Tea occupies only about 9 per cent of the cultivated land of this region.

By expanding the area, improving the varieties, and mechanizing the picking, the Soviets have done an admirable job of attempting to become self sufficient in tea. By 1955 they were providing 87 per cent of their tea consumption. However, since that date the consumption has been expanding more rapidly than production so that considerable quantities of tea are still being imported from such countries as India, China, and Sri Lanka.[10]

Forage Crops

One of the major emphases during the last two decades has been the expansion of production of forage crops to sustain the expansion of livestock products. These crops occupy much land throughout the agricultural territory of the country. Perennial hay crops, primarily clover and alfalfa, occupy about 35 million

[10] For a more detailed discussion of citrus and tea growing in the Transcaucasus, see Lydolph, 1977, pp. 267–270.

Figure 9–14   The kolkhoz market in Bukhara. Photo by Toni Crane.

hectares; annual hay crops, such as timothy and other grasses, occupy around 17 million hectares; and a considerable amount of wild hay is harvested from natural meadows, mountain foothills, and so forth. Silage corn now occupies about 18 million hectares, and root vegetables used for feed, such as sugar beets and potatoes, occupy about 2 million hectares. Since the corn and root crops yield much more weight per area than hay crops, their portions in feedstocks are much greater than in areas sown. On the average during the period 1971–1975, annual supplies of livestock fodder consisted of approximately 224 million tons of corn silage, 119 million tons of hay, and 40 million tons of feed roots. Within the hay category, wild hay made up 47 million tons, perennial hay 44 million, and annual hay 29 million.

The corn planted for silage and green fodder is generally located north of that planted for dry grain, although there is a great deal of corn harvested for silage even in the southern parts of the country. Corn for silage is planted in much of the wooded steppe zone of European U.S.S.R. extending eastward to southwestern Siberia and northern Kazakhstan. Scattered plantings are also found in mixed forest areas farther north in European U.S.S.R. and southern parts of Eastern Siberia and the Far East. Some silage corn is now being grown in Central Asia under irrigation.

Clover is grown most intensively in the northern parts of the Agricultural zone of European U.S.S.R. The extent is approximately coincident with the mixed forest zone. Much of the alfalfa is grown farther south in the wooded steppe and steppe zones extending from the western Ukraine into Eastern Siberia. As mentioned before, alfalfa is a major rotation crop in all the irrigated cotton growing areas of Central Asia and the eastern Transcaucasus.

er in the world. It regularly produces about 20 per cent of the world's raw cotton, and raw cotton has become one of the two main Soviet agricultural exports, along with sunflower seed oil. In recent years the Soviet Union has been accounting for 15 per cent or more of the world's exports of raw cotton. Cotton is the leading fiber crop in the Soviet Union, and it occupies more irrigated land than any other crop. All the cotton grown in the Soviet Union is grown under irrigation in the oases of Central Asia and the eastern Transcaucasus. Therefore, its yields are very high. The area planted to cotton has risen to more than 2.9 million hectares.

The Uzbek Republic alone, which contains most of the Fergana Basin, the Tashkent region, the Hungry Steppe, and much of the Khiva area, has more than half the cotton acreage in the country. (Fig. 9–15) Yields are highest in the southern part of the Tadzhik Republic where the growing season is warmest and long staple cotton is grown. Cotton cannot be grown in all the oases of Central Asia and Kazakhstan, for in the north the growing season becomes too short. The cotton area lies southwest of the small Talas River which flows northward out of the Kirgiz Republic into southern Kazakhstan along the northeastern edge of the Karadag Mountains.

Much of the cotton growing has been accomplished during the Soviet period in a drive to make the Soviet Union self sufficient in raw cotton. The rapid expansion of cotton growing in Central Asia displaced much grain growing and necessitated an exchange of goods with the rest of the country. Grain now has to be shipped southward from northern Kazakhstan and Western Siberia to feed the cities of Central Asia, and much of the raw cotton is shipped northwestward to the Central Region for fabrication.

Fiber Crops
Cotton

During the early 1970s the Soviet Union passed the U.S.A. as the leading cotton produc-

Flax

Flax is the other large fiber crop in the Soviet Union. Unlike cotton, flax was an established crop long before the Bolshevik Revolu-

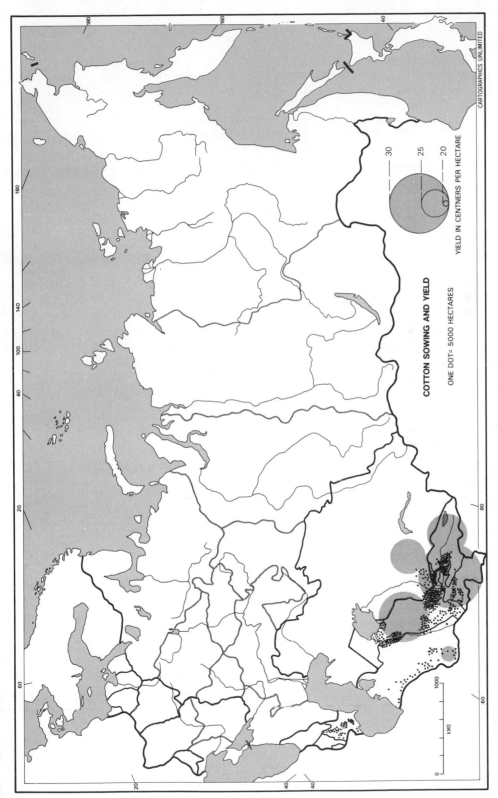

Figure 9–15 Distribution of cotton sowing and yield. Source same as Figure 9–9.

Figure 9–16   Piles of cotton in Bukhara. Photo by Toni Crane.

tion. It is ideally suited to the cool, humid climate of northwestern European U.S.S.R. which is conducive to its growth and to the process of removing the fiber from the pulp. For many years it has been the main cash crop in this area which has been characterized primarily by subsistence farming based on a mixture of livestock, hay, and small, hardy grains. It is nutrient exhausting and requires heavy fertilization in the soils of the northwest which are not very rich in minerals.

The U.S.S.R. produces about two-thirds of the world's flax for fiber, and some seed flax is grown for linseed oil used in the manufacture of paints and varnishes. Although the area planted to flax has declined over the years, increased yields have nearly doubled production since 1950. The Soviet Union accounts for 10–15 per cent of the world's flax fiber exports. The Central Region contains by far the greatest area of flax, and within it Kalinin Oblast northwest of Moscow contains the most of any single political unit. Smolensk Oblast farther south is second. (Fig. 9–17) The flax

growing area extends southwestward through Belorussia and into the Polesye of the northwest Ukraine. Most of the seed flax is grown farther south in the grain growing areas of the steppe. The highest yields of flax fiber are achieved in the Ukraine and Belorussia. The Central Economic Region ranks high also, and since it has much more area sown to flax, it is the major producing region.

Other Fibers

Hemp was introduced into Russia during the reign of Catherine the Great to provide raw material for rope making and exports. It has traditionally been concentrated in the Central Chernozem Region south of Tula. In recent years there has been some dispersal into such areas as irrigated regions of the North Caucasus.

Jute also has been introduced, although not in very large amounts. Most of this is raised in irrigated oases of Central Asia, particularly around Tashkent.

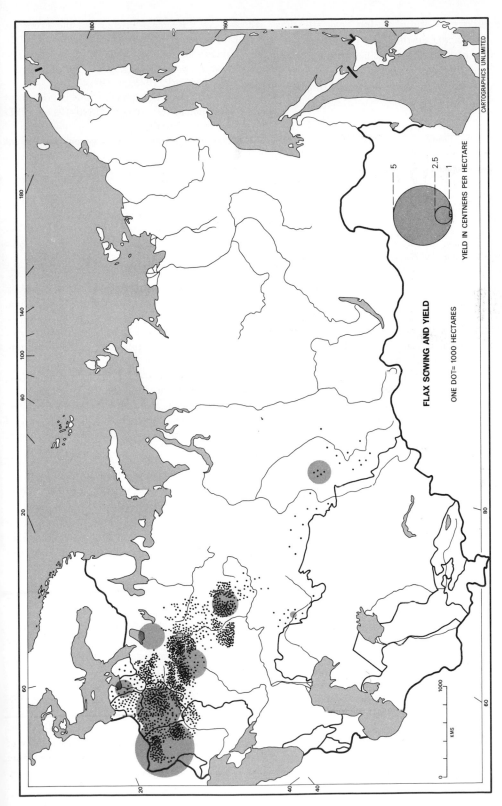

FLAX SOWING AND YIELD

ONE DOT = 1000 HECTARES

YIELD IN CENTNERS PER HECTARE

CARTOGRAPHICS UNLIMITED

Figure 9–17   Distribution of flax sowing and yield. Source same as Figure 9–9.

The silkworm industry for real silk has always been active in the cities of Central Asia and parts of the Transcaucasus where silkworms are fed on the leaves of the mulberry trees that are grown along irrigation ditches.

Reading List

1. Atkinson, Dorothy, "The Statistics on the Russian Land Commune, 1905–1917," *Slavic Review,* December 1973, pp. 773–787.
2. Bradley, Michael E., and Clark, M. Gardner, "Supervision and Efficiency in Socialized Agriculture," *Soviet Studies,* January 1972, pp. 465–473.
3. Bush, Keith, *Soviet Agriculture: Ten Years Under New Management,* Radio Liberty Research Paper, August 21, 1974, 39 pp.
4. Carey, David W., "Soviet Agriculture: Recent Performance and Future Plans," *Soviet Economy in a New Perspective,* Joint Economic Committee, Congress of the United States, Washington, 1976, pp. 575–599.
5. Denton, Elizabeth, "Anatomy of Soviet Agricultural Trade," paper presented at annual meetings of American Association for Advancement of Slavic Studies, Washington, October 1977, 15 pp.
6. Diamond, Douglas B., "Comparative Output and Productivity of US and Soviet Agriculture," paper presented at conference on Soviet Agriculture, Kennan Institute, Washington, November 1976, 12 pp.
7. Dienes, Leslie, "Pasturalism in Turkestan: Its Decline and its Persistence," *Soviet Studies,* July 1975, pp. 343–365.
8. Fulchino, Ralph Albert, "A Study of the Economic Role of the Machine-Tractor Stations and the Impact of their Abolition on Soviet Agriculture," PhD Dissertation, Georgetown University, 1971.
9. Gray, Kenneth Royal, "The Efficient Location and Specialization of Soviet Agricultural Procurement," PhD Dissertation, University of Wisconsin, 1976.
10. Jackson, W. A. Douglas, ed., *Agrarian Policies and Problems in Communist and non-Communist Countries,* University of Washington Press, Seattle, 1971, 497 pp.
11. Jensen, Robert G., "Regionalization and Price Zonation in Soviet Agricultural Planning," *Annals of the Association of American Geographers,* June 1969, pp. 324–347.
12. ———, "Regional Pricing and the Economic Evaluation of Land in Soviet Agriculture," in Bandera, V. N., and Melnyk, Z. L., eds., *The Soviet Economy in Regional Perspective,* Praeger, New York, 1973, pp. 305–327.
13. Kazmer, Daniel Raphael, "The Agricultural Development of Siberia, 1890–1917," PhD Dissertation, MIT, 1973.
14. Krueger, Constance, "A Note on the Size of Subsidies on Soviet Government Purchases of Agricultural Products," *ACES Bulletin,* Fall 1974, pp. 63–72.
15. Laird, Roy D., Hajda, Joseph, and Laird, Betty, A., eds., The Future of Agriculture in the Soviet Union and Eastern Europe: The 1976–1980 Five-Year Plans, Westview Press, Boulder, 1977, 242 pp.
16. Leversedge, Francis M., and Stuart, Robert C., "Soviet Agricultural Restructure and Urban Markets," *The Canadian Geographer,* Spring, 1975, pp. 73–93.
17. Lewin, M., *Russian Peasants and Soviet Power: A Study of Collectivization,* W. W. Norton, New York, 1975, 539 pp.
18. Lydolph, Paul E., "The Agricultural Potential of the Nonchernozem Zone," in Laird, Roy D., Hajda, Joseph, and Laird, Betty A., eds., *The Future of Agriculture in the Soviet Union and Eastern Europe,* Westview Press, Boulder, 1977, pp. 49–77.
19. Male, D. J., *Russian Peasant Organization before Collectivization: A Study of Commune and Gathering, 1925–1930,* Cambridge University Press, 1971, 253 pp.
20. Micklin, Philip P., "Irrigation Development in the USSR During the 10th Five-Year Plan (1976–80)," *Soviet Geography: Review and Translation,* January 1978, pp. 1–25.
21. Millar, James R., ed., *The Soviet Rural Community,* University of Illinois Press, Urbana, 1971, 420 pp.
22. Mote, Victor L., "The Cheliabinsk Grain Tariff and the Rise of the Siberian Butter Industry," *Slavic Review,* June 1976, pp. 304–317.
23. Osofsky, Stephen, *Soviet Agricultural Policy: Toward the Abolition of Collective Farms,* Praeger, New York, 1974, 300 pp.
24. Raup, Philip, "Soviet Agriculture," *The Economic Performance of the Soviet Union and Eastern Europe in 1976,* Harvard Faculty Club, Boston, February 7, 1977, pp. 1–7.
25. Schoonover, David M., "Prospects for Soviet

Grain Trade," Economic Research Service, U.S. Department of Agriculture. Paper presented at annual meetings of the American Association for Advancement of Slavic Studies, Washington, October 13, 1977, 28 pp.

26. ———, "Soviet Agricultural Trade and the Feed — Livestock Economy," in *Soviet Economy in a New Perspective,* Joint Economic Committee, Congress of the United States, 1976, pp. 813–821.

27. ———, "Soviet Agriculture and Grain Trade in the 1976–1980 Plan, Economics, Statistics, and Cooperative Service," U.S. Department of Agriculture Paper presented at Corporate Sponsor Seminar, Harvard University, February 6, 1978, 22 pp.

28. ———, "Soviet Agriculture in the 1976–80 Plan," paper presented at annual meeting of American Association for Advancement of Slavic Studies, St. Louis, October 1976, 20 pp.

29. ———, "Trip Report, U.S. Team to Study USSR 1976–80 Livestock Plans," U.S.-U.S.S.R. Agricultural Agreement, May 17–June 5, 1976, 49 pp.

30. Severin, Barbara S., and Carey, David W., "The Outlook for Soviet Agriculture," in Hunter, Holland, ed., *The Future of the Soviet Economy: 1978–1985,* Westview Press, Boulder, 1978, pp. 100–132.

31. Shaffer, Harry G., ed., *Soviet Agriculture: An Assessment of its Contributions to Economic Development,* Praeger, Boulder, 1977, 188 pp.

32. Stuart, Robert C., *The Collective Farm in Soviet Agriculture,* D. C. Heath, Lexington, Mass., 1972, 255 pp.

33. Symons, Leslie, *Russian Agriculture: A Geographic Survey,* Wiley, New York, 1972, 348 pp.

34. *USSR Agricultural Situation: Review of 1977 and Outlook for 1978,* U.S. Department of Agriculture, Washington, April 1978, 47 pp. (This excellent summary is published annually.)

35. *USSR Agriculture Atlas,* Central Intelligence Agency, Washington, 1974, 58 pp.

36. *USSR Grain Statistics: National and Regional, 1955–75,* Statistical Bulletin No. 564, Economic Research Service, U.S. Department of Agriculture, Washington, 1977, 42 pp.

37. Wädekin, Karl-Eugen, "Income Distribution in Soviet Agriculture," *Soviet Studies,* January 1975, pp. 3–26.

38. ———, "The Place of Agriculture in the European Communist Economies," *Soviet Studies,* April 1977, pp. 238–254.

39. ———, The Private Sector in Soviet Agriculture, 2nd revised and enlarged edition, University of California Press, Berkeley, Los Angeles, London, 1973, 407 pp.

10

Energy

The Soviet Union is in the enviable position of being the only large developed country in the world with ample energy resources of all kinds for the foreseeable future. It has been estimated that the Soviet Union has about two-thirds of the world's coal reserves and undoubtedly more gas reserves than any other country. It might eventually prove to have the largest oil reserves in the world, although large areas are still not prospected adequately. Although many of these resources are located in remote areas of Siberia and the Far East, and therefore may never be exploited fully, they nevertheless are resources that will be available if ever needed.

For many years the Soviet Union has been the largest coal producer in the world. During the early 1970s it became the largest oil producer. In 1975 the Soviet Union produced 491 million metric tons of petroleum, while the second producer, the U.S.A., produced 410 million metric tons. That same year, the U.S.S.R. produced 645 million metric tons of all types of coal, while the United States produced 560 million metric tons, although more of it was hard coal. The Soviet Union produces large quantities of lignite for power production and heating purposes. The Soviet Union is the second largest producer of natural gas and electricity after the United States. In the mid 1970s it was producing about half as much of each of these commodities as the

United States was, but it was well above any other country in the world. (Table 8-2) The production of both of these items has been increasing very rapidly, and with its great reserves of recently discovered natural gas, undoubtedly the Soviet Union will soon become the largest producer of that commodity.

It is only since 1955 that the Soviet Union has been producing much natural gas. At that time, discoveries of large deposits in Central Asia, the North Caucasus, and the eastern Ukraine stimulated the industry, as did the change in governmental policy after the death of Stalin which switched the emphasis from coal to oil and gas. All through the Stalin era, oil was looked upon as a special fuel which should be conserved for special uses, and there was no knowledge of large natural gas resources in the Soviet Union so the production of that commodity was almost negligible. In 1950 coal comprised two-thirds of the total fuel production of the Soviet Union, while oil made up only 17.4 per cent and natural gas only 2.3 per cent. (Table 10-1)

Coal made up a much larger share of total fuel production in the 1950s than it did way back before the Revolution in 1913. Although oil production had increased considerably since 1913, its share of total fuels had dropped to little more than half of what it had been. But in the mid 1950s this trend was totally reversed as the Soviets began to realize that they had large

Table 10–1   Fuel Production by Type, in Million Metric Tons of Standard Fuel (1 ton = 7 million kilocalories of heat) and Per Cents of Total

	1913	1940	1950	1955	1960	1965	1970	1975	1976	1980[1]
Total	48.2	237.9	311.2	479.9	692.8	966.6	1221.8	1571.3	1649.3	2120
Oil (Including Gas Condensates)	14.7	44.5	54.2	101.2	211.4	346.4	502.5	701.9	743.1	914
Per Cent	30.5	18.7	17.4	21.1	30.5	35.8	41.1	44.7	45.0	43.1
Gas	—	4.4	7.3	11.4	54.4	149.8	233.5	342.9	380.3	519
Per Cent	—	1.8	2.3	2.4	7.9	15.5	19.1	21.8	23.1	24.5
Coal	23.1	140.5	205.7	310.8	373.1	412.5	432.7	471.8	479.0	551
Per Cent	48.0	59.1	66.1	64.8	53.9	42.7	35.4	30.0	29.0	26.0
Peat	0.7	13.6	14.8	20.8	20.4	17.0	17.7	18.5	11.3	19
Per Cent	1.4	5.7	4.8	4.3	2.9	1.7	1.5	1.2	0.7	0.9
Shale	—	0.7	1.3	3.3	4.8	7.4	8.8	10.8	11.0	11
Per Cent	—	0.3	0.4	0.7	0.7	0.8	0.7	0.7	0.7	0.5
Firewood	9.7	34.2	27.9	32.4	28.7	33.5	26.6	25.4	24.6	13
Per Cent	20.1	14.4	9.0	6.7	4.1	3.5	2.2	1.6	1.5	0.6

Source: Narkhoz SSSR za 60 let, p. 204.

[1] 1980 planned data are from Energetika SSSR v 1976–1980 godakh, p. 149. They include all forms of energy. In addition to percentages for the various fuels, the 1980 plans include 3.0 per cent from hydro energy and 1.4 per cent from nuclear energy.

reserves of both oil and natural gas and that the exploitation of these reserves would enhance their total economy and defense posture in many ways. Differences in production costs alone were enough to convince the Soviets that they should emphasize the use of oil and gas as much as possible. For equivalent amounts of heat, Soviet production costs for coal average about 6 times those for oil and as much as 35 times those for natural gas. (Table 10–3) In addition, there were economies in the transport of the fluid fuels, and as pipelines have been built this has greatly relieved the heavily overburdened railroads. The conversion of railroad locomotives from steam to diesel and diesel-electric traction has greatly reduced the needs for long coal hauls and has increased the efficiency and power of the locomotives which can now handle heavier trains at faster speeds. In addition, the expansion of the oil and gas industries has provided a broad new base for a

Table 10–2   Heat Equivalents of Various Kinds of Soviet Fuels, in Thousand Kilocalories per Metric Ton and Per Cents of One Metric Ton of Standard Fuel (7,000,000 Kilocalories)

Fuel	Heat Equivalent 1000 kcal/ton	Per Cent of Standard Fuel
Coal:		
Donets	6500	0.93
Kuznetsk	7000	1.00
Karaganda	5600	0.80
Pechora	6300	0.90
Moscow	2900	0.42
Petroleum Products		
Crude Oil	9800	1.40
Diesel Oil	10000	1.43
Gas (1000 Cubic Meters)		
Natural	8400	1.20
Coke	4000	0.57
Blast Furnace	910	0.13
Shale	1610	0.23
Peat	2800	0.40
Firewood	1750	0.25

Source: Zverev, N. P., and Polikarpov, A. A., *Statistika zheleznodorozhnogo transporta* (Statistics of railroad transport), Transport, Moscow, 1976, p. 219.

Table 10–3   Production Costs of Specific Fuels per 7 Million Kilocalories of Energy, in Rubles

Coal	12.10
Oil	2.04
Natural Gas	0.38
Peat	5.70
Shale	14.83
Wood	24.50

Source: Dienes, 1973, p. 4.

wide range of chemical industries. During the 1970s, with rapidly rising world prices for petroleum and natural gas, the Soviets have found it most advantageous to export as much of these commodities as possible in order to make up some of their hard currency trade deficits.

Thus, by 1976, in terms of equivalent heat units, oil was accounting for 45 per cent of total fuel production in the Soviet Union, coal was accounting for only 29 per cent, and gas was accounting for 23.1 per cent. Although there is some concern now in the Soviet Union, as there is in the rest of the world, about the finite reserves of oil and gas and their conservation for specific needs, it appears that current trends cannot be turned around very fast because of financial and technological difficulties of converting existing facilities and the physical impossibility of increasing coal production as rapidly as the Soviets would like. Thus, it is planned that in 1980 oil will still account for 43.1 per cent of the energy production in the country, gas will rise to 24.5 per cent, and coal will fall to 26.0 per cent. There is planned to be increased emphasis on hydro and nuclear energy, but in 1980 these will still remain relatively insignificant. (See footnote, Table 10–1)

The consumption pattern of energy in the Soviet Union is considerably different from that in the United States. Whereas in the United States a great share of energy is used by private individuals for heating their homes and other domestic purposes and for running millions of automobiles, in the Soviet Union industry takes the lion's share. The percentages shown in Table 10–4 have not varied significantly for the last 20 years, since the Soviet buildup of industry. It might be concluded that there is a large nascent domestic demand that has not yet surfaced which in the future, if awakened, might place tremendous stress on Soviet ability to satisfy its own needs, let alone maintain export commitments to the socialist countries of Eastern Europe and exports to Western countries to defray many of the Soviet hard currency trade deficits. Compared to the United States, consumer demands for energy have hardly begun to develop in the Soviet Union.

Table 10–4   Soviet Energy Consumption by Branches of the Economy, 1975, in Per Cents of Total

Industry	54.1
Transport	12.0
Agriculture	6.5
Domestic	20.3
Other	7.1

Source: Dienes, 1976, p. 114.

OIL

In 1974 Soviet oil production exceeded that of the United States and became first in the world. In 1975 the Soviet Union produced 491 million metric tons of oil and gas condensates, as compared to 410 million in the United States. In recent years Soviet oil production has been increasing at the rate of about 7 per cent per year, or 29–31 million tons per year. During the tenth five-year plan, 1976–1980, the rate of growth is to fall to 5.4 per cent per year, but the absolute growth will still be about 30 million tons per year. In 1976, this growth was essentially achieved, 29 million tons of new oil, which brought the 1976 total production to 520 million metric tons.

The position of leading oil producer in the world is not new to the area. Back in 1901, Tsarist Russia produced more than 50 per cent of the world's oil. Of course, at that time, world production was only a drop in the bucket compared to what it is today, and only a few countries were producing. In 1901, Russia and the U.S.A. together produced 91.2 per cent of the world's oil. At this time, Russia was the largest exporter of oil in the world, a role which the U.S.S.R. has been striving to regain in recent years. During the 1970s the Soviet Union has been exporting about one-fourth of its oil production, which has made it third largest oil exporter in the world, after Saudi Arabia and Iran.

As Soviet production has mushroomed in total amount, the geographical distribution of production has changed radically. As late as 1937, the Caucasus region produced more than 90 per cent of the Soviet Union's oil. Main areas were at Baku in Azerbaydzhan and at Groznyy and Maykop on the north slope of the Caucasus. (Table 10–5) Other small producers were the old Emba fields at the northern end of the Caspian Sea in Kazakhstan, the Nebit Dag field in western Turkmenia, the Fergana field in the Fergana Basin of Uzbekistan, and the fields on the northern end of Sakhalin Island in the Far East. In addition to these old fields, in 1937 production was already beginning in the newly discovered fields between the Volga River and the Urals, particularly in the Bashkir A.S.S.R., Perm Oblast, and Kubyshev Oblast, as well as in the newly discovered Komi field in the European north.

In the two decades after World War II the big development took place in the Volga-Urals fields, which quickly surpassed the famous old producer at Baku. After declining during the war, production at Baku slowly rose back to what it had been before the war as deeper drilling into older rock structures and offshore drilling in the Caspian compensated for dwindling production in older areas. However, Baku never regained its preeminence in the total country's production, as the Volga-Urals fields expanded rapidly far beyond Baku.

The expansion of total production was particularly rapid during the 1955–1965 period after the death of Stalin when policies were reversed to stress oil as a primary fuel. By 1965

Table 10–5   *Geographical Distribution of Soviet Oil Production, Including Natural Gas Liquids, in Million Metric Tons*

	1937	1945	1955	1965	1970	1975	1976	1977 Plan	1980 Plan
U.S.S.R.	28.5	19.4	70.8	243	353	491	520	550	640
R.S.F.S.R.					285	411	445		554
Europe					227	221	219		
Komi A.S.S.R.	0.4		0.6	2.2	7.6	11			
Tatar A.S.S.R.	0.0	—	14.6	76.4	101.9	103.7		98.9	
Bashkir A.S.S.R.	1.0	1.3	14.2	43.9	39.2	40	40	40	
Kuybyshev Oblast	—	1.0	7.2	33.4	35			31.7	
North Caucasus	4.3		6.5	20.9	34.2	25.0			
Urals					24	40	42		
Perm Oblast	—	0.2	0.6	9.7	16.1	22.3		24.7	28–30
Orenburg Oblast	0.0		0.5	2.6	7.4	12.2		12.9	
Siberia					33.8	150	184		300
West Siberia	0.0	0.0	0.0	1.0	31.4	148	181.7	214.5	
Sakhalin	0.4		1.0	2.4	2.4	2.5	2.5		
Ukraine		0.2	0.5	7.6	13.9	12.8	11.6		8.6
Belorussia	0.0	0.0	0.0	—	4.2	7.95	6.2		
Azerbaydzhan	21.4	11.5	15.3	21.5	20.2	17.2	16.5		19.7
Georgia	—	—	—	—	0.02	0.26	0.88	1.4	3.0
Kazakhstan	0.5	0.8	1.4	2.0	13.2	23.9	23.3		26.9
Turkmenia	0.5	0.6	3.1	9.6	14.5	15.6	14.8	13.9	
Uzbekistan	0.4	0.5	1.1	2.1	1.8	1.4	1.3		1.0
Tadzhikistan					0.18	0.27	0.31		0.4
Kirghizia					0.30	0.23	0.23		

Source: Various issues of *Soviet Geography: Review and Translation.*
— means less than 50,000 tons.

the Volga-Urals fields were producing two-thirds of a greatly expanded total production in the country, and were credited with at least two-thirds of the total reserves of the country. At the same time, production had expanded significantly in the Turkmen Republic and had reached significant proportions in the Ukraine where new fields in north-central Ukraine had been added to the older producing fields in southwestern Ukraine along the northern slopes of the Carpathian Mountains. Oil production in the old Groznyy fields was also revived in the late 1950s and 1960s as drilling went deeper into older rock structures. Production at Groznyy had diminished from its early peak of about 7.1 million metric tons in 1930, when it was second producer in the country,

after Baku, to only about 2 million tons per year in the mid 1950s. But the added investment of drilling deeper into older rocks raised the production to 21.6 million tons in 1971. However, oil production in these deeper horizons has declined sooner than anticipated, and since 1971 the production at Groznyy has decreased constantly. In 1976 the production at Groznyy amounted to about 8 million tons.

During the 1950s, the Tatar A.S.S.R. shot into first place among all political units in oil production. The adjacent Bashkir A.S.S.R. ranked second, and adjacent Kuybyshev Oblast third. All of these political units within the Volga-Urals oil fields individually outproduced the Baku fields in Azerbaydzhan, the Groznyy fields in the Chechen-Ingush A.S.S.R. in the

North Caucasus, and the Maykop field in Krasnodar Kray in the western part of the North Caucasus. (Fig. 10–1)

Since the mid 1960s oil production has experienced another major geographical shift as the huge West Siberian fields have been brought into production rapidly. In one decade production in the Ob Plain increased from practically nothing to 182 million metric tons in 1976, a rate of increase more than twice that achieved in the Volga-Urals fields earlier, in spite of the fact that the natural environment in Western

Siberia posed incomparably greater obstacles to development than the Volga-Urals area had. Almost all the West Siberian oil comes from huge Tyumen Oblast which has surpassed the production of any other single political unit. Annual production in the Tatar A.S.S.R. peaked around the mid 1970s at around 104 million metric tons and apparently is due to go into a slow decline. The Bashkir A.S.S.R. has plateaud at around 40 million tons, and Kuybyshev Oblast is declining slowly after peaking around 35 million tons in 1970.

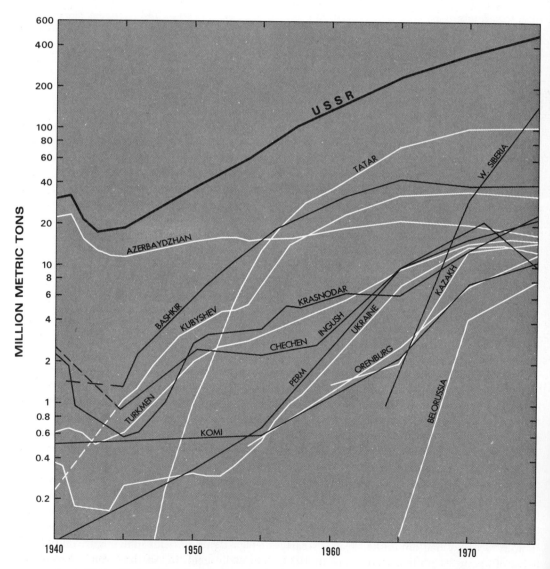

Figure 10–1   Oil production by major producing regions in the U.S.S.R., 1940–1975.

Western Siberia is now credited with the largest share of the country's reserves, and is scheduled to produce about 300 million metric tons in 1980. (Fig. 10–2) It will then be producing almost half the country's oil. Most of this will come from Tyumen Oblast, with only a small amount from adjacent Tomsk Oblast. In 1976 Tomsk Oblast produced about 5 million metric tons. During 1971–1975 most of the output gains in Western Siberia were derived from a single giant field, Samotlor near Nizhnevartovsk, which in 1976 yielded more than 110 million tons, or 60 per cent of the West Siberian production and 20 per cent of all Soviet production. Samotlor, however, is expected to level out at about 130 million tons, and therefore it will be necessary during the current five-year plan, 1976–1980, to register a similar rate of increase from more widely scattered fields. This may be more difficult to do.

The major oil field to be developed in Western Siberia during 1976–1980 is Kholmogory 200 kilometers north-northeast of Surgut along the railroad which is being extended from Surgut to the huge developing gas fields far to the north at Urengoy near the Arctic coast. Production started at Kholmogory in July 1976, and a pipeline has been laid to Surgut. The railroad is expected to be finished to Kholmogory in 1978. Kholmogory is the twentieth producing field to be put into operation in Western Siberia since its first commercial output in 1964.

The spectacular West Siberian development during the last decade has overshadowed what had been anticipated as a major development in the Mangyshlak Peninsula of western Kazakhstan on the eastern shore of the Caspian Sea where exploration and development got underway a couple of years before it did in Western Siberia. Although development there has increased production in Kazakhstan from only 2 million tons in 1965 from the old Emba oil fields farther north to 23.3 million metric tons in 1976, the Mangyshlak fields have proved to be nowhere near the size of the West Siberian fields, and the Mangyshlak crude has presented special problems to exploitation,

transportation, and refining. The crude is about 30 per cent paraffin which solidifies at a temperature of 32°C (90°F). Fourteen heating stations had to be installed on the Mangyshlak-Kuybyshev pipeline to keep the crude oil at a temperature of 60°C (140°F). To facilitate extraction of the high paraffin crude, water has to be brought 150 kilometers from the Caspian Sea, desalted, and brought to the boiling point and injected at high pressure into the oilbearing horizons. The high wax crude requires special refinery treatment, for which most refineries are not equipped. Conveniently, the Baku refinery, which has been processing similar local crude, has been able to take on some of the Mangyshlak oil as Baku oil production has decreased. In fact, in 1976 the Baku refinery complex received a new straight-run unit to process Mangyshlak oil being shipped across the Caspian.

In addition to recent activities in Western Siberia and the Mangyshlak Peninsula, small oil developments have been dispersed into many parts of the country. The Soviets are particularly eager to expand development in the European part of the country where most of the market is. A significant increase in oil production has taken place in Perm Oblast as more effort has been expended in this oldest, but minor, producing area of the Volga-Urals fields. Production increased from 9.7 million metric tons in 1965 to 22.3 million in 1975. A goal of 28–30 million tons has been set for 1980 because of new discoveries in the northern portions of the region. Since 1969 the Volga-Urals oil development has been expanding westward into the Udmurt A.S.S.R. The first oil was discovered in the southeast corner of the republic across the Kama River from the Neftekamsk oil district of northern Bashkiria, but more recent discoveries have been made in the middle of the republic around the small town of Igra. Total Udmurt production in 1975 was around 3.5 million tons.

Farther north the Komi oil fields have been expanded northwestward and southward from the center of Ukhta to Usinsk and Vozey. In addition, about half of the Soviet's natural gas liquids are produced in the gas fields of Vuktyl

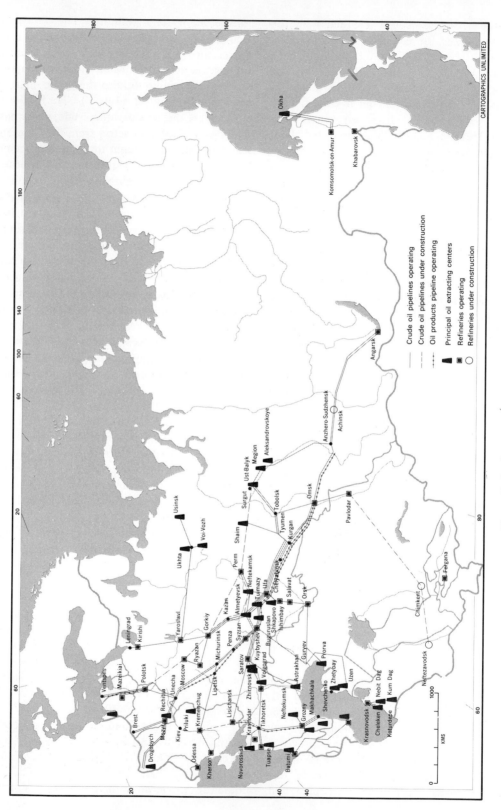

Figure 10-2   Oil production, refineries, and pipelines.

nearby. Oil production in this region amounted to 7.1 million tons in 1975 and is scheduled to increase to 25 million tons in 1980. Natural gas liquids peaked at 4.5 million tons in 1973 and have been running about 4 million tons per year since then.

Ukrainian oil production took a spurt in the early 1960s as the fields in north-central Ukraine were added to those of southwestern Ukraine along the northern slopes of the Carpathian Mountains. Total Ukrainian production peaked at 14.5 million tons in 1972 and has been on the decline since. The goal for 1980 has been set at 8.6 million tons. In adjacent Belorussia, production began in the mid 1960s in the southeast corner of the republic around the town of Rechitsa near Mozyr, where a major refinery and chemical complex has developed at the fork of the Friendship oil pipeline that carries oil northwestward to Poland and East Germany and southwestward to Czechoslovakia and Hungary. Belorussian production peaked around 8 million tons in

1975 and dropped to 6.2 million tons in 1976. The Belorussian oil administration is also overseeing the development of some small fields in Kaliningrad Oblast to the northwest. Commercial production started in 1975 with 290,000 tons of crude oil which were moved by tank car train to the Novopolotsk refinery in northern Belorussia. It appears that the Kaliningrad fields will be only minor producers.

In the south the oil producing fields of Azerbaydzhan and Turkmenia continue to decline after an earlier revival, in spite of all-out efforts to drill more deeply and to extend farther into the Caspian. Turkmenian output peaked at 16.2 million tons in 1973, and the 1975 production of 15.6 million tons was far short of the 22 million-ton goal originally set. Azerbaydzhan production was down to 16.5 million tons in 1976, but a little gain is envisioned by 1980. Some of the Azerbaydzhan decline has been compensated for by a small new development in adjacent Georgia. A new oil field has been opened about 25 kilometers

Figure 10–3   Oil derricks in Caspian off Baku. Photo by Irving Cutler.

northeast of Tbilisi. However, this appears to be a very minor development. Expectations were that Georgia's total production in 1977 would be about 1 million tons.

As declines in production take place in older fields and the better deposits of Western Siberia begin to peak, the Soviets are eager to expand production into still unexploited areas. They are exploring such remote regions as the Arctic coastal shelf of the Barents and Kara Seas and the continental shelf around Sakhalin Island in the Far East. The capital of the Nenets Autonomous Okrug, Naryan-Mar, has become the base for oil and gas exploration in the northern part of European Russia. In

January, 1976 the Soviets announced the first oil well to be completed in this area in the region of Varandey northeast of Usinsk. Farther east development has started on the Russkaya oil field on the right bank of the Taz River in the Arctic tundra between the Ob and Yenisey Rivers. It is thought that eventually large oil fields may prove to lie under the large gas fields of this region. Farther south in the central Ob Basin where the great expansion of oil production has taken place during the last decade in Mesozoic rocks, the Soviets hope to find new commercial deposits in deeper Paleozoic strata.

The Soviets are hopeful of eventually finding

Figure 10–4   Pumping oil in the karst valleys of the Zhiguli Hills near Kuybyshev. Photo by Irving Cutler.

large deposits of oil in the thick sedimentary strata of the Central Siberian Upland, although so far they have not expended much effort on exploration in this region. Some time ago they did announce that oil had been found near the village of Markovo on the Lena River.

Refinery and Pipeline Development

Prior to World War II when most of the oil production of the Soviet Union was located in the Caucasus, most of the refineries were located in oil producing areas such as Baku, Groznyy, and Maykop. A pipeline was built westward from Baku up the synclinal valley of the Transcaucasus to Batumi on the coast of the eastern end of the Black Sea where crude was refined to ship products across the Black Sea to the ports of the southern Ukraine. Similarly, a short pipeline was built from Maykop southwestward across the low northwestern end of the Caucasus Mountains to the small refinery at Tuapse on the Black Sea coast to serve the same function. But the big oil movement was by marine tanker across the Caspian from Baku to Astrakhan up the Volga to the Central Region. In all of these movements, oil products were distributed over wide areas at their destinations by railroad transport.

In the Far East the small oil production on the northern end of Sakhalin Island was serviced by refineries that were built in Khabarovsk in 1935 and Komsomolsk in 1942. Originally the oil moved by rail all the way. In 1953 a pipeline was extended southward to Komsomolsk utilizing a below-sea pipeline that had been built across the Tatar Strait in 1943. In 1969 a second line was laid across the strait.

After the war, as the Volga-Urals fields developed rapidly, the pattern of oil refining and transportation changed drastically. In the initial stages refineries were still concentrated in producing areas, particularly in clusters around Ufa in the Bashkir A.S.S.R. and Kuybyshev on the Samara Bend of the Volga. But as time has progressed, refineries have come to be located more and more in market areas. During the 1950s pipelines were laid primarily east and west from the oil producing areas of Bashkiria and Tataria to carry Volga-Urals oil into southern Siberia to new refineries established at Omsk and Angarsk near Irkutsk and westward into European Russia to serve new refineries in such cities as Gorky, Ryazan, Moscow, Yaroslavl, and Kirishi near Leningrad.

During the 1960s the pipeline systems were greatly expanded with branches to broaden the zone of delivery, particularly in European Russia, as new refineries were established in many towns. The Friendship Pipeline system was built west-southwestward from the great Romashkino oil producing pool near Almetyevsk in the Tatar Republic to carry crude oil through the Central Chernozem Region to Mozyr in southeastern Belorussia where it split, with lines going northwestward to Poland and Eastern Germany and southwestward to Czechoslovakia and Hungary. Later a branch line was built to lead oil off the Friendship Pipeline from Unecha northwestward to a new refinery at Polotsk in northern Belorussia and on to the port city of Ventspils on the Baltic coast of Latvia for export to west European countries. (Fig. 10–2) A pipeline was built southwestward from Ukhta to provide an outlet for the developing oil producing area of the Komi A.S.S.R. in northeastern European Russia to refineries at Yaroslavl and Moscow.

During the later half of the 1960s and the first half of the 1970s, as oil production developed rapidly in Western Siberia and the Mangyshlak Peninsula of western Kazakhstan, pipelines were laid from these new fields to join up with existing pipeline systems. Now West Siberian oil flows both eastward and westward along the pipeline system that originally was built to carry Volga-Urals oil. In addition to the old lines, two new lines have been built from the West Siberian oil producing region directly to hookup points in European Russia, one completed in 1973 from the Ust-Balyk field near Surgut to the Tatar oil center of Almetyevsk and the second completed in 1976 from Nizhnevartovsk at the site of the giant

Samotlor field to Kuybyshev on the Volga where it connects both with the Friendship Pipeline system to Eastern Europe and with the line completed in late 1974 from Kuybyshev to the Black Sea tanker terminal of Novorossiysk. In 1977 the Soviets were preparing to construct a third direct pipeline leading westward from the West Siberian oil fields around Surgut to refineries at Perm, Gorky, Ryazan, Moscow, Yaroslavl, and Polotsk in northern Belorussia. Both crude and products pipelines now run from Polotsk to Ventspils for export. West Siberian oil now has export outlets in both the Baltic Sea at Ventspils and the Black Sea at Novorossiysk.

In addition, in 1977 a pipeline was being completed from Kuybyshev to a new oil refinery at Lisichansk in the Donets Basin of the Eastern Ukraine. This pipeline will be extended westward to Kremenchug, the largest Ukrainian refinery, on the Dnieper River. Kremenchug had been provided earlier in 1974 with West Siberian oil brought by a pipeline that branched off the Friendship Pipeline at the town of Michurinsk in the Central Chernozem Region and ran southward to Kremenchug and a refinery at Kherson. During 1977 a short pipeline was to have been completed from Snigirevka on the Kremenchug-Kherson oil pipeline westward to an old refinery at Odessa in the southwestern Ukraine where it would also provide another marine outlet for West Siberian oil through the large port of Odessa.

A large oil refinery was to have been completed in 1977 at Pavlodar in northeastern Kazakhstan. This will be connected by pipe from Omsk, and eventually the pipeline will be built southwestward from Pavlodar across Kazakhstan to new refineries that are to be built in Chimkent in southern Kazakhstan and Neftezavodsk in eastern Turkmenia. Thus, West Siberian oil will also be used to augment Central Asian oil to satisfy needs in that region. Other refineries that are to be completed in the late 1970s or early 1980s include Mazeikiai in Lithuania and Achinsk in southern Siberia just east of the Kuznetsk Basin.

Thus, refineries are continuing to be dispersed into market areas where petroleum products are needed. This process, together with the construction of pipelines to serve outlying refineries, has provided increasing flexibility for planners to locate all sorts of manufacturing plants in market areas of the country. The fluid fuels, moving through pipes, have revolutionized industrial plant location practices, and have facilitated the further concentration of industrial production in large metropolitan areas of the country.

All this development in the oil industry during the last twenty-five years has necessitated a tremendous construction of pipelines. Although pipelines for tha gas industry have been given priority, oil pipelines have increased in length from only 5,400 kilometers in 1950 to 56,900 in 1975. Most of the long distance pipelines that have been laid during the last few years have been 48 inches in diameter, the same as the Alaskan pipeline. Most recently, some lines from Western Siberia are 56 inches in diameter. During some of the most feverish periods of pipeline laying from the West Siberian fields, the Soviets have built an equivalent of the Alaskan pipeline every 4–5 weeks.

All this has put a strain on the Soviet ability to produce pipe fast enough. Large diameter pipe plants have been opened at Novomoskovsk in the Ukraine, Chelyabinsk in the Urals, Volzhskiy, across from Volgograd on the lower Volga, and Khartsyzsk in the Donets Basin of the eastern Ukraine. Another is under construction in Vyksa southwest of Gorky. In 1975 steel pipe production in the Soviet Union had risen to 16 million tons, of which more than 3 million tons was of large diameter, 40 inches or more. Imports in 1975 totaled 2.7 million tons, including 1.7 million tons in larger diameters. In recent years, about two-thirds of the Soviet requirements in large diameter pipes have been met by domestic production and one-third through imports, notably from West Germany, Italy, France, and Japan. Many of these imports have been parts of compensatory deals whereby companies in the Western countries will be repaid in oil over a period of time.

In spite of the remarkable buildup of pipelines in the Soviet Union, pipeline construction has not been able to keep up with the expansion of the oil industry, and large quantities of oil are still carried on railroads, particularly refined products. In 1975 oil products still were second only to coal in the composition of railroad freight. Railroads moved 58.3 million metric tons of crude oil and 329.4 million metric tons of refined products, while pipelines moved 458.0 million metric tons of crude oil and 39.6 million metric tons of refined products. Little relative change is expected by 1980, all quantities increasing absolutely. Probably railroad haulage of crude oil cannot be reduced much further, since the small volume of movement along certain lines does not warrant the building of pipelines. Also, some crude oil is moved by rail in order to avoid mixing certain kinds of crude oil in pipelines. The crudes of Baku and Mangyshlak with their high paraffin base are used for special high distillate fuels and lubricating oils, so products from these regions move to all parts of the country, while fuel oil and other more common products are shipped into the Caucasus to conserve the use of the special crude in that area. Thus, the nature of different oil fields necessitates some cross hauling.

While the movement of crude oil by pipeline has been facilitated about as much as possible, movement of products has lagged. Product pipelines have not been stressed, and they are not to be greatly expanded during the current five-year plan, 1976–1980. Railroads are still scheduled to carry 86.7 per cent of all oil products in 1980. Of course, it is more difficult to concentrate the movement of oil products than it is crude oil, products being dispersed to many cities in the country. The transport of products has been minimized as much as possible by decentralizing the refining industry, and this appears to be the primary policy of the future.

Oil Exports

Since 1963 the Soviet Union has allocated at least 25 per cent of its oil production for export. This has been necessary because of its large commitments to the East European countries, some of which get all of their oil from the Soviet Union, and its need in recent years to generate hard currency in order to pay for large balance of payment debts with industrialized Western countries. In 1975 Soviet oil exports amounted to 130 million metric tons. 77.7 million tons of this went to other socialist countries, and 52 million tons went to West European countries, Japan, and the United States. Hard currency earnings from oil in 1975 amounted to 3.2 billion dollars. In 1976 oil exports made up 51 per cent of the value of all Soviet exports to the industrialized Western countries. Primary purchasers were West Germany, France, Austria, the United Kingdom, Denmark, Italy, Sweden, and Finland. (Table 17–5)

Although there is a ground swell underway in the Soviet Union to conserve oil for domestic use in the future, short run needs to balance trade deficits seem to have taken precedence. Since world prices for petroleum have increased so rapidly during the early 1970s, the Soviets have found petroleum exports to be about the only way they can increase export values. They are chagrined by the fact that they are committed for such large oil exports to East European countries where they have agreed to prices well below world market prices. Although they have effected some changes in the price structure with East European countries since 1975, they are still not getting the prices they could get on the world market.

GAS

As was shown in Table 10–3, natural gas is by far the cheapest type of fuel to produce. It also has the advantage of being the cleanest fuel presenting the least hazards to the environment. Therefore, it is most adaptable to domestic uses and power generation within large metropolitan areas. It has increasingly been substituted for other fuels in industry and electrical power generating stations in heavily populated areas where air pollution is of great concern. Although it has been estimated that about 150 million of the 260 million people in the Soviet Union now have gas supplied to their homes, household and communal services account for only 15 per cent of the natural gas consumption in the country. Industry takes 60 per cent, the iron and steel and chemical industries alone consuming 22 per cent, and power stations another 25 per cent.

Since the mid 1950s when the Soviets began to discover large deposits of natural gas in their country, the production of this fuel has increased at a faster rate than any of the other fuels. This will continue during the present five-year plan, 1976–1980; the production of natural gas is scheduled to increase 50 per cent, while the production of oil will increase only 30 per cent and coal will increase less than 17 per cent. The share of gas in the total fuel consumption of the Soviet Union increased from 2.4 per cent in 1955 to 23.1 per cent in 1976 and is scheduled to increase to 24.5 per cent by 1980. (Table 10-1) During the early 1980s gas will surpass coal as the second most important fuel, after oil.

Simultaneously with the rapid expansion of the production of natural gas has been the rapid expansion of proven reserves. Before 1955, few reserves of natural gas were known. Most of the small amount of gas production was associated with oil production. About the only known dry gas fields were located near Saratov and Volgograd on the lower Volga and at the old gas producing area of Dashava along the northern foothills of the Carpathians which was added to the western Ukraine as a result of World War II. Then, in rapid succession in 1956 and 1957, large gas deposits were discovered along the northern slopes of the Caucasus, particularly around Stavropol and Krasnodar, at Karadag southwest of Baku in the Transcaucasus, and in the eastern Ukraine around the small town of Shebelinka southeast of Kharkov. For a few years the North Caucasian fields were the largest producers in the country, but they were soon surpassed by the eastern Ukraine, which in turn was surpassed by Central Asian fields in the early 1970s. The

first large field in Central Asia, Gazli, near Bukhara, began large-scale production in 1959–1960. (Table 10-6) Now the production of all these fields is scheduled to be surpassed by the huge deposits along the Arctic coast of Western Siberia. At the same time, a smaller but continual expansion of production has been taking place in the gas fields of the Komi A.S.S.R. in northeastern European Russia, and most recently a huge new gas field has been discovered and opened up in 1974 in the vicinity of Orenburg in the southern Urals which promises to be second only in importance to the West Siberian fields.

As one after another of these discoveries have been made, estimated gas reserves have continually increased. Figures are still extremely tentative, but in 1975 the Soviets claimed that the explored gas reserves amounted to 24.5 trillion cubic meters, which was about 40 per cent of all the gas reserves in the world. These compared to approximately 7 trillion cubic meters in the United States. The Soviets estimated that potential reserves in the U.S.S.R., based on geological structure but not actual exploration, might amount to as much as 150 trillion cubic meters. Of the 24.5 trillion cubic meters of supposedly proven reserves, Western Siberia, primarily Tyumen Oblast, was credited with 14 trillion, Central Asia and Kazakhstan with 3.3 trillion, and Orenburg with 2.9 trillion. In Western Siberia the great Urengoy field, the largest in the country, alone was credited with 6 trillion cubic meters, and in Central Asia, Shatlyk field west of Mary in the Turkmen Republic, the largest in Central Asia, was credited with 1.5 trillion.

It is thought that the potential reserves of Western Siberia may be in the order of 70 trillion cubic meters, the Nadym-Pur region, including the large Urengoy and Medvezhye fields, alone having perhaps 26 trillion. It is thought that the Turkmen Republic in Central Asia might eventually prove to have as much as 9 trillion cubic meters. In the Far East, the Lena-Vilyuy lowland in Central Yakutia might have as much as 12.3 trillion cubic meters, although this region is still very little known. 1–2 billion cubic meters of gas have

Table 10–6   Geographical Distribution of Soviet Gas Production, in Billion Cubic Meters

Region	1955	1965	1970	1972	1974	1975	1976	1980 Plan
U.S.S.R.	9.0	127.7	198	221	261	289	321	435
R.S.F.S.R.	4.5	64.3	83.3	87	100	115	136	251
Europe	4.1	63.7	70		59	53	50	45
Komi	1.1	0.6	6.9	12.8		18.5	19.6	22
Orenburg			—	4	11.3	18	31	45
North Caucasus	0.6	39.0	50			16		
Krasnodar	0.3	22.3	26 [1]	14.3	6.7	5.5		
Stavropol	—	15.1	23	15.2	11.0	10.5		
Chechen-Ingush		1.4	4.3		4.0			
Volga-Urals	2.4	24.0						
Saratov	0.8	6.2						
Volgograd	—	6.6						
Siberia			11.0		29	40	51	155
Medvezhye			—	—	19	30	40	
Urengoy								30
Punga-Igrim							4	
Surgut area								14
Ukraine	2.9	39.4	60.9	67	68.3	68.7	68.7	53.8
Dashava	2.8	9.5						
Shebelinka	—	26.2	31			23		
Kretishche			—			27		
Azerbaydzhan	1.5	6.2	5.5	6.9	9.2	9.9	11.0	11.9
Kazakh			2.1	3.5	5.4	5.2	5.2	5.9
Uzbek	—	16.4	32.1	33.7	37.2	37.2	36.1	36.3
Gazli	—	16.4		33.1				
Turkmen			13.1	21.3	39.3	51.8	62.6	75
East (Dry Gas)				19.8		47		
Shatlyk					6	16	30	
West (Oil Well Gas)				1.5		3		

Sources: Various issues of *Soviet Geography: Review and Translation,* and Shabad, Theodore, *Basic Industrial Resources* of the U.S.S.R., Columbia, 1969, p. 25.
[1] 1969.
—, Small amounts. Blank spaces indicate no information.

been produced there annually since the mid 1960s.

As these new developments have taken place in the eastern parts of the country, production in some of the older fields in the west has peaked and declined. The old gas fields of Dashava in the western Ukraine have already been exhausted, and the evacuated rock structures are now being used as storage reservoirs for gas that is being piped in from Shebelinka, the Komi A.S.S.R., and Western Siberia for transmission to countries in eastern and western Europe. Annual production in the gas fields of the North Caucasus peaked at around 50 billion cubic meters in the late 1960s and amounted to only 16 billion cubic meters in 1975. Originally the Stavropol and Krasnodar fields were credited with reserves amounting to 690 billion cubic meters. By the mid 1970s about two-thirds this amount had been used. In an effort to maintain gas production in Krasnodar Kray, drilling is underway along the coast of the Sea of Azov where one well already has been brought into production.

The decline in gas production on the northern slopes of the Caucasus has been compensated to a small extent by increases in the Baku area of Azerbaydzhan on the southern side of the great Caucasus where the downward trend in oil production has been associated with an upward trend in gas production. The Karadag gas field southwest of Baku, which was brought into production simultaneously with the Krasnodar and Stavropol areas in the mid 1950s, depleted very early, and now the evacuated rock structures in the area are being used as storage reservoirs for Iranian gas which is being piped into the Transcaucasian pipeline system to service the Baku area, Tbilisi, and Yerevan. However, offshore drilling in the Bakhar gas field 30 kilometers southeast of Baku has allowed gas production in Azerbaydzhan to reach 11 billion cubic meters in 1976.

The Ukraine is still the largest producer in European U.S.S.R. It has been holding steady at about 67–68 billion cubic meters per year for the last five years. However, within the eastern Ukraine Shebelinka peaked at about 31 billion cubic meters in 1970–1971 and declined to 23 billion in 1975. Its production has been surpassed by the Kretishche field which was opened in 1970.

Most of the gas deposits in the Soviet Union are not associated with oil deposits. In 1973, out of a total U.S.S.R. gas production of 236 billion cubic meters, only 25 billion cubic meters were recovered from oil producing areas. The Soviets estimate that as much as 40 billion cubic meters might have been recovered from oil production, but they were not adequately equipped to use the gas, and in many oil fields it was being flared off. Of the 25 billion cubic meters recovered, 12 billion were processed in gas plants and yielded 2 million tons of liquid gas condensates. Since 1973, a number of large gas processing plants have been brought into production, and the amount of gas condensates produced annually amounts to about 8 million tons. The Vuktyl gas fields in the Komi A.S.S.R. are producing

about half of these condensates. Other fields with large amounts of "wet gas" are Orenburg in the southern Urals and Urengoy in Western Siberia, but production is only getting under way in those areas. However, in 1976, the first two stages of the Orenburg gas processing plant yielded 2.5 million tons of liquids, as well as 690,000 tons of sulfur, which represented about one-sixth of the total Soviet sulfur production. The Orenburg gas is high in H_2S and must be desulfurized before pipeline transmission to avoid corrosion. Another 160,000 tons of sulfur were recovered from the Mubarek gas fields near Bukhara in Central Asia.

Gas Processing and Transmission

The expansion of the gas industry depends on the ability to handle the gas through processing plants and pipelines, and it has been the limitations on the ability to construct these facilities fast enough that has limited the expansion of the use of natural gas. Although the use of natural gas has grown more rapidly than that of any other fuel during the last two decades, the utilization of gas might have grown even faster could the transport of gas have been effected by existing facilities, such as railroads and river routes, as was the case for oil. In the gas producing areas, often some processing has to be done through gas processing plants before the gas can be transmitted to users. In so-called "dry gas" wells this may not be necessary, but in "wet gas" wells and in gas associated with oil wells the gas should first be processed to separate out any liquid constituents and perhaps some noxious mineral constituents, such as the sulfur at Orenburg. These then can be used as by-products to provide a base for various kinds of chemical industries. In some cases, the liquid constituents of natural gas can be utilized directly as high octane distillate fuels in automobiles and other vehicles without refining.

Although the construction of gas processing plants has still not caught up with the expansion of gas production, large plants are being built, generally in the oil and gas producing areas of the country. Older gas plants date back to the 1950s when they were built in Caucasian oil producing areas such as Baku and Groznyy and in the Volga-Urals oil fields, particularly around Tuymazy and Shkapovo in the Bashkir A.S.S.R. and Minnibayevo near Almetyevsk in the Tatar A.S.S.R. The Minnibayevo plant is the largest processing plant in the Soviet Union, but it will eventually be surpassed in capacity by giants being built in Western Siberia. Newer plants have been built around Ufa, Ishimbay, and Salavat in the central part of the Bashkir A.S.S.R. and Nevinnomyssk and Krasnodar in the North Caucasus. There are now three processing plants in the Groznyy area of the North Caucasus alone. In addition, plants have been constructed in some of the consumer gas collecting areas such as Moscow, Yaroslavl, Volgograd, and Odessa.

A huge new plant was in the process of being completed at Nizhnevartovsk near the Samotlor oil field in the central part of Western Siberia in 1977. This will provide feedstocks to a large petrochemical plant being completed in Nizhnevartovsk and dry gas to the thermal electric station in nearby Surgut. Other large gas processing plants being built in Western Siberia at Pravdinsk and South Balyk near Surgut will provide feedstocks to the huge petrochemical plants being built in Tobolsk and Tomsk.

Plants are also being built at Novyy Uzen in the Mangyshlak oil field of western Kazakhstan, Gnedintsy in the Ukraine's Priluki oil field, and at the Rechitsa oil field in southeastern Belorussia. During the 1960s gas plants were built in the Volga region at Otradnyy and Neftegorsk in the Kuybyshev region and at Kstovo in the Volgograd region. Also in the mid 1960s a plant was opened at Sosnogorsk in the Komi A.S.S.R. Two small plants have been built in the western Ukraine.

Gas pipelines are being constructed at a tremendous pace in ever increasing diameters. Since the completion of the first long distance gas pipeline, 800 kilometers, from Saratov to Moscow in 1947, the total length of gas mains in the U.S.S.R. has increased to 103,500 kilometers at the end of 1976. The long distance mains are concentrated on bringing North Caucasian, east Ukrainian, Central Asian, and West Siberian gas to the central part of European Russia, the Urals, and the western Ukraine for export to eastern and western Europe. (Fig. 10–5) Many feeder lines distribute gas from main distributing points such as Torzhok northwest of Moscow and Yelets west of Lipetsk in the Central Chernozem Region to most of the cities in the European part of the country. Underground storage reservoirs for great quantities of gas have been created in porous sandstones in southern Novgorod Oblast northwest of Torzhok, in the exhausted gas-bearing strata of Karadag southwest of Baku in the Transcaucasus, and at Dashava in the western Ukraine.

As of 1977, four pipelines had been laid northwestward from the North Caucasus through the eastern Ukraine to the Moscow region, four lines had been laid from Central Asian gas fields to Moscow, two lines had been laid from Central Asia to the Urals, and a fourth line was being completed from the eastern Ukraine to the western Ukraine for export. A line was completed in 1977 all the way from Nadym in the West Siberian fields to the Punga fields on the lower Ob River and across the northern Urals to hook up with the "Northern Lights" pipeline system running southwestward from Ukhta in the Komi A.S.S.R. through Torzhok, Minsk, and Ivatsevichi to the Czechoslovak border. This line comprised the fourth line between Nadym and Punga, the first line between Punga and Ukhta, the third line between Ukhta and Torzhok, and the second line between Torzhok and the Czechoslovak border.

Also in 1977 a line was completed from Nizhnevartovsk in the central Ob Basin to carry oil well gas southeastward to Novosibirsk and the Kuznetsk Basin. Earlier, two lines had been completed southward from the West Siberian oil fields to supply the industrial middle Urals and hook up with lines that ran westward across the south-central Urals to such cities as Perm, Izhevsk, Kazan, Gorky, and Moscow. The Bratsvo ("brotherhood") Pipeline has been built across European Russia

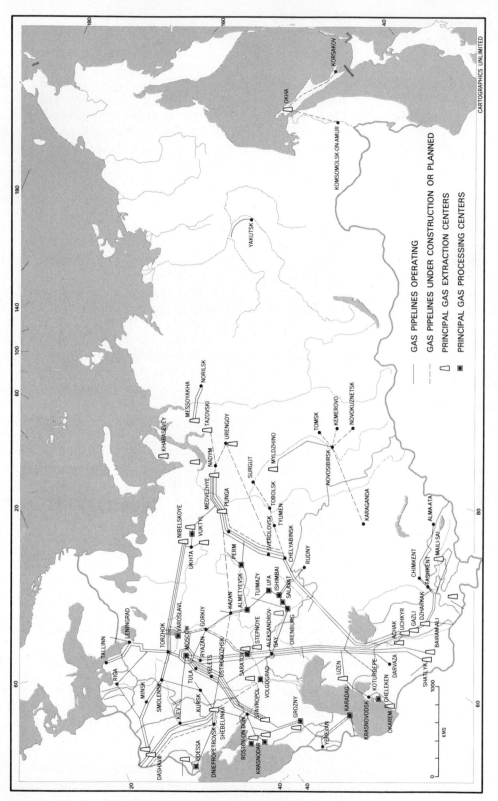

Figure 10-5 Gas production, processing plants, and pipelines.

to the western Ukraine to hook up with pipelines going to eastern and western Europe. A second larger string of this pipeline system, 56 inches in diameter, is under construction.

Most of the long distance pipelines now being constructed are of 56-inches diameter, whereas previously during the 1960s most of them were of 48-inches diameter. Although the U.S.S.R. still has only about one-third the length of pipelines that the U.S.A. has, most of the Soviet pipes are newer and their diameters are larger. In 1972, 29.5 per cent of the Soviet pipelines had diameters in excess of 32 inches while in the United States only 0.6 per cent were of that size.

Gas from the Uzbek and Turkmen fields of Central Asia is now being transmitted northwestward through a four-pipeline system to Moscow, northward through a two-pipeline system to the Urals, and eastward through a single pipeline to the major cities of Central Asia and southern Kazakhstan along the northern foot of the Tien Shan Mountains. About 21 per cent of the Central Asian gas is being used within the local region, 26 per cent moves to the Urals, and 53 per cent to European U.S.S.R.

The largest pipeline under construction at the present time, and perhaps the largest single pipeline construction project ever undertaken in the world, is the Orenburg gas line leading southwestward from the large Orenburg gas field through the pipeline junction of the Central Asian-Center pipeline system at Aleksandrov-Gay, Sokhranovka, and Kremenchug to the western Ukraine to supply gas for export to Poland, East Germany, Czechoslovakia, and Hungary. A branch line leads south from the central Ukraine through Rumania to supply Bulgaria. This pipeline extends for 2750 kilometers (1859 miles) and is 56 inches in diameter. By comparison, the Alaskan oil pipeline is 785 miles long and 48 inches in diameter and the Medvezhye-Moscow gas pipeline that was completed in 1977 is 1500 miles long and is 56 inches in diameter.

The Orenburg pipeline will be equipped with 22 compressor stations that will maintain pressures of 75 atmospheres which will give the pipeline a capacity to carry 28 billion cubic meters of gas annually. The construction of the line has necessitated moving 30 million cubic meters of earth and laying pipes across 170 streams, including the Volga, the Don, the Dnieper, and the Southern Bug, as well as over the Carpathian Mountains. Three hundred excavators and 500 pipe-laying machines have been operating simultaneously. About 20,000 men are employed on the project by four other member countries of COMECON besides the U.S.S.R. Construction has been proceeding under the flag of the Council for Mutual Economic Assistance. When the project was first discussed in the COMECON Council in June 1974, all seven European members were to be involved, and each country was given a separate portion of the pipeline to build. Rumania was to supply equipment and expertise. Although Hungary and Czechoslovakia later dropped out of the project, the other countries have gone ahead, and completion is scheduled for late 1978. East Germany, Poland, Rumania, and Bulgaria are to be paid for their efforts by deliveries of natural gas through the pipeline system over a period of years.

The exploitation of the West Siberian gas fields present particularly difficult problems because of the severity of the climate and the swampyness of the ground. In the main fields along the Arctic coast strong winds occur much of the time which in mid winter may drop wind chill factors below −150°C. During the thaw period throughout Western Siberia the earth is so swampy that roads and other construction work are difficult to maintain. The general lack of roads and railroads in the area necessitates the use of waterways to a great extent for the delivery of bulky supplies to establish settlements, construct gas field equipment, and lay pipelines. All materials and equipment for the large Medvezhye and Urengoy gas fields have had to be transported during the brief summer shipping season, May–October, from Trans Siberian rail terminals at Omsk and Tobolsk and, since 1975, at Surgut, by water down the Ob River to the Kara Sea and then up the shallow Nadym and Pur Rivers, a total water distance of up to 4000 kilometers. The water is so shallow in the Ob and Taz Gulfs and around the Yamal Peninsula that in many places boats cannot approach the immediate shoreline. The mouths of rivers are typically filled by sand bars which limit drafts of boats to 1–2 meters. Because of the shallowness of the water, ice breakers convoyed supply vessels along the Northern Sea Route in April of 1976 and 1977 before the breakup of the ice around the Yamal Peninsula to a new gas development at Kharasavey on the west coast of the Yamal Peninsula where supplies were unloaded on the fast ice about eight kilometers from shore.

Farther south gas fields being opened up along the northern fringes of the oil fields in central Western Siberia have to be approached from the base at Surgut where materials move up the Ob River to the mouth of the Agan, a right tributary, and then up the Agan to a supply settlement named Novoagansk, from which they are hauled overland northward, mostly by road during winter when the ground is frozen. Typically, the frozen streams are used in winter as roadbeds. In an effort to improve access to the gas fields, work is being pressed on a 700-kilometer Surgut-Urengoy Railroad, which is to become a key north-south transport route in Western Siberia. Work began on the new line in the spring of 1976, and Kholmogory oil field is supposed to be reached in 1978. Eventually the rail line is to be extended to the projected town of Yagelnyy which is a workers' settlement to be built on the Urengoy gas site consisting of high-rise buildings of eight and nine stories. A floating power station, manufactured in Tyumen, has been moored in the Pur River near the Yagel-nyy site to provide a temporary source of electricity to the area. This type of temporary electrical source has been used time and again in the remote northern areas before permanent facilities could be installed.

Gas Exports and Imports

Soviet exports of natural gas have been increasing rapidly in the last few years as pipelines have been extended from the western Ukraine across the border into Czechoslovakia, Poland, East Germany, Hungary, Bulgaria, Austria, Italy, West Germany, and France, and in the north from Leningrad into Finland. A considerable quantity of gas exports have been repayments for gas pipeline, pumping, and processing facilities supplied by East and West European countries. In 1975 the Soviet Union exported a total of 19.3 billion cubic meters of gas, 17.5 billion of which went via pipeline through the western Ukraine. The big customers were Czechoslovakia with 3.7 billion cubic meters, East Germany with 3.3 billion, West Germany with 3.1 billion, Poland with 2.5 billion, Italy with 2.3 billion, and Austria with 1.9 billion. (Table 10–7)

The Soviets have also been importing considerable quantities of gas from Iran and Afghanistan. In both cases, the foreign gas supplies adjacent Soviet areas via pipeline more cheaply

Table 10–7 U.S.S.R. Gas Exports and Imports, in Billions of Cubic Meters

	1965	1970	1974	1975
EXPORTS				
Total	0.4	3.3	14.0	19.3
To Eastern Europe	.4	2.3	8.5	11.3
Bulgaria	0	0	.3	1.2
Czechoslovakia	0	1.3	3.2	3.7
East Germany	0	0	2.9	3.3
Hungary	0	0	0	.6
Poland	.4	1.0	2.1	2.5
To Western Europe	0	1.0	5.5	8.0
Austria	0	1.0	2.1	1.9
Finland	0	0	.4	.7
Italy	0	0	.8	2.3
West Germany	0	0	2.2	3.1
IMPORTS				
Total	0	3.6	11.9	12.4
Afghanistan	0	2.6	2.8	2.8
Iran	0	1.0	9.1	9.6
Net hard currency earnings, million dollars				$52.5

Source: Jack, *et al.*, p. 476.

than remote domestic fields could supply these areas. In 1975 the Soviets imported 9.6 billion cubic meters of Iranian gas and 2.8 billion cubic meters of gas from Afghanistan.

The Soviets helped Iran build a trans-Iranian gas pipeline northward to the Azer-baydzhan border where the Iranian gas is stored in the exhausted gas-bearing strata of the Karadag fields southwest of Baku for future pumping into the Transcaucasian gas line system to Tbilisi and Yerevan. Eventually the Iranian gas is to cross the Great Caucasus via the pipeline that was built originally to carry North Caucasian gas southward. Iranian gas may flow further northwestward to join the gas flow into central European Russia.

In early 1976 an agreement was signed whereby natural gas from Iran would be transported across Soviet territory to west European countries. Under the agreement, 13.4 billion cubic meters of gas will be supplied by Iran annually from January 1981 through the year 2003. West Germany will get about 50 per cent of the gas, France 33 per cent, and Austria 17 per cent. The Soviets anticipate large capital investments for this project in their territory, and for this purpose banks in West Germany, France, and Austria have granted credits to the Soviet Union of 650 million rubles in hard currency which will be paid off by receipts from payments for transit.

In the Far East, American and Japanese firms signed a general agreement with the Soviets on November 22, 1974 which would provide for delivery on credit equipment and materials for the surveying of the Yakut gas deposits with expectations that subsequent deliveries of Soviet gas will be made to the U.S.A. and Japan. This would entail liquifying the gas somewhere on the Pacific coast before shipment to the west coast of the United States.

COAL

The Soviet Union is credited with about one-third of the world's proven coal reserves and almost two-thirds of the potential reserves based on geological structures.[1] Total coal reserves of the U.S.S.R. have been estimated at 5,527,983,000,000 metric tons, two-thirds of which are hard coal (bituminous and anthracite) and one-third of which is brown coal (lignite). At the current rate of production these reserves would last 7764 years. Hence, the Soviet Union is in no immediate danger of running out of coal. This is a comforting thought to the Soviets in a world which is rapidly running out of energy. And in their concern for future energy supplies, they have emphasized the need in their tenth five-year plan, 1976–1980, to reemphasize coal production and, along with expanded hydroelectric and nuclear power, as much as possible substitute these sources of energy for petroleum.

Therefore, it appears that the Soviets intend to emphasize the expansion of coal production again after 20 years of relative neglect as the oil and gas industries have expanded rapidly. However, this might not be too easy to achieve, since 90 per cent of the coal reserves lie in the eastern parts of the country far from major markets, long lead times are usually necessary for coal mining operations, and generally coal is much more expensive to mine and transport than are the liquid fuels. (Table 10–3) In addition, coal is a dirtier fuel that adds more to air pollution than fluid fuels do. Since so many power generation stations and other heavy fuel users are located within large metropolitan areas, coal might not be acceptable there because of environmental considerations. More than half of all thermal electric generating stations today, representing 37 per cent of the total conventional steam plant capacity, supply both heat and power, and to fulfill such joint functions most of them are located inside city limits.

During the tenth five-year plan, annual coal production is to increase 13 per cent, as compared to 12.3 per cent during the ninth five-year plan. Hence, no great increase in the rate of growth of coal production is scheduled

[1] Beamish-Crooke, J. A. E., "The role of coal in the Siberian and World Energy Markets," in Laulan, M. Yves, editor, *Exploitation of Siberia's Natural Resources*, NATO, Brussels, 1974, p. 181.

for the current five-year plan. Most western analysts conclude that it would be hard for the Soviets to alter their fuel balance very much before the 1990s. Therefore, the share of coal in total fuel consumption will probably continue to decrease through much of the 1980s, although perhaps at a continually declining rate. The share of coal in total energy consumption is scheduled to decrease from 30 per cent in 1975 to 26 per cent in 1980. The 1976 share of 29 per cent seems to be in line with these plans. (Table 10–1)

In spite of its declining relative role during the last two decades, coal production has increased absolutely at a rate of 2–3 percent per year. The Soviet Union for many years has been the leading coal producer in the world, regularly accounting for about one-fourth of the total world production. Coal is still the bulkiest freight on railroads, and, of course, it cannot be replaced by other fuels in many of the metallurgical industries. In the mid 1970s, coal still accounted for just under half of all boiler uses in the country and a little more than half of the electricity generation. Power stations consumed 34 per cent of the coal used in the U.S.S.R., coking plants 27 per cent, other industrial uses and households 35 per cent, and exports accounted for about 4 per cent of the production.

Regional Distribution of Reserves and Production

As can be seen in Figure 10–6, coal deposits are dispersed widely throughout the Soviet Union. They cover huge areas in the Central Siberian Upland between the Yenisey and Lena Rivers as well as in the southern part of Siberia, the south and central European regions of the country, and scattered deposits in northeast European U.S.S.R., the Urals, and Kazakhstan. By far the largest reserves are in the Tunguskan and Lena Basins in Eastern Siberia and the Far East. (Table 10–8) However, these deposits are so far from civilization that they will probably never be used to any significant extent. These coals are only

Table 10–8   Geological and Commercial Reserves of Coal by Generalized Basins, in Billions of Metric Tons

	Geological	Commercial
Tunguska	2345	<5
Lena	1647	<5
Kuznetsk	725	60
Kansk-Achinsk	601	73
Pechora	214	8
Donets	128	40
Irkutsk	76	7
Central Asia	68	<5
Turgay	61	6.3
Karaganda	51	7.5
South Yakut	23	<5
Moscow	20	<5
Sakhalin	12	<5
Ekibastuz	10	7.5
Dnieper	6	<5
Lvov-Volyn	<5	<5
Urals	<5	<5
Raichikhinsk (Amur Oblast)	<5	<5
Suchan (Maritime Kray)	<5	<5

Source: Gregory, J. S., Editor, *Geography of the USSR,* Collet's, London, 1975, p. 33.

mined locally to provide the needs of some remote mining, lumbering, or hunting settlements, and aggregate production is so small that the coal industry has not even been organized in these regions and statistics are not reported. The Kuznetsk Basin in Western Siberia, on the other hand, which has the third largest reserves, is the second most productive basin in the country, after the Donets Basin in the eastern Ukraine. (Table 10–9)

The Donets Basin in the eastern Ukraine and adjacent Rostov Oblast of the Russian Republic has consistently been the leading coal producing basin in the country since its development in the 1880s. This is in spite of its difficult geology and generally great depths which have made it one of the more costly producing basins. (Fig. 10–6) Although it does not produce nearly the share of total production that it did earlier, its absolute amount has been steadily increasing. At the present time it produces about one-third of the country's coal and about half its coking coal. The reason it is

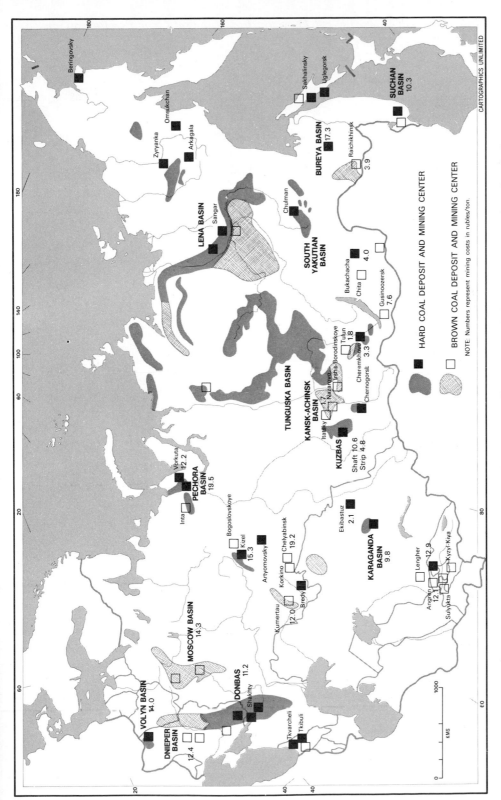

Figure 10–6   Coal and lignite basins and mining locations. Numbers next to basin names represent estimated production costs in rubles per standard ton (7,000,000 kilocalories). Modified from Dienes, 1973, p. 14.

Table 10–9   Geographical Distribution of Soviet Coal Production, in Million Metric Tons

	1970	1975	1976	1980 Plan
U.S.S.R.	624	701	712	805
anthracite	75.8	77.0		
coking coal	165	181		
other bituminous	235	280		
lignite	147.7	163.6		
shaft-mined	457.5	475.5		515
strip-mined	166.6	225.8		290
R.S.F.S.R.	345	381	387	436.5
coking coal	65	76.6		
Europe	99			
Moscow Basin	36	34		
Pechora Basin	21.5	24.2	25.8	31
coking coal	12.7	14.4		
Urals	47	36		
Siberia	199			
Kuznetsk Basin	110	139		162
coking coal	46.9	56.2		
Kansk-Achinsk	19	29		44
Ukraine	207	216	218	229
coking coal	80.7	84.7	84.3	
Donets Basin [1]	216	222	224	
coking coal [1]	84.3	88.5		
Georgia	2.3	2.05	1.93	2.17
coking coal	1.8	1.7	1.7	
Kazakhstan	61.6	92.2	93.7	126.1
Karaganda Basin	38.6	46.3	47.4	52
coking coal	16.9	18.1	19	
Ekibastuz	22.8	45.8	46.2	72
Uzbekistan	3.7	5.3	5.4	
Kirghizia	3.7	4.1	4.3	
Tadzhikistan	0.89	0.87	0.80	

Source: Soviet Geography: Review and Translation, April 1977, p. 264.
[1] Includes eastern portion of Donets Basin in Rostov Oblast (R.S.F.S.R.).

producing so heavily, of course, is because of its advantageous location close to the markets of European U.S.S.R. and the Krivoy Rog iron ore, which together with the Donbas coal has provided the basis for the primary buildup of heavy industry in the country.

The other important coking coal producing basins in the country are Kuznetsk, Karaganda, and Pechora. Of these, Karaganda is the most economically producing basin, but its coals are hampered by high ash contents and must be mixed with higher grade coals in blast furnaces. Therefore, the Kuznetsk coal, which is of considerably higher grade, is utilized more and shipped farther. In fact, the Kuznetsk coal is shipped farther than any other coal in the country, some of it finding its way almost to the western border in the southwestern Ukraine and completely to the eastern border where it is exported through Pacific ports. (Fig. 10–7)

On a delivery cost basis the Kuznetsk Basin commands a market area that includes the

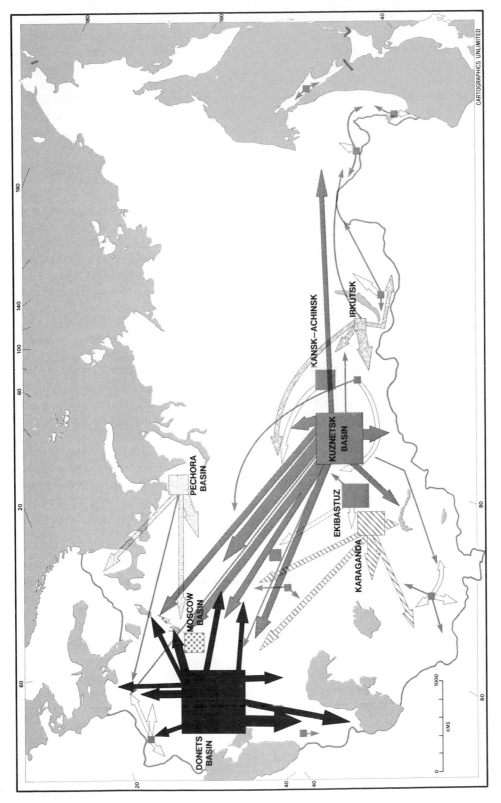

Figure 10-7   Coal production and flows from major basins.

Central Region around Moscow eastward to at least Krasnoyarsk in Eastern Siberia. According to Soviet calculations, the combined mining and transport costs of Kuznetsk coal are 2.45 rubles per ton lower than Donets coal in Moscow and even 1.44 rubles per ton lower in the Northwest around Leningrad. The Kuznetsk coals are nearer to the surface and lie in much thicker, more horizontal seams than the Donets coal does, and more of the Kuznetsk coal is subject to cheaper strip mining. Delivery prices of Kuznetsk coal in central and northwestern European Russia may be reduced even more by transshipping the coal from rail to water at Volga river terminals for western transportation by water via the Volga River and its extensions through the Moscow Canal and Volga-Baltic Canal systems. The Kuznetsk coal supplies about two-thirds of the coking coal used in the Urals, while the lower grade Karaganda coal supplies only about one-third, in spite of the fact that Karaganda is significantly closer to the Urals than Kuznetsk is.

The Pechora Basin has some of the highest mining costs in the country, but in spite of that production continues to expand because of the high quality of the coal. About 60 per cent of the Pechora production is coking grade, compared with 39 per cent in the Karaganda basin. The production costs of Pechora are high mainly because of the severe climate and remote location. If the Pechora-Vychegda-Kama Diversion Project is ever completed in northeast European Russia, this could supply an all-water route for Pechora coal to the industrial Urals and other parts of European U.S.S.R. which might completely change the cost effectiveness of the Pechora Basin. In general the Pechora coals are of as high quality as the Donets coals, and the Pechora Basin is credited with more geological reserves, although the reserves thus far readied for commercial production are smaller than in the Donets Basin. (Table 10–8)

A number of lesser coal fields have been producing for a long time because of their proximity to markets. Outstanding among these is the Moscow brown coal basin, which in spite of its low quality and high production

costs is located so advantageously that large quantities are mined for local heating and power generation. In fact, for many years the Moscow coal basin was third in production after the Donbas and the Kuzbas. But in recent years it has decreased both relatively and absolutely. At the present time the Moscow Basin ranks fifth in production after the Donbas, Kuzbas, Ekibastuz, and Karaganda. Other old producing minor fields are Volyn in the western Ukraine, Tkibuli and Tkvarcheli in Georgia, Kizel and Chelyabinsk in the Urals, Angren in Central Asia, Cheremkhovo near Irkutsk in Eastern Siberia, the Bureya fields in the southern part of the Far East, and scattered fields on Sakhalin Island, as well as some other scattered fields in the vicinity of the Trans Siberian Railroad in Eastern Siberia and the Far East. Of these, the Georgian coal mines contain some coking coal which is used in the blast furnace of the iron and steel plant that was established at Rustavi in eastern Georgia during the 1950s to supply iron and steel to the Transcaucasus. The small Kizel basin in the Urals partially finds a market for its coal in a mixture with Kuznetsk coal in some of the blast furnaces of the Urals.

A new hard coal development is underway at Neryungri in southern Yakutia in the Soviet Far East, primarily for export to Japan. Unlike most of the better coals of the country which are located deep underground and must be mined in deep shafts, the Neryungri coking coal is close enough to the surface to be strip mined. The Japanese have extended credits to the Soviet Union and supplied equipment for the development of this area in return for shipments of coking coal which will amount to about 13 million tons per year after 1983. The area was reached by branch railroad in 1977 which connects it southward to the Trans Siberian Railroad and eventually will connect with the Bykal-Amur Railroad when it is built through the region.

The cheapest mining costs in the country can be achieved in some of the lower grade coal fields that lie at or near the surface in eastern Kazakhstan and Eastern Siberia. (Fig. 10–6) Cheapest of all is the huge Kansk-Achinsk field that stretches for about 700 kilometers along the Trans Siberian Railroad on either side of the big city of Krasnoyarsk. This field is credited with the fourth largest reserves in the country. However, the coal is of very low quality, crumbly and hard to transport, and subject to spontaneous combustion so storage is a problem. Development here has lagged behind plans because of these problems which have not yet been adequately solved. The Soviets intend to build huge minehead power plants in the Kansk-Achinsk area to utilize the coal locally and transport the electricity over ultrahigh voltage transmission lines westward to European Russia. However, they seem to be having problems with the perfection of long distance electrical transmission technology. Although original plans called for the Kansk-Achinsk field to become the largest producing basin in the country, producing 300–400 million tons per year by 1990, at the present time it is producing only around 30 million tons per year, and not much is being said these days about specific plans for the future.

A similar brown coal field which lies at the surface that has been much more amenable to exploitation is the much smaller Ekibastuz deposit in northeastern Kazakhstan. The quality is a little higher than that at Kansk-Achinsk, and it is not so crumbly and is easier to move and store. Production there has soared during the last two decades, expanding more rapidly than at any other coal producing area in the country. In 1977 the Ekibastuz production surpassed that of Karaganda, which made Ekibastuz the third largest producing basin in the country. Seams of lignite lie right at the surface and extend downward for ten meters or more. Mining is accomplished by huge rotary excavators that can fill an entire train in one hour. Ekibastuz coal is now being used for heating and power generation purposes as far west as the Urals. Future plans for the field are similar to those for the Kansk-Achinsk area, involving the construction of huge power plants at mineheads to transmit electricity westward over high voltage lines.

Another development of a surface deposit of brown coal has taken place in the Azey Basin

west of Cheremkhovo in Irkutsk Oblast in Eastern Siberia as the old Cheremkhovo deep mines have been phased out and even the strip mines at Cheremkhovo have become depleted. By 1975, the Azey Basin accounted for 44 per cent of all Irkutsk Oblast coal production, and the Cheremkhovo Basin for 56 per cent.

Development has been renewed in the South Urals lignite basin which straddles the boundary between the Bashkir A.S.S.R. and Orenburg Oblast around the town of Kumertau. Production began there in 1952, but proceeded only very slowly through the 1960s as the role of coal diminished in the total energy development of the country. By 1974 Kumertau produced only 8.2 million tons. Now, as the pendulum is beginning to swing back toward coal once more, exploitation has been accelerated in this area, and it is planned to raise the annual production eventually to around 15 million tons.

In recent years Soviet geologists have discovered many deposits of brown coal in the Turgay Lowland in Kustanay Oblast of northern Kazakhstan. These are near the surface and suitable for strip mining and are situated only 200–500 kilometers from big power stations in the Urals. Tentative plans have been announced for some of these deposits, as well as another deposit south of Ekibastuz.

Coal Exports and Imports

The Soviets have been exporting about 4 per cent of their bituminous coal production and 6 per cent of their anthracite production. In 1975 this amounted to 26.1 million metric tons, 14.8 million of which went to Eastern Europe, particularly Bulgaria and East Germany who have no significant high grade coal resources of their own. 5.5 million tons went to Western Europe, mainly France and Italy, and 3.3 million tons went to Japan. The export of 9.6 million tons to non-communist countries earned $385,000,000 worth of hard currency during 1975. Practically all of these exports came from the Kuznetsk Basin, since the European export of Donetsk coal has been curtailed as the Soviets become more conservative about the use of this limited coal field. Eventually it is planned that Neryungri in southern Yakutia may supply as much as 40 million tons per year, much of which may be exported. Long-term export intentions of the Soviets regarding this coal are indicated by the construction of a specialized coal loading terminal at the new port of Wrangel (Vostochnyy) on the Pacific coast.

Part of the Soviet coal exports are balanced by imports from Poland into adjacent parts of the western Soviet Union. In 1975 these imports amounted to 9.8 million metric tons. In addition to net coal exports, the Soviet Union has been exporting about 4.5 million tons of coke per year. Most of this goes to East European countries that have large iron and steel industries and poor coking coal bases, such as East Germany, Rumania, and Hungary. Since the Soviet coke producing capacity is limited and domestic needs are growing rapidly, it cannot be expected that coke exports will increase significantly. It is more likely that coking coal exports will grow and that the coal will be coked at its destinations.

SHALE

Shale production has persisted in eastern Estonia and adjacent parts of Leningrad Oblast in the Russian Republic for many years in spite of the fact that the cost of production of energy from shale is more expensive than from any other fuel except firewood. In recent years the Soviet Union has been producing 30–40 million tons of oil shale per year, almost all of which comes from the Estonian-Leningrad region. Production of shale has been expanding at a rate commensurate with that of total fuel expansion. Since the mid 1950s oil shale has accounted for about 0.7 per cent of energy output in the country. Shale deposits are scattered about the eastern part of the European plain also, particularly around Syzran, near Kuybyshev, and large deposits exist in the northern part of the Central Siberian Uplands. However, none of these deposits have been

exploited, except for the Syzran deposits occasionally. Although shale production makes up less than one per cent of total energy production in the Soviet Union, the Estonian mining area is the largest shale operation in the world, and is very important to the Baltic Region.

Considerable amounts of gas used to be produced from the shale processing at Kohtla-Jarve, and a pipeline was built westward to Tallinn and eastward to Leningrad to transmit this shale gas. However, with the coming of abundant supplies of natural gas through pipeline systems into Leningrad, the gas flow on the Tallinn-Leningrad pipeline has been reversed and natural gas now supplies the entire area. At present about two-thirds of the shale production is utilized in large electric power generating plants at the mines, and the other third is used for various chemicals and refined shale products. The little bit of shale that is produced in the Syzran area on the Volga is utilized for power generation.

PEAT

About 50 million tons of peat are produced annually in the Soviet Union. This fluctuates drastically year by year. During recent years it has reached as much as 61.2 million tons in 1972 and as little as 32.8 million tons in 1976. However, over the years the absolute amount has been increasing slowly while peat's share of total energy production in the Soviet Union has been constantly declining. In 1976 it provided 0.7 per cent of the country's energy, exactly the same as shale.

Almost all the peat is dug in the bogs in the western part of the country, particularly Belorussia, the Baltic Republics, and adjacent parts of the Russian Republic. Most of it is used for heating and power generation, but some is now being processed chemically to produce artificial products, even margarine.

FIREWOOD

As late as 1955, firewood was the third most

important fuel in the Soviet Union, after coal and oil. But since that time, the production of firewood has diminished slowly absolutely and rapidly relatively, as other fuels, particularly natural gas and oil, have expanded rapidly. In 1976 firewood accounted for only 1.5 per cent of the energy production of the Soviet Union; however, its importance should not be underestimated, as it is still the primary fuel for heating homes in rural areas. A common site throughout the Soviet Union in the rural areas is the huge, neat stack of split firewood outside each cottage.

ELECTRICITY

About one-fourth of the gross energy supply in the Soviet Union is converted into electricity. During the early 1970s one-fourth of all petroleum products and over two-fifths of the natural gas were burned for the generation of electricity, steam, and hot water, often in the same power stations. Lenin early emphasized the importance of electricity to the economy when he coined his famous equation: "Communism equals Soviet power plus electrification of the whole country." Since that time, the production of electricity has increased about four times as rapidly as the production of industry in general. However, the rate of growth recently has been slowing until now it is about equal to that of the entire economy. The Soviets still have a way to go to satiate their needs for electricity. In 1976 they produced 1,111,420,000,000 kilowatt-hours of electricity, which was roughly half that produced by the United States. On a per capita basis, then, the Soviet Union is producing only about 42 per cent as much electricity as the United States is. And in the Soviet Union more of the electricity is used for industrial and construction purposes and less in households than in the United States. The pattern of consumption in the Soviet Union is shown in Table 10–10.

Soviet electricity is overwhelmingly produced by thermal stations. In 1976 only 18.9 per cent of the electrical generating capacity in

Table 10–10   Soviet Consumption of Electricity by Branch of the Economy, in Billion Kilowatt-Hours

	1975	1980 Plan
Industry	582	740
Construction	20	27
Transportation	74	99
Households	124	170
Agriculture	73	130
Operating Losses	152	194
Exports	11	20
Total	1038	1380

Source: Shabad, "News Notes," *Soviet Geography: Review and Translation,* December 1976, p. 719.

the Soviet Union was in hydroplants, and these produced only 12.2 per cent of the country's electricity. Nuclear plants produced 2 per cent of the electricity, and thermal plants produced more than 85 per cent. A small percentage was also produced by Diesel installations, which, of course, also burned fossil fuels.

From 1965 to 1975, the share of electricity produced by hydropower diminished from 16 per cent to 12.1 per cent. This trend seems to be slowly changing now, as the general world energy crunch has induced the Soviets to put more emphasis on the future use of hydro and nuclear power and the utilization of cheap, low grade coal that can be strip mined in such areas as Ekibastuz and Kansk-Achinsk. However, it will be difficult technically to reconvert thermal power stations from gas and oil to coal or other solid fuels, and it may be impossible environmentally to effect this change since so many of the thermal stations produce not only electricity but also centralized heating for large metropolitan areas and therefore are built within the metropolitan areas themselves. A conversion of these plants to coal would not meet air pollution standards that have been set in these areas. Also, the planning process needs a rather long lead time. Nevertheless, there is some indication that during the present five-year plan, 1976–1980, more emphasis will be placed on coal, hydroelectricity, and nuclear power than was true during the 1971–1975 plan. As compared to 1971–1975, the growth in new power generating capacity during 1976–1980 will be only 94 per cent as much in thermal stations, as against 360 per cent as much in nuclear stations and 158 per cent as much in hydroelectric stations. By 1980 it is planned that hydroelectric stations will generate 14.3 per cent of the country's electricity and nuclear stations will generate 6 per cent, while thermal and Diesel output will decline to 79.7 per cent.

In the thermal and Diesel stations, coal will account for 42.5 per cent of the fuel consumption, oil 28 per cent, and gas 25.1 per cent. This is a small decline in the shares of oil and gas and a small gain in the share of coal over 1975. (Table 10–11) But oil and gas will still be emphasized much more than prior to 1965. In 1960 coal accounted for 70.9 per cent of thermal electricity generation and peat accounted for 7 per cent, almost as much as oil. During the 1960s and first half of the 1970s there was a rapid changeover in thermal electric generation from solid fuels to oil and gas. This changeover was even more rapid than it had been in the United States. Now it appears that the Soviets would like to treat oil and gas as special fuels and limit their use in stationary boilers as much as possible. But it is going to be hard to revert back to previous fuel balances in boilers and furnaces.

Hydropower

Although the Soviet Union boasts 12 per cent of the world's hydropower resources, more than any other country, much of this resource cannot be realized. At present only 13 per cent is being utilized. About 50 per cent of the potential is located north of 60 degrees latitude where the climate is forbidding, the population sparse, the river runoff extremely irregular, and construction problems enormous due to permafrost, poor drainage, and lack of transportation facilities. 82 per cent of the hydro potential lies in the large rivers of Siberia, the Far East, and Central Asia, while 80 per cent

of the market for electricity is in European U.S.S.R., and so far the Soviets have not been able to consummate their long-talked about extra-long-distance transmission of electricity over extra-high-voltage transmission lines. Apparently they have not yet solved the technological problems entailed in such transmissions. In this light, it appears significant that the Soviets cut back on the ultimate capacity of the Ust-Ilimsk station on the Angara River as it was being completed in 1977 during the critical period of reassessment of the feasibility of transmitting electricity all the way from Eastern Siberia to European Russia. The plant had originally been designed for a generating capacity of 4320 megawatts, which entailed the installation of 18 generating units of 240 megawatts each. But after the installation of the fifteenth unit in 1977, the Soviets decided to call the plant complete with a total capacity of 3600 megawatts. It will be instructive to see during the next few years whether the Soviets cut back on other electrical construction projects in the eastern regions. It appears already that construction is lagging way behind original plans for huge minehead thermal power plants in the Ekibaskuz and Kansk-Achinsk surface deposits of brown coal in northeastern Kazakhstan and Eastern Siberia.

Of course, the share of hydropower in electrical generation varies a great deal from one part of the country to another. In European Russia it accounts for less than 10 per cent of total electrical production, while in Eastern Siberia it contributes 64 per cent of the total. From the Urals westward, close to half the economically exploitable hydropower capacity is already installed or under construction, and the rest is sorely needed for peaking during hours of the day when uses are greatest. Much of the present hydroelectric capacity is used for peaking purposes, for that matter. This means that hydroplants are utilized only during times of day when extra loads of electricity are needed, and the basic electrical production is accomplished by thermal plants. Thus, hydroplants are often used very inefficiently. During the mid 1970s it was reported that hydroelectric stations were turned on only about 23 per

Table 10–11   Fuel Uses in Thermal Electric Stations, 1960–1980 Plan, in Per Cents of Total

Fuel	1960	1965	1970	1975	1980 Plan
Gas	12.3	25.6	26	25.7	25.1
Fuel Oil	7.5	12.8	22.5	28.8	28
Coal	70.9	54.6	46.1	41.3	42.5
Peat	7	4.5	3.1	2	2.6
Shale	1	1.5	1.7	1.7	1.4
Other	1.3	1	0.6	0.5	0.4

Source: Nekrasov and Pervukhin, p. 151.

cent of the time in the European part of the country and 46 per cent of the time in the Asiatic part. And much of the time they were running, they were using only about half their installed capacity. Part of this limited use of installed hydroelectric capacity is due to restricted water flow in many streams such as the Volga which would not have enough water to meet peak load needs if the water were not conserved in the reservoirs behind the dams for the periods when it was most needed. Also, other uses such as navigation require conservation of the water. The multipurpose use of water generally has meant that substantially less water is available for power generation than would be if that were the only use of the river. Conflicting demands on water usage will be dealt with thoroughly in Chapter 14.

During the mid 1970s, about 60 hydroelectric stations of various sizes were under construction in all parts of the country. As these are now coming into production, they are causing a small increase in the share of total electricity produced by hydropower. But after this wave of new construction has been completed, probably the share of electricity produced by hydroplants will decline once more as production from nuclear and thermal plants increases more rapidly. It has been estimated that sometime after 1980 the share of electricity generated by hydropower will probably decrease to less than 10 per cent.

As early as 1957, when Premier Khrushchev was dedicating the newly completed Kuybyshev dam on the Volga, he made the statement that although over the long term hydropower generally produces electricity more cheaply than any other source of power, the construction of hydroplants ties up capital investments for many years before any returns are realized. And at that time he pointed out that time was of the essence, as well as costs, in Soviet efforts to catch up with the West. He pointed out that whereas thermal power plants could be constructed on a standard plan and set down most anywhere they are needed, hydroplants must be planned individually, each one being unique and tied to a certain location. Although in subsequent years many hydroplants have been constructed, the changing fuel usage in thermal plants during the past two decades has swung the cost factors more to favor the thermal plants as time has gone on. The large-scale conversion of thermal plants to gas and oil has reduced the costs of fuels in thermal plants to as little as one-twelfth that of the original coal. And the recent opening up of cheaply operating strip mines in brown coal areas with large minehead thermal power plants has greatly increased the cost effectiveness of coal burning plants. Thus, on a cost basis, hydropower plants do not have as much advantage as they used to, and they still have time and location disadvantages.

Since most of the hydroelectric stations in the Soviet Union are integral parts of multipurpose water construction projects and water basin developments, individual projects will be discussed in their entirety in Chapter 14. But the main hydroelectric plants that have been completed or are under construction are listed here in Table 10–12. These do not include many smaller stations that are scattered about the country for which there is little information.

Table 10–12   Data on Selected Hydroelectric Projects

	Height of Dam Meters	Length of Dam Meters	Reservoir Area in Square Kilometers	Ultimate Power Capacity Megawatts	Date Construction Started	Date Production Started
Volga River						
Ivankovo				300	1932	1937
Uglich				110	1935	1940
Rybinsk			4,550	330	1936	1941
Gorky			1,591	520	1947	1955
Cheboksary				1,400	1969	1980?
Kuybyshev	80	4,400	6,450	2,300	1950	1955
Saratov	13		1,950	1,290	1956	1967
Volgograd	48	6,000	3,117	2,563	1950	1958
Kama River						
Kama (Perm)			1,915	504	1939	1954
Votkinsk			1,120	1,000	1954	1961
Nizhnekamsk			2,850	1,080	1963	
Don River						
Tsimlyansk			2,700	164		1952
Dnieper River						
Kiev				370	1961	1964
Kanev				420	1963	
Kremenchug			2,250	625	1954	1959
Dneprodzerzhinsk				350	1956	1963
Dnieproges (Zaporozhye)				1,400 [a]	1927	1932
Kakhovka	20		2,160	343	1951	1955
Dniester River						
Dniester				702	1978?	1985?
Western Dvina River (Daugava)						
Kagums				68		1953
Plavinas				825	1961	1965
Riga				384		1975
Sulak River						
Chirkey	230			1,000		1974
Rioni River						
Rioni				48		1933
Gumati (2 stations)				66.5		1956–1958
Ladzhanuri				118		1960
Vartsikhe (4 stations)				176		1976
Inguri River	300					
Main Underground Plant				1,300	1961	1977
Four Smaller Plants				340		1971–1972
Kura River						
Mingechaur				400		1955

	Height of Dam Meters	Length of Dam Meters	Reservoir Area in Square Kilometers	Ultimate Power Capacity Megawatts	Date Construction Started	Date Production Started
Sevan-Razdan Cascade						
(6 stations)				600		1960
Vorotan River						
Tatev				157		1970
Shamb and Spandaryan				250		1980?
Vakhsh River						
Rogun	345			3,600	1978	
Nurek	315	1,000		2,700		1972
Perepadnaya				29.6		1958
Tsentralnaya				18		1964
Golovnaya				210		1962
Naryn River						
Toktogul				1,200		1975
Chirchik River						
Bazsu-Chirchik						
(16 stations)				320		1926–1960
Charvak				600		1972
Khodzhikent				165		1967
Gazalkent				120	1977	
Ili River						
Kapchagay	50			434		1970
Ob River						
Novosibirsk			1,070	400	1957	1959
Irtysh River						
Bukhtarma			5,510	675	1953	1960
Ust-Kamenogorsk				330	1939	1952
Yenisey River						
Krasnoyarsk	130	1,100	2,340	6,000	1956	1967
Sayan-Shushenskoye	240			6,400	1964	1978–1980
Angara River						
Irkutsk		2,363		660	1950	1956
Bratsk	100		5,470	4,500	1956	1961
Ust-Ilimsk				3,600	1962	1974
Boguchany				4,000	1974	1983?
Zeya River						
Zeya	115			1,290	1964	1975
Bureya River						
Talakan	140			2,000	1976	1983?
Vilyuy River						
Vilyuy (Chernyshevskiy)				648	1964	1967
Khantayka River						
Snezhnogorsk				440		1970

Sources: Data are from scattered Soviet sources; Shabad "News Notes" in various issues of *Soviet Geography: Review and Translation;* Michel and Klain, p. 208; and Nikolskiy, I. V., *et. al., Geografiya vodnogo transporta SSSR,* Moscow, 1975, p. 69.

[a] Destroyed during World War II and reconstructed in 1949. Second stage completed in 1977.

? Speculative.

As can be seen, such rivers as the Volga, the Kama, the Don, the Dnieper, and some other smaller streams on the European Plain have been pretty well developed in their entirety. Significant amounts of electricity are now being generated along the Rioni and Inguri Rivers in western Georgia, the Kura River in Azerbaydzhan, and the Vorotan River and Sevan-Razdan Cascade in Armenia, but these by no means exhaust the potentials in the Transcaucasus. Large power potential exists in the mountains of Central Asia, but since so many of the water construction projects there are primarily for the purpose of irrigation, many of them do not include hydroelectric installations. The main hydroelectric plants have been built on the Vakhsh, Naryn, Chirchik, and Ili Rivers.

Huge hydroelectric plants have been built in Siberia, particularly on the Yenisey River and its main right-bank tributary, the Angara. The largest power plants in the world are found in this Eastern Siberian area. Smaller plants are found on the Ob and Irtysh Rivers in Western Siberia and the Zeya and Bureya Rivers in the Soviet Far East. The Soviets are beginning to develop some of the rivers of the north, such as the Vilyuy and Khantayka Rivers to provide power bases for some of the mining activities such as the diamonds and platinum group metals in the west-central portions of the Central Siberian Uplands. However, much hydropower potential still remains to be realized throughout the eastern regions. Its development will have to await the development of markets.

Though the list of hydroelectric stations is long and the capacity of some of the stations is huge, the list of thermal stations in the country would be much longer, and the capacity of individual stations is becoming just as large as the hydro stations. Many of the thermal power plants scattered about the more populated parts of the country now have capacities on the order

Figure 10–8   The Bratsk Dam on the Angara River in Eastern Siberia generates more electricity than any other plant in the world because of the steady flow of water originating in Lake Baykal. Photo by Henry A. Coppock.

Figure 10–9   Generator room of the Bratsk Dam. Photo by Henry A. Coppock.

of 3–4 thousand megawatts, and stations for as much as 6000 megawatts are planned for mine-head locations in such coal basins as Ekibastuz and Kansk-Achinsk. As can be seen in Table 10–13 Eastern Siberia with its huge hydro-electric plants produced only 97.2 billion kilowatt-hours of electricity in 1975 out of a U.S.S.R. total of 1,039. The bulk of the electrical production is in the European Plain of the R.S.F.S.R., the Ukraine, and adjacent republics in the western part of the country, and the bulk of the production there is thermal production. There is a great areal discrepancy between the locations of hydropower and the market for electricity, and until very-long-distance electrical transmission technology can be perfected, the Soviets are going to have to make use of whatever resources they have in the populated parts of the country. These are primarily the fossil fuels. If they do ever overcome major electrical line losses on long distance transmissions, they hope eventually to form an all-Union grid out of existing lines which can then feed electricity from any part of the country to any other part. Among other things this would take advantage of the instantaneous differences in daily peak loads among the eleven time zones of the country, so that when one region is at its peak another region a long distance away can supply electricity to it during its period of minimum use. The Soviets estimate that they can save considerable amounts of wasted electrical capacity this way.

Nuclear Power

With much of the demand for electricity in the European part of the country where hydropower is limited and fossil fuels generally entail long distance hauls, the Soviets are attempting to turn to other forms of electrical generation to solve their problems. Chief

Table 10–13 *Geographical Distribution of Soviet Electric Production, 1975, in Billion Kilowatt-Hours*

U.S.S.R	1039
R.S.F.S.R.	640
Europe	339
Northwest	52.3
Central	114.6
Volgo-Vyatka	14.9
Central Chernozem	15.0
Volga	101.9
North Caucasus	39.1
Urals	112.1
Siberia	189
West Siberia	70.1
East Siberia	97.2
Far East	21.9
Ukraine	195
Donets Basin	58
Moldavia	13.7
Belorussia	26.7
Baltic:	28.6
Lithuania	9 0
Latvia	2.9
Estonia	16.7
Transcaucasia:	35.5
Armenia	9.2
Azerbaydzhan	14.7
Georgia	11.6
Kazakhstan	52.5
Central Asia:	47.2
Kirghizia	4.4
Uzbekistan	33.6
Tadzhikistan	4.7
Turkmenia	4.5

Source: Soviet Geography: Review and Translation, April 1977, p. 272.

among these at the present time is nuclear power. Although the world's first nuclear reactor for the production of electrical energy was activated at the Obninsk Research Center southwest of Moscow in 1954, progress in the development of nuclear energy in the Soviet Union lagged during the 1950s and 1960s while other countries, notably the United States, were developing nuclear electrical generating plants rapidly. By 1975 the Soviet Union had installed a generating capacity of 5500 megawatts in nuclear stations. By comparison the United States had 39,600 megawatt capacity in nuclear stations. The Soviet nuclear capacity represented only 2.5 per cent of the country's total electrical generating capacity.

However, during the 1970s, as the United States and West Germany have questioned their commitment to nuclear energy and Sweden has totally abandoned it, the U.S.S.R. has moved ahead with the intent to make nuclear energy a main component in the electrical generating industry of the country. By 1980 they plan to have installed 19,400 megawatts of nuclear capacity. This is a major scaling down of their original plan of 30,000 megawatts by 1980, which indicates that they are having problems with nuclear development as well as other forms of energy. Nevertheless, the Soviets plan eventually to establish many large nuclear plants around the country and in some of the neighboring countries as well. They have already contracted for nuclear stations in East Germany, Bulgaria, Finland, Hungary, Czechoslovakia, Poland, and their Caribbean partner, Cuba.

A list of plants already constructed in the Soviet Union along with names of plants that are projected for the near future is presented in Table 10–14. Their locations are shown on Figure 10–10. Since the region east of the Urals has an abundance of hydroelectric potential and fossil fuels, no more nuclear stations are planned for that part of the country. The only stations there now are the Beloyarsk plant near Sverdlovsk on the east side of the Urals, the unlocated "Siberian" plant, probably at Troitsk in the southern Urals, and the small, 48-megawatt, station in the gold mining center of Bilibino along the Arctic Coast of the Chukotsk Peninsula in the Far East. Nuclear stations are particularly useful in remote areas where mining activity requires considerable amounts of electrical power but has no adequate transport and settlement infrastructures to provide the basis for conventional types of power stations.

Most of the turbines for nuclear power plants so far have been built in the city of

Figure 10–10   Atomic power stations in the U.S.S.R., after Pryde, p. 78. Professor Pryde graciously provided an updated version of the map.

Kharkov, but during the tenth five-year plan a huge construction project has been initiated to build a factory to mass-produce reactor vessels of 1000 mcgawatts each to supply units for the large new stations planned for the near future. This huge plant, known as "Atommash" is being built along the Don River near the city of Volgodonsk. The plant will occupy a site 1600 acres in size. The main assembly plant will be one-half mile long, one-fourth mile wide, and 150 feet high. It is expected that the plant will begin producing nuclear reactors in 1978 and reach full-scale production by 1980 or shortly thereafter. In addition, a new nuclear engineering college, to be known as the Atomic Power Institute, is being created at the research

Table 10–14   Nuclear Power Reactors in the U.S.S.R.

Station Name and Reactor Number	Station Site	Reactor Designation [a]	Began Operation	Capacity Megawatts [b,c]
Obninsk	Obninsk	AM-1	1954	5 [c]
Siberian	Troitsk (?)	?(Graphite)	1958	600
Obninsk	Obninsk	BR-5	1959	12 [c]
Novomelekess — 1	Dimitrovgrad [d]	VK-50	1962	50–70 [c]
Beloyarsk — 1	Beloyarsk	AMB-1	1964	100
Novovoronezh — 1	Novovoronezh	VVER-1	1964	210–280
Beloyarsk — 2	Beloyarsk	AMB-2	1967	200
Novovoronezh — 2	Novovoronezh	VVER-2	1969	365
Novomelekess — 2	Dimitrovgrad	BOR-60	1969	12 [c]
Novovoronezh — 3	Novovoronezh	VVER	1971	440
Shevchenko	Shevchenko	BN-350	1972	150
Novovoronezh — 4	Novovoronezh	VVER	1972	440
Bilibino — 1, 2, 3	Bilibino	VK-12	1973–1975	36
Kola — 1	Polyarnyye zori	VVER	1973	440
Leningrad — 1	Sosnovyy bor	RBMK-1000	1973	1000
Kola — 2	Polyarnyye zori	VVER	1974	440
Leningrad — 2	Sosnovyy bor	RBMK-1000	1975	1000
Bilibino — 4	Bilibino	VK-12	1976	12
Kursk — 1	Kurchatov	RBMK-1000	1976	1000
Armenian — 1	Metsamor	VVER	1976	405
Kursk — 2	Kurchatov	RBMK-1000	(1977–1980)	1000
Armenian — 2	Metsamor	VVER	(1977–1980)	405
Novovoronezh — 5	Novovoronezh	VVER	(1977–1980)	1000
Beloyarsk — 3	Beloyarsk	BN-600	(1977–1980)	600
Chernobyl — 1	Chernobyl	RBMK-1000	(1977–1980)	1000
Chernobyl — 2	Chernobyl	RBMK-1000	(1977–1980)	1000
Smolensk — 1	Desnogorsk	RBMK-1000	(1977–1980)	1000
Smolensk — 2	Desnogorsk	RBMK-1000	(1977–1980)	1000
West Ukraine (Rovno)	Rafalovka	VVER	(1977–1980)	440
West Ukraine (Rovno)	Rafalovka	VVER	(1977–1980)	440
Kalinin — 1	Udomlya	VVER/RBMK [e]	(1977–1980)	1000
Kalinin — 2	Udomlya	VVER/RBMK [e]	(1977–1980)	1000
Drukshai — 1	Ignalina	RBMK-1500	(1977–1980)	1500
Drukshai — 2	Ignalina	RBMK-1500	(1977–1980)?	1500
South Ukraine — 1	Konstantinov	VVER	(1977–1980)	1000
South Ukraine — 2	Konstantinov	VVER	(1977–1980)?	1000
Leningrad — 3	Sosnovyy bor	RBMK-1000	(1977–1980)	1000
Leningrad — 4	Sosnovyy bor	RBMK-1000	(1977–1980)?	1000

complex at Obninsk. It is planned that up to 3500 students can be accommodated simultaneously for training there.[2] Obviously, with such installations underway, the Soviets have unequivocally committed themselves to a sustained large-scale development of nuclear energy in the country. This is being underpinned by widely publicized propaganda conceived to reassure the Soviet people that nuclear energy is perfectly safe.

In some of the remote mining and exploration areas, particularly in the north, a temporary electrical power supply is now being provided by a newly developed floating nuclear power plant that is being produced in the Tyumen shipyards in Western Siberia which can be floated down streams and along the Northern Sea Route of the Arctic coast into ports that service developing areas. These so-called "severnoye siyaniye" (northern lights) plants are four-story ships that contain power stations with capacities of 24,000 kilowatts and living quarters for crews of 30 people. They generally are being utilized only temporarily

[2] Much of the information on nuclear plants has been derived from Pryde.

while permanent power plants are built in adjacent areas.

Other Sources of Energy

The Soviets are eager to develop such things as tidal power, geothermal, and solar energy, but with present levels of technology these sources of energy are limited and expensive. The Soviets have already experimented with a small tidal electrical generation unit in a narrow fjord of the Barents Sea along the Murman coast of the Kola Peninsula, and they intend to build much larger stations along western portions of the Arctic coast in the near future. One planned for the estuary of the Mezen River in Archangel Oblast has a projected capacity of 14,000 megawatts.

Geothermal heat is being used in an experimental power station on Kamchatka which was inaugurated in 1966. Although this is the only power station so far to use this source of energy, geothermal heat has been used for some time to heat homes, water, and hothouses in volcanic areas of the Dagestan and Chechen-Ingush A.S.S.R.s in the North Caucasus,

Source: Pryde, Philip R., "Nuclear Energy Development in the Soviet Union," *Soviet Geography: Review and Translation,* February 1978, p. 80.

Other sites frequently mentioned for future construction, but which will certainly not be brought into commercial operation prior to 1980, include Aktash (Crimea), Saratov, Khmelnitsky, Tsimlyansk, Yaroslavl, Gorky, Ulyanovsk, Segozero (Karelia), Pavilosta (Latvia), Krasnodar, Chograi (Stavropol), Sangachaly (Azerbaydzhan), Tuzly (Odessa), Zaporozhye, Otashev (Kiev), Rozhnyatov (Carpathians), and Olkhovatka (Kremenchug?). Of these, only Aktash had undergone initial site preparation as of 1/1/77. Additionally, a third unit is planned at Rovno, and third and fourth units eventually at Kalinin, Konstantinov, and Ignalina; all would be 1000 MW in size except Ignalina which would be 1500 MW.

[a] Reactors designated "AM," "AMB," and "RBMK" are graphite moderated-water cooled; those designated "VK" are boiling water reactors; those designated "VVER" are pressurized water reactors; and those designated "BR" and "BN" are fast breeder reactors.

[b] A second figure indicates the result of improvements in technical efficiency.

[c] Except for Bilibino, reactors of less than 100 MW are experimental and are not included in the total figure for commercial installed capacity.

[d] Dimitrovgrad is the new (1972) name for Melekess.

[e] Both types of reactors have been mentioned at the Kalinin site in different Soviet sources.

? Indicates doubt as to whether this reactor can be brought into operation by 1980.

Georgia in the Transcaucasus, and Kamchatka in the Far East.

In August, 1977 the Soviets announced the nearing completion of the first solar power station in the Kara-Kum desert of Turkestan near the foothills of the Kopet Dag Mountains. Its capacity is to be 100 megawatts. A solar powered unit has been operating for several years in the same general vicinity to desalt ground water to provide drinking water and irrigation for sheep pastures in the region. The Soviets are eager to use solar energy in this sunny Central Asian part of the country for such purposes as well as to provide heat to hothouses that will be operated around the year for the growing of such things as tomatoes, cucumbers, and melons out of season.

Exports of Electricity

The Soviets are already exporting energy in the form of electricity, as well as in other forms such as oil, gas, and coal. With the completion of the Mir (Peace) electricity grid to Eastern Europe via a 400-kilovolt transmission line through Mukachevo to Czechoslovakia, Hungary, and Rumania, the Soviet Union has established the third energy link that provides Druzhba (Friendship) oil pipeline, Bratsvo (Brotherhood) gas pipeline, and Mir (Peace) electricity transmission line to other CMEA countries. In addition a 400-kilovolt line was completed in 1972 from the Moldavian Regional Power Station at Dnestrovsk to Bulgaria. The Soviets plan to complete a 750-kilovolt line from the Vinnitsa power system in western Ukraine to Hungary in 1978. In the mid 1970s Hungary, the largest consumer of Soviet electricity, imported about 4 billion kilowatt-hours per year, Bulgaria imported about 3.5 billion, Czechoslovakia 1 billion, and Poland 300,000 kilowatt-hours. All this amounts to less than one per cent of the Soviet output. But the Soviets plan to export much larger amounts in the future. In 1976 the 2400 megawatt Gusinoozersk thermal power station in the Buryat A.S.S.R. east of Lake Baykal began producing electricity, some of which

is already being exported southward to Mongolia.

Reading List

1. Bernstein, Lev B., "Russian Tidal Power Station is Precast Offsite, Floated into Place," *Civil Engineering*, April 1974, pp. 46–49.
2. Campbell, Robert W., *Trends in the Soviet Oil and Gas Industry*, Johns Hopkins, Baltimore, 1976, 125 pp.
3. Denisova, T. B., "Types and Stages of Economic Development in the New Pioneering Regions of the Northern U.S.S.R. (with particular reference to the gas-producing regions of West Siberia)," *Soviet Geography: Review and Translation*, December 1976, pp. 679–690.
4. Dienes, Leslie, "Energy Self-Sufficiency in the Soviet Union," *Current History*, July/August 1975, pp. 10–14, 47–51.
5. ———, "Geographical Problems of Allocation in the Soviet Fuel Supply," *Energy Policy*, June 1973, pp. 3–20.
6. ———, "Issues in Soviet Energy Policy and Conflicts over Fuel Costs in Regional Development," *Soviet Studies*, July 1971, pp. 26–58.
7. ———, "Soviet Energy Resources and Prospects," *Current History*, October 1976, pp. 114–118, 129–132.
8. ———, "The Soviet Union: An Energy Crunch Ahead?" Problems of Communism, September/October 1977, pp. 41–60.
9. Elliot, Iain F., *The Soviet Energy Balance: Natural Gas, Other Fossil Fuels, and Alternative Power Sources*, Praeger, New York, 1974, 277 pp.
10. Haberstroh, John R., "Eastern Europe: Growing Energy Problems," *East European Economics: Post-Helsinki*, Joint Economic Committee, Congress of the United States, Washington, 1977, pp. 379–395.
11. Jack, Emily E., Lee, J. Richard, and Lent, Harold H., "Outlook for Soviet Energy," *Soviet Economy in a New Perspective*, Joint Economic Committee, Congress of the United States, Washington, 1976, pp. 460–478.
12. Kazmer, Daniel R., "A Comparison of Fossil Fuel Use in the U.S. and U.S.S.R.," in *Soviet Economy in a New Perspective*, Joint Economic Committee, Congress of the United States, Washington, 1976, pp. 500–534.

13. Kosnik, Joseph T., *Natural Gas Imports from the Soviet Union: Financing the North Star Joint Venture Project,* Praeger, New York, 1975, 236 pp.

14. Lee, J. Richard, "The Soviet Petroleum Industry: Promise and Problems," in *Soviet Economic Prospects for the Seventies,* Joint Economic Committee, Congress of the United States, Washington, 1973, pp. 283–290.

15. Lvov, M. C., *Resursy prirodnogo gaza SSSR* (Natural Gas Resources in the U.S.S.R.), Nedra, Moscow, 1969, 220 pp.

16. Matrusov, N., "Western Siberia Offers Energy," *The Geographical Magazine,* June 1976, pp. 548–552.

17. Nekrasov, A. M., and Pervukhin, M. G., eds., *Energetika SSSR v 1976–1980 godakh* (Energy in the U.S.S.R. During 1976–1980), Energiya, Moscow, 1977, 288 pp.

18. Pryde, Philip R., "Nuclear Energy Development in the Soviet Union," *Soviet Geography: Review and Translation,* February 1978, pp. 75–84.

19. Sawyer, Herbert L., "Soviet Oil and Eastern Europe," *ACES Bulletin,* Spring, 1977, pp. 53–78.

20. Shabad, Theodore, "News Notes," *Soviet Geography: Review and Translation,* April 1977, pp. 262–277.

21. Thomas, Trevor M., "World Energy Resources: Survey and Review," *Geographical Review,* April 1973, pp. 246–258.

22. *Ugolnaya promyshlennost SSSR (1917–1967 gg.)* (The Coal Industry of the U.S.S.R., 1917–1967), Nedra, Moscow, 1969, 419 pp.

23. Wright, Arthur W., "Contrasts in Soviet and American Energy Policies," *Energy Policy,* March 1975, pp. 38–46.

11

Metallurgy and Chemicals

Other than energy, modern industrial societies are based on a multitude of products derived from the metallurgical and chemical industries. These are often found in conjunction with one another since in many cases by-product tars and gases from such things as coking industries associated with heavy metallurgy form the basis for a wide variety of chemical industries. Russia, and subsequently the Soviet Union, started earlier and progressed more rapidly in metallurgical industries, particularly the iron and steel industry, than it did in chemical industries, although during the last two or three decades emphasis has been placed on chemicals. Consequently, the Soviet Union at present has reached first rank in the world in the iron and steel industry, whereas it lags considerably in most chemical production.

In 1971 for the first time Soviet steel production topped American steel output, as American production went into a decline. This was the first time since 1895 that the United States had not been the world's largest steel producer. Soviet production has continued to expand steadily as production in the United States and Western Europe has fluctuated with world economic conditions. By 1975, Soviet production had risen to 233 million metric tons of usable iron ore, 103 million metric tons of pig iron, and 141 million metric tons of steel. This compared to 85 million tons of iron ore, 75

million tons of pig iron, and 106 million tons of steel in the second largest producer, the United States. (Table 8–2) Soviet steel production rose 4.3 per cent in 1975 while world production dropped 8.2 per cent, U.S. production dropped 20 per cent, Japan dropped 13 per cent, and West Germany dropped 24 per cent. In 1975 the Soviet Union produced almost 22 per cent of the world's crude steel. In the chemical industry the Soviet Union has reached first rank only in the production of cement and potash fertilizer.

IRON AND STEEL

Historical Background

The iron industry had its beginnings in central European Russia during the seventeenth century when centers like Bryansk and Tula established rudimentary iron smelters based on local small deposits of high grade iron ore smeltered by charcoal derived from the surrounding forests. During the eighteenth century much larger iron deposits were found in the Urals, and the iron industry underwent a major expansion at this time which by the middle of the eighteenth century made the Urals the world's leading producer of pig iron. But this lead was soon lost to such countries as Britain and Germany as Russia failed to modernize the industry by shifting from charcoal to coke until after 1870.

As the shift took place during the last two decades of the nineteenth century, Russia's iron and steel industry once more moved to a new resource base in what is now the eastern Ukraine where the Donets coal basin provided the needed coking coal and the Krivoy Rog iron deposits the needed iron ore. In between the Donets coal and Krivoy Rog iron lay Nikopol, the world's largest deposit of manganese, and in the surrounding region was abundant limestone for fluxing. Thus, as Russia began a belated industrial revolution in the last two decades of the nineteenth century, the eastern Ukraine presented the most conveniently located resources for the development of a modern iron and steel industry.

As the Donets-Dnieper region rapidly became the leading iron and steel producer in the country, the Urals went into a period of stagnation that it did not come out of until the establishment of the Urals-Kuznetsk Combine in the early 1930s instigated by the desire to disperse the industry into the eastern regions as the threat of war with Germany became more imminent. At this time the largest, most modern steel plant in the country was built at Magnitogorsk in the southern Urals next to the newly discovered "magnet mountain" on the upper Ural River, and a secondary plant was constructed at Stalinsk (Novokuznetsk) in the coal rich Kuznetsk Basin of Western Siberia more than 2000 kilometers to the east. The Urals-Kuznetsk Combine was conceived to shuttle coking coal westward to the Urals and iron ore eastward to the Kuznetsk Basin, thereby making use of railroad cars in both directions.

Although this long-distance haul of bulky materials initially had to be rendered economically feasible by arbitrarily setting an exceptionally low freight rate along the West Siberian section of the Trans Siberian Railroad, the Urals-Kuznetsk Combine proved its worth during World War II when the Ukraine was knocked out by the Germans. At the same time, the Urals were revitalized by an expansion of old plants and relocation of some plant and equipment from the west, so that during the height of the war the Urals and Western Siberia became the sole producers of iron and steel in the Soviet Union. After the war, costs of raw materials rose so much faster than costs of rail transport that the freight costs in steel production became relatively less significant, and the Urals-Kuznetsk Combine was rendered economically efficient without further state subsidies.

However, during the 1950s the combine began to separate into its two terminal nodes as local ore sources were found for Novokuznetsk and Karaganda coal was substituted partially for Kuznetsk coal in the Urals. In addition, as plants in the west were rehabilitated immediately as the German armies retreated, even before the end of the war, the pendulum began to swing back to the west as large, modernized plants became established in the Donets-Dnieper region and other parts of European U.S.S.R. near sources of iron ore and the rapidly expanding market. The Urals then went into another slump which has lasted to this day.

For a time during the late 1950s it looked as though production in the Urals was going to have to be cut back, since the Urals were running out of iron ore and hence would have neither coal nor iron ore to support the industry. However, during the 1960s large deposits of near-surface, low-grade iron ores were discovered up and down the eastern slopes of the Urals from Kachkanar in the north southward to Kustanay Oblast of northern Kazakhstan. Although these iron ores are universally low grade, some with no more than 16 per cent iron content, large concentrators and beneficiators have rendered their use feasible and thus supplied the Urals, and to some extent Western Siberia and northern Kazakhstan, with a seemingly inexhaustible supply of cheap surface-mined ore. Consequently plant expansion has continued in the Urals and Western Siberia, and new plants have been brought into production at Novotroitsk in the southern Urals, Novokuznetsk (the new West Siberian plant) in Western Siberia, and Karaganda in north-central Kazakhstan.

However, during the last two decades there has been a much larger expansion in the European part of the country, not only in the old Donets-Dnieper region but also in the newly exploited area of the Kursk Magnetic Anomaly in the Central Chernozem Region where new plants have been established at Lipetsk and Tula and are under construction at Staryy Oskol. In addition, rapid growth has taken place at Cherepovets which was established in the Northwest Region in 1955 to utilize iron ore from the Kola Peninsula and coal from the Pechora Basin in northeast European Russia.

Hence, through time, the locational emphasis on the iron and steel industry has shifted with changing relative cost factors, technology, and security. Originally, until about 1870, when the market was small and the fuel was fairly ubiquitous charcoal, iron and steel plants were located primarily next to iron ore. As the market expanded rapidly with the construction of the railroad network in the late nineteenth century and technology shifted to coking coal as a fuel base, new iron and steel plants were located primarily next to coking coal, specifically the Donets Basin. During the early part of the Soviet Period, coal continued to be the leading locational factor for the steel industry, and market began to exert some pull also. But strategic considerations, plus an ideological drive toward the east, initiated a dispersal of new plants toward iron ore and coal in the Urals, Western Siberia and northern Kazakhstan. The onslaught of World War II consolidated these eastern gains absolutely, but since the war the relative emphasis has returned to the west as transport costs have been minimized relative to the costs of raw materials, and changing technology has reduced the amount of coal necessary for the production of pig iron and steel. Modern iron and steel plants now use about three times as much ore, by weight, as they do fuel, and the coke share of fuel has been steadily declining. The conversion of steel production partially to electric furnaces where the electricity is generated primarily by natural gas, and the substitution of gas for coal in some other processes of the industry have reduced the industry's dependence on coal and allowed a closer location of new plants to iron ore. This process is well illustrated by the recent rapid expansion of steel plants in such areas as Krivoy Rog, Lipetsk, and Cherepovets, as well as the new plant under construction at Staryy Oskol. In addition the ever-increasing size of blast furnaces and other producing units, as well as the increasing specialization of plants on certain types of steel and steel forms, has favored the further concentration of the industry in giant plants to the detriment of dispersion of the industry across the country. At the present time it appears that the relative importance of locational factors has gone full circle and now is back to iron ore as the most decisive locational pull, perhaps with some help from market. Since by far the largest iron ore resources are situated in the southern part of densely populated European U.S.S.R., both the iron ore and the market tend to exert influences in approximately the same direction.

The Resource Base

As was the case in energy resources, the Soviet Union is blessed with the world's greatest resources of all the ingredients of the iron and steel industry. The Soviets claim to have about 50 per cent of the world's coking coal, 50 per cent of the iron ore, 80 per cent of the manganese, and 35 per cent of the chromite, as well as abundant supplies of other alloy metals such as nickel, tungsten, cobalt, and molybdenum.

Coking Coal

As was seen in the preceding chapter, huge coking coal reserves lie in the Tunguskan and Lena coal fields of Eastern Siberia and the Far East, the Kuznetsk Basin of Western Siberia, the Karaganda Basin of Kazakhstan, the Pechora Basin in northeast European Russia, and the Donets Basin in the eastern Ukraine. Of these, the Donets Basin produces about 49 per cent of the country's coking coal, the

Kuznetsk Basin produces about 31 per cent, the Karaganda Basin about 10 per cent, and the Pechora Basin about 8 per cent.

The Donets Basin produces almost half of the country's coking coal in spite of the fact that its mining costs are the highest of any coking coal basin in the country because it is so advantageously located next to iron ore, manganese, and markets. The Kuznetsk Basin, on the other hand, has some of the largest quantity, highest quality, lowest-cost coking coals in the country, but is hampered by distance from most markets. Nevertheless, because of its high grade and low mining costs Kuznetsk coal moves farther than any other coal in the country, supplying steel plants as far west as Moscow. (Fig. 11-1) The Karaganda coal is hampered by high ash and sulfur contents which necessitate mixing with higher grade Kuznetsk coal in blast furnaces at a ratio of about two parts Kuznetsk to one part Karaganda. Thus, Karaganda serves less of the needs of the Urals than Kuznetsk does, even though it is much closer to the Urals than the Kuznetsk Basin is. The Pechora Basin has larger reserves and generally higher quality coking coal than the Donets Basin, but it is so far off base and in such a severe climatic region that its mining costs are very high, and its production has been expanding at only a very slow rate. It supplies coking coal only to the single iron and steel plant at Cherepovets.

Coal coking capacity has not kept pace with coal mining or coke utilization in the eastern regions. As a result, coking coal from the Kuznetsk Basin and Karaganda has been moving westward while blast furnace coke has been moving eastward from coke plants in the Ukraine and at Cherepovets to the Urals and Kazakhstan. Additional coke batteries are to be built in the Kuznetsk and Karaganda coal basins, and a coke chemical plant is nearing completion at Zarinskaya in Altay Kray.

Iron Ore

The Soviet Union undoubtedly contains the largest iron-ore resources in the world. Unlike most other mineral resources in the country,

the largest and richest resources of iron ore are conveniently located in the European part of the country. (Fig. 11-2) According to a recent estimate 76 per cent of the iron-ore reserves are located in European U.S.S.R., including the Urals. This is almost an exact reverse of coking coal reserves, 68 per cent of which are located in the eastern regions. By far the largest iron-ore reserves are located in fairly close juxtaposition to one another at Krivoy Rog in the Dnieper Region of the Ukraine and in the Kursk Magnetic Anomaly (KMA) in the Central Chernozem Region just to the north. Although Krivoy Rog is the oldest and most developed iron mining region, the Kursk Magnetic Anomaly is now credited with at least twice as much recoverable reserves and perhaps ten times as much ultimate reserves as Krivoy Rog.

The KMA is now credited with about 50 billion tons of high grade iron ore averaging 35-37 per cent iron. This represents about one-fourth of all the industrial reserves of iron ore in the country. The rich ores alone of the KMA could supply all the iron-ore needs of the country for 150 years at the present rate of consumption. The KMA deposits stretch northwest-southeast for about 850 kilometers from Smolensk to Rostov, but most of the reserves are in Belgorod and Kursk Oblasts in the southern part of the Central Chernozem Region.[1]

The next largest concentration of iron ore lies in a north-south zone east of the Urals. The main deposits in this area are concentrated around the new town of Rudnyy in Kustanay Oblast of northern Kazakhstan. These are all near-surface, low-grade ores that must be beneficiated before use.[2] Many other iron deposits are scattered about the country, as can be seen in Figure 11-2.

If the U.S.S.R. is divided into five main iron and steel bases, as shown in Figure 11-1, the iron ore reserves of the country break down as

[1] For a detailed description of the Kursk Magnetic Anomaly, see Lydolph, Paul E., *Geography of the U.S.S.R.*, third edition, Wiley, New York, 1977, pp. 91-94. For details on Krivoy Rog, see the same book, pp. 106-108.
[2] Lydolph, *ibid.*, pp. 358-359.

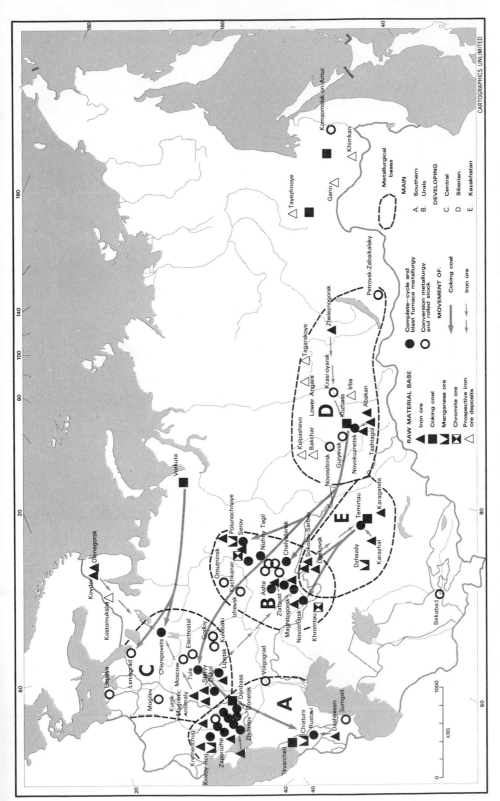

Figure 11–1   The iron and steel industry. Modified from Mints, A.A., The Geography of the U.S.S.R., Novosti, Moscow, 1975, pp. 58–59. Flow arrows are not shown between juxtaposed locations.

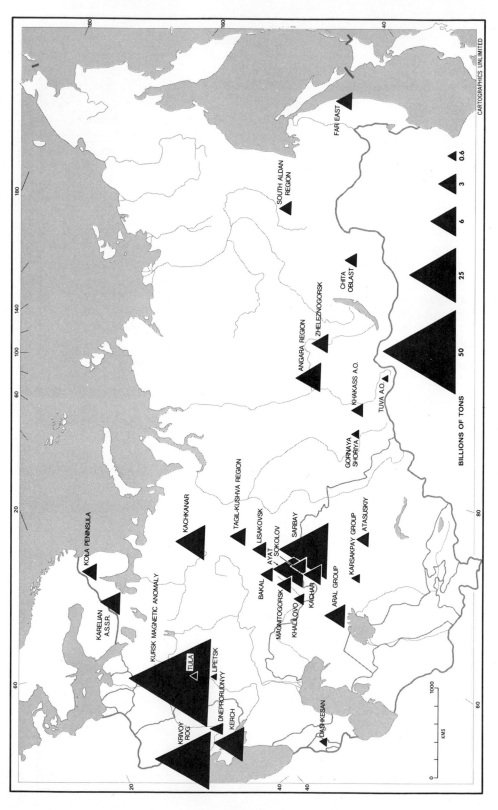

Figure 11-2   Iron ore reserves.

shown in Table 11–1. Here it can be seen that the so-called "center," which contains the Kursk Magnetic Anomaly and other scattered deposits in the Central Chernozem Region as well as a number of minor but significant deposits in the Kola Peninsula-Karelian area of the Northwest Economic Region, is credited with 42 per cent of the recoverable iron ore reserves of the country, while the "south" (Krivoy Rog and Kerch) is credited with 21 per cent, Kazakhstan with 15 per cent, the Urals with 13 per cent, and Siberia (mainly the Angara River area) with 8 per cent.

Not only does the "center" have the greatest reserves, but it also has the richest ore, averaging 52 per cent iron. This then gives the center, mainly KMA, more than half of all the extractable iron in the country. Unfortunately, most of this great reserve of ore lies deep beneath the surface and under thick water-bearing rocks which make exploitation very difficult. This largely explains why the KMA ore has not been exploited to any extent previously. Although much of the mining in the KMA region is now being done by open-pit methods, if the bulk of the ore ultimately is used it will have to be taken out by deep shaft mines. The South, Urals, and Kazakhstan, on the other hand, lend themselves much more to cheaper open-pit mining. Nevertheless, the center has a much larger portion of its ore that can be used directly or with easy beneficiation, while Kazakhstan, with its very low-grade ore, needs difficult beneficiation. Even so, the very low-grade surface ores of Kazakhstan are being used in larger and larger quantities as the Soviets are going more and more to open-pit mines wherever possible. At present more than 80 per cent of the iron ore produced in the country comes from strip mines.

The Soviet Union is by far the largest iron-ore producer in the world. In 1976 it produced 239 million tons of usable ore. Of this about 80 million tons was direct shipping ore derived from higher grade, deep mined material. The rest was derived from low grade, surface mined ore that had to be concentrated. Thus, the Soviet Union produced 460 million tons of crude ore, but this was concentrated down to only 239 million tons of usable ore. Iron concentrates from the beneficiation of low grade ores now contain a higher metal content than the direct shipping ores. Although the average iron content of surface mined ores is

Table 11–1 Regional Characteristics of Recoverable Iron-Ore Reserves

Characteristics	Main Iron and Steel Regions				
	Center	South	Urals	Siberia	Kazakhstan
1. Iron-ore reserves (% of U.S.S.R.)	42.0	21.0	13.0	8.0	15.0
2. Mean metal content (%)	52.0	38.6	19.7	41.3	39.1
3. Extractable iron (% of U.S.S.R.)	53.5	20.5	5.5	8.0	13.0
4. Percentage of ore suitable for openpit mining	35.0	87.0	87.0	40.0	67.0
5. Beneficiation classes (in % for each region)					
(a) direct-shipping	44.0	10.0	8.0	10.0	10.0
(b) easy beneficiation	45.0	67.0	87.0	56.0	32.0
(c) difficult beneficiation	11.0	23.0	5.0	34.0	58.0

Source: Rom, p. 123.

about 34 per cent, and in Kustanay Oblast it is as low as 16 per cent, concentrates derived from these ores generally contain 61–64 per cent iron, while direct shipping ores from Krivoy Rog average about 55 per cent and from the high grade Bakal mines of the Urals only 43 per cent. Overall, the marketed iron ore in the Soviet Union averages about 60 per cent iron.

As can be seen in Table 11–2, the Ukraine still produces more than half the country's ore. Most of this comes from Krivoy Rog, which in 1976 alone produced 53 per cent of the country's iron ore. The percentage was down a little from previous years, but absolutely the production was larger than at any time previously, and it is anticipated that production here will continue to expand. Not only does the Krivoy Rog ore serve the huge local needs of the Donetsk-Dnieper Region, but some also moves

north to Lipetsk and Tula and southeastward to Rustavi in the Transcaucasus, as well as westward for export. Krivoy Rog still provides most Soviet iron exports, which go primarily to East European iron and steel industries. In 1974 the Soviet Union exported 43.3 million metric tons of iron ore, about 20 per cent of its total production, 11 million tons of which went to Czechoslovakia, 11 to Poland, 6 to Rumania, 4 to Hungary, 2.6 to East Germany, and 2 to Bulgaria. In addition, Italy, Britain, and Japan each purchased more than 1 million tons.

The Kursk Magnetic Anomaly is now the second most important producing iron ore region, although it is still a poor second to Krivoy Rog. Development here has been expanding slowly since World War II, but it is scheduled to expand faster than any other region during the current five-year plan, and eventually it might become the leading ore

Table 11–2   Iron-Ore Production in the U.S.S.R. by Major Producing Regions, 1940–1980, in Million Metric Tons of Usable Ore

	1940	1955	1965	1970	1975	1976	1980 Plan	Ultimate
U.S.S.R.	30	72	153	195	233	239	275	
R.S.F.S.R.				65	87	89	100	
Europe	1.1	2.2	18	26	47	49	60	
KMA	—	0.3	12	18	37	39	52	
Kola	—	0.4	5.5	8	10	10	10	
Tula-Lipetsk	1.1	1.5	0.6					
Urals	8.1	25	28	26	26	26	25	
Siberia	0.5	3.6	8.3	13	15	15	15	
Kuzbas	0.5	3.6	7.5	8	9			
Irkutsk O.	—	—	0.8	5	6			
Ukraine	20	40	84	111	123	127	145	
Krivoy Rog	19	37	79					
Kerch	1.3	2.6	4.6					
Kazakhstan	—	0.2	14	18	21	23	26	
Rudnyy	—	—	11	15	16		24	
Lisakovsk				—	2			21
Karazhal	—	—	2.6	3	3			
Azerbaydzhan	—	0.8	1.5	1.4	1.4	1.4	1.3	

Sources: Shabad, Theodore, *Basic Industrial Resources of the U.S.S.R.*, Columbia University Press, New York, 1969, p. 36, and various issues of *Soviet Geography: Review and Translation*.

—, Negligible amounts. Blank space, no information.

producer in the country. The Soviets are eager to shift their export burdens to KMA in order to conserve the Krivoy Rog ore for local needs. KMA ore now serves most of the needs of the large Lipetsk integrated iron and steel plant in the local area and supplements the ore needs of Cherepovets in the north as well as Magnitogorsk, Chelyabinsk, and Novotroitsk in the Urals. Soviet planners are calling for much larger quantities of KMA ore to be shipped to the Urals utilizing empty train cars that are returning eastward in a trade exchange that is heavily overbalanced toward the west. In addition, a large new steel complex is being established in the Central Chernozem Region to utilize the KMA ore locally, and more plants are projected for the future. More will be said about iron-ore production and movements in conjunction with individual iron and steel producing areas later in the chapter.

Ferroalloys

The Soviet Union is also well endowed with most of the ferro alloys. Manganese is used in the greatest quantity, and the Soviet Union contains by far the world's greatest reserves of manganese. These are concentrated primarily at Nikopol in the Ukraine and Chiatura in Georgia, the two largest known manganese deposits in the world, as well as in scattered deposits in such places as the Urals, the Kuznetsk Basin, central Kazakhstan, and the Mangyshlak Peninsula in western Kazakhstan. (Fig. 11–3) Although the Nikopol deposit is by far the largest, the Chiatura deposit has richer ore and was the major producer until the middle 1960s when the rich ore began to run out. Since then much expansion has taken place in the Nikopol region with the construction of concentrators to use the lower grade ore. At present the U.S.S.R. is producing about 8.4 million tons of manganese per year, which is almost one-third of the world's supply. Nikopol produces 6.5 million tons, and Chiatura about 1.8. Hence, these two deposits account for practically all of the U.S.S.R. production. In 1974, the Soviet Union exported 1.5 million tons of manganese, or 18 per cent of total production, primarily to the East European steel producing countries. Poland and Czechoslovakia took 55 per cent of the exports.

The Soviet Union is the second largest producer of chromite after South Africa. It normally produces about one-fourth of the world's supply. Almost all of this comes from Khromtau (chrome mountain) at the southern end of the Urals in northwestern Kazakhstan. In 1975 Soviet chromite production amounted to 4 million metric tons. 1.1 million tons of this was exported. The United States is normally the largest buyer of Soviet chromite, averaging about 300,000 tons per year. Lesser amounts go to Poland, Czechoslovakia, Sweden, East Germany, and Japan.

The Soviet Union is the third leading producer of nickel after Canada and New Caledonia, normally producing about one-sixth of the world's supply. Primary producing areas are the Pechenga area of the Kola Peninsula that was taken over from Finland during World War II and the Norilsk-Talnakh area along the lower Yenisey River in Eastern Siberia which began nickel production in 1942. In addition, small nickel deposits are scattered up and down the Urals. The major one is in the new mining area of Orsk-Khalilovo in the southern Urals where it is found in association with iron.

The Soviet Union has now surpassed the United States in tungsten production and become the second largest producer after China. It is now producing more than one-fifth of the world's supply. Although it is still a net importer of tungsten, primarily from China, it is increasingly supplying its own needs. Major Soviet producing centers are at Tyrnyauz in the Caucasus, Akchatau in central Kazakhstan, Koytash and Ingichka in Uzbekistan, Zakamensk in the Buryat A.S.S.R., and Iultin in the Chukchi Autonomous Okrug in the far northeastern part of the country. In 1977 the Soviets opened a new tungsten mine and concentrator in the northern part of Maritime Kray at a site they named Vostok-2 after one of the early manned space missions. They claim this is one of the largest tungsten deposits so far discovered in the Soviet Union. Much of the tungsten

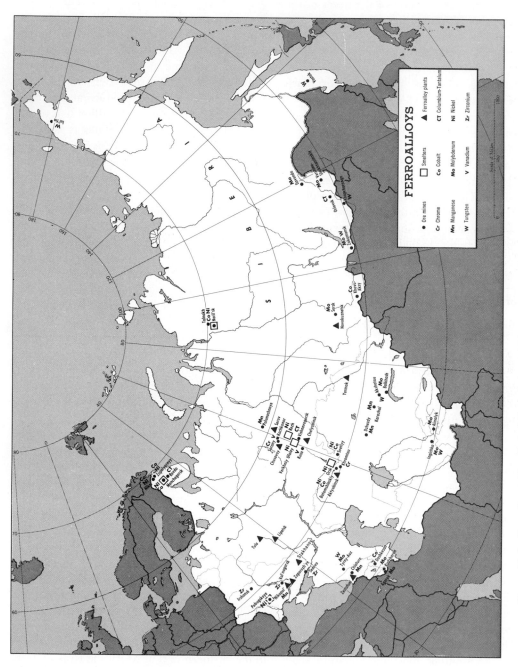

Figure 11–3   Ferroalloys. After Shabad, Basic Industrial Resources of the U.S.S.R., Columbia University Press, 1969, pp. 46–47.

in the Soviet Union is found in conjunction with molybdenum and tin.

The largest deposits of molybdenum are found in the Kabardino-Balkar A.S.S.R. in the North Caucasus. Lesser deposits, often in conjunction with tungsten, are scattered through the Urals, the mountains of Central Asia, Kazakhstan, southern Siberia, and the Far East. (Fig. 11–3) The U.S.S.R. is now the number four producer of molybdenum, after the U.S.A., Canada, and Chile. In 1975 it produced approximately one-ninth of the world's supply.

Titanium is also scattered rather widely in the Urals. But since the late 1950s, alluvial placers in the Ukraine have become the major sources of titanium for the Soviet Union. These river gravels also are the main source of Soviet zerconium, a metal that has growing applications as a structural material in nuclear reactors as well as in chemical processing plants and refractory alloys. The titanium and zerconium gravels are located near Irshansk west of Kiev and at Volnogorsk west of Dneprodzerzhinsk. More recently zerconium has been derived as a by-product from the tailings of the iron mine near Kovdor on the Kola Peninsula, as has magnesium silicate, which is used as a molding sand in foundries and as a refractory material.

Processing plants for ferroalloys are shown in Figure 11–3. Besides those established in cities with major iron and steel industries, such as Tula, Lipetsk, Zaparozhye, Stakhanov, Serov, Chusovoy, Chelyabinsk, and Novokuznetsk, there are separate plants at Nikopol and Zestafoni to process the manganese of the deposits at Nikopol and Chiatura respectively, at Aktyubinsk to process the chromite from nearby Khromtau, and at Yermak near Pavlodar in eastern Kazakhstan which produces ferrosilicon, ferrochrome, and other alloys.

Pig Iron and Steel Production

The Soviets now recognize five iron and steel districts that have evolved in the U.S.S.R. (Fig. 11–1) Two of these, the "south" (Ukraine and Georgia) and the Urals, are the primary districts which have been the main bases of heavy industry for many years, and the other three, the so called "central," Siberian, and Kazakhstan, are in developing stages. As can be seen in Table 11–3, as late as 1976 the Donets-Dnieper region of the Ukraine produced 47 million metric tons of pig iron out of a U.S.S.R. total of 105. This was a smaller percentage than had been true in the past, but absolutely the Ukrainian region has been expanding continuously and is planned to do so in the future. The Urals produced 28 million metric tons of pig iron in 1976, the European part of the R.S.F.S.R., 16 million, Siberia 9 million, Kazakhstan 4.6 million, and Georgia 0.8 million.

Steel production is somewhat more dispersed than pig iron and not so closely tied to raw materials. (Table 11–4) Steel plants are often found in many of the larger cities of the country as works auxilliary to major machine construction plants and so forth. Nevertheless, most of the steel is turned out by large integrated pig iron and steel plants that process the full cycle from iron ore and alloy materials through pig iron to steel and rolled and cast steel products. In 1976 the Ukraine produced 53 million metric tons of the country's 145 million tons of steel. The Urals, again, was second with 43 million tons. The other major metallurgical bases in European R.S.F.S.R., Siberia, and Kazakhstan produced much of the rest of the steel, but small quantities were produced in Georgia, Azerbaydzhan, Latvia, and Uzbekistan.

The five metallurgical districts and their outstanding individual plants are discussed below along with their resource connections.

The South

The southern region of iron and steel production consists primarily of the Donets-Dnieper region in the eastern Ukraine with the addition of small steel plants at Taganrog in Rostov Oblast and Volgograd in Volgograd Oblast in the adjacent Russian Republic and the small integrated iron and steel plant at Rustavi in eastern Georgia in the Transcau-

Table 11–3   Pig Iron Production, by Region, 1940–1980, in Millions of Metric Tons

	1940	1955	1965	1970	1975	1976	1980 Plan
U.S.S.R.	15	33	66	86	103	105	122
R.S.F.S.R.				42	52	53	62
Europe	1.0	1.9	7.5	12	16	16	22
Cherepovets	—	—	3.1				
Tula-Lipetsk	1.0	1.9	4.4				
Urals	2.7	12	19	23	28	28	29
Siberia	1.5	2.4	4.8	7	9	9	12
Ukraine	9.6	17	33	41	46	47	54
Donets	5.2		15				
Dnieper	3.9		17				
Kazakhstan	—	—	1.6	1.8	3.6	4.6	5.3
Georgia				0.8	0.8	0.8	1.0

Sources: Shabad, *op, cit.,* Table 11-2, p. 38, and various issues of *Soviet Geography: Review and Translation.*
—, Negligible amounts. Blank spaces, no information.

Table 11–4   Crude Steel Production, by Region, 1940-1980, in Million Metric Tons

	1940	1955	1965	1970	1975	1976	1980 Plan
U.S.S.R.	18	45	91	116	141	145	169
R.S.F.S.R.				64	80	83	94
Europe	12	24	53	19	23	25	33
North	0.6	0.9					
Central	1.5	2.6					
Volga (Volgograd)	0.9	1.5					
N. Caucasus	0.5	0.9					
Urals	4	16	30	36	43	43	45
Siberia	1.9	4.5	6.7	9	14	14	16
Ukraine	9	17	37	47	53	53	63
Kazakhstan (Karaganda)	—	0.2	1.1	2.2	4.9	5.6	6.7
Georgia (Rustavi)	—	0.6	1.4	1.4	1.5	1.5	1.6
Azerbaydzhan (Sumgait)	—	0.4	0.8	0.7	0.8	0.8	0.9
Latvia (Liepaya)	—	0.1	0.1	0.4	0.5	0.5	
Uzbekistan (Bekabad)	—	0.2	0.4	0.4	0.4	0.4	1.1

Sources: Shabad, *op. cit.,* Table 11-2, p. 43 and various issues of *Soviet Geography: Review and Translation.*
—, Negligible amounts. Blank spaces, no information.

casus. (Fig. 11-1) Within this general region, the Donets-Dnieper Economic Region produces the overwhelming share. This region contains the Donets coal basin, the Krivoy Rog iron basin, and the Nikopol manganese deposit, all within 250 kilometers of one another. There is probably no other region in the world that contains such large supplies of all the ingredients of the iron and steel industry in such close proximity to one another. Although neither the Donets coal basin nor the Krivoy Rog iron basin are the largest in the country, they are by far the largest producers. In 1976 the Ukraine, which included the large Krivoy Rog Basin as well as the smaller basins at Kerch on the eastern Crimea and Dneprorudnyy south of Zaporozhye, produced 53 per cent of the country's iron ore. This was down from earlier years when it amounted to as much as 72 per cent, but in recent years the Ukraine has been holding its own in iron ore production as new areas have been opened up. According to Table 11-1 the southern metallurgical region is now credited with 21 per cent of the country's iron ore reserves, 87 per cent of which are suitable for inexpensive open pit mining and 67 per cent of which are suitable for easy beneficiation. Add to this low transportation costs, and one can see that the southern region is well endowed with iron ore that can be efficiently utilized. On the other hand, the Donets coal, in spite of its advantageous location, has some of the highest mining costs in the country.

The Krivoy Rog ore exists in a narrow strip of land 1-6 kilometers wide that stretches north-south for about 100 kilometers. High grade ores averaging about 60 per cent iron content total about 2 billion tons, and iron quartzites averaging about 35 per cent have reserves of 9-13 billion tons. Much of the rich ore lies at considerable depths and must be mined underground, while much of the quartzite lies near the surface and is all mined by open pit methods.

Large scale iron mining began in the Krivoy Rog Basin simultaneously with the development of the Donets coal around 1880. The region rapidly developed into the major iron and steel producing area of the country and has held this distinction ever since. In 1976 the Ukraine was still producing 45 per cent of the country's pig iron and about 38 per cent of the steel.

Before World War II all the iron mining in the Krivoy Rog basin produced rich ores through shaft mines, but as the iron content decreased to about 55 per cent it was found to be more economical to produce ore from lower grade quartzites by open pit methods and concentrated into iron content of about 65 per cent. Large open pit mines came into operation in 1955, and they are now producing well over half the usable ore. In 1976, the Ukraine produced 127 million metric tons of usable iron ore, of which Krivoy Rog, together with its northern and southern extensions, probably produced around 122 million, and Kerch produced about 5 million. Most of the Krivoy Rog ore is used locally in the many iron and steel plants of the Donets-Dnieper economic region, and significant amounts are exported westward, as discussed earlier. The Kerch iron ore moves northward across the Sea of Azov to Zhdanov on the northern shore.

The third major ingredient of the iron and steel industry, manganese, is found at Nikopol on the west bank of the Dnieper River southwest of Zaporozhye. This deposit is credited with about four-fifths of the reserves of the Soviet Union, and is by far the largest manganese deposit in the world. Mining operations began here with the building of the iron and steel industry in the eastern Ukraine in the 1880s. Originally production came mainly from shaft mines in deep rich ores, but beginning in the early 1950s a great expansion of mining operations took place, primarily in open pits with lower grade ores. By 1974 production in the Nikopol area had increased to about 6.3 million tons out of a U.S.S.R. total of 8.1 million tons. Most of this is used domestically in the iron and steel plants scattered over much of the U.S.S.R.

The happy juxtaposition of major deposits of coal, iron ore, and manganese, plus abundant limestone for fluxing, has prompted the construction of many large iron and steel plants in the Donets-Dnieper region. Initially two major clusters of plants were built, one in the coal mining area of the Donets basin, and the other in the Dnieper Bend area between the iron and the coal. Coal moved westward from the Donets cluster and iron ore moved eastward from Krivoy Rog to serve all of these plants at the two ends of the railroad shuttle. The Donets cluster consists of a considerable number of small-to-medium-sized plants in a number of different cities. Apparently the largest at present is Kommunarsk, which in 1976 turned out 7 million metric tons of pig iron and had its capacity raised to 9 million metric tons. (Table 11–5) Other large integrated plants of the Donets Basin exist in Donetsk, Yenakiyevo, and Makeyevka. Somewhat smaller integrated iron and steel plants are located in Konstantinovka, Kramatorsk, and Stakhanov (Kadiyevka). In addition, there are a number of cities producing only steel. (Fig. 11–1)

In the Dnieper Bend area plants are located in Dneprodzerzhinsk and Zaporozhye. The Dneprodzerzhinsk plant, which dates from 1889, was the first to be built in the area, and until the major expansion of the new Krivoy Rog plant in the 1960s it was the biggest single producer of pig iron in the Ukraine. It is scheduled for the construction of an additional capacity of 4–5 million tons during 1976–1980. In 1976 the Zaporozhye plant turned out about 5 million tons of steel.

During Soviet times two large iron and steel plants have been developed outside these two clusters. During the early 1930s a plant was built in Krivoy Rog itself west of the Dnieper Bend, and another plant, the Azovstal plant, was built at Zhdanov on the coast of the Sea of Azov to utilize the high phosphorus iron ore coming across the Sea of Azov from the Kerch Peninsula on the Crimea. During the last two decades, the Krivoy Rog plant has been expanded into the second largest iron and steel plant in the country, after Magnitogorsk in the southern Urals. At present its pig iron and steel capacities are on the order of 10–12 million metric tons, and these are to be expanded to about 18 million tons of pig iron and 22 million tons of steel sometime during the 1980s. The

steel production at Zhdanov recently has been expanded to about 8 million tons. The plants at Zhdanov and Dneprodzerdzhinsk account for two-thirds of the steel capacity increase in the Ukraine during the current five-year plan, 1976–1980.

During the early 1950s a small integrated iron and steel plant came into being in eastern Georgia in the new town of Rustavi to utilize nearby iron deposits at Dashkesan in western Azerbaydzhan and coal and manganese in the foothills bordering the Colchis Lowland in western Georgia. The Tkvarcheli coking coal is rather low grade and must be mixed with Donets coal in the Rustavi blast furnaces. Therefore, about 1.5 million metric tons of Donets coal are shipped annually to Rustavi. The Chiatura manganese deposit in western Georgia is second in the world only to Nikopol in the eastern Ukraine. Production started there in 1879, and for many years the rich ores of Chiatura were the primary manganese producing ores in the world. Much of the ore was exported through the nearby port of Poti to other countries, as it still is. However, as the rich ores have declined, and open pit mines have expanded at Nikopol, the Chiatura production has diminished to around 1.8 million tons in 1974. As was pointed out earlier, since 1933 part of the Chiatura manganese ore has been smelted at the Zestafoni ferroalloys plant nearby for use in steel industries throughout the country.

The Rustavi iron and steel development has been plagued with various difficulties, and still gets about one-third of its ore from the Krivoy Rog basin in the Ukraine. The capacity of the pig iron and steel production at Rustavi now is around 1 million tons each. This serves about 60 per cent of the steel requirements of the Transcaucasus, mainly for steel pipe for gas and oil development, and a steel plant at Sumgait on the northern shore of the Apsheron Peninsula north of Baku provides the other 40 per cent.

The Central Metallurgical Region

As here defined, the central metallurgical

Table 11–5   Major Iron and Steel Plants and Their Specifications, by Metallurgical Regions

	Date Initiated	Pig Iron Capacity, Million Tons (Date of Information)	Steel Capacity, Million Tons (Date of Information)	Sources of Supply and Remarks
South				
Dnepropetrovsk Oblast		20 (1976)	20 (1976)	
Krivoy Rog		9 (1973)	11 (1973)	
		18 (1980s)	22 (1980s)	
Dneprodzerzhinsk			Additional 4–5 m. T. 1976–1980	Coal from Donbas, Iron ore from Krivoy Rog (Kerch for Zhdanov), and Manganese from Nikopol
Zaporozhye Oblast				
Zaporozhye			5 (1976)	
Donetsk Oblast		20 (1976)	22 (1976)	
Zhdanov			8 (1977) More to be added	
Donetsk				
Yenakiyevo				
Voroshilovgrad Oblast				
Kommunarsk		9 (1977)	6 (1976)	
Georgia S.S.R.				
Rustavi		0.8 (1976)	1.6 (1976)	Coal from Tkvarcheli and Donbas, Iron Ore from Dashkesan (⅔) and Krivoy Rog (⅓), Manganese from Chiatura
Center				
KMA				
Lipetsk		6.5 (1976)	7 (1975)	Coal, Donbas (⅔)
		9 (1980)	12 (1980)	Kuznetsk (⅓) increasing
		15 (during 1980s)	15	Iron ore, KMA Manganese, Chiatura
Staryy Oskol				
Direct Conversion Plant			3.5 (1980s)	Under Construction with W. German Assistance
Conventional Plant		8 (?)	8 (?)	Problematical
Cherepovets	(1955)	5.5 (1976)	6 (1976)	Coal, Pechora and Kuznetsk.
		9 (1980)	12 (1979)	Iron ore, Olenegorsk-Kovdor (75%), KMA (25%). Eventually also Kostamuksha

Table 11–5   (Continued)

	Date Initiated	Pig Iron Capacity, Million Tons (Date of Information)	Steel Capacity, Million Tons (Date of Information)	Sources of Supply and Remarks
Urals				Coal, Kuzbas (⅔), Karaganda (⅓). Iron ore, Local (50%), Rudnyy, KMA, Kola.
Magnitogorsk	(1932)	10 (1973)	16 (1976)	Iron Ore, Rudnyy (50%), Magnitnaya, KMA
Chelyabinsk	(1942)	3–4 (1970)	7 (1975)	
Nizhniy Tagil	(1940)	4–5 (1970)		Iron Ore, 50% of Karazhal Production
Novotroitsk	(1955)	3.5 (1973)		
Siberia				Coal, Kuzbas
W. Siberian	(1964)	6 (1977) 7.2 (1980)	5.7 (1975) 7 (1980) 20 (?)	Iron Ore, Zheleznogorsk, (85%), Gorniya Shoriya-Abakan
Kuznetsk	(1933)	4.2 (1975) 4.3 (1980)	5.4 (1975) 5.5 (1980)	Iron Ore, Zheleznogorsk, Gorniya Shoriya-Abakan
Kazakhstan				
Karaganda	(1960)	4.6 (1976) 5.3 (1980)	5.6 (1976) 6.7 (1980)	Coal, Kuzbas and Karaganda Iron Ore, Rudnyy (50%), Karazhal. Eventually Lisakovsk. Manganese, Dzhezdy.

Sources: Many scattered sources, mostly Shabad, "News Notes" from various issues of *Soviet Geography: Review and Translation.*

region combines two nodes of activity, one around the Kursk Magnetic Anomaly in the Central Chernozem Economic Region, and one around the iron and steel city of Cherepovets in the Northwest Economic Region. Some KMA ore is moving northward to Cherepovets, and some coke produced from Pechora and Kuznetsk coals at Cherepovets is moving southward to the iron and steel plant at Lipetsk. However, except for these two links, the two nodes operate independently of one another.

The Kursk Magnetic Anomaly The Kursk Magnetic Anomaly (KMA) of the

Central Chernozem Economic Region is now credited with 42 per cent of the U.S.S.R.'s iron ore reserves with an average iron content of 52 per cent, 44 per cent of which is direct shipping ore. (Table 11–1) This puts the reserves of the KMA at approximately double those of Krivoy Rog, and the iron content more than 2.5 times as much. The main drawback of the KMA ores is their great depth below the surface and the presence of thick water-bearing aquifers overlying much of the ore. Therefore, only about 35 per cent is suitable for open pit mining.

The existence of a huge deposit of iron ore in this area had been expected ever since 1783 when it was observed that compasses did not respond correctly to the earth's magnetic field. Hence, the name "Magnetic Anomaly." But it was not until 1923 that iron ore was actually discovered in Kursk Oblast. During the next decade many separate ore deposits were discovered that together outlined an ore bearing region consisting of an area approximately 200,000 square kilometers in size that stretched 850 kilometers northwest-southeast all the way from Smolensk to Rostov. The parent rock is a thick quartzite which averages about 35 per cent iron content. The top portion of the quartzite has been leached of much of its silica by groundwater action which has left rich ores averaging 56–66 per cent iron content on top of the quartzite. Generally as one progresses from north to south in the ore body the quartzite plunges to greater depths, increases in quantity, and eventually becomes totally replaced by rich ores. Thus, Belgorod Oblast in the south has the largest reserves and richest ores, but at the greatest depths.

Development finally got underway in 1932 in northern Belgorod Oblast with the establishment of the new town of Gubkin, named after the leader of the geological survey team that had discovered ore in 1923. The first experimental shaft mine ran into insurmountable problems of flooding from saturated aquifers, and then in 1941 the Nazis invaded and interrupted the program. Development did not resume until the 1950s. In 1959 the Lebedi strip mine of high grade ore was opened up, and since then two other open pit mines have been developed, the Stoyla mine in the Gubkin area and the Mikhaylovka mine near Zheleznogorsk in Kursk Oblast. Although other open pit mines and shaft mines have been initiated, most of the development so far has taken place in the Lebedi mine of the Gubkin area and the Mikhaylovka mine of the Zheleznogorsk area. In 1975 the Gubkin region produced 23 million tons of usable ore and Zheleznogorsk produced 14 million tons. By 1980 the Lebedi mine alone is to be producing 40 million tons, and by 1990 perhaps 80 million tons, which will make it one of the world's largest open pit iron mines.

In addition to the iron, the KMA ore averages 1.2–1.7 per cent alumina, which could provide an adequate base for a significant aluminum industry in the area. Also, great amounts of cement can be derived from the chalk overburden that is being removed in huge quantities from open pit mines. The city of Belgorod for years has been one of the biggest cement producers of the country, and already a large cement plant has been constructed at Staryy Oskol, the old town that is now receiving a large new steel plant.

Although open pit mining is most economical, great concern is now being expressed about the tremendous amount of damage that is being done to the rich chernozem soil cover in this region. It has been pointed out that already more than 15,000 hectares of fertile land have been despoiled by open pits, spoil banks, and tailing piles of concentrators. Even under the best conservation methods, only the spoil banks, which constitute about 40 per cent of the despoiled area, can be rehabilitated for farming. Thus, the future of open pit mining in this area is now uncertain.

The Soviets intend greatly to increase iron and steel production in the Central Chernozem Region. There have also been suggestions that some intermediate locations in the Volga-Kama region might be ideal sites for new iron and steel plants which could feed off the traffic bringing in coal from the east and iron ore from the west. This would serve the huge steel needs of the burgeoning machine building industries in the Volga-Kama region, such as the Togliatti automotive plant and the Kama truck plant. Already the Lipetsk plant has been built into one of the largest plants in the country.

Lipetsk got its first iron and steel plant, the Svobodnyy Sokol ("free falcon"), in 1899 to produce high phsophorus foundry iron from small local iron ore deposits. The plant has been in continuous operation ever since and specializes in cast iron pipe. The first five-year plan, 1928–1932, called for the transformation of Lipetsk into one of the main iron and steel centers in the Soviet Union. Work got underway on a new large plant, the Novolipetsk iron and steel plant, which was finally inaugurated in 1934. With the opening of the KMA mining district in the 1950s, the Novolipetsk plant underwent a major expansion program that is still continuing. By the middle 1970s, the pig iron capacity at Lipetsk had reached about 6.5 million metric tons and the steel capacity about 7 million tons. It is planned that by 1980 these will be expanded to 9 and 12 million tons respectively, and further expansion will raise them to about 15 million tons each sometime during the 1980s. (Table 11–5) The Lipetsk plant receives practically all of its iron ore from the KMA deposit, its manganese from Chiatura in Georgia, and all its coking coal from the Donets Basin, although a considerable amount of coke is shipped in from Cherepovets which uses a mix of Pechora and Kuznetsk coals. The coking plant at Novolipetsk is under expansion and eventually will take care of all the coke needs of the local plants. When this takes place, some of the Donets coal will probably be replaced by considerable amounts of Kuznetsk coal.

Some expansion has taken place in the old iron and steel plant at Tula, also, but no information has been released on current iron and steel capacities there.

A new steel plant is now under construction with the aid of a consortium of four West German firms at the old town of Staryy Oskol in the Gubkin area on the Moscow-Donbas Railroad. This is to be the Soviet's first and the world's largest direct reduction electric furnace plant that bypasses the blast furnace stage. The first stage of the plant, with a capacity of about 2 million tons of semi finished steel and 1.5 million tons of finished products is now under construction, and a second stage is to be completed around 1980. Apparently this is to undergo successive expansions in the future, although plans are not clear on this. For a number of years the Soviets talked about a second plant in this area of a conventional integrated iron and steel type which they hoped would be built largely by cooperating COMECON countries and perhaps be based on Polish coal. The initial plans for this conventional plant stipulated two 5000 cubic meter blast furnaces with an annual pig iron capacity of 8 million tons and an oxygen converter with a steel capacity of 8 million tons. However, since the beginning of construction on the direct reduction plant by the German firms, little mention has been made of the conventional COMECON plant.

There have been some statements to the effect that eventually iron and steel production at Staryy Oskol will be expanded to 2.5 times that at Magnitogorsk, the largest plant in the country at present. As a result of this, the old town of Staryy Oskol, which had a population of about 70,000 in the mid 1970s, is planned to increase to 300,000 by 1980 and ultimately to 800,000 sometime during the 1990s. This will probably make it the fastest growing large city in the country and eventually one of the largest industrial cities in central European Russia. In addition, the mining center of Gubkin only 25 kilometers away will experience rapid growth.

All this industrialization and urbanization in the Staryy Oskol-Gubkin node will put great stress on the water supply of the area. Iron and steel plants use tremendous quantities of water, as do burgeoning cities, and there are no large rivers in the Central Chernozem Economic Region. Lack of adequate water supply has been one of the main constraints on full-scale planning for the industrialization of this area which otherwise has the advantages of intermediate location between the two main industrial nodes of the country, a highly developed infrastructure, relatively abundant labor, and the largest iron ore reserves in the country. The immediate water needs of the Staryy Oskol area will be supplied by a small reservoir created by a dam on the Oskol River, but eventually this is to be augmented by an Oka-Don-Oskol waterway which will divert water from the Oka and Don Rivers to the Oskol.

Cherepovets During the mid 1950s a new iron and steel integrated plant was built in Cherepovets at the northern end of the Rybinsk Reservoir to provide the steel needs of the Northwest Economic Region, particularly Leningrad. Iron ore was derived from deposits around Olenegorsk and Kovdor on the Kola

Peninsula about 1200 kilometers to the north and coal was derived from the Pechora fields. Although the long transports of basic resources to Cherepovets exceed those of any other plant in the country, the plant has undergone continual expansion. In 1976 it produced about 5.5 million metric tons of pig iron and 6 million metric tons of steel. By 1980 its capacities are to be expanded to 9 million tons of pig iron and 12 million tons of steel. Thus, Cherepovets is one of the largest single iron and steel plants in the country. At present it is getting 75 per cent of its iron ore from the Olenegorsk-Kovdor area and about 25 per cent from the Kursk Magnetic Anomaly, which is actually closer to Cherepovets. A new iron mining district is currently being opened up in the central-western Karelian area at the small settlement of Kostamuksha near the Finnish border, with the cooperation of Finland, in return for which Finland will receive some of the ore for its iron and steel works at Raahe. Production at Kostamuksha was scheduled to begin in 1978 to supplement the dwindling ore supplies at Olenegorsk and Kovdor. In addition, it is assumed that increasing amounts of KMA ore will be shipped northward to Cherepovets. All the ores in the north are low grade, 30–35 per cent, and must be concentrated before use. It is planned to build a concentrator at Kostamuksha that will be the basis for a town with an ultimate population of about 45,000 people.

Urals

The Urals was the first area in the Russian Empire to develop large scale ferrous metallurgy. Although rudimentary plants had already been established at Bryansk and Tula in the Central region, these were nowhere near the scale of what was to follow in the Urals. Development in the Urals began in the early part of the eighteenth century during the reign of Peter the Great. The iron industry was based on a number of localized iron deposits and charcoal from the local forests. A great expansion took place during the latter half of the eighteenth century during the reign of Catherine the Great, when estate owners from central European Russia were encouraged to diversify their farming economy by establishing industrial plants in the Urals and manning them with excess serfs from their farms. By 1800 the Urals had become the largest iron producing area in the world. But as technology shifted from charcoal as a fuel to coal and coke, during the nineteenth century the location of new plants shifted to the eastern Ukraine, and the Urals went into a relative decline. The share of Russian pig iron produced by the Urals dropped from 70 per cent in 1860 to 20 per cent on the eve of World War I. There was some rejuvenation of the iron industry in the Urals during the early 1930s when the Urals-Kuznetsk Combine was established, but the real revitalization came with World War II when whole plants were relocated in the area from the western regions. During the war years the Urals once again became the primary metallurgical base, as the Ukraine was occupied and largely destroyed by the Germans.

After the war it became evident that the higher grade ores were running out at Magnitnaya, which fed the giant blast furnaces of Magnitogorsk, and at Blagadat and Vysokaya on either side of the other large iron smelting center of Nizhniy Tagil farther north. The old iron mines of Bakal, which for years had supplied the highest grade ore to the fine steel center of Zlatoust west of Chelyabinsk, had always been a relatively small operation and could not be expected to take up the slack. For several years Soviet planners contemplated the phasing out of some of the iron industry in the Urals and the building of new plants in other regions of the country. Then, in the mid 1950s seemingly inexhaustible supplies of low grade iron ore were discovered in widespread deposits in northern Kazakhstan and Western Siberia immediately adjacent to the Urals and within the Urals themselves. This transformed the picture for the future, and plans were changed to develop rapidly large open pit mines equipped with huge concentrators to process ore that ranged in iron content from only 17 per cent to 35 per cent. All of these low grade deposits lie near the surface and can be exploited by inexpensive open pit mining.

Within the Urals, the most outstanding new iron deposit is at Kachkanar northwest of Nizhniy Tagil. The Kachkanar deposit is now credited with half the reserves in the Urals. Iron content averages only 17 per cent, but it is low in sulfur and phosphorus, which makes it easy to process, and it contains vanadium as a by-product. The Kachkanar concentrator was opened in 1963 and has become the principal source of vanadium for the iron and steel industry throughout the entire Soviet Union. Much of the vanadium is made usable for the steel industry at the nearby Chusovoy plant. Expansion at Kachkanar has not proceeded as rapidly as anticipated because of lack of processing capacity for the vanadium slag. Nevertheless, by 1975 the capacity of the Kachkanar iron ore concentrator complex had expanded to about 45 million tons of crude ore per year which was concentrated into 8 million tons of usable ore. The principal consumer of the Kachkanar concentrate is the Nizhniy Tagil iron and steel plant nearby.

Larger deposits of iron ore are strung in a north-south line through Tyumen Oblast in Western Siberia, Kurgan Oblast in the Urals region, and Kustanay Oblast in northern Kazakhstan. The largest deposits are centered on the new mining town of Rudnyy in Kustanay Oblast of Kazakhstan.

In spite of the discovery of these extensive ore bodies nearby, the need for iron ore in the Urals has kept ahead of supply, and during recent years Urals iron and steel plants have found it necessary to import ore from the Kursk Magnetic Anomaly, the Kola Peninsula, and the Karazhal deposit southwest of Karaganda in central Kazakhstan. In 1977 the Urals produced about 26 million tons of usable iron ore and shipped in 14–15 million tons from the Kursk Magnetic Anomaly and about 1.5 million tons from Karazhal. The KMA ore went to Magnitogorsk and Chelyabinsk, and the Karazhal ore to Nizhniy Tagil.

Ferrous alloys such as manganese, nickel, tungsten, and chrome are found in the Urals. Chrome and nickel are particularly abundant in the Orsk-Khalilovo area in the south. Apparently the largest deposit of chrome in the

world lies across the Kazakh border at Khromtau. Some iron ore also exists in this Orsk-Khalilovo area, and a new steel plant was established at the new town of Novotroitsk in the mid 1950s to utilize the naturally alloyed iron-chrome-nickel ores. However, the Soviets have found the local ore difficult to utilize, and most of the iron ore for Novotroitsk is now being shipped in from Rudnyy.

The largest iron and steel plant in the Urals, and in the entire U.S.S.R., is at Magnitogorsk. This plant has undergone continual expansion since its inception in 1932, and by 1976 its steel capacity had been expanded to 16 million tons. (Table 11–5) Now that the Magnitnaya ores next door are running out, Magnitogorsk is receiving 50 per cent of its ore from Rudnyy in northwestern Kazakhstan and significant quantities from the Kursk Magnetic Anomaly.

The second largest integrated iron and steel plant in the Urals is at Chelyabinsk. This was established during World War II when it was based on Bakal ores. Now that the Bakal ores are running out, after 200 years of mining, the expanded plant at Chelyabinsk is using ore primarily from Rudnyy and some from the Kursk Magnetic Anomaly. In 1975 the steel capacity of Chelyabinsk was reported to be about 7 million metric tons. Chelyabinsk also has one of the main steel pipe plants in the country. Both Magnitogorsk and Chelyabinsk are expected to use increasingly greater amounts of Kursk ore in order to make use of empty freight cars returning from the west.

The third largest integrated iron and steel plant in the Urals is at Nizhniy Tagil. This began in 1940, based on an older, smaller plant, and by the early 1970s it had reached a capacity of 4–5 million tons. It takes much of the ore from Kachkanar nearby and in addition receives about 50 per cent of the output of Karazhal ore southwest of Karaganda, in spite of the fact that Karaganda has to ship in ore from farther away.

The fourth largest integrated iron and steel plant in the Urals is the Orsk-Khalilovo iron and steel plant located in Novotroitsk, which began operations in 1955. It had reached a pig iron capacity of 3.5 million tons by 1973.

The above four plants produce about 80 per cent of the Urals pig iron and 70 per cent of its steel. Smaller integrated plants that turn out both pig iron and steel exist in Alapayevsk, Beloretsk, Serov, Chusovaya, Asha, and Verkhniy Ufaley. Pig iron only is produced at Satka, Nizhnyaya Salda, and Staroutkinsk. Steel and rolled steel products only are produced at Lysva, Izhevsk, Zlatoust, Revda, Nizhniye Sergi, Verkh-Iset (part of Sverdlovsk City), Verkhnyaya Salda, and Minyar. Steel pipe is produced in Chelyabinsk, Pervouralsk, Kamensk-Uraliskiy, and Polevskoy.

Siberia

In the mid 1970s about 9 per cent of the U.S.S.R.'s pig iron and steel were being produced in the Kuznetsk Basin of Western Siberia. Production began here in the early 1930s when the Kuznetsk integrated iron and steel plant was constructed at the new town of Novokuznetsk at the eastern end of the rail shuttle of the so called Urals-Kuznetsk Combine. The Kuznetsk plant underwent successive expansions, and then in 1964 was joined by a second larger plant that was built in Antonovo, about 16 kilometers northeast of downtown Novokuznetsk. This new plant has been called the West Siberian Plant, or "Zapsib" for short. In 1975 it was reported that the West Siberian Plant had a pig iron capacity of 5–6 million tons per year and a steel capacity of about the same amount. The older Kuznetsk plant had a pig iron capacity of 4–5 million tons and a steel capacity of 5–6 million tons. Most of the future expansion is to take place in the West Siberian Plant. It is planned that by 1980 it will have pig iron and steel capacities each around 7 million tons. Eventually the steel capacity may be expanded to about 20 million tons.

Although the Kuznetsk plant originally was planned to derive iron ore from Magnitogorsk, it soon found local supplies, and now gets about 60 per cent of its ore from local mines in the Gornaya Shoriya district along the southern rim of the Kuznetsk Basin and at other mining areas in the Khakass Autonomous Oblast in the Kuznetsk Alatau to the east along the railroad that has been built to Abakan in the Minusinsk Basin. The other 40 per cent of the ore comes from Zheleznogorsk east of Bratsk in Irkutsk Oblast of Eastern Siberia. A railroad was completed from Abakan through Tayshet to Zheleznogorsk in 1964. Ore is also supplied by scattered mines along this railroad in southern Krasnoyarsk Kray. Open pit mines exist in this area at Abaza, Vershina Tei, Irba, and Krasnokamensk. The Zheleznogorsk complex has become the major ore supplier to the West Siberian Plant. The ore contains 32 per cent iron and is concentrated at the mine before it is shipped to the Kuzbas. Most of the steel manufactured in the Kuznetsk Basin is marketed in central Siberia stretching from Omsk to Irkutsk.

In addition to the iron and steel plants of the Kuznetsk Basin, a small steel plant has operated for years in Eastern Siberia east of Lake Baykal at the town of Petrovsk-Zabaykalskiy. Steel is produced here from scrap metal and some pig iron shipped in from the Kuznetsk Basin. The steel capacity is only about 1 million tons per year and does not come very close to satisfying the steel needs of Eastern Siberia, most of which have to be supplied from the Kuznetsk Basin.

In 1972 the Soviets announced the beginning of the construction of a coke-chemical plant in the town of Zarinskaya east of Barnaul in Altay Kray. A coke-chemical plant is ordinarily the beginning of an iron and steel complex, and there have been some hints that the Soviets are seriously considering another large iron and steel complex at this location. In the past there have been serious talks of iron and steel plants in other locations in Siberia, particularly at Tayshet at the fork of the Trans Siberian Railroad and the newly constructed Baykal-Amur Mainline. However this is not being mentioned much anymore. With the planned large expansion of the West Siberian steel plant in the Kuznetsk Basin, it appears that plans for the immediate future intend for the steel needs of Siberia to be supplied from the Kuznetsk Basin.

Figure 11-4   Scrap metal for steel mill at Petrovskiy Zavod.

Kazakhstan

The city of Karaganda came into being in the early 1930s when a large development of coal mining was initiated. A small steel plant, the Kazakh Metallurgical Plant, which used long haul pig iron, was completed during World War II in the northern satellite city of Temirtau ("iron mountain"). This steel plant reached a production of 400,000 tons by 1960. However, in the 1950s the Karaganda area was selected as the site of one of the Soviet Union's new integrated iron and steel complexes. Although it was called the Karaganda Metallurgical Plant, it also became part of the city of Temirtau. The first blast furnace was opened in 1960. Since then continual expansion has taken place, and in 1976 it produced 4–5 million tons of pig iron and 5–6 million tons of steel. It is planned to continue to expand this plant slowly, so that by 1980 it will be producing around 5 million tons of pig iron and 6–7 million tons of steel.

The iron ore source for Karaganda original-ly was planned to be the Atasu deposit in the town of Karazhal about 250 kilometers southwest of Karaganda. However, Karazhal now is supplying only about 20 per cent of Karaganda's needs, and at least half of Karazhal ore, for some reason, is being shipped to the Urals. The Karazhal ore consists of 55 per cent direct shipping ore that is mined in an open pit. The better ores are beginning to run out, and as costs rise, more and more of Karaganda's needs are being supplied from northwestern Kazakhstan.

The main exploitation of iron ore in Kustanay Oblast so far has been in the Sokolov and Sarbay deposits near the new town of Rudnyy. These two deposits consist of magnetite ore with about 45 per cent iron content. Both deposits lie near the surface at depths of about 65 meters and are exploited in open pit mines. Exploitation of the Sokolov mine began in 1957 and the Sarbay mine in 1960. Initially the total output was shipped westward to the Urals, but now some of the ore is being shipped eastward to Karaganda.

Two more large deposits are being opened up in the Kustanay area at Lisakovsk and Kachar. So far the Lisakovsk deposit has developed faster in spite of its high phosphorus content which presents technical problems for processing. However, an intermediate product can yield phosphatic fertilizer, which helps make the use of the ore economically feasible. The iron content here averages about 36 per cent. Ultimately the Lisakovsk deposit is expected to support two very large mining and concentrating complexes and to become the main supplier to Karaganda, which now gets about 50 per cent of its ore from the Rudnyy area. During the current five-year plan, 1976–1980, the Kachar deposit will experience the main expansion. In 1975 Kazakhstan produced 21 million tons of usable ore out of a total U.S.S.R. production of 233 million tons. Sixteen million tons came from the Rudnyy area, 2 million from Lisakovsk, and 3 million from Karazhal. (Table 11–2)

In addition to the iron, considerable quantities of ferrous alloys are also found in Kazakhstan. Already mentioned is the chromite at Khromtau in the Mugodzhar extension of the Urals. This deposit produces about 85 per cent of the Soviet Union's chromite and exports about 40 per cent of its production to the United States, Japan, West Germany, France, and Sweden. Development began in Khromtau in 1943 coincident with the establishment of a ferroalloys plant at nearby Aktyubinsk to which most of the chromite ore was shipped. Also in the Aktyubinsk area, nickel-cobalt ores are mined and shipped northward to a refinery at Orsk in the southern Urals. A manganese mine was developed at Dzhezdy during World War II when Ukrainian and Transcaucasian manganese sources were cut off. It declined after the war but has been revived since the mid 1960s as a source of manganese for the new ferroalloys plant at Yermak on the Irtysh River in eastern Kazakhstan.

Other Plants

In addition to the five large metallurgical regions already described, two small steel plants are situated in outlying areas. The first to be established was the small steel plant at Komsomolsk-on-Amur which began operations in 1942. The new city of Komsomolsk, named after the Young Communist League that built it, was established around this steel plant. Since that time, the plant has consistently produced about 1 million tons of steel per year utilizing scrap iron and some pig iron from the Kuznetsk Basin. This "Amurstal" plant provides only about 30–40 per cent of the steel needs of the Soviet Far East. It specializes in tin plate for fish canning and ship plating for local shipyards.

The second small steel plant was established in 1944 in the new town of Bekabad (originally Begovat) at the western entrance to the Fergana Basin in the Uzbek Republic in Central Asia. This plant produces about 400,000 tons of steel per year from scrap metal and pig iron from the Kuznetsk Basin, which meets only about 15–20 per cent of the steel needs of Central Asia. It is planned that by 1980 steel production here will expand to 1.65 million tons with the completion of an electric furnace.

Relative Production Costs and Location Factors

Costs of production of pig iron and steel vary with costs of mining and transportation, mineral constituents of ingredients, stage of development, level of technology, and size of plant. A Soviet study based on data from 1964 shows that the cost of coke and iron ore is lowest at Magnitogorsk and highest at Tula and Lipetsk among the major plants in the country. (Table 11–6) Despite the use of long-haul Kuznetsk and Karaganda coal, all the iron and steel plants in the Urals produce cheaper coke than the plants of the South, situated near the Donets Basin. And the Cherepovets plant, 1900 kilometers from the Pechora coking coal, yielded coke at lower costs than the plants in central Russia situated far closer to the Donbas, or the Rustavi plant close to its coking coal supply in Transcaucasia. Cheap mining

Table 11–6 Grouping of Iron and Steel Plants by Level of Ore and Coke Costs

Cost of Coke (rubles per ton)	Cost of Ore Used at the Plants (Rubles per Ton)		
	Low (under 5.50)	Medium (5.50 to 8.00)	High (over 8.00)
Low (under 18)	Magnitogorsk	Novotroitsk Chelyabinsk Chusovoy	Nizhniy Tagil Kuznetsk Serov West Siberian Karaganda
Medium (18 to 22)	Dnepropetrovsk Konstantinovka Kramatorsk Donetsk	Zaporozhye Zhdanov Dneprodzerzhinsk Yenakiyevo	Cherepovets
High (over 22)	Krivoy Rog	Rustavi	Tula Lipetsk

Source: Rom, p. 124.

costs and relative purety of the Kuznetsk coal accounts for the cheap production of coke in the Urals. The Donetsk coal has a sulfur content four times greater than either the Kuznetsk or Pechora coals. This necessitates a 10–12 per cent rise in coke consumption based on Donets coal. Because of these factors, during the mid 1970s Kuznetsk coke was becoming more economical than Donets coke in the iron and steel plants of central Russia, and Pechora coke was almost as cheap.

The pig iron produced in southern plants using Donets coal ends up with a higher sulfur content than plants in the Urals and Siberia or at Cherepovets, which has the lowest sulfur content of all the large plants. Thus, it appears that the Cherepovets iron and steel plant, which in its initial stages was plagued by very high costs, has now become as economical as many of the plants in the central and southern regions.

It appears that all new plants suffer from high production costs in their early stages. The cost of pig iron at the West Siberian Plant was more than twice as high as the neighboring Kuznetsk plant in the mid 1960s even though they both had the same supply relationships. The high initial costs are due to break-in

problems, lower labor productivity, and high costs of subsidiary operations. But as plants approach their design capacity, the cost of pig iron declines rapidly to a mean level.

Concentration of production, which usually goes hand-in-hand with modernization, tends to reduce costs and reduce regional differences in costs. Steel production costs show a steady decline from around 45–50 rubles per ton in plants with capacities of less than 1 million metric tons to only 25 rubles per ton in plants with capacities of 10 million tons or more. Costs also tend to decline as the degree of metallurgical processing increases. For instance, in 1964 the cost of production for pig iron in Cherepovets was still somewhat higher than at some other major plants, but the cost of open hearth steel was roughly the same, and the cost of finished products was in fact somewhat lower.

Over the years, the share of transport costs in total costs of production has declined significantly. This has been advantageous to plants such as Cherepovets which ship in supplies over long distances. As transport costs have declined relative to costs of raw materials, the importance of regional differences in transport costs has declined.

As was pointed out near the beginning of this chapter, as transport costs have diminished in importance, and as newer technology has alleviated some of the need for coke, iron ore costs have increased relative to the other costs and have become more important in the determination of the location of new plant capacity. These cost relationships have swung the pendulum back toward central and southern European Russia with their large supplies of iron ore. In addition, the large markets of this area provide a further strong impetus for location of new capacity here. In a few instances, such as the Bekabad steel plant in Central Asia and the Komsomolsk steel plant in the Far East, market has been the determining locational factor.

NONFERROUS MINERALS

Although the Soviet Union is a major producer of many of the nonferrous minerals, the greatest paucity of Soviet data exist for these ores, and production statistics can only be gleaned from bits and pieces of information that appear in Soviet literature of one kind or another. Much of the information that follows has been derived from the various writings of Theodore Shabad in his 1969 book on *Basic Industrial Resources of the USSR,* in the reports of the Joint Economic Committee, Congress of the United States, in the *New York Times,* and in the "New Notes" of *Soviet Geography: Review and Translation.*

Aluminum

Aluminum is the second most used structural metal, after steel. For a number of years now, the Soviet Union has ranked second in aluminum production after the United States. It has been estimated that in 1975 the Soviet Union produced 1,500,000 tons of aluminum, while the United States produced 4,373,200, and Japan, the third leading producer, 1,439,200. The Soviet production constituted 12.5 per cent of the world's supply. Like the United States,

the Soviet Union is short on aluminum resources, particularly bauxite, and long on electrical power to convert the intermediary product, alumina, to aluminum. The lack of abundant resources of high grade bauxite is one of the Soviet Union's main metal deficiencies. In 1975 the U.S.S.R. produced 4,400,000 metric tons of bauxite, which was more than twice the production of the U.S.A., but only one-fifth that of the leading producer, Australia. The U.S.S.R. ranked fifth, with about 6 per cent of the world's production.

The Soviet aluminum industry began in 1932 with the opening up of the low grade bauxite deposit at Boksitogorsk east of Leningrad. A small alumina-aluminum plant began operation at Volkhov nearby utilizing hydroelectricity from a small station that had been built on the Volkhov River. A year later a somewhat larger alumina-aluminum plant was brought into operation at Zaporozhye to utilize electricity from the newly completed hydroelectric station on the Dnieper. This plant also used bauxite ores from Boksitogorsk. In 1938 an alumina plant was opened at Boksitogorsk itself. Meanwhile, a much larger, richer bauxite deposit had been discovered in the northern Urals, the so-called Krasnaya Shapochka (Red Riding Hood) mines near the town of Severouralsk (Northern Urals). In 1939 a combined alumina-aluminum plant was opened at Kamensk-Uralskiy farther south to utilize the Krasnaya Shapochka bauxite, and in 1943 a second combined plant was opened at Krasnoturinsk near the mines. Also, during World War II whatever equipment could be evacuated from the threatened plants at Zaporozhye and Volkhov was installed in a new aluminum plant built at Stalinsk (Novokuznetsk) in the Kuznetsk Basin of Western Siberia.

Since the bauxite reserves at Boksitogorsk were inadequate to last very long, even for the small plants in the Northwestern Region, the Soviets began considering the use of nepheline associated with apatite ore in the central Kola Peninsula which was being discarded on tailing piles during the apatite mining and concentrating process. A nepheline concentrator was built at Kirovsk in the contral Kola Peninsula in 1939, but World War II intervened, and the first shipment of nepheline concentrates was received in Volkhov only in 1949. The process was judged successful, and was introduced at the new Pikalevo alumina plant which came into production in 1959. The nepheline process was made economical by yielding not only alumina, but also byproduct cement, soda ash, and potash. A mix of 4.5 tons of nepheline concentrate with about 9 tons of limestone yielded 1 ton of alumina, 1 ton of soda ash and potash, and 7 tons of cement. The nepheline process in the northern region was also rendered economically efficient because it was a by-product of the apatite mining industry which was in great demand as a base of phosphate fertilizers in European Russia. The apatite operation is now large enough to make available about 10 million tons of nepheline per year. But because of the limited processing capacity in the Northwestern Region, no more than 1.5 million tons per year have been used. Thus, the apatite tailing piles containing waste nepheline are still piling up at a rapid rate.

After World War II the Volkhov and Zaporozhye plants were reconstructed, and five new aluminum reduction plants were put into operation in the European part of the country. Plants were opened at Kandalaksha on the Kola Peninsula in 1951 and at Nadvoitsy in Karelia in 1954 to utilize alumina from the old Volkhov plant and the newer Pikalevo plant. (Fig. 11-5) In the south, aluminum plants were established at Yerevan in Armenia in 1950, at Sumgait in Azerbaydzhan in 1955, and at Stalingrad (Volgograd) in 1959. The southern plants were now deriving most of their bauxite and alumina from the Urals, although Zaporozhye began receiving some imported bauxite, initially from Hungary, and later from Greece.

During the mid 1950s the Soviets began a concerted attempt to develop an adequate resource base for the aluminum industry in the Transcaucasus. An alumina plant was completed in 1965 at Kirovabad in the middle Kura Valley of the Azerbaydzhan Republic to utilize alunite ores at nearby Zaglik. Use of the alunite ore was justified by the by-products of sulfuric acid and potassium sulfate (a fertilizer). However, the breaking-in process proved to be long and difficult, and only after a decade of operation has the Kirovabad alumina plant been described as working normally. The current five-year plan, 1976–1980, includes an expansion of the Kirovabad alumina process utilizing imported bauxite from Guinea in West Africa. This bauxite-based alumina operation is due to start in the late 1970s and will supply alumina to the Tursunzade (Regar) aluminum plant near the Nurek hydroelectric plant on the Vakhsh River in the Tadzhik Republic of Central Asia which went into operation in 1975, apparently using imported alumina.

Another effort to establish a local base of alumina in the Transcaucasus has been attempted at Razdan north of Yerevan in Armenia. This was to have been based on a local nepheline deposit. However, after sporadic construction work over a period of 18 years, it was announced in 1978 that the project had been abandoned.

As larger and larger hydroelectric plants came into operation in Siberia during the 1960s huge new aluminum plants were established at Shelekhov, near Irkutsk, in 1962, at Krasnoyarsk in 1964, and at Bratsk in 1966. These, along with the expanded Novokuznetsk plant initially derived their alumina all the way from the Urals. However, there was not enough alumina to serve the needs of these large aluminum plants, and the Soviets began looking around for new sources of alumina for the Siberian area. Consequently, in 1964, an open pit operation began production of high silica bauxite at Arkalyk in north-central Kazakhstan. An alumina plant was established at Pavlodar in eastern Kazakhstan in 1964, and Arkalyk bauxite was hauled 1000 kilometers by rail eastward to Pavlodar. Alumina then moved eastward to the aluminum plants in Siberia. But the Arkalyk ore is limited in quantity, probably about twenty years supply if used at full capacity, and so the Soviets have developed other poorer grade ores in the same general area of northern Kazakhstan to mix

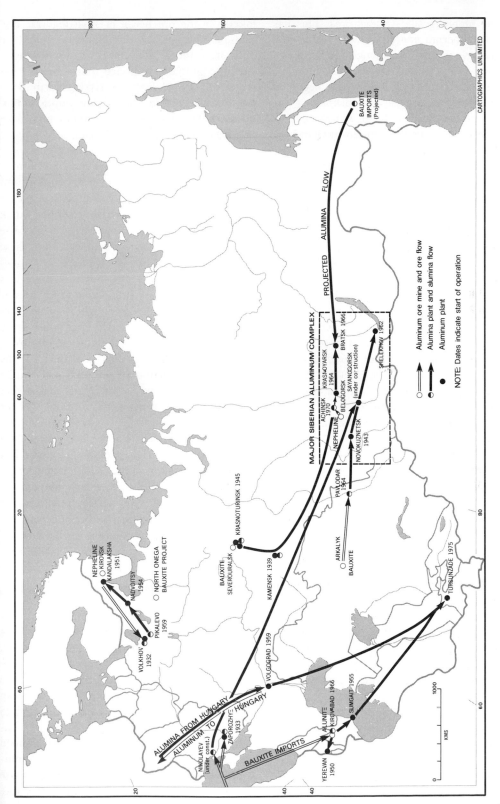

Figure 11–5   The aluminum industry. Modified from Shabad, Resources Policy, December, 1976, p. 224.

with the higher grade Arkalyk ores. This has made the Siberian operation more costly, and still has not assured it of a long-term supply of resources.

During the mid 1950s construction began on a new alumina plant at Achinsk along the Trans Siberian Railroad west of Krasnoyarsk to utilize local nepheline deposits at Belogorsk 200 kilometers southwest of Achinsk. Construction dragged on for 15 years here, and only in 1970 did alumina production begin. However, even now, it is only operating at about two-thirds of its 800,000-ton capacity, since there is some difficulty in using the ore, and there is not enough market in southern Siberia to use the great quantities of cement that are produced as a by-product.

Now another large aluminum plant is nearing completion near the giant hydroelectric project at Sayanogorsk on the upper Yenisey River in Eastern Siberia. So it appears that adequate domestic sources of alumina for all these huge aluminum complexes in Eastern Siberia will be hard to come by. Therefore it is projected that sometime during the 1980s an alumina plant will be constructed somewhere on the Pacific coast to utilize bauxite imports from the Pacific area, perhaps from Australia. The Soviets have looked at other aluminum ores such as the kyanite in the central Kola Peninsula, the sillimanite at Kyakhta in southeastern Siberia on the Mongolian border, and kaolin clay overburden in the lignite strip mines of Angren east of Tashkent in Central Asia. However, it now appears that attempts to use other than bauxite ores have been abandoned.

In 1977 it was announced that bauxite shipments had started from the North Onega mine near Plesetsk on the Onega River in the Northwest Economic Region. This had been under development for more than ten years and was initially thought to be a major bauxite deposit that might alleviate some of the resource needs of the aluminum industry. However, the bauxite lies under a water saturated overburden, and it took seven years to drain the area enough to produce a 60-meter-deep pit. Originally it was projected that this deposit might

take over the ore needs of Boksitogorsk, and that perhaps a new alumina plant might be built near the North Onega deposit itself. It was also intitially projected that a future city, tentatively called Severorossiysk (North Russia) was planned for an ultimate population of 100,000. However, in recent years very little has been said about this development and its future is in doubt. Future domestic bauxite prospects are now focusing on the Timan Ridge in northeastern European Russia and the Belgorod district of central Russia where bauxite is mixed with the iron ore of the Kursk Magnetic Anomaly. However, no definite plans have yet been announced for these sources of bauxite.

In the mid 1970s the Soviet Union was producing about 1.5 millions tons of aluminum, about 60 per cent of which came from domestic materials and 40 per cent from imported materials. Of the domestic resources, bauxite accounted for 37 per cent of the production, nepheline 19 per cent, and alunite 4 per cent. The imported materials consisted of bauxite, 19 per cent, and alumina, 21 per cent.

Since alumina production has not kept pace with aluminum capacity, the Soviet Union has found it necessary to import larger and larger quantities of partially processed ores in the form of alumina. The largest amounts are imported from Hungary, which go primarily to the Volgograd aluminum plant. In 1975, out of a total alumina import of 1,029,000 tons, Hungary supplied 405,000, Jamaica 169,000, Guyana 121,000, the United States 114,000, Italy 76,000, India 47,000, and Turkey 38,000. Bauxite imports totaled 3,477,000 tons, of which Guinea supplied 1,844,000, Yugoslavia 947,000, Greece 611,000, and Turkey 75,000. Imported bauxite is going primarily to the Zaporozhye and Kirovabad plants.

It appears that in the future the Soviets plan to import more bauxite and alumina and to discontinue attempts to expand uses of nonbauxite domestic ores. No expansion is planned even for the nepheline ores of the Kola Peninsula, which apparently are economical to use because of their association with the apatite that is being mined anyway and the realization of the by-product cement and soda ash. The decision to curtail use of the Kola nepheline has prompted some dissension between apatite mining interests and the management of the aluminum industry.

With the emphasis now being placed on imported materials, it appears that many of the alumina and aluminum plants already built in the Soviet Union are poorly located. They would better have been located nearer seaports. This is partially being corrected after the fact by the construction of a new alumina plant at Nikolayev on the northern coast of the Black Sea and a projected alumina plant somewhere on the Pacific coast to be built probably sometime during the 1980s. In early May, 1976 a French steel and aluminum group announced that they had signed an initial agreement with Soviet officials to build a major alumina facility near Odessa on the Black Sea to process about 1 million tons of alumina annually. Under the agreement, the French consortium would buy 50,000 tons of aluminum annually over a ten year period to help cover the costs of constructing the new plant. The Soviets have not made mention of this arrangement.

The main pattern of distribution of the aluminum industry is already set and cannot be changed much by new construction. The aluminum capacity has already been overbuilt, and most of that now lies in the deep interior of the country in the southern part of Siberia and Central Asia. To get alumina to these plants from foreign sources is going to be a major transportation problem. Part of the strategy to construct a new alumina plant on the Pacific coast undoubtedly is tied in with the completion of the Baykal-Amur Railroad, which, it is anticipated, will carry freight whose flow is heavily overbalanced from west to east. Thus, there will be empty returning cars available to haul alumina from the Pacific plant westward to the aluminum plants in Eastern Siberia.

The construction of the huge aluminum plants in Eastern Siberia and Central Asia has been prompted by the availability of a super-abundance of hydroelectric power that has recently been made available by the completion

of several of the largest hydroelectric power plants in the world. The Soviets would now like to put all this aluminum capacity to work for their benefit, and it appears that they would like to import raw materials and export finished aluminum, thereby realizing a profit on their electrical and other manufacturing imputs. Already some finished metal is being exported. The Hungarian alumina imports are paid for largely by aluminum exports to Hungary. In 1974, the Soviet Union exported 351 million dollars worth of aluminum. This more than compensated for the 97.5 million dollars worth of raw material imports for the aluminum industry. But at least two-thirds of the aluminum exports went to East European countries while more than two-thirds of the raw material imports were bought outside the ruble bloc. Therefore, as far as hard currency was concerned, the trade was not so lucrative. If the Soviets do build the projected alumina plant on the Pacific coast, they hope to balance imports of bauxite from the Pacific basin with exports of aluminum to the Pacific basin. The most likely trading partner would be Australia.

Copper

The Soviet Union with apparently about 1.4 million metric tons of refined copper production per year, ranks second in the world, after the United States with 1.6 million tons. The U.S.S.R. produces more than one-sixth of the world's supply. Copper production was initiated in the Urals by Peter the Great during the early eighteenth century and remained concentrated there until the Soviets began opening up large deposits in Kazakhstan and Uzbekistan. Early mining and smelting centers were located at Kirovgrad, Karabash, and Baymak, and an electrolitic refinery was located at Kyshtym. During the 1930s these were joined by mining and smelting operations at Krasnouralsk, Revda, and Mednogorsk and a second electrolitic refinery at Verkhnyaya Pyshma. After World War II as some of the old copper deposits were beginning to play out, new mines were opened at Sibay and Uchaly in the Bashkir A.S.S.R. and Gay in Orenburg Oblast. (Fig. 11–6)

A smelter began operations in 1938 at Balkhash on the north shore of Lake Balkhash in southern Kazakhstan to process local Kounrad deposits, and it later expanded its raw material base eastward to the Sayak copper deposit. At the same time, mining began at Dzhezkazgan in central Kazakhstan, reported to be the largest copper ore deposit in the country. An old smelter existed at Karsakpay near Dzhezkazgan, but much of the Dzhezkazgan ore was shipped to smelters in the Urals and at Balkhash. Finally, an electrolitic refinery was opened at Dzhezkazgan in 1972, and this was joined in 1973 by the completion of a long-delayed smelter. Now Dzhezkazgan, which has become the largest copper ore producer in the country, smelts and refines some of its ore locally and ships concentrates to the Balkhash copper complex and to the Urals smelters. The significance of the Dzhezkazgan operation was highlighted in 1973 with the creation of Dzhezkazgan Oblast out of the large southern portion of what had been Karaganda Oblast, and the city of Dzhezkazgan was made the administrative seat. This new oblast also includes the copper city of Balkhash.

In eastern Kazakhstan, a relatively new expansion of copper production has taken place at Orlovka in the mineral rich district of the Rudnyy Altay along the upper Irtysh River near the cities of Leninogorsk and Ust-Kamenogorsk. An old copper smelter at Glubokoye is being supplemented by a new larger smelter and refinery that will process copper-zinc ores.

In northeastern Kazakhstan initial preparation is being made to open up the Boshchekul copper-molybdenum deposit 90 kilometers west of the coal mining center of Ekibastuz. Ore was discovered there in early 1930, but the deposit has not been developed because of low metal content and the absence of water supplies and transport access. However, new technology has made the working of the deposit economically feasible, the construction of the Irtysh-Karaganda Canal nearby has provided a source of water, and the construction of the Pavlodar-Tselinograd railroad has provided transport access. The Boshchekul deposit is said to rate second only after Dzhezkazgan. In addition to copper and molybdenum, Boshchekul will yield cobalt, gold, silver, and pyrite. It is assumed that the Boshchekul ore will be shipped to the Balkhash smelter.

Copper is often found in association with other metals, both nonferrous and ferrous, in the same ore. Copper is a coproduct with nickel in the mining centers of Norilsk and Talnakh east of the lower Yenisey River in Eastern Siberia and in the central and northwestern parts of the Kola Peninsula. The Norilsk metallurgical complex came into being in the late 1930s. It first produced electrolitic nickel in 1942, cobalt in 1944, and copper in 1950. Platinum group metals, gold, silver, tellurium, and selenium are important by-products. The Norilsk complex underwent a major expansion in the late 1960s following the discovery of a similar metallic deposit at Talnakh 25 kilometers to the northeast. During the mid 1970s a new nickel and copper smelting complex was constructed at Nadezhda 15 kilometers west of the city of Norilsk to process tailings not previously used for the mining operation. Nickel, copper, cobalt, platinum metals, and sulfur will be realized from this operation.

In spite of its remote location, the mining and smelting operations in the Norilsk area have stimulated an urban growth at Norilsk from nothing in the early 1930s to 168,000 in 1976. The Yenisey River port of Dudinka has grown to 22,000. This port, which is joined to Norilsk by a 100-kilometer electrified railroad, handles all the mineral products coming out of the Norilsk district, which are shipped to other parts of the country via the Northern Sea Route during the open season. The Murmansk-Dudinka segment of the Northern Sea Route is now being kept open by means of ice breakers from mid June to the end of December, and plans have been announced to try to prolong the Arctic navigation season into April.

Fuel for the Norilsk complex was first provided by local low grade coal mines, but

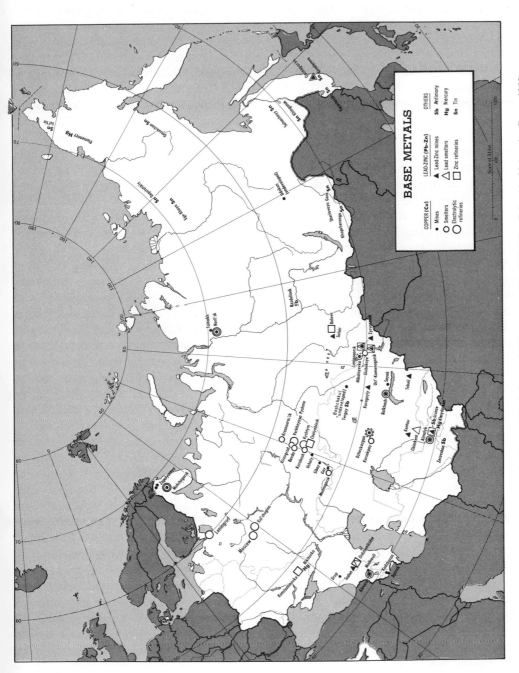

Figure 11–6 Base metals. After Shabad, Basic Industrial Resources of the U.S.S.R., Columbia University Press, 1969, pp. 54–55.

much of the operation has now been switched to natural gas which is being brought in from fields to the west via three pipelines. In addition, in 1970 a hydroelectric station was completed at Snezhnogorsk on the Khantayka River to provide electricity to the Norilsk area.

In the Kola Peninsula, copper mining and smelting began at Monchegorsk in 1938 and was revived after the war and supplemented by the Pechenga (Petsamo) mines in the northwestern portion of the Peninsula acquired from Finland during the war.

In Transcaucasia, old copper mines at Kafan and Alaverdi in Armenia have been supplemented by new developments during the Soviet period at Kadzharan, Dastakert, and Agarak, where the copper is found in association with molybdenum. In 1974 copper production began at the new Madneuli copper mining complex in Georgia.

During the early 1960s a new copper complex was developed at Almalyk in Uzbekistan in Central Asia. With the construction of an electrolitic refinery in 1964, Almalyk has become a major producer. Before completion of the Almalyk refinery, the Soviet Union had been a net importer of copper metal, primarily from Zambia, Britain, and West Germany. After 1964, imports virtually ceased, while exports to Eastern Europe and other countries rose to more than 100,000 tons per year.

One of the big developments for the future is to take place at the large Udokan copper deposit in northern Chita Oblast in Eastern Siberia which will be provided with adequate transportation by the completion of the Baykal-Amur Railroad in the early 1980s. It is planned to have a pilot concentrator in operation by the time the railroad arrives. Apparently reserves here rival those at Dzhezkazgan, and high expectations are associated with this development, primarily for export to Japan.

Lead and Zinc

These two metals are usually found together in complex ores which may also include such things as copper, gold, silver, and a variety of other rare metals. The largest concentrations of lead-zinc ores are found in two places in Kazakhstan, in the Ust-Kamenogorsk—Leninogorsk area of eastern Kazakhstan and the Chimkent area of southern Kazakhstan. These are followed by the mining complex at Almalyk in Uzbekistan, already mentioned in conjunction with copper production. Smaller mines exist in other scattered places in Central Asia, as well as at Dalnegorsk (Tetyukhe) in the Far East, near Ordzhonikidze in the North Caucasus, and in the Salair Ridge west of the Kuznetsk Basin. (Fig. 11–6) The oldest producing areas are in eastern Kazakhstan where production started as early as the late eighteenth century, and in the North Caucasus where mining began in the middle nineteenth century.

Most of the mining areas process both lead and zinc ores in their own concentrators, but then the concentrate travels separately to lead smelters and zinc refineries. Lead concentrates from southern Kazakhstan and Central Asia are smelted at the Chimkent lead plant, opened in 1934, which reportedly is the largest in the country. The east Kazakhstan lead concentrates are smelted at Leninogorsk, dating from 1926, and Ust-Kamenogorsk, opened in 1952. A smaller lead smelter operates at Ordzhonikidze in the North Caucasus to process local ores as well as concentrates that are brought by rail all the way from Dalnegorsk in the Far East. A small lead smelter has also been built at Dalnegorsk.

The lead smelters are few in number and are concentrated in lead mining areas. Zinc refineries on the other hand are more widely scattered because of their large energy requirements which causes them to be located near coal sources or hydroelectric power. Although Kazakhstan traditionally has accounted for about half the zinc concentrate production of the country, before World War II the absence of an electric power base in the republic necessitated shipment of zinc concentrates thousands of kilometers to refineries in other parts of the country. Early refineries were located at Konstantinovka in the Donets Basin and Belovo in the Kuznetsk Basin. Both of these operations began in 1930. Zinc refineries were opened at Ordzhonikidze in the Northern Caucasus in 1934 and at Chelyabinsk in the Urals in 1935. After construction of the hydroelectric plant at Ust-Kamenogorsk and subsequently at Bukhtarma on the Irtysh River in eastern Kazakhstan, zinc refineries were opened in Ust-Kamenogorsk in 1947 and Leninogorsk in 1966. Finally, a zinc refinery was included in the Almalyk complex in Uzbekistan during the late 1960s.

Apparently the lead smelter production in the Soviet Union is around 480,000 metric tons per year, which is second after the United States with 1,107,300 tons. The Soviet production amounts to about one-seventh of the world's supply. The Soviet Union has been a net lead exporter for many years. Zinc output is on the order of 690,000 metric tons per year, which puts the Soviet Union in first place, with about one-seventh of the world's supply. The U.S.S.R. is a net exporter, shipping zinc to East Germany and Czechoslovakia and importing zinc from Poland and North·Korea.

Tin

The Soviet Union has been trying to become self-sufficient in tin production since its Chinese imports ceased in the early 1960s. Apparently it is now producing about 25,000 tons per year which is little more than half its needs. Most of the production comes from the Far East, particularly in the southern portions around the old producing area of Dalnegorsk and the newer producing area of Solnechnyy 40 kilometers northwest of Komsomolsk on the lower Amur River. (Fig. 11-6) Apparently a significant development is now taking place in the very far northeastern part of the country at Iultin, and since 1974 dredging operations have been carried out in an underwater deposit in Vankina Gulf of the Laptev Sea off the Arctic coast of Eastern Siberia.

So far tin concentrates have all been moving to smelters at Podolsk and Ryazan south and southeast of Moscow and a newer smelter in Novosibirsk in Western Siberia. During the mid 1970s construction was underway on a new smelter at Solnechnyy to smelt that ore locally, and it is assumed that ore from other mining areas in the Far East will move to this smelter also. This signifies the importance of this deposit as probably the largest tin resource in the country. The first tin concentrator went into operation at Solnechnyy in 1963, and in 1973 the area also began yielding copper and tungsten concentrates as by-products. The new smelter will produce tin and blister copper as well as by-product sulfuric acid.

Gold

The U.S.S.R. apparently is the world's third ranking gold producer, after South Africa and Canada. This has proved to be a very handy commodity for paying off trade deficits in a world of hard currency which does not accept the ruble in exchange. Gold mining has been carried on since the eighteenth century at scattered deposits in the Urals and Siberia. (Fig. 11-7) In Siberia gold mining began in the Altay Mountains in the eighteenth century and in the Vitim Plateau of Eastern Siberia, around the urban center of Bodaybo, in the nineteenth century. During the Soviet period, production shifted eastward to Chita Oblast and the Aldan Plateau of Yakutia in the 1920s. During the mid 1930s political prisoners were shipped northeastward to the Kolyma gold district inland from the port of Magadan on the north coast of the Sea of Okhotsk. During the last fifteen years gold mining has spread continually northward into the far northeastern part of the country, and new mining activities have been opened up in the southwest in the Transcaucasus and Central Asia.

In the Chukchi Autonomous Okrug of the remote northeastern part of the country gold lode operations have been opened up in the Cape Shmidt area of the Arctic coast and around the urban settlement of Bilibino. To signify the importance of the development of this region, in 1974 Shmidt Rayon was created out of a portion of Iultin Rayon which had

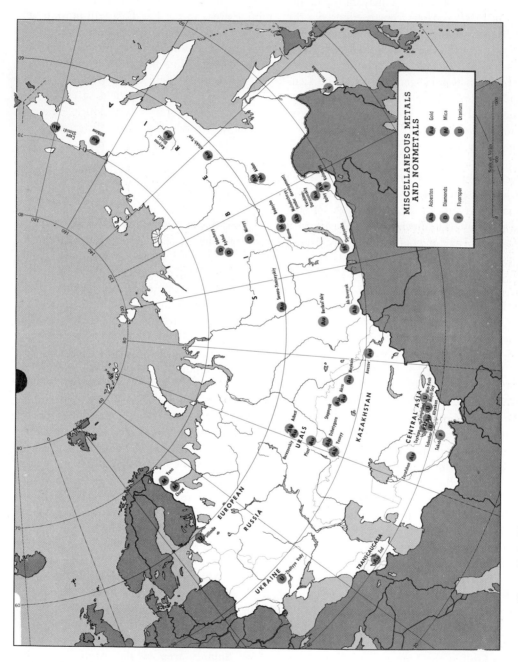

Figure 11–7   Miscellaneous metals and nonmetals. After Shabad, Basic Industrial Resources of the U.S.S.R., Columbia University Press, 1969, pp. 68–69.

Figure 11 8 Tailings of gold dredging on the Ingoda River near Chita, Eastern Siberia. Photo by Toni Crane.

been centered around the town of Iultin, the tin-tungsten mining center. In 1976 a floating power station was moved into place to provide electricity to Shmidt Rayon. The gold lode center of Polyarnyy is reported to now have a population of about 3000. Farther west, Bilibino is now credited with about 12,000 population. Bilibino also originally was supplied with electrical power from a floating power station, but in 1976 a small nuclear power plant with a capacity of 48,000 kilowatts was completed. This is the only nuclear power plant east of the Ural Mountains, and apparently will remain the only one for many years to come. It is the first Soviet nuclear plant to provide steam heat as well as power generation.

During the 1960s gold lode deposits have been opened up at Auezov in eastern Kazakhstan, at the new desert town of Zarafshan in the Kyzyl Kum Desert of the Uzbek Republic, at the new town of Altynkan on the southern slopes of the ore rich Kurama Mountains in the Fergana Valley of Uzbekistan, and at Zod northeast of Lake Sevan in Armenia. This has shifted gold production southwestward into more accessible areas of the country. The Zod complex, under construction since the mid 1960s, was finally brought into operation in 1976 with an associated ore treatment plant at the town of Ararat in an unpopulated part of the steppe of the Araks Valley 280 rail kilometers to the south. The ore treatment plant had to be located where it would not pollute Lake Sevan or the Araks River.

Other Minerals

The Soviet Union produces other minerals which are important to its economy. In some cases it is among the top producers in the world, but little information is available.[3]

[3] For more complete details refer to appropriate sections of Shabad, Theodore, *Basic Industrial Resources of the USSR*, Columbia University Press, 1969, and Lydolph, Paul E., *Geography of the USSR*, 3rd edition, Wiley, 1977.

Silver

The Soviets produced 1340 metric tons of silver during 1975, which placed them first in the world a little ahead of Canada, Mexico, Peru, and the United States. The U.S.S.R. accounted for one-seventh of the world's supply. Most of the silver in the Soviet Union is produced in conjunction with other metals, particularly gold.

Diamonds

Diamond production is a recent development in the Soviet Union. Old placer deposits in the Urals yielded small amounts of diamonds for many years, but in the mid 1950s Kimberlite pipes were discovered in Yakutia which shot the Soviet Union into the position of one of the leading diamond producers in the world. It now ranks second behind South Africa in gem diamonds and second behind Zaire in industrial diamonds. In 1975 it produced 23 per cent of the world's diamonds by weight. Diamond production began at the town of Mirnyy in 1957, Aykhal in 1964, and Udachnyy in 1968. (Fig. 11-7) To supply power to this remote part of the Central Siberian Upland, the Vilyuy Hydroelectric Station was completed at Chernyshevskiy on the Vilyuy River during the period 1967-1975 with a generating capacity of 648,000 kilowatts. About 20 per cent of the diamond output is of gem quality, and the other 80 per cent is used in industry. Considerable quantities are now being exported. Britain takes most of the gem diamond exports.

Uranium

Uranium, the key metal of the nuclear age, has been under intensive development in the Soviet Union, but very little is known about its magnitude and location of production. Principal mining areas are believed to be in the Central Asian Mountains and around the town of Zheltyye Vody in the Krivoy Rog iron basin of eastern Ukraine. A secondary operation may be associated with the Estonian oil shale production.

Asbestos

During the mid 1960s, Soviet production of asbestos moved ahead of Canada and now amounts to about 40 per cent of the world's supply, almost 2 million tons per year. About one-sixth of the production is exported, primarily to eastern and western Europe, but also to the United States and Japan. The oldest producing area, and still the largest, is at the town of Asbest in the Urals, which apparently produces about three-fourths of the Soviet supply. (Fig. 11-7) Farther south, production was initiated at Dzhetygara in northwestern Kazakhstan in 1965 and at nearby Yasnyy across the border in Orenburg Oblast several years later. Dzhetygara is now producing much of the rest of the asbestos of the country. A small production has developed at Ak-Dovurak in the Tuva A.S.S.R. in Eastern Siberia where production began in 1964. Although small in production, the Tuva complex produces a special spinning fiber, whereas the Dzhetygara mine yields only short fibers for asbestos-cement board.

Mercury and Antimony

The Soviet Union is a significant producer of mercury and antimony, generally in association with one another in ores located primarily in the Kirgiz Republic of Central Asia and the Donets Basin of the Ukraine. Before World War II the entire mercury supply came from a mine at Nikitovka in the Donets Basin, but during the war when this was lost to the Germans, larger operations were developed in the mountains of Central Asia, and primary production has remained there. More recently new mercury complexes have gone into operation southeast of Lake Sevan in Azerbaydzhan in the Transcaucasus and in the Chukchi National Okrug in the far northeastern part of the country. (Fig. 11-6) The Soviet Union is now the largest producer of mercury, with almost one-fifth of the world's supply.

CHEMICALS

Since the mid 1950s the Soviets have been

sustaining a concerted drive to expand and modernize their chemical industries in order to supply a wide range of components to other industries and rapidly growing demands of the consuming public for synthetics, plastics, and a great variety of gadgetry. Large inputs of new capital and labor have been allocated to this sector of industry. One unique aspect of the program has been the reliance on foreign capital and technology. Although foreign capital and technology have actively been imported for the economy as a whole during recent years, they have been integral parts of the expansion of the chemical industry from its inception in 1958. The Soviets have made a practice of importing whole plants from countries in Western Europe, Japan, and the United States, as well as from some of the more industrialized countries of Eastern Europe, in order to get head starts on technologies that are completely new to the Soviet scene. Recently the Soviets have been trying to set up reciprocal arrangements whereby they can gain the technology and raw materials from abroad and use their own energy sources and other inputs to process materials in foreign-aided plants to produce semifinished and finished products that can be exported to equipment-supplying countries and elsewhere in the world, as well as serve domestic needs. One of the larger examples of this kind of arrangment during recent years has been the agreement with the Occidental Petroleum Corporation in the United States to help construct chemical plants in the port cities of Grigoryevska on the Black Sea coast and Ventspils on the Baltic coast that will import Florida phosphates controlled by Occidental Petroleum and export ammonia. The actual exchange of materials began in February, 1978. Among the chemical industries, the chemical fertilizer industries have probably received more foreign help than any other industries in the country. Out of 64 major mineral fertilizer plants in the Soviet Union, fully 27 have utilized some Western plant.

The growth of the chemical industry has been facilitated by the rapidly expanding exploitation of oil and natural gas which can serve as feedstocks for many processes that originally were based on limited supplies of plant materials, such as potato and grain alcohol, by-product tars and gases of coal coking, and various nonmetallic minerals. As the fluid fuels have become more abundant and the pipeline network more sufficient, oil refineries and gas processing plants have been dispersed into new locations that have tended to serve the markets of the country better and have allowed the establishment of chemical complexes in market areas that turn out large quantities of wide varieties of associated products. In most cases the processes involved are so intertwined among various chemical raw materials and products, often associated with other industrial processing such as metallurgy, that it is difficult if not impossible to separate out individual chemical products, or even raw materials, and discuss their geographical distributions one at a time.

Likewise, the raw materials, processes, and finished products of the chemical industries are so varied that it is difficult to grasp the overall level of development of the chemical industries in a given country in order to compare it with other countries. The basic raw materials for most chemical processing are natural gas and gas condensates, oil and by-product gases of oil refining, coal tars and gases, sulfur and pyrites, phosphorite and apatite, potassium salts, sodium chloride and sodium sulfate, calcium carbonate (lime), wood wastes, cotton linters, and other vegetable products such as potato and grain alcohol. From these raw materials are made such major categories of finished products as mineral fertilizers, synthetic rubber, artificial and synthetic fibers, plastics, paints and dyes, soaps and detergents, insecticides and herbacides, pharmaceuticals, and various products for use in oil refining and metallurgy. Between the raw materials and the finished products, generally lie some intermediate products that can serve many needs for further processing.

It is often most instructive to look at quantities of production of such intermediate substances as sulfuric acid, nitric acid, hydrochloric acid, ammonia, soda ash, caustic soda, chemical pulp, and various polymers.

Unfortunately, of these only sulfuric acid, caustic soda, soda ash, and chemical pulp are reported regularly among Soviet production statistics in terms that can be compared with the production of other countries. Among the finished products, about the only country-wide statistics available concern the mineral fertilizers (nitrogen, phosphate, and potash) and cement. Information on other components of the chemical industry is scattered and incomplete and does not allow for valid comparisons between the Soviet Union and other countries or for good geographical distribution analyses within the Soviet Union. Since the chemical industries are usually associated with other industries and are sensitive to market locations, the overall distribution of chemical industries in the U.S.S.R. corresponds very closely to the distribution of total industry, with concentrations in the Central industrial region; the heavy metallurgical areas in eastern Ukraine, the Urals, and the Kuznetsk Basin; and in areas of oil refining and gas processing. Outside these general areas, individual chemical complexes may be situated next to specific sources of raw materials, such as salt deposits, sulfur, phosphates, and limestones.

Sulfuric Acid

Perhaps the best single indicator of relative world position in the chemical industry is the production of sulfuric acid. Large quantities of this intermediate product are used in the production of chemical fertilizers; the metallurgical processing of copper, cobalt, nickel, platinum, and silver; in the production of rayon; in the production of galvanizing elements; in the production of oil products; in the processing of starches and sugar; in the production of dyes; in the tanning of hides; and for many other uses. In the mid 1970s the Soviet Union was producing about two-thirds as much sulfuric acid as the United States was. This was a great leap forward from the mid 1960s when the Soviet Union produced only about one-third as much as the United States. The Soviet production is now a strong second

in the world, being more than three times as much as its next leading competitor, Japan. (Table 8-2)

Native sulfur is now produced at two major places in the Soviet Union, the Rozdol-Yavorov mines in the northern foothills of the Carpathians in the western Ukraine which began production in 1959 and at Gaurdak along the Upper Amu Darya near the Afghan border of Soviet Central Asia, where production began in 1964. (Fig. 11-9) A small amount of production is still taking place in an older mining area at Alekseyevka in the Volga region near Kuybyshev. But most of the sulfuric acid production in the U.S.S.R. does not come from native sulfur. In the mid 1970s native sulfur accounted for only 13.3 per cent of the sulfuric acid production. By far the largest amount came from iron pyrites in the Urals. These accounted for 56.7 per cent of the sulfuric acid. Smelter gases, particularly from copper, lead, and zinc operations, accounted for 23.3 per cent, and hydrogen sulfite, a by-product of oil and gas processing, accounted for 6.1 per cent. At least 40 per cent of the sulfuric acid is now being used to produce superphosphate, and since sulfuric acid is hard to transport, much of it is being produced at superphosphate plants, whose distribution will be discussed a little later. Iron pyrites from the Urals are shipped all over the country to these plants.

Soda and Salts

Another important intermediate chemical material is soda. Calcined soda, or soda ash, is used in the production of a wide array of chemical products as well as in the production of soap, glass, textiles, leather, paper, and many other things. Caustic soda is used in the production of such things as artificial fibers and organic dyes. Soviet production of soda ash by the ammonia-ash process is located in areas that combine salt, limestone, and coal resources. Such combinations are found in the Donets Basin and the Urals-Volga region. Until recently, most of the soda ash production in the Soviet Union took place at the towns of

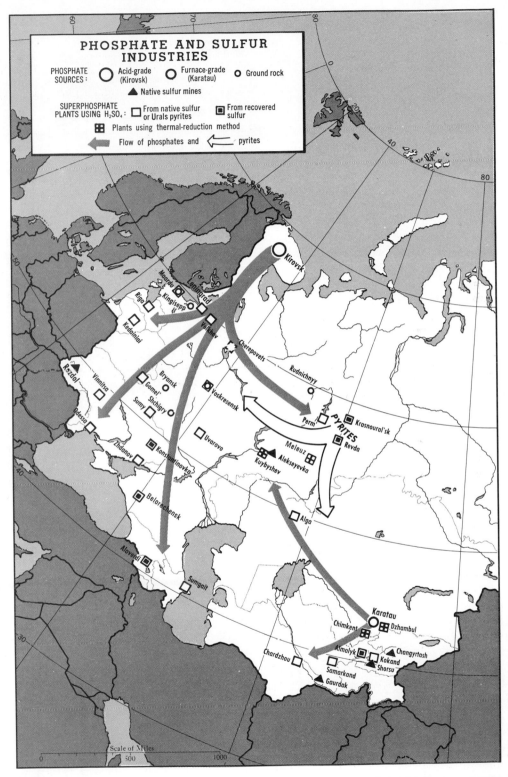

Figure 11–9 Phosphate and sulfur industries. Updated from Shabad, Basic Industrial Resources of the U.S.S.R., *Columbia University Press, 1969, p. 74.*

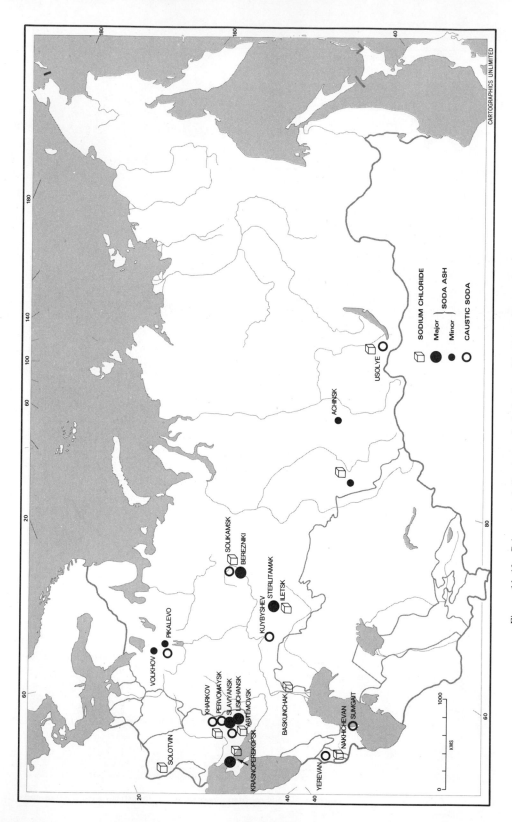

Figure 11–10 Primary producing areas of salt (sodium chloride), soda ash, and caustic soda.

Slavyansk and Lisichansk in the Donets Basin of the eastern Ukraine and the Berezniki and Sterlitamak areas in the western Urals. (Fig. 11–10) The Donets plants utilize the rich underground deposits of rock salt at Artemovsk, and the Berezniki plant in the Urals utilizes the Solikamsk salt deposits. The Sterlitamak complex was established in 1951 to utilize the salt deposits at Iletsk. In addition small amounts of soda ash are being obtained as by-products of nephelite processing at Volkhov and Pikalevo in the Northwest. A small amount of soda ash has been derived from various soda lakes in the Kulunda Steppe, and in 1970 soda ash production was initiated at Achinsk in Eastern Siberia as a by-product of the nephelite-alumina plant.

In 1974 another large soda ash plant went into operation at Krasnoperekopsk on the Perekop Isthmus which connects the Crimean Peninsula to the mainland in the southern Ukraine. This plant is part of the growing chemical complex that has been established at Krasnoperekopsk to utilize salt-rich brines from the stagnant Sivash Sea and to use the sea as a dumping ground for waste materials. An ammonium phosphate fertilizer plant was established at Krasnoperekopsk in 1972, and a year earlier a titanium pigment plant went into operation there. The first unit of the soda plant in 1974 produced disodium phosphate, a feed additive. Eventually the plant is to turn out 675,000 tons of soda ash per year, which will make it one of the largest plants in the country. In 1975, the U.S.S.R. produced about 4.7 million metric tons of soda ash, which was almost twice the production of the United States. (Table 8–2) Of this, 1.8 million tons came from Sterlitamak, 0.9 million from Berezniki, 1.2 million from the Ukraine, 0.6 million from Siberia, and 0.3 million from the Northwest Economic Region.

Caustic soda can be produced from soda ash, but in recent years more and more of it has been produced by electrolysis of salt, which also yields chlorine. Caustic-chlorine plants require large amounts of electricity. Therefore they tend to be located near large sources of low cost electricity and salt deposits. The Donets-Dnieper Region has been one of the leading caustic-chlorine producing areas of the country, together with the Volga, Volgo-Vyatka, and Urals regions. In 1975 the Soviet Union produced 2.4 million tons of caustic soda, which ranked it fourth behind the United States, Japan, and West Germany. (Table 8–2) About 50 per cent of the Soviet production originated in the Volga Valley, mostly around Kuybyshev, 10 to 15 per cent each in central European Russia, the Ukraine, Transcaucasia (Sumgait and Yerevan), and Siberia (Usolye, near Irkutsk), and about 6 per cent in the Urals.

In 1975 a new large caustic soda-chlorine unit went into operation at Pervomaysk, a chemical complex 70 kilometers south of Kharkov. This uses local salt deposits and natural gas via pipeline to produce caustic soda and a wide range of chlorine products. Future expansion is planned at Pavlodar in northeastern Kazakhstan to utilize cheap electric power based on Ekibastuz brown coal, at Zima west of Irkutsk in Eastern Siberia to utilize local salt and coal, and at Yavan in Central Asia to utilize local salts and cheap electricity from the Nurek Dam on the Vakhsh River.

Total Soviet salt production in 1975 was about 20 million metric tons, 13.5 million of which were produced under the auspices of the food industry and 6.5 million under the auspices of the chemical industry for the production of soda ash and caustic-chlorine. Among the salt deposits used by the food industry, Lake Baskunchak east of the lower Volga, the principal lake salt source, and Artemovsk in the Donets Basin, the principal rock salt source, each account for about 35 per cent of production. (Fig. 11–10) Artemovsk has been producing salt since the 1870s. Most of it is extracted by room-and-pillar mining, but some is extracted by solution mining, in which water is injected into the deposit, forming an artificial brine, which is then pumped to the surface.

Lake Elton, north of Lake Baskunchak, produced sodium chloride mixed with magnesium and potassium salts during the eighteenth century and first half of the nineteenth century, but with the establishment of cheap Volga River transportation from the Baskunchak salt, Lake Elton could not compete and went out of operation. The salt port of Akhtubinsk was founded on the lower Volga River in 1936 and has become one of the Soviet Union's principal salt suppliers for canning and meat packing industries.

The salt needs of Siberia and the Far East, with its large fishing industry, are provided by the Sol-Iletsk rock salt complex in Orenburg Oblast in the southern Urals, the lake salts in Altay Kray, and the Kalkaman lake salt in Kazakhstan. The Solotvin rock salt mine in Transcarpathia in the western Ukraine produces mainly for export to Eastern Europe. In 1976, the Soviets announced the discovery of a gigantic salt deposit in southeastern Turkmenia, which according to them is enough to meet the needs of the entire earth's population for the next 200 years. No plans have been announced for the development of this salt deposit.

Other Intermediate Materials

Most other chemical materials are derived from various gases. These initially came primarily from the coking of coal, and therefore formed large chemical complexes in major producing coal basins, particularly the Donets and Kuznetsk basins. The primary basis for these industries was methanol, which was derived from coke-based water gas. Now synthetic methanol is derived from natural gas at Shchekino in Tula Oblast south of Moscow, at Severodonetsk (Northern Donetsk) in the Ukraine, and Nevinnomyssk in the North Caucasus. Nevinnomyssk in recent years has become one of the major chemical complexes in the country, producing gas-based nitrogenous fertilizers and derivatives in addition to the synthetic menthanol. Methanol from Nevinnomyssk moves northward to plants in Orekhovo-Zuyevo east of Moscow and Nizhniy Tagil in the Urals for the production of formaldehyde for phenoic resins, to Togliatti for isoprene rubber synthesis, and to Chapayevsk southwest

of Kuybyshev to produce dyes and explosives.

In addition to methanol, major natural gas derivatives for chemical industries include ethylene and polyethylene, ammonia, and urea. Much of this is derived from natural gas liquids which must be separated from the dry gas at gas processing plants before being fed into chemical complexes. The utilization of wet gas condensates has been slowed, particularly in areas like the Orenburg and West Siberian gas developments, by the lack of gas processing plants. These are being built as fast as possible, but the Soviets have not been able to keep up with the expansion of the oil and gas industries, and much gas is being flared off wastefully in the fields.

Until recently, gas processing and chemicals based on it have been concentrated very much in the Volga-Urals area where natural gas liquids from the Minnibayevo plant at Almetyevsk move by pipeline to major petrochemical complexes at Kazan, Nizhnekamsk, Novokuybyshevsk, Salavat, Ufa, Sterlitamak, and Perm. An ethylene pipeline system has been completed to connect many of these complexes. In addition, petrochemical plants have grown up around Groznyy in the North Caucasus, and individual plants have been established at Guryev at the north end of the Caspian, the Novopolotsk refining center in Belorussia, Sumgait north of Baku in the Transcaucasus, and Severodonetsk in the eastern Ukraine.

In Siberia the first petrochemical complexes were established with oil refineries in Omsk in the west and Angarsk, near Irkutsk in the east, which were initially based on petroleum brought in by pipeline from the Volga-Urals fields. Now gas processing plants are beginning to be established in the West Siberian oil producing area around Surgut. The first opened in 1975 at the new town of Nizhnevartovsk near the largest producing oil field, Samotlor, to recover natural gas liquids from oil field gas. These natural gas liquids will be used as petrochemical feedstocks at Omsk and at two large new petrochemical centers that are being established at Tomsk and Tobolsk, all in Western Siberia. The Tomsk complex which is to be completed during the early 1980s is to have an initial polyethylene capacity equal to the total Soviet capacity in 1974, about 350,000 tons. And there is to be a second stage further doubling that capacity sometime in the future.

Mineral Fertilizers

One of the largest chemical industries in the country is constituted by the various mineral fertilizers, primarily phosphate, nitrogen, and potash. These industries alone now utilize 40–50 per cent of all the sulfuric acid produced in the country. Mineral fertilizer production has been expanded tremendously during the last 15 years as the post-Khrushchev regime has mounted a crash program greatly to improve agricultural production. The production of mineral fertilizers of all types, in standard fertilizer units, has increased from 5.5 million tons in 1950 to 31.3 million tons in 1965 and 115 million tons in 1976. This makes the Soviet Union now the largest mineral fertilizer producer in the world. Its closest competitor, the United States, produces about 80–85 million tons per year. The Soviet Union is particularly outstanding in potash production, apparently possessing the largest potassium salt resources in the world.

Phosphate

The early phosphate industry in Tsarist Russia relied on imported phosphate from north Africa and the United States, as well as some low grade phosphate rock in locations such as Vinnitsa in the western Ukraine, Perm in the western Urals, Rudnichnyy near Kirov and Dzerzhinsk in the Volgo-Vyatka Region. The opening of the Kola apatite deposits in 1929 soon replaced all imports of phosphatic ores and became almost the sole supplier to all the new superphosphate plants that were cropping up in European Russia. In addition, ground phosphate rock to be applied directly as fertilizer began to be produced at Voskresensk southeast of Moscow, near Bryansk, at Shchigry, a chemical town east of Kursk, and later at Maardu in Estonia and Kingisepp near Lenin-

grad. (Fig. 11–9) A superphosphate plant was established at Konstantinovka in the Donets Basin to use sulfur gases from an adjoining zinc refinery to produce sulfuric acid to be applied to Kola apatite shipped into the area. In 1935 the Voskresensk plant switched to Kola apatite, and in the 1960s it added a new ammonia unit which derives necessary hydrogen from natural gas brought in by pipe from Central Asia. The Voskresensk plant has expanded into one of the largest superphosphate producers in the Soviet Union.

The apatite deposit in the Khibiny Mountains of central Kola Peninsula is one of the largest sources of phosphate in the world. It contains 17–19 per cent P_2O_5, which is concentrated to about 40 per cent before shipment to plants all over European Russia and for export. Production began in 1929 at the new settlement of Kirovsk, which since has become the primary commercial city of the central Kola Peninsula mining region. In 1963 a new concentrator was opened at the new town of Apatity, and there is now talk about opening a third concentrator at Titan rail station half way along the 20-kilometer rail line linking Kirov and Apatity. In 1975 the Kola Peninsula produced 15.5 million tons of apatite concentrate, 3.8 million tons of which came from Kirovsk and 11.7 million tons from Apatity. The 1980 plan calls for a total production of 18.2 million tons.

In the past, about half the Kola apatite has been exported to countries such as East and West Germany, various East European countries, and Finland. This all moves through the port of Murmansk to the north. The nearly 10 million tons of apatite used for domestic purposes in 1975 was shipped to 26 superphosphate plants and served as the raw material for more than 80 per cent of all the phosphatic fertilizer produced in the Soviet Union. Out of 90.2 million tons of all fertilizers produced in 1975 in the Soviet Union, phosphatic fertilizers accounted for 23.8 million tons, of which about 20 million were based on Kola apatite. The apatite concentrate moved to sulfuric acid production centers for decomposition by acid treatment to superphosphate.

Much of the other 20 per cent of phosphatic fertilizers are produced from the lower grade phosphate rock produced in the Karatau district in southern Kazakhstan. This began to develop after World War II and instigated the construction of four superphosphate plants in Central Asia and adjacent southern Kazakhstan at the cities of Kokand in the Fergana Basin, Dzhambul, Samarkand, and Chardzhou. In the initial years, the lower grade Karatau phosphate had to be supplemented by apatite coming all the way from the Kola Peninsula, but in recent years the Karatau phosphate process has been switched to thermal reduction that yields elemental phosphorus which can then be shipped to fertilizer manufacturing plants to be used in mixed fertilizers such as ammonium phosphate, as well as to produce certain feed additives. This has allowed for greater utilization of the Karatau phosphates and their wider shipment across the country.

In 1975 it was announced that the Gomel phosphate fertilizer plant in Belorussia had added an ammonium phosphate unit which was shipping in elemental phosphorus all the way from the Chimkent and Dzhambul plants in southern Kazakhstan and that the cost of this shipment of elemental phosphorus over this distance was only about 30 per cent of the cost of shipping Kola apatite to the Gomel plant. Yellow phosphorus plants now exist at both Chimkent, opened in 1966, and Dzhambul, opened in 1973, and a second plant is under construction at Dzhambul. The elemental phosphorus derived from the Karatau phosphate rock by the thermal reduction method in electrical furnaces requires great quantities of electricity, which at present are being derived primarily from the Dzhambul power station based on Central Asian gas.

In 1969 the first ammonium phosphate complex was established at Almalyk, the copper smelting town in Uzbekistan. The ammonium phosphate is produced by combining phosphoric acid and ammonia. The phosphoric acid is obtained at Almalyk by treating Karatau phosphorite concentrate with sulfuric acid derived from local smelter gases. The

ammonia for the process is shipped in from nearby Chirchik, a gas-based nitrogen chemical center. This process, along with the processing of phosphate by phosphoric acid, has allowed for the establishment of a triple superphosphate industry (confusingly called double superphosphate by the Soviets) which has raised the P_2O_5 content of the single superphosphate form 18–21 per cent to 42–50 per cent. This has greatly decreased costs of transport of phosphate materials around the country and made possible longer shipments of fertilizers to outlying areas.

In 1975 the Soviet Union was the second largest producer of phosphate fertilizers, with about two-thirds the production of the United States and one-sixth of the world's supply. The application of fertilizer per acre of cultivated land is still not up to par compared to most of the developed countries of the world, and the Soviets intend to continue to expand the industry. However, they are beginning to worry about running out of Kola apatite sometime in the distant future, and consequently they are arranging for foreign imports of phosphate ores and phosphoric acid. The arrangement with Occidental Petroleum Corporation to provide for imports of phosphate and phosphoric acid from Florida has already been mentioned. In addition, agreements are now being worked out with Morocco to revive imports of phosphate from that area. Thus, the Soviet Union now seems to have gone full circle in its phosphate industry. In the future the Soviets will be importing phosphates from Morocco and the United States just as Tsarist Russia did many years ago. On the other hand, the Soviets are committed to continue large exports of Kola apatite to certain East European countries, West Germany, and Finland.

Nitrogenous Fertilizers

Nitrogenous fertilizers are commonly made by the synthetic ammonia process which combines nitrogen from the air with hydrogen to produce ammonia. The major location factor of the industry is the source of hydrogen. Until the late 1950s, almost all the hydrogen was obtained from coal by water-gas reaction and from coke oven gases, so that nitrogenous fertilizer plants tended to be concentrated in coal basins or coke-chemical centers. Some of the main coking centers that produced hydrogen for ammonia synthesis were Gorlovka in the Donets Basin, Dneprodzerzhinsk on the lower Dnieper River, Magnitogorsk in the southern Urals, and Kemerovo in the Kuznetsk Basin. In addition, plants established at Novomoskovsk near Tula in the Moscow Coal Basin and at Berezniki in the coal basins of the western Urals used water-gas reaction. In Central Asia, Chirchik near Tashkent derived hydrogen from the electrolosis of water. (Fig. 11–11)

As the gas industry expanded rapidly, beginning in the late 1950s, and natural gas pipelines were built from raw material areas to many distributing points in the country, the nitrogenous fertilizer industry became much more dispersed and shifted to natural gas as a cheaper, cleaner source of raw materials. In addition to new plants based on gas, many of the old coal and coke-based plants switched to gas. In Central Asia, natural gas from Gazli near Bukhara became the basis for a large new chemical complex at the new town of Navoi nearby and another plant at the town of Fergana in the Fergana Basin which was receiving Gazli gas by pipe. In the Transcaucasus, plants were established at the steel city of Rustavi and at Kirovakan to utilize gas from Karadag southwest of Baku and from Stavropol and Krasnodar in the North Caucasus, at Nevinnomyssk in the North Caucasus to use Stavropol gas, and at Grodno in Belorussia and Jonava in Lithuania to use gas from the north Carpathian foothills in the western Ukraine. In addition, the Novomoskovsk complex, founded in 1933 and originally based on Urals coke to derive hydrogen for ammonia synthesis, switched to natural gas in 1959 when a pipeline reached the area from the North Caucasus. As a result of all this activity, as early as 1965 51 per cent of all the ammonia synthesis in the country was based on natural gas, 39 per cent on coal, and 10 per cent on water electrolosis.

The Novomoskovsk plant has undergone a continual program of expansion and modernization and has become one of the largest fertilizer producing centers in the country. In 1975 it produced about 10 per cent of the total Soviet nitrogen fertilizer. Over the years it has shifted increasingly from simple ammonium nitrate fertilizer to more concentrated urea and complex fertilizers combining all three, nitrogen-phosphorus-potash. Some of the expansion has been aided by American expertise to design larger ammonia units. Similar units are also being added at the large chemical complexes at Nevinnomyssk in the North Caucasus, Severodonetsk in the Donets Basin and Novgorod in the north.

The conversion of another large nitrogen complex is taking place at the large steel city of Cherepovets in the Northwest Economic Region. Beginning in 1970 a new ammonium nitrate process was added to the older plant which had been limited to coking by-products. Hydrogen for ammonia synthesis is being derived in the new plant from natural gas transmitted from the Vuktyl fields in the Komi A.S.S.R. to the northeast. In addition, a double superphosphate plant using Kola apatite is also planned for Cherepovets. A mixed fertilizer section was already added in 1976.

Most recently, in 1976 work began on a large new nitrogenous fertilizer complex at Rossosh in the southwestern part of Voronezh Oblast in the Central Chernozem Region. This plant, which will use some Japanese equipment, will be based on natural gas taken from the North Caucasus-Central Russia transmission system nearby. It will supply fertilizer to the rich farming areas of the Central Chernozem Region, the North Caucasus, and the Volga Valley. The Soviet Union is now a close second to the United States, producing about one-fifth of the world's nitrogenous fertilizers.

Potash

The Soviet Union contains the world's largest known reserves of potash, and is currently producing about one-third of the world's supply. In terms of K_2O content, in 1975–1976 the

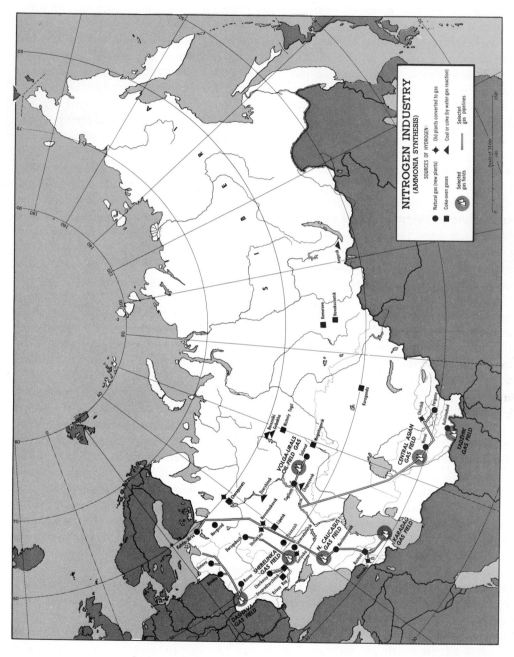

Figure 11–11   The nitrogen industry. After Shabad, Basic Industrial Resources of the U.S.S.R., Columbia University Press, 1969, pp. 78–79.

U.S.S.R. produced 7,944,000 metric tons of potash, which compared to 4,841,000 for its nearest competitor, Canada, and 2,099,000 in the fourth ranking U.S.A. Most of the production takes place in two primary producing areas and a third secondary area, In 1975 the Solikamsk-Berezniki area on the upper Kama River on the western slopes of the Urals produced 9.47 million tons (of 41.6 per cent K_2O), the Soligorsk area in Belorussia produced 8.33 million tons, and the Stebnik-Kalush area in the north Carpathian foothills in the western Ukraine produced 1.07 million tons. Another 0.23 million tons was produced as a potassium sulfate by-product of the alunite-based alumina plant at Kirovabad in Azerbaydzhan. Out of the total production of 19.1 million tons, 5.98 million tons were exported, primarily to countries in Eastern Europe, Austria, Italy, and Finland. Potash production has been expanding consistently during the last twenty-five years, from 0.75 million tons in 1950 to 9.82 million tons in 1970 and 19.1 million tons in 1975. Exports have been running about one-third of production.

In the late 1960s, 62.3 per cent of the Soviet potash reserves were estimated to be in the Solikamsk-Berezniki area, 18.9 per cent in Belorussia, 7.5 per cent in the Kalush-Stebnik area, and 11.3 per cent in Kazakhstan and Central Asia. The Solikamsk-Berezniki deposit was opened in 1934 and was the largest producer in the country until it was surpassed by the new Belorussia deposits in the late 1960s. The Soligorsk deposit in south-central Belorussia was opened up in 1963 and was the leading producer from the late 1960s until the Urals regained first place in 1975. The Stebnik-Kalush area was gained from Poland in 1939 and underwent a major expansion in the 1960s as a large chemical complex came into being at Kalush in 1967 which produced not only potassium-sulfate fertilizer but also magnesium metal and chlorine and its derivatives, all of which were derived from the sulfates in the area. Although the Carpathian deposits are not as large as those in Belorussia and the Urals, they have special uses, since they consist

of potassium sulfates, unlike the Urals and Belorussian deposits which consist of chlorides only. Sulfate fertilizers can be used on crops that do not tolerate chlorine, such as potatoes, flax, alfalfa, tobacco, citrus fruit, and vineyards. Kalush is one of five main Soviet plants producing magnesium. The others are at Zaporozhye, Solikamsk, Berezniki, and Ust-Kamenogorsk. The Kama River potassium deposits consist of both sylvite, the potassium ore, and carnallite, a magnesium ore, that is the principal source of magnesium metal in the Soviet Union.

In 1975 it was announced that the Soviets were testing a pilot plant for the solution mining of potash at Karlyuk, a deep potash deposit in the southeastern part of the Turkmen Republic near the Uzbek border.

Cement

With the tremendous amount of construction of buildings, dams, highways, and many other huge projects during the Soviet period, the production of cement has had to expand astronomically, from only 1,845,000 tons as late as 1945 to 122,057,000 tons in 1975. The U.S.S.R. is now the leading cement producer in the world, producing about 18 per cent of the world's supply and twice as much as its leading competitors, Japan and the United States. (Table 8–2) At the same time its production has been dispersed geographically from a few old centers such as Novorossiysk on the Black Sea coast and Belgorod in the southern part of the Central Chernozem Region to many different locations scattered throughout much of the settled parts of the country.

The materials necessary for the production of 1 ton of Portland cement amount to about 1.5 tons of calcium carbonate (limestone), 0.4 tons of clay, and 0.3 tons of coal or equivalent other fuel. Since most of these materials are widely found and the economics of production is primarily related to transportation costs of such bulky products, most of the industry has tended to be market oriented. The substitution of gas technology for much of the coal in recent years has further stimulated the market orientation of the industry.

The Novorossiysk cement complex, utilizing pure chalk limestone along the Black Sea coast, is still one of the major producers in the country with a current capacity of about 4.5 million tons per year. This has been joined in the North Caucasus by the Ust-Dzheguta plant established near the construction headworks of the Kuban-Kalaus-Kuma irrigation system, with an ultimate capacity of 2.6 million tons, and the Chiryurt plant near Groznyy with a capacity of 1.2 million tons. The old Belgorod (white city) plant, also based on a chalky limestone escarpment, which now has a capacity of 2 million tons per year, is being joined by a 3.6-million-ton plant at Staryy Oskol in conjunction with the large steel plant that is being built there. The cement plant is using chalk overburden in open pit iron ore mines in the area. It is also using some blast furnace slag which is being shipped from the Urals on return cars carrying KMA iron ore to Urals iron and steel plants. Farther northeast the Alekseyevka cement plant has been established in the Mordvinian A.S.S.R. to serve the Volga-Vyatka Economic Region containing the large industrial district of Gorky. The cement plant, built on a local limestone deposit, started operation in 1956, and now has a capacity of 3.5 million tons per year. Old cement plants based on the limestone of the Zhiguli Hills in the Samara Bend of the Volga have constantly undergone expansion.

In central Kazakhstan the Karaganda cement plant, which was expanded to 2 million tons capacity in the mid 1970s, is planned to have an ultimate capacity of 6 million tons, which will provide much of the needs for Kazakhstan. In the Far East, the cement center of Spassk-Dalniy, on the Vladivostok-Khabarovsk railroad, uses local deposits of limestone and clays to produce much of the cement needs of the Soviet Far East. It is being expanded to a capacity of about 3.7 million tons.

In addition to some of the major plants just mentioned, large quantities of cement are being turned out in many of the alumina producing areas of the country as a by-product. As mentioned before, alumina plants produce about 4–5 times as much cement as they do alumina.

Synthetic Rubber

After experimenting for several years with the cultivation of such latex-bearing plants as kok-sagyz, a dandelion-like plant, the Soviets finally gave up the effort to develop some sort of natural rubber-producing crop of their own, and, faced with uncertain natural rubber supplies from Malaysia, turned to synthetic rubber as the way to become self sufficient in an industry that was going to become very important for industrial modernization. Thus, during the 1930s, the Soviet Union became the first major producer of synthetic rubber, at that time based on grain and potato alcohol. Early plants were established in 1932 and 1933 at Voronezh and Yefremov in the Central Chernozem Region, and at Yaroslavl in 1932 and Kazan in 1936 in the upper Volga valley. These early rubber factories were situated close to the tire plants of Moscow, Voronezh, and Yaroslavl and the rubber footwear industry of central European Russia, Leningrad, and Kazan. In 1940 a chloroprene rubber plant was opened in Yerevan based on acetylene derived from local limestone. (Fig. 11–12)

During the 1950s, as the oil and gas industries expanded, the synthetic rubber industry expanded and diversed as it switched from a vegetable alcohol base to ethylene, an oil refinery by-product gas, as the major feedstock. A synthetic plant opened in the new chemical city of Sumgait north of Baku in 1957 to make use of oil refining gases from Baku, and other synthetic rubber plants became attached to oil refineries at Orsk, Ufa, Saratov, and Novokuybyshevsk. In 1956 a synthetic rubber plant based on hydrolosis of wood cellulose was established at Krasnoyarsk in Eastern Siberia.

As the production of synthetic rubber shifted increasingly to oil refinery gases, huge new plants were opened at the major petrochemical centers of Sterlitamak in 1960, Togliatti in 1962, Omsk in 1964, and Volzhskiy in 1966.

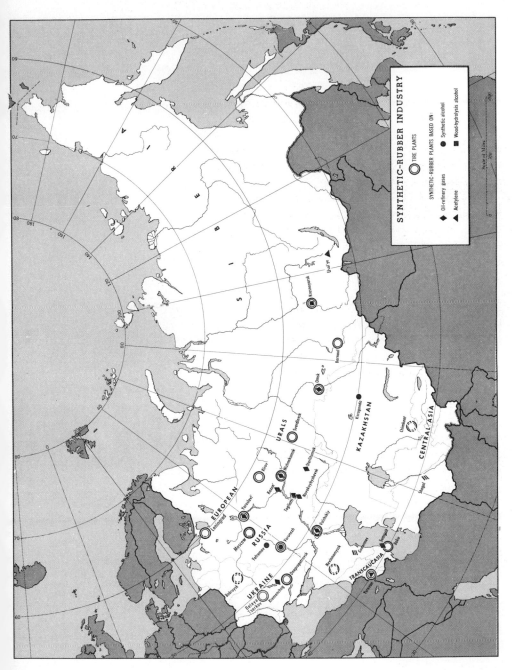

Figure 11–12 Synthetic rubber industry. Updated from Shabad, Basic Industrial Resources of the U.S.S.R., Columbia University Press, 1969, pp. 84–85.

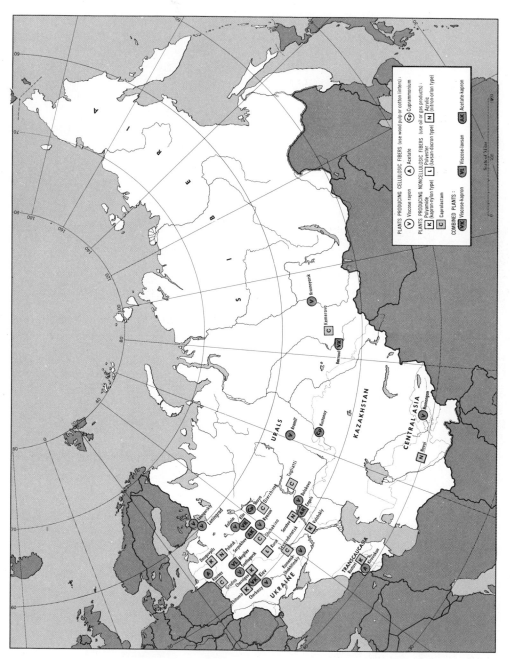

Figure 11–13 Production of chemical fibers. Updated from Shabad, Basic Industrial Resources of the U.S.S.R., Columbia University Press, 1969, pp. 88–89.

In the late 1960s a synthetic rubber plant was completed at Nizhnekamsk to supply a local tire plant that had been built to service the huge Kama Truck Plant nearby and the Togliatti car plant downstream on the Volga. The tire industry, for various kinds of vehicles, utilizes much of the synthetic rubber produced in the country. There are now 16 tire factories in the country either completed or in the near stages of completion. (Fig. 11–12) Synthetic rubber now accounts for more than 90 per cent of tire production.

Man-Made Fibers

The Soviet Union has been lagging in the development of man-made fibers, particularly synthetic fibers derived from non-cellulosic materials. True synthetics make up only about 40 per cent of the man-made fibers in the country, while rayon and other fibers derived from cellulose make up the rest. By comparison, in the United States non-cellulosic fibers account for about 80 per cent of all man-made fibers. In 1975 the U.S.A. produced about 8 times as much non-cellulosic fibers as the U.S.S.R. did.

Most of the synthetic production is based on ammonia synthesis which now is based mainly on natural gas or coal products. Therefore, large new synthetic plants are coming into being either in coal working complexes or along natural gas pipelines. The recent construction of caprolactam plants well illustrates this. (Fig. 11–13) Caprolactam is the intermediate product in the manufacture of capron (a type of nylon). Caprolactam plants have been established in the large chemical cities of Dzerzhinsk near Gorky and at Togliatti, as well as at Grodno in western Belorussia, all three on natural gas pipelines, and at Shchekino in the Moscow coal basin, Severodonetsk in the Donets coal basin, and Kemerovo in the Kuznetsk Basin. The major producing man-made fiber centers, with their types of production, are shown in Figure 11–13.

Synthetic Resins and Plastics

The Soviets have also lagged in development of synthetic resins and plastics, and they do not report statistics on their production. They are now trying to catch up in these industries in order to be able to produce a wide variety of consumer products without cutting into their metals industries. However, they still have a long way to go to catch leading producers such as the United States, West Germany, and Japan. Urea resins, on which many of their plastics are based, are derived from ammonia production, which is usually associated with nitrogenous fertilizer plants. Vinyl resins are associated with chlorine production at such places as Novomoskovsk near Tula, Sterlitamak in the Bashkir A.S.S.R., and Usolye in Irkutsk Oblast of Eastern Siberia. They are also associated with acetylene-based industries in places such as Yerevan in the Transcaucasus. Polyolefins are being produced from oil refinery gases in such places as Groznyy, Salavat, Novokuybyshevsk, Novopolotsk, and Guryev.

Reading List

GENERAL

1. Shabad, Theodore, *Basic Industrial Resources of the USSR*, Columbia University Press, New York, 1969, 393 pp.

FERROUS METALS

1. Braun, G. A., *Zhelezorudnaya baza chernoy metallurgii SSSR* (The Iron Ore Base for Heavy Metallurgy in the USSR), Nedra, Moscow, 2nd ed., 1970, 309 pp.
2. Khrushchev, A. T., "Formation of the Gubkin-Staryy Oskol Industrial Node (in the Kursk Magnetic Anomaly)," *Soviet Geography: Review and Translation*, December 1976, pp. 690–695.
3. ———, "The Formation of the Industrial Complex of the Kursk Magnetic Anomaly," *Soviet Geography: Review and Translation*, April 1975, pp. 239–248.
4. Korostik, V. P., "A Comparative Analysis of the Iron Ore Basins of Krivoy Rog and the Kursk Magnetic Anomaly," *Vestnik Moskovskogo Uni-*

versiteta, seriya geografiya, 1978, No. 1, pp. 78–83.

5. Nikitina, S. A., "The Iron and Steel Industry of the Lipetsk Industrial Node," *Soviet Geography: Review and Translation,* March 1974, pp. 128–134.

6. Rodgers, Allan, "A Visit to the Kuznetsk Basin," *Soviet Geography: Review and Translation,* December 1976, pp. 695–698.

7. Rom, V. Ya., "Geographical Problems in the Iron and Steel Industry of the USSR," *Soviet Geography: Review and Translation,* March 1974, pp. 121–128.

8. Sidorova, V. S., and Vadyukhin, A. A., "New Technology and the Location of the Iron and Steel Industry in the Eastern Portion of the USSR," *Soviet Geography: Review and Translation,* January 1977, pp. 33–38.

NONFERROUS METALS

1. Shabad, Theodore, "Raw Material Problems of the Soviet Aluminum Industry," *Resource Policy,* December 1976, pp. 222–234.

2. ———, "Raw Material Problems of the Soviet Aluminum Industry," *Soviet Economy in a New Perspective,* Joint Economic Committee, Congress of the United States, Washington, October 14, 1976, pp. 661–674.

3. ———, "Soviet Experiment in Aluminum Fails," *The New York Times,* May 9, 1976.

CHEMICALS

1. Abouchar, Alan, "Postwar Developments in the Soviet Cement Industry," in *Soviet Economy in a New Perspective,* Joint Economic Committee, Congress of the United States, Washington, 1976, pp. 558–574.

2. Dienes, Leslie, *Locational Factors and Locational Developments in the Soviet Chemical Industry,* The University of Chicago, Department of Geography, Research Paper No. 119, Chicago, 1969, 262 pp.

3. Rushing, Francis W., "Soviet Chemical Industry: A Modern Growth Sector," in *Soviet Economy in a New Perspective,* Joint Economic Committee, Congress of the United States, Washington, 1976, pp. 535–557.

4. Woods, Louis Alan, *The Soviet Chemical Fiber Industry and Locational Doctrine,* PhD Dissertation, University of North Carolina, 1972.

12

Manufacturing

Some of the manufacturing industries are the oldest industries in Russia, and they still employ by far the most people in the country. If one uses the definition of manufacturing literally to mean the manual alteration of materials, then they are distinguished as a group by their high input of labor. In this chapter, discussion will be limited to the machine building and metal-working industries, light industries (textiles, leather working, and so forth), and food industries, which use 65 per cent of all industrial labor. (Table 8-11)

MACHINE BUILDING AND METAL-WORKING

Of all the major categories of industry in the Soviet Union machine building and metal-working ranks first, by far, in most respects. This category of industry occupies fully 40 per cent of all labor in industry, accounts for almost 28 per cent of the gross product of industry, and has shown the greatest growth during the Soviet period. (Tables 8-9, 8-10, and 8-11) Machines are the basis of all industrial production. In the early stages of the Soviet period the machine building industries had to be expanded first before any other industries could be initiated. Therefore, in the early stages of industrial development, 1913–1940, the largest investments and the largest resultant growths of all industries occurred in the machine construction and metal-working category. (Table 8-9) Later, 1940–1955, as a great amount of construction took place all over the country to rehabilitate the destruction of World War II and continue the expansion of urbanization and industrialization of the country, the construction materials industries grew fastest. (Table 8-8 and 8-9) During 1956–1960, oil and gas industries expanded the fastest, and during 1961–1965, chemical industries, many of which were based on the previous expansion of oil and gas, expanded most rapidly. But since 1970, machinery has jumped into the forefront again, along with chemicals. (Table 8-8) During the entire period, 1913–1975, machine industries grew at almost twice the rate of their nearest competitor, chemicals. (Table 8-9)

The machine building industries range all the way from fine tools, instruments, and computers through industrial machines of all sorts, transportation and communications equipment, agricultural machinery, and mining equipment to such exotic things as space vehicles. The Soviets, by putting the first sputnik into space in the 1950s, demonstrated their ability to create the most complicated types of machinery, and on occasion, such as the recent crash program in tractor production, they have demonstrated their ability to overcome quantitative deficits in the production of selected items. However, their perennially tight capital throughout their economy has forced them to make hard choices between various kinds of machine production, so that they still have not reached their desired level in certain sectors of machine building, and in recent years they have turned increasingly toward the more industrialized countries of eastern and western Europe, the United States, and Japan for the importation of some of the more sophisticated machine technology.

The machine building industries developed in Tsarist Russia in the heavily populated central European part of the country and later in the metal-producing areas of the Urals and the eastern Ukraine. These three industrial nodes still turn out the bulk of the machinery of the country, but the industry has dispersed greatly during the Soviet period, and since most machine building industries are labor intensive, generally the distribution of machine production matches the distribution of population. Therefore, it is rather useless to talk about the distribution of the machine building industry as a whole, and data for most individual industries are not available. In the following pages some qualitative information will be given for major branches of the industry, and more specific information will be presented for the two most rapidly expanding machine building industries during the last decade, the automotive and tractor industries.

Machine Tools

The production of all sorts of machine tools is absolutely essential to the rest of industry. More than 100 enterprises in the Soviet Union now manufacture annually 250,000 metal cutting machines, forges and presses, and lathes. The primary role in these industries is retained by Moscow and its environs and Leningrad, but such industries are now dispersed throughout the country, particularly in such old manufacturing centers as the Gorky region, the Urals, and the Ukraine, and more recently the Volga Valley, Belorussia, and Lithuania. The production of the most metal

consuming of these machines is centered in such metallurgical areas as the Donets-Dnieper Region and the Urals, while the most labor consuming are in more diversified large cities, such as Moscow, Leningrad, Kiev, and Kharkov.

Instrument Making

Since World War II the production of all sorts of instruments has expanded at a growth rate 3.5 times that of machine building industries as a whole. Instrument-making plants turn out a great assortment of goods, including control mechanisms and computers which are absolutely essential to modern spheres of material production, management, and research institutions. The decisive location factor in instrument making is the availability of skilled manpower. The production of computers and electronic analyzers has been developed in such cities as Moscow, Leningrad, Minsk, Penza, Kursk, Ryazan, and various centers in the Urals and Lithuania, as well as many other parts of the country.

Heavy Machines

Heavy machine building includes plant and equipment for such industries as ferrous and nonferrous metallurgy, large electric power stations, and cement plants. This production is characterized by high metal consumption, and so is generally located near metallurgical bases such as the Donets-Dnieper region and the Urals. Two huge plants, Uralmash at Sverdlovsk in the Urals and Kramatorsk in the Donbas, have become the leading suppliers for the whole country in metallurgical equipment and powerful excavators. In the same areas Kharkov and Sverdlovsk turn out large turbines, generators, and steam boilers.

Some heavy machine building has developed in market areas because the machines are so bulky to transport. For instance, Novosibirsk turns out electric furnaces, hoisting cranes, equipment for hydroelectric power stations, and so forth primarily for the Kuznetsk Basin nearby and the large hydroelectric plants being installed in Siberia. Similarily, the smaller towns of Barnaul and Biisk in Western Siberia are turning out boilers for various uses in the east. Farther east, Krasnoyarsk and Irkutsk turn out a great array of market-oriented heavy machinery. In the central European region Moscow and satellite cities such as Podolsk and Elecktrostal, as well as the Gorky region, turn out a wide range of heavy machines for local consumption.

In some cases the deciding locational factor has been the presence of a trained labor force. Leningrad is probably the best case in point to illustrate this. Until the Revolution, St. Petersburg served as the prototype city which tried out new technology in pilot plants before other plants were built in other parts of the country. Although it has largely lost this function to Moscow during the Soviet period, it still retains virtually a monopoly on certain items, such as large turbines for hydroelectric plants. Most of the large turbines installed in the huge hydroelectric plants of Eastern Siberia have been manufactured in Leningrad and floated into place on ships along the Northern Sea Route and up the Yenisey and its tributaries because the components are too large to carry on railroad cars.

Chemical Equipment

During the last quarter century the production of chemical equipment has been growing twice as rapidly as that of machine building as a whole, as the entire chemical industry and its major suppliers, the petroleum and gas industries, have expanded at rapid rates. Principal areas of domestic production of chemical equipment and the building of pumps and compressors coincide with the main areas of the chemical industry itself, the Central Region, Ukraine, the Urals, and the Volga Valley. As was mentioned in the section on chemical industries, chemical equipment, including entire plants, have been one of the major technological imports by the Soviets from more indus-

trially advanced East European countries, Western Europe, the United States, and Japan.

Plant and Equipment for the Textile and Food Industries

Leningrad traditionally has been the largest producer of textile machinery, and other traditional centers are Moscow and old textile producing cities in the Central Region, particularly around the major centers of Moscow, Ivanovo, and Kostroma. Newer textile machine industries have been set up in Penza, Kuznetsk, Orel, and Taganrog, as well as in some outlying cities such as Tashkent.

Since the food industry is the most dispersed industry of all, the building of equipment for food processing plants is also dispersed, primarily in the main food producing areas of the country. The greatest number of machine building plants in the food processing industry are found in the Ukraine.

Transport Engineering

Train Locomotives and Railroad Rolling Stock

Since the railroads carry much of the freight and passenger traffic in the country the manufacture of locomotives and rolling stock has occupied the leading position in transport engineering in the country. Locomotive plants were established during the period of rapid railroad building in the latter half of the nineteenth century in Kolomna, at the juncture of the Moscow and Oka Rivers south of Moscow, and at Kharkov and Lugansk (Voroshilovgrad) in the eastern Ukraine, greatly aided by foreign investments. During the 1930s, the Bolsheviks built a second plant in Voroshilovgrad which since then has grown to the largest locomotive manufacturing plant in the country. All these plants have been fully reconstructed and converted from steam engines to diesels. Most of this conversion took place during the mid

1950s when most of the switch from steam to diesel and electric locomotion took place on the railroads. During that time also the first large plant producing electric locomotives was constructed in Novocherkassk northeast of Rostov-On-Don. Electric locomotives are also now being turned out at plants in Tbilisi and Kharkov. In addition, locomotives are built in Murom and Lyudinovo in the Central Region. In 1976 the Soviet Union produced 1455 diesel and 410 electric locomotives.

A number of railway car building plants, each specializing on certain types of railroad rolling stock, have developed over the years in the European part of the country, and one plant exists in the Altay region of southwestern Siberia. Of particular importance are plants in Bryansk and Kalinin. Other CMEA countries have been cooperating in the construction of these plants, and have been exporting railroad rolling stock to the Soviet Union, as well. The construction of a huge railroad car plant is an integral part of the plan for the industrialization of the Minusinsk Basin in Eastern Siberia that is to take place with the completion of the Sayan Dam on the upper Yenisey. This plant is specifically to serve the needs of the new Baykal-Amur Railway, as well as the continued heavy use of the Trans Siberian Railway as a "land bridge" between Japan and western Europe. It will turn out primarily flat cars for carrying large containers, which will also be manufactured in this area. In 1976 the Soviet Union produced 71,900 freight cars, 2078 passenger cars, 1113 streetcars, and 308 subway cars. Subway cars are manufactured in Mytishchi, a northern suburb of Moscow. Engles, east of Saratov in the Volga Valley, is the main trolley bus manufacturing center.

Shipbuilding

Ocean-going vessels traditionally have been built in Leningrad on the Baltic and Nokolayev at the mouth of the Southern Bug River on the north coast of the Black Sea. These shipbuilding yards have been reconstructed and modernized, and new yards have been built in Riga, Klaipeda, and Kaliningrad in the Baltic area,

Archangel on the White Sea in the north, and at certain ports on the Pacific coast. Several small shipyards have developed on the Black and Azov Seas, including the ports of Batumi, Poti, and Kerch. Batumi and Poti now produce hydrofoil ships. Some sea-going vessels are also built in inland shipyards such as those at Gorky, Astrakhan, and Baku.

Soviet shipyards now turn out vessels of all types including multipurpose dry cargo ships, timber carriers, supertankers, refrigerator ships, large passenger liners, powerful nuclear and conventional ice breakers, fishing boats and cannery ships, and so forth. Many ships have been imported in the last few years from such countries as East Germany, Poland, Finland, Sweden, Yugoslavia, Bulgaria, Hungary, Denmark, and France. In total tonnage, the maritime fleet of the Soviet Union now ranks fifth in the world.

With its great use of waterways, Russia has always been a major river boat manufacturer. Most of the river craft in the country are built in the Volga-Kama river basin. River craft of all kinds built in these shipyards can be found all over the country from the Danube in the west to the Amur in the east, and significant numbers are now being exported. The oldest river craft shipyard in the country, and still the leading enterprise, is the Krasnoye Sormovo Shipyard in Gorky. Other major river boat manufacturing centers are Moscow, Rybinsk, and Kostroma. The Soviets have been pioneers in the development of hydrofoil vessels for rapid transport on rivers and lakes.

Motor Vehicles

Until the last decade, the motor vehicle industry in the Soviet Union has been minimal, and priority has been given to the production of trucks. But during the mid 1960s, the Soviet leaders apparently made the decision to increase the availability of passenger cars along with other large consumer durables to abate the inflationary pressures generated by steady growth in spendable personal income and to increase worker incentive. Since then large new automobile plants have been brought into production, and older plants have been expanded and modernized. It now appears that the Soviets are heading down the primrose path of rapid "automobilization" of the country. The Soviet people, as they become more affluent, apparently have the same burning desire for private ownership of motor vehicles that has occurred in most of the rest of the developed world. Thus, we now see the Soviets rapidly expanding car production and all that goes with it: highway building and the establishment of gas stations and repair garages. The largest construction project in the entire Soviet Union during the eighth five-year plan, 1966–1970, was the Volga Motor Vehicle Plant at Togliatti, and the largest construction project during the ninth five-year plan, 1971–1975, was the Kama River Truck Plant in Naberezhnyye Chelny.

Soviet passenger car production increased slowly during the 1950s from 65,000 in 1950 to 139,000 in 1960. The pace picked up somewhat in the 1960s as passenger car production increased to 344,000 in 1970. There was a quantum leap in the one year between 1970 and 1971 as the Togliatti plant began to produce Fiat-type cars, and simultaneously the Renault-aided Izhevsk plant came into operation, and a large expansion program, using Renault aid, went into effect in the Moscow plant. The Soviet production of cars in 1971 was 529,000. The production increased at a rapid rate as all these new facilities came into capacity production by 1975 when total production was 1,201,000 passenger cars. Since then, growth has tapered off somewhat as no significant expansions to plant have taken place. In 1976, the passenger car production amounted to 1,239,000 and the plan for 1977 was 1,274,000.

In spite of this rapid increase in passenger car production, the Soviet Union still lags way behind other industrial countries in the world. In 1976 the United States produced about 15,000,000 passenger cars and light trucks which are being used by young studs as passenger vehicles. Whereas at the beginning of 1975 the U.S.S.R. had 3,782,000 passenger cars registered in the country, the United States had 104,898,000. West Germany, France, the United Kingdom, and Italy each had approximately 4 times as many registrations as the Soviet Union. Whereas these west European countries had from 240 to 278 vehicles per 1000 population, and the United States had 502, the Soviet Union had only 15, which was lower than all the East European countries except Rumania. Thus, the Soviet Union is only now emerging into the automobile age, and has a long way to go if it indeed intends to go this route.

In 1976 the Soviet Union exported 344,743 passenger cars, 31,944 trucks, and 2088 buses. Most of these went to East European countries and secondarily to other socialist countries, but sales are dispersing to many countries of Europe and the Middle East, and even a few to Africa and South America. In return the Soviet Union is importing a great number of parts, primarily from East European countries, and some assembled trucks and buses. In 1976, the Soviet Union imported 11,775 trucks, mainly from West Germany, Poland, Czechoslovakia, and East Germany, and 11,105 buses from Hungary and Poland. Soviet imports of automotive products from the East European countries have been running about two-thirds the value of Soviet exports of automotive products to these countries, which in 1975 amounted to almost 600 million dollars.

The Volga Valley has emerged as the overwhelming concentration of the motor vehicle industry in the country. Except for the small Zaporozhye plant on the Dnieper River of the Ukraine and a plant under construction at Lutsk in the northwestern Ukraine, all car assembly takes place within the drainage basin of the Volga system. In addition, the largest truck and bus plants are situated in the Volga Basin, and many of the supplier plants producing parts for these assembly plants are also located in this region. (Table 12–1)

Much of the new plant has been constructed with the aid of foreign technology and equipment, particularly from such companies as Fiat of Italy, Renault of France, Daimler-Benz of Germany, and a wide variety of other compa-

Table 12–1 *Automotive Plants in the U.S.S.R.*

PASSENGER CARS

Location	Plant	Production Began	Model	Characteristics	Production 1975 or 1976	1980s
Togliatti	Volga (VAZ)	1970	Zhiguli	4 cylinder, 60 HP Fiat 124 and 125	660,000	1,320,000
Moscow	Moscow Leninskiy Komsomol (AZLK)		Moskvich ZIL	4 cylinder, 75 HP Limosine, 8 cyl. 300 HP	162,000	300,000
Izhevsk	Izhevsk Motor Vehicle (ZIMA)	1971	Moskvich Kombi	4 cylinder	150,000	300,000
Zaporozhye	Zaporozhye Motor Vehicle (ZAZ)		Zaporozhets	Small, 4 cyl., 40 HP air cooled	142,500	
Gorky	Gorky Motor Vehicle (GAZ)		Volga Chaika	4 cylinder, 98 HP Limosine, 8 cyl. 195 HP	80,000	
Ulyanovsk			Military Jeeps			
Lutsk		Under construction	Volynyanka	6 passenger or half-ton cargo		
				Total, 1976	1,239,000	

BUSES

Location	Plant	Production Began	Model	Characteristics	Production 1975 or 1976	1980s
Moscow	Likhachov (ZIL) ⎫		Chassis and Engines for All Buses			
Gorky	⎬				(1972)	
Lvov	LAZ ⎭		City and Intercity		10,000	
Likino	LiAZ		City Transit		6,000	
Pavlovsk	PAZ		City Transit		22,000	
Riga	(Yelgava) RAF		Microbuses		4,000	15,000
Kurgan	KuAZ		School Buses		10,000	
				Total, 1976	73,400	

TRUCKS

Location	Plant	Production Began	Model	Characteristics	Production 1975 or 1976	1980s
Naberezhnyye Chelny	Kama	1976	Heavy Transport Semitrailer Dump	Up to 16 Tons Up to 20 Tons 7 Tons ⎫⎬	5,000	150,000
Neftekamsk		1977	Dump	10 Tons		
Gorky	Gorky Motor Vehicle (GAZ)	1932	Medium Transport	2.5–4 Tons	300,000	
Moscow	Likhachov (ZIL)		Medium Transport	5 Tons	157,000	200,000
Ulyanovsk	(UAZ)		Panel Trucks	1 Ton	25,000	150,000
Minsk	Minsk Motor Vehicle (MAZ)		Heavy Transport	4.5–14 Tons ⎫		
Zhodino	Belorussia (BelAZ)		Off-Highway Dump	27–120 Tons ⎬	37,000	
Mogilev				⎭		
Kremenchug	Kremenchug Motor Vehicle (KrAZ)		Heavy Transport Semitrailer Dump	12–14 Tons up to 30 Tons ⎫⎬⎭	25,000	
Miass	Ural Motor Vehicle (UAZ)		Heavy Transport	7.5 Tons	200,000(?)	
Yerevan			Off Highway Dump		8,245	
Kutaisi	Kutaisi Motor Vehicle (KAZ)		Medium Transport	4.5 Tons	19,300	
Saransk Frunze Bryansk	⎫⎬⎭		Off Highway Dump		30,000	
				Total, 1976	716,000	

Sources: Derbinova, *et. al.;* Edwards; Kalesnik and Pavlenko, p. 206; *Narkhoz SSSR za 60 let,* p. 227; and other scattered sources, especially Shabad, "News Notes," in various issues of *Soviet Geography: Review and Translation.*

nies in many countries producing foundry equipment, forges and presses, conveyor systems, and the like. A lively trade has developed between the Soviet Union and various East European countries for the exchange of automobile parts. Thus, the automotive industry has become dispersed, specialized, and integrated among many plants, not only in the European part of the Soviet Union, but also in East European countries.

Relations among suppliers and assembly plants probably play larger roles in the automobile industry than in any other machine building industry. The automotive industry is a major consumer of steel products, tires, and many chemical and machine products. Manufactures and parts from supplier plants account for more than 60 per cent of the production of finished vehicles in assembly plants. The automobile plants in Moscow and Gorky each have more than 40 supplier plants, and that at Togliatti more than 30. Some of the supply linkages are very far flung. The Moscow automobile plant has suppliers in eleven of the economic regions of the country, Togliatti in twelve, and the Kama Truck Plant in nine. The Moscow and Gorky plants have their suppliers predominantly within a radius of 200–800 kilometers from them, but Togliatti's suppliers are mostly between 800 and 3000 kilometers away, and the Kama Truck Plant suppliers are generally 1500–3000 kilometers away, as are the suppliers of the small Yerevan truck plant in the Transcaucasus.

The Fiat plant at Togliatti exchanges parts with plants in Poland and Yugoslavia, which also have Fiat automobiles. Poland supplies headlights, backup lights, shock absorbers, circuit breakers, bulbs, direction indicators, and bumpers, while Yugoslavia supplies batteries, radiator grills, piston rings, electrical parts, switches, mirrors, axles, and steering wheels. In addition Bulgaria, Czechoslovakia, East Germany, and Hungary supply parts that are universal in use, such as batteries, generators, starters, coils, condensors, oil filters, air filters, carburetors, headlights, horns, radios, panel instruments, door locks, door handles, tire gauges, and the like. In addition, parts are sometimes acquired from the Fiat home production facilities in Turin, Italy when they cannot be produced locally.

The Volga Automobile Plant at Togliatti is now by far the largest passenger car producer in the country, producing more than all other plants put together. (Table 12–1) This plant was designed by Fiat of Italy and built with the help of Fiat and other Western technology and equipment, including about 10 per cent of foreign expenditures made in the United States. The plant began production in late 1970 and reached its full capacity of 660,000 cars per year in late 1973. More than 50,000 people are employed in two shifts. There are plans eventually to expand the plant to double its present size. The plant turns out a variant of the Fiat 124 and Fiat 125 which have been modified to withstand the rough roads and cold climate of the East European Plain. The domestic models are named the Zhiguli after the Zhiguli Hills in the Samara Bend of the Volga nearby. The cars are five passenger, and the engines are four cylinder, 60 horsepower.

Since no support facilities for the Fiat car existed in the Soviet Union, the plant had to incorporate foundry, forging, stamping, pressing, engine production, assembly, and tooling sections in a highly integrated plant. In addition a number of supplier plants have been built in other towns in the surrounding region. All this construction activity in the automotive industry, as well as earlier development of industries such as cement, synthetic rubber, phosphorus chemicals and nitrogen fertilizer, have caused the new town of Togliatti to be one of the fastest growing cities in the U.S.S.R. during the last twenty years. Its predecessor town, Stavropol, which had to be moved when the area was flooded by the Kuybyshev Reservoir in the mid 1950s, had a population of only about 15,000. On January 1, 1977, Togliatti had a population of 479,000. The city now consists of seemingly endless rows of identical concrete apartment buildings, as well as the low-slung automotive plant itself, which covers many hectares of land.

The Moskvich car, turned out by the Moscow Motor Vehicle Plant, was the most popular mass-produced car in the country before the entrance on the market of the Zhiguli. The Moscow plant is still the second largest producer in the country, having expanded in the late 1960s with the technical assistance of Renault of France. It now has a production capacity of 200,000 cars per year, but in 1976 it still only produced 162,000. It is planned that it will be expanded to a capacity of about 300,000 per year. The plant is now primarily an assembly facility, depending on a large number of specialized supplier plants for components, including engines from Ufa in the Bashkir Republic.

Moskvich cars are also being built in the new Izhevsk plant which came into being in 1971. This is now the third largest producer in the country, having turned out 150,000 in 1976. The Izhevsk plant was also designed and equipped by Renault.

The fourth largest passenger car plant is now Zaporozhye on the lower Dnieper, which turned out 142,500 vehicles in 1976. This Zaporozhet car is a small, four cylinder, 40 horsepower, air cooled vehicle, which is cheap to operate but not very popular among buyers, and the Zaporozhye plant has probably been the most neglected plant in the country in recent years. The old Gorky plant, which used to turn out by far the greatest number of cars in the country, now is relegated to fifth place, with only 80,000 automobiles produced in 1976. A few large limosines called the "Chaika" (Seagull) are also produced here, as are the ZIL limosines in the Moscow Plant. These are the two prestige automobiles in the country.

The Gorky motor vehicle plant has become mostly a medium-weight truck-producing plant, and is now the largest truck producer in the country, with approximately 300,000 units in 1976. Similar trucks are turned out in the second largest truck plant, the Likhachov plant in Moscow, a separate plant from the car plant at Moscow. A variety of trucks are also assem-

Figure 12–1   The new automobile town of Togliatti. Photo by Robert M. Hordon.

bled in about a dozen other cities in the country, as shown in Table 12-1. The heaviest transport trucks in the country are being produced at Minsk in Belorussia, Kremenchug in the Ukraine, and Miass in the Urals. Huge off-highway trucks are being produced in the new plant at Zhodino just to the east of Minsk. In 1976 this plant turned out 37,000 dump trucks with capacities of 27 and 40 tons. It has now been announced that the plant is beginning production of trucks with capacities of 75 and 120 tons. Such trucks are used in large construction projects such as dam building.

The truck plant of the future, and the one that has been attracting most attention during the last decade, is the Kama Truck Plant at Naberezhnyye Chelny on the Kama River. This is to become the world's largest heavy transport truck producing plant. At full capacity it will turn out 150,000 three-axle trucks per year and 250,000 diesel engines. By comparison, the United States in the early 1970s was building 93,000 trucks with three or more axles per year. Eight models of trucks using three basic variants are to be produced. One is a truck with a stake-and-platform body which can pull a trailer with a combined capacity of up to 16 tons. Another is a truck tractor for pulling semitrailers up to 20 tons capacity, and the third is a dump truck with 7 tons capacity.

The complex, which is comprised of six major production plants, various support facilities, and housing for a labor force of 80,000, covers an area of 100 square kilometers. The site was selected for several reasons. Plenty of open land and surplus laborers were available. Railroads and waterways already existent in the area linked the project to raw material sources and markets. And large scale industrial cooperation could be arranged with related enterprises fairly nearby in Yaroslavl, Gorky, Ulyanovsk, and Togliatti. The complex was built with extensive foreign assistance, although the Soviets could not get any one company to act as general contractor. The Likhachov Plant in Moscow developed the overall configuration of the trucks to be produced. The two largest foreign-supplied components, the engine plant and foundry, were subcontracted to Renault of France and a large U.S. engineering firm respectively. Forty U.S. companies eventually were involved in the KAMAZ project.

As was the case with the growth of Togliatti after the construction of the Fiat plant, with the development of the Kama Truck Plant the old town of Naberezhnyye Chelny has increased its population from 38,000 in 1970 to 253,000 in 1977. Nearby the Nizhnekamsk Hydrostation with a designed capacity of 1.24 million kilowatts is scheduled to go into operation in 1978. And in 1977 it was announced that an assembly plant for trucks had been opened up at nearby Neftekamsk to assemble components from the Kama plant.

A major deficiency of the Soviet truck industry has been the poor performance of truck engines. All light and medium trucks, and even some heavy trucks, are powered with gasoline engines. Only heavy cargo trucks and off-highway trucks are powered by diesel engines. Most of the gasoline engines use low octane fuel and thereby achieve only low compression ratios. Most of the gasoline engines have traditionally been built in the two major truck producing plants, the Moscow-Likhachov and Gorky plants. In recent years some of the Gorky engines have been made at subsidiary plants in Zavolzhye and Arzamas, which now produces engines for jeeps manufactured in Saransk nearby. Most of the diesel engines have been produced at the Yaroslavl Engine Plant, and this plant designed the engine to be produced in the new Kama Truck Plant.

The Gorky Motor Vehicle Plant and the Likhachov Plant in Moscow used to turn out most of the buses of the country, but now it appears that they are producing all the chassis and engines, and the bus assembly is taking place in other plants scattered about the country, as is shown in Table 12-1. Bus production was always in direct competition with truck production in the Moscow and Gorky plants, and usually was given low priority as compared to the truck production. Therefore, the assembly of buses has been moved to other cities, but the bus-producing industry still has to compete with truck-producing industries for chassis and engines from the Moscow and Gorky plants. Therefore, the Soviet Union generally imports a fairly large percentage of its buses.

Perhaps the major location factor for new motor vehicle assembly plants has been the need to bolster the economy of certain areas and provide work for excess laborers. This is well illustrated by the recent buildup of automotive industries in the Bashkir A.S.S.R. where oil production is now on the decline and there is a need to diversify industry in order to maintain the health of the general economy of the region. In addition to the truck assembly plant that has gone into operation at the oil production center of Neftekamsk in the northern part of the republic, there is a Moskvich engine plant in Ufa in the central part of the republic and parts plants at Belebey and Oktyabrskiy, another oil collection center. The recent establishment of the Moskvich plant in Izhevsk, the capital of the Udmurt Republic next door, also illustrates this process. Soviet planners have taken pains in recent years to point out the advantages of locating more automotive industry in the Udmurt Republic. The establishment of the large truck plants in Minsk, Zhodino, and Mogilev in Belorussia have also no doubt been located there primarily to bolster the economy of that chronically economically depressed western part of the Union. The recent shifting of some truck assembly operations from Gorky to Saransk, the capital of the Mordovian Republic to the south, is also a good example.

In other cases, perhaps the main location factor for automotive assembly plants has been the necessity to serve outlying markets. Such are the plants at Kutaisi and Yerevan in the Transcaucasus, the Miass plant in the Urals, and the Kremenchug truck plant and Zaporozhye car plant in the Ukraine. The new car plant now under construction at Lutsk in the northwestern corner of the Ukraine, probably combines the location advantages of surplus labor in an undeveloped area with markets in an outlying region of the Soviet Union as well as in Eastern Europe next door.

Aircraft

The Soviets have developed their aircraft industry to the highest degree. They have been pioneers in the field of commercial jet planes and various space ships. They have apparently been able to expand production of aircraft as rapidly as they have expanded their aviation transport, essentially without foreign aid. Although little is known about specific locations and types of plants, it appears that the industry is dispersed widely throughout most of the larger cities of the country, particularly in the heavy industrial areas of the Central region, Ukraine, the Volga Valley, and the Urals. The Soviets export large numbers of planes and helicopters and aviation equipment of all sorts.

Agricultural Machinery

About 300 agricultural machine building plants in the Soviet Union turn out more than 70 different kinds of agricultural implements and equipment. The distribution of various branches of the farm implement industry are oriented primarily toward principal consuming areas because the finished products are so cumbersome to transport. For instance, grain harvesting machinery is produced primarily in the lower Don area, the Ukraine, and West Siberia-north Kazakhstan. The first harvester plant, named "Kommunar," was set up in Zaporozhye in 1930. In 1932 the huge agricultural machinery plant, "Rostselmash" (Rostov agricultural machinery), was opened in Rostov-on-Don, and soon developed into the largest harvester plant in the country. It now cooperates with another plant at Taganrog nearby to turn out about 80 per cent of the Soviet self-propelled grain harvesters. Other harvester enterprises are located in Syzran, Tula, Lyubertsy, Gomel, Krasnoyarsk, and Birobidzhan.

Implements for planting and harvesting potatoes are produced in Belorussia and the Central Region. One of the main plants is at Tula. Equipment for producing flax is manufactured in the same general area. A large flax harvester plant is located at Bezhitsa. Cotton harvesters are produced primarily in Tashkent. Plants in Georgia manufacture tea harvesters. Production of soil cultivating implements and tools required for all zones is more dispersed.

Tractor production is concentrated in nine huge plants which account for more than four-fifths of all tractors produced in the country. In 1975, these were Minsk, with 16 per cent of the total production, Volgograd 14 per cent, Kharkov 12 per cent, Dnepropetrovsk 10 per cent, Lipetsk 10 per cent, Rubtsovsk 7 per cent, Pavlodar 5 per cent, Vladimir 5 per cent, and Chelyabinsk 5 per cent. (Table 12–2) Smaller tractor plants exist in Bryansk, Tashkent, Kishinev, and Kutaisi. The Kishinev and Kutaisi plants specialize in small tractors for truck gardening purposes. Powerful tractors for logging are produced at the Kirov plant in Leningrad, the Onega plant in Petrozavodsk, and the Minsk plant. A new plant has been opened up in Cheboksary to turn out large industrial tractors, primarily to act as the focal point for the provision of bulldozers and drainage equipment to facilitate the up-grading of agriculture in the nonchernozem zone of European Russia. As was the case in the recent dispersal of the automotive industry, some of the tractor plants have probably been located in order to bolster the economy of chronically depressed areas. Undoubtedly the Minsk, Kishinev and Lipetsk tractor plants would fall into this category.

During the late 1950s, as tractor production in the United States declined, the U.S.S.R. put on an intensive drive to become the largest tractor producer in the world. By 1960 they had achieved that goal, and they have continued to expand their production rapidly since. In 1975 they produced 550,000 tractors, which was more than twice the production of the United States and one-fourth the production of the world. The average horsepower of the U.S. tractor is somewhat greater than that in the U.S.S.R., so the Soviet production in terms of total horsepower is about 60 per cent more than the United States. Since 1970, the main effort in the Soviet Union has been to modern-

ize the tractor industry and concentrate more on wheeled tractors which are more adaptable to the cultivation of row crops. In 1975 wheeled tractors made up about 55 per cent of the total production and track-laying tractors made up about 45 per cent. This is still a very different mix from the United States whose production is about 90 per cent wheel tractors and 10 per cent track-laying tractors.

Although track-laying tractors are more expensive to produce and operate, and lack the speed and mobility of wheeled types, they have better traction in most soils, compact the soil less, consume less fuel per hectare, and are more easily adapted to non-agricultural uses. The Soviets do not produce many specialized types of tractors for industrial purposes, and therefore they like to keep their tractors as versatile as possible. On the other hand, as more and more of the agriculture of the country has turned to row-type crops, wheel tractors have come into more use. Also, tractors pulling trailers are the main transport means on farms, taking the place of the ubiquitous pickup truck on American farms, and wheel tractors are much handier for that purpose.

Most tractor engines are produced in seven major specialized plants located in Barnaul, Kharkov (2 plants), Minsk, Rybinsk, Yaroslavl, and Volgograd. In addition, the Bryansk, Chelyabinsk, and Vladimir tractor plants produce engines for their own tractors. The Vladimir plant produces far more engines than tractors, and supplies engines to other wheeled tractor plants.

The first tractor plants in the Soviet Union were built during the early 1930s at Chelyabinsk, Kharkov, and Stalingrad (Volgograd) with extensive assistance from U.S. firms. The Soviet tractor industry has depended upon United States design technology for much of its production ever since, but the new Cheboksary plant seems to have deviated from U.S. design and is being built on an innovative Soviet design that bears no resemblance to U.S. track-laying models.

The greatest share of tractors goes to agriculture in the U.S.S.R., as it does in the United States. In spite of the fact that the Soviets are

Table 12–2   Production of Tractors, by Model, 1974

Model	Horsepower	Number of Tractors	Producing Plant
Total		531,100	
Tracklaying		239,500	
DET-250M	300	500	Chelyabinsk Tractor Plant
T-180, T-180G	175	400	Bryansk Motor Vehicle Plant
D-804M	175	100	Bryansk Motor Vehicle Plant
T-150	150	500	Kharkov Tractor Plant
T-130	140/160	Few	Chelyabinsk Tractor Plant
T-4A	110	22,100	Altay Tractor Plant (Rubtsovsk)
TT-4	110	5,000	Altay Tractor Plant (Rubtsovsk)
T-100M, T-100MB	108	27,500	Chelyabinsk Tractor Plant
DT-75M	90	84,100	Volgograd Tractor Plant; Pavlodar Tractor Plant
DT-75, DT-75A	75	8,000	Volgograd Tractor Plant
DT-75B	75	10,000	Volgograd Tractor Plant
T-74	75	47,700	Kharkov Tractor Plant
TDT-75	75	2,000	Altay Tractor Plant (Rubtsovsk)
TDT-55, LKhT-55	62	7,000	Onega Tractor Plant (Petrozavodsk)
T-54V, T-54L, T-54S	55	8,600	Kishinev Tractor Plant
DT-54A	54	100,000	Altay Tractor Plant (Rubtsovsk)
TDT-40M	50	5,100	Onega Tractor Plant (Petrozavodsk)
T-38M	48	900	Lipetsk Tractor Plant
Wheeled		291,600	
K-700, K-700A	215	19,600	Plant Imeni Kirov (Leningrad)
T-150K	165	15,500	Kharkov Tractor Plant
MTZ-80/82	80	1,000	Minsk Tractor Plant
YuMZ-6M/6L	60	53,000	Southern Machine Building Plant (Dnepropetrovsk)
MTZ-50M/501	55	61,600	Minsk Tractor Plant
MTZ-52M/521	55	19,000	Minsk Tractor Plant
MTZ-50Kh	55	2,500	Minsk Tractor Plant
T-28Kh4	50	21,600	Tashkent Tractor Plant
T-40/40M	50	8,200	Lipetsk Tractor Plant
	40	8,200	Lipetsk Tractor Plant
T-40A/40AM/40AN	50	16,800	Lipetsk Tractor Plant
	40	16,800	Lipetsk Tractor Plant
T-25A	25	28,000	Vladimir Tractor Plant
T16M	20	19,800	Kharkov Tractor Assembly Plant

Source: Rubenking, p. 616.

currently turning out more than twice as many tractors as the United States, the tractor park on farms in the Soviet Union amounts to only about 2.4 million tractors, as compared to 4.2 million in the United States. This is due to several facts. First of all, the United States used to produce many more tractors than the Soviet Union. In fact, in 1950, the United States production was about equal that of the 1975 U.S.S.R. production. Therefore, there is a large residual tractor park on U.S. farms, and most of the current production is simply for replacements. In addition, the attrition rate of U.S. tractors has been much less than that of Soviet ones. About 5 per cent of the U.S. inventory is retired annually, whereas about 12 per cent of the Soviet inventory is retired annually. The tractor park in the United States has been slowly but consistently declining for the last 20 years or more, and currently the annual retirement of tractors amounts to 152 per cent of the annual deliveries to farms. This has been made possible by consolidation of farm operations into larger units and the production of larger and larger tractors. Thus, while the U.S.A. is now well supplied with farm tractors, the Soviet Union is still trying to catch up. A recent Soviet estimate says that about 3.2 million tractors are needed for optimal agricultural exploitation in the U.S.S.R. Thus, about 800,000 additional tractors are needed. At the present rate of delivery and attrition, it would take about 10 years for this addition to be made.

The parts problem in the Soviet Union has always been a bugaboo. In spite of the fact that the Soviets are spending about two-thirds as much on spare parts as they are on the output of new tractors, while in the United States the production of spare parts amounts to a little over one-fourth the value of new tractors, various ingredients of the socialist administrative network result in a chronic shortage of spare parts. It has been estimated that 30 to 40 per cent of the entire tractor park in Soviet agriculture is constantly in a stand-down position waiting for spare parts for repair. In addition, other tractors may be grossly underutilized because of low inventories of complementary farm machinery. For example, thousands of newly produced heavy duty wheel tractors have not been utilized because they do not have commensurately large plows, harrows, and other machinery to equip them.

The U.S.S.R. has made only slow progress in satisfying the tractor needs of highly specialized industrial producers. Although about 28 per cent of all tractors produced annually in the U.S.S.R. are allocated to industrial consumers, most of these tractors have been designed primarily for use in agriculture. In the mid 1970s the U.S.S.R. produced only about 20,000 specially designed tractors per year for industrial application, and almost all of these were logging tractors. The Soviets are particularly in need of specially designed bulldozer equipment for heavy construction work. Most of their bulldozers consist of track-laying farm tractors with blades mounted in front. Thus, in spite of their large tractor production, the Soviets have found it necessary to import some bulldozers and other types of heavy tractors for gas pipe laying purposes, and so forth. One of the main suppliers for such equipment has been the International Harvester Company in the United States.

Because of its large domestic need, the U.S.S.R. has been exporting only 6–7 per cent of its tractor output. Nevertheless, this has made it one of the world's largest exporters of tractors. In 1974 it exported about 40,000 units, which was about 88 per cent of the export of the United States, and about one-third that of the United Kingdom, the world's leader. About three-fourths of the Soviet tractor exports go to communist countries, primarily in Eastern Europe and Cuba. In recent years Soviet sales to industrialized countries have begun to expand, even in the United Kingdom, Canada, and the United States. Soviet tractors are being offered in the United States at roughly four-fifths the price of comparable U.S. tractors. The Soviets seem to have solved their quality and spare parts problems for their export tractors, and they are finding ready markets in some of the more advanced countries in the world because of their reasonable prices and availability in countries such as the

United States which during the last decade or more has had fewer tractors on the market than farmers have wanted to buy. The Belarus (Belorussia) model turned out by the Minsk plant has been the main export item. This tractor has been given an A-1 rating by the tractor testing station at the University of Nebraska.

Consumer Durables

During the last couple of decades, the Soviets have mounted a crash program to expand greatly the production of all sorts of household gadgets, appliances, and personal machines such as bicycles, musical instruments, and watches. The Soviets now claim to be the largest producers in the world of bicycles and motorcycles. They are third in the production of both televisions and radios, after Japan and the United States. Whereas they used to be a country almost devoid of watches, they now have a great abundance of watches for export. Large household appliances, such as refrigerators, washing machines, and vacuum cleaners, are now becoming commonplace. Much of this type of production is located in the Baltic Republics and to a certain extent in Belorussia, where the Soviets have poured large sums of money since World War II in order to rehabilitate the economy and utilize the skills of the people of the area.

TEXTILES AND CLOTHING

The Soviet Union leads the world in the quantity of production of all kinds of textiles. In 1975 it produced 1,572,600 metric tons of cotton yarn, which put it well ahead of its second place competitor, the U.S.A., with 1,141,700 million, third place India with 989,300, and Japan with 431,700. It was a little behind India in woven cotton fabrics, but still produced about 14 per cent of the world's supply. It is by far the largest producer of linen. In 1975 it produced 260,000 metric tons of linen yarn, as compared to second place

Poland with 54,000. It produced 416,900 metric tons of woolen yarn, as compared to its leading competitor, the United Kingdom with 187,500, France with 134,900, Japan with 114,300, and Poland with 102,000. It produced 956 million square meters of woven wool and fabrics, as compared to Japan with 357 million, United Kingdom with 151, and Poland with 124. It produced 44,258,000 square meters of natural silk woven fabrics, which was second to Japan with 168,472,000.

In man-made fibers, the Soviet Union leads in rayon and acetate, but lags rather badly in synthetic fibers from non-cellulosic materials. In 1975, it produced 281,000 metric tons of rayon and acetate, which was about one-fourth of the world's output. Second ranked U.S.A. produced 166,000, and third ranked Japan 113,200. It produced only 230,330 metric tons of non-cellulosic continuous filaments, which ranked it fourth in the world behind the U.S.A. with 1,455,700 metric tons, Japan, and West Germany. And it produced 134,260 metric tons of non-cellulosic discontinuous fibers, which ranked it only seventh in the world. The U.S.A. produced almost ten times as much. Thus, the Soviet Union is a jump behind the rest of the industrialized world technologically in the production of man-made fibers. While the rest of the world has moved away from cellulose-based rayon and acetate, the Soviet Union has been expanding production.

Textiles were one of the first groups of industries to be developed in Tsarist Russia, primarily during the eighteenth century. These developed initially as cottage industries in the most densely populated parts of European Russia, particularly around the Central Region including Moscow. The people served both as labor, which is the major input in textile industries, and as market. Labor and market are normally much stronger locational factors in textile industries than raw materials are. Very early, Ivanovo, northeast of Moscow, became known as the "Manchester of Russia" for its heavy concentration on cheap cotton fabrics. Kostroma, in the same general region, became the primary city for linens. At the time, much of the raw cotton for the textile industries in the Central Region was imported, from such places as Egypt, India, and the United States. Since the Revolution, the Soviet Union has become self sufficient in raw cotton, utilizing irrigation agriculture for the crop in the oases of Central Asia and the Kura Lowland of the Transcaucasus. A little cotton is still imported from places such as Egypt, but this is primarily a political import which is accepted by the Soviet Union in payment for construction projects and military goods that the Soviets have extended to the Egyptians in the past. This cotton might never enter the Soviet Union, but go directly to countries such as Poland which have standing arrangements with the Soviets for supplies of raw cotton. Some Soviet cotton is also exported, so that on balance cotton production in the Soviet Union just about satisfies domestic demands.

Although the cotton is grown in Central Asia and neighboring Transcaucasia, and the Soviets have made some effort to establish cotton textile plants in these producing areas, the overwhelming share of the cotton textile industry still remains in the Central Economic Region of European Russia. Moscow, Ivanovo, and a great number of lesser cities in the area still produce about 75 per cent of the national output of cotton fabrics. This is by far the largest cotton fabric producing region in the world, producing more than twice as much as all of Japan. The industry has been dispersed a little bit into certain outlying centers to serve markets far from either the major textile producing centers in European Russia or the major raw materials producers in Central Asia and the Transcaucasus. Thus, in the 1930s, a large cotton textile factory was built in Barnaul in the Kulunda Steppe of southwestern Siberia to receive raw cotton from Central Asia over the newly constructed Turk-Sib Railroad in return for grain and timber that were moving from the Altay Region southward. A little later a major cotton textile center was established at

Figure 12-2   Inside a textile factory in Tashkent. Photo by Edward Furstenberg.

Kansk in Eastern Siberia just east of Krasnoyarsk.

The large woolen industry in the Soviet Union is also centered in the Central Economic Region. Most of it is based on domestically produced raw wool, which like the cotton is mostly produced far away in the mountains and deserts of Central Asia, Kazakhstan, and the Transcaucasus, as well as parts of southern Siberia and the Far East. Early centers of the woolen industry were Ivanovo, Kalinin, Bryansk, Sverdlovsk, and Krasnodar. The industry has been dispersed somewhat in recent years into Siberia and the Far East where the long, severe winters necessitate wearing woolen clothing much of the year. The Karakul sheep of Central Asia provide skins from the new born lambs for a thriving karakul industry, the products of which bring high prices on the world markets. In addition, artificial karakul is being turned out in cities such as Tashkent.

The linen industry is also located primarily in the Central Economic Region, but in this case the raw material, flax, is near at hand. The largest flax producing political unit in the country is Kalinin Oblast just to the northwest of Moscow, and the entire northern part of the Central Economic Region plus the adjacent regions of Belorussia, and the Baltic Republics are the largest flax producing area in the world. Kostroma and Yaroslavl northeast of Moscow are the major centers for the production of linen, and many other cities in the immediate surroundings are also important. In later years the industry has been dispersed somewhat into the Baltic Republics and Belorussia.

Silkworms are fed on mulberry trees grown along irrigation ditches in Central Asia and the eastern part of Transcaucasia. Cities such as Tbilisi in Georgia and Samarkand in Central Asia have long been known for their silk production. Unfortunately, Soviet statistics lump silk production with synthetic fibers, and since silk is only a small portion of the total, its distribution of production is obscured. The

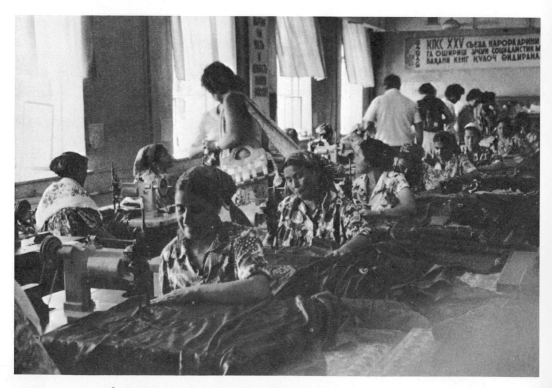

Figure 12–3   Inside an embroidery factory in Bukhara. Photo by Toni Crane.

geographical distribution of man-made fibers has already been discussed under the section on chemicals in Chapter 11. (See Fig. 11–13)

The knitted goods and clothing industries are much more dispersed than are the basic textile industries. The consumer is the key location factor behind the distribution of inexpensive clothing, and most large cities of the country contain some clothing factories.

Leather and Footwear

Tsarist Russia was traditionally a major producer of leather goods. At that time the industry was concentrated in cattle growing areas and trading centers along the Volga. For many years Kazan dominated the industry. Under the Soviets, the industry has been greatly expanded and dispersed into 150 different cities of the country. The Soviets must import considerable quantities of hides from countries such as the United States and India in order to sustain their large leather industry. The Soviets now claim to lead the world in leather footwear production. In 1975 they turned out 698 million pairs of shoes, as compared to 400 million in the United States, their nearest competitor.

FOOD INDUSTRIES

Since the initiation of the Khrushchev farm program in the mid 1950s and its continuation by the post-Khrushchev regime, a great effort has been made to improve the diet of the Soviet people by greatly expanding and improving animal products of all kinds. The Soviet Union now leads the world in milk and butter production, but still lags behind rather seriously in meat and egg production. In 1975 the Soviet Union produced 13,440,000 metric tons of meats of all kinds, as compared to 16,690,000 in the United States. Since the Soviet Union has about 50 million more people than the United States, the per capita consumption in the Soviet Union was considerably less. Also the kinds and qualities of meat were very different from those in the United States. There is little pure beef industry in the Soviet Union. Most of the beef is derived from dairy or dual-purpose stock which have been used for dairying. The meat is derived either from older cows that no longer are efficiently producing milk or from young bull calves that are used for veal. The Soviet Union has long been a major area of swine raising, and recently there has been a great push on poultry raising, both for meat and for eggs. In 1976 the meat products reported in official statistics consisted of 53 per cent of beef and veal, 25.1 per cent of pork, 8.3 per cent of poultry, 4.5 per cent of mutton, and 9 per cent of other various products derived from the above. Since much meat is consumed on collective farms by the collective farmers themselves, from animals that they have raised on their private plots, the official statistics are probably very incomplete.

In spite of the fact the Soviet Union is the world's largest producer of butter, more than twice as much vegetable oils are produced as butter. The Soviets claim that they now produce about 15 per cent of all the world's vegetable oils. These oils are used as cooking oils, margarine, and so forth. As was mentioned in Chapter 9, by far the largest source of vegetable oil in the Soviet Union is the sunflower, which also is the "Soviet peanut." Sunflower seeds are roasted and salted and sold in small cellophane bags in all the stores of the country. People go about munching them all the time. In 1976, sunflower seeds accounted for about 44 per cent of all the vegetable oil in the Soviet Union. Next in rank was cotton seed oil, which accounted for about 17 per cent. The rest was made up by such plants as soybeans, arachia, flax seed, hemp seed, castor seed, mustard seed, and tung nuts.

The main branches of the food industries are flour milling, sugar processing, meat processing, canning, vegetable oil production, and fishing. These, of course, are all based on agriculture, except fishing, which is primarily an exploitative industry and will be taken up in the next chapter. Although food industries around the world tend to be ubiquitous, wherever one finds people, certain types of food and food processing lend themselves to certain localities with respect to raw materials and markets. Locational choices are based on degrees of bulkiness and perishability. If the raw material is very bulky and the final product is not perishable, then the processing industry will likely be located in the areas producing the raw materials. The sugar industry is a good example of this. Each ton of granulated sugar requires about nine tons of sugar beets. In the Soviet Union all domestically produced sugar is derived from sugarbeets, which are grown primarily in the northern half of the Ukraine and southern half of the Central Chernozem Region and secondarily in such areas as the Kuban district of the North Caucasus, the Volga Region, the northern part of the Kirgiz Republic in Central Asia and the adjacent southeastern part of Kazakhstan, Belorussia, the Baltic Republics, the Far East, and Western Siberia. In addition, some raw cane sugar is imported from Cuba and processed in the Soviet Union in some other regions that do not grow beets. Thus, the outstanding regions for sugar production are the Ukraine, the Central Chernozem Region, and the North Caucasus, with various other regions producing minor amounts. (Table 12–3)

Like the sugar industry, the vegetable oil industry utilizes bulky raw materials and turns out a much reduced quantity of fairly durable products. Therefore, processing plants are located in the growth areas of the oil bearing crops. Since sunflowers are grown primarily in the droughty Donets-Dnieper Region of the Ukraine and in the North Caucasus, vegetable oil production is outstanding in those two regions. The Uzbek Republic also produces a lot of vegetable oil, but this is all from cotton seed. Most of the flax grown for linseed oil is also produced in the droughty southern parts of the country, as opposed to the fiber flax used for linen which is grown in the cool, humid northwestern regions of European Russia.

The processing of bulky vegetable commodities, such as sugar beets and sunflower and cotton seeds, as well as such operations as flour mills, creameries, and alcohol and vodka distil-leries, result in huge quantities of waste vegetable matter that can be fed to animals or turned into by-products for animal feed such as bran, oil cake, molasses, and malt residue. Thus, the processing of these crops in areas where they are grown has the added advantage of sustaining important livestock operations in these rich farming areas. Therefore, the distribution of meat production of all kinds is closely correlated with the distribution of the best crop lands of the country. (Table 12–3)

Flour milling makes up about one-fourth of the gross output of the entire Soviet food industry. Initially flour mills were built almost entirely in the major grain producing areas of the Ukraine, the North Caucasus, the Central Chernozem Region, the Volga Region, and Western Siberia. Since flour is much more difficult and expensive to transport than the original grain and is more susceptible to spoilage, it would make more sense to build flour mills in areas of consumption and ship the grain to them. New flour mills have generally tended to be placed in consuming areas, but still a large part of the flour milling industry is located in the grain producing areas of the country. This does, however, facilitate the use of by-products of milling for animal feeds.

Raw materials that are perishable that can be turned into products that are not perishable are processed locally as quickly as possible before they spoil or lose their taste. Such things as grapes, fruit, fresh vegetables, and meat are immediately turned into canned products, wines, and so forth in their areas of growth. Since there is still a lack of adequate refrigeration and transport facilities for such agricultural products, most of them are processed immediately to preserve in one form or another. There is very little in the way of frozen foods in the Soviet Union, so most things are canned. Most of the meat that is sold in state stores is canned or cured in one form or another. Fresh meat supplies are dependent almost entirely on kolkhoz markets where farmers daily bring in their slaughtered animals, and the meat is purchased and consumed before it spoils.[1] This is also true of most of the fresh fruit and vegetables as well as certain other perishable

Table 12–3   Regional Production of Selected Food Industries, 1976, in Thousands of Tons

	Sugar	Meat	Butter	Vegetable Oil	Canning (Million Standard Tins)
U.S.S.R.	9249	8368	1263	2775	14520
R.S.F.S.R.	2725	4131	615	945	5901
Northwest	—	308	30	23	411
Central	96	726	100	22	469
Volgo-Vyatka	22	260	53	6	94
Central Chernozem	1221	406	79	172	469
Volga	217	575	102	131	638
North Caucasus	995	571	45	499	2203
Urals	—	363	63	14	115
West Siberia	50	495	93	21	329
East Siberia	—	260	26	11	179
Far East	125	132	14	46	786
Ukrainian S.S.R.	5032	1858	341	907	3474
Donets-Dnieper[1]	1237	785	132	683	727
Southwest[1]	3444	784	152	83	1407
South[1]	351	290	57	141	1342
Baltic Region					
Lithuanian S.S.R.	198	325	55	4	281
Latvian S.S.R.	251	189	37	20	382
Estonian S.S.R.	—	137	31	—	277
Kaliningrad Oblast	—	40	10	—	208
Transcaucasian Region					
Georgian S.S.R.	43	78	1	9	355
Azerbaydzhan S.S.R.	—	60	4	40	377
Armenian S.S.R.	12	46	2	13	347
Central Asian Region					
Uzbek S.S.R.	—	160	8	439	526
Kirgiz S.S.R.	249	97	9	21	128
Tadzhik S.S.R.	—	46	4	94	223
Turkmen S.S.R.	—	27	3	57	48
Kazakh S.S.R.	154	538	47	82	372
Belorussian S.S.R.	224	537	94	21	551
Moldavian S.S.R.	339	140	14	124	1277

Sources: *Narkhoz SSSR za 60 let,* pp. 258–265, and *Narkhoz RSFSR za 60 let,* pp. 112–120.

[1] Estimated from proportions reported in previous years.

farm products such as cottage cheese. The distribution of the canning industry, as shown

[1] The state has been getting into the fresh meat, milk, and egg business recently by establishing large urban-oriented state farms specializing on few products in the immediate vicinities of most large cities, as was discussed under Agriculture in Chapter 9.

in Table 12–3, corresponds to regions of origin of such things as vegetables, fruit, meat, and fish. It can be seen that the rich farming areas of the Ukraine, Moldavia, and the North Caucasus are outstanding in the canning industry. These areas would be processing primarily vegetables, fruits, and meat. The Belorussian

Republic, Uzbek Republic, and the Central Chernozem Region are also notable in this respect. The Far Eastern and Volga regions have large canning industries, which are primarily based on fish. In 1976 vegetables, tomatoes, fruits, and their juices made up two-thirds of all canned goods. Fish made up 16.4 per cent, canned milk 10 per cent, and meat and vegetable mixtures 6.3 per cent.

In cases where the raw material is not perishable and can be shipped in bulk more readily than in smaller packages of high value, the packaging is usually done in transport focal points that serve market hinterlands. Good examples of this are the tea and tobacco industries. Often these undergo two-stage processing. Primary processing is done in raw material producing areas and final blending and packaging in consumer areas. In addition to being located in the tea growing area of Georgia, large tea packaging operations are located in cities that handle imports of tea, which is a primary source of the product for the large tea drinking population of the Soviet Union. The city of Irkutsk in Eastern Siberia has long been a tea processing center, utilizing tea that comes across the border from China and maybe even as far away as India and Sri Lanka (Ceylon).

Food products that take a good deal of manufacturing and that turn out either very bulky or very perishable products are always located next to large markets, and therefore can be found in all cities of significant size. Such food industries would be bakeries, macaroni factories, liquor and vodka distilleries, breweries, enterprises producing soft drinks, milk bottling, and so forth. Their products are either difficult to transport or significantly heavier than their ingredients. The processing of such things as soft drinks and beer involve the addition of large quantities of water, which can be derived anywhere; therefore it is needless to transport such a commodity long distances.

The dairy industry presents an interestingly complex picture. The fresh milk industry, of course, has to be located near large markets, and in recent years major efforts have been made to establish huge industrial-type dairy operations next to large cities throughout the country. However, dairying has also been traditionally a major part of agriculture in areas such as Western Siberia and the Northwest Economic Region of European Russia where the natural environment is more conducive to the growing of hay crops and pasture than it is to cash grains or industrial crops. In these areas, farmers naturally have turned to the dairy cow as the source of cash income, and the cropping pattern has been devised to serve the dairy industry. In these regions there are large surpluses of milk, which cannot be shipped to far-away markets in time for them to be consumed without souring. Thus, the milk either has to be canned or turned into less perishable products, such as cheese and butter. Such considerations brought about the decision to produce large quantities of butter during the settlement of Western Siberia in the late nineteenth and early twentieth centuries when many of the original farms were dairy farms based on natural hay and pastures and there were no local markets for dairy products. At this time Western Siberia became the main supplier of butter to Tsarist Russia, and "Siberian Butter" became a trade name known throughout the food markets of the world.[2] Although butter is no longer exported from this area, Western Siberia is still one of the major butter producing regions of the U.S.S.R.

The wine making and liquor and vodka industries have similar end products, but they use different raw materials and therefore are located in different parts of the country. Wine making is located where grapes are grown, while alcohol and liquor and vodka industries are mostly located in the potato growing areas of the central European part of the Soviet Union. Ripe grapes rapidly lose their taste and other properties, and so the primary materials of wine making are obtained in the grape growing areas, primarily Moldavia, Ukraine, including the Crimea, the Transcaucasian Republics, the North Caucasus, and Central Asia. The intermediate materials may then be

[2] Mote, Victor L., "The Cheliabinsk Grain Tariff and the Rise of the Siberian Butter Industry," *Slavic Review,* June, 1976, pp. 304–317.

shipped considerable distances to wine distilleries where they are processed further and bottled. Historically, many of the distilleries have been concentrated where wine materials are produced, but it would make more sense if the materials were shipped to consuming areas in large vats instead of shipping finished wine in millions of small bottles. In recent years the Soviets have been trying to correct this situation by building several large distilleries in consumer areas. The Soviet Union has become one of the major wine producing countries of the world, now surpassed only by Italy, France, and Spain.

Salt is an irreplaceable food product, as well as a key raw material in many industries, particularly the chemical industries, as already discussed in Chapter 11. The current production of salt goes slightly more than half into industry, a little less than one-fourth into human consumption, and also about one-fourth in the consumption of livestock. The common table salt that is used for human and livestock consumption is produced mostly at the rock salt mining center of Artemovsk in the Donets Basin of the eastern Ukraine and in the lake salt deposit of Lake Baskunchak east of the lower Volga.

Reading List

MACHINE BUILDING

1. Derbinova, M. P., Karneyeva, Ye. D., and Chebanova, L. A., "Economic-Geographic Aspects of Supplier Relations in the Soviet Automotive Industry," *Soviet Geography: Review and Translation,* January 1978, pp. 49–54.
2. Edwards, Imogene U., "Automotive Trends in the USSR," *Soviet Economic Prospects for the Seventies,* Joint Economic Committee, Congress of the United States, 1973, pp. 291–314.
3. Edwards, Imogene, and Fraser, Robert, "The Internationalization of the East European Automotive Industries," *East European Economies: Post-Helsinki,* Joint Economic Committee, Congress of the United States, 1977, pp. 396–419.
4. Kalesnik, S. V., and Pavlenko, V. F., *Soviet Union: A Graphical Survey,* Progress Publishers, Moscow, 1976, pp. 203–210, 225–234.
5. Rubenking, Earl M., "The Soviet Tractor Industry: Progress and Problems," *Soviet Economy in a New Perspective,* Joint Economic Committee, Congress of the United States, Washington, 1976, pp. 600–619.

TEXTILES AND LEATHER WORKING

1. Gately, Michael O., *The Development of the Russian Cotton Textile Industry in the Pre-Revolutionary Years, 1861–1913,* PhD Dissertation, University of Kansas, 1968.
2. Gorlin, Alice W. C., "Soviet Firms and the Rationalization of the Shoe Industry of the USSR," PhD Dissertation, University of Michigan, 1973.
3. Moskoff, William, *The Soviet Hide-Leather-Footwear Sequence in the Post-Stalin Period,* PhD Dissertation, University of Wisconsin, 1970.
4. Pryde, Philip R., "The Areal Deconcentration of the Soviet Cotton-Textile Industry," *Geographical Review,* 1968, pp. 575–592.

13

Fishing, Forestry, and Furs

Fishing, forestry, and the derivation of furs from animals will be considered together as industries based on biological resources which are mainly extractive in nature, but are now all becoming in part cultured industries based on sustained yields through farming. Historically these extractive industries of biological resources have been very important to Russia and subsequently the Soviet Union, and the area has ranked high in the world's supply of these items.

FISHING

Russia and the Soviet Union has always been a country where fish have been a major portion of the diet. Until about 1955 much of the fish catch came from immediate surrounding seas, particularly the Caspian, the Black-Azov, the Barents, and the Okhotsk, as well as the many inland lakes and rivers, and, more recently, myriads of small ponds constructed on farms to control erosion and so forth. But during the last two decades, the Soviets have made a major effort greatly to expand their pelagic fishing fleet and fish the seas of the world. As a consequence, they have expanded their operation rapidly, diversified it, and increased their total catch by more than four times since 1955. In 1975 the Soviet catch amounted to 10,311,000 metric tons, which

was second only to Japan, with 10,500,000, and about one-seventh of the world's total catch. The previous leader, Peru, diminished from 10,529,000 tons in 1971 to only 3,448,000 in 1975. 88.3 per cent of the Soviet catch came from marine fisheries.

Marine Fisheries

Modern, well equipped Soviet fishing vessels now fish all parts of the world and are a common sight off the coasts of most continents. They often have challenged the integrity of territorial waters set by various countries off their coasts and have repeatedly damaged lobster gear, oyster beds, and so forth on the immediate shelves of places like the Grand Banks off the eastern United States and Canada. In addition, the Soviets have been accused frequently of exceeding quotas of certain types of catch that they have agreed upon with adjacent countries. Canada went so far in 1975 to close its ports at St. Johns, Newfoundland and Halifax, Nova Scotia to the provisioning of Soviet trawlers that had provided these two communities with considerable amounts of income. About 400 Soviet trawlers had habitually been purchasing food, fuel, repairs, and recreation from these communities in recent years, but the Canadian government announced that the income from such activities did not make up for the loss of fish and lobster gear to the Canadian economy. In a similar incident in April, 1976 the United States seized a Soviet trawler and accused the captain of illegal lobster fishing. After the captain pleaded no contest he was fined $10,000 and the Soviet government was required to pay an additional $400,000 to get the ship released. In most cases such incidents seem to have been the fault of the ship captains themselves and not the policy of the Soviet government. In all cases the Soviet government has reported that they have dealt severely with individuals that have violated international waters and agreements.

Whaling

Another controversy has involved whaling. After the major whaling nations of the world had agreed to restrict the slaughter of two endangered species of whales in 1974, the two leading whaling countries, the Soviet Union and Japan, announced they would not go along with the agreement. These two countries, both equipped with modern whaling fleets that use spotter planes, factory ships, and sonar-equipped catch boats, kill 85 per cent of the whales currently taken from the seas. As the whale population of the world has diminished and the total whale catch has declined, there has been a rapid shifting in position of countries in the whaling industry. Whereas Norway used to be the biggest whaling country, by the early 1960s the lead had passed to Japan and the U.S.S.R. By the mid 1970s the U.S.S.R. was clearly in the lead, although its catch too was down by about one-third from the mid 1960s. Between 1965 and 1975 the world catch declined from 57,891 whales to 29,164, the Soviet catch declined from 21,313 to 14,456, and the Japanese catch declined from 21,856 to 9450. Much of the catch now takes place in the sea surrounding Antarctica. South Africa has emerged as a weak third in whaling countries, due to its close proxmity to the southern ocean. Soviet whaling vessels, mainly based in Vladivostok, range to the Antarctic during the Southern Hemisphere summer and to the Bering Straits during the Northern Hemi-

sphere summer. Some of the Soviet whale catch is used for human food, but much is used on fur farms to feed mink and sables.

North Atlantic

As can be seen in Table 13–1, the north Atlantic is by far the most important Soviet fishing area. In 1975 it accounted for 5,580,000 metric tons or 54.2 per cent of the total Soviet catch. The Soviets traditionally have fished the northeast Atlantic, particularly the Barents Sea, but since the late 1950s they have expanded their activities to the northwest Atlantic, particularly off the coasts of Nova Scotia, New England, and Norfolk, Virginia, and the east-central Atlantic off the west coast of Africa. Each of these three regions accounted for roughly 11 per cent of the Soviet fish catch in 1975.

Baltic   Much of the Atlantic fishing fleet is

Table 13–1   Changing Distribution of Soviet Fish Catch, in Thousand Metric Tons

	1940	1950	1960	1970	1975
Total	1309	1655	3511	7783	10311
Marine fisheries	565	945	2736	6704	9109
NE Atlantic	243	402	1128	1566	2406
NW Atlantic	—	—	285	812	1167
West Central Atlantic	—	—	—	—	69
East Central Atlantic	—	—	44	613	1166
SE Atlantic	—	—	—	423	421
SW Atlantic	—	—	—	421	9
Pacific Ocean	322	484	856	2195	3367
Indian Ocean	—	—	—	47	37
Inland fisheries	744	709	775	1079	1202
Inland seas	628	589	561	746	718
Azov-Black Sea	238	234	153	294	350
Caspian	352	319	367	438	357
Aral	38	35	42	14	12
Freshwater fisheries	116	120	214	333	484
Lakes	106	108	167	76	104
Rivers				139	173
Reservoirs	2	7	29	55	70
Ponds	8	6	18	63	138

Source: Shabad, Theodore, "News Notes," *Soviet Geography: Review and Translation*, June 1978, p. 426.

based at ports along the Baltic, which in 1975 accounted for 25 per cent of total Soviet fishing fleet and fish catch. Kaliningrad has become the largest Soviet fishing port on the Baltic; in 1975 it alone accounted for nearly 10 per cent of the Soviet fish catch. Latvian ports, mainly Riga, Liepaya, and Ventspils, ranked second with 6 per cent of total catch. Also important were Klaipeda in Lithuania, Tallinn in Estonia, and Leningrad in the Russian Republic. Of the fish processed at these ports, about 19 per cent came from the Baltic itself, 35 per cent from the northern part of the Atlantic, 23 per cent from the western part of the Atlantic, 8 per cent from the southeastern part of the Atlantic, and 15 per cent from the Arctic. Main species within the Baltic area are the herring and sprat.

Northwest Ports along the Barents and White Seas account for 17 per cent of Soviet fish catch. Murmansk is by far the largest, with 13 per cent of the catch, and Archangel is second. Ships based in Murmansk range the Barents Sea and large sections of the north Atlantic.

Pacific

In 1975 the huge Pacific basin accounted for 35 per cent of the Soviet fishing fleet and fish catch. Vladivostok is by far the largest fishing port and fish processing center, but there are many other ports scattered along the mainland coast as well as on the Island of Sakhalin and the Peninsula of Kamchatka that are very important fish processing centers. Ships from these ports range the Pacific from the Bering Stratis to the Antarctic and the west coast of North America. Fish collectives have been established all along the lower Amur River from Khabarovsk to Nikolayevsk; along the shores of Maritime Kray, especially around Peter the Great Bay in the vicinity of Vladivostok; the southern part of Khabarovsk Kray, particularly around the mouth of the Amur River; along the northern coast of the Sea of Okhotsk; around Sakhalin Island; and around Kamchatka Peninsula.

The cold waters of the Sea of Okhotsk provide one of the richest fishing grounds in the country. In 1975 it provided 1,330,000 tons of fish out of a Pacific total of 3,340,000. It is especially known for its salmon, which are caught either in the lower Amur River as the fish enter for their annual spawning or in the Gulf of Penzhina next to Kamchatka. Since the Soviets acquired the southern half of Sakhalin and the Kuril Island chain as a result of World War II, they consider the Okhotsk Sea to be a Russian lake, and the Japanese have had a hard time negotiating fishing rights in the area. Now that most countries have enacted a 200-mile offshore territorial limit, the Soviet Union, Japan, and Korea have found themselves in various disputes concerning parts of the Sea of Japan.

The fisheries of Kamchatka account for about 60 per cent of the salmon catch of the U.S.S.R. Another product in the Kamchatka area that is of world renown is the Kamchatka crab. Other common species in the area are herring, flounder, smelt, mackerel, cod, and sea animals (whales, walruses, and seals). Seal rookeries are maintained on the Commander Islands off the east coast of Kamchatka. Walruses and seals are also caught along the coasts of the Bering Straits.

The Amur River is populated by about 100 fish species, some of which are unique to the region. Most outstanding among these is the so-called "Amur Queen," the Kaluga Sturgeon (Huso Dauricus) which is the world's largest fresh water fish. Fully grown specimens may reach six meters in length and one ton in weight. Their life span is about 300 years; females do not reach adulthood until they are 22 years old. The fish never leave the Amur River throughout their entire life cycles. Twenty years ago the U.S.S.R. decreed a complete ban on the catching of these fish because they were being depleted so rapidly, but now it has been announced that their numbers have doubled since that time and about 70 tons per year will be allowed to be removed from the river. To assure a steady supply of fish in the future, the Soviets have planned to build a large fish breeding farm on the bank of the Amur where they can release about three million fry per year into the river. It has also been announced that the Soviets are building a fish farm in Peter the Great Bay near Vladivostok which will produce about 11 million young sea cucumbers, scallops, oysters, and plaice per year.

Inland Fisheries

During 1940–1975 catch from marine fisheries increased 16 times while catch from inland fisheries increased only 51 per cent. However, the burgeoning imposition of 200-mile territorial limits by many countries in recent years has aroused Soviet concern about the future of marine fisheries and renewed efforts to develop inland sources of supply. But this is going to take some doing. Traditionally the largest inland sources of fish products have been the Caspian, Black-Azov, and Aral Seas in the dry southern part of the country which have been experiencing great difficulties due to falling water levels, pollution, and increases in salinity because of competing economic activities such as expansion of irrigation for agriculture, construction of dams and reservoirs, and rapid urbanization and industrialization. These problems will be taken up in a general way in the following chapter on water.

Caspian

The Caspian, which used to be the major fishing ground of Russia, has maintained a fairly stable catch over the years, but there has been a great shift in fish species caught and areas from which they are taken. The falling water level has affected mainly the shallow northern end of the sea which is the main spawning grounds of valuable species such as sturgeon, shad, and Caspian roach. As supplies of these fish have dwindled, efforts have turned to a small pelagic fish called the kilka (clupeonella) which is used mainly for fish meal for fur farms and other animal feeds. Consequently, many operations have shifted to the use of large freezing vessels and factory ships produc-

ing fish meal that operate out of more southerly ports along the shores of the Turkmen and Azerbaydzhan Republics. Although Astrakhan is still by far the largest fish processing center on the Caspian, and Guryev at the mouth of the Ural River on the northern coast of the Caspian is still of intermediate importance, the new fishing port of Gousany next to Baku, Makhachkala on the Dagestani coast, and Krasnovodsk on the Turkmen coast have become even more important than Guryev, and Bautino on the Mangyshlak Peninsula is of almost the same importance as Guryev.[1]

Of special significance to the Caspian fisheries have been the huge Caspian Sea sturgeon which are the main source of the world's caviar. These fish may live for 200–300 years and reach lengths of 7–8 meters and weights of up to 1.5 tons. A single female commonly produces 25 kilograms (55 pounds) of roe and sometimes as much as 35 kilograms which at present on the world market may bring as much as $225 per kilogram. In addition, the meat of the sturgeon is prized. The sturgeon catch dwindled from 28,300 metric tons in 1913 to only 10,400 tons in 1960. Various corrective measures have increased the Soviet catch of sturgeon back up to 23,400 tons in 1975, but there is still a severe shortage of caviar. Of the 96 tons of gray-black sturgeon eggs produced annually during the mid 1970s, the Soviet Union exported almost all in order to gain hard currency, and the delicacy has almost disappeared from stores and restaurants in the Soviet Union. Leading Soviet restaurants may now charge as much as $20 an ounce for the princely food. A caviar substitute has now appeared on the domestic market. This is made out of casein from curdled milk and treated with gelatin, sturgeon sperm, tannin, and a salt bath to produce small gray beady masses that simulate the look and taste of caviar.

Azov-Black and Aral Seas

As the inflow of water from the Don, Kuban, and smaller streams to the Sea of Azov

[1] Carré, 1978, p. 24.

has dwindled, the water balance in the sea between inflow and evaporation has changed from slightly positive to slightly negative so that the flow through the Kerch Strait has reversed, and now saltier Black Sea water is entering the Sea of Azov. This has upset the ecological balance for many fish species that originally inhabited the Sea of Azov. Also, pollution has increased steadily along the small tributary streams flowing in from the north from the heaviest industry area in the country. The result has been a drastic reduction in Azov fish catch. During its peak productivity the Azov Sea used to contribute half to two-thirds of the catch in the Azov-Black basin. In 1975 it contributed only 5700 tons out of a total of 350,000 tons.

The Aral Sea has been undergoing similar consequences as more and more inflow from the Amu and Syr Darya has been diverted for irrigation. But unlike the Sea of Azov, the Aral Sea has no source of water replenishment. Therefore, its level has been dropping and the water has become saltier and more polluted. As a consequence the fish catch has declined drastically since 1960.

Freshwater Fisheries

The Soviets are putting more and more effort into the exploitation of inland lakes and streams and the establishment of fish farms utilizing small erosion control ponds and irrigation reservoirs and ditches. There are now 320 freshwater fish farms in the Soviet Union with a total water surface close to 150,000 hectares. Fishing has generally been organized as a part of the agricultural operation, and many farms now report fish statistics along with crop and other animal products. By adding adequate supplies of nutrients to small bodies of water, the Soviets have been able to yield as much as 100 kilograms of fish per square meter of water surface per year. This amounts to much more protein yield than could be achieved by growing crops on a similar area and feeding them to animals.

The inland fisheries also provide a great deal of recreation for Soviet workers during week-ends and other short periods of leisure. Along most of the streams and lakes of the country, one can observe fishermen's tents and lean-tos, and small fishing boats are constantly plying the streams. The Soviet authorities reported in 1974 that recreational fishermen had hooked 70 million pounds of fish in the middle Volga Region that year, which was seven times the catch of the state industry in the area. Amature fishermen in this region bought 15,000 new motor launches as well as a good deal of other fishing gear. Thus, recreational fishing has become a large business. Not only does the activity provide recreation for the people engaged in it, but also supplies them with a considerable amount of their meat intake. Many private individuals fish not only for recreation but to augment the diet.

Lake Balkhash now leads all other lakes in fish production, 13,500 tons in 1975, mostly carp. This serves the two large population centers of Alma Ata to the south and Karaganda to the north. Although Lake Balkhas is not strictly fresh, its fish statistics are included with freshwater lakes. Fish yield in Lake Baykal has declined from 12,500 tons in 1940 to 3500 in 1975 due to restrictions placed on the over-fishing of the preferred omul, a species of whitefish. The Siberian roach is now the leading commercial species taken from the lake. The Great Lakes region of northwestern Russia, including lakes Ladoga, Onega, Chudskoye, and Ilmen, now yields about 20,000 tons per year.

WOOD INDUSTRIES

Resources

The Soviet Union contains by far the world's largest forest resources and is the largest producer of wood products. It is estimated that the Soviet Union accounts for about one-third of the forested area of the earth which constitutes about 22 per cent of all forest resources of the world. Forests cover more than half the territory of the Soviet Union. Although the Soviet Union, and Tsarist Russia before it, has long exploited its forests, the industry now apparently has been placed on a sustained yield basis, and in fact in recent years more area has been forested than deforested. During the five-year plan, 1966–1970, trees were felled on an area of 10,200,000 hectares and planted on an area of 11,200,000 hectares, an area equal to Belgium, Denmark, and Holland, put together.

Huge new timber processing complexes that are being established in newly opened regions of Siberia, the Far East, and the Euorpean North are being put on a sustained yield basis from the beginning. Large enough tracts of land are allotted to individual wood working complexes so that under natural conditions the cutover areas can reforest themselves by the time the industrial complexes get around to using the same areas again. In much of the north this means setting aside enough timber land to supply associated complexes for about 80 years, since it takes approximately 80 years for the forests to regenerate themselves in these regions of short, cool growing seasons.

Not only are the Soviets replanting forests in areas of commercial timber production, but they have done an admirable job of afforestation in previously unforested areas in the form of shelterbelts to cut down the action of the wind and thereby diminish soil erosion and conserve precious soil moisture. Throughout much of the steppe and wooded-steppe regions of south-central European U.S.S.R., shelterbelts have been planted both around fields in rectangular patterns and in long, broad strips running across certain sections of the landscape. In most of the arable land shelterbelts have been planted around cultivated plots of about 40–60 hectares size. An extensive broad shelterbelt runs for miles along the western side of the Volga River all the way from Rostov-on-Don to Ulyanovsk. Expansive shelterbelts have also been planted in the virgin lands of Western Siberia and northern Kazakhstan. A national forest strip now runs from Slavgorod to Rubtsovsk in the Kulunda Steppe west of the Altay.

The Soviets also have initiated a program to reforest steep slopes along stream banks and gullies in many farming regions of the country where rural villages have for centuries cut down the trees for firewood. In the subhumid and semiarid forest-steppe and steppe regions in the better farming areas, most of the few trees that originally grew were on river embankments where they could derive constant supplies of groundwater, and most of the rural villages have historically been located in these same valleys. Consequently, a great deal of overcutting has taken place on these steep slopes, primarily to heat rural cottages. This has led to excessive soil erosion, gullying, and the caving of banks of streams and reservoirs.

There has also been a huge tree planting program going on in all the cities of the country, both for esthetic and recreational purposes and to combat air pollution.

Production

In 1975 the U.S.S.R. produced about one-sixth of all the world's roundwood. (Table 13-2) Except for China, the leading countries produced mostly coniferous softwoods. The U.S.S.R. produced four times as much coniferous wood as broadleaf. The second leading producer, the United States, lying at a lower latitude, had more hardwood production from broadleaf trees such as oak and maple. Much of the hardwood from broadleaf trees in the Soviet Union is birch. The Soviet Union produced almost one-third of the coniferous wood in the world.

Much of the roundwood in the Soviet Union goes into sawnwood, whereas in countries such as the United States and Canada with more advanced development of wood materials and wood chemical industries, large portions of roundwood are used for these industries. During the 1960s, about 60 per cent of the industrial roundwood in the Soviet Union was converted into lumber, more than 20 per cent was consumed domestically in unprocessed form (for log cabins in rural areas, telephone and electric poles, and so forth), about 3 per cent was exported, and only about 6 per cent went into pulp and paper industries. In the

United States and Canada, on the other hand, the production of chemical and groundwood pulp accounted for about half of the industrial timber cut. The production of every branch of the American wood processing industry, except lumber, exceeded that of the U.S.S.R. In 1964, the U.S.A. produced approximately 6 times more paper, 10 times more pulp, and 16 times more paperboard than the U.S.S.R. Canada produced about the same amount of these products as the U.S.S.R. did.

Table 13-2   Roundwood Production of Leading Countries, 1975, in Million Cubic Meters

	Coniferous	Broadleaf	Total	Per Cent
World	1056	1365	2421	100
U.S.S.R.	324	64	388	16
U.S.A.	226	69	295	12
China	86	102	188	8
Canada	110	11	121	5
Sweden	46	7	53	2
Japan	20	17	37	2
Finland	23	8	31	1

Source: UN Statistical Yearbook, 1976.

The Soviet Union is attempting to modernize its wood industry and utilize more of the roundwood for processed wood products other than sawn lumber in order to conserve much of the waste that is now being tolerated. But in 1975, the United States and Canada were still producing more than 2 and 3 times respectively the amount of mechanical wood pulp than the U.S.S.R. was, and 5.2 and 1.4 times as much respectively of chemical pulp. Japan and Sweden produced more chemical pulp than the U.S.S.R., and Finland produced more than half as much as the U.S.S.R. Canada produced more than 5 times as much newsprint as the U.S.S.R., and the U.S.A. produced about 2.5 times as much. In the production of other paper and paperboard products, the U.S.A. was by far the largest producer in the world, producing more than 6 times as much as the

U.S.S.R. Japan produced almost twice as much as the U.S.S.R.

The U.S.S.R., of course, is outstanding in sawnwood. (Table 13-3) In 1975 it produced almost one-third of the world's supply, well ahead of the second producer, the United States, which produced less than one-fifth of the world's supply. The third producer, Japan, is notable because most of its sawn lumber is derived from imported roundwood. A large share of Soviet roundwood still goes into firewood, which is still the primary fuel to heat rural homes. In recent years firewood has been consuming about 21 per cent of the total roundwood production in the U.S.S.R. Probably this is an underestimate, since official statistics probably would not include lots of firewood that is cut by individuals in collective farm woodlots.

Table 13-3   Production of Sawnwood by Leading Countries, 1975, in Million Cubic Meters

	Coniferous	Broadleaf	Total	Per Cent
World	303.6	89.2	392.8	100
U.S.S.R.	101.5	13.5	115.0	29
U.S.A.	62.5	13.0	75.5	19
Japan	28.0	10.3	38.3	10
Canada	26.1	1.0	27.1	7
China	11.0	6.2	17.2	4
Sweden	10.0	0.3	10.3	3

Source: UN Statistical Yearbook, 1976.

The wood industry in the Soviet Union has had a fairly low priority for investment capital, as compared to such industries as metallurgical, chemical, and machine building. Therefore, its output has not been expanding very rapidly, and it is not planned that it will in the foreseeable future. In fact, as improved technology has cut waste, the production of roundwood declined from 395 million cubic meters in 1975 to 385 million in 1976. Although a slight recovery is planned for 1977, to 389 million cubic meters, this still will not match 1975.

Sawnwood has declined in recent years from a high of 119 million cubic meters in both 1971 and 1972 to only 113 million in 1976, and the plan for 1977 is a further reduction to 111 million. In contrast, the production of various wood products has been on the increase. Total cellulose production is up from 5,110,000 tons in 1970 to 7,204,000 tons in 1976. That of paper is up from 4,185,000 tons in 1970 to 5,389,000 in 1976, and the production of cartons is up from 2,516,000 tons in 1970 to 3,527,000 tons in 1976. Substantial increases are planned for all these products for 1977. Plywood, on the other hand, has been gaining unevenly. 1976 saw a slight decrease, but an increase is planned again for 1977.

Of the 302,900,000 cubic meters of commercial roundwood produced in the Soviet Union in 1976, 17,892,000 were exported, primarily to Japan, Finland, Hungary, East Germany, Italy, Bulgaria, Yugoslavia, France, Poland, Czechoslovakia, Belgium, Great Britain, The Netherlands, and West Berlin, in that order. Japan alone took almost 45 per cent of the roundwood exports. Of the 113,000,000 cubic meters of sawnwood produced in the Soviet Union in 1976, 9,905,000 were exported. Japan took 77 per cent of this. Other leading countries were Finland, China, Bulgaria, Hungary, and Sweden. From 300 to 600 tons each of the following products were exported, primarily to the same countries as listed above: plywood, cellulose, paper, newsprint, and cartons. The Soviets would like to reduce their exports of roundwood and greatly increase those of processed products in order to derive income from the processing, particularly from hard currency countries such as Japan. But, so far the Soviet processing industries have lagged well behind the timber industry itself.

Regional Distribution

Almost all the forest resources of the U.S.S.R. are located in the Far East, East Siberia, West Siberia, Northwest, and Urals regions of the Russian Republic. (Table 13-4) The other republics contain only small areas.

The huge Far East and East Siberian economic regions contain by far the largest forested areas. The East Siberian Region also leads in percentage of total area covered by forests. But generally these eastern regions do not have as dense stands nor as high quality wood as the Northwest Economic Region and portions of the Urals. The best quality timber generally is found in Archangel Oblast and the Karelian and Komi A.S.S.R.s in the Northwest Economic Region, Sverdlovsk and Perm Oblasts in the Urals, Irkutsk Oblast in Eastern Siberia, and certain parts of Maritime and Khabarovsk Krays in the Far East. Good stands also exist in places on the slopes of the Altay Mountains and in Tyumen and Tomsk Oblasts in Western Siberia.

The better stands of timber in places such as Archangel, Perm, Tomsk, and Irkutsk Oblasts, and Khabarovsk Kray have much of their timber in such species as pine and spruce which are preferred for lumber production. But large areas of Siberia and the Far East, as well as portions of northern European Russia are forested primarily by larch, which is less desired. The wood is heavy and tends to waterlog and sink in streams, thus making log floating very difficult, clogging streams with debris, and causing pollution of lakes. The larch is ideally suited to growing over permafrost, since it has a shallow, wide-spreading root system which can sustain the plant in a few feet of active soil layer during the summer. Recently there have been experiments to improve the floatability of larch logs by coating the butt ends of logs with water repellent substances.

In total standing wood resources of commercial grade, Eastern Siberia ranks first, the Far East second, Western Siberia third, the Northwest economic region fourth, and the Urals fifth. These five economic regions contain 90 per cent of the country's standing commercial wood resources. In addition to these regions in the Russian Republic, the Baltic Republics, Belorussia, and even Georgia in the Transcaucasus, have about one-third of their territories covered by forests, a great deal of which is being exploited in one way or another, but

Table 13–4   Regional Distribution of Forest Resources in the
U.S.S.R. as of January 1, 1973

	Forested Area Million Hectares	Per Cent of Area Covered by Forests	Wood Resources Billion m.^{3}
U.S.S.R.	769.8	34.4	81.78
R.S.F.S.R	728.0	42.7	78.51
Northwest	83.1 (4)	49.7 (2)	8.60 (4)
Urals	29.1	42.7 (3)	3.49 (5)
W. Siberia	84.9 (3)	34.8	10.31 (3)
E. Siberia	227.9 (2)	54.9 (1)	28.58 (1)
Far East	257.2 (1)	41.8 (4)	22.34 (2)
Ukraine	8.5	14.1	0.97
Belorussia	6.8	32.7	0.61
Lithuania	1.7	26.4	0.18
Latvia	2.4	38.3	0.30
Estonia	1.6	36.1	0.18
Moldavia	0.3	8.0	0.02
Georgia	2.7	38.8	0.38
Azerbaydzhan	0.9	11.0	0.12
Armenia	0.3	3.3	0.31
Kazakh	9.1	9.9	0.03
Uzbek	1.2	2.7	0.01
Kirgiz	0.7	3.3	0.02
Tadzhik	0.4	2.9	0.01
Turkmen	3.2	6.6	0.01

Source: Narkhoz SSSR, 1975, p. 269.
Numbers in parentheses indicate ranks.

these republics are so small compared to the Russian Republic that the total wood resources are minimal.

The regions of large forest resources are generally the leading regions of wood products production also, but not necessarily in the order of resources. Traditionally the Northwest Economic Region, which ranks only fourth in wood resources, has ranked first in all forms of wood production, including roundwood, sawnwood, plywood, paper, and cartons. (Table 13–5) It is so much closer to the main markets of the Soviet Union than the Siberian and Far Eastern regions are, that it has been exploited more rapidly. Also, as was pointed out before, it has some of the best quality forests. However, in recent years, as huge wood processing complexes have been established in certain parts of Siberia and the Far East, these eastern regions have gained on the Northwest in total production. During the last decade, Far Eastern production increased by 45 per cent, Eastern Siberia by 21.2 per cent, and Western Siberia by 11.9 per cent, while production in the Northwest increased only 4.5 per cent. Khabarovsk Kray in the Far East Economic Region increased more than 97 per cent, by far the highest increase of any political unit. Tyumen Oblast in Western Siberia was second with an increase of 71 per cent, and Maritime Kray in the Far East and Irkutsk Oblast in Eastern Siberia each had more than 30 per cent increases. The Komi A.S.S.R. in the Northwest showed a large increase, 29 per cent, and Volodga Oblast in the same region showed a significant increase, 15 per cent, but the Kare-

Table 13–5   Wood Products Production by Major Regions, 1975

	Roundwood Million m.³	Increase 1975/1965 %	Sawnwood Million m.³	Plywood 1000 m.³	Paper 1000 Tons	Cartons 1000 Tons
U.S.S.R.	395.1	4.5	116.2	2196	5215	3368
R.S.F.S.R.	366.9	6.4	93.5	1559	4318	2514
Northwest	97.3 I	4.5	18.5 I	417 I	1875 I	790 I
Archangel O.	27.2 (2)	3.0	7.1 (2)		329 (4)	561 (1)
Komi A.S.S.R.	23.6 (6)	29.0 (5)	2.6	74	164	37
Vologda O.	17.4 (7)	15.2	2.0	75	130	11
Karelian A.S.S.R.	15.8	−18.1	3.0		877 (2)	41
Leningrad O.	6.8	6.2	2.1	100 (5)	150	68
Central	29.7	0.0	9.7	360 II	172	457 II
Kostroma O.	8.6	−12.2	1.9	126 (1)		
Kalinin O.	5.4	1.9	1.5	75		
Moscow O.			1.9			168 (3)
Volgo-Vyatka	30.3	−4.4	8.2	92	612	171
Kirov O.	17.3	−9.5	3.9	73		24
Gorky O.	7.7	−2.5	2.5	19	466 (3)	124 (5)
Volga	11.3	−13.1	6.7	239 III	81	214
Bashkir A.S.S.R.	4.6		1.4	108 (4)		
Tatar A.S.S.R.	1.9		1.4	94 (6)		
N. Caucasus	3.2	−28.9	3.0	53	33	115
Krasnodar Kray	1.9		1.5	52		103
Urals	58.4 III	−5.8	13.5 III	233 IV	1028 II	137
Sverdlovsk O.	25.3 (4)	−5.9	6.3 (4)	115 (2)	79	17
Perm O.	24.2 (5)	−3.2	3.7	112 (3)	949 (1)	119
W. Siberia	33.0	11.9 III	8.8	68	2	56
Tyumen O.	14.2	71.1 (2)	2.1	29		
Tomsk O.	8.6	−1.1	1.9			
E. Siberia	69.2 II	21.2 II	17.3 II	50	133	394 III
Irkutsk O.	32.5 (1)	32.7 (4)	7.7 (1)	50	14	216 (2)
Krasnoyarsk Kray	25.4 (3)	16.0	6.9 (3)		120	153 (4)
Buryat A.S.S.R.	5.8	0.0	1.5			
Far East	33.2	45.0 I	6.6	47	229	134
Khabarovsk Kray	14.6	97.3 (1)	2.4	16		43
Maritime Kray	6.3	37.0 (3)	1.7	30		
Sakhalin O.					216 (5)	91
Ukraine	9.6	−23.2	9.5	n.a.	235	n.a.
Belorussia	6.2	−13.9	3.2	n.a.	178	n.a.
Baltic Region	9.4	−5.1	3.1	n.a.	535	n.a.
Kazakhstan	2.2	10.0	2.6	n.a.	18	n.a.

Sources: *Narkhoz SSSR* and *Narkhoz RSFSR*, 1975. (1976 editions contained only incomplete data) n.a. = not available. Blank space indicates the region was not the next largest producer. Roman numerals indicate ranks of economic regions. Arabic numerals in parentheses indicate ranks of political subdivisions.

ian A.S.S.R. in this region showed a loss of 18 per cent.

Since the establishment of the huge Bratsk timber processing complex, Irkutsk Oblast has been the leading wood producer among all political units, both in total roundwood production and in sawnwood production. Also in Eastern Siberia, huge Krasnoyarsk Kray ranks third in the country in both roundwood and sawnwood production. However these two political units in Eastern Siberia do not equal the total production of such important producing areas as Archangel Oblast, the Komi A.S.S.R., Volodga Oblast, the Karelian A.S.S.R., and Leningrad Oblast in the Northwest Economic Region. In the near future, of course, the picture might change considerably. Among other things, it is envisioned that after the Baykal-Amur Railroad is completed through the East Siberian and Far Eastern regions, its zone of influence, which has a forest area commensurate in size with that of Archangel Oblast, Volgoda Oblast, and the Karelian A.S.S.R. combined, will soon be providing about 10 per cent of the total Soviet production of timber products.

Sawmilling traditionally has been concentrated in timber producing areas or along routes of transport between timber producing and consuming areas. Thus, sawmilling towns are often lined up along streams and railroads and are particularly bunched where railroads cross timber floating streams. (Fig. 13–1) Some major concentrations have developed at major wood export ports, such as Archangel on the White Sea and Igarka on the lower Yenisey which collects wood from Krasnoyarsk Kray to export via the Northern Sea Route. A number of other lumber ports carry on sawmilling along the shores of the Baltic, White, and Barents Seas in the Northwest and the Pacific coast of Maritime Kray and Sakhalin Island in the Far East.

But other wood processing industries are more dispersed; generally the more the processing, the more the dispersion. In the past, pulp and paper mills traditionally have been small separate enterprises that have been concentrated along the Kama River district of Perm Oblast on the western slopes of the Urals and in Karelia and adjacent regions. The metropolitan area of Gorky, with its primary paper producing satellite city, Pravdinsk, has been a separate node of concentration for paper making, as has been Sakhalin Island in the Far East. But various kinds of paper are made in many different regions of the country, as is the manufacture of cartons, which not only is concentrated in timber producing areas such as Archangel and Irkutsk Oblasts, but also in market regions such as Moscow Oblast.

Newsprint comprises about one-fourth of all paper production in the Soviet Union. Three major centers produce almost all the newsprint in the country. Solikamsk in Perm Oblast contributes about 40 per cent, Pravdinsk in Gorky Oblast about 30 per cent, and Kondopoda in Karelia about 30 per cent. Nearby Segezha turns out about 60 per cent of all the brown paper bags in the Soviet Union. In 1970 it produced about 550,000,000 bags which weighed 268,000 tons. An expansion program now under way is to add a capacity of about 700 million more bags per year.

Other woodworking industries of many sorts, such as furniture making, are found in many of the large cities of the country, and their geographical distribution closely corresponds to the population distribution. (Fig. 13–1)

As rivers such as the Volga and Dnieper have been dammed, log rafting has become more difficult, generally involving towing rather than free floating, and more and more roundwood has been shifted to rail transport. The railroads now move more than twice as much roundwood as rivers do. This has increased transport costs and induced further concentration of primary processing, such as sawmilling, in timber producing areas in order to reduce volume and hence transportation costs. Sawnwood effects as much as a 40 per cent saving in transportation costs over roundwood. As more and more of the new expansion of the timber industry has taken place in the eastern regions, rail hauls of wood have continued to lengthen. In 1975 the average length of rail haul of wood products was 1640 kilome-

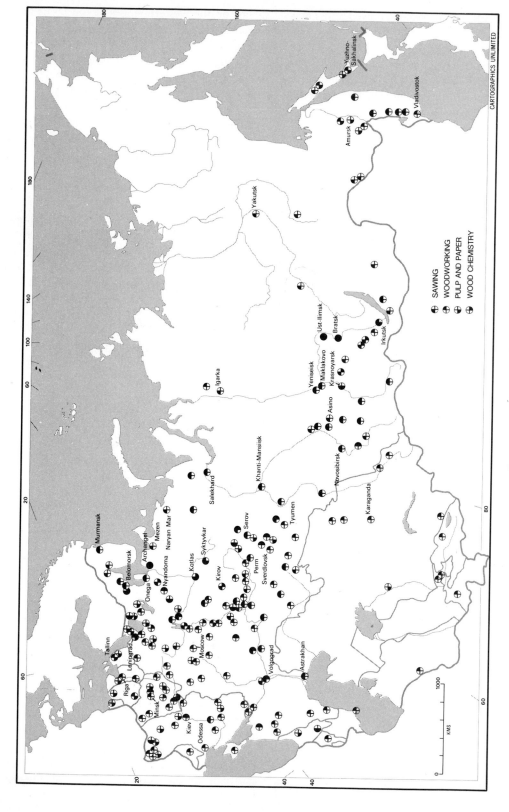

Figure 13–1 Wood Industries.

Figure 13-2   Log rafting on the Volga. Photo by Irving Cutler.

ters, by far the longest rail haul of any commodity. To counterbalance increasing rail costs, more of the primary processing has become concentrated in large integrated plants in the timber producing areas of the east. This is true not only of sawmilling but also of pulp production, both for mechanical and chemical purposes, and the production of plywood, fiber board, and container board.

The Bratsk complex in Eastern Siberia apparently is the largest single wood processing complex at the present time. In the mid 1970s, Bratsk was producing about one million tons of wood pulp, 40 million square meters of fiber board, 280,000 tons of container board, 600,000 cubic meters of sawn wood, and had a capacity to produce 200,000 cubic meters of plywood, reportedly the second largest plywood producing unit in the world. For all these wood products, the complex of plants at Bratsk are utilizing about 6 million cubic meters of roundwood per year. An even larger wood processing complex reportedly is being constructed downstream from Bratsk at Ust-Ilmsk near the site of the new hydroelectric plant.

A large new wood processing complex came into being in the Soviet Far East in 1967 at the town of Amursk south of Komsomolsk. This is to become the largest wood processing plant in the Soviet Far East. In the mid 1970s it was turning out about 160,000 tons of pulp and 139,000 tons of paperboard, with an ultimate capacity of 278,000 tons of paperboard. As a result of the construction of this plant, the town of Amursk became the fastest growing city in the Far East during the early 1970s. By 1974 it had reached a population of 32,000.

The largest lumber producing center in Western Siberia is Asino, established in 1946 at the end of a Trans Siberian rail spur northeast of Tomsk near the Chulym River, a major logging stream. It now processes about one million cubic meters of roundwood per year to produce sawnwood and prefabricated

Figure 13–3   Wood processing complex at Bratsk. Photo by Henry A. Coppock.

housing. A fiber board plant has just been added, and a wood chip plant is under construction. The ultimate capacity of this complex is eventually to utilize about 3 million cubic meters of roundwood per year. A railroad has been extended to Belyy Yar on the Ket River, to open up new timber lands for Asino in one of the highest quality stands of timber in Western Siberia. The population of Asino has now grown to more than 30,000.

FURS

Russia has always been a large producer of furs, which come primarily from its forests in the north. Fur trading was the impetus for the opening up of Siberia in the sixteenth and seventeenth centuries, and many of the early towns of Siberia were primarily fur trading centers. Slobodskoy, a suburb of Kirov in the Volga-Vyatka Region, eventually became the primary center for fur collection and processing. It is situated in the southern part of the forest of northeastern European Russia where some of the best fur bearing animals live and is situated at the intersection of the Vyatka River with the ancient trading and cattle driving road leading from Siberia westward to the European part of the country. The fur industry and sheepskin coat industries here are as old as the town itself. The major factory is the Belka factory, which is the largest in the country. It turns pelts of squirrel, fox, polar fox, hare, and mole into beautiful fur coats and other items. It also has developed the manufacture of immitation sea lion and otter from sheep skins. Other large fur industry centers are Kazan, Uralsk, Chita, and Beltsy in Moldavia.

Although sable and mink have been the most prized pelts, their numbers have diminished and they are now protected. Some are being raised on fur farms. But the species trapped in largest numbers today are squirrel and

Figure 13–4   Rolls of brown paper inside Bratsk wood processing complex. Photo by Henry A. Coppock.

muskrat, which was introduced from Canada during the early part of the Soviet period and quickly acclimated to its familiar swamps and streams of the northern forests.

Furs traditionally have supplied valuable exports for Tsarist Russia and the Soviet Union. In 1975 they constituted the 22nd most valuable export to industrialized western countries, amounting to $55,971,000. The United Kingdom and West Germany took by far the largest shares.

Reading List

FISHING

1. Carré, Francois, "Les Pêches de la Baltique," (Fish in the Baltic Sea), *Revue Norois*, October–December 1975, pp. 575–593.
2. ———, "Les Pêches en mer Caspienne" (Fish in the Caspian Sea), *Annales de Geographie*, January–February 1978, pp. 1–39.
3. Low, Loh Lee, *A Study of Four Major Ground-fish Fisheries of the Bering Sea*, PhD Dissertation, University of Washington, Seattle, 1974.
4. Sysoev, N. P., *Ekonomika rybnoy promyshlennosti SSSR* (Economics of the Fishing Industry in the USSR), Pischevaya promyshlennost, Moscow, 1977.
5. Vasileva, E. V., and Runova, N. V., *Problemy effektivnogo ispolzovaniye osnovnykh fondov pishchevoy promyshlennosti* (Problems of effectively utilizing the resources of the fishing industry), Pischevaya promyshlennost Moscow, 1974, 350 pp.
6. Vinogradov, L. G., *et al.*, "Significance and Immediate Tasks of Soviet Fisheries," Gerasimov, I. P., *et. al.*, eds., *Natural Resources of the Soviet Union: Their Use and Renewal*, Freeman, San Francisco, 1971, pp. 303–336.

FORESTRY

1. Barr, Brenton M., "Regional Variation in Soviet Pulp and Paper Production," *Annals of the Association of American Geographers*, March 1971, pp. 45–64.
2. ———, *The Soviet Wood-Processing Industry,*

Research Publications in Geography No. 5, University of Toronto Press, Toronto, 1970, 135 pp.

3. Gorovoy, V. L., and Shlykov, V. M., "Basic Trends in the Development of the Forest Industry Along the Baykal-Amur Mainline," *Soviet Geography: Review and Translation,* February 1978, pp. 84–98.

4. Privalovskaya, G. A., "The Impact of Raw-Material Factor on the Territorial Production Structure of Primary Processing Industry" (A Case Study of the Lumbering and Forest-Products Industries), *Soviet Geography: Review and Translation,* February 1973, pp. 78–91.

5. Vasilyev, P. V., "Forest Resources and Forest Economy," in Gerasimov, I. P., Armand, D. L., and Yefron, K. M., eds., *Natural Resources of the Soviet Union: Their Use and Renewal,* Freeman, San Francisco, 1971, pp. 187–215.

14

Water Resources and the Transformation of Nature

A basic tenet of Marxian doctrine is the principle of "man over nature." Once a communist society has become fully established, man is supposed to have the wherewithal to subject nature to his own will completely and no longer be a victim of his environment. The Soviets have subscribed to this doctrine, and it is evident that it has had strong influence in the formulation of policies that determine the development of the country. Of course, the nature of the environment in much of the Soviet Union is such that it needs massive amelioration in order to be utilized fully, especially for agriculture. Therefore, through dire necessity, the Soviets have mounted large scale amelioration programs such as irrigation, drainage, afforestation, construction of reservoirs, and interbasin transfers of water. But in some cases, particularly the construction of huge hydroelectric plants on eastern rivers, it appears that ideology might have taken the upper hand and construction projects have been completed without the impetus of demonstrable necessity.

Practically all the attempts to improve on nature in the Soviet Union have had to do with altering the water balance. Measures have ranged all the way from such subtle things as the adaptation of farming methods and the planting of shelterbelts that enhance soil moisture to such grandiose construction projects as the Volga cascade of reservoirs and the Kara-Kum canal in Central Asia.

Overall, the Soviet Union has ample water resources. (Table 14–1) Average annual river flow alone amounts to about 4700 cubic kilometers, almost 13 per cent of the earth's total, which places the Soviet Union first in the world. It also contains huge water resources in its lakes, swamps, and subsurface aquifers. Lake Baykal alone is credited with one-sixth the earth's fresh water supply. The Caspian and Aral Seas, both inland salt lakes, respectively rank first and fourth in surface area among the lakes of the world. (Table 14–2)

Unfortunately about 84 per cent of the runoff in rivers flows through sparsely inhabitated regions of northern European Russia, Siberia, and the Far East. (Fig. 14–1) The densely populated, industrially and agriculturally developed portions of the nation in the drainage basins of the Azov-Black and Aral-Caspian Seas, which encompass 29 per cent of the territory of the U.S.S.R., have only 12 per cent of the river flow. The remaining 4 per cent of runoff flows through the rivers within the drainage basin of the Baltic Sea which has significant population and industrial development but adequate water for foreseeable needs.

Where water is abundant, primarily in the north and east, settlement has been limited by other factors: cold temperatures, poor drainage, and infertile soils. The best agricultural land

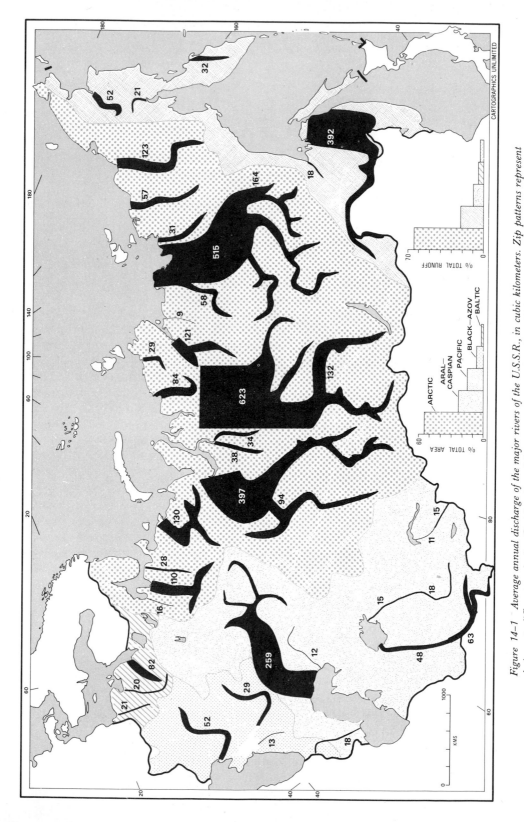

Figure 14-1 Average annual discharge of the major rivers of the U.S.S.R., in cubic kilometers. Zip patterns represent drainage to different sea basins. Graph at lower left represents percentages of total U.S.S.R. territory drained into specified basins. Graph at lower right represents percentage of total runoff drained into specified basins. From Nikolskiy, et. al., p. 65.

Table 14–1   Rivers of the U.S.S.R. With Lengths Greater Than 1000 Kilometers, in Order of Length[1]

River	Length, Kilometers		Area of Basin km.^{2}	Average Flow at Mouth m.^{3}/sec.
	Total	Navigable		
Lena	4400	4125	2,490,000	17000
Irtysh	4248	3779	1,643,000	2830
Ob	3650	3650	2,867,000	12700
Volga	3531	3194	1,360,000	7710
Yenisey	3487	3487	2,580,000	19800
Lower Tunguska	2989	—	473,000	3680
Amur	2824	2824	1,855,000	10900
Vilyuy	2650	—	454,000	1480
Ural	2428	1230	237,000	—
Aldan	2273	—	729,000	5110
Olenek	2270	—	219,000	1210
Syr Darya	2212	—	219,000	—
Dnieper	2200	1869	504,000	1700
Kolyma	2129	1986	647,000	3900
Don	1870	1578	422,000	935
Stony Tunguska	1865	—	240,000	1750
Vitim	1837	—	225,000	2200
Pechora	1809	1547	322,000	4000
Ishim	1809	—	177,000	—
Kama	1805	1507	507,000	3770
Chulym	1799	—	134,000	785
Angara	1779	1558	1,039,000	5100
Indigirka	1726	—	360,000	1850
Amga	1650	—	69,300	—
Khatanga	1636	—	364,000	3320
Ket	1621	—	94,200	560
Argun	1620	—	164,000	340
Tobol	1591	—	426,000	805
Alazeya	1520	—	64,700	300
Oka	1500	1170	245,000	1300
Olekma	1436	—	210,000	1950
Belaya	1430	—	142,000	970
Amu Darya	1415	1415	309,000	—
Taz	1401	—	150,000	1450
Kura	1364	539	188,000	575
Dniester	1350	—	71,800	295
Vyatka	1314	—	129,000	890
Zeya	1242	—	233,000	1900
Uda	1203	—	56,800	300
Markha	1181	—	238,000	405
Anadyr	1150	—	191,000	1680
Desna	1130	—	88,900	361
Vychegda	1130	—	121,000	1160
Omolon	1114	—	113,000	700
Konda	1097	—	72,800	310
Vasyugan	1082	—	61,800	345

Table 14–1   (Continued)

River	Length, Kilometers		Area of Basin km.²	Average Flow at Mouth m.³/sec.
	Total	Navigable		
Araks	1072	—	102,000	—
Maya	1053	—	171,000	1175
Selenga	1024	—	447,060	970
Western Dvina	1020	723	87,900	678
Northern Donets	1016	—	98,900	—
Biryusa	1012	—	55,800	365
Tura	1009	—	80,400	—
Ili	1001	—	140,000	—
Chunya	1000	—	70,500	435

Sources: Domanitskiy, *et. al.*, Nikolskiy, *et. al.*, p. 63, and *Sovetskiy Soyuz: Obshchiy Obzor,* Mysl, Moscow, 1972, p. 744.

[1] The longest river systems in the U.S.S.R. are the Ob-Irtysh (5410 km.) and Amur-Shilka-Ononom (4416 km.). The Yenisey-Biy-Khem is 4092 km., the Syr Darya-Naryn is 2991 km., and the Amu Darya-Pyandzh is 2600 km.

—, Not available.

lies in the subhumid and semiarid zones in the drainage basins of the Black and Caspian Seas. Thus, the problem is to make use of every drop of moisture available in the dry south while trying to get rid of the excess moisture on the land in the north and east. Not only is the water poorly distributed geographically, but the supply also fluctuates widely seasonally and from year to year. Seasonal fluctuations cause water deficits in both the south and the north. In south European U.S.S.R. lowest water stages are generally reached during late summer, while in the north minimum stream flow usually occurs in late winter due to freeze-up. Many of the streams in the north freeze solid to the bottom. Thus, the flow through hydroelectric turbines is often curtailed, and a great deal of winterkill of fish may be experienced. And, of course, frozen streams are not available for navigation.

Both the north and the south may experience floods during spring when rains combine with melting snow to overflow the banks of streams. This is particularly severe in the north where streams flowing to the Arctic thaw first in their southern headwaters while the lower portions of the streams farther north are still jammed with ice. A great deal of water is lost during this time of year as harmful runoff which will not be available later when it is needed. The only way to remedy this is by inpoundment in reservoirs, but reservoirs themselves have their drawbacks, as will be seen later. The spring runoff in the south might be reduced somewhat by correct farming procedures and afforestation of steeper slopes, as well as the building of many small ponds on small streams and gullies. A great deal of this has already been done. It has been estimated that the runoff of the Don and other rivers in the southern European plain has been reduced by these means by as much as 15–20 per cent. This reduction of surface runoff signifies greater utilization of the moisture resources by better infiltration into the soil and transpiration through plants.

The best seasonal coincidence between water supply and water need occurs in Central Asia where snow that has fallen in the high mountains during winter reaches its greatest volume of melt during middle and late summer at the

Table 14–2 Lakes in the U.S.S.R. With Surface Areas of More Than 800 Square Kilometers, in Order of Size

Lake	Area km.²	Elevation m.	Maximum Depth, m.	Volume km.³
Caspian Sea	371,000	−28	1025	—
Aral Sea	64,100	52	68	1023
Baykal	31,500	455	1741	23000
Balkhash	18,300	339	26	112
Ladoga	17,700	4	230	908
Onega	9,720	33	127	285
Issyk-Kul	6,280	1609	702	1730
Zaysan	5,510	395	30	53
Taymyr	4,560	6	26	13
Khanka	4,190	68	10.6	16.5
Chudskoe-Pskov	3,550	30	15	25
Alakol	2,650	350	54	59
Chany	1,990	105	9	4.3
Tengiz	1,590	304	8	—
Sevan	1,360	1900	90	—
Beloe	1,290	113	20	5.2
Vyg-ozero	1,140	89	18	7.1
Top-ozero	986	—	—	—
Ilmen	982	18	4-10	1-12
Khantayskoe	822	73	—	—
Imandra	876	—	—	—
Seg-ozero	815	—	—	—

Source: Domanitskiy, *et. al.*

—, Not available

very time that agriculture on the plains to the north most needs irrigation water that is being derived from the rivers flowing down the mountains. But, of course, in this desert region a shortage of water exists all the time. Thus, in spite of the fact that rate of flow generally coincides with greatest need, thereby limiting wasteful runoff, the whole area needs interbasin transfers of water from the north in order to realize its fullest potential.

MAJOR WATER CONSTRUCTION PROJECTS

Since the most obvious man-made transformation of natural conditions are huge dams, reservoirs, and canal systems, with their associated irrigation and drainage districts, major water basin development programs will be dealt with in some detail individually and plans for future large-scale water diversions will be discussed. This will be followed by an analysis of the various advantages and disadvantages realized by such projects and possible alternative means of more efficiently utilizing water resources.

The Volga-Kama-Don Cascade

First attention has been given to water construction projects in the areas of greatest need, the south European part of the Soviet Union and Central Asia. Among these, the Volga-Kama-Don basin development probably constitutes the greatest transformation of nature. When completed this cascade will consist of twelve reservoirs with a combined area of 28,000 square kilometers and a useful water capacity of 100 cubic kilometers. (Table 10–12) (Also see folded physical map inside back cover.) These reservoirs have completely transformed the entire landscape along the valley into a vast inland waterway that provides not only one of the greatest sources of hydroelectricity in the country, but also an improved navigational channel that carries from half to three-quarters of all the river traffic in the country, and almost unlimited recreational facilities in the form of beaches and camping grounds along the banks and in the islands among the channels, as well as boating and fishing in the waters themselves.

The principal benefit derived from the reservoirs on the Volga and Kama Rivers is the replenishing of water resources during dry years and the evening out of seasonal fluctuations. On the lower Volga the stream flow has been increased by 2–3 times during low water stage, which is an important achievement, since it is the low water level that decides the base for economic utilization. The evening of the flow has been beneficial not only for power generation, but also for municipal and industrial water supplies, irrigation, navigation, and the improvement of water quality in river segments with little or no gradient where the discharge of additional water during low stage improves effluent dilution and aeration.

Actually the present operating regime of the reservoirs fails to make full use of the potential for adding to downstream flow during low water stage. Although this system is considered to be a multipurpose one, power generation has generally taken precedence except in the irrigated districts of the south. Since the hydropower plants are used primarily for peaking, they operate sporadically and are mostly shut down during weekends when power demands are low. Therefore, the flow of water through the dams on weekends is often less than it was in the natural river stage. (Fig. 14-2) During weekends the flow of water through the Kuybyshev Dam is only 10-15 per cent of the weekday level.

Many water basin planners in the Soviet Union have decried the fact that in almost all the water construction projects in the country, except for strictly irrigation projects in the southern regions, the interests of power generation have taken precedence over other uses and considerations for environmental impacts. This has been an inevitable consequence of the fact that it has usually been the ministry for electrical power that has footed the bill and hence administered the construction of projects. In spite of the fact that projects are planned as multipurpose works, when it comes to the actual building, some agency within the bureaucracy has to budget the project, and it has usually been the electrical power industry.

The earliest construction works on the Volga were smaller projects in the north that were prompted primarily by the need to provide additional domestic water and a more navigable channel to the burgeoning Moscow area. The Moscow Canal, completed in 1937, joins

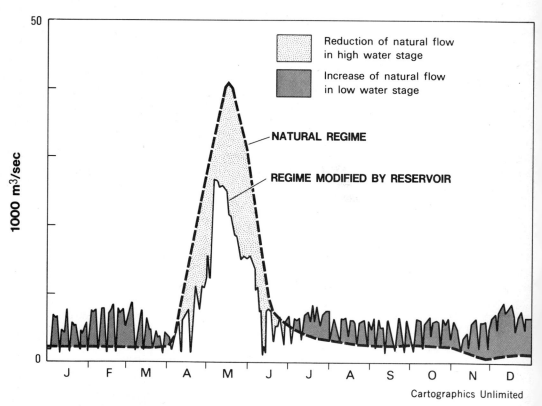

Cartographics Unlimited

Figure 14-2   Volga River flow below Kuybyshev Dam before and after the hydro-construction project. After Lvovich, 1977, p. 564.

the Moscow River in the city of Moscow through a system of eight locks with the Volga 128 kilometers to the north. A dam with a hydroelectric plant of 300,000 kilowatts capacity was constructed on the Volga River near Ivankovo which backed up the Volga 100 kilometers beyond the city of Kalinin to form the Volga Reservoir. One-third of the water collected in the reservoir is used to feed the Moscow Canal and the rest goes down the Volga into the Uglich Reservoir and eventually the large Rybinsk Reservoir which was filled in 1941. These reservoirs have regulated the flow of the upper Volga and supplied additional water to the Moscow River via the Moscow Canal to provide a six-meter-deep water route for navigation from the city of Moscow to the Volga River. The reservoirs and canal also have assured recreational facilities and a domestic water supply for the city of Moscow. Moscow's expanding industries and population use more than half of all the additional water being dumped into the canalized river. Although the canal was conceived originally to improve transportation, the function of supplying domestic water to Moscow has transcended the original purpose. At present the Volga provides two-thirds of Moscow's water, and the original flow of the Moscow River provides only one-third. In late 1977, the Moscow water supply was augmented by the completion of a reservoir and canal system that brings in water from the Vazuza River a tributary of the upper Volga in Smolensk and Kalinin oblasts.

It is planned eventually to construct a shipping canal that will skirt Moscow on the east. Also planned is an Oka-Moscow Canal to provide a navigational channel southeastward from Moscow to the Oka River and the Volga at Gorky. The Oka River in this vicinity has an even greater flow than the upper Volga.

Navigation along the upper Volga was greatly enhanced in the early 1960s when the 150-year-old Mariinsk canal system was revamped to handle Volga-sized steamers on a waterway that runs north from the Rybinsk Reservoir to Lake Onega where it connects with a canal system going westward down the Svir River between Lakes Onega and Ladoga

and on down the Neva River to the Gulf of Finland at Leningrad. It also connects northward through the Baltic-White Sea Canal that was opened in 1933 and reconstructed after World War II. Thus, the central Russian plain is connected by good waterways to the Black, Azov, Caspian, Baltic, and White Seas.

The first project to be completed on the lower Volga was the Volga-Don Canal in order to provide an outlet for Volga traffic to the sea, rather than in the dead end of the Caspian. Completed in 1952, the canal starts along the west bank of the Volga a few miles below Volgograd and follows a looping course for approximately 100 kilometers across the lowest part of the divide where the Don and Volga Rivers bend toward each other. Thirteen locks, each with a lift of about 10 meters, raise the water 45 meters above the Don and drop it 95 meters to the Volga. To provide water for the canal and to improve the channel on the lower Don, an earthen dam was strung for more than 11 kilometers across the broad, shallow valley of the Don River at the town of Tsimlyansk. The Tsimlyansk Dam raised the water 26 meters and backed it up the Don valley 360 kilometers to form the Tsimlyansk Sea, which at the time it was built was the largest man-made body of water in the world.

During recent years four low-head dams have been projected for the lower Don below the Tsimlyansk Dam in order to facilitate irrigation and fish spawning. The Nikolayevsk Dam was put into operation in 1975, and the construction on the Konstantinovsk Dam was started in 1976. Also, the long talked-about Volga-Ural Canal reportedly is under construction to carry water from the Volgograd Reservoir eastward to irrigate large portions of the Volga-Ural watershed. It would appear that if this is to be achieved, more water is somehow going to have to be found for the Volga system.

The Kuybyshev Reservoir is the water monitor for the entire Volga River downstream from the dam. The Saratov and Volgograd dams are mainly flow-through structures, although the Volgograd Reservoir does control flooding on the river below Volgograd. If the

Volga receives additional water from the north, then the Volgograd Reservoir will become the discharge regulator for distribution of water to the Azov, Caspian, and Aral Seas.

Not all the results of the transformation of the Volga have been positive. In addition to the flooding of huge acreages of prime agricultural floodplain land, which also necessitated the removal of thousands of villages and some large city installations, the transformation of a flowing stream into a series of relatively stagnant reservoirs while greatly deepening navigational channels has presented various hazards to navigation. No longer can log rafts be floated freely down the stream; they must be tugged through or loaded onto boats. This has greatly increased the cost and time of transport. The elaborate series of locks at the various dams form bottlenecks at which ships must line up and wait for passage. And the large surfaces of the reservoirs under the influence of storm winds generate waves that capsize small boats, break up barge trains, and often necessitate laying over for extended periods in storm shelters specifically provided along the route.

The early completion of the Volga Cascade has provided a natural laboratory during the last twenty years for the study of impacts of large reservoirs on environment in natural zones ranging from steppe in the south through forest steppe and mixed forest into the taiga zone of the north. The rise in water level in the reservoirs has flooded the lower concave slopes of surrounding hillsides and exposed the convex upper slopes to direct wave action at the high water level. The ground water table in the surrounding landscape has also risen so that slopes that were stable in their semi-dry state have often become mobile under the lubricating action of water. In addition, it has been found that water levels in the man-made reservoirs fluctuate much more seasonally and from year to year than do water levels in natural lakes in the same areas. The water level in the Tsimlyansk Reservoir fluctuates 5–6 meters during the year which is three times as much as the average fluctuation of natural lakes in the steppe zone. As a result of these three changes, bank erosion, landslides, and karstification all

were speeded up in the initial years after the filling of the reservoirs as new concave bank profiles were developing to adjust to the new water levels. Over a broader shore zone, often extending several kilometers inland, the rising ground water table has caused the expansion of swamps in northern humid areas and secondary salinization of soils in southern dry areas. Along the east bank of the Saratov Reservoir five years after its filling it was noticed that although a narrow shoreline strip 0–200 meters wide showed a decrease in water soluble salts, farther from the bank soil mineralization had increased from 0.9 parts per thousand to 7.5–16.0 parts per thousand.

The large surfaces of shallow water presented by the reservoirs, which get quite warm during summer compared to running streams and deeper water bodies, has greatly increased the evaporation of runoff which previously had drained into interior basins such as the Caspian Sea. Since 1929 the Caspian has dropped about three meters and is currently dropping about 6.25 centimeters every year. This has detrimentally affected shipping, fishing, and salt industries along the shores of the Caspian which has caused great concern to Soviet planners. A discussion of this, along with similar occurrences in the Aral and Azov Seas, will be discussed in conjunction with the possibilities of interbasin transfers of water from the north.

The existence of stagnant, shallow embayments along the edges of man-made reservoirs has led to the accumulation of pollutants and subsequent eutrophication. This has been combatted in some cases by controlled flooding which allows surges of water to pass through dams to flush out downstream sections of rivers without overflowing their banks. This process has been used on a regular basis on the Moscow River and was being experimented with on the lower Volga during the summer of 1976 when the author was participating in a study cruise along the Volga from Rostov to Kazan. At that time the Volga reservoirs were filled to the brim, but during normal summers there would not be sufficient excess water to continue this practice on a regular basis.

Ice generally remains as much as two weeks longer on the large reservoirs than it did on the original river. This has altered the microclimate in the immediate vicinity, particularly during spring. During summer reservoirs with widths of greater than 2 kilometers have been shown to depress convective precipitation over the water surface itself and on its downwind side. On the other hand, it is thought that the increased evaporation might enhance precipitation farther from the reservoirs, but this hypothesis is difficult to prove. The rising groundwater table, as well as the intermittent existence of shallow surface waters, have significantly altered vegetation in immediate shore areas. In some cases, particularly in the north, this has been very detrimental to forests over broad regions, sometimes covering areas twice the size of reservoirs themselves. As a consequence, the Soviets are now thinking of using large estuaries, such as the Ob Gulf, to impound fresh water rather than building reservoirs on land. The Arctic coast of the Kara, Barents, White, and Baltic Seas abound in such embayments. The Soviets have not explained how they are going to do this, but it is assumed they would build dams somewhere near the outer limits of estuaries which would keep salty sea water from mixing with fresh water brought in by rivers. Such constructions would preserve the natural hydrological regimes of the river systems as well as avoid flooding more land and raising the water table under the land.

Other Projects on the European Plain

The Dnieper River has been changed into a miniature Volga system with the construction of six dams which have converted the stream into a stairway of reservoirs all the way from the Belorussian-Ukrainian border southward to nearly the Black Sea coast. (Table 10–12 and the physical map at the end of the book) This has enhanced navigation along the stream, created 3500 megawatts of electrical generating capacity, and provided for large areas of irrigation, particularly in the south

where a major canal system leads water southeastward from the Kakhovka Reservoir across the Perekop Isthmus onto the northern plain of the Crimea and eastward all the way to the city of Kerch. The Kakhovka irrigation project has already provided water to irrigate 400,000 hectares of land which, among other things, has provided for another major rice growing region in the country.

Smaller dams and electrical generating units have been installed on some other rivers of the European plain, particularly the Western Dvina in Latvia, but such constructions have not created large reservoirs that have significantly altered the landscape.

Siberia and the Far East

Huge power stations and reservoirs have been created on some of the rivers of Siberia, although none of the river systems yet have been harnessed to the extent that the Volga and Dnieper Rivers have. Work has proceeded farthest on the Yenisey system, particularly its tributary, the Angara, in Eastern Siberia. The upper half of the Angara has been transformed into a series of three reservoirs by the Irkutsk, Bratsk, and Ust-Ilimsk Dams which were constructed primarily to generate electricity. Construction of the Boguchany Dam farther downstream will continue the process of the complete transformation of the river from head to mouth. Since the Angara drains the inexhaustible waters of Lake Baykal, it has a large and consistent flow which is ideal for power generation purposes. Even during winter, the generating stations are little hampered by ice as water from beneath the ice flows through the turbines. The consistency of flow throughout the year allows the Bratsk Dam to generate more electricity annually than any other installation in the country in spite of the fact that its capacity is only about two-thirds that of the Krasnoyarsk Dam on the Yenisey. Although at present no provisions have been made for ship locks or fish ladders along the Angara, eventually navigational aids are to be constructed which will allow navigation along the entire length of the stream.

On the upper Yenisey River, the Krasnoyarsk and Sayan hydroelectric stations are the biggest installations in the world. They have created elongated reservoirs that have flooded much of the upper portion of the stream from Krasnoyarsk southward into the Tuva A.S.S.R. Plans have been projected for other stations downstream, but until the need for more hydroelectricity in this region is evident, it appears that construction will be delayed indefinitely.

In Western Siberia the Novosibirsk Dam has been constructed on the Ob River which has created an extensive reservoir running southwestward up one of the broad, flat glacial rills described in Chapter 3. The dam was created primarily for electrical generation, but also serves some purposes for irrigation and navigation.

During the 1950s the Russians and Chinese

Figure 14–3   The Bratsk dam (top-left) has backed water up the Angara River (east and south) and its major left bank tributary, the Oka River (south). Landsat imagery.

Figure 14–4   The diabase gorge of the Angara River downstream (north) from the Bratsk dam. Photo by Henry A. Coppock.

collaborated on a plan for the complete development of the Amur River and its tributaries to reduce flooding caused by monsoon rains in late summer, enhance navigation, and generate electricity. However, with the falling-out between the two countries, the international scheme has gone to naught, and the only construction project so far realized is the Zeya Dam and hydroelectric plant on the Zeya River, a left-bank tributary of the Amur. This is one of the worst flooding streams in the region, and the dam will greatly alleviate flood damage in the agriculturally settled Zeya Plain to the south. In 1976 a similar dam of a somewhat smaller scale was under construction on the Bureya River just to the east. Additional construction works have been projected for these two streams.

In western Yakutia, the Vilyuy Hydroelectric Plant was established on the Vilyuy River near the settlement of Chernyshevskiy to provide power to the diamond mines around the town of Mirnyy. This has created an extensive reservoir on the upper Vilyuy and its main right-bank tributary, the Chona. Another hydroelectric project has created a sizeable reservoir on the Khantayka River in the far north near the lower reaches of the Yenisey to supply power to the Norilsk mining and processing area. The Khantayka Reservoir has added to the natural finger lakes that occupy the glacial valleys along the western slopes of the Putorana Mountains in the northwestern portion of the Central Siberian Upland.

The Caucasus

Many small hydroelectric stations have been established on streams in the Caucasus where steep gradients and consistent flows from melting glaciers and mountain snows provide ideal conditions for development of hydroelectric power even on small streams. But, again, most of these construction projects have not altered the landscape over extensive areas. On the North Caucasian plain reservoirs on the Kuban and Turek Rivers have provided for extensive areas of irrigation. In the Transcaucasus the outstanding multipurpose projects are the Mingechaur Reservoir on the Kura River and the Sevan-Razdan Cascade already mentioned in Chapter 10 in conjunction with power generation. (Table 10–12)

The Sevan-Razdan Cascade was conceived during the 1930s to provide hydroelectricity, irrigation, and domestic water supplies to the Razdan Valley including the basin around Yerevan, the capital of the Armenian Republic. The plan envisioned draining down the lake and eliminating the shallower southeastern portion of the lake to reduce the loss of water through evaporation which accounted for 92 per cent of the outgo. After completing a tunnel through a low mountain range at the western end of the lake to increase outflow and constructing six small power stations along the river totaling a generating capacity of 600,000 kilowatts, the project was dropped in 1961 on two grounds: (1) the retreating shoreline of the lake exposed bottom sediments that were not as easy to cultivate as had been originally anticipated and the drop in the water table intensified erosion of the surrounding mountain slopes, and (2) the availability of natural gas piped into the area ended the Armenian Republic's dependence on hydroelectric power. Subsequently it has been decided that only enough water will be drained through the hydroelectric plants to serve the needs of irrigation. The water withdrawal from the lake has been reduced from a maximum of 1750 million cubic meters in 1962 to 400–500 million at present. This has reduced electrical generation along the cascade from a peak of 2500 billion kilowatt-hours in 1961 to only 1 billion at the present time. An effort is now being made to raise the water level of the lake part of the way back up to its original level by driving a 50-kilometer-long tunnel through the mountains at the south end of the lake in order to divert some of the water from the Arpa River from its normal southward flowing course northward into the lake.

Central Asia and Kazakhstan

In dry Central Asia and Kazakhstan, many construction projects have been completed to provide irrigation water for broad areas. (Fig. 9–1) Most of these are single-purpose projects, but some of them have hydroelectric purposes as well. This is particularly true of major streams that head in the high mountains. On the plains the streams are too shifting in unconsolidated sediments and the flows are too uncertain for hydroelectric plants. The primary streams for power generation are the Vakhsh River in southwestern Tadzhikistan, the Naryn River in the Kirgiz Republic, the Chirchik River northeast of Tashkent, and the Ili River in southeastern Kazakhstan. (Table 10–12)

The most extensive reservoirs have been created by the Kapchagay installation on the Ili River, the Chardara installation of the Syr Darya downstream from the Hungry Steppe west of Tashkent, the Kayrak-Kum project on the Syr Darya at the western end of the Fergana Basin which formed the so-called Tadzhik Sea, and the Toktogul installation on the Naryn River upstream from the Fergana Basin.

Huge main canal systems and thousands of feeder canals have been created to irrigate large sections of intermontane basins and foothill areas, as was elaborated in Chapter 9. Most notable is the Kara-Kum Canal, the most extensive in the world, which stretches for 900 kilometers along the southern fringes of the Kara-Kum desert in the Turkmen Republic. The canal was completed from Kerki on the upper Amu Darya to Ashkhabad in 1962, and an extension toward the northwest is apparently under construction. Plans are that eventually this will be extended all the way to Krasnovodsk on the east shore of the Caspian with a branch running southward to the Atrek River along the international boundary with Iran.

The Kara-Kum runs through the old irrigated oases around Mary on the Murgab River and Tedzhen on the Tedzhen River and supplements the water from these two small streams.

Other major canals circle the Fergana Basin. The Great Fergana Canal was built during the 1930s and became one of the three great construction projects in the country at that time, along with the Dnieper Dam and the Magnitogorsk steel plant, on which young volunteers were used during their spare time on weekends without pay. Later the North Fergana Canal, Andizhan Canal, and Namangan Canal were completed in the basin.

In northeastern Kazakhstan the Bukhtarma and Ust-Kamenogorsk Dams create two reservoirs on the upper Irtysh River. The Bukhtarma Dam raised the water 67 meters and backed it up the Irtysh 600 kilometers to create the Large Irtysh Sea, which engulfed Lake Zaysan and raised its water level six meters. Recently a dam has been constructed at Yermak about 30 kilometers south of Pavlodar to provide water for the Irtysh-Karaganda Canal which has recently been constructed to supply water to the growing industries in central Kazakhstan. It will also provide irrigation water along the way. The canal runs southwestward for 480 kilometers and utilizes 23 pumping stations to raise the water to an elevation of 520 meters at the divide between the headwaters of the Shiderty River and the Karaganda area. Work has begun on a 480-kilometer extension westward to the copper mining complex of Dzhezkazgan. Eventually this canal may serve as the initial stage of a longer system to divert water from the upper Irtysh and other rivers of Western Siberia to central Kazakhstan. The Kulunda Steppe Canal now being constructed westward from the Ob River at Kamen might eventually be extended to Pavlodar on the Irtysh so that Ob River water can be added to the flow of the Irtysh-Karaganda Canal.

Large areas (about 6 million hectares in 1975) have been brought under irrigation in Central Asia and southern Kazakhstan by the projects that have just been mentioned and by

many other water construction projects too numerous to mention. This has transformed large sections of the desert floor, particularly the loess-covered foothills where soils are better and sources of mountain water are nearer. In addition to the beneficial effects of raising crops, there have been some harmful effects such as secondary salinization over broad areas. Two extensive brackish lakes have been formed by the drainage of excess irrigation water into low spots west of major irrigation districts. One of these lies in the Arnasay Depression to the west of the Hungry Steppe southwest of Tashkent and stretches for more than 150 kilometers east-west. The other has gathered in the Sarykamysh Depression west of the Khorezm oasis along the lower Amu Darya. Together these cover an area that averages about 1500 square kilometers and evaporate about 2.6 cubic kilometers of water per year.[1] In addition, considerable seepage has taken place from certain sections of the Kara-Kum Canal that has created a ridge in the rising water table next to the canal and swampy saline water conditions farther away from the canal.

MAJOR WATER PROBLEMS

From the foregoing discussions it can be surmised that the basic problem of water resources in the Soviet Union is the surplus in the north and the deficit in the south. The four great rivers, Yenisey, Lena, Ob, and Amur carry 44 per cent of all the fresh water. Thus, the water is concentrated in few large streams and needs to be dispersed more widely, and most of these large streams flow through sparsely populated or empty areas. The southern part of the country where 80 per cent of the population and industrial and agricultural production are located has only 14 per cent of all the river water and 80 per cent of this is concentrated in 11 rivers: the Volga, Dnieper, Dniester, Don, Kuban, Ural, Terek, Sulak, Kura, Amu Darya, and Syr Darya. Thus,

[1] Micklin, 1978, p. 19.

while the south generally has moisture deficits, it also suffers from over concentration in few streams.

Water construction projects created thus far include 205 large reservoirs with a combined capacity of 400 cubic kilometers for regulating river runoff. 90 of these reservoirs, whose effective capacity totals 361 cubic kilometers, have been built in conjunction with hydropower stations. This huge volume of storage increases the low base runoff by 20–25 per cent. A total length of 3740 kilometers of interbasin canals provide for transfers of river runoff. Hundreds of thousands of other canals have been built for irrigation purposes. The Aral Sea basin alone, which includes most of Central Asia and southern Kazakhstan where about 50 per cent of the country's irrigated lands are located, has more than 250,000 kilometers of irrigation canals and 90,000 kilometers of drainage canals to carry off salinated excess irrigation water.

But all of these construction works are still not sufficient to bring together adequately water sources and water needs. Most of the construction projects so far have been built to utilize local water resources for local needs. Those interbasin transfers that have been completed so far, such as the Amu-Bukhara and Zeravshan-Kashka Darya transfers in Central Asia, are of local scale also, as is even the largest artificial river in the world, the Kara-Kum Canal. What will be needed in the future to correct the mistakes of nature are much larger interbasin diversion projects to transport massive volumes of water from the water abundant areas of the north to the water deficit areas of the south.

The problem centers around three drainage basins, the Azov, Caspian, and Aral seas, all of which have been experiencing rapid drops in water level and deterioration of water quality as their drainage basins have become more economically developed. Many of their problems are similar to each other, and solutions for each ultimately involve the others in a single water economy system ("SWES"). But at present the Sea of Azov is most critical, although the Caspian has received more publicity.

The Azov Sea Basin

The severity of the Azov Sea problem stems from two facts: (1) the Azov drainage basin, which consists of a watershed of more than 500,000 square kilometers in area, contains about one-sixth of the Soviet population and the most polluted region in the entire country, the Donets coal basin with its heavy metallurgy and chemical industries, and (2) the Azov Sea is small and shallow and located in a droughty region. With a surface area of 38,000 square kilometers it has a volume of only 320 cubic kilometers, which indicates that its average depth is only 8.5 meters. Although about two dozen short rivers drain into the sea, the only two of much consequence are the Don and Kuban, both of which are now being heavily used for irrigation and other purposes.

Prior to 1952 when the Tsymlyansk Reservoir on the Don River was completed, the annual inflow to the sea amounted to about 41 cubic kilometers which was barely enough to give the sea a positive water balance so that there was a little outflow through the Kerch Strait into the Black Sea. But since that time water consumption in the Azov basin has risen to 23 cubic kilometers annually with an irreversible consumption of about 15 kilometers, so that the inflow into the Sea of Azov has dropped precipitously to 22 cubic kilometers in 1975. Most of this decrease in inflow has taken place since 1970. As the inflow has diminished, the water balance in the sea has changed from positive to negative which has reversed the flow through the Kerch Strait, and now saltier and, in summer, colder Black Sea water enters the Sea of Azov. At present about 60 million tons of salt move from the Black Sea to the Sea of Azov annually. Consequently, the average salinity of the Sea of Azov has climbed from a long-term average of about 10.5 parts per thousand to 13.8 parts per thousand in 1976. In the Don estuary, one of the more important fish spawning grounds, salinity has risen from 6.5 parts per thousand to 10 parts per thousand. The colder water from the Black Sea has settled beneath the warmer water of the Sea of Azov and produced extreme vertical stability in the water which has reduced mixing and accelerated sedimentation of suspended organics which has enlarged the bacterial population on the bottom of the sea by several orders of magnitude and greatly increased the biochemical oxygen demand (BOD).

The high tropic status of the Azov Sea and its partial oxygen starvation has caused periodic appearances of toxic products which have been very detrimental to the rich fish population. The Azov Sea, with its high influx of nutrients from intensively farmed land in its drainage basin, has always been characterized by a high density of fish population but low numbers of species. The limited number of species that are adaptable to changing salt, oxygen, and toxic conditions explains why the biotic system in the Sea of Azov is so vulnerable to change. The deterioration of the oxygen regime has also decreased the potential for self purification from organic pollutants. And the rise in salinity appears to be in inverse relation to the decay rate for oil products, detergents, and pesticides.

Increasing salinity in the Sea of Azov has induced the immigration of Black Sea and Mediterranean types of fish including the harmful stinging Black Sea jellyfish whose biomass in the Sea of Azov now exceeds eight million metric tons. Wherever they compete with fish for food the jellyfish gain dominance. As a consequence, the breeding and feeding grounds of valuable commercial species have diminished. This has been reflected in a rapid decrease of annual commercial fish catch. According to past records, the Sea of Azov should produce 90–100,000 tons of fish per year. Instead, the 1975 catch was only 5700 tons. In addition to the damage done by salinification, dam construction along the Don and Kuban Rivers have destroyed spawning beds, reduced the flow of waterborn nutrients to the sea, and altered temperature regimes in the rivers where fish normally spawn.

Since water consumption in the Azov Sea basin can only be postulated to increase with increasing development of industry and agriculture, the plight of the Sea of Azov can only be projected to deteriorate even farther left to its own devices. Consequently, two solutions have been offered: (1) the addition of about 30 cubic kilometers per year of fresh water to the inflow of the sea, which would have to be brought in from northern rivers via the Volga-Don system. (The magnitude of this transfer is based on the assumption that by the year 2010 the yearly influx of river water into the Sea of Azov from its own drainage basin will be reduced to approximately 10 cubic kilometers per year because of increased water consumption in the farms and cities of the drainage basin.) Soviet planners have not elaborated how northern waters coming down the Volga would be transmitted to the Don River. This would be a major fete, since the divide between the two rivers lies about 90 meters above the level of the Volga which at the entrance to the canal is approximately at sea level. Obviously such a transfer of water would require expensive pumping. The Soviets have not faced up to this hurdle yet because a transfer of such magnitude from the north to the Don Basin at present seems unlikely in light of the extreme need for this fresh water elsewhere. This will be elaborated later. (2) The alternative suggestion has been the construction of a long dam across the Kerch Strait to regulate the exchange of water between the Black and Azov Seas. The proposed dam would be 5.2 kilometers long and consist of an earthen spillway composed of 40 million cubic meters of land fill and a million cubic meters of reinforced concrete. 46 sluice gates, each 14 × 8 meters, would regulate the flow of salt water from the Black Sea into the Azov and would allow for the migration of fish between the two seas. Two locks for ocean-going river and fishing vessels would provide for passage through the dam, and railroad and highway shortcuts from the North Caucasus to the Crimea would be built on the crest of the dam.

In the early 1970s the dam project seemed to be the only feasible solution to the immediate deterioration of the Azov Sea, but now closer scrutiny of basic facts regarding the relative salinities of the Black and Azov Seas and the rate of influx of water from various sources indicates that perhaps the dam would not be the solution after all. Assuming a continuation of the present average annual river influx of 22 cubic kilometers until the completion of the dam, supposedly around 1985, and thereafter some improvement in inflow as a result of more efficient water use in the drainage basin, the dam structure might ultimately achieve the goal of reducing the salinity of the Azov Sea back down to around 10 parts per thousand. But this would take about 50 years! And, in fact, probably the natural inflow to the sea would diminish in the years that the dam is being constructed, so that the goal would never be reached. In addition to the salt problem, the dam might serve as a giant stopper plugging some very dirty water that is coming in from such rivers as the Don and Donets whose basins are plagued with the worst soil erosion in the country.

The Caspian Sea Problem

Practically everything that has been said about the Sea of Azov can be multiplied several times for the Caspian Sea, although the deterioration of the entire sea is not so imminent since the Caspian has an incomparably larger volume of water than does the Sea of Azov. However the shallow northern end of the sea has been experiencing problems similar to those of the Azov Sea for a much longer time than the Azov Sea has, and the Caspian problem in the past has attracted much more attention.

Long-term sea level changes in the Caspian apparently are part of its natural regime, perhaps due to long-term climatic fluctuations in the basin of the Volga River, which supplies 80 per cent of the inflow to the sea, or even to tectonic movements on the sea floor which in its southern portion lies in a very tectonically active area. Old shorelines of the sea extending as far northward as Saratov and beyond attest to the fact that at times in the past the water level in the Caspian has been much higher, and in fact during the Pleistocene rose above sea level and spilled northwestward through the Manych Depression to the Sea of Azov and the

world's oceans. Now the water level in the Caspian stands at about 28 meters below sea level. On the other hand, many ancient sea terraces lie beneath the present water surface, and skin divers have found foundations of walls of drowned ancient cities and have brought up many pieces of glazed dishes, jugs, coins, and small ornaments. All these attest that at times the Caspian has had a water level much below that of the present. Thus, the Caspian level has fluctuated up and down drastically under natural forces of magnitudes that might rule vain any attempts by the Soviets to regulate the level of the water.

However, the Soviets are concerned about the more recent short-term severe fall in water level, which since 1929 has amounted to about 3 meters, and which at present seems to be going on at a rate of about 6 centimeters per year. It has been estimated that during the last half century evaporation from the Caspian has exceeded inflow by an annual amount of about 26 cubic kilometers. During the early stages of this period the drop in water level was undoubtedly due primarily to a trend toward drier climate in the Volga basin, but since the mid 1950s much of the fall has been caused by man-made constructions. The huge reservoirs created in the Volga basin provide much larger evaporation surfaces than the original river did. It has been calculated that additional evaporation losses amount to 7–8 cubic kilometers per year even after one accounts for the fact that evaporation from reservoirs in the humid northern parts of the basin is less than the transpiration losses typical for those areas before they were submerged. Also, a great deal of water has been drawn off for irrigation as well as for rapidly increasing domestic and industrial uses in the burgeoning cities along the streams. Such uses can only be forecasted to increase.

The reduction of inflow and drop of water level in the Caspian has caused great harm to the fishing industry which is situated primarily in the shallow northern end where the water surface has shrunk about 25 per cent over the last four decades, the salinity has increased by about 30 per cent, and pollution has increased from soil erosion and domestic, industrial, and agricultural wastes. The large Volgograd Dam has kept many of the fish from migrating upstream to spawn in spite of the fact that a fish ladder has been provided. The fishing industry in the north Caspian has been so important because it accounts for about 90 per cent of the world's sturgeon catch which, among other things, is the source of Beluga caviar.

Shipping has also suffered because of the drop in water level. This is particularly true in the shallow northern end where the Volga-Caspian Canal has had to be dredged repeatedly as the shoreline has receded southward and ports such as Astrakhan have been left farther inland. In addition, port facilities everywhere around the sea have had to be relocated continuously to lower levels.

Sulfate extraction based on the brines of Kara-Bogaz-Gol has suffered also because of the Caspian drop as diminished flow into the gulf has led to increased salinity and resultant precipitation of unwanted salts along with the desired mirabilite. This has forced the industry to turn from salt deposits occurring naturally along the shore to more costly buried brines.

Although the dropping sea level has perhaps made underwater exploitation of oil around Baku a little easier, the pollution of water by oil seeps in the area plus leaks from oil tankers going across the sea has become even more severe in imbayments which are constantly becoming shallower.

Remedies for the falling level of the Caspian Sea have been discussed in all-Union conferences and other meetings especially called to consider the Caspian Sea problem since the early 1930s. Initially it was tacitly assumed that it was desirable to raise the Caspian back up to the level it had in 1929 or before. But as discussion progressed it became obvious that it would be neither feasible nor desirable to work toward this goal since it would require an unwarranted addition of water to the Caspian and would necessitate the relocation once more of all facilities around the Caspian. In recent years discussion has centered more on the possibility of stabilizing the Caspian at some level, perhaps lower than it has now, and, on the disposition of fresh water if it is brought in from the north. Perhaps it would be wiser to use it for irrigation in the North Caspian Lowland where the value of crops raised might far exceed the benefits realized from fisheries improved by dumping the fresh water into the Caspian.

Schemes to regulate the level of the Caspian have fallen under two groups: (1) measures taken within the Caspian Sea itself, and (2) importation of additional water, either from the European North, Siberia, or the Sea of Azov. All of these schemes are grandiose in scope and would be very costly and time-consuming to achieve. Within the Caspian Sea, it has been suggested that a 375-kilometer-long earth-and-rock dike be built to separate the shallow northern end from the rest of the sea, and thereby allow water to accumulate in the north and maintain that end of the sea at a higher level than the rest of the sea. A less ambitious scheme is to block off Kara-Bogaz-Gol on the eastern side of the Caspian, which is one of the main evaporating surfaces for the Caspian, thereby preventing approximately four cubic kilometers of evaporation each year. Also, it has been suggested that the northeastern part of the Caspian be blocked off. It is estimated that this would save about 37 cubic kilometers from being evaporated each year.

The suggestion to divert water from the head of the Sea of Azov through the Manych Depression to the Caspian would necessitate pumping over a 28-meter divide and might serve the purpose of stabilizing the level of the Caspian, but it would run into the problem of further salinization of the northern Caspian as well as the necessity to do something to stabilize salinity conditions in the Sea of Azov. Thus, it does not seem to be a plan that can realistically be discussed without consideration of auxiliary major diversion projects.

The other alternative, bringing in fresh water from the north via the Volga system, either from northern European Russia or Siberia, seems to hold the most promise in the long run, but this involves a huge system of interconnecting reservoirs and canals that would be exceedingly expensive to construct and gets into all sorts of environmental problems, particularly in the northern regions from which the water is to be derived. These will be discussed in a later section.

At present it seems that the most imminent thing that might be done for the Caspian is to close off Kara-Bogaz-Gol and thereby reduce some of the evaporation from the Caspian.

The Aral Sea Basin

Since 1961 the level of the Aral Sea has lowered by about three meters, and the sea is experiencing deterioration similar to that which is taking place in the Azov and Caspian Seas. However, unlike the Caspian, which has a huge volume of water, and the Azov Sea, which is connected to the world's oceans, the Aral Sea faces the very immediate prospect of drying up completely. Its average depth is only 16 meters, and the present volume is around 1000 cubic kilometers. If current trends are not reversed soon the lake could dry up within the next couple of decades, or at least be reduced to a salty stagnant pool along the deeper western side of the basin. The sea is maintained by the two largest rivers of Central Asia, the Amu Darya and the Syr Darya, and as more and more of their water has been devoted to irrigation and domestic and industrial uses of cities, less water has been available to feed the lake.

Since there is not nearly enough water in Central Asia and Kazakhstan to develop fully the agricultural land available and serve the needs of the rapidly growing population and expanding urban economy, it appears that the preservation of the Aral Sea in its present form must be given a low priority. At the present time about 6–7 million hectares of land are irrigated in Central Asia and southern Kazakhstan, and it has been estimated that at least 50 million additional hectares of land are suitable for irrigation if enough water can be found. Such an expansion would require about 300–400 cubic kilometers of water per year, and the total runoff of streams in Central Asia and southern Kazakhstan amounts to only

about 117 cubic kilometers per year. Therefore, it is obvious that to realize the potentials of this area huge quantities of water are needed, and many uses will take precedence over the preservation of the Aral Sea, as well as many other smaller water bodies in the area. Lake Balkhash, for instance, presents various problems, which might be partially solved by cutting the lake in two and allowing the eastern end to dry up. The only alternative that seems to come anywhere near solving the water needs of this region seems to be the massive diversion of water southward from the Ob and Yenisey river systems in Siberia. This will be discussed, along with other diversion schemes, in the next section.

INTERBASIN TRANSFERS OF WATER

For a long time the Soviets have been looking longingly to the cool, humid northern slope of European Russia and Siberia for additional water supplies to bring to the dry southern slope. But all projects involve such massive construction works and such complex environmental problems that none have come to fruition yet and none are even on the final drawing boards. Nevertheless, as time has gone on and more and more thought has been given to the subject, ideas have become more focused and some general guidelines have evolved.

In initial stages of the thought process little concern was expressed for effects that diversion projects might have on donor regions of the north which were sparsely settled and looked upon as undevelopable areas. Almost all attention was centered on how to get the water southward and how to use it once it was there. Construction projects in the north were conceived as consisting of a relatively simple pattern of large dams that would impound immense reservoirs on such rivers as the Pechora and Vychegda in the European North and the middle Ob in Western Siberia. But now planners pretty much agree that they can no longer afford to flood large tracts of floodplain land that represent about the only land suitable for pastures and rudimentary cultivation in these remote areas of the country. In addition, it is now understood that large reservoirs in cool, swampy regions such as the European north and Western Siberia would cause even more waterlogging in wide surrounding areas. It has been pointed out that already the West Siberian plain is the world's largest swamp and that under natural conditions the swamps have been expanding at a fairly rapid rate ever since the Pleistocene period. Any construction of extensive shallow reservoirs in this area would greatly accelerate this process. What should be done is to reverse the trend by pumping water out of rivers and thereby divert some of the flow southward without the use of reservoirs.

The following general principles have pretty much been agreed upon: (1) North-south transfers of water should be so designed as to benefit both the northern region from which the water is withdrawn and the southern region where water resources are to be enhanced. (2) Noneconomic criteria, such as environmental impacts of water transfers, esthetics, and recreation, should be given as much attention as economic and engineering criteria. (3) It has been the experience that each transformation introduces new problems which then must be tackled after the fact. For instance, fisheries generally have not been provided for adequately. After the dams have been built and the damage done, then half-hearted attempts have been made to remedy the situation. Everything should be anticipated about 20 years ahead of time so that preventative measures can be taken at the time of the initial construction. This would be much cheaper and would avoid the initial deterioration of environmental factors and consequent losses of economic activity. Provision must be made for periodic controlled flooding to flush out pollution along streams, particularly in their delta areas and along shorelines of recipient seas. (4) Any program of interbasin transfers of water should be accompanied by a program of intensification of water use. Wherever possible, more subtle means of enhancing local water supplies should be utilized before huge construction projects are undertaken. (5)

Smaller, short-term construction projects that can be added to sequentially should be preferred over grandiose single-stage projects that commit one to huge investments over long periods of time that must be carried through to their ultimate conclusions even though at some intermediate stage it might become evident that the course of action should follow a different direction. In other words, there must be flexibility in plans. Since most of these projects are so large that their completion requires decades, one must not be locked into a single course of action. (6) It is generally agreed that the next stage of water resource development must be the interbasin transfer of water. Most of the rivers of Europe have been developed to their fullest, and most of the usable water resources in Central Asia and Kazakhstan are now being utilized. The next logical stage is the correction of the mistakes of nature to bring the water where it is needed. This represents a quantum jump in scale and complexity over previous construction works. Imminent disaster, perhaps of an irreversible nature, in such water bodies as the Azov, Caspian, and Aral Seas prompt the necessity to put into actual effect some of these diversion projects now.

Over the years so many different projects and different variants of the same projects have been proposed that it is hardly worth outlining them in detail until firmer plans have been announced. Detailed analyses of various plans during various stages of their development can be read in the literature cited at the end of this chapter. At the present time it appears that there are tentative agreements on several major projects that are now being elaborated in various preparatory stages by various design agencies. Plans still include a large number of possible alternative courses of action. Figure 14–5 schematically illustrates what intentions are.

In recent years there has evolved a so-called "Northwestern Project" that calls for the transfer of 31 cubic kilometers of water per year from the Sukhona and Onega Rivers and Lake Onega into the Rybinsk Reservoir and down the Volga. Although this is a relative newcomer among projects, it appears most feasible for the

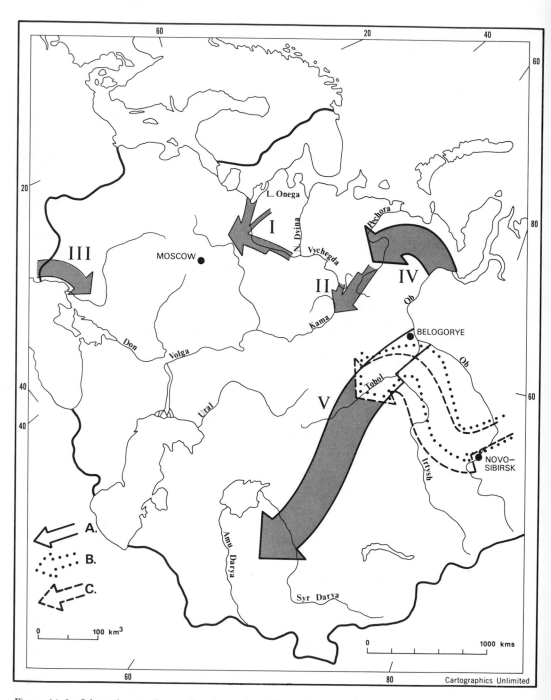

Figure 14–5   Schematic map of water diversion projects. Width of arrow proportional to volume of transfer. I Northwest Project, II Northeast, III Danube to southern Ukraine, IV Lower Ob to Pechora-Kama, V Western Siberia to Kazakhstan and Central Asia. A. From Tobol Reservoir and Ob River at Belogorye. B. From Tom and Chulym Rivers and Novosibirsk Reservoir. C. From both A and B. After Lvovich, 1977, p. 560.

immediate future since it involves smaller construction works and less disruption of donor streams. It would also feed water into the Volga hydroelectric cascade at a point far up the Volga where it could benefit most of the plants already on the Volga.

In the northeastern part of European Russia there is the long-standing proposal to divert water from the Pechora and Vychegda Rivers to the Kama and down the Volga. But the details of this scheme have been changed greatly since it was first proposed. Instead of a huge reservoir on the Pechora-Vychegda-Kama divide equal in area approximately to Lake Ladogda, the largest fresh water lake in European Russia, the scheme now envisions smaller dams at various places, perhaps limited to the Pechora River, with much reduced reservoirs, in order to preserve floodplain agricultural lands and reduce waterlogging in surrounding areas. This would necessitate more pumping to get the water over the divide to the Kama River, but would avoid many objections from local residents in the north. The northeast diversion project is probably second most feasible after the northwest. Initially about 34 cubic kilometers per year could be diverted from this northeastern system, and a second stage could add another 20 cubic kilometers.

Eventually the diversion from the Pechora might be added to greatly by a diversion from the lower Ob westward along the flat Arctic coastal plain around the northern end of the Urals. This is a relatively new idea which is part of a group of somewhat smaller schemes than the original Ob scheme to form a huge reservoir in Western Siberia and divert all the water southward through the Turgay Gate into Central Asia. By diverting water from the lower Ob into the Volga system great quantities of Ob River water would be made available in the lower Volga to be dispensed to the drainage basins of the Caspian, the Azov, and the Aral Seas, using the Volgograd Reservoir as the monitoring waterbody. These choices would add much flexibility to the system allowing it to adjust to needs that vary from year-to-year according to the weather in different areas. The Volga-Ural Canal which is now

under construction could be the beginning of a canal system that could lead water eastward into south-central Kazakhstan.

It is even envisioned that in the long run Ob water might be brought via the Volga system as far west as the Dnieper River which eventually is going to need additional water. However, an alternative to this could be a diversion eastward of water from the lower reaches of the Danube which flows through the Soviet Union. About 30 cubic kilometers per year might be channeled across the lower courses of the Dniester and Southern Bug Rivers to the Dnieper. This, again, is a relatively new idea, and details for it have not been worked out. But it appears that diversion of Danube water eastward to the Dnieper might be more economically feasible than diversion of Ob water westward through the Volga and Volga-Don Canal system.

The grandest scheme of all, and probably the one that will be left to last, is the southward diversion of Ob River water through the Turgay Trough into the Aral Sea basin. There are many variants that have been proposed for the southward diversion of Ob water. These have been boiled down now to about three alternative projects. They all involve a trunk canal running almost due north-south through the Turgay Trough toward the interfluve between the Syr Darya and Amu Darya rivers. The length of the canal would be 2000–2500 kilometers and its annual stream flow would be roughly equivalent to that of the Dnieper River!

The different variants involve the way that the water is to be diverted from the Ob and its tributaries. One variant envisions the withdrawal of water from the lower reaches of the Irtysh, the Tobol, and the Ob below the confluence with the Irtysh at Belogorye. A second variant envisions the withdrawal of water from the Chulym and Tom Rivers farther east as well as from the Novosibirsk Reservoir on the Ob, with a westward transfer of the water through a canal to a proposed reservoir on the Irtysh and onward by canal to Kurgan, from whence it would be diverted southward through the Turgay Trough. The third alternative combines the first two with the withdrawal of water from the Novosibirsk Reservoir on the Ob River and transfer by canal to a reservoir on the Irtysh as well as withdrawal from a proposed reservoir on the Tobol River.

In all variants, reservoirs would be kept to minimum sizes and much pumping would be substituted for some gravity flow that might be derived from larger reservoirs. In the first stage of development it is assumed that about 25 cubic kilometers might be diverted from the Ob system and during a subsequent stage about 60 cubic kilometers, for a total of 85 cubic kilometers. This is a much reduced estimate over the initial plan which called for a Caspian-sized reservoir in the middle Ob Basin with a Volga-sized canal flowing through the Turgay Trough. In the distant future there is a possibility that Yenisey water might be brought into the Ob system to augment the flow southward, but this is very conjectural.

At the south end of the Turgay canal there are a multitude of variants for the dispersal of water for various uses. One would be a canal southwestward to the Iranian border near the southeastern end of the Caspian Sea. This would provide additional water for the lower Syr-Darya and Amu-Darya as well as for various spots through the Kara-Kum Desert, augment the flow of the Kara-Kum Canal between Ashkhabad and the Caspian, and supply water to the sheltered Atrek River valley along the Iranian border. It would also provide an all-water route from the Caspian northward through Central Asia, Kazakhstan, and Western Siberia to the Arctic. Branch canals could lead off from this major canal southeastward to the Tashkent area and the Zeravshan Valley.

Another major variant is a canal that takes off to the southeast from the Turgay Trough and brings water into the oases along the northern slopes of the Tien Shan south of Lake Balkhash as far east as the Ili River near Alma Ata. Still a third variant is a canal that loops southwestward from the Turgay Trough toward the north end of the Aral Sea and then proceeds northwestward to the Ural River area. Branch canals would go southwestward into the lowlands along the northeastern edge

of the Ustyurt Plateau. The most westerly canal would extend into the Mangyshlak oil producing area.

ALTERNATIVE REMEDIES OF A MORE SUBTLE NATURE

In recent years Soviet hydrologists, apparently becoming more sensitive to the tremendous cost of grandiose projects and the environmental disruptions they might cause, have been calling more and more for different parts of the country to draw upon their own resources, to utilize water more efficiently, and to cut back on its use in general. In the cities they are calling for industrial recycling of water and the conversion to completely dry processes in plants where that is feasible. They are urging the population to conserve water in their households. In the countryside, farms for a number of years now have been doing such things as cutting the grain high to leave tall stubble on the fields to hold snow in place and keep it from blowing into huge drifts in certain parts of fields, fall plowing which will allow more of the spring meltwaters to seep into the soil and convert useless or damaging runoff to valuable subsurface water for summer use, digging of millions of small ponds, particularly in the steppe zone to impound water in place on all the little gullies which will further enhance seepage into the soil and provide the basis for a large fish farming operation, and planting of thousands of kilometers of shelter belts.

The Soviets have done an admirable job of planting trees, in the cities as well as in the countryside. They line every street and road, and in the drier zones of the south they have generally been planted along all field margins. In the steppe lands they have been planted primarily to reduce the effects of the wind, thereby conserving moisture and preventing soil deflation, but everywhere trees have added to the esthetics of the land and have benefited the microclimate by aiding in the purification of pollutants and the transpiration of moisture. It has been found that they are most effective if planted in rectangular plots around the edges of all fields, but in some of the drier zones broad expanses of shelterbelts have been run across many kilometers of countryside perpendicular to the prevailing wind systems, regardless of the pattern of farmland. Where the climate is too dry to grow trees without the aid of irrigation, shelterbelts have been planted on all the canal systems of irrigation projects as well as along field boundaries. Although it would seem that all these trees would use a lot of irrigation water, it appears that the Soviets believe that the resultant transformation of the microclimate over the fields, the reduction of surface temperatures, increase of atmospheric humidity in the lower layers, and the reduction of back radiation and reflection of heat from the earth's surface, more than offset the use of the water by the trees themselves.

The reduction of useless heat loss from the earth's surface through back radiation and reflection is an important by-product of many of the measures taken to improve the water balance. In general heat is in as short supply for agricultural purposes as moisture is, and in many cases has been a limiting factor on the selection of crops before the moisture balance comes into play. Even in the southern parts of European U.S.S.R. summers are relatively cool and short, with only occasional hot spells, comparable more to southern Canada and the northern tier of states of the United States than to the corn belt of the Midwest. The conversion of a dry steppe or desert surface to a dry farmed or irrigated field surrounded by shelterbelts with attendent decreases in surface soil and air temperatures, increase in surface atmospheric humidity, and formation of a good vegetative cover act to reduce the albedo and terrestrial radiation and convert sensible heat into the latent heat of evaporation, primarily in the form of transpiration through plants. And the reduction of surface temperatures and increase of atmospheric humidities reduces the transpiration rate of each plant growing in the region so that water is utilized more conservatively per plant. Reduced rates of transpiration are generally beneficial to plants since only a little transpiration is needed to carry nutrients upward from the soil to feed the plants and

most transpiration serves only as a coolant to protect the plant under heat stress. If the plant is put under great heat stress, it is called upon to transpire more moisture from its leaves than it can take up through its roots and therefore must take on protective measures such as wilting which over prolonged periods of time are detrimental to its growth and ultimate production. Thus, the creation of an extensive irrigated oasis generally benefits all plants in the region, the more so the larger the irrigation area because of the increasing effect on the microclimate.

Not much has been said about drainage. But in the Soviet Union, as in many countries of the world, drainage is just as important or more so than irrigation. Roughly as much land has been drained in the northwestern parts of the country as have been irrigated in the southeast. (Fig. 9-1) And as much land still remains to be drained, as it does to be irrigated. Drainage systems generally are not as grandiose and obvious on the landscape as irrigation systems are, which require huge dams in rivers that form extensive reservoirs whose waters are led out through lengthy canal systems. But for the same monetary investment, drainage systems generally yield more results than irrigation systems. Drainage areas lie in cool, humid regions where large applications of fertilizers can yield large results without damaging crops, as might be the case in dry regions. The long-range plan now under way for agriculture has called for more development of the so-called "nonchernozem" zone of the European north. It has been pointed out that due to reduced transpiration rates in this region grain uses only one-third to one-half as much water for the same yield as it does in the steppe zone of the south. Therefore, whatever crops can be adapted to the north-central part of European Russia should be, and agriculture should be intensified in that region. With a better areal distribution of crops and a reduced dependency on the drought-ridden regions of the south, crop production in the Soviet Union might be increased and stabilized from year-to-year without any interbasin transfers of water. Hydrologists are now calling for every measure possible to be taken to utilize existing water resources better before interbasin transfers are attempted. Hence, interbasin transfer is now being looked upon as a last resort after every other measure has been exhausted.

Soviet hydrologists are calling for the complete utilization of water in the mountains of Central Asia and Transcaucasia in order to reduce the need for large transfers of water over long distances from the north. They point out that there are still large water reserves in the mountains of the southern regions which could be impounded behind dams in deep reservoirs with small surface areas in the mountains themselves rather than trying to impound the rivers on the plains as generally has been done in the past. Unitl these water resources are exhausted, along with huge reserves of ground water in such regions as south-central Kazakhstan and adjacent portions of Central Asia, water should not be brought in from the north.

Planners are paying more and more attention to ground water reserves and the improvement of these reserves through measures that have already been mentioned, such as snow retention and fall plowing which will convert surface runoff to ground water. It has been pointed out that during the middle and late summer periods when the rivers on the European plain are at their lowest ebb, it is the ground water table that determines the minimum flow, and it is the minimum flow on which plans must be predicated, for this is the only reliable base. It has already been mentioned that better farming methods have decreased the surface runoff in such streams as the Don River by as much as 15–20 per cent. This part of the surface runoff has largely been converted to subsurface reserves.

Desalination

The Soviets are looking to water desalination to provide fresh water in some of the arid regions of Central Asia and Kazakhstan, particularly along the eastern fringes of the Caspian where concentrations of industry have

developed, such as in the oil fields of Mangyshlak and Nebit Dag. By 1969 they had completed ten desalination plants in the Kazakh and Turkmen S.S.R.s with a total daily capacity of 54,800 cubic meters of fresh water. Five more installations were under construction with a combined capacity of 61,400 cubic meters. Most of the capacity so far has been installed in the cities of Krasnovodsk and Shevchenko. The first dual purpose nuclear power plant has been established in Shevchenko with an electrical capacity of 150,000 kilowatts and a daily water distillation capacity of 120,000 cubic meters. Even larger dual purpose plants have been projected for the cities of Zhdanov on the Azov coast of the Donets Basin and Sumgait north of Baku in Azerbaydzhan. How these plants are faring is not known. The Soviets predict that in the near future they can make desalination costs competitive with other means of bringing fresh water to remote areas of resource exploitation in such regions as Central Asia.

Reading List

1. Avakyan, A. B., "Some Problems in the Creation of Reservoirs in the USSR," *Soviet Geography: Review and Translation,* February 1973, pp. 117–124.
2. Averyanova, A. G., "The Volga Drainage Basin and Its Regional Water-Management Significance," *Vodnyye Resursy,* 1974, No. 6, pp. 17–28.
3. Azernikova, O. A., "The Water Balance of Lake Sevan based on New Data," *Soviet Geography: Review and Translation,* September 1976, pp. 456–467.
4. Bronfman, A. M., "The Azov Sea Water Economy and Ecological Problems: Investigation and Possible Solutions," in White, Gilbert F., *Environmental Effects of Complex River Development,* Westview, Boulder, 1977, pp. 39–58.
5. Bykov, V. D., and Kalinin, G. P., "The Prospects of Use and Preservation of the Water Resources of the USSR," *Vestnik Moskovskogo Universiteta, Seriia Geografiia,* September–October 1971, pp. 3–7.
6. Davydov, M. M., "The Water Resources of the Ob River Basin," *Soviet Geography: Review*

and Translation, November 1972, pp. 618–621.

7. Domanitskiy, A. P., Dubrovina, R. G., and Isayeva, A. I., *Reki i ozera Sovetskogo Soyuza* (Rivers and Lakes in the Soviet Union), Gidrometeoizdat, Leningrad, 1971, 104 pp.

8. Dreyer, N. N., "Water Resources of Major Economic Regions of the RSFSR and the Other Union Republics," *Soviet Geography: Review and Translation,* March 1969, pp. 137–144.

9. Editorial Board, *Vodnyy Resursy,* "The Future Water Supply for Moscow and Moscow Oblast," *Soviet Geography: Review and Translation,* May 1975, pp. 302–307.

10. Gabriyelyan, G. K., "The Future of Lake Sevan," *Geografiya v Shkole,* 1977, No. 2, pp. 14–15.

11. Gangardt, G. G., "On the Question of Diverting Part of the Unused Runoff of Northern and Siberian Rivers into Regions Suffering from a Shortage of Water Resources," *Soviet Geography: Review and Translation,* November 1972, pp. 622–628.

12. Gerasimov, I. P., and Gindin, A. M., "The Problem of Transferring Runoff from Northern and Siberian Rivers to the Arid Regions of the European USSR, Soviet Central Asia, and Kazakhstan," in White, Gilbert F., *Environmental Effects of Complex River Development,* Westview, Boulder, 1977, pp. 59–70.

13. Gerasimov, I. P., Vendrov, S. L., Zonn, S. V., Kes, A. S., Kuznetsov, N. T., and Neyshtadt, M. I., "Large-Scale Research and Engineering Programs for the Transformation of Nature in the Soviet Union and the Role of Geographers in their Implementation," *Soviet Geography: Review and Translation,* April 1976, pp. 235–245.

14. Gorodetskaya, M. Ye., "The Geomorphology of the Turgay Trough in Connection with the Problem of Diverting the Water of West Siberian Rivers to Central Asia," *Soviet Geography: Review and Translation,* November 1972, pp. 629–642.

15. Grin, A. M., and Koronkevich, N. I., "Principles of Construction of Long-Term Water Management Balances," *Soviet Geography: Review and Translation,* March 1969, pp. 118–136.

16. Kolodin, M. V., "Progress in Water Desalination Technology," *Soviet Geography: Review and Translation,* December 1970, pp. 858–864.

17. Korenistov, D. V., Kritskiy, S. N., Menkel, M. F., and Shimelmits, I. Ya., "The Aral Sea Problem," *Vodnyye resursy,* 1972, No. 1, pp. 138–162.

18. Kornilov, B. A., and Timoshkina, V. A., "The Impact of the Kara-Kum Canal on the Environment," *Soviet Geography: Review and Translation,* May 1975, pp. 308–314.

19. Kudritskiy, D. M., "The Morphometry of the Caspian Sea Based on Contemporary Data," *Soviet Geography: Review and Translation,* April 1978, pp. 265–273.

20. Kuznetsov, N. T., "Geographical Aspects of the Future of the Aral Sea," *Soviet Geography: Review and Translation,* March 1977, pp. 145–163.

21. ———, "Principles for Forecasting Environmental Change as a Result of the Drop of the Aral Sea Level," *Izvestiya akademii nauk SSSR, seriya geograficheskaya,* No. 5, 1977, pp. 41–47.

22. Lvovich, M. I., "Geographical Aspects of a Territorial Redistribution of Water Resources in the USSR," *Soviet Geography: Review and Translation,* October 1977, pp. 557–574.

23. ———, *Mirovyye vodnyye resursy i ikh budushcheye* (The World's Water Resources and Their Future), Mysl, Moscow, 1974.

24. ———, *Reki SSSR* (Rivers of the U.S.S.R), Nauka, Moscow, 1971.

25. ———, "Scientific Principles of the Complex Utilization and Conservation of Water Resources," *Soviet Geography: Review and Translation,* March 1969, pp. 95–118.

26. ———, ed., *Vodnyy balans SSSR i ego preobrazovanie* (The Water Balance of the U.S.S.R. and its Transformation), Nauka, Moscow, 1969, 338 pp.

27. Lvovich, M. I., and Chernogayeva, G. M., "Transformation of the Water Balance Within the City of Moscow," *Soviet Geography: Review and Translation,* May 1977, pp. 302–313.

28. Lvovich, M. I., and Tsigelnaya, I. D., "Control of the Aral Sea Water Balance," *Izvestiya Akademii Nauk SSSR, seriya geograficheskaya,* 1978, No. 1, pp. 42–54.

29. Micklin, Philip P., "Dimensions of the Caspian Sea Problem," *Soviet Geography: Review and Translation,* November 1972, pp. 589–598.

30. ———, "Environmental Costs of the Volga-Kama Cascade of Power Stations," *Water Resources Bulletin,* June 1974, pp. 565–572.

31. ———, "International Environmental Implications of Soviet Development of the Volga River," *Human Ecology,* June 1977, pp. 113–135.

32. ———, "Irrigation Development in the USSR During the 10th Five-Year Plan (1976–80)," *Soviet Geography: Review and Translation,* January 1978, pp. 1–25.

33. ———, "NAWAPA and Two Siberian Water-Diversion Proposals: A Geographical Comparison and Appraisal," *Soviet Geography: Review and Translation,* February 1977, pp. 81–99.

34. Minayeva, Ye. N., and Kuznetsov, N. T., "Changes in the Structure of Evaporation in the Aral Sea Basin," *Soviet Geography: Review and Translation,* December 1977, pp. 769–778.

35. Mote, Victor L., and ZumBrunnen, Craig, "Anthropogenic Environmental Alteration of the Sea of Azov," *Soviet Geography: Review and Translation,* December 1977, pp. 744–759.

36. Neyshtadt, D. I., "The Contemporary Swampiness of West Siberia and the Problems Likely to Arise if Streamflow is diverted from the Region and its Swamps are Reclaimed," *Izvestiya Akademii Nauk SSSR, seriya geograficheskaya,* No. 5, 1977, pp. 26–35.

37. Nikolskiy, I. V., Tonyaev, V. I., and Krasneninnikov, V. G., *Geografiya vodnogo transporta SSSR* (Geography of Water Transport in the U.S.S.R.), Transport, Moscow, 1975, 224 pp.

38. Pecherin, A. I., "On the Inadvisability of the Projected Dam Across Kerch Strait," *Soviet Geography: Review and Translation,* December 1977, pp. 760–763.

39. Petrov, G. N., "Hydrologic-geographical Study of Water Resources in the Middle Volga Basin," *Voprosy Geografii,* Vol. 102, 1976.

40. Saushkin, Yu. G., *Velikoye preobrazovaniye prirody SSSR* (The Great Transformation of Nature in the U.S.S.R.), Geografgiz, Moscow, 1952.

41. Selivanov, R. I., "The Mechanism of Development of the Volga Delta and Its Growth Prospects," *Soviet Geography: Review and Translation,* May 1978, pp. 333–344.

42. Vendrov, S. L., "Problems in the Spatial Redistribution of Streamflow," *Soviet Geography: Review and Translation,* June 1976, pp. 415–420.

43. ———, *Problemy preobrazovaniye rechnykh sistem* (Problems of Transformation of River Systems), Gidrometeoizdat, Leningrad, 1970.

44. Vendrov, S. L., and Avakyan, A. B., "The Volga River," in White, Gilbert F., ed., *Environmental Effects of Complex River Development,* Westview, Boulder, 1977, pp. 23–38.

45. Vendrov, S. L., and Dyakonov, K. N., *Storage Reservoirs and the Environment,* Nauka, Moscow, 1976.

46. Vendrov, S. L., and Glukh, I. S., "On Some Problems of Transformation of the Drainage Net in the Russian Plain," in *Voprozy priobrazovaniya prirody Russkoy ravniny* (Problems of Transformation of the natural environment of the Russian plain), Ak. Nauk, Institut Geol., Moscow, 1974.

47. *Vodnyye Resursy* (Water Resources), bimonthly journal begun in 1972. Contents listed in issues of *Soviet Geography: Review and Translation.*

48. Voznesenskiy, A. N., "Water, Its Resources and Consumption," *Vodnyye Resursy,* 1972, No. 1, pp. 3–14.

49. Voznesenskiy, A. N., Gangardt, G. G., and Gerardi, I. A., "Principal Trends and Prospects of the Use of Water Resources in the USSR," *Soviet Geography: Review and Translation,* May 1975, pp. 291–302.

50. Yegorov, A. N., Zybina, L. N., Ivanova, V. P., Istoshin, B. Yu., Podolskiy, Ye. M., Teodoronskaya, E. Ye., Frolov, A. Ye., Vukolova, T. P., and Fomicheva, Ye. N., "Marginal Cost Estimates of the Water Resources of the USSR," *Soviet Geography: Review and Translation,* June 1974, pp. 333–341.

51. Zektser, I. S., Kudelin, B. I., and Popov, O. V., "Study of Subsurface Water Resources in the USSR," *Vodnyye Resursy,* 1972, No. 1, pp. 42–51.

52. Zonn, S. V., "Problems of Land Development in the Southern Part of the Russian Plain in Conjunction with Interbasin Diversion," *Izvestiya Akademii Nauk SSSR, seriya geograficheskaya,* No. 5, 1977, pp. 36–40.

53. ZumBrunnen, Craig, "Water Pollution in the Black and Azov Seas," in Singleton, F., ed., *Environmental Misuse in the Soviet Union,* Praeger, New York, 1976, pp. 33–59.

15

Transportation and Domestic Trade

The transportation system is the lifeline of the economy in the Soviet Union, as it is in any country. It moves the traffic that is generated by a disparity between production and consumption in each locale, and is the critical factor in keeping materials supplied to industrial and agricultural concerns. The transportation system not only has the function of providing services to the general economy; its operations constitute a significant portion of that economy. The transport system of the U.S.S.R. regularly consumes about one fourth the fuel and steel production of the country and employs about eight percent of the labor.

Since the Soviet Union is such a huge country, commodities generally are moved longer distances, and freight traffic is therefore much greater than it is in any other country in the world. Much of this has been generated by economic development during the Soviet period. Total freight traffic on all carriers has increased from 126 billion ton-kilometers in 1913 to 5201 billion in 1975. It is now approximately 160 per cent that of the United States. This great amount of traffic in the Soviet Union is carried by a transport system that is significantly different from that of the United States and countries of Western Europe, and some understanding must be had of the underlying geographical factors and governmental policies controlling the system before it can be understood and appreciated.

NATURE OF THE SOVIET TRANSPORTATION SYSTEM

Since the transportation system of the Soviet Union is government-owned it is unusually closely integrated with the overall resources and investment policies of the total economy. Since the Soviet leadership looks upon transportation as a necessary evil to keep the economic machine turning and not a sector of the economy to be developed for its own sake, concerted efforts are made to limit investment in transportation, eliminate overlap and competition, and minimize traffic. This policy has resulted in an unusually heavy reliance on railroads for intercity movement of freight and passengers at the expense of other forms of transport such as automotive, which suffers from high line haul costs, or waterways which suffer from various physical disabilities that will be elaborated later. The broad plains of the U.S.S.R. are unusually favorable for the construction and low cost operation of railroads. 96 per cent of the total main track operated has ruling gradients of less than one per cent, 60 per cent of the line has gradients below 0.5 per cent, and 25 per cent of the lines are horizontal. Railroad operation is hampered to some extent by climate, extreme cold and snow in winter, and lack of water in the southern deserts, but the seasonality induced in railroad traffic by climatic factors is much less than that induced in the traffic of other carriers. And generally rail traffic moves more quickly and more directly to its destinations than does traffic on other carriers in this country where highways are poorly developed. Therefore, until the mid 1950s, railroads typically carried 80–85 per cent of the freight traffic of the country and 90 per cent or more of the passenger traffic. Since that time railroads' share has been decreasing as pipelines and the merchant marine have been developed to carry freight, buses have been introduced heavily in commuter traffic, and airlines have

been greatly expanded for intercity passenger transport. Nevertheless, in 1975, the railroads still carried 62 per cent of all the freight traffic and 42 per cent of all the passenger traffic. (Table 15–1 and 15–12) This is accomplished on a railroad trackage that is expanded only under the pressure of dire need with a resultant intensity of total railroad plant operation that is unheard of in the rest of the world.

This obviously leads to considerable frustration on the part of shippers who are required to adjust their operations to the transport system rather than vice versa, as is usually the case in

Table 15–1   Freight Traffic by Means of Transport, U.S.S.R., Selected Years, and U.S.A., 1974, in Billion Ton-Kilometers and Per Cents of Total

	U.S.S.R. (Within Present Boundaries) [a]							U.S.A.
	1913	1928	1940	1950	1960	1970	1975	1974
Total, billion ton-kilometers	126.0	119.5	487.6	713.3	1,885.7	3829.2	5200.8	3219
Railroad, billion ton-kilometers	76.4	93.4	415.0	602.3	1,504.3	2494.7	3236.5	1251
Per cent	60.6	78.2	85.1	84.5	79.8	65.1	62.2	38.9
Sea, billion ton-kilometers	20.3	9.3	23.8	39.7	131.5	656.1	736.2	—
Per cent	16.1	7.8	4.9	5.6	7.0	17.1	14.2	—
River, billion ton-kilometers	28.9	15.9	36.1	46.2	99.6	174.0	221.7	506 [b]
Per cent	22.9	13.3	7.4	6.5	5.3	4.5	4.3	15.8
Oil pipeline, billion ton-kilometers	0.3	0.7	3.8	4.9	51.2	281.7	665.8	736
Per cent	0.3	0.5	0.8	0.7	2.7	7.4	12.6	22.9
Automobile, billion ton-kilometers	0.1	0.2	8.9	20.1	98.5	220.8	338.0	720
Per cent	0.1	0.2	1.8	2.8	5.2	5.8	6.5	22.4
Airplane, billion ton-kilometers	0.0	0.0	0.02	0.14	0.56	1.9	2.6	5.7
Per cent						—	—	—

Sources: Computed from data in *Narkhoz SSSR*, 1975, p. 455, and *Statistical Abstract of the United States*, 1976, p. 583.

[a] U.S.S.R. statistics include foreign trade.

[b] Includes Great Lakes and coastal shipping.

Table 15–2 Per Cent Growth of Freight Turnover by Types of Transport, 1955–1975

	U.S.S.R.	U.S.A. [a]
Total	346.4	70.4
Railroads	233.4	31.3
Marine	968.5	60.4
River	227.5	
Automobile	695.3	122.0
Oil Pipelines	4429.3	149.0
Airlines	936.0	550.0

Source: Computed from data in *Narkhoz SSSR,* 1975, p. 455, and *Statistical Abstract of the United States,* 1976, p. 583.
[a] 1955–1974.

Table 15–4 Total Lengths of Rail Lines, U.S.S.R. and U.S.A., at Ends of Selected Years, in Thousands of Kilometers

Year	U.S.S.R. [a]	U.S.A.
1950	116.9	358.4
1960	125.8	353.6
1965	131.4	337.6
1970	135.2	329.6
1975	138.3	320.0 [b]

Sources: Narkhoz SSSR, 1975, pp. 458 and 463, and *Statistical Abstract of the United States,* 1976, p. 604.
[a] Figures include only wide-gauge railroads operated by the Ministry of Transport. At the end of 1975, the U.S.S.R. also had 88.3 thousand kilometers of other railways operated by individual industries and other organizations.
[b] 1974.

Table 15–3   Loadings of Main Commodities by Modes of Transport, 1975 in Millions of Tons [a]

	Railroad	Sea	River	Pipeline
Total	3621.1	200.0	475.5	
Coal	716.9	9.2	23.4	
Coke	35.2			
Oil	389.0 [b]	91.4	39.0	497.6 [c]
Ores	307.8	17.9	8.9	
Metals	183.1	10.0	3.6	
Mineral Construction Materials	946.8	17.9	281.0	
Mineral Fertilizers	106.1	6.3	2.9	
Timber	187.0	18.3 [d]	85.5 [d]	
Firewood	12.3			
Grain	122.0	9.1	6.0	
Other	627.2	19.9	25.2	
Gas (Billion m.³)				279.4

Source: Narkhoz SSSR, 1975, pp. 460, 464, 467, 474, 475, and 488.
[a] Commodity breakdown for freight hauled by trucks and airplanes is not available. In 1975 trucks loaded 21 billion tons of freight, but hauls averaged only 16.1 kilometers in length. Airplanes loaded only 2.5 million tons, much of which was mail.
[b] Three-fourths refined products.
[c] Mostly crude.
[d] On seas, timber moved 0.4 million tons by raft, 11.4 million tons by boat; on rivers, 65.3 million tons by raft, 20.2 million tons by boat.

western countries where private companies and different modes of transport offer lavish alternative opportunities to shippers in order to solicit their business. Shippers in the Soviet Union are frequently required to hold shipment until entire trainloads or shiploads can be sent to single destinations. In order to relieve the overworked railroads, shippers are urged to use waterways or mixed modes of transport involving transshipments between waterways and railroads, even though this means added time and expense for transshipment and much bureaucratic red tape between ministries. And shippers are penalized for tying up transport facilities longer than necessary. Whereas in the United States and Western Europe railroad boxcars often sit idle for weeks on railroad sidings serving as warehouses for industrial plants until they get around to using the contents, in the Soviet Union shippers are required to unload the cars immediately upon arrival so that they can get rolling again. Such measures lead to service conditions that would be intolerable in the Western World, but they certainly make for efficient use of transport equipment. Thus, while the Soviet transport system suffers from lack of investment, it is, by necessity, catered to by the rest of the economy.

THE RAILROADS

Rapid industrialization during the Soviet period coupled with a rising average length of haul has produced a 42-fold increase in rail freight turnover and more than a 10-fold increase in railroad passenger traffic. During this time the length of line operated has less than doubled. The average rail density for the entire country has risen very slowly to 6.2 kilometers of line per thousand square kilometers of territory in 1975. Of course, the rail net is very uneven across the country, as is the population density and other economic factors. The rail net is most adequate in the Ukraine and the Baltic Republics where rail densities are 36.1 and 35.2 kilometers of line per thousand square kilometers of territory respectively. In the Center the density is only 21.3, and in the Urals 12.1.

Freight movement in the Baltic Republics and other western fringes of the country that were gained as a result of World War II has been hampered by the necessity to transship goods on some lines which are of narrower West European gauge to Russian lines that are all wide gauge. This has been facilitated by lifting entire railroad cars off their chassis with cranes and setting them down on other chassis on the different gauge lines. Also, a gradual replacement of narrower gauge lines by wide gauge lines has been nearly completed in some areas.

The Soviet rail system now carries more than half the world's railroad freight traffic on a little more than ten per cent of the world's railroad trackage. Freight traffic density on the railroads during the Soviet period has increased from 1.1 million ton-kilometers per kilometer of line operated to 23.4 million ton-kilometers per kilometer of line. By comparison, average freight traffic density on railroads in the United States in 1974 was 3.9 million ton-kilometers per kilometer of line.

The Soviet rail network is minimal, whether considered in relation to land area, population, or traffic volume. It is a planned system of main routes without competitive overlap and with feeder lines developed sufficiently to provide only necessary minimum service to major sources of tonnage.

The urgency for speed of industrialization and the benefits of economy of scale, which have led to gigantomania in industrial plant construction, have also led to trunklining of railroads between a few major producing areas at the expense of extending new lines into underdeveloped areas.

Industrial plant locations often have been determined by railroad location, and farms have been forced to convey their produce to rail heads, usually by primitive means. Although it has been attempted all along to locate industrial plants so that the average length of haul could be decreased, in actuality, the average length of haul has consistently increased, mainly because of regional specialization and the extension of economic activities into far flung parts of the country. The latter has been particularly true of mining and timber operations which provide some of the bulkiest goods on the railroads. In 1928 the average length of rail haul was 598 kilometers. This increased steadily to 794 kilometers in 1945. It appeared to have shortened during World War II, but after the war it increased again to a plateau of about 800 kilometers during the 1960s. During the first half of the 1970s it has risen again to 894 kilometers in 1975.

The increasing traffic densities and lengths of haul have been accommodated by technological advances in locomotive traction and block signaling. Almost all steam engines have been replaced by more powerful electric and diesel-electric engines which allow for heavier train loads to be pulled at faster speeds. The Soviet Union has been leading the world in length of electrified railroads since 1958. As of the beginning of 1976, there were 38,874 kilometers of electrified lines in the Soviet Union, which were 28.1 per cent of the total rail net. These lines handle a little more than half of all freight hauls. Almost all the rest is handled by diesel-electric locomotives. In 1975 less than one per cent of the railroad freight in the country was moved by steam traction. This conversion has been accomplished largely since 1955 when steam traction still operated on 90 per cent of the Soviet rail net. An improved block signaling system has allowed for more frequent trains to move on the same tracks. Many lines in the Soviet Union now have train frequencies that are unthought of in the rest of the world. On the most highly traveled line in the country, the Trans Siberian, the author during the summer of 1977 observed train frequencies as great as one every three minutes on certain segments of line during certain hours of the day.

New Railroad Construction

Some railroad construction continues all the time. Much of this is double tracking of existing lines to handle increasingly heavy flows of traffic between major concentrations of population and industry. The Soviets report about 75 per cent more track length than they do line length, which signifies the amount of double tracking in the country. During 1970—1975, about 3100 kilometers of new track were commissioned. These lines were built for very specific purposes in response to urgent demands that already existed or were imminent. It has not been the practice of the Soviets to extend rails into remote areas of the country with the vague purpose of stimulating settlement, as has so often been the case in the past in many other countries of the world, particularly the United States during the nineteenth century. Current railroad construction in the U.S.S.R. is being made in response to three types of needs: to facilitate the exploitation of large new mineral deposits and timber in areas that have not been served by railroads previously; to complete links in existing lines that will provide necessary alternative routes for heavy flows of traffic between major regions; and to provide adequate access into and out of newly settled areas whose population densities and aggregate production have generated adequate demands for market outlets and incoming supplies.

During the last decade the two most outstanding examples of the first type of railroad building have been the railroad to the Mangyshlak Peninsula and the Tyumen-Tobolsk-Surgut Railroad in Western Siberia, both in response to the discovery and rapid exploitation of large oil deposits. Another such line is the Arctic Railroad running about 100 miles eastward from Salekhard, near the mouth of the Ob River, to Nadym to serve a new collecting and supply center for the large West Siberian gas fields that are being developed in this area. In the European north a similar railroad is being laid eastward from Archangel to the Pinega River to open up new timber areas. Also a 105-kilometer line has been built to provide a more direct route from the iron mines at Zheleznogorsk in the Kursk Magnetic Anomaly to Orel. Other short lines of this type have been extended northward from the Trans Siberian Railroad in central Siberia to new hydroelectric sites.

The best example of completion of an alternate route to relieve heavy flows of traffic between major regions is the Beyneu-Kungrad line across the Ust Yurt Plateau in western Kazakhstan which linked up sections of line to form a new direct route between Central Asia and European Russia. Another such alternate route was opened between Omsk and Barnaul in Western Siberia. This line runs southeastward from Omsk to Barnaul and eastward to the Kuznetsk Basin, and thereby provides an alternate route to the Omsk-Novosibirsk section of the Trans Siberian Railroad, which, linking the Kuznetsk heavy industry with the Urals heavy industry, carries the heaviest traffic of any railroad in the world.

The "Land Bridge"

In 1971 the Soviets began handling foreign freight on the Trans Siberian Railroad on what they had promoted as a "land bridge" alternative to sea routes between countries of the Far East, such as Japan and South Korea, and countries of Western Europe, such as West Germany and France. In order to break into established trade agreements, they offered 25 per cent lower costs, and, since the Suez Canal was still blocked at that time, considerably faster deliveries. The mixed water-rail route from Japan to Europe is 13,000 kilometers, as compared to 27,000 kilometers by the all-water route around Africa and 20,000 kilometers via the Suez Canal.

Although initially the route was plagued by transit delays and erratic handling due to crude terminal facilities, the Soviets rapidly built port facilities at Nakhodka and Vostochnyy in the Far East and Tallinn on the Baltic to handle van-sized containers. This has greatly improved services. In addition, since the reopening of the Suez Canal, the Soviets have started offering rebates of as much as half of freight charges if equivalent transit times of sea passages are not matched. All this has captured about 20 per cent of the 500,000 freight-laden containers that move between the Far East and Europe each year.

The route has become so successful that the service has been extended to Poland, Hungary,

and Iran. The Iran movements involve imports not only from Europe but from the U.S.A. as well. Container handling facilities have also been installed at Ilyichevsk, a port near Odessa on the Black Sea, so that the western end of these land bridges can be originated or terminated either in the Baltic or the Black Sea. A plant to manufacture twenty-ton containers, the first in the Soviet Union, has been constructed at Ilyichevsk, to augment the containers leased from foreign countries. In addition a huge new container and specialized flat car building plant is now arising north of Abakan in the Minusinsk Basin of southern Krasnoyarsk Kray in Eastern Siberia. The first flat cars were turned out in 1976. Ultimately 5000 cars are to be produced each year. The container plant is scheduled to begin operation in 1978 with an ultimate capacity of 40,000 units per year.

All this movement of foreign goods to bring in hard currency has placed another heavy burden on the Trans Siberian Railroad which was overloaded before. Particularly bothersome is the overbalance of traffic toward the west. In 1976 50,000 containers moved westward while only 18,000 moved eastward. The Soviets are seeking to correct this situation.

The BAM

By far the most important rail construction taking place at the present time is the Baykal-Amur Magistral (Mainline). This is a new route across Eastern Siberia and the Soviet Far East lying from 200 to 300 kilometers north of the existing Trans Siberian Railroad. It has been conceived as an alternative route to this section of the Trans Siberian which will relieve the Trans Siberian of some of the expanding freight traffic. In addition, it is being built to facilitate the movement of West Siberian oil eastward to the Pacific coast for domestic use and foreign shipments. Although this route will require transshipment of oil at both ends of the rail line, it has been favored over the extension of a pipeline all the way to the Pacific because it will serve many other purposes. It will make accessible large new mineral and timber resources and perhaps stimulate settlement in an area that has been largely empty of population. In addition, should military conflict develop in this region between Russia and China or some other power the BAM will provide a more inland route that can be more easily defended.

Construction began on the BAM in 1974 and is supposed to be completed around 1983. The organization for the bulk of the work has been turned over to the Komsomol (Young Communist League) which is in charge of enlisting students and other recruits who are mostly in their late teens or early twenties. A zionistic fervor has taken hold of the project reminiscent of that which sparked the building of the Dnieper Dam and the Magnitogorsk steel plant in the early 1930s, the opening of the Virgin Lands in the 1950s, and the building of the Kama truck plant in the 1960s.

The proposed line will be about 3150 kilometers long. Together with already completed sections on either end it will total more than 4200 kilometers. It will extend from the Lena River in the west at the end of the Tayshet—Ust-Kut spur line leading off from the Trans Siberian, and continue eastward through Nizhneangarsk at the northern end of Lake Baykal, Chara, Tynda, and Urgal to Komsomolsk-on-Amur where it will hook up with the Komsomolsk—Sovetskaya-Gaven Railroad across a new bridge over the Amur River completed in 1975. (Fig. 15-1) About 500 kilometers of this distance runs through country underlain by permafrost. The line will have to cross seven mountain ranges and a number of large rivers such as the Lena, Olekma, Zeya, Selemdzha, and Amur. Four tunnels are to be dug, one more than 1500 meters long, and 140 bridges will have to be built ranging in length from 100 to more than 1000 meters. Approximately 100,000 workers eventually will be employed on the project. In addition a great number of support personnel will have to be moved into the region.

The route east of Lake Baykal will pass through nickel-copper deposits near Nizhneangarsk, the large Molodezhnyy asbestos deposit in the northern part of the Buryat A.S.S.R., the huge Udokan copper deposit in the northern part of Chita Oblast — perhaps the largest copper deposit in the Soviet Union — and through the rail junction of Tynda, where it will cross a north-south railroad already built from Bam station on the Trans Siberian Railroad north through Tynda to Berkakit in the Chulman (Neryungri) coking coal district in southern Yakutia, and perhaps eventually on to Yakutsk. The BAM will also pass near iron ore, manganese, and mica deposits in southern Yakutia as well as the operating coal fields around Urgal, where it will connect another north-south line already built. The new line will also cross through regions of great timber reserves which will be exploited to transport large quantities both westward to domestic markets and eastward to the sea ports of Nakhodka, with its new outer port of Wrangel (Vostochnyy), and Vanino, the new port near Sovetskaya-Gavan, where the wood will be loaded on seagoing vessels for export, primarily to Japan.

The construction of the BAM should greatly enhance the prospects of trade between the Soviet Far East and Japan. The Soviets have decided that it might be more logical to try to integrate the economy of the Soviet Far East with the rest of the Far East rather than with the rest of the Soviet Union, whose main markets and supply areas are so far to the west. Shortly after the announcement of the plans to go ahead with the BAM, the Japanese signed a contract in June, 1974 to start buying coal from the Chulman district in the late 1970s at the rate of about five million tons per year over a twenty year period. It is assumed that similar contracts will be signed in the near future for the delivery of much larger quantities of Soviet timber and West Siberian oil.

Commodity Structure on Railroads

Coal and coke have dominated rail traffic since 1907 when they surpassed grain in tonnage transported. They reached a peak of 37 per cent of all rail traffic in 1947, and in 1975 they still accounted for 16.3 per cent of

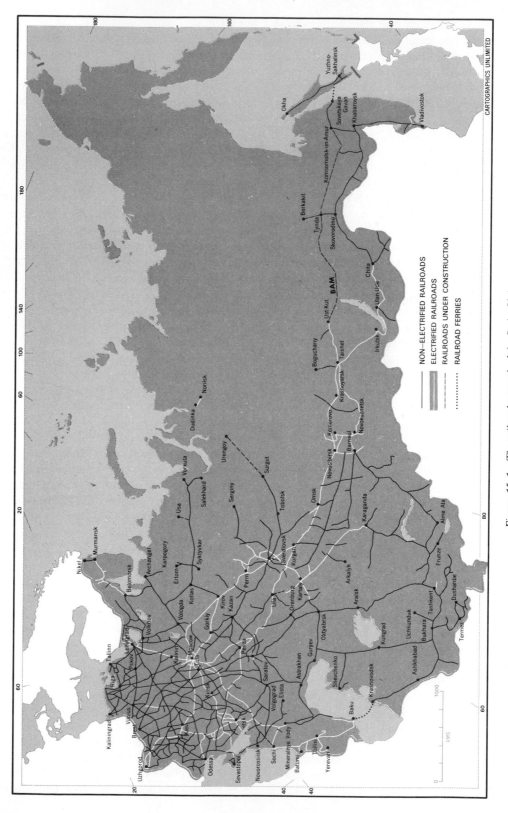

Figure 15–1   The railroad network of the Soviet Union.

Figure 15–2　The Trans Siberian Express chugs its way across the Yablonovyy Mountains, Eastern Siberia. Photo by Toni Crane.

the traffic. (Table 15–5) Their role is diminishing as industries and power stations switch to oil and gas for fuels and steam locomotives are replaced by electric and diesel-electric. In the past the railroads themselves consumed as much as one third of the coal production of the country.

In rail traffic, coal and coke are followed in order by petroleum and petroleum products, mineral construction materials, timber, metals, ores, grain and mineral fertilizers. Short hauls of mineral construction materials have been the most rapidly expanding type of railroad traffic in recent years, and mineral fertilizers in significant amounts are relatively new commodities on railroads. In 1975 mineral construction materials actually led in tons of railroad freight originated, but the short average length of haul dropped them behind coal and petroleum in ton-kilometers of traffic. Timber, metals, and oil move farthest of all railroad freight.

By comparison, railroad traffic in the United States is more diversified, although it is also dominated by coal and coke. Mineral construction materials and ores make up a larger percentage of the total, and petroleum products make up very little percentage. Most of the fluid fuels in the United States move by pipeline.

Railroads in the Soviet Union in 1975 transported almost all the coal, coke, metals, and ores, 89 per cent of the grain, 76 per cent of the mineral construction materials, 64 per cent of the timber, and almost 50 per cent of the petroleum and petroleum products. (Table 15–3)

Main coal flows move out of the Donets Basin in all directions to the Dnieper Bend, Moscow, the North Caucasus, and other destinations in European Russia; from the Kuznetsk Basin westward to the Urals and the Volga Region; from Karaganda westward to the Urals and southward to Middle Asia; and from Pechora southwestward to Cherepovets and Leningrad. (Fig. 15–3) Oil on the rail-

Table 15–5   Railroad Freight Traffic Composition, 1975

U.S.S.R.

Commodity	Million Tons	Average Haul in Kilometers	Billion Ton-Kilometers	Per Cent of Traffic
Total	3621.1	894	3236.5	100
Coal	716.9	695	498.0	15.4
Coke	35.2	835	29.4	.9
Petroleum and Petroleum Products	389.0 [a]	1240	481.4	14.9
Ores	307.8	75	232.0	7.2
Metals	183.1	1410	258.3	8.0
Mineral Construction Materials	946.8	465	440.5	13.6
Mineral Fertilizers	106.1	1060	112.2	3.5
Timber	187.0	1640	307.7	9.5
Grain	122.0	1050	127.9	4.0
Other	627.2	1190	749.1	23.1

Source: Narkhoz SSSR, 1975, pp. 459–460.

[a] 89 million tons of crude oil and 300 million tons of refined products. Most crude oil moves by pipeline, whereas most refined products move by rail.

roads moves both east and west from the Volga-Urals fields and the West Siberian fields and from Baku northwestward to the Ukraine. The heaviest flows of ferrous metals move out of eastern Ukraine northward to the Central Region, out of the Urals westward to the Volga, and out of the Kuznetsk Basin westward along the Trans Siberian Railroad. Lesser flows move primarily out of these three regions to all parts of the country.

With the continued development of lumbering areas in the European North, the Urals, and Siberia, the average rail haul of timber has increased from 415 kilometers in 1913 to 1640 kilometers in 1975. 60 per cent of all sawn wood is processed in the wood consuming areas, 20 per cent of which is in the Center. Consequently 72 per cent of railroad traffic in forest products is raw timber. The heaviest flow moves southward from Archangel on the northern railroad. (Fig. 15–4) It is joined at Konosha by wood coming from the northeast on the Pechora Railroad and at Danilov by wood coming from the east on the Kirov-Buy Line. From Danilov it flows to Moscow and fans out to the south beyond. There is also a very heavy flow along the Trans Siberian in Eastern Siberia westward from Irkutsk to the Kuznetsk Basin.

Large grain flows move out of Ukraine, the North Caucasus, and the Volga Region to the Center, the Northwest, and Belorussia. Since the opening of the Virgin Lands in 1953 there has been a sharp increase in grain flow from the southern Urals, Western Siberia, and northern Kazakhstan to European Russia. Grain loadings on the railroads of northern Kazakhstan and Western Siberia increased 20 times between 1953 and 1956. Grain accounts for about 30 per cent of all loadings on the Omsk Railroad, 25 per cent on the Orenburg Railroad, and 10 per cent on the South Urals Railroad. The heaviest flow moves from Novosibirsk westward to Chelyabinsk. Cotton flows primarily northwestward from Central Asia and eastern Transcaucasia to the European Center and Northwest and northward from Central Asia to Western Siberia. (Fig. 15–5)

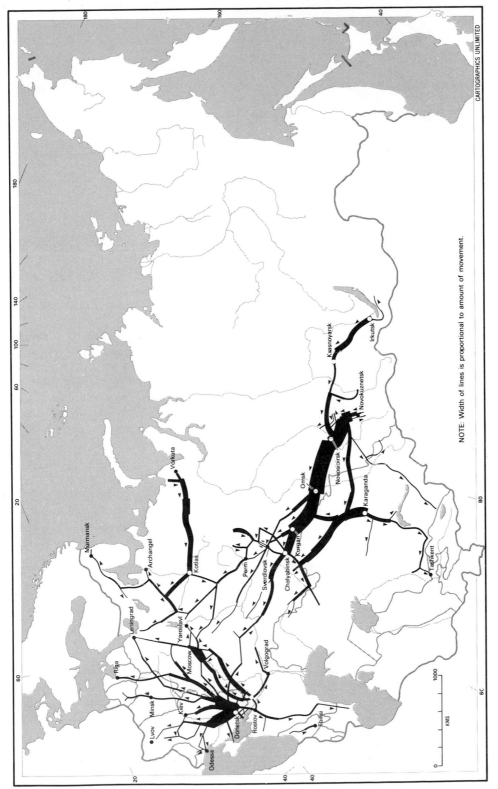

Figure 15–3   Coal movements. Adapted from Nikolskiy, Toryaev, and Krasheninnikov, pp. 53 and 54.

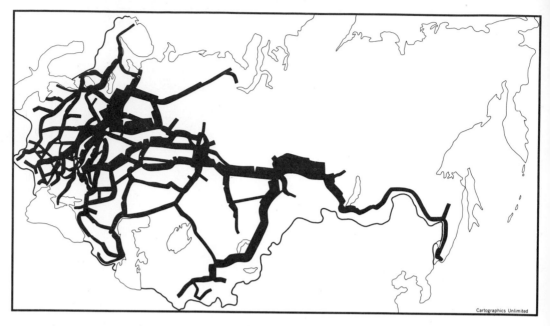

Figure 15–4   Wood movements. After Nikolskiy, Tonyaev, and Krasheninnikov, p. 56.

INLAND WATERWAYS

In spite of the great to-do often made about Soviet rivers in general and the Volga River in particular, the truth of the matter is that all Soviet waterways suffer from a number of disabilities, and over the years the rivers' share of total Soviet freight traffic has dwindled to less than 5 per cent. (Table 15–1) This has been in spite of rather heroic efforts by the Soviet government to increase traffic on rivers and to reduce it on railroads. During the last four decades the Soviets have put into operation a great number of huge water construction projects, the likes of which were not even dreamed about in Tsarist times. The great Volga scheme, the Dnieper Cascade, the rejuvenated Mariinsk Canal System (Volga-Baltic Waterway), the White Sea-Baltic Canal, to mention only a few of the major navigational channels, include some of the largest reservoirs of water in the world with lengths totaling thousands of kilometers and almost innumerable locks and wintering and repair facilities that represent large investments in money, time, and energy.

In addition, in the late 1950s laws were passed that arbitrarily guaranteed freight rates on waterways to be no more than those on railroads for identical shipments. According to these laws, penalties as high as 100 per cent could be levied against rail shipments that paralleled navigable waterways during the navigation season, and discounts of as much as 30 per cent could be awarded for mixed shipments utilizing combinations of water and rail carriers. All these measures have increased water freight turnover absolutely by more than seven times, from 28.9 billion ton-kilometers in 1913 to 222.8 billion ton-kilometers in 1975. But as can be seen in Table 15–2, traffic on rivers has been increasing at a slower rate than on any other type of carrier, and its share of total traffic decreased from 22.9 per cent in 1913 to only 4.3 per cent in 1975. The Volga, which still accounts for about 60 per cent of river traffic in the entire country, is working at only about one-fifth capacity, whereas paralleling railroads work at nearly full capacity.

Some of the obvious drawbacks of river transportation are winter freezing, slow speeds, and circuitous routes. On the Volga, the aver-

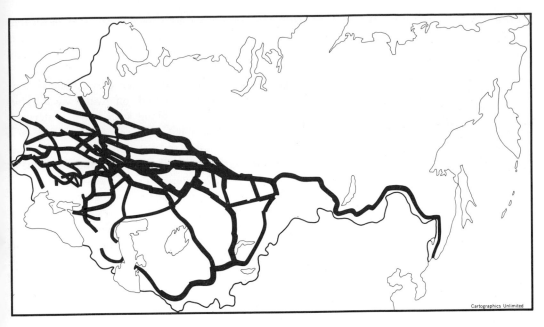

Figure 15–5   Grain flows.

age speed of commodities is about 80 kilometers per day as compared to a commodity speed on the paralleling railroad of about 200 kilometers per day. And in a circuitous section of the river such as that between Gorky and Saratov, the river distance is 1290 kilometers, as against a rail distance of 546 kilometers. On the average, Volga freight travels 50 per cent farther than it would by rail. And even at the mouth of the Volga, the river is closed by ice more than 3 months of the year. In the Moscow area it is closed 5 months and more. (Table 15–6)

The river construction projects have not been entirely beneficial. Initial construction costs entailed capital investments per additional ton-kilometers of freight traffic capacity that were 2 to 2.5 times as high as they would have been for railroad construction, and the years involved in the completion of these projects tied up capital and labor that could have yielded returns far more quickly in other types of endeavor. Once the construction projects were completed, this was not the end of expenditures, either. Docking and port facilities have to be maintained, and in many cases along the

shallow gradients of the European streams frequent dredging is required. So the Soviets are finding out, as other countries have, that a waterway is not free to operate once it is in existence.

The huge reservoirs themselves have proved to be more of a hazard to transportation than an asset. The wind over them is often so great that huge waves are generated during storms which tend to capsize self-propelled vessels and render the towing of barges impossible. It has been estimated that along the Volga tows and barges lose 15 to 20 per cent of the navigational season laying over in wave shelters. This no doubt accounts for the seemingly irrational Soviet effort to place more and more self-propelled vessels on their waterways. Storm waves and wide seasonal fluctuations of water levels in the reservoirs also cause extreme erosion along the banks which has led to serious landslides in areas such as Ulyanovsk along the Volga. The lack of perceptible currents in reservoirs makes the rafting of timber impossible. Either the rafts have to be escorted by tugs, frequently fore and aft, or the wood has to be loaded on self-propelled vessels.

Table 15–6   Average Annual Length of Shipping Season, U.S.S.R., at Major Rivers and Ports

Location	Length of Season (Days)	Percentage of Time Navigable
River		
Dnieper at Kiev	267	73.2
Lower Volga	264	72.3
Upper Volga	224	61.4
Western Dvina	236	64.7
Northern Dvina	177	48.5
Ob at Salekhard	152	41.6
Irtysh at Tobolsk	189	51.8
Yenisey at Krasnoyarsk	197	54.0
Southern (Upper) Lena	145	39.7
Northern (Lower) Lena	88	24.1
Seaport		
Odessa	328	89.9
Zhdanov	288	79.8
Taganrog	252	69.0
Astrakhan	238	65.2
Tallin	383	77.5
Leningrad	200	54.8
Murmansk	365 [a]	100.0
Archangel	175	47.9
Nizhne-Kolymsk	110	30.1
Vladivostok	255	69.9

Source: Holland Hunter, *Soviet Transportation Policy*, 1957, p. 13.

[a] Kept open by icebreaker for 50 days.

Ice remains on the reservoirs 12 to 14 days longer than it did on the original rivers, which further shortens the navigational season. And, finally, the locks that are necesary for boats to change water levels at each dam have become bottlenecks as ships back up to await passage.

Although water channels along the Volga and other major waterways are now adequate, river craft and port facilities are not. Ports are poorly mechanized, and transshipments are costly and time consuming. Large industries located directly on river floodplains along navigable waterways, such as the Volgograd tractor plant and the Moscow automobile plant, do not even have docks. Obviously they are making no use of the river as a means of transport for their bulky supplies and products. Less than two percent of refined petroleum products move by water even though many refineries are located on waterways. Thus industrialization along such major waterways as the Volga has not been accompanied by a corresponding construction of river facilities and growth of river traffic. Since the major rivers of the country flow off to the edges of the land mass and fail to join together the major concentrations of natural resources and economic activity, use of waterways would usually entail transshipments to and from rail at points where rivers cease to flow in right directions. Since transshipping facilities are poor and bureaucratic red tape between ministries of railroad transport and river transport are involved, most shippers despair of mixing modes of transport. Soviet economists ruefully joke that many shippers suffer from "hydrophobia."

There seems to be some increase during the last few years in the use of mixed modes of transport. There has been a noticeable increase in the use of river tankers to move refined products from the Volga Basin refineries. More products also seem to be moving through the Volga-Baltic Waterway and the Baltic-White Sea Waterway to northern markets such as Petrozavodsk and Kandalaksha. It has been reported that traffic along the Volga-Baltic Waterway rose from 10 million tons in 1970 to 14 million tons in 1975. The Baltic-White Sea Waterway, which dates from the early 1930s, is now being reconstructed to eliminate a large number of small-sized locks with wooden gates and walls, replacing them with reinforced concrete sections. A growing share of coal shipments westward from the Kuznetsk Basin are now being transshipped to water at points where rail lines from the east cross the Kama and Volga Rivers. The volume of such rail-water transshipments rose from 3.1 million tons in 1970 to 4.5 million in 1975. Similarly, coal from the Karaganda Basin is being transshipped at the Volga Waterway. Most Karaganda coal terminates in the Urals, but some actually moves as far as the Donets Basin to be burned in power stations. This Karaganda coal moves by rail to Kuybyshev and then via the Volga River, Volga-Don Canal, Don River, and Sea of Azov to the port of Zhdanov, where it is transshipped to rail once more for the last leg to power stations in the Donets Basin. In addition, some Inta steam coals from the Pechora Basin in northeast European Russia have been moving by rail to the Volga River port of Yaroslavl, then by water down the Volga, across the Volga-Don Canal, and down the Don River to the Sea of Azov coal terminal at Zhdanov, from where rail shipments resume to coal fired power stations near Zaporozhye and even in the western Ukraine. Such long hauls of coal into areas that normally would be regarded as Donbas marketing areas have been necessitated by the fact that the Donets Basin has not been able to meet growing demands in its own market area. Round-about water shipments have made the cost of these far away coals competitive with the Donets coals which are more costly to mine.

Iron ore from the Kursk Magnetic Anomaly has been traveling by rail to the lower Don where it is transshipped to the Volga-Don Canal and up the Volga and Kama Rivers to Perm, where it is transshipped once more to rail to continue to steel plants at Chelyabinsk and Nizhniy Tagil. Ore has also been moving from the Olenegorsk and Kovdor mines on the Kola Peninsula via rail-water-rail routes to Cherepovets and Magnitogorsk.

In spite of all this renewed activity, the use of expensive canals has been disappointing. The White Sea-Baltic and Volga-Don Canals have been the most expensive to construct and the least remunerative in their operations. Perhaps the Moscow canal is the only one that has paid for itself, and its function as an additional supplier of domestic water to Moscow has transcended its navigational function. The Volga-Baltic Waterway may eventually pay for itself since it connects the important industrial areas of Moscow and Leningrad with each other and with resource regions of bulky materials such as apatite, iron ore, coal, and timber. If the Pechora-Vychegda Diver-

sion Project is ever built, it might greatly enhance water movements of bulky freight in northern European Russia. Particularly it would provide an all-water route for Pechora coal to move southward to the industrialized part of the Urals.

The huge river systems of Siberia unfortunately flow northward rather than east-west and hence do not provide direct connection with European Russia. Before the coming of the Trans Siberian Railroad in the late nineteenth century, the east-west portions of streams in Siberia were about the only means of transportation moving through the region. However, they constituted round-about routes that had to be connected with frequent portages. Connection of these streams by way of the Northern Sea Route, from their mouths westward to Archangel and Murmansk is severely limited by the short shipping season and the high cost of navigating the northern seas. The Amur River in the Soviet Far East has proved to be of slight value in developing the territory around it. Water transport has been fostered to some extent in recent years in Siberia by the development of certain areas north of the Trans Siberian Railroad such as the oil and gas development in the Ob River Basin, the expansion of the Norilsk nickel and platinum metals complex along the lower Yenisey, the development of Yakutia in the Lena River Basin, and most importantly, the construction needs of the BAM rail project. Although the BAM Railroad is being constructed to alleviate the necessity to move goods on rivers, during its construction huge amounts of bulky materials are being moved by river to construction sites.

Commodity Structure on Rivers

River transport has long been dominated by timber and firewood, and this dominance increased until 1960 at the expense of the second most important item, oil and oil products. (Table 15-7) Since then the gap has been narrowed. In 1975, 88.5 million tons of timber were shipped on river transport facilities, but only 39 million tons of oil and oil products. The average length of haul for timber, however, is only one third that for oil, so that total freight turnover is about the same for both products. The short hauling of mineral construction materials by river barge has increased rapidly since 1940, and they now constitute by far the largest freight originations. But because the average haul is only about 150 kilometers, they make up less than 20 per cent of river traffic. Coal and grain make up minor portions.

European rivers typically have carried most of the river traffic of Russia, the Volga system alone accounting for about 60 per cent of total traffic. In terms of tonnage, the Northern Dvina is second only to the Volga, because of large-scale floating of timber, but since the distance is relatively short, its freight turnover is not as large as some other streams. (Figure 15–6)

MARINE TRANSPORT

Domestic maritime shipping in the Soviet Union suffers from many of the same ills as river transportation does. The borders of the U.S.S.R. total approximately 95,000 kilometers, 70 per cent of which are bounded by water. Yet only a small fraction of the surrounding water is suitable to the carriage of freight between points of the U.S.S.R. Except for canal connections on Soviet territory, which are closed by ice during winter, commodity movement between north and south European U.S.S.R. by sea require trips around the whole circumference of Western Europe, and sea passage from southern ports along the Black Sea to the Soviet Far East entails a voyage almost half way around the world by way of the Suez Canal, skirting India and China. Thus the movement of commodities by seas between major producing and consuming areas

Table 15–7   River Transport

	1913 (Within Present Boundaries)	1940	1960	1970	1975
Length of navigable waterways in thousand kilometers	64.6	107.3	137.9	144.5	145.4
Freight turnover in billion ton-kilometers	28.9	36.1	99.6	174.0	221.7
Freight originations, in millions of tons	35.1	73.1	210.3	357.8	475.5
Oil and oil products	5.4	9.7	18.5	33.5	39.0
Timber and firewood	11.0	40.2	89.4	91.2	85.5 [a]
Coal and coke	0.9	2.2	11.0	17.6	23.4
Ore	—	0.1	2.0	5.2	8.9
Mineral construction materials	1.5	7.6	70.3	180.9	281.0
Metals and metal scrap	0.6 [a]	0.5	1.0	2.0	3.6
Grain	6.1	5.2	6.8	6.8	6.0
Chemicals and mineral fertilizers				1.7	2.9
Average length of haul in kilometers	823	494	474	486	466
Passenger turnover, in billion passenger-kilometers	1.4	3.8	4.3	5.4	6.3
Number of passengers, in millions	11.5	73.0	118.6	145.2	161.4
Average length of trip, in kilometers	125	52	36	37	39

Source: Narkhoz SSSR, 1975, p. 467.

[a] 65.3 in rafts, 20.2 in boats.

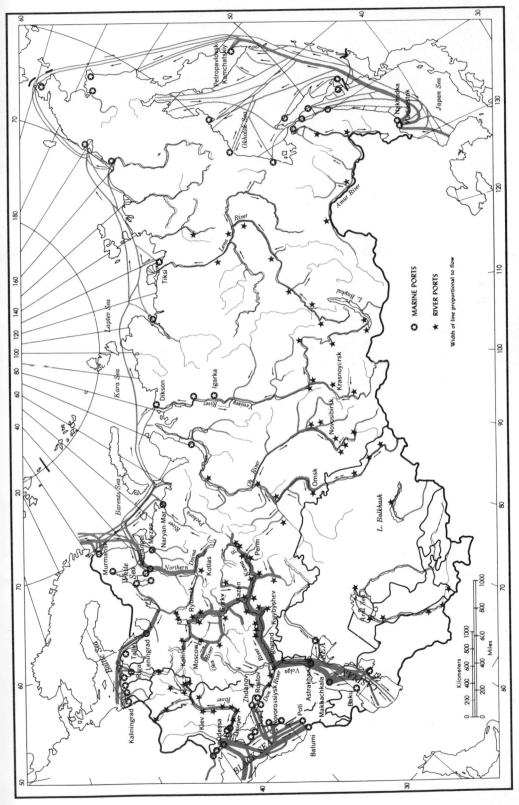

Figure 15–6 Freight flows on waterways. After Galitskiy, et al., pp. 73–74.

Figure 15–7   Lock on Volgo-Don Canal. Photo by Irving Cutler.

in the Soviet Union entails extremely circuitous routes which involve unwarranted periods of time for shipment. The more direct route between European Russia and the Far East, the Northern Sea Route, is closed by ice as much as 9 months of the year, and during the short navigational season can only be navigated by the use of ice breakers moving ships in convoy aided by aircraft, floating weather stations, and other support equipment to survey ice conditions and chart the course ahead of the ships. So far, traffic along it has been nominal, and it appears that it will remain so. This, in spite of the fact that the Soviet nuclear powered ice breaker, *Arktika*, reached the North Pole on August 17, 1977 by crashing through ice crust as thick as four meters. This has prompted the Soviets to announce plans to create a shipping route through the middle of the Arctic which would be considerably shorter than moving along the shore of Siberia. There has been talk of extend-ing the navigational season in the Arctic to nearly the entire year. However, if this were physically feasible it would probably be too costly to be economically practical. In the South, the Caspian Sea was landlocked until 1952 when it was joined with the Black Sea by the Volga-Don Canal. But even now this canal is closed by ice five months of the year.

In view of all these difficulties, sea traffic was allowed to lapse during the early part of the Soviet period. (Table 15–1) In 1940 sea traffic was barely more than it had been in 1913 and its share of total traffic had dwindled from 16.1 per cent in 1913 to 4.9 per cent in 1940. However, it appears that sometime after 1940 the decision was made to increase sea movements. During the period 1955–1975, marine transport was the second most rapidly increasing mode of traffic after pipelines. (Table 15–2) Relative to other modes of freight transport, sea traffic reached a peak of 17.1 per cent of total turnover in 1970. Since then its

Figure 15–8   River port at Volgograd. Photo by David Kromm.

share has decreased to 14.2 per cent in 1975, although absolutely it is still growing slowly. (Table 15–8) Much of this increase has been in foreign trade. Sea transport handles more than 50 per cent of Soviet foreign trade.

Undoubtedly the reason behind this growth in sea traffic has been the stress during the past two decades on the building of a Soviet Merchant Marine, which has both commercial and strategic implications. The fleet has grown from about 650 ships totaling 4 million tons dead weight in 1960 to around 6,500 sea vessels totaling a dead weight of almost 14.7 million tons in 1975. Most important, it is the youngest fleet in the world and hence one of the most modern. More than 80 per cent of Soviet vessels have been launched within the last 15 years. Many of these have been built in Soviet shipyards, but also many have been bought from countries in eastern and western Europe and Japan.

Prior to 1960 much of the small Soviet

foreign trade was carried in foreign bottoms, and no doubt the Soviets were loath to carry any domestic trade in this way. But during the last fifteen years, as foreign trade has expanded rapidly, the Soviets have built up their merchant marine to the point where they not only carry almost all their own foreign trade but also have actively solicited business from foreign shippers in order to generate hard currency. More than 90 per cent of all Soviet sea loads are now foreign transportation. This is true for passenger traffic as well as freight traffic. For instance, in 1977 Soviet liners provided the main trans Atlantic services between Britain and the United States. Fares on new, well equipped passenger liners have been set arbitrarily at prices competitive with cheap air fares across the Atlantic.

Now with a greatly expanded merchant marine of their own, the Soviets probably are willing to devote significant portions of space in their own ships to domestic trade if this

Table 15–8   Marine Transport

	1940	1965	1970	1974	1975
Freight turnover, billion ton-miles	13.4	209.9	354.3	420.2	397.5
Freight loadings, million tons	32.9	119.3	161.9	192.2	200.0
Average length of haul, miles	409	1,759	2,188	2,186	1,988
Passenger traffic, million passenger-miles	480	796	859	1,127	1,153
Passengers, millions	9.7	37.2	38.5	48.9	51.6
Average length of trip, mile	50	21	22	23	22

Source: *Narkhoz SSSR*, 1975, p. 464.
Note: Miles are nautical miles.

happens to coincide with directions of movement of foreign trade. For instance, domestic trade between such regions as European Russia and the Soviet Far East might well be integrated with foreign trade between Russia or Western Europe with Japan. The same ships could stop off at Soviet Pacific ports that continue on to Japan or some other country in the Far East.

To keep pace with the growth of the fleet and expanding trade, seaports are being expanded and modernized rapidly. Particularly, handling facilities for transshipments are being improved. A major shift to containerization has taken place in all large ports.

Geographical Distribution of Marine Shipping

The Black and Azov Seas

In 1975, the Black-Azov Sea basin accounted for 46 per cent of marine loading. Major commodities in this area are oil, coal, ores, grain, cement, timber, and sugar. This region also handles about 80 per cent of all marine passenger transport in the Soviet Union. The largest commercial ports in this area are Odessa and the newer Ilyichevsk nearby. This port complex handles by far the greatest amount of

marine freight traffic in the Soviet Union. It is now being augmented by the construction of a brand new port just to the east of Odessa in Grigoryevsky Bay. This will be a deeper water port than either Odessa or Ilyichevsk and will be able to handle oil supertankers with displacements of as much as 180,000 tons. A large chemical complex is to be built at the new port in conjunction with planned phosphoric acid shipments from the United States and exports of ammonia. Cargo handling will be mechanized and automated. A new plant in Ilyichevsk to mass produce 20-ton containers has already been mentioned. (Figure 15–9)

Novorossiysk on the northeastern Black Sea Coast of Krasnodar Kray has developed into the second largest port complex in this sea basin. Among other things, it now includes a large oil terminal to facilitate foreign shipments of West Siberian oil brought into Novorossiisk via a new pipeline from Kuybyshev. It also has the largest cement loading dock in the Soviet Union. Other ports of national significance are Nikolayev at the mouth of the Southern Bug River, Kherson up the estuary of Dnieper River, and Tuapse, Poti, and Batumi on the eastern end of the Black Sea in the Caucasus. Nikolayev has been known for a long time for its construction of ocean-going vessels. The largest port on the Sea of Azov is the iron and steel city of Zhdanov, which

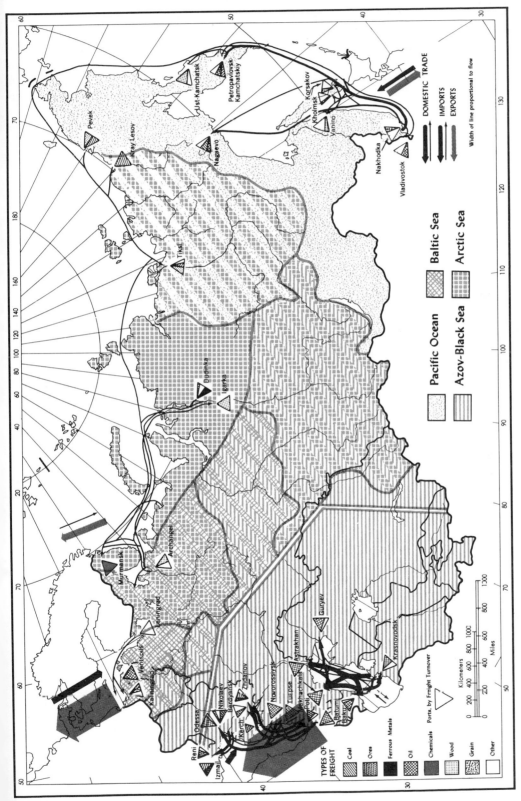

Figure 15-9 Marine transport. After Atlas razvitiya khozyaystva i kultury SSSR, p. 81.

handles large quantities of Donets coal and Kerch iron ore, among other things. Smaller ports in the Black Sea area include Izmail and Reni up the mouth of the Danube which were acquired along with the Izmail District from Rumania during World War II, Kerch at the eastern end of the Crimean Peninsula which has a shipbuilding yard that is building super-tankers for oil transport, and other minor ports in the Crimea such as Feodosiya. In the western Crimea is the old port of Sevastopol which has been developed into one of the main naval ports of the country, along with Kronshtadt on an island in the Gulf of Finland near Leningrad and Vladivostok in the Far East.

The Caspian

The Caspian Sea, which used to carry the heaviest marine traffic in the Soviet Union, still carries about 23 per cent of all inland sea cargoes, mainly oil products from Baku, Turkmenia, Mangyshlak, and Emba oil producing areas. Other Caspian Sea cargoes are grain, timber, cotton, and salt. The largest port is Baku with its great oil loadings, followed by Astrakhan which handles all the Caspian-Volga River shipping including large amounts of fish products and salt as well as oil from the areas just mentioned. Other ports of significance are Makhachkala, the capital of Dagestan A.S.S.R. on the western coast of the Caspian, Krasnovodsk on the eastern coast, Guryev at the mouth of the Ural River in the north, and Shevchenko on the Mangyshlak Peninsula in the northeast. Guryev and Shevchenko handle primarily oil from the Emba and Mangyshlak oil fields respectively. Krasnovodsk is the western terminus of the Trans Caspian Railroad which is linked with Baku across the Caspian by railway ferry.

The Baltic

Baltic ports load about 14 per cent of Soviet marine freight. They ship coal, timber, metal, oil products, grain, flour, and machinery. The principal port is Leningrad, and the old port of Riga is second. But of growing importance are such ports as Tallinn, Ventspils, Klaipeda, Kaliningrad, and Liepaya. During recent years the Latvian port of Ventspils has been singled out as one of the two main oil exporting ports of the Soviet Union along with Novorossiiysk in the eastern Black Sea. Exports from Ventspils have been facilitated by the construction of a crude oil pipeline and an oil products pipeline from the refinery town of Polotsk in northeastern Belorussia which receives petroleum via a spur off the Friendship oil pipeline from the Volga-Urals and West Siberian oil fields. More recently a large chemical marine terminal has been completed in Ventspils to handle ammonia and potash exports and receive superphosphoric acid imports. A fertilizer manufacturing complex is being established in the area. All this chemical buildup is similar to that going on at the new port of Grigoryevka east of Odessa in the Black Sea in conjunction with foreign trade agreements with the Occidental Petroleum Corporation in the United States. Oil exports at Ventspils began on a small scale in 1961 and greatly expanded when the port was reached by pipeline in 1968. A deep water oil pier accommodating 100,000 ton tankers opened in 1974. During 1975 oil exports through Ventspils amounted to about 15 million tons. This rapid buildup of handling facilities for bulky commodities such as oil and chemicals is rapidly converting Ventspils into one of the major foreign trade ports in the Soviet Union.

It appears that the trade of Baltic ports is concentrated more on foreign trade than are ports in any other part of the country. This area handles primarily transit goods that are passing to and from more interior parts in the northern half of European Russia, including the Moscow region. The main port of Leningrad is hampered by ice in the narrow eastern Gulf of Finland from December through May. And during that time some of the traffic is diverted far north through Murmansk, which, in spite of its northerly location, is ice free much of the time because of the northeasterly extension of the Gulf Stream. Some of the more open ports farther west, such as Ventspils, are far less hampered by ice. The most western port, Kaliningrad, would appear to be the most logical location for future port expansion, but apparently the Soviets are loath to invest much capital in this area until they are sure the post World War II boundaries are permanent.

Far East

The seas of the Soviet Far East account for about 11 per cent of all Soviet marine trans-port. In contrast to other seas, most of the domestic shipping is intraregional traffic. There is little connection by ship with other parts of the country except for the narrow stream of traffic flowing northward through the Bering Strait along the Northern Sea Route during the short shipping season. A growing share of maritime traffic in the Far East is occupied by foreign trade, as the Soviet Union increases trade with Japan and other Far

Figure 15–10   The southwest-trending ridges of the Sikhote-Alin Mountains in southern Maritime Kray trail into the Sea of Japan to form a series of peninsulas, islands, and embayments that provide sheltered harbors. Vladivostok sits in the middle of the long peninsula between two prongs of Peter the Great Bay in the lower-left quadrant of the picture. The Nakhodka-Wrangle embayment is in the lower-right. Landsat imagery.

Figure 15-11   Passenger dock, port of Nakhodka. Photo by Toni Crane.

Eastern countries. Primary commodities loaded at Far Eastern ports are coal, ore, timber, oil, grain, building materials, and fish.

The largest commercial port on the Pacific is Nakhodka about 80 kilometers east of Vladivostok which has taken over much of the commercial shipping originally handled by Vladivostok. Nakhodka sits in a more open water area and is not hampered by ice as Vladivostok is. This port now handles about seven million tons of cargo a year, which apparently makes it second in the Soviet Union after Ilyichevsk in the western Black Sea. The port of Nakhodka has been developed since 1950, and a city of 140,000 inhabitants now stretches across 30 kilometers of wooded hillside back from the port. The port has been connected by rail to the Ussuri Mainline north of Vladivostok where the line runs north to Khabarovsk to connect with the eastern terminus of the Trans Siberian Railroad. Thus it serves as the port facility for the eastern terminus of Trans Siberian freight traffic. It recently has installed a large container

handling facility to serve the "land bridge" between Japan and Europe. It also provides a large ship repair yard and services the Soviet Pacific tanker and fishing fleets. Several passenger liners weekly ply the route to Yokohama and Hong Kong.

The Nakhodka port area has recently been greatly expanded by the construction of a new port, Vostochnyy (east) on Wrangel Bay, an eastern inlet of the Gulf of Nakhodka, which was officially renamed from the Gulf of Amerika in 1972. It is envisioned that this new port which lies about 20 kilometers southeast of Nakhodka, will eventually merge with Nakhodka and ultimately handle about five times as much freight as Nakhodka now does. A roundwood timber terminal opened in 1974 and a wood chip terminal in 1975 to facilitate wood movements to Japan. A container terminal was opened in 1976 which is now handling 75,000 containers a year and is ultimately to handle about 140,000. A coal loading terminal is under construction which eventually is to handle about ten million tons of coal exports a year. Wrangel (Vostochnyy) is being built with the aid of 14 Japanese companies and 80 million dollars worth of Japanese credits which are supplying advanced technology and equipment.

Another large new port that is being readied as the eastern terminus of the BAM Railroad is Vanino near the older port of Sovietskaya-Gavan. Like Wrangel, Vanino eventually will handle great quantities of timber, oil, and coal, as well as other minerals from the BAM region. The importance of the port of Vanino has recently been enhanced by the establishment of the Vanino-Kholmsk train ferry which carries trains from Vanino across the Tatar Strait to Sakhalin.

The older port of Vladivostok, which sits at the head of Peter the Great Bay and is severely hampered by ice from December through May, has lost much of its commercial significance and today serves primarily as one of the three main naval bases in the country and as the center for the Pacific fishing fleet which ranges all the way from the Bering Strait to the Antarctic. Because it is a main naval base, the port of Vladivostok is closed to foreigners.

Other major ports in the Pacific basin are Nikolayevsk at the mouth of the Amur River, Korsakov and Kholmsk on Sakhalin Island, Nagayevo (Magadan) on the northern coast of the Sea of Okhotsk, and Petropavlovsk-Kamchatsky.

The Northern Sea Route

The Arctic seas along the northern coast of the Soviet Union carry about six per cent of all Soviet sea traffic. Much of this plies the more open western end of the route in the Barents Sea. Here the main commodities are iron and apatite ores from the Kola Peninsula that are being shipped to northern European U.S.S.R. In addition great quantities of timber are exported from the White Sea port of Archangel, the main timber exporting port in the Soviet Union. The largest port on the route is the western terminus, Murmansk, which connects the Northern Sea Route with routes westward to the Atlantic and serves as a main

fishing port for the rich fishing industry of the Barents Sea and adjacent Norwegian Sea. The second largest port on the Northern Sea Route, Archangel, is frozen over about half the year in the enclosed White Sea, while Murmansk remains open through the winter because of its position on the eastern extension of the Gulf Stream. Naryan Mar near the mouth of the Pechora River in the Nenets National Okrug is also significant as a lumber port and is becoming a focus for oil and gas explorations on the continental shelf in the Barents and Kara Seas.

Farther east the Northern Sea Route becomes increasingly hampered by ice, and only minor roles are played by the ports of Dikson, Dudinka, Igarka, and Tiksi. Dudinka near the mouth of the Yenisey serves the large metal producing area around Norilsk, and Igarka farther upstream on the Yenisey is the major exporting port of timber from the East Siberian Region. Tiksi near the mouth of the Lena River and Dikson near the mouth of the Ob Gulf play much more reduced roles. Way to the east, Pevek on the shore of the East Siberian Sea is becoming important as an outlet for gold and other mining activities in this remote section of the country.

The Soviets now claim to keep the Northern Sea Route open six months of the year and say that this can be expanded to eight or nine months. However, this entails usage of such costly equipment as ice breakers, floating weather stations, and air support to plot the progress of navigational routes through the ice. As mentioned earlier the Soviets recently have navigated to the heart of the ice pack at the North Pole with the recently constructed 75,000-horsepower atomic ice breaker, *Arktika*. The Northern Sea Route is also served by two other nuclear ice breakers, the *Sibir* which was launched in 1976, and the *Lenin* which has been in successful operation since 1960. In addition there are 36,000-horsepower diesel ice breakers, such as the *Yermak* and *Admiral Makarov*. Whether an extended shipping season along the Northern Sea Route can be made economically feasible remains to be seen.

Commodity Structure of Marine Transport

In total marine transport, petroleum has long dominated the scene, particularly on the Caspian and Black Seas. Although its relative role has diminished somewhat with the development of the Volga-Urals and West Siberian oil fields, statistics show that liquids, which must be predominately oil products, still made up 41 per cent of total marine freight in 1975. Among the solid commodities, mineral construction materials and ores have shot well ahead of other commodities, and they are now followed by timber and firewood, metals, coal, grain, and chemical products, primarily mineral fertilizers. (Table 15-9)

AUTOMOTIVE TRANSPORT

Since motor transport entails both high initial outlays and high line costs, the Soviets have neglected this form of transportation except for short hauls where it is most efficient in dispersing products to many different points. Trucks are used almost exclusively for construction work and to augment other forms of transport, collecting produce and taking it to railheads or water terminals or taking it from rail and water terminals to its ultimate destinations. Construction and excavation materials make up much of the freight loaded on trucks. (Table 15-10) Intercity truck traffic does not really exist. The average length of truck haul in 1975 was only 16.1 kilometers. At the beginning of 1975, the U.S.S.R. had about 4 million trucks in civilian use, whereas the United States had about 24.8 million. Many of the United States trucks were large semitrailers which hauled goods long distances between major cities, whereas most of the Soviet trucks were of the small military type performing only collecting and disseminating functions.

Concrete, blacktop, and gravel highways in 1975 totaled only 660,500 kilometers in the U.S.S.R. By comparison, the United States had

Table 15-9   Marine Freight Loadings, Million Tons

	1940	1965	1970	1975
Total	32.9	119.3	161.9	200.0
Liquids (Oil and Gas)	19.6	53.5	75.1	91.4
Timber and Firewood	1.9	6.9	11.0	.11.8 [a]
Coal	2.7	8.2	9.3	9.2
Ores	.5	10.4	13.6	17.9
Mineral Construction Materials	0.8	13.0	15.3	17.9
Metals and Scrap	0.2	4.6	6.7	10.0
Machinery and Equipment	0.2	1.7	2.5	3.8
Chemicals and Mineral Fertilizers	0.2	3.6	5.5	6.3
Salt	0.3	0.4	0.6	0.7
Grain	1.6	6.7	6.4	9.1
Fish Products	0.1	0.2	0.3	0.3

Source: *Narkhoz SSSR*, 1975, p. 464.

[a] In 1975, 0.4 million tons of timber moved in rafts and 11.4 million tons moved in ships.

Table 15–10 Freight Loadings on Trucks by Main Commodities, 1970, in Millions of Tons

Total	2675.7
Coal and Coke	77.0
Oil	31.2
Ores	13.0
Metals	109.6
Chemicals and Mineral Fertilizers	5.9
Construction Materials	1322.9
Cement	16.9
Excavation Materials	894.2
Wood	55.0
Grain	116.3
Industrial Goods	33.7

Source: Transport i svyaz SSSR, 1972, pp. 228–229.

more than 6 million kilometers of surfaced roads on only 40 per cent as much territory. The areas having the densest road nets, the Center, Ukraine, Baltic, Transcaucasia, and Volga-Urals, have only about 100 kilometers of surfaced roads per thousand square kilometers of territory. Over most of the country the density is less than 10 kilometers of road per thousand square kilometers. Hugh areas have no roads at all. (Fig. 15–12) Those roads designated as major highways are usually only two-lane blacktop. Although the U.S.S.R. recognizes that the lack of good roads is a real handicap to its economy, particularly in the critical agricultural sector, the tightness of investment resources has forced the Soviets to progress slowly in the grading and surfacing of roads. During the last decade the surfaced road system has been expanding at a rate of about 30,000 kilometers per year. Now that the huge Kama truck plant is coming into production, perhaps the picture will change significantly.

PIPELINES

Until the mid 1950s, the relatively small volume and geographical dispersion of oil movements did not warrant the construction of many pipelines for the transport of petroleum and petroleum products, and the use of natural gas was virtually undeveloped. The only relatively concentrated oil movement was that from Baku across the Caspian up the Volga to the Central Region, which moved by lake and river steamers. There was also considerable waterborne oil traffic on the Black Sea as tankers picked up oil and refined products at the Batumi end of the pipeline that traversed the Kura-Rioni synclinal valley, and also at Tuapse at the end of a short pipeline that traversed the low western end of the Caucasus from Maykop, and carried them to markets in the Ukraine. But the rest of the distribution of oil products to markets was done almost entirely by railroads.

With the policy trend started in 1955 to develop rapidly the usage of oil and natural gas, the Soviets realized that such an expansion of bulky products would probably completely break down the already overworked railway system, and therefore they concomitantly decided upon a rapid construction of trunk pipelines. This is still going on, and pipes are continually being constructed in larger and larger diameters. By the end of 1975, oil pipelines in the U.S.S.R. totaled 56,900 kilometers, and gas pipelines totaled 99,200 kilometers. (Figs. 10–2 and 10–5) During 1971–1975, the oil pipeline system expanded at the rate of approximately 4000 kilometers per year, and the gas pipeline system expanded at more than 6000 kilometers per year. Oil pipelines alone now account for about 13 per cent of total freight traffic in the Soviet Union, whereas in 1950 they accounted for less than 1 per cent. Priority during the last few years has been given to the construction of gas pipelines as part of a drive to substitute cheap natural gas for coal. Gas pipeline technology is somewhat more complicated than oil pipeline technology since gas is transmitted under much higher pressures than oil products. And since the expansion of gas production depends almost entirely on pipeline transmission, the Soviets have been actively entering into agreements with foreign countries, such as West Germany and Italy, as well as other CMEA countries to

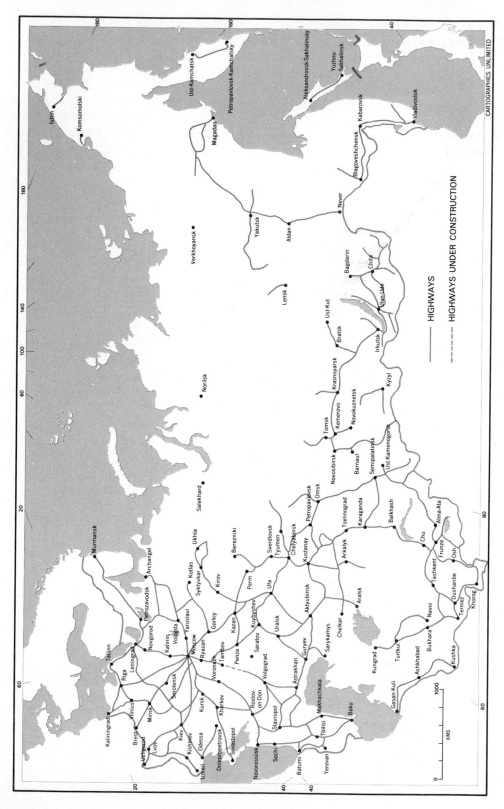

Figure 15–12   Main highways. After Atlas razvitiya khozyaystva i kultury SSSR, pp. 86–87.

provide pipeline equipment and help construct major pipelines westward to Europe which will deliver supplies of gas to various countries in eastern and western Europe.

The Soviets still must lay much pipeline if they are going to exploit fully the huge resources of oil and gas in such areas as Western Siberia and the Central Asian deserts. Refined petroleum products still are moved primarily by rail, and significant amounts of crude petroleum are still being moved on railroads. These oil products constitute the second most bulky freight traffic on railroads. As long as this situation exists, the rate of expansion of petroleum and natural gas industries will be determined to a great extent by the adequacy of transport facilities.

THE PATTERN OF COMMODITY MOVEMENT

The geographical pattern of commodity movements, of course, fits to a great extent the geographical pattern of population distribution in the country. In continuously populated European U.S.S.R., large movements of commodities radiate out from focal points such as Moscow, Leningrad, Kharkov, Kiev, Minsk, Odessa, and Donetsk, to all parts of the area. These flows developed very early as the grain-growing south augmented the industrialized north, and as the mining of coal, iron ore, and oil developed in the south and timber developed in the north. Later a southward extension of this European mass exchange developed into the Caucasus, and during the late nineteenth century and continuing up to the present time an increasing flow of commodities has developed across southern Siberia all the way to the Pacific. Southerly branches take off from this eastward flow southward into Kazakhstan and Central Asia. (Fig. 15-13) This basic pattern cannot be expected to change much in the future, although of course offshoots to primary producing areas like the oil fields of Western Siberia and the BAM region of Eastern Siberia and the Far East will continue to complicate the pattern. But the primary development will be the intensification of density of movement in the pattern already existent and the incorporation into the origination and termination of products from intervening areas that are already crossed by transportation lines. A good example of this is the Volga Region which before World War II was primarily a transit region between the three primary producing areas, the Center, the Ukraine, and the Urals. During and since the war it has developed into a freight originator and terminator in its own right, greatly intensifying the movement of freight in the region.

In all freight originations on railroads, rivers, and seas, the Donets-Dnieper region of Ukraine is by far the most important. (Table 15-11) The Urals are second, but with only about half as much as the Donets-Dnieper region. These two regions have been originating more freight than any other region for many years. Now the Volga Region has surpassed the Center to become the third most important freight originator. In recent years Western Siberia has increased its freight originations very significantly, and the Northwest Region has increased significantly, so that these two are now tied with the Center for fourth place. Except for the Center, it is obvious that each of these regions ships some bulky products. The Donets and Western Siberia ship coal and ores, the Urals ship ores, oil, and timber, the Volga ships oil, and the Northwest ships timber and coal. All ship considerable quantities of mineral construction materials.

In total freight terminations, the Donets-Dnieper region ranks first again. The Urals are a weak second and the Center a close third. These are followed at some distance by the Northwest and the Volga Regions. Thus, those regions originating the most also receive the most, although in slightly different order.

The greatest net exporter by far is also the Donets-Dnieper Region. This is followed by Western Siberia, Kazakhstan, the Volga, and Eastern Siberia. It must be remembered that these imbalances are computed only in terms of weight, not value. Thus, Eastern Siberia may be a net exporter of weight, but it is a rather significant net importer of value of products.

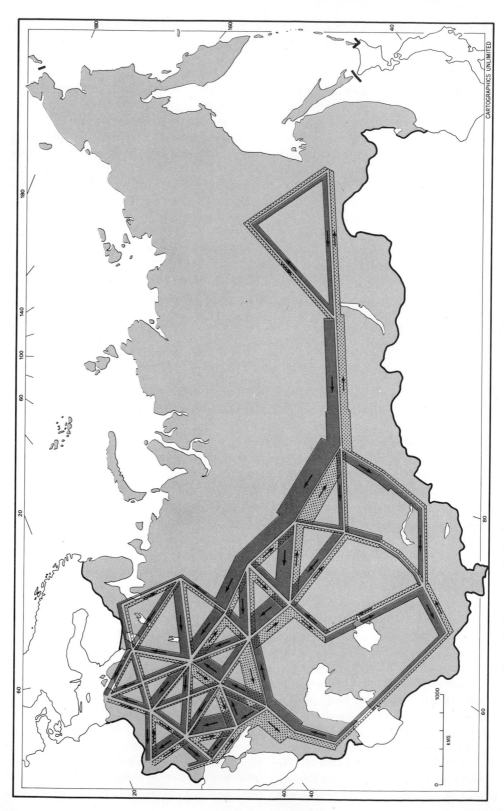

Figure 15–13 Schematic of commodity flow. Width of line represents volume of traffic. Adapted from Kalesnik, S.V. and Pavlenko, V.F., Soviet Union: A Geographical Survey, Progress Publishers, Moscow, 1976, pp. 246–247.

Table 15–11   Regional Movements of Freight on Railroads, Rivers, and Seas, 1970, in Millions of Tons

Economic Reporting Regions	Freight Originations	Freight Terminations	Intra-regional Movements	Regional Exports	Regional Imports	Net Exports (+) or Imports (−)
Northwest	265	247	185	80	62	+ 18
Center	265	306	178	88	128	− 41
Volgo-Vyatka	71	90	33	38	57	− 19
Central Chernozem	79	96	40	39	56	− 17
Volga	272	232	135	137	97	+ 40
North Caucasus	171	165	90	81	75	+ 7
Ural	332	331	196	136	135	+ 1
Western Siberia	265	220	158	107	62	+ 46
Eastern Siberia	158	121	96	62	25	+ 38
Far East	99	121	92	8	29	− 22
Donets-Dnieper	621	493	401	220	92	+128
Southwest	150	209	95	55	114	− 59
South	71	115	37	34	78	− 44
Baltic	68	108	49	19	59	− 40
Transcaucasia	89	103	67	22	36	− 14
Central Asia	86	102	64	21	37	− 16
Kazakhstan	196	153	104	92	49	+ 43
Belorussia	60	90	39	21	51	− 32
Moldavia	13	23	8	5	15	− 10

Source: Transport i svyaz SSSR, Moscow, 1972, pp. 68–69.

The largest net importers are the Southwest, South, Center, Baltic, and Belorussia. These are all heavily populated regions whose industries concentrate mainly on the manufacture of finsihed products of great variety and require large quantities of raw materials. Therefore in these regions tons terminated greatly exceed tons originated. The Urals have the highest imports of any region, but its exports are almost exactly the same as imports so its interregional trade is nearly balanced. The Center is the second greatest importer, but since it exports much more than regions such as the Southwest and the South its net imports are not as great. There was not much shifting of position in net exports and imports between the two reporting years 1965 and 1970. In general, imbalances increased; those regions having net exports increased their exports and those having net imports increased their imports.

The Donets-Dnieper region also has by far the greatest intraregional movements. No other region is even close. Intraregional movements in the Donets-Dnieper region make up about two-thirds of all freight originations and terminations in the area. The heaviest rail traffic in the country flows between the two nodes of the Donets-Dnieper heavy industrial region, with the Donets Basin sending great quantities of coal westward and Krivoy Rog and Nikopol sending large quantities of iron ore and manganese eastward. However, no single railroad in this region has traffic equal to that which moves along the Omsk-Novosibirsk section of the Trans Siberian Railroad. The Urals are a very weak second in intraregional movements, having less than half those of the Donets-

Dnieper Region, and the Northwest and Center are close third and fourth. These are followed by Western Siberia and the Volga Region.

In addition to eastern Ukraine and the West Siberian section of the Trans Siberian Railroad, very heavy rail traffic moves along the three main lines connecting the Donets Basin with the Central Region. Northbound freight predominates on all these lines since heavy raw materials and steel move northward to the Center and light finished goods move southward out of the Center.

Four main rail lines connect the Center eastward with the Urals and Western Siberia. Westbound traffic dominates on all these rail lines. Since the mid 1950s, the heavy westbound movement of coal, ores, and steel between Western Siberia, the Urals, and European Russia have been augmented by large movements of grain from the new lands of Western Siberia and northern Kazakhstan.

The Soviets have published 1970 data on the movement of only the following bulky goods: coal and coke, oil and oil products, ores, wood products, and cement. Cement generally moves short distances and therefore does not figure significantly in interregional trade. As for coal, the greatest originations by far were in the Donets-Dnieper region, 236 million tons. Western Siberia originated 119 million tons, Kazakhstan originated 59 million tons, and other regions were significantly less. The Donets-Dnieper region exported 71 million tons and imported 6 million tons, probably from the adjacent eastern end of the Donets Basin lying in the North Caucasus region in the Russian Republic, for a net export of 65 million tons. Coal exports accounted for almost one-third of the total exports of the Donets-Dnieper Region. Almost all of this went by rail. Only 5 million tons were exported via water, which attests to the underuse of the Volga-Don waterway, which might be expected to carry major portions of such bulky commodities. Western Siberia had a net export of 53 million tons of coal, which constituted half the exports of that region. All of this went by rail. The only other two regions with signif-

icant net exports of coal and coke were Kazakhstan with 18 million tons and the North Caucasus with 15 million tons. Kazakhstan had a fairly high activity of coal movements, with 28 million tons exported and 10 million tons imported. Since the Kazakhstan coals are not of the highest quality, considerable amounts of Kuznetsk coal must be brought in for the metallurgical industry in Karaganda.

Imports of coal and coke were dispersed more evenly among regions. The Urals were by far the largest importer, with 50 million tons coming into the region and 7 million tons going out of the region. The net import of 43 million tons constituted about one-third of all Urals regional imports. Other than this, regions such as the Center, the Central Black Earth Region, the Volga, the Southwest, and the South each had net regional imports of 15–16 million tons.

The oil transport data are clouded by the fact that they include both crude oil and oil products, so that some regions with high refinery capacity show large originations even though they may not be producing any crude oil. Since many of the new refineries have been placed in market areas, this distorts the picture considerably. Also, the data do not include movement by pipeline which has become very important for the major producing regions such as the Volga Region and Western Siberia. Of course, the 1970 data do not reveal the great increase in production in Western Siberia that has taken place since that time. In 1970 the largest loadings of oil and oil products on railroads, rivers, and seas, was largest by far in the Volga Region which loaded 96 million tons. 71 million went by rail and 25 million by water. The "Volgoneft" oil tankers are very noticeable to anyone traveling on the Volga-Don waterway. The North Caucasus region was the second highest originator with 39 million tons. Third was the Central Region, with 31 million tons, all of which, of course, consisted of refined products. The Volga region was the only region that showed very high net exports of oil products in 1970, 51 million tons. The adjacent Urals region had a net export of 6 million tons and Western Siberia 6 million tons. The North Caucasus Region was second to the Volga in total oil transport activity, importing 27 million tons and exporting 21 million tons, but the net import was not outstanding. The Baltic region had the largest net import of oil, with 21 million tons, followed by the South Region with 17 million tons. The Far East had a net import of 10 million tons. Other than that, net imports were not very large in any particular region. This was probably due to dispersed refining which caused movements of oil products in various directions, both in and out of regions.

In 1970 the Donets-Dnieper Region had by far the largest loading of ores, 111 million tons. Practically all of this was on railroads. A poor second and third were Kazakhstan and the Urals with 37 and 30 million tons respectively. Iron ore obviously accounted for most of this. Since three-fourths of the Donets-Dnieper iron ore is used within the region, net exports among regions do not show such great discrepancies. The Donets-Dnieper region exported 41 million tons and imported 9 million tons, probably mainly from Kerch in the South Economic Region and the KMA in the Central Chernozem Region. Thus, the Donets-Dnieper Region had a net export of ores of 32 million tons. Next was Kazakhstan with 21 million tons. The Urals, on the other hand, imported much more ore than they exported. They imported 30 million tons and exported 7 million tons, for a net import of 23 million tons. These were the largest net ore imports of any economic region. The Urals were followed closely in this respect by the Southwest which had net ore imports of 22 million tons. A poor third was Western Siberia with net imports of 10 million tons, probably all iron ore from adjacent Kazakhstan and Eastern Siberia.

The biggest net exporters of wood products were the Northwest with 28 million tons, Eastern Siberia with 25 million tons, the Urals with 19 million tons, and the Volgo-Vyatka Region with 11 million tons. Wood exports constituted more than one-third of the net exports of the Northwest Region and about 40 per cent of the net exports of the West Siberian Region. The biggest importers were the Donets-Dnieper Region with 16 million tons and the Southwest Region with 13 million tons. Some other areas with many wood processing industries showed very high wood transport activities but did not figure significantly in net imports and exports. For instance, the Central Region loaded 15 million tons and unloaded 18 million tons, but had net imports of only 3 million tons. Most of the interregional wood exports from the Northwest must move by rail, since the rivers in the region flow northward and do not serve domestic markets. The Urals, on the other hand, make considerable use of the Kama-Volga waterway. About two-thirds of the Urals wood exports go by rail and one-third by water.

PASSENGER TRAFFIC

Railroads traditionally have also carried the bulk of passenger traffic of the U.S.S.R., but this is changing now. The railroads' share of total passenger-kilometers has diminished from 90 per cent in 1950 to less than 42 per cent in 1975. (Table 15–12) Most of this relative decrease has been due to the exceedingly rapid increase of bus traffic and, to a lesser extent, air traffic. Buses have displaced many railroads in suburban commuting. Bus traffic increased twelve-fold from 1950 to 1960 and almost five times again between 1960 and 1975. The relative share of total passenger traffic increased from 5.3 per cent in 1950 to 40.6 per cent in 1975.

Air passenger transport has had an equally phenomenal growth. It increased ten times between 1950 and 1960, and since then has increased ten times again. In 1950 airlines provided a little over 1 per cent of the total passenger transport, but by 1975 this portion had risen to over 16 per cent. Of course, all of this is intercity transport. If one deducts commuting by bus and train, then the share of airplane traffic rises to 28.8 per cent of total, trains rise to 52.6 per cent, and buses decline to 16.5 per cent. In 1975 Aeroflot, the official Soviet airline, carried more than 98 million passengers, which was five times the number it

Table 15–12   Passenger Traffic by Type of Carrier, U.S.S.R., Selected Years, and U.S.A., 1973, in Billions of Passenger-Kilometers and Per Cents of Total

	U.S.S.R.						U.S.A.
	1913	1928	1950	1960	1970	1975	1973 [a]
Total	32.7	26.9	98.3	249.5	553.1	747.1	2171
Per Cent	100	100	100	100	100	100	100
Railroad	30.3	24.5	88.0	170.8	265.4	312.5 [b]	14.4
Per Cent	92.7	91.1	89.6	68.4	48.0	41.8	0.7
Bus	—	—	5.2	61.0	202.5	303.6 [c]	41.6
Per Cent	—	—	5.3	24.4	36.6	40.6	1.9
Air	—	—	1.2	12.1	78.2	122.6	229
Per Cent	—	—	1.2	4.8	14.1	16.4 [d]	10.5
River	1.4	2.1	2.7	4.3	5.4	6.3	6.4 [e]
Per Cent	4.3	7.8	2.7	1.7	1.0	0.8	0.3
Sea	1.0	0.3	1.2	1.3	1.6	2.1	—
Per Cent	3.1	1.1	1.2	0.5	0.3	0.3	—
Private Car	—	—	—	—	—	—	1878
Per Cent	—	—	—	—	—	—	86.5

Sources: Computed from *Narkhoz SSSR,* 1975, pp. 456, 460, and 481, and *Statistical Abstract of the United States,* 1976, p. 583.

[a] Intercity only.

[b] Long-distance passenger traffic involving 340,000,000 passengers averaging 658 kilometers per trip accounted for 223,800,000,000 passenger-kilometers and commuting involving 3,130,000,000 passengers traveling an average of 28 kilometers accounted for 88,700,000,000 passenger-kilometers.

[c] Intercity traffic involving 1,891,000,000 passengers averaging 37.2 kilometers per trip accounted for 70,300,000,000 passenger-kilometers, and commuting involving 7,716,000,000 passengers traveling an average distance of 10.8 kilometers accounted for 83,600,000,000 passenger-kilometers.

[d] 28.8 per cent of intercity traffic.

[e] Includes rivers, Great Lakes, and coastal traffic.

carried in 1960. This compares to 205 million passengers carried by U.S. airlines in 1975. At the end of 1975 Aeroflot operated over 827,000 kilometers of scheduled routes, of which 182,000 kilometers were international. (Fig. 15–14) The international routes have been the fastest growing part of the network.

Since 1955 average air trips have shown a sharp decrease in length because of the burgeoning development of local air lines in virtually every region of the Soviet Union, which have given a great impetus to air travel over medium distances. These local lines now handle more than half of the total air passengers and have cut deeply into the expected increase of passenger traffic on railroads for medium-length hauls. In most cases air rates

have been set arbitrarily at levels comparable to first-class rates on the railroads, which puts them within the financial reach of many of the ordinary workers in the country. On most domestic routes, all airplanes are jammed to capacity with citizens and their families who are moving from one job to another or are going on scheduled vacations.

The Soviet Union has been a pioneer in the field of jet propulsion and the development of large high-speed transport planes. People in remote areas that used to be almost inaccessible because of vast distances or lack of surface transport facilities now find themselves within easy reach of the main centers of the country through only a few hours' flight by jet aircraft. Although the line-haul costs of airplanes are

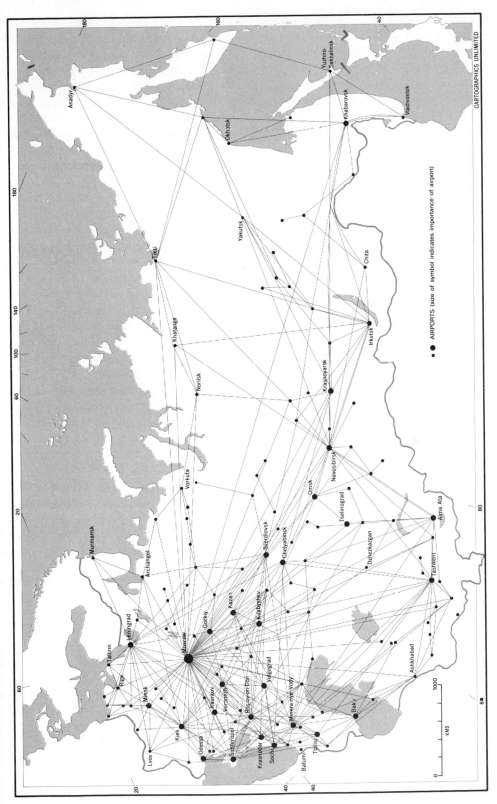

Figure 15–14 Airline routes.

high, the initial outlays of capital for facilities and equipment are low, and this consideration has proved to be of most importance in the Soviet Union's desire to overcome the time factor in catching up with the West.

At the other end of the scale, the initial capital outlays for automotive traffic are exceedingly high, involving the construction of hundreds of thousands of kilometers of good roads and the production of millions of automobiles. The strict competition for investment capital in the Soviet Union has thus relegated automotive traffic to a low priority, and intercity automobile traffic is practically undeveloped. In contrast, in the United States the private automobile accounts for 86 per cent or more of all passenger traffic. The number of passenger automobiles registered in the Soviet Union in 1975 was 3,782,000, which for a country of 253,000,000 people was a very small stock of passenger cars indeed. Whereas the ratio of the population to automobile registrations in the United States is about 2 to 1, and in West Germany, France, and the United Kingdom about 5 to 1, in the Soviet Union it is more than 66 to 1. If one realizes that this limited stock of automobiles in the Soviet Union is to a large extent in the hands of state organizations rather than private individuals, and that approximately one-fifth of the existing stock is always out of service awaiting repairs, then it appears that there are more than 165 people for every car in unrestricted private use in the U.S.S.R.

In 1975 the production of passenger cars in the U.S.S.R. was 1,201,000 of which 215,000 were exported, mostly to east European countries. Taking into account normal depreciation, the addition of cars to the total fleet in the Soviet Union has been taking place at a rate of only about 500,000 per year. Not only are cars in short supply, but also filling stations and garages.

Passenger traffic on the waterways of the country, which many years ago was very significant, has remained at about the same absolute level throughout the Soviet period, and thus relatively has almost dropped out of the total picture. In view of the slowness of this type of transport, no resurgence of its importance can be expected. At the present time much of the river passenger traffic is for commuting or pleasure purposes within cities such as Moscow, where the Moscow River has been canalized and lined with frequent river stations. These are often combined with amusement facilities to provide pleasure-seeking citizens the opportunity to take a short evening cruise of a few kilometers length and combine it with an evening of dining and dancing on one of the old river boats lashed to the bank to serve as a combination river station and amusement hall. Longer cruises of several days duration have been organized on some of the canal and waterway systems, such as the Volga-Don.

Since the private automobile is a negligible factor in passenger traffic in the Soviet Union, public transportation systems within cities are crowded by swarms of urban dwellers who are either commuting to work, going shopping, or simply killing time. Since most living quarters are cramped, and frequently more than one family is living in the same apartment, leisure time is not easily spent at home, and many people simply wander the streets trying to amuse themselves when they are not on the job. Very cheap fares on public conveyances induce people to ride indiscriminantly. At any time of day, it seems the buses, streetcars, trolleys, and subways are jammed to capacity. In recent years there has been a rapid conversion from streetcars and trolleys to buses. Subways exist in Moscow, Leningrad, Kiev, Kharkov, Tbilisi, Baku, and Tashkent. Subways are under construction in Yerevan, Minsk, and Gorky and they are planned for Novosibirsk, Sverdlovsk, Kuybyshev, Riga, Dnepropetrovsk, and Volgograd.[1]

The subways of Moscow are world-renowned not only for their good service but for their beauty and cleanliness. Built far underground to cross beneath the Moscow River, they are well lighted and ventilated and are lined with large murals and chandeliers. The

[1] For more details on subways, see *Soviet Geography: Review and Translation*, June 1978, p. 429.

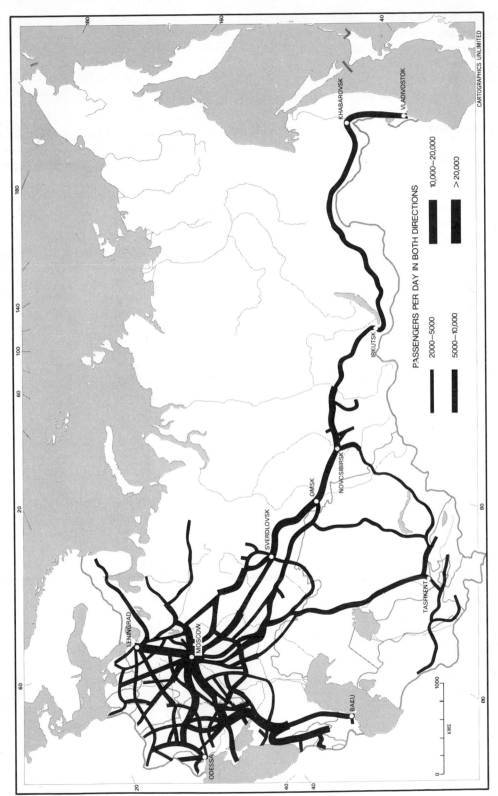

Figure 15–15 Main intercity passenger flows. After Nikolskiy, Tonyaev, and Krasheninnikov, p. 60.

escalators leading down into the subways themselves are something at which to marvel; they pitch at angles of 45 degrees and go so deeply into the earth that one cannot see the bottom when he enters the top.

Intercity passenger flows resemble freight flows. (Fig. 15–15) The heaviest movement by far is between the Center and eastern Ukraine. Part of this flow continues southeastward to the Caucasus. Moderately heavy flows also move eastward from the Center along the Trans Siberian Railroad, particularly between Omsk and Novosibirsk in Western Siberia.

Reading List

1. Alexander, Jean, *Russian Aircraft Since 1940,* Putnam, London, 1975, 555 pp.
2. *Atlas Avtomobilnykh dorog SSSR* (Highway Atlas of the U.S.S.R.), Glavnoe upravlenie geodezii i kartografii pri SM SSSR, Moscow, annually, about 170 pp.
3. "The Baykal-Amur Mainline," *Voprosy Geografii,* No. 105, 1977.
4. Beloglazova, O. A., and Mikhaylenko, V. Ya., eds., *Atlas skhem zheleznykh dorog SSSR* (Railroad Atlas of the U.S.S.R.), G.U.G.K., Moscow, 1976, 101 pp.
5. Edwards, Imogene U., "Automotive Trends in the USSR," in *Soviet Economic Prospects for the Seventies,* Joint Economic Committee, Congress of the United States, June 1973, pp. 291–315.
6. Edwards, Imogene, and Fraser, Robert, "The Internationalization of the East European Automotive Industries," in *East European Economies, Post-Helsinki,* Joint Economic Committee, Congress of the United States, August 25, 1977, pp. 396–419.
7. Galitskiy, M. I., Danilov, S. K., and Korneev, A. I., *Ekonomicheskaya geografiya transporta SSSR,* Moscow, 1965, 303 pp. Translated into English by Joint Publications Research Service, JPRS 31647, August 23, 1965.
8. Gohstand, Robert, *The Internal Geography of Trade in Moscow from the Mid-Nineteenth Century to the First World War,* PhD Dissertation, California, Berkeley, 1973.
9. Grava, Sigurd, "Politics and design of the Moscow Metro," *EKISTICS,* March 1977, pp. 174–178.
10. Gudkova, G. N., and Moskin, B. V., "The Development of Motor Roads in the USSR," *Soviet Geography: Review and Translation,* November 1974, pp. 573–581.
11. Kalesnik, S. V., and Pavelenko, V. F., *Soviet Union: A Geographical Survey,* Progress, Moscow, 1976, pp. 245–265.
12. Kibalchich, O. A., "The Baykal-Amur Mainline and the Integrated Economic Development of the Eastern Regions of the USSR," *Soviet Geography: Review and Translation,* June 1976, pp. 384–394.
13. ———, "The Territorial-Production Structure of the Zone of Influence of the Baykal-Amur Mainline," *Soviet Geography: Review and Translation,* June 1976, pp. 394–401.
14. Kovaleva, M. Z., and Shklovskaya, T. S., *Ekonomicheskiy analiz khozyaystvennoy deyatelnosti predpriyatiy morskogo transporta* (An Economic Analysis of Undertakings in Marine Transport), Transport, Moscow, 1976, 206 pp.
15. MacDonald, Hugh, *Aeroflot, Soviet Air Transport Since 1923,* Putnam, London, 1975, 323 pp.
16. Markov, A. N., *Transport SSSR i osnovnye etopy ego razvitiya* (Transport in the U.S.S.R. and Basic Stages in its Development), Nauka, Moscow, 1977, 231 pp.
17. Miller, Elisa B., "The Trans-Siberian Landbridge, a New Trade Route Between Japan and Europe: Issues and Prospects," *Soviet Geography: Review and Translation,* April 1978, pp. 223–244.
18. Molodykh, I. A., *Passazhirskiy transport v prigorodnoy zone krupnogo goroda* (Passenger Transport in the Suburban Zones of Main Cities), Transport, Moscow, 1976, 144 pp.
19. Nikolskiy, I. V., "Problems in the Study of Domestic Commerce of the USSR," *Soviet Geography: Review and Tranlation,* October 1973, pp. 526–531.
20. Nikolskiy, I. V., Tonyaev, V. I., and Krasheninnikov, V. G., *Geografiya vodnogo transporta SSSR* (Geography of Water Transport in the U.S.S.R.), Transport, Moscow, 1975, 224 pp.
21. Parker, W. H., *Motor Transport and the Motor Industry in the Soviet Union,* Westview Press, Boulder, 1978, 190 pp.
22. Popova, Ye. I., *Transportnyye zatraty v obshchestvennom proizvodstve* (The Costs of Transportation in Social Production), Nauka, Moscow, 1972. Pages 10–94 have been translated into English and published as "The

Transport Industry in the Western and Eastern Zones of the USSR," *Soviet Geography: Review and Translation,* April 1974, pp. 187–243.

23. Shabad, Theodore, and Mote, Victor L., *Gateway to Siberian Resources (The BAM),* Scripta Publishing Company, New York, 1977, 189 pp.

24. Shoemaker, Michael M., *The Great Siberian Railway,* G. P. Putnam and Sons, New York and London, 1904.

25. Sochava, V. B., "Problems in Applied Geography in Connection with the Baykal-Amur Mainline Rail Project," *Soviet Geography: Review and Translation,* March 1976, pp. 159–172.

26. Symons, Leslie, "Soviet Aviation Reviewed," *Soviet Studies,* July 1977, pp. 460–464.

27. Symons, Leslie, and White, Colin, eds., *Russian Transport: An Historical and Geographical Survey,* G. Bell and Sons Ltd., London, 1975, 192 pp.

28. *Transport i svyaz SSSR* (Transport and Communications in the U.S.S.R.), Statistika, Moscow, 1972, 319 pp.

29. Tupper, Harmon, *To The Great Ocean,* Little, Brown and Company, Boston, 1965, 536 pp.

30. Zverev, N. P., and Polikarpov, A. A., *Statistika zheleznodorozhnogo transporta* (Railroad Transport Statistics), Transport, Moscow, 1976, 264 pp.

16

Prospects for Regional Development[1]

It has been demonstrated in previous chapters that natural resources, population, agriculture, industrial production, and transportation facilities are distributed very unevenly across the territory of the Soviet Union. This is true, of course, in any large country with diverse landscapes and climate. Almost 90 per cent of the territory of the U.S.S.R. is unsuitable for cultivation because it is too cold or too dry or too ill drained or too mountainous. Agriculture can be carried on profitably primarily in the so-called "fertile triangle" which stretches from the western border in a tapering wedge eastward across the southern Urals into the southern part of Western Siberia. Other than this, about the only significant agriculture is found in outliers such as the Caucasus, the oases of Central Asia, and the southern basins of Eastern Siberia and the Far East. Since initially most people were engaged in agriculture, the agricultural potentials of the land largely determined the original settlement pattern. As industrialization proceeded, manufacturing plants generally were attracted to the already populated portions of the country with their developed infrastructures. Metallurgical

plants wherever possible exploited mineral deposits located within the settled ecumene. Only extractive activities utilized outlying resources of minerals, timber, etc. Thus, such things as mineral resources have played only minor roles in the broad areal location of industry, limited primarily to the intensification of nodes of settlement and economic activity within the overall pattern of development. As late as 1976, a Soviet analysis concluded that the correlation between the distributions of industrial resources and industrial output was practically nil, while the correlation between the distributions of population and industrial output was close to 1.00.[2]

Such an uneven distribution of settlement and economic activity does not satisfy Soviet ideology. Marxian doctrine requires that in order for a country to be socialist, all its regions must be highly developed, otherwise it becomes illogical that the developed regions in the same country should be considered socialist when the undeveloped regions are not. Social justice can only be achieved if citizens in all regions have the same opportunities to be employed at good wages and as a result enjoy good standards of living. In a multinational state such as the Soviet Union, political and cultural equality cannot be attained without economic equality among regions inhabited by different nationalities.

---

[1] In addition to publications cited at the end of the chapter, some of the concepts presented here have been drawn from unpublished manuscripts by Donald W. Green and Herbert S. Levine, George A. Huzinec, Robert G. Jensen, Theodore Shabad, Hans-Jurgen Wagener, and Douglas Whitehouse.

[2] Runova, p. 84.

Such a doctrine confronts Soviet regional planners with the needs to: (1) develop densely populated, industrially undeveloped regions, (2) integrate harsh pioneer areas rich in natural resources into the mainstream of the country's economic life, (3) placate opposing nationality and regional interests, (4) erase the differences between rural and urban life, and at the same time (5) rejuvenate or diversify old industrial areas with the attraction of growth industries.[3]

These needs for development have generally been in opposition to economic realities which stem from two overriding objectives that have emerged in all socialist countries: (1) emphasis on overall growth of industry, primarily producer goods, and (2) haste to create a strong base for defense. In addition, so far these two overriding objectives have had to be achieved within the constraints of severe limitations of capital and, more recently, of labor. Therefore, the primary principle that has emerged in the development process of socialist countries is most rapid growth of industrial development with maximization of returns on capital and labor inputs. This has required that: (1) natural resources be exploited in a way that minimizes the social costs of their production, including transport, and (2) manufacturing industries be located either near natural resources or consumer markets, again according to minimal costs of production, including transport.

In the regional apportionment of industry, the Soviets have generally tried to achieve both regional specialization on the one hand, to take advantage of peculiarly favorable conditions for given industries, and, on the other hand, complex development of each region to achieve regional autarky which would be invaluable for the defense of the country during times of stress. The balance between these two opposing objectives has shifted through time, primarily according to the international situation. For instance, between 1940 and 1957 there was a two-tier hierarchy of economic regions, thirteen major economic regions for planning and reporting purposes and many more minor regions for the management of industry and agriculture. One of the main functions of the major economic regions was to plan in such a way that each region would be somewhat self-sufficient in case of national emergency. This, of course, was a direct result of the Soviet experience in World War II when many of the factories had to be hastily reassembled in the eastern regions. After the war, until about 1960, the overriding fear of the Soviets was a repeat of this situation, and they wanted to be prepared for it by making outlying regions semi-independent of the western regions of the country so that they could carry on if the western regions were lost. Since 1960 it appears that the Soviets have not been so fearful of this event. In 1961 they divided the country into 19 economic regions without any subdivisions, and investment capital was reallocated regionally to some extent so that the disproportionate shares of outlying areas were pared down somewhat.

Whatever the regional subdivision, planning has continued to be done primarily from the center. Throughout much of Soviet history, economic regions have not been provided with planning bodies, and on occasions when they have, these bodies have been rather ineffective.[4] Therefore, any push for greater regional development in a given area has had to be initiated by local authorities. The precedence of branch over territorial authority in industry necessitates any regional effort for a larger share of total investment to struggle through a bureaucratic maze of separate ministries. Therefore, the establishment of an optimally efficient industrial structure for each region has been most unlikely. In addition, branch authority has mitigated against cooperative utilization of common regional installations such as power supplies, water and sewer systems, and transportation equipment. Each ministerial enterprise in a given region has usually set up its own separate facilities. This tendency for

---

[3] Dienes, 1972, p. 437.

[4] Dewdney, 1967, pp. 25–28.

industrial and ministerial autarky has compounded the problem of placing industrial investments rationally among regions.

It appears that over time the rates of development of various regions in the Soviet Union have not corresponded very closely to economic principles. There has been considerable directive from the center to invest capital in undeveloped regions, primarily to exploit large natural resources, despite low returns on such capital investments. To get some idea of the extent of the deviation of Soviet practice from purely economic considerations, let us take a look at the results of some studies that involve the evaluation of the regional distribution of both the natural resource base in the country and the distribution of people and their cultural infrastructures, and compare these with regional patterns of investment and production.

DISTRIBUTION OF THE RESOURCE BASE

An attempt has been made to assess the natural resource base of the Soviet Union according to the nineteen economic regions.[5] This assessment has been based on coal, oil, natural gas, iron ore, hydroelectric power, timber, arable land, natural forage, and a category called "other" which allows emphasis of such things as chemical raw materials, nonferrous metals, and the like where they are particularly significant in a region. Although this list excludes such things as nonmetals, some ferrous metals, some plant resources, resources of the animal world, and water resources other than those used for power generation, it is a more complete assessment than most because it attempts to include the agricultural resources of the land, particularly soil, heat, and moisture, which are usually the most important resources of any long-settled area. The results are shown in Table 16-1.

Using these criteria, the European part of the U.S.S.R., including the Urals, accounts for more than 40 per cent of the total potential of

the counry, and Siberia and the Far East about 33 per cent. The agricultural component of the resource potential represents more than 69 per cent of the total resources of Kazakhstan, 65 per cent of the European south, 64 per cent of the middle and northern latitudes of European U.S.S.R., and 61 per cent of Central Asia. Only in Siberia and the Far East does it play only a modest role, around 15 per cent.

As can be seen in Figure 16-1, the greatest natural resource density per unit area is found in the southern agricultural regions of the wooded steppe, the steppe, and the desert oases, particularly where they are associated with large mineral and hydroelectric resources, such as in the Donets Basin, the Dnieper Valley, the Middle Volga, and the mountains of Central Asia. In the eastern regions only the Kuznetsk Basin is distinguished by a high resource density. Of course, if some of the huge eastern regions had been divided into smaller territorial units other regions of resource concentrations might have become visible, for instance the oil region in central Tyumen Oblast. But unfortunately data have not been made available for sub-oblast regions. In terms of resource potential per capita, the eastern regions rank higher. (Fig. 16-2) Thus, the southern half of the European part of the U.S.S.R. has the greatest concentration of natural resources, but since this area is much more heavily populated than the eastern regions, opportunities for individuals in certain categories of work might be greater in the east.

The foregoing discussion on natural resources, of course, does not take into account such economic considerations as level of development, transport infrastructure, accumulations of capital, and so forth which might play just as large roles or even more dominant roles than natural resources in projecting returns on capital investments and hence optimal locations for new economic activity. Market potentials and transport costs are enormously important in such a vast country where the bulk of the population is concentrated in only a small portion of the area and where levels of economic development show such great regional disparities.

[5] Mints and Kakhanovskaya.

Table 16–1   Natural Resource Potential by Economic Regions of the U.S.S.R.

Economic Region	Total Potential in % of U.S.S.R.	Coal	Oil, Gas	Iron Ore	Hydro	Timber	Arable	Forage	Others	Total
					Percentage of Each Resource Group in Total Potential					
Northwest	3.2	14.0	4.3	3.5	10.5	30.5	11.3	5.6	20.3	100.0
Central	2.6	3.1	—	0.4	1.4	10.6	73.9	10.6	—	100.0
Volga-Vyatka	1.3	—	—	—	5.2	18.5	69.5	6.8	—	100.0
Central Chernozem	3.1	—	—	28.6	0.1	0.4	67.8	3.1	—	100.0
Volga	7.0	0.3	37.9	0.0	5.3	2.5	50.4	3.6	—	100.0
North Caucasus	4.8	8.3	14.2	—	7.4	0.6	65.1	4.4	—	100.0
Urals	5.4	5.3	27.8	5.1	1.6	9.5	35.7	4.3	10.7	100.0
West Siberia	15.8	18.5	49.8	0.4	5.3	6.3	16.8	2.9	—	100.0
East Siberia	10.1	28.8	0.1	1.7	29.2	15.4	10.4	2.8	11.6	100.0
Far East	5.1	13.7	3.9	1.4	40.3	18.8	5.6	3.3	13.0	100.0
Donets-Dnieper	7.2	39.1	3.1	12.3	0.9	0.0	43.3	1.3	—	100.0
Southwest	3.6	1.6	4.8	—	1.8	1.3	86.7	3.8	—	100.0
South	1.5	—	0.7	5.9	2.1	0.1	89.1	2.1	—	100.0
Baltic (with Kaliningrad)	1.0	—	—	—	6.2	6.0	75.8	12.0	—	100.0
Transcaucasia	1.7	1.1	26.1	1.1	30.4	0.8	30.1	10.4	—	100.0
Central Asia	10.1	2.1	14.5	0.0	19.6	0.0	47.6	14.0	2.2	100.0
Kazakhstan	14.7	9.9	3.8	3.2	3.0	0.2	27.5	41.6	10.8	100.0
Belorussia	1.2	—	5.5	—	1.8	4.0	78.0	10.7	—	100.0
Moldavia	0.6	—	0.1	—	1.2	0.3	96.7	1.7	—	100.0
Total U.S.S.R.	100.0	12.4	15.9	3.1	10.2	6.0	37.0	10.6	4.9	100.0

Source: Mints and Kakhanovskaya, p. 560.

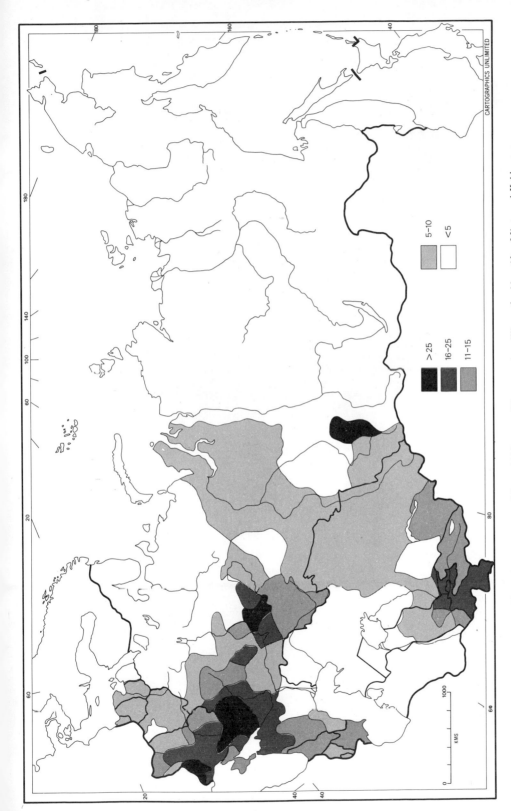

Figure 16–1 *Natural resource potential per 1000 square kilometers, in millions of rubles. After Mints and Kakhanovs-kaya, 1974, p. 562.*

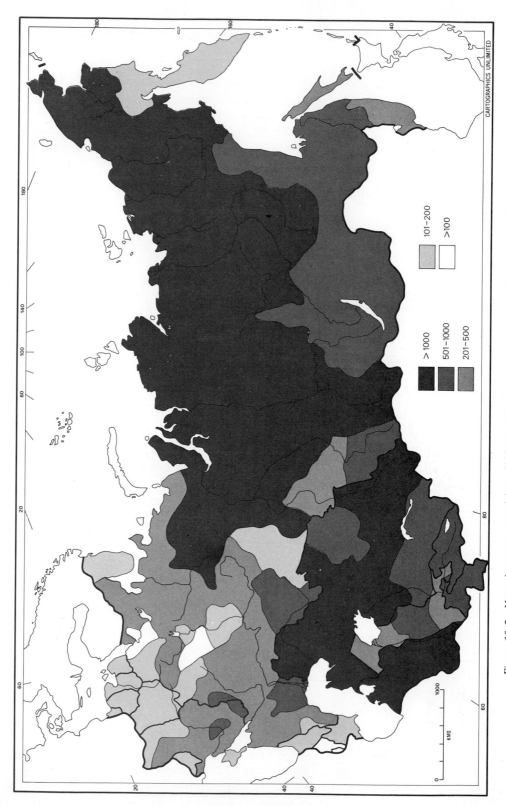

Figure 16–2   Natural resource potential per 1000 population, in thousands of rubles. After Mints and Kakhanovskaya, 1974, p. 563.

MARKET POTENTIAL AND TRANSPORTATION COSTS

The market potential for most industrial goods produced in the Soviet Union is greatest around Moscow in the heart of the heavily populated European portion of the U.S.S.R. and diminishes fairly rapidly outward in all directions in a somewhat concentric pattern. Of course, it diminishes much more rapidly toward the empty lands of the northeast than toward the continuously populated area southward. The market potential falls off least rapidly eastward along the tapering wedge of population that pushes into southern Siberia. (Fig. 16–3) Thus, as would be expected, the market potential for industrial goods in the Soviet Union pretty well matches the population distribution. From this factor alone, it might be concluded that the best place to locate industries to serve the national market would be in Moscow, and choices for location become progressively less favorable away from that point.

Since much of the advantage of industrial location is related to transportation costs, it is instructive to look at Figure 16–4 which approximates potential transportation costs, in per cents greater than those of the least cost center to serve a given market. The top map shows that Moscow is the cheapest center from which to service the entire national market. Transportation costs away from Moscow increase rapidly northeastward and southward, with a less rapid increase directly eastward along main trunk lines of railroads running into Western Siberia. However, by the time one reaches Novosibirsk in Western Siberia, transportation costs to serve the national market are 80 per cent higher than those of Moscow, and at Irkutsk in Eastern Siberia they are more than twice as high. The Far East would experience costs four times as high as Moscow.

The advantage of the Central Economic Region in European Russia increases as the percentage of national market to be served decreases. Thus, the Central Region has an even greater advantage in serving that part of the national market that one would normally expect it to serve within a reasonable distance. At the 50 per cent market level, the least-cost center shifts from Moscow to Bryansk in the southwestern portion of the Central Economic Region. Costs increase rapidly outward from this center, and by the time one gets to the Far East costs have jumped ten times. When the market to be served is only 25 per cent of the national market, the least-cost center shifts back to Moscow, and transport costs increase even more rapidly outward, reaching 15 times in the Far East. It is obvious that in densely populated European Russia, one does not have to go nearly so far to serve 25 per cent of the national market as one does in the Far East and Siberia where population density is low.

PROFITABILITY

Aside from the mere distance relationships of market potential and transportation costs, there is a wide regional variation in returns on inputs that relates to conditions within regions themselves. As was shown at the end of Chapter 8, fixed industrial capital per capita is highest in the outlying areas of the country. (Table 8–14) The Far East and Eastern Siberia are the most highly capitalized regions in the country. It is obvious that it costs more to establish industries in these regions than in already established industrial areas of European U.S.S.R. But these regions have some of the lowest percentage returns on capital and the lowest labor productivity of any of the economic regions. (Table 16–2) Industrial wages must be kept high in the eastern regions in order to attract labor there at all.

The Far East average industrial wage is 66 per cent higher than the average for the country, but even this is not enough to compensate for the higher costs of living and general lack of amenities in this remote area, so that labor is still not enticed into the region in sufficient quantities. (Table 16–3) What labor is drawn (or sent) into these outlying areas is often transitory in nature and results in a high level of labor turnover in industry. Thus, in spite of

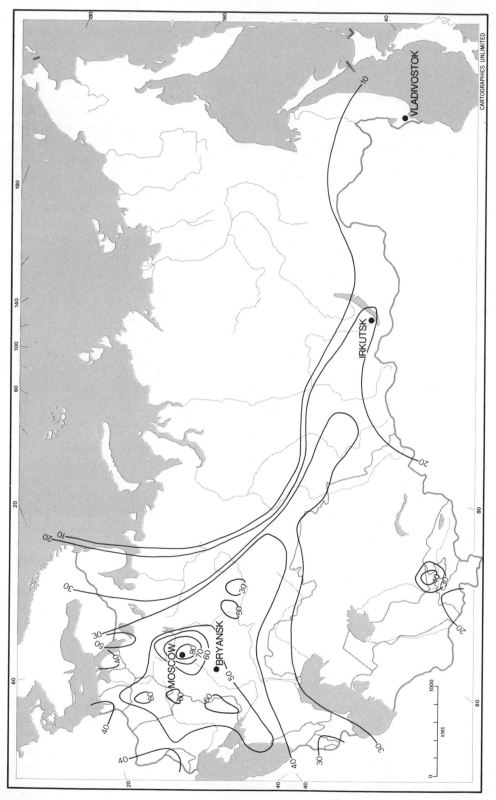

Figure 16–3   Market potential of all points in the U.S.S.R., as percent of Moscow. Based on urban population weighted by retail sales per capita by republic. After Houston, Cecil, "Market Potential and Potential Transportation Costs: an Evaluation of the Concepts and their Surface Patterns in the U.S.S.R.," The Canadian Geographer, Vol. 13, 1969, p. 221.

the capital-intensive nature of industry in the eastern regions, the wages bills generally constitute larger percentages of value added by manufacture than in other regions of the country. (Table 16–2) In Kazakhstan the wages bill amounts to as much as 48 per cent of the value added, in the Far East 45 per cent, and in Eastern Siberia 43 per cent. These three highest regions in the country compare to an average percentage for the U.S.S.R. of only 35. In the Volga-Vyatka and Central Regions, which together with the Southwest Region have the lowest wages bills of the country, the wages bills constitute only 27 and 28 per cent respectively of the value added.

In addition to paying significantly higher wages in the eastern regions, the Soviets must provide necessities of life such as housing, schools, medical facilities, and transport systems in these underdeveloped areas in order to establish a labor force at a new industrial site. In these outlying areas often new industries must incur such auxiliary costs themselves, while in established areas, where infrastructures already exist, new plants are relieved of much of this cost. It has been stated that it costs 7500 rubles per worker more to establish new housing and service facilities in southern Siberia than it does in the western populated areas, and the direct cost of resettlement of a family is no less than 1000 rubles.[6]

Transport, of course, is the major problem in these outlying regions. The index of transport infrastructure is only 20–35 per cent that of the country average in such regions as Eastern Siberia, the Far East, and Kazakhstan. (Table 16–2) The transport infrastructure in the most poorly supplied region, Eastern Siberia, is only 4 per cent as well endowed as that of the best supplied region, the Baltic. In general there is a great dichotomy in the development of the transport system, particularly the railroads, between the European part of the country on the one hand and the eastern-Central Asia regions on the other hand.

The regional discrepancies in returns on capital and labor inputs are not limited to comparisons between east and west. There are very significant discrepancies within the old established industrial areas themselves. Returns on fixed capital are more than twice as high in the Volgo-Vyatka and Central regions as they are in the Donets-Dnieper and Urals regions. This relates primarily to differences in amounts of labor and the level of labor skills used in the industrial process. In the Volgo-Vyatka and Central regions large amounts of skilled labor constitute much of the industrial input, while in the heavy industry areas of the Donets-Dnieper and Urals regions much more capital is employed. Generally labor productivity is greatest in the Central, Volgo-Vyatka, and Northwest industrial regions, also. Therefore, the highest returns on fixed capital are realized in the Central and Volgo-Vyatka regions.

However, these regions do not necessarily realize the largest returns on new capital investments. During the 1960s the highest marginal capital product in industry (growth of industrial output resulting from a given increase of fixed investment over a time period) was experienced in the Transcaucasus, North Caucasus, Southwest, and Southern regions where large supplies of cheap labor coupled with rapidly changing technologies provided maximum returns on investment capital.[7] (Table 16–2) In contrast the old industries of the Central Region showed returns on new investments that were slightly less than the average for the entire country, and Eastern Siberia was exceedingly low. The Far East was a little above the national average, but again it must be realized that the establishment of labor in these frontier areas entails large additional costs that are not included in the industrial investment figures taken into account here.

RECENT INVESTMENT TRENDS AND PROSPECTS FOR THE FUTURE

In light of generally poor returns on capital

[6] Ivanchenko, A. A., "Trudovye resursy i razmeshcheniye promyshlennosti," in *Planirovaniye i ekonomiko-matematicheskiye metody,* Nauka, Moscow, 1964, pp. 214–215.

[7] Dienes, 1972.

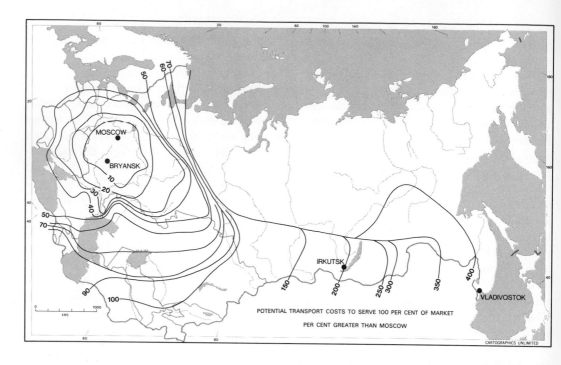

POTENTIAL TRANSPORT COSTS TO SERVE 100 PER CENT OF MARKET

PER CENT GREATER THAN MOSCOW

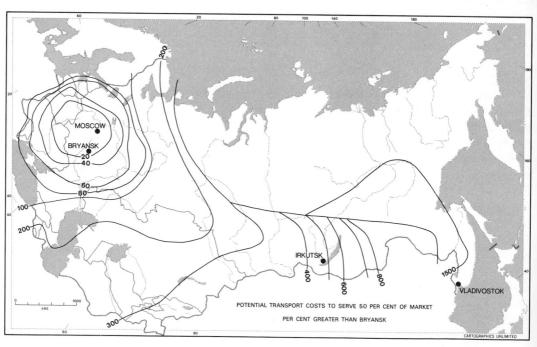

POTENTIAL TRANSPORT COSTS TO SERVE 50 PER CENT OF MARKET

PER CENT GREATER THAN BRYANSK

inputs, low labor productivity, high wages bill, and problems with labor shortages and high labor turnover in the eastern regions, it would seem that the Soviets would be unwise to place more than necessary investments in these areas of the country. Yet, over the years the Soviets generally have poured disproportionate amounts of investment into the eastern regions.

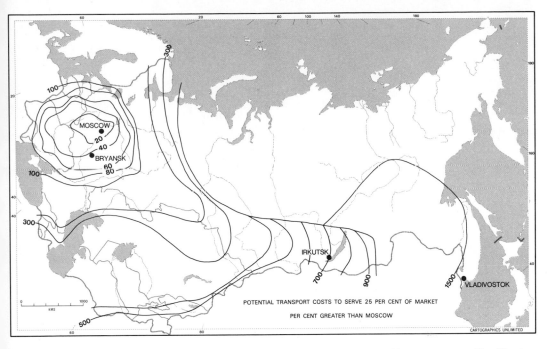

Figure 16-4   Potential transportation costs of all points in the U.S.S.R., as percent of least cost center. After Houston, Cecil, "Market Potential and Potential Transportation Costs: an Evaluation of the Concepts and their Surface Patterns in the U.S.S.R.," The Canadian Geographer, Vol. 13, 1969, pp. 222 and 233.

This subsidization of Eastern Siberia and the Far East, as well as most northern regions of the country, apparently is motivated by the continuance of a pioneering spirit which has always propelled the Russians to push the frontier of their ecumene farther and farther into the wilderness, as well as ideological inertia which clings to the principle to develop all parts of the country. These rather vague urges are undoubtedly buttressed by such things as strategic apprehension, a northern vision aspect of the national image, and to some extent Great Russian chauvinism. In the latter respect it appears significant that most of the investment capital that has been poured into the economic development of outlying regions has been applied largely to the outlying parts of the Russian Republic rather than to outlying other republics.[8]

The "man-over-nature" tenet of Hegelian-Marxian doctrine, as well as the natural appeal to the Soviets of grandiose projects,

[8] Hooson, p. 553.

must not be overlooked either. In some cases, particularly hydroconstruction projects, it appears that such things as dams have been built simply because the rivers were there. The physical feasibility of reordering natural conditions, such as streamflow, to more nearly suit the needs of human occupancy appears to be a propelling force that the Soviets have found hard to resist even though individual projects might not have been justified economically. Although such projects might be rejected time and again on economic grounds, eventually they frequently end up getting done. As one well-known Soviet economic geographer has said, "These proposals, once drawn up, tend to take on a life of their own, circulating for a long time, then vanishing, only to reappear at a later stage."[9]

Investment in larger construction projects in some of the eastern and northern regions has already been so great that it is now difficult to discontinue capitalization. For instance, the

[9] Saushkin, p. 294.

Table 16–2 Regional Indices for Development

	Return as Percentage of Fixed Capital 1968	Marginal Capital Product in Industry 1960–1968	Labor Productivity 1968 U.S.S.R. = 100	Monthly Wages in Industry 1968 100 = 116.7 Rubles	Wages Bill as a Percentage of Value Added	Composite Index of Transport Infrastructure U.S.S.R. = 100	Index of Per Capita State Investment 1959–1967 U.S.S.R. = 100
U.S.S.R.	43	1.33	100.0	100.0	35	100	100
R.S.F.S.R.							
Northwest	51	1.13	114.3	115.7	35	51	174
Central	84	1.03	117.7	95.7	28	293	128
Volgo-Vyatka	89	1.35	115.3	93.6	27	181	80
Central Chernozem	47	1.37	86.7	88.5	31	193	77
Volga	29	1.36	81.7	97.8	39	121	129
North Caucasus	42	1.64	91.3	94.2	34	223	96
Ural	39	1.41	97.1	107.1	37	113	132
Western Siberia	45	1.31	101.0	110.7	35	44	143
Eastern Siberia	25	1.06	83.3	125.7	43	22	197
Far East	31	1.47	94.2	157.2	45	29	207

Ukraine S.S.R.	44				34	
Donets-Dnieper	32	1.32	94.8	109.2	39	441	118
Southwest	78	1.55	104.5	87.8	27	372	58
South	53	1.65	102.7	95.7	33	244	113
Baltic Region	63	1.32	105.4	102.8	29	570	110
Lithuania S.S.R.							91
Latvia S.S.R.							116
Estonia S.S.R.							137
Transcaucasus	25	1.70	81.1	93.5	39	367	83
Georgia S.S.R.							73
Azerbaydzhan S.S.R.							83
Armenia S.S.R.							101
Central Asia	33	1.28	86.7	95.0	36	58	77
Uzbek S.S.R.							74
Kirgiz S.S.R.							68
Tadzhik S.S.R.							72
Turkmen S.S.R.							115
Kazakh S.S.R.	22	1.47	82.0	112.8	48	32	157
Belorussia S.S.R.	71	1.42	105.2	88.5	30	299	74
Moldavia S.S.R.	n.a.	n.a.	n.a.	n.a.	n.a.	399	54

Source: Dienes, Leslie, "Investment Priorities in Soviet Regions," *Annals of the Association of American Geographers*, September, 1972, pp. 440, 442, 444.

Underlined names are the nineteen official Soviet economic regions for planning and statistical reporting.

Table 16–3   Average Industrial Wage by Economic Region, as a Percentage of the Center, Circa 1970

Center	1.00
Northwest	1.22
Volgo-Vyatka	0.97
Central Chernozem	0.92
Volga	0.99
North Caucasus	0.98
Urals	1.10
Western Siberia	1.15
Eastern Siberia	1.33
Far East	1.66
Donets-Dnieper	1.13
Southwest	0.91
South	1.00
Baltic	1.07
Transcaucasus	1.00
Central Asia	1.00
Kazakhstan	n.a.
Belorussia	n.a.
Moldavia	n.a.

Source: Feshbach, pp. 58–59.

Soviets found the lure of the great rivers of Siberia to be too enticing to ignore, so they built a number of huge hydroelectric plants on such rivers as the Yenisey and the Angara. Then they had to look around for a market for the electricity they were capable of producing, and finally decided that they should establish some high-energy, low-labor using industries such as aluminum in these areas to utilize the electricity. Once the aluminum plants were built, however, planners had to look around for sources of alumina to feed them. In most cases they had to go far to get this resource. After the fact, it has become evident to them that probably they would better have placed their aluminum plants near seacoasts where they could depend upon imported sources of alumina and bauxite. However, now they have large aluminum plants in Siberia, and so they must continue to pour money into the development of resources for these plants. The whole process has been one of placing the cart before the horse. They built the hydroelectric stations on the rivers because the rivers were there. But

they did not bother at that point to make a well balanced economic analysis to determine whether this was the best thing to do with their scarce investment capital.

Some unstated change of attitude seems to have taken place during the late 1950s when it was finally realized that no amount of wage differentials or other commonly used incentives could induce adequate labor supplies to move into the eastern regions and stay there. Curiously enough in this totalitarian state, it has been the population that seems to have broken the back of party doctrine to settle the eastern regions. The people simply refuse to move into frontier areas and stay there for any length of time. It has finally been decided by planners that it is more expensive to establish population in remote undeveloped areas and provide them with all the amenities necessary to maintain them there than it is to move raw materials to established settlements.

Nevertheless, during the 1960s Eastern Siberia and the Far East received twice as much investment per capita as the average for the entire country and 3 to 4 times as much as such heavily populated underdeveloped regions close to the industrial center as the Central Chernozem Region, Belorussia, the Southwest, and Moldavia. (Table 16–2) This pattern has continued into the 1970s. (Table 16–4) Thus, it appears that the Soviets still are not investing their industrial capital in the parts of the country where they can expect the greatest returns. It also appears significant that of the seven regions leading in per capita industrial investment during 1971–1975, six are in the Russian Republic, and the seventh, Kazakhstan, has a majority of Russians in its population. Among the other republics, only two of the Baltic states exceeded the national investment average.

There really are two growth patterns going on in the Soviet Union: One that involves skill-intensive manufacturing, and one that involves extractive industry. The growth of skill-intensive manufacturing has tended to cluster in old industrial centers such as Moscow, Leningrad, and the Baltic Republics in response to agglomeration economies, while

Table 16–4   Per Capita Fixed Industrial Investment, 1971–1975, in Rubles, Based on Population as of the 1970 Census

U.S.S.R.	1719
R.S.F.S.R.	1962
Northwest	2301 (4)
Central	1781
Volgo-Vyatka	1333
Central Chernozem	1321
Volga	1972 (6)
North Caucasus	1424
Ural	1864 (7)
Western Siberia	2509 (3)
Eastern Siberia	2659 (2)
Far East	3485 (1)
Ukraine S.S.R.	1316
Donets-Dnieper	1590
Southwest	958
South	1618
Baltic Region	1844 (8)
Lithuania S.S.R.	1697
Latvia S.S.R.	1929
Estonia S.S.R.	2033
Transcaucasus	1126
Georgia S.S.R.	1094
Azerbaydzhan S.S.R.	999
Armenia S.S.R.	1445
Central Asia	1282
Uzbek S.S.R.	1280
Kirgiz S.S.R.	1109
Tadzhik S.S.R.	1081
Turkmen S.S.R.	1797
Kazakh S.S.R.	2214 (5)
Belorussia S.S.R.	1455
Moldavia S.S.R.	1118

Source: Narkhoz SSR, 1922–1972 and 1975, Narkhoz RSFSR, 1975, and Narkhoz UkSSR, 1975.
Underlined names are the nineteen official Soviet economic regions for planning and statistical reporting.
Numbers in parentheses indicate ranks.

the growth of extractive industry has been dispersed into the eastern regions and Central Asia. This dichotomy is not an uncommon phenomenon. The same sort of separation emerged earlier in the developed economies of the West, although much of their extractive capital was invested in underdeveloped parts of the world outside their own countries.

The two patterns of growth have somewhat separate and mutually exclusive regional extents. It would appear that Siberia and northeastern Kazakhstan represent the most economic location for energy-oriented industries because of the large amounts of cheap oil, gas, coal, and hydroelectricity in these regions that overcome the distance factor from the main markets in the west, while the economies of the further development of manufacturing seem to accrue to the western regions with their high densities of settlement, developed infrastructures, accumulated capital, and availability to skilled labor and markets.

The growing eocnomic cooperation between the Soviet Union and its east European satellites exerts an additional strong westward pull on industry in the Soviet Union. As more and more oil and gas pipelines and electrical transmission lines cross the international boundary of western U.S.S.R. and more joint efforts are contracted for with the east European countries to develop Soviet minerals and timber, the economies of the CMEA countries become more individually specialized and integrated with each other. Therefore, the Soviets increasingly find it more convenient and remunerative to locate certain industries closer to the western margins of the country in order to interact most efficiently with their east European satellites. In addition, as Soviet trade rapidly expands, the Soviets are beginning to realize the value of having industries located near coasts in order to facilitate imports and exports of raw materials and finished goods. This generally means more orientation toward the Black and Baltic Seas and to a small extent the southern portion of the Soviet coast of the Pacific.

As the Soviet economy has become more sophisticated, the extractive industries suitable for development in Siberia contribute less and less to the total production and growth of the country. The structural change in Soviet industry toward more consumer goods, synthetics, and engineering products tends to work against the eastern territories. The Soviet Union has entered a mature stage of industrial development where further industrial expansion depends more on an established critical mass of investment capital, infrastructure, and population than on raw materials. This all further enhances the advantages of the western part of the country.

A shortage of industrial labor looms as the most serious problem for continued economic growth in the next decade or two. This should finally force the issue of what to do with the burgeoning population reserves in Central Asia and Transcaucasia. At the present time, except for natural gas piped northwestward out of Central Asia, the industrial contribution of these two regions is not one of national significance. The continuing high birth rate and reluctance of these native populations to move out of their regions, along with continuing inmigration of Russians into these regions, might well provide an irresistible incentive in time of labor shortage to promote labor-intensive industries of national importance in these areas. However, political and strategic considerations might well cause these predominantly non-Russian areas to experience more difficulties in building truly powerful industrial bases than is the case in such overwhelmingly Russian components of the country as Siberia and the Far East.[10]

The meager information so far released on the tenth five-year plan, 1976–1980, has not given a clear indication of future regional distributions of investment capital, but some major thrusts have been specifically mentioned. In order of importance they are: (1) the rehabilitation, both agriculturally and culturally, of the nonchernozem zone of European Russia, (2) the further exploitation of the fuel resources of the Timan-Pechora Ridge in northeastern European Russia, (3) the further development of the Kursk Magnetic Anomaly, (4) the continued exploitation of West Siberian oil and gas, and (5) the completion of the Baykal-Amur Mainline. The plan states that during the five years Siberia, the Far East, Kazakhstan, and Central Asia will account for all the growth in oil and gas production and the

smelting of aluminum, more than 90 per cent of the growth of coal production, 80 per cent of the growth of copper production, and 45 per cent of the growth of cellulose production. It mentions certain other specific projects that are mainly in the eastern regions. It is planned that Siberia as a whole is to achieve a 50 per cent increase in industrial production, as compared to 36 per cent for the entire country.

THE PROCESS OF LOCATIONAL CONCENTRATION[11]

On a local scale, the ideological goals to fill up undeveloped portions of the country and improve the economy of undeveloped nationality groups can be ignored, and the primary goal becomes the achievement of the highest productivity of socialist labor with minimum outlays of capital. This generally means further concentration of economic growth in large cities, since skilled labor is generally concentrated there and the recoupment period for capital is shorter. Although as early as 1931 the Central Committee of the Communist Party of the Soviet Union declared itself against the further growth of big cities, and from time to time has tried to take definite steps to restrict the further industrial growth of such cities as Moscow and Leningrad, in actuality large cities have continued to grow, and usually at faster rates than smaller cities. (Table 6–16) The usual process of "stepping stone" migration from smaller to larger cities results in labor skills increasing with size of city. Thus, sophisticated industries with advanced technologies can better be located in large cities with high labor skills than in small cities which have just received influxes of untrained industrial laborers from surrounding farms.

Soviet planning has tended to emphasize projects with high payoffs in immediate growth. A characteristic feature of such planning is the relative neglect of economic infra-

[10] Hooson, p. 554.

[11] Some of the basic concepts included in this section were first presented in unpublished manuscripts by George A. Huzinec.

structures, particularly the transport network. Railroads have a high capital-to-output ratio and thus do not result in a high payoff in immediate growth. Fixed capital in transport and communications has increased at about half the rate of the increase of fixed capital in the economy as a whole.

The minimization of transport routes means that transport accessibility in the Soviet Union is very uneven. Also, since rolling stock is minimized as well, there is a need to minimize movement over the routes. This creates a tendency for agglomeration in space. Soviet rate setting practices have tended to mask the importance of location and distance by favoring longer hauls and larger shippers. This has created conditions amenable to the concentration of production in large units that serve wide markets.

A planning environment whose main success criterion is the fulfillment of production quotas inevitably emphasizes the expansion of existing facilities or the development of new plants in areas that already provide support services. Existing production capabilities are supported by powerful industrial and governmental organizations. Decision makers often view space distorted toward their own office locations. They are not fully aware of the complete range of opportunities, and since the political sector of society has been given such an inflated role in economic decision making, there is a tendency for investment funds to flow to areas of political importance. The status of a local official obviously is enhanced if his administrative unit is economically strong. Thus, local party officials can be expected to exert much pressure for economic investment funds, and it is logical to conclude that the more politically powerful economic administrative units would be able to influence more investment decisions and therefore secure more for themselves. Thus, there is a never-ending sequence of larger agglomerations becoming even larger.

From the viewpoint of industrial production, the high degree of product specialization in giant plants that seems to be characteristic of Soviet development also enhances the need for agglomeration, since such plants have to be near one another in order to exchange necessary components. In addition, a trend toward automation and improved efficiency has released workers from older industrial enterprises and necessitated the building of new industries in the same cities so that people can be put to work without moving them to other parts of the country.

Reading List

1. Bandera, V. N., and Melnyk, Z. L., eds., *The Soviet Economy in Regional Perspective,* Praeger, New York, 1973, 368 pp.
2. Barr, B. M., "The Changing Impact of Industrial Management and Decision-Making on the Locational Behavior of the Soviet Firm," in Hamilton, F. E. I., ed., *Spatial Perspectives on Industrial Organization and Decision-Making,* Wiley, New York, 1974, pp. 411–446.
3. Burghardt, Andrew F., ed., *Development Regions in the Soviet Union, Eastern Europe and Canada,* Praeger, New York, 1975, 212 pp.
4. Conolly, Violet, *Siberia Today and Tomorrow: A Study of Economic Resources, Problems, and Achievements,* Collins, London, 1975, 248 pp.
5. Dienes, Leslie, "Basic Industries and Regional Economic Growth: The Soviet South," *Tijdschrift voor economische en sociale geografie,* January/February 1977, pp. 2–15.
6. ———, "Investment Priorities in Soviet Regions," *Annals of the Association of American Geographers,* September 1972, pp. 437–454.
7. ———, "Issues in Soviet Energy Policy and Conflicts Over Fuel Costs in Regional Development, *Soviet Studies,* July 1971, pp. 26–58.
8. ———, "Regional Variations of Capital and Labor Productivity in Soviet Industry," *Journal of Regional Science,* December 1972, pp. 401–406.
9. Feshbach, Murray, "Regional and Branch Wage Differentials in the Soviet Union," *ACES Bulletin,* Winter 1975, pp. 57–60.
10. Fitzgerald, John Hoyt, *The Interaction of Demographic Trends in Siberia and Developmental Policy as a Problem for the Soviet Government, 1959–1975,* PhD Dissertation, University of Notre Dame, 1977, 374 pp.
11. Hooson, David, "The Outlook for Regional

Development in the Soviet Union," *Slavic Review*, September 1972, pp. 535–554.

12. Houston, Cecil, "Market Potential and Potential Transportation Costs: An Evaluation of the Concepts and their Surface Patterns in the USSR," *Canadian Geographer*, No. 3, 1969, pp. 216–236.

13. Huzinec, George A., "A Reexamination of Soviet Industrial Location Theory," *The Professional Geographer*, August 1977, pp. 259–265.

14. ———, "Some Initial Comparisons of Soviet and Western Regional Development Models," *Soviet Geography: Review and Translation*, October 1976, pp. 552–566.

15. ———, "The Soviet Strategy for Economic Development: Its Economic and Geographic Spaces," PhD Dissertation, Ohio State University, 1973.

16. Jensen, Robert G., "Soviet Regional Development Policy and the 10th Five-Year Plan," *Soviet Geography: Review and Translation*, March 1978, pp. 196–202.

17. Kalashnikova, T. M., and Khrushchev, A. T., "Territorialnyy aspekt desyatogo pyatiletnego plana razvitiya narodnogo khozyaystva SSSR," (Spatial Aspects of the 10th Five-Year Plan 1976–1980), *Vestnik Moskovskogo Universiteta, geografiya*, 1976, No. 2, pp. 3–9.

18. Khrushchev, A. T., "The Formation of Industrial Complexes in the Eastern Regions of the USSR in the 10th Five-Year Plan (1976–80)," *Geografiya v Shkole*, 1977, No. 2, pp. 6–13.

19. ———, "The Formation of New Industrial Complexes of the USSR in the Ninth Five-Year Plan (1971–75)," *Geografiya v Shkole*, 1972, No. 2.

20. ———, "A Taxonomic Model of Industrial Regionalization of the USSR," *Vestnik Moskovskogo Universiteta, geografiya*, 1976, No. 5, pp. 3–11.

21. Kochetkov, A. V., and Listengurt, F. M., "A Long-Term Plan for Settlement in the USSR," *Izvestiya akademii nauk SSSR, seriya geograficheskaya*, 1976, No. 5, pp. 60–71.

22. Koropeckyj, I. S., "Industrial Location Policy in the USSR During the Postwar Period," *Economic Performance and the Military Burden in the Soviet Union*, Subcommittee on Foreign Economic Policy of the Joint Economic Committee, Congress of the United States, Washington, 1970, pp. 232–295.

23. ———, "Regional Resource Allocation, Growth, and Income Inequality Under Social-

ism," in Bandera, V. N., and Melnyk, Z. L., *The Soviet Economy in Regional Perspective*, Praeger, New York, 1973, pp. 45–62.

24. Lonsdale, Richard E., "Regional Inequity and Soviet Concern for Rural and Small-Town Industrialization," *Soviet Geography: Review and Translation*, October 1977, pp. 590–602.

25. Lydolph, Paul E., and Pease, Steven R., "Changing Distributions of Population and Economic Activities in the USSR," *Tijdschrift voor economische en sociale geografii*, July–August 1972, pp. 244–261.

26. Mazanova, M. B., *Territorialnye proportsii narodnogo khozyaystva SSSR* (Territorial Appointment of the Economy of the U.S.S.R.), Nauka, Moscow, 1974, 206 pp.

27. McAuley, Alastair, "The Distribution of Earnings and Incomes in the Soviet Union," *Soviet Studies*, April 1977, pp. 214–237.

28. Mints, A. A., and Kakhanovskaya, T. G., "An Attempt at a Quantitative Evaluation of the Natural Resource Potential of Regions of the USSR," *Soviet Geography: Review and Translation*, November 1974, pp. 554–565.

29. North, Robert N., "Centralization and the Soviet Regional Economy," in British Columbia Geographical Series, No. 16. *Occasional Papers in Geography*. Contemporary Geography: Research Trends, 1972, pp. 103–110.

30. Orlov, B. P., "Tendencies of Economic Development in Siberia and Promotion of the Region's Role in the National Economy," *Soviet Geography: Review and Translation*, January 1970, pp. 1–13.

31. Privalovskaya, G. A., "The Role of the Raw-Material Sectors in the Shaping of Industrial Production," *Soviet Geography: Review and Translation*, January 1975, pp. 7–19.

32. Rodgers, Allan, "The Locational Dynamics of Soviet Industry," *Annals of the Association of American Geographers*, June 1974, pp. 226–240.

33. Runova, T. G., "The Location of the Natural Resource Potential of the USSR in Relation to the Geography of Productive Forces," *Soviet Geography: Review and Translation*, February 1976, pp. 73–85.

34. ———, "The Role of the Resource Base in the Location of Extractive Industry," *Soviet Geography: Review and Translation*, May 1972, pp. 282–293.

35. Saushkin, Yu. G., "Stages and Methods of Economic-Geographic Prediction," *Soviet Geog-*

raphy: Review and Translation, May 1973, pp. 285–295.

36. Schroeder, Gertrude E., "Soviet Wage and Income Policies in Regional Perspective," *ACES Bulletin,* Fall 1974, pp. 3–20.

37. Shabad, Theodore, "Some Geographic Aspects of the New Soviet Five-Year Plan," *Soviet Geography: Review and Translation,* March 1978, pp. 202–206.

38. Telepko, L. N., *Urovni ekonomicheskogo razvitiya rayonov SSSR* (Levels of Economic Development in the Regions of the U.S.S.R.), Ekonomika, Moscow, 1971, 207 pp.

39. Wagener, Hans Jürgen, "Recent Development Patterns in Soviet Economic Regions," *Ostereuropa-Institut Munchen, Forschungobericht 1971,* Munchen, 1971, pp. 139–172.

40. ———, "Rules of Location and the Concept of Rationality: The Case of the USSR," in Bandera, V. N., and Melnyk, Z. L., *The Soviet Economy in Regional Perspective,* Praeger, New York, 1973, pp. 63–103.

41. Whitehouse, F. Douglas, "Demographic Aspects of Regional Economic Development in the USSR," in Bandera, V. N., and Melnyk, Z. L., editors, *The Soviet Economy in Regional Perspectives,* Praeger, New York, 1973, pp. 154–166.

42. Woroniak, Alexander, "Regional Aspects of Soviet Planning and Industrial Organization," in Bandera, V. A., and Melnyk, Z. L., editors, *The Soviet Economy in Regional Perspective,* Praeger, New York, 1973, pp. 261–304.

43. Yevstigneyev, Viktor P., "The Location of Metal-Intensive and Labor-Intensive Industries in the Eastern Regions," *Soviet Geography: Review and Translation,* May 1976, pp. 314–324.

17

Trade, Aid, and International Relations

Coauthored by Robert M. Cutler

The Soviet Union is a young country but the revolutions in 1917 did not change its geography. That legacy, inherited from Tsarist Russia, had given the country a pivotal position straddling Europe and Asia for more than 1000 years. During this time the Empire of all the Russias and its political antecedents had relations with many peoples, from the Livonian Knights, the Tatar Hordes, and the Persian Empire long ago to the British, the French, and the Germans in modern times. The Empire expanded over the centuries to include territories occupied by diverse groups of peoples. Russia thus became international externally and multinational internally. The tensions of this dynamic together with the domestic contrast between a small urban population and a great peasant mass, have created a Soviet Russian policy characterized by insulation from the rest of the world and a desire for self-sufficiency.

In general, the foreign trade of the Russian Empire and the Soviet Union has been limited not only in total value and in number of commodities exchanged, but also in number of trading partners. This pattern has been interrupted several times by short periods of increased foreign trade, motivated by the need to develop the country economically and characterized by the importation of significant amounts of technology. The Russian/Soviet state has felt this need for economic develop-

ment most keenly under military pressure. Peter the Great made the first major approach toward the Western world at the beginning of the eighteenth century. His 25-year venture was followed by 160 years of State isolation and Imperial stagnation, save possibly for a few contacts with the West under Catherine the Great, during the second half of the eighteenth century. The next period of international contact came during the 1890s, when foreign investment in Russia's industrialization drive was encouraged by the Russian minister of finance, Count Witte. During that decade foreign capital, notably from France and Belgium, accounted for about 50 per cent of all new capital invested in Russia. By the turn of the century foreign companies owned more than 70 per cent of the capital in the mining, metallurgical, and machine building industries in Russia. Foreign technology was imported not only in the form of equipment but also in that of trained personnel.

The third historical period of major involvement in the world economy occurred during the 1920s and early 1930s, when the Soviets sought to import foreign machinery and technology through a program of foreign concessions. The Soviets took advantage of the Western economic depression which made Western corporations eager to sell their expertise and equipment at low prices wherever possible. During this period imports of capital goods amounted to almost 15 per cent of gross investment in the Soviet Union. However, this foreign trade tapered off quickly after the end of the first Five-Year Plan in 1933, for the terms of trade worsened for the Soviets. Again they aimed for self-sufficiency.

Soviet trade is now in the midst of another period of expansion, under the aegis of detente and peaceful coexistence. The Soviet Union seems to have decided not only to attempt to increase its rate of industrial growth by importing huge amounts of advanced Western technology but also to provide its citizens with incentives to work more effectively by importing Western consumer goods. The value of Soviet trade during the five years 1971–1975 was 87 per cent above its level during the five years 1966–1970. Trade turnover increased more than 28 per cent from 1974 to 1975 and more than 12 per cent from 1975 to 1976. Some of this increase in value can naturally be attributed to the general global inflation, which has particularly affected petroleum products and gold, the two main Soviet exports to hard currency countries. Even in terms of fixed prices, however, Soviet trade turnover in 1975 was 232 per cent that of 1965.

In spite of this recent rapid increase, Soviet trade is still well below what one might expect of an economy the size of that of the Soviet Union. In 1975 the Soviet Union ranked seventh in the world in total trade turnover, but on a per capita basis it was nowhere near the leading trading countries in the world. (Table 17–1) It has been estimated that Soviet trade would be about 3.5 times what it is now if it had a market economy. It remains to be seen whether the current rise in trade volume is another crash effort to catch up technologically with the West, to be followed by a diminution of trade, or whether it marks the beginning of a Soviet program to maintain foreign exchanges at a level commensurate with the economy of the country.

RECENT CHANGES IN THE STRUCTURE OF TRADE

Significant changes in the structure of Soviet trade have occurred during the postwar period, particularly during the last decade of rapid growth. The number of trading partners has greatly increased, and the proportions of trade among primary trading partners have shifted. Commodites have also shifted in relative importance, and the Soviets have begun to import more than they export, particularly from hard currency developed and developing countries. To cover their debts the Soviets have been extended long-term credits by those countries.

By 1976 Soviet trade had grown to 56.8 billion rubles carried on with 117 different countries. 55.6 per cent of that trade was conducted with other socialist countries, of which 50.8 per cent was with members of the Council for Mutual Economic Aid (German Democratic Republic, Poland, Czechoslovakia, Hungary, Romania, Bulgaria, Mongolia, and Cuba). 32.9 per cent of Soviet trade was with industrialized capitalist countries, and 11.5 per cent with developing countries.

During the last decade Soviet trade has grown most rapidly with the United States, Japan, and leading trade partners in western Europe. This has occurred at the expense of trade with other communist countries and with developing countries, although Soviet trade with most of the countries of the world has continued to increase slowly in absolute terms. Between 1965 and 1976, the fraction of total Soviet trade conducted with the Industrialized West increased from 19 per cent to 31 per cent, while the fraction conducted with Eastern Europe decreased from 57 per cent to 48 per cent. Soviet trade with the developing world decreased from 12 per cent to 11.5 per cent during the same time period, after having increased to 15 per cent in 1973 and 1974. The two Germanies have emerged as the largest Soviet trading partners, each within its respective bloc.

Though the Soviets have had some success in selling manufactured goods on the world market, they have had a hard time finding ready markets in industrialized countries for what usually have been inferior consumer products. Consequently the 1970s have seen an

Table 17–1   Foreign Trade of Leading Countries, 1975

	Imports	Exports	Turn-over	Per Capita Trade (Dollars)
	(Millions of U.S. Dollars)			
U.S.A.	102,984	106,157	209,141	979
Federal Republic of Germany	74,208	90,021	164,229	2656
Japan	57,881	55,844	113,725	1025
France	54,247	52,214	106,461	2017
United Kingdom	53,262	43,760	97,022	1734
Italy	38,366	34,821	73,187	1311
U.S.S.R.	36,969	33,310	70,279	276
Netherlands	34,573	35,075	69,648	5101
Canada	34,306	31,881	66,187	2899

Source: Computed from data in *United Nations Statistical Yearbook,* 1976.

expansion of the export of fuels, electricity, ores, and metals, as prices for these items have skyrocketed. In recent years there has been renewed emphasis on an export profile that maximizes raw materials at the expense of consumer goods, while the portion of industrial goods remains essentially constant. In 1976 fuels, electric power, ores, and metals accounted for 49.5 per cent of Soviet exports; wood and paper goods and raw materials of animal origin accounted for 8.5 per cent; machinery and equipment accounted for 19.4 per cent; and consumer goods accounted for 6 per cent. Other types of exports accounted for the remaining 16.6 per cent.

Imports since 1960 have emphasized machinery and equipment — although not to the degree evident during the 1930s — and consumer goods, which now constitute their highest portion of total imports ever. In 1976 Soviet imports were comprised of machinery and equipment, 36.3 per cent; consumer goods, 35.4 per cent; metals, ores, and fuels, 14.7 per cent; wood and paper products and raw materials of animal origin, 4.1 per cent; and other goods, 9.5 per cent.

The structure and quantity of Soviet trade are determined by Soviet planners' priorities for bolstering the domestic economy. On the one hand they are after advanced technology to improve their industrial productivity, and on the other hand they are after special types of consumer goods to satisfy the Soviet citizen. Most of the advanced technology has to be purchased from the industrialized capitalist countries, whereas consumer goods are purchased wherever they may be, often being taken in exchange as payment for Soviet aid projects in developing countries. In years of poor harvests the Soviet Union has had to go to the West to purchase grain. This has become a continuing import item, and the Soviets signed in the early 1970s an agreement with the United States to purchase at least 6 million tons of grain per year.

Like the foreign trade of all powerful countries, Soviet foreign trade has political overtones. After World War II the Soviets swung the bulk of their trade for the first time to the countries of Eastern Europe and in 1949 established the Council for Mutual Economic Assistance (CMEA) in an attempt to consolidate their political and economic gains in that area. In the mid 1950s the Soviets began granting foreign aid to developing countries in the Near and Middle East and north Africa, as well as to emerging new nations in sub-Saharan Africa and to politically critical areas such as Korea, Vietnam, and Cuba. In many countries a great deal of this aid was military aid, for which statistics are frequently unavailable save by assuming that payments by these

Table 17–2   Soviet Trade Turnover by Principal Countries, 1976, in Millions of Rubles and Per Cents of Total

	Million Rubles	Per Cent
Total	56,755	100.0
Socialist Countries	31,552	55.6
German Democratic Republic	5,997	10.6
Poland	5,235	9.2
Czechoslovakia	4,543	8.0
Bulgaria	4,466	7.9
Hungary	3,492	6.2
Cuba	2,872	5.1
Yugoslavia	1,821	3.3
Romania	1,600	2.9
Mongolia	615	1.1
China	314	0.6
North Korea	301	0.5
Vietnam	296	0.5
Industrially Developed Capitalist Countries	18,658	32.9
Federal Republic of Germany	3,009	5.3
United States of America	2,205	3.9
Japan	2,121	3.7
Finland	1,979	3.5
Italy	1,778	3.1
France	1,697	3.0
Great Britain	1,233	2.2
Other (19 countries)	4,636	8.2
Developing Countries	6,545	11.5
Iraq	715	1.3
India	648	1.1
Egypt	531	0.9
Brazil	446	0.8
Iran	445	0.8
Syria	235	0.4
Algeria	190	0.3
Other (69 countries)	3,335	5.9

Source: Computed from *Vneshnyaya torgovlya SSSR v 1976 g.*

countries of consumer goods and raw materials to the Soviet Union represent reimbursement therefor.

The countries with which the Soviet Union maintains trade and diplomatic relations can be divided into several categories roughly on the basis of geographic area. These groups of countries are discussed in the following pages.

EAST EUROPE

Soviet troops, in the process of defeating Nazi Germany, came to occupy territory westward beyond Berlin and southward beyond the Danube. The various countries in this area were characterized to different degrees by discontinuities in political institutions, by physical destruction from war, and by class tensions. Immediately after the war, Soviet objectives in eastern Europe were basically three; to deny the area to other powers, to use the area to promote Soviet economic recovery from the war, and to prevent anti-Soviet elements from coming to power there. By February 1948 Poland, Rumania, Bulgaria, Hungary, Czechoslovakia and Yugoslavia all had communist governments. In the first four countries the communist parties (CPs) had limited indigenous support and promoted themselves by advocating nationalism (especially regarding territorial issues), by introducing popular social and economic reforms (especially land reform where there had been none in the interwar period), by expropriating private industry, and by undermining generally the legal opposition.

In Czechoslovakia the Communists had strong domestic roots and soon became the leading party. The head of the Czechoslovak CP became the country's premier in 1946 and the party thereafter consolidated its influence generally by legitimate means, though the final takeover in 1948 came on the eve of national elections. In Yugoslavia the communist revolution was the outcome of a civil war which had raged simultaneously with World War II. As early as November, 1945 a single slate of candidates had been presented to the Yugoslav electorate. The Yugoslav CP had extensive indigenous support and was thus able to introduce reforms faster than any other CP in eastern Europe.

After the war was over the U.S.S.R. concluded reparations agreements with the states of eastern Europe for alleged "collaborationist" behavior, agreements which in 1945–1946 permitted it to extract as much as 20 billion dollars from that region. Beginning in 1948, the Soviet Union concluded a series of long-term bilateral foreign trade agreements with the states of eastern Europe even though national reconstruction had barely begun there. These agreements became a basic part of the process of reconstruction. By 1950 these countries conducted the majority of their trade with the U.S.S.R. and with each other. The extremes were Poland, whose imports from and exports to the Soviet Union and other bloc members comprised 58 per cent of its total trade turnover, and Bulgaria, whose trade with other communist states was fully 90 per cent of its total turnover.

In January, 1949, in response to the Marshall Plan, the U.S.S.R., Poland, Czechoslovakia, Hungary, Rumania, Bulgaria, and the Mongolian Peoples Republic formed the Council for Mutual Economic Assistance (CMEA). East Germany and Albania joined in 1950. Yugoslavia remained aloof and was rewarded with an embargo. Although CMEA's purpose was said to be the promotion of economic development with member states, its major function was to coordinate their trade. In 1950 the ruble became the standard currency of CMEA transactions, making the Soviet Union the ultimate arbiter of rates of exchange.

CMEA remained relatively dormant until 1955, when it was revived in response to the formation in the preceding year of the North Atlantic Treaty Organization (NATO). NATO also resulted in the creation of the political and military organization called the Warsaw Treaty Organization (WTO), also called the Warsaw Pact. Until 1955 resources flowed primarily from eastern Europe to the U.S.S.R., but Stalin's death in 1953 had opened the way for reforms in CMEA's organization. The strain in the Stalinist system of post-war political and economic relations in eastern Europe had become unbearable, and the East Berlin uprising of 1953 and the

Hungarian and Polish revolts in 1956 demonstrated drastic needs for reform. Such events induced the Soviets to extend credit to these national regimes in late 1956 and 1957. The purposes of CMEA were redefined to include (1) the facilitation of mutual exchanges of experiences and techniques, (2) the promotion of an international division of labor and of specialization in industrial production, and (3) the coordination of investment in the subsequent five-year plans. By 1958, the year after Khrushchev's consolidation of his power, genuine economic integration had become Soviet and CMEA policy in the region. The existing price system, which favored the Soviets heavily, was reformed in 1963, and the International Bank for Economic Cooperation (IBEC) was created for the purpose of multilateralizing interbloc trade.

However, the notion of economic integration began to take on disquieting supranational tones, and Rumania opposed the Soviet plan for integration during the CMEA sessions in 1962. With the support of East Germany and Czechoslovakia, the two most industrially developed states of eastern Europe, Rumania declared that international economic efficiency within the world Communist system would mean not only that the less industrialized countries (such as Rumania) would develop more slowly, but also that they would have to provide raw materials and agricultural support for the further expansion of already industrialized national economies. The Soviets could not effectively threaten Rumania with an economic boycott because western Europe could offer alternate trade arrangements to the Rumanians. Further, China was using the issue in her dispute with the Soviets, which by then had become an open polemic. The argument raged for three years, the Rumanians becoming ever more defiant and independent. In the end bilateral agreements of shorter terms became once more the preferred economic instrument throughout CMEA. Only with changes in leadership upon the death of the Rumanian leader in 1965 and the ouster of Khrushchev in 1964, was the Soviet Union able to mollify its discontented ally.

Trade among the countries of eastern Europe themselves increased markedly between 1966 and 1968, and they even collaborated with each other and without the Soviets on joint-stock enterprises. Despite IBEC, the trade behavior of the CMEA countries was not multilateralized; however, bilateral ties that excluded the Soviet Union proliferated. Khrushchev's heirs were still interested in integrating CMEA, but the invasion of Czechoslovakia in 1968 had the side effect of quelling renewed moves to confer supranational economic power on CMEA; another side effect was to halt any incipient disintegration of CMEA.

In the late 1960s the Soviet Union still supplied most of East Europe's imports of raw materials, and in return it purchased a large fraction of the latter's total exports of machinery. As raw materials became more valuable on the world market and hard currency more desirable, the U.S.S.R. grew dissatisfied with this commodity structure of trade among the CMEA countries. As the 1970s began, the Soviet Union started asking other CMEA member states to purchase more Soviet machinery and to deliver more consumer goods to the U.S.S.R.

In 1971 CMEA adopted a Comprehensive Program of Socialist Economic Integration, i.e., international economic cooperation, just in time for Cuba's entrance into CMEA in 1972. The Comprehensive Program was essentially a set of proposals dealing, in a time frame of 15 to 20 years, with an enormous array of problems concerning the coordination of programs to increase the international division of labor, foreign trade flows, and joint investment projects. But the program is only a set of proposals and contains few suggestions for their implementation. The increased activity of IBEC and the establishment of a new International Investment Bank (IIB) have been two major attempts to realize those goals.

The CMEA Council instituted two further structural changes in 1974, against what is believed to be strong opposition by the East European states. The principal of unanimity was eliminated as a requirement for certain actions, in order to prevent Rumania's opposition from holding up certain projects; and CMEA constituted itself a single legal entity, better to deal directly with the Common Market of western Europe and with the United States. This latter move drew especially strong opposition from the countries of eastern Europe because it limits their independence in matters of trade and cooperation with the West. Two further proposals to promote integration were pressed in 1975. The first revised intra-CMEA pricing policies to Soviet advantage and initiated monetary reforms. The second altered planning procedures and provided for the investment by the East European countries of up to 10 billion rubles in extractive and primary manufacturing projects in the U.S.S.R. In spite of these measures, the individual countries of CMEA (including the U.S.S.R.) have over the last ten years turned more and more toward developed western countries for commodities that the CMEA countries cannot supply each other, sophisticated industrial technology and grain in particular. Indicative of this trend is the statistic that between 1965 and 1976 the East European share of total Soviet trade declined from 57 per cent to 48 per cent.

The Soviet Union continues to export mainly raw materials and energy to CMEA partners, although the amount of machinery and equipment is increasing. In the mid 1970s more than a quarter of all Soviet exports to other socialist countries were fuels and electrical energy, about a fifth were ores and concentrates, and between a fifth and a quarter were machinery and equipment. Exports of oil, natural gas, and electricity to the east European countries have been facilitated by the construction of the Druzhba (Friendship) oil pipeline, the Bratstvo (Fraternity) gas pipeline, and the Mir (Peace) and a number of other high-voltage electrical transmission lines across the western border of the Soviet Union. These will be enhanced in the near future by the completion of the Orenburg gas pipeline, which will connect the newly discovered large gas fields of Orenburg Oblast in the southern Urals with several East European countries.

During the mid 1970s, half of all Soviet oil and oil products exports went to Poland, Czechoslovakia, Bulgaria, Hungary, and the German Democratic Republic. Rumania had its own oil supplies.

Soviet imports from eastern Europe consist largely of consumer goods and machinery and equipment. During the mid 1970s, about one-fifth of all Soviet imports from eastern Europe were food products, one-fifth were manufactured consumer goods, and two-fifths were machinery and equipment. During the mid 1970s eastern Europe supplied close to 60 per cent of all the machinery and equipment imports of the Soviet Union. This statistic is down from levels it had attained before the Soviet Union began substantial imports from West Germany, the United States, Japan, and other capitalist countries. East Germany supplies by far the largest portion of machinery and equipment imports to the Soviet Union; Czechoslovakia and Poland are next in importance among East European countries, but now both of these have been surpassed in absolute figures by West Germany.

Rapidly rising world market prices for energy and raw materials during the first half of the 1970s caught the Soviet Union at a disadvantage, for its customary trade relations with the CMEA countries provided that prices be set only every five years. When the price of crude oil on the world market, for example, more than quadrupled between 1972 and 1974, the Soviet Union was caught between its desire to export more oil to the Industrialized West in return for hard currency and its commitment to sell the oil to its CMEA partners near the old price.

This experience, combined with declining rates of economic growth in the U.S.S.R. and exceedingly poor harvests in 1972 and 1975, convinced the Soviets to revise intra-CMEA pricing policies to their own advantage. Intra-CMEA prices were increased ahead of schedule, and the countries involved agreed to set intrabloc oil prices annually at a level equalling the average world market prices over the three most recent years. The Soviet Union still sold oil to the CMEA countries at a price lower than the world market, but it raised the price of oil appreciably and avoided major economic and political dislocation in the countries concerned.

The Soviets, although they have encouraged the East European countries to look elsewhere for oil, have decided to meet the bulk of CMEA's energy requirements at least during the current (1976–1980) Five-Year Plan, because any significant energy shortfall in eastern Europe would create a severe, possibly insurmountable, balance of payments problem that would hamper further economic development. In return for supplying East Europe with fuels and other raw materials at favorable prices, the Soviet Union has convinced the East European countries to increase significantly their investment in Soviet extractive industries. Various East European countries have agreed to help construct the Orenburg gas pipeline, the Ust-Ilim cellulose factory, an iron and steel complex at Kursk, the Kiyembay asbestos plant, and a plant to produce ferroalloys. For these projects the East Europeans have already promised 9 billion transferable rubles (over 13 billion dollars). They are extending this credit at the low interest rate of about 2 per cent per year. In effect the East Europeans are subsidizing Soviet industry. The East European countries will be repaid over a period of about 20 years in the form of products produced by the projects for which they are now supplying equipment, machinery, and personnel.

Over the years, the primary concerns of the Soviet Union with regard to eastern Europe seem to have been: (1) stability of economic and political relations, (2) quality and mix of products that can be supplied to the Soviet Union, and (3) favorable terms of trade for the Soviet Union. More recently, to these have been added: (4) good economic performance by the planned economies of eastern Europe, (5) modernization of the Soviet and other CMEA economies, and (6) insulation from capitalist business cyles. Through the years the Soviets have been faced with the difficult task of assuring the stability of supplies from the East European countries while helping them modernize and attain high product quality. It now appears that joint ventures, such as the ones mentioned in the previous paragraph, might help resolve this dilemma. The Soviets want to continue to promote integration of the national economies of eastern Europe with their own, and it appears that the joint ventures may be the way to do so without causing political upsets. However, the process is proceeding very slowly in practice.

OTHER SOCIALIST COUNTRIES

China

For the first decade of the existence of the People's Republic of China, through the late 1950s, the U.S.S.R. rendered fraternal socialist aid. Ideological conflict, however, appeared between the two, and Khrushchev's famous "secret speech" in 1956, which began his destalinization campaign, made the breach irrevocable. As interparty relations worsened, interstate relations became likewise strained. By 1960 Khrushchev had recalled to the U.S.S.R. all Soviet technicians in China and terminated all economic aid, leaving factories half-built and tractors idle for want of spare parts.

The polemics between the Chinese and the Russians are not now as vituperous as they were in the 1960s. While interparty relations remain poor, the interstate relations have improved. Most stable in this regard is the establishment of a navigation commission to govern river traffic on the Ussuri, where Chinese and Soviet troops clashed in 1968. The underlying territorial questions, however, have not been resolved. The Chinese still claim much land under the Soviet flag, north of the Amur River and east of the Ussuri River in the Far East as well as along the international border in Turkistan. Although at present the Chinese are not pushing these claims vigorously, the Soviets maintain a considerable troop buildup along their common border. China also continues to compete with the Soviet Union for influence in many Third World areas, particu-

larly in Africa and southern Asia, and occasionally even in eastern Europe and Cuba.

Trade between China and the Soviet Union has declined ever since the peak of over 2 billion dollars in 1959. Now it barely exceeds Soviet trade with North Korea or Vietnam. In 1976 China accounted for only 0.6 per cent of Soviet trade. Primary exports from the Soviet Union to China are machinery and energy resources, whereas primary exports from China to the Soviet Union are consumer goods, especially items of clothing and food.

North Korea and Vietnam

The Soviet Union has had experiences in Korea and Vietnam similar to those of the United States: much involvement and little result. As early as 1964 North Korea changed its allegiance from the Soviet Union to China, and shortly thereafter set out on a course independent from both of them. During recent years North Korean government officials seem to have been engaging in questionable international monetary maneuvers such as the South Koreans have in an attempt to pull themselves out of the hole of a large hard currency debt. An interesting episode occurred in December, 1976, when nearly a third of the North Korean embassy personnel in Moscow were expelled in the wake of a scandal involving black marketeering in Scandinavia.

The Soviets created a steel industry in North Korea — just as the United States did in South Korea — and Soviet imports from North Korea include large amounts of steel, other metal products, ores, and machinery. Most Soviet exports to North Korea are also products of heavy industry. However, this trade is small in relative terms. In 1976, North Korea accounted for only 0.5 per cent of the total Soviet trade turnover.

Since the fall of the Thieu regime in South Vietnam, relations between the Soviet Union and the unified Vietnam have rapidly cooled. The Soviets no longer supply massive amounts of equipment to Vietnam, and the amount of trade has dwindled to even less than that with

North Korea. What trade remains is still much more Soviet exports to Vietnam than vice versa. In June 1978, Vietnam became a member of CMEA. This might rapidly expand trade with the Soviet Union.

Cuba

The U.S.S.R. has subsidized the Cuban economy for many years by purchasing huge amounts of raw sugar, often above the world market price. The absolute value of this trade, however, has not historically been high. In 1972, however, Cuba joined the CMEA organization, and Soviet-Cuban trade has increased significantly since then, to such an extent that in 1976 Cuba accounted for 5.1 per cent of Soviet trade. This was a higher portion of total Soviet trade than some of the East European countries had and was almost as much as the share of West Germany, which is the top western trader with the Soviet Union. The Soviets generally import more from Cuba than they export, possibly indicating that the Soviet Union continues to supply Cuba with significant amounts of military aid. Almost all Soviet imports from Cuba remain raw sugar, some of which is eventually reexported after it has been refined in the Soviet Union. Soviet exports to Cuba are primarily machinery of various sorts and petroleum.

THE INDUSTRIALIZED WEST

The national economies of western Europe, the U.S.A. and Japan complement that of the Soviet Union. The Federal Republic of Germany (FRG), Great Britain, and Japan in particular import large amounts of raw materials from the U.S.S.R. and supply industrial technology in return. This pattern continues the historical tradition in which Germany and Britain were major trading partners with the Russian Empire.

Since the Bolshevik Revolution, in 1917, trade between the West and the Soviets has had its ups and downs, usually because of political considerations. In the years immediately following the civil war in Bolshevik Russia, Western corporations hesitated to enter into trade agreements with the Soviets because the Soviets had renounced all Tsarist debts, leaving many such corporations with unpaid accounts. However, as the Western world plunged into an economic depression during the late 1920s and early 1930s, and as the Soviets proved to be trustworthy trading partners, Western corporations became eager to supply goods and skilled personnel to the Soviets in order to bolster their sagging profits and keep labor forces busy. Such trade flourished throughout most of the 1930s in spite of difficult monetary arrangements (the Soviet ruble being unconvertible into Western currency).

The Soviets chose to conduct trade primarily on a bilateral basis with other countries and has sometimes had to undersell established suppliers of various items in order to gain the necessary barter deals that it needs. This is often interpreted as a form of "dumping" on the world market, necessary for the Soviets to break into long-established trade relations among other countries, and has sometimes resulted in punitive measures by the countries whose trade such methods have hurt.

During World War II the Soviet Union received considerable quantities of lend-lease materials from the West, particularly from the United States, but exported little in return. After the second World War, as the Cold War intensified during the 1950s, the United States enforced embargoes against the U.S.S.R. and trade between the Soviet Union and the West diminished. Soviet trade began to expand again in the late 1950s as some of the Western countries defied the U.S. and began to relax their export restrictions. Since the mid 1960s the Soviets have sought to expand trade on all fronts, the United States has greatly relaxed restrictions in the face of growing domestic economic difficulties, and Soviet trade with the West has burgeoned. Between 1966 and 1976, the share of Soviet trade with the West jumped from 21 per cent to almost 33 per cent. The increase has been especially rapid since 1972, although it is in part due to the rapidly inflating prices of raw materials and agricultural commodities.

Soviet efforts to promote trade with the West have been prompted primarily by their need for advanced technology to keep their domestic economy growing at a respectable rate and by their decision to import considerable quantities of consumer goods, including foodstuffs.

In order to facilitate trade with the Soviet Union, many Western countries have had to extend substantial credits to the Soviets over periods of ten to fifteen years. In many cases Western corporations have entered into so-called "compensatory agreements" which call for them to supply certain equipment to the Soviet Union to exploit natural resources, deferred payments being made over a period of time in the form of products from the projects supported. One example of such an arrangement is the provision by the Federal Republic of Germany of the gas pipelines which will be used to supply natural gas from the Soviet Union to the FRG and other countries. The Japanese have also negotiated such deals in the Soviet Far East where they have helped build ports, cut timber, and provide equipment and know-how for the exploration and exploitation of coal, oil, and natural gas.

In spite of such compensatory arrangements, the Soviets have run large trade deficits with the West. Those deficits have been exacerbated by the need to import large quantities of grain during the bad harvest years of 1972, 1975, and 1977. The grain trade has not only created large debts for the Soviet Union, but also produced large swings in commodity prices in the supplying countries, particularly the United States. In order to alleviate these difficulties, an agreement was reached between the Soviet Union and the United States in the mid 1970s for the United States to supply a fairly constant amount of corn and wheat to the Soviet Union over the five-year period 1976–1980. Although the wheat imports have been attracting the most attention from the world, imports of corn, soybeans, and other feed grains have been just as important. Thus, the U.S.S.R. has become a consistent grain import-

er, and this will remain the case in the foreseeable future.

The Soviets' need to import grain stems not so much from thier inability to produce as much grain as they want to eat as from their need to provide animal feedstocks and to honor standing export commitments to socialist partners. These imports have come largely from the West, particularly from the United States, Canada, Australia, Argentina, Brazil, and France. (Table 17–3) Much of the grain purchased from Canada has been delivered directly to Cuba, and the grain the Soviets buy from Australia is usually shipped to their Far East.

Over the last two decades the U.S.S.R.'s major Western trading partners, in terms of total amounts of trade with the Soviet Union have changed several times. In the 1950s and early 1960s her major partners were typically the United Kingdom and neighboring Finland, but as time has gone on and political rapprochements have been struck with West Germany, Japan, and the United States, these latter countries have jumped into the forefront. During the mid 1960s Japan several times occupied first place in Soviet trade with the West. But it now appears that the Federal Republic of Germany has become consistently the largest Western trading partner. British trade has relatively dwindled, primarily because of domestic economic difficulties in Britain. In 1976 the United States jumped into second place with its large grain exports, but American trade fluctuates most from year to year because it is relatively concentrated on a few agricultural commodities, the scale of which depends much on weather conditions in the Soviet Union. The recent agreements between the Soviet Union and the United States that six to eight million tons of U.S. grain should be exported to the Soviet Union each year should stabilize these annual fluctuations somewhat. For the Soviet Union to purchase more than this would require prior permission from the U.S. government.

Among the industrialized Western countries export trade shares to the U.S.S.R. are greatest in the Federal Republic of Germany, the

Table 17–3   Soviet Grain Trade, 1970–1976, in Thousands of Metric Tons

	1970–1971 Average	1972–1973 Average	1974	1975	1976
Total Exports	7,169	4,707	7,030	3,578	1,468
Cuba	562	546	570	533	537
Czechoslovakia	1,434	1,092	669	587	56
GDR	1,755	1,022	1,425	720	187
North Korea	200	169	181	212	213
Poland	1,603	1,125	1,898	1,015	269
Total Imports	2,850	19,700	7,131	15,909	20,638
Argentina	98	—	c670	1,764	1,261
Australia	134	662	581	1,186	1,263
Brazil	—	—	288	749	535
Canada	1,720	4,443	c500	3,007	3,099
France	219	1,362	c145	205	339
Hungary	—	322	137	854	421
U.S.A.	—	11,305	4,143	7,141	11,962
Grain Trade Balance	+4,319	−14,993	−101	−12,331	−19,170

Source: Radio Liberty Research Bulletin, August 22, 1977.
Figures exclude groats, flour, and soybeans.

United States, and Japan. (Table 17–4) In 1976 the Soviet Union took 23 per cent of West Germany's exports, 19.8 per cent of United States' exports, and 19.3 per cent of Japan's exports. No other country approached these proportions. The import picture is quite different. The Federal Republic of Germany ranked first again, and Japan was also prominent, but the United States was way down the list. Countries having the largest portions of their imports coming from the Soviet Union are West Germany, Italy, the United Kingdom, Japan, and France. As mentioned earlier, the West European countries and Japan have a much greater need for Soviet raw materials — especially oil, timber, and a variety of mineral commodities than does the United States. Such raw materials make up the bulk of Soviet exports to the Industrialized West. The second largest Soviet export to the West was timber, followed by cotton, natural gas, and coal.

The top 25 individual commodity exports from the U.S.S.R. to the West in 1975 are shown in Table 17–5, in rank order along with the percent shares taken by individual Western countries. Here one can see the importance to the U.S.S.R. of West Germany, Japan, the United Kingdom, Italy, and France for the purchase of oil products, natural gas, and timber. In 1975 these five countries imported the most Soviet products in absolute terms. The United States, however, the second largest Western exporter to the Soviet Union, imported only nominal amounts of metals such as platinum, nickel alloys, and chrome ore. Recently petroleum products have been added to this list. In 1976 residual fuel oil became the second most important Soviet export to the U.S.A. after platinum, and that year the value of Soviet fuel exports to the United States was twice that of chrome ore. These commodity exports to the United States were followed by aluminum waste and scrap, nonindustrial diamonds, and collectors items (predominantly metal coins). Nonindustrial diamonds have become a large export item from the Soviet Union to the West, most of them taken by the United Kingdom.

Table 17–4 Soviet Shares of Trade of Industrialized Western Countries, 1976, in Per Cents

Country	Exports	Imports
Federal Republic of Germany	23.0	19.4
United States of America	19.8	2.5
Japan	19.3	13.3
France	9.6	10.4
Italy	8.4	15.5
Canada	4.7	0.6
United Kingdom	3.7	13.6
Belgium-Luxembourg	2.6	3.4
Sweden	2.4	5.4
Austria	2.0	4.8
Switzerland	1.7	3.0
Netherlands	1.5	4.4
Norway	0.7	1.0
Denmark	0.6	2.7

Source: Journal of the US-USSR Trade and Economic Council, August/September 1977, pp. 4 and 6.

As can be seen from Table 17–5, in 1975 the Soviets ran a trade deficit of more than 3.5 billion dollars with the Industrialized West. The biggest trade deficit was with the United States, and the second largest was with the Federal Republic of Germany. Much smaller, but still significant, was the trade deficit with Canada. The Soviets ran moderate trade surpluses with most other Western countries, though the surplus with the United Kingdom was considerable. Although trade balance between the Soviet Union and the Industrialized West has generally fluctuated from year to year between deficit and surplus a pattern of large, growing deficits has emerged over the last decade, due primarily to trade with the United States and West Germany.

The Soviets are eager to expand their exports to the West to remedy this imbalance; they would like in particular to sell more machinery and other finished goods to the West. However, their technology is in most cases a step behind that of the West, so their manufactured goods have a hard time finding markets in the West. To make up for this in the short run they have rapidly expanded their exports of petroleum and other primary commodities. Yet, though the prices for such goods have risen rapidly, the Soviets have become net importers from the West, and the further expansion of exports of such primary items as petroleum is questionable. Already they are caught between the desire to expand hard-currency petroleum exports to the West at world market prices and their commitment to continue supplying their East European allies with reduced-priced oil.

The Soviets have frequently sold domestically mined gold to reduce their hard currency deficits, but the values of these sales are never disclosed. It is believed that in 1976 Soviet gold sales totaled about 1.4 billion dollars. The East European allies of the U.S.S.R., however, are running hard currency deficits and have no gold or oil or natural gas to sell. Their deficits affect the U.S.S.R.'s ability to export to the West, because the Soviets do not want to risk the potential political unrest in eastern Europe that might result from a reduction of low-price exports of oil and other basic commodities. Such a move would force the countries of eastern Europe to rely even more heavily on high-price imports from other sources in the world. Preliminary reports indicate that during 1976 and 1977 the Soviets reduced their hard currency debt to just over one billion dollars by drastically curtailing imports of Western technology. Thus, it appears they have sacrificed some economic growth in order to reduce their debt. It also appears that they have placed East European political stability ahead of hard currency gains by discontinuing expansion of oil exports to the West in favor of continued shipments at reduced prices to eastern Europe. The Soviets plan to reduce oil exports from 146 million tons in 1976 to "over 120 million" in 1978.

Since Soviet trade with Western countries has been almost entirely bilateral, often of a barter type, trade relations with some individual Western countries are discussed below in order of trade turnover in 1976.

Taken by Each Western Country

1975 Rank	Export Item	Dollar Value (Thousands)	Canada	United States	Japan	Belgium/Luxembourg	France	Federal Republic of Germany	Italy	Netherlands	Austria	Norway	Sweden	Switzerland	United Kingdom	Denmark
1	Distillate fuels	878,881	—	2.5	—	4.5	9.4	36.5	7.0	9.6	0.1	0.7	13.4	6.7	3.2	6.3
2	Crude petroleum	585,736	—	—	0.6	.3	16.7	48.6	—	—	16.0	.6	—	—	10.4	6.8
3	Residual fuel oil	510,675	—	10.5	11.1	1.3	8.1	2.5	18.9	1.8	.1	.7	41.0	.5	.3	3.3
4	Diamonds, nonindustrial, unset	481,512	—	2.7	1.6	13.2	.1	3.1	—	—	.1	—	.1	.1	79.1	—
5	Coal (anthracite, bituminous)	438,200	—	—	37.4	2.3	22.0	1.0	16.6	(1)	10.6	—	6.6	—	(1)	3.4
6	Sawlogs and veneer logs	392,224	—	—	99.2	—	.1	.2	(1)	.2	.2	—	.2	—	—	—
7	Motor spirit (gasoline)	364,461	—	—	—	10.8	4.3	8.0	20.3	31.8	1.9	2.9	2.7	5.5	11.5	.2
8	Raw cotton	339,992	—	—	50.3	1.1	24.3	8.2	5.6	.4	1.6	—	.2	.3	7.8	—
9	Lumber, sawn lengthwise	314,255	—	—	2.3	10.2	6.8	16.4	10.8	6.2	—	(1)	(1)	(1)	45.9	1.3
10	Platinum	200,940	—	29.9	58.0	—	2.5	6.7	.2	.1	—	—	(1)	1.2	1.4	—
11	Natural phosphates	158,204	—	—	—	7.9	(1)	41.0	—	1.9	9.9	14.3	19.8	—	—	5.1
12	Gas, natural	142,477	(1)	(1)	—	.1	11.5	—	31.6	—	56.7	—	—	8.5	.1	.1
13	Sunflower seed, oil	116,747	—	—	—	.1	46.8	38.0	—	5.3	.5	—	.1	—	—	.6
14	Ores and chromium	97,043	—	25.2	14.5	.8	13.8	19.2	2.8	—	—	1.7	22.9	—	23.9	—
15	Iron ore and concentrates	83,822	—	3.0	26.0	14.6	.5	3.3	28.4	3.6	14.1	.2	—	—	15.8	—
16	Chemical potassic fertilizer	77,398	—	1.5	37.1	18.0	5.5	25.3	6.6	11.5	—	3.2	9.8	4.4	12.3	2.3
17	Passenger motor vehicles	76,239	—	—	—	4.2	9.4	.1	.2	6.8	3.1	4.2	4.3	—	.3	7.3
18	Pulpwood	75,019	—	—	24.5	2.8	19.0	5.7	25.1	.1	(1)	1.2	18.7	—	19.0	—
19	Aluminum alloys	63,990	7.4	.1	44.9	(1)	14.5	28.9	2.1	—	.7	8.4	1.8	.4	—	—
20	Radioactive elements	60,717	—	—	—	—	63.6	41.4	—	10.5	.1	—	—	—	2.0	—
21	Copper, refined	56,066	—	—	4.5	—	25.6	32.3	4.3	.4	.9	.1	11.3	—	41.4	—
22	Fur skins, undressed	55,971	1.8	6.3	4.9	.7	5.4	1.6	3.2	—	—	—	2.5	—	—	(1)
23	Iron and steel scrap	54,320	—	—	22.8	—	—	22.7	52.0	—	—	—	23.6	(1)	—	—
24	Nickel alloys, unwrought	52,287	—	28.7	17.3	.2	16.6	97.5	2.5	1.4	—	—	8.6	2.1	—	—
25	Nonlubricating oils	49,941	—	—	—	—	—	—	—	—	—	—	—	2.5	—	.6
	Total exports to Industrialized Western countries	7,131,446	.4	3.6	16.4	4.2	10.8	18.2	12.3	4.3	4.5	1.2	7.4	1.7	12.7	2.4
	Total imports from Industrialized Western countries	10,714,789	3.8	17.1	15.2	3.3	10.7	26.4	9.5	1.9	2.0	.9	2.7	1.7	4.3	.6

Source: Lenz and Kravalis, p. 1067.
(1) Small amount, rounding to zero.

West Germany

In 1970 the U.S.S.R. and the Federal Republic of Germany signed a treaty which in effect let the bygones of World War II be bygones, and since then the Federal Republic of Germany has become the largest trading partner of the Soviet Union among the industrialized Western countries. Much of West Germany's exports to the Soviet Union consist of machinery and equipment to aid the Soviets in exploiting their natural resources, the products of which Germany is interested in buying. West German companies have made long-term agreements with the Soviets to supply gas and oil pipe equipment so that pipelines can be built westward from the Soviet Union, supplying West Germany and other European countries with Soviet oil and natural gas. Also, West German companies have become involved in the construction of a large iron and steel complex in the Kursk Magnetic Anomaly, and earlier they were involved in part of the construction work on the Kama truck plant. Cooperation is also taking place in the development of machine tools and other metal processing equipment in the U.S.S.R. A plan for West Germany to build a 600-million dollar nuclear power plant in the Soviet Union, however, was abandoned in 1976 after three years of discussion, when the U.S.S.R. refused to let the power lines be routed so as to supply West Berlin with electricity. The Soviet Union has interpreted the Quadripartite Agreement of 1973 on West Berlin to mean the city is totally unrelated to the Federal Republic of Germany. West Berlin remains a deterrent to better political relations between West Germany and the Soviet Union, although trade relations seem not to suffer greatly.

The United States

Potentials for Soviet-American trade have been aggressively pursued since the Nixon-Brezhnev summits in the early 1970s which made *detente* a household word. Soviet trade with the United States jumped almost three hundred percent between 1971 and 1972, largely due to massive grain sales after the disastrous Soviet grain harvest in 1972. They more than doubled again in 1973, and although they dropped in 1974 after the bumper Soviet grain harvest of 1973, they have risen again since. In 1976 American grain sales to the U.S.S.R. were 12 times as large as they had been in 1971.

It is ironic that the recent increase in exports from the United States to the U.S.S.R., the two largest industrial economies in the world, has been due to the Soviet need for foodstuffs. In 1976 food, feeds, and beverages made up 64.2 per cent of U.S.A. exports to the U.S.S.R. Capital goods exports, by comparison, were only 26.5 per cent. Because of the large grain exports to the Soviet Union, the U.S.A. has run a larger trade surplus with the Soviet Union than has any other country, and much of the U.S.S.R.'s hard currency debt is to American companies, even though the Soviets have more difficulty getting trade credits from the United States than from many other Western countries. The Trade Act which the United States Congress passed in 1974 denied the Soviets the status of most favored nation so long as they restricted emigration from their country. The U.S.S.R., as a result, could not get Eximbank credits, but this does not seem to have greatly affected the amount of Soviet imports from the United States. The effect of the 1974 Trade Act has in this regard been more political than economic.

Though much of the U.S.-U.S.S.R. trade turnover consists of grain exports from the United States to the Soviet Union, a few major deals have been consummated for American companies to supply plant and equipment to various Soviet industries (examples of which have been mentioned in previous chapters), and there has been a burgeoning of agencies established in the United States, both governmental and private, to attempt to facilitate the establishment of such deals in the future.

Since doing business with centrally planned, non-market economies presents unique problems, and since much of this trade has political overtones, the U.S. government has taken steps to enhance and control it. The first step taken in the early 1970s was to set up cabinet-level joint commercial commissions with the U.S.S.R., Poland, and Rumania. These government-to-government commissions serve as mechanisms for negotiating bilateral trade agreements, and through them mutual credits can be arranged and commercial disputes settled. The full commissions meet annually.

Persuant to the 1974 Trade Act, the East-West Foreign Trade Board was established to monitor trade, credits, and technology transfers between the U.S.A. and non-market countries to ensure that such trade would be in the U.S. national interest. This board is primarily a policy oriented body and is not directly concerned with day-to-day problems of trade. In addition, a private group of corporate business executives has established the U.S.-U.S.S.R. Trade and Economic Council, which also involves some governmental officials as *ex-officio* members.

To assist U.S. businessmen in more basic operational matters, the Bureau of East-West Trade was created in the Department of Commerce in December, 1972. The aim of the Bureau has been to help American firms learn how to deal successfully with a relatively new and unfamiliar market. The assistance programs established by the Bureau for American companies supply market information, arrange participation in foreign trade missions and exhibitions, facilitate commercial contacts and assist companies in contract negotiations, provide specialized information on each socialist country, and publish studies on trade policies and practices as well as on the economic plans of individual socialist countries. In addition to promoting and facilitating trade, the Bureau of East-West Trade is responsible for regulating exports to socialist countries of materials which have strategic importance or are in short supply.

Between 1969 and 1973 the U.S. Congress passed several amendments to the Export Administration Act that reduced the list of controlled exports from 550 to 73, allowing U.S. corporations to compete more successfully with West European and Japanese companies for Soviet trade.

The Soviet Union likes to deal with U.S. corporations because they often offer technology available nowhere else, and because they usually have experience building large industrial plants, on a scale commensurate to those the Soviet Union favors. The Soviets thus perceive the United States as a great supermarket where goods may be selected from a wide variety and purchased in large quantities.

Technology transfer has not been exclusively unidirectional. American oil and gas companies, for example, have bought licenses to methods that the Soviets developed while exploiting their Siberian resources. By mid 1975 twenty American firms had licensed Soviet technology, much of it of high quality. And projects for scientific cooperation abound in the fields of medicine, transportation, oceanography, energy, and the environment.

For some technology the Soviet Union does not have to go to the United States; it can buy from western Europe or Japan. But the technology for which it cannot go elsewhere is precisely that which the U.S. Government may hesitate to approve for export on the grounds of national security. Thus, the U.S. cancelled an agreement that had been worked out for the sale of computer technology to Intourist, the Soviet state travel agency, because the eleven-million-dollar system could have been used for keeping track of missiles just as easily as for keeping track of hotel reservations.

In the strategic arena, the U.S.S.R. and the United States survived many localized conflicts in the 1960s, including the Cuban missile crisis, the Bay of Pigs, several Berlin crises, American intervention in the Dominican Republic, and wars in the Middle East and Indochina. The two giant powers are not willing to allow localized conflicts to erupt into a mutually destructive direct confrontation.

Japan

Like West Germany, Japan overcame the bad feelings from World War II, normalizing relations and expanding trade with the U.S.S.R. Japanese authorities remain unable to negotiate satisfactory fishing rights in the Sea of Okhotsk or to secure the return of the Kurile Islands, but these political difficulties have not deterred the rapid expansion of mutually beneficial Japanese-Soviet trade. Japan needs oil, natural gas, timber, coal, iron ore, and other raw materials which the eastern parts of the Soviet Union can furnish, while the Soviets need Japanese expertise and capital in order to exploit such resources. The Soviets also realize the difficulty of attempting to integrate their Far Eastern economy with the distant European U.S.S.R. and would like to link it rather with the Far East, where Japan is a natural customer for primary materials.

Three major development projects in the Soviet Far East currently involve Soviet-Japanese cooperation. The first concerns natural gas reserves in northern Yakutia. These reserves are now being explored and, if adequate reserves are proven, then the U.S.S.R. will begin negotiating with Japanese and American companies for their exploitation. Such a long-term project could require Western credit to finance the design, research, and construction work and to purchase pipe and other materials. The second project involves coking coal in southern Yakutia. In exchange for the machinery, materials, and other goods to develop and transport the coal, Japan will receive 100 million tons of it over the last two decades of this century. This project appears to be proceeding normally. The third development project involves the exploitation of gas and oil reserves on and near Sakhalin Island. Long negotiations were required before exploration began in mid 1975.

The exploitation of the Tyumen oil fields in Western Siberia has been the subject of long and tortuous Soviet-Japanese negotiations. Proposals and counter proposals have been offered since 1966 and made conditional on unspecified participation by American companies. The volatile world energy market in the early 1970s prompted the U.S.S.R. to revise downward its estimate of the quantities of petroleum that could be supplied to Japan, and as a result the Japanese began to lose interest. When the Soviet Union proposed that Japan assist in the construction of the Baykal-Amur Mainline (BAM) for transporting the fuel eastward, the Japanese let the entire project die quietly, in response to Chinese objections regarding its strategic and political overtones. The Soviets are nevertheless proceeding with the BAM on their own (with tractors and other equipment from U.S. companies). The railroad should enable the U.S.S.R. to expand Japanese markets for oil, timber, coal, copper, and other raw materials when it is completed around 1983. It will also siphon off from the overloaded Trans Siberian Railroad some of the Japanese-West European trade, as was discussed in Chapter 15.

Finland

The geographical juxtaposition of Finland to the Soviet Union has enabled it to become a major Western trading partner of the Soviet Union. In the 1950s and early 1960s it was often the leading trading partner in the West. During the 1970s it has fluctuated between third and fourth rank, as Soviet trade has expanded more rapidly with other countries. Finland has long been a major purchaser of crude oil from the U.S.S.R., although the volume of this item has decreased slightly in recent years. Natural gas imports from the Soviet Union, however, are on the increase. The Soviet Union is not supplying all the gas that Finland could take, and so the world energy crisis has drawn Finland, at least temporarily, into a position of greater dependence on the U.S.S.R. than has been in the past. If Norwegian development of oil and gas deposits in the North Sea continues, Finland might turn to this source to satisfy her demand and thus relieve her dependence on the Soviet Union.

Because of a long history of tense relations with the U.S.S.R., and previously as a part of the Russian Empire, Finland has followed a political course of strict neutrality and nonparticipation in military alliances. However, this has not prevented her activity in the Nordic Council and associate membership in the European Free Trade Association. Finland is also a member of the Organization for Economic Cooperation and Development, and in 1973 she became an associate member in the CMEA organization. At the present time about 20 per cent of Finland's trade is with the U.S.S.R. and other East European countries.

Italy

Despite the Italians' precarious financial position, they have been among the most persistent west Europeans in pursuing trade and investment with the Soviet Union. Along with France, Italy was a pioneer in deals with both the U.S.S.R. and Eastern Europe. Fiat, Olivetti, and Motecatini-Edison were among the first Italian firms to sign deals with the Soviet Union. The largest Italian construction project in the Soviet Union has been the Fiat plant at Togliatti on the Volga, which is now the largest car manufacturing plant in the Soviet Union. Italian firms have also constructed chemical plants, textile factories, canning factories, blast furnaces, and other enterprises for the Soviet Union.

Italy has been most interested in importing large amounts of oil and gas from the Soviet Union. To that end she has entered into agreements whereby Italian companies supply pipeline equipment in return for shipments of oil and gas over extended periods of time. In return for supplying gas pumping stations to the Soviets, Italy began in 1974 to receive Soviet natural gas via the Czechoslovak-Austrian pipeline. In 1974 another deal was reached for the Italians to supply 1.5 billion dollars worth of pipe to construct West Siberian oil and gas pipelines and be paid in coal and iron ore which they would use to expand their domestic steel production. Italy's imports of Soviet oil in 1976 were double those of 1975, making Italy the biggest Soviet oil market in the West.

The Communist Party of Italy, the strongest in western Europe, may have played a role in the early, rapid expansion of Soviet-Italian trade. It is true that the Italian communists have benefited financially from the conclusion of Italio-Soviet trade agreements, but at the same time it must be noted that when many of these agreements were being made in the 1960s other Western concerns either were restrained by their interests in the U.S. from getting involved in Soviet trade or were unable to take on huge projects because of physical limitations and other commitments. It is interesting that the site of the Fiat plant on the Volga was renamed from the previous settlement of Stavropol to Togliatti in honor of the leader of the Italian Communist Party at that time.

France

France was the first capitalist country to increase its trade with the U.S.S.R. as a matter of policy. That began in 1966, when the two states signed a treaty for that purpose. Valery Giscard d'Estaing, now President of France, was Minister of Finance at the time, and the Soviets' long familiarity with him is one factor in their preference for his government over one headed by the Communist Party of France.

The most striking trade deal between the U.S.S.R. and France is the agreement allowing Renault to participate in building the huge Kama River Truck Plant. Renault has also supplied equipment for other car plants in the Soviet Union such as those at Moscow and Izhevsk. Agreements also exist between France and the U.S.S.R. for joint development of color television systems and for Soviet licensing of French telephone and other electronic patents. In reciprocation, the U.S.S.R. has supplied equipment to France and Soviet engineers have helped build industrial complexes including an oil refinery and an iron and steel plant in France.

The United Kingdom

The United Kingdom's trade with the Soviet Union has diminshed relatively over the last decade as trade with other leading European countries, the United States, and Japan have expanded more rapidly. In the past the United Kingdom was frequently the leading trading partner of the Soviet Union in the West, often alternating this first rank with Finland. The United Kingdom has traditionally been a buyer of large amounts of Soviet timber and other raw materials, which recently have included increasing amounts of oil.

Part of the decline in Anglo-Soviet trade during the early 1970s was due to an espionage scandal which, in September, 1971, resulted in the expulsion of 105 Soviet citizens from Britain. Much of the relative decline in British trade with the U.S.S.R. has, however, been due to Britain's weak national economy. In recent years Great Britain has been running a large trade deficit with the Soviet Union, an import-export ratio on the order of 4 to 1. In an attempt to increase British exports to the U.S.S.R., Prime Minister Wilson agreed, in February 1975, to extend 2.2 billion dollars worth of credits to the U.S.S.R. at the relatively low annual interest rate of 7.5 per cent. This might stimulate some Soviet purchases in the future, but in 1975 the Soviet Union still bought only about one-third as much from the United Kingdom as the United Kingdom bought from the Soviet Union. Recently some British companies, including Rolls-Royce, have signed contracts with the U.S.S.R. to develop and supply new technology in such fields as airplane engines and agricultural fertilizers.

Effects of East-West Trade

The rapid expansion of trade between the Industrialized West and the Soviet Union during the last decade or more has occasioned many commentaries on the advantages and disadvantages of trading with the Soviet Union. Proponents of the "linkage" conception of *de'tente* have asserted that expanded economic relations with the Soviet Union will reduce international tensions, restrain Soviet behavior in crisis situations, and deepen the Soviet Union's integration into the world economy. That, in turn, is believed to make for more responsible Soviet participation in efforts to solve global economic problems. But there is some fear that the transfer of advanced technology to the Soviet Union will strengthen the Soviet's military capabilities, either directly by military use of imported manufactures or indirectly by making it possible for the Soviets to shift to military sectors resources that would otherwise be required in the industrial sector. Also, shipments to the Soviet Union of things like American grain strengthen Soviet economic capability to export grain to India and other parts of the world where they are trying to curry favor.

It is generally agreed that exports of goods and technology to the Soviet Union relieve the Soviet leadership of certain constraints that are inherent in the shortcomings of the Soviet economy, but it is not generally agreed whether this will result in advantages or disadvantages for the West. It is an open question whether an economically isolated Soviet Union, if the West could achieve such a thing, would become more quiescent or reckless in world affairs. It is argued by many that involvement of the Soviet Union in a network of relationships with the world economy is more likely to encourage a long-term evolution of the Soviet system in the direction of international responsibility than would its isolation.

Among possible disadvantages it has been argued that a great degree of dependency by the West upon Soviet sources of minerals or petrochemicals, or the deepening of the Soviet debtor relationship to Western countries, could give the Soviet Union a greater capability for political manipulation than it now has. It has been contended by various U.S. economists that the United States could not as effectively deal politically with a Soviet Union that owed it, say, 50 billion dollars as it could with a Soviet Union that was not in debt to the United States.

Spokesmen for American corporations that desire to do business with the Soviet Union cite the following economic benefits to the United States: (1) It has been estimated by the Department of Commerce that each billion dollars of exports generates between 35,000–40,000 jobs in American industry. (2) The large trade surplus that the United States generates with the Soviet Union helps to balance U.S. trade in other portions of the world where it is running deficits. (3) The United States derives important raw materials from the Soviet Union. In 1975 52 per cent of the platinum group metals consumed in the United States were imported from the Soviet Union, as was 22 per cent of the chrome ore, 5 per cent of the nickel, and 26 per cent of the titanium. In the last few years imports of petroleum and petroleum products have been growing rapidly. (4) There is actually a considerable flow of technology from the Soviet Union to the United States. American corporations have licensed Soviet technology in the areas of power transmission, underground gasification of coal, above-ground processing of oil shale, atomic and magneto-hydrodynamic generation of power, and in various aspects of metallurgy, mining, and medicine. The number of patents granted by the U.S. Patent Office to the Soviet Union has increased from 66 in 1966 to 382 in 1973 and continues to rise. (5) The agreement providing for annual Soviet purchases of between 6 and 8 million metric tons of American grain is expected to stabilize the American grain market.

DEVELOPING COUNTRIES

The Soviet Union and the Russian Empire before it have always carried on some trade with the "Third World," mainly to purchase certain consumer commodities that are not produced at all or not produced in sufficient quantities in the Soviet Union, particularly some of the luxury fruits and beverages such as cocoa, tea, oranges, and so forth. Before the mid 1950s this trade was never very large nor very vital to the Soviet Union, although some of it had political overtones that were important to the Soviets in the strip of countries along their southern margins stretching from the eastern Mediterranean to India.

In 1954, after the death of Stalin, Khrushchev's government entered into an aid program, both civil and military, which with time has expanded and become intertwined with increasing trade and political aspirations in various countries of the Third World. This has stimulated Soviet trade in these countries to the point where during recent years it has been occupying around 11–12 per cent of total Soviet trade.

In many cases Soviet trade and aid agreements have taken the form of the extension of credit to less developed countries (LDCs). Such agreements last an average of 12 years at interest rates of about 2.5 per cent. Their purpose is to finance, in the recipient countries, development projects which the Soviets largely construct and equip. The Soviets are usually repaid in kind with export products from the recipient countries, often the products of the aid projects themselves. Such projects have included mining and other raw material extraction, and the construction of major dams and other hydro-works, steel mills, roads and other transport facilities. The Soviets try to fit the type of project undertaken to the stage of development in each country and to take into account both the major needs of the economy of the recipient country and the level of skills of its labor force. Thus, in India the Soviets have helped build steel mills, oil refineries, and other sophisticated industries, whereas in Afghanistan such things as the construction of highways into remote parts of the country have been emphasized to open up these areas to trade and communication with the rest of the country.

Such development projects have involved the presence in the recipient countries of Soviet engineers and other skilled workers and technical advisors. They first set up the projects and then remain for a while to train their counterparts in recipient countries to run and maintain the equipment. By 1975 the number of Soviet technicians in LDCs had risen to about 18,000. Also by 1975 Moscow had trained about 23,000 technical personnel from various countries in the Soviet Union and about 450,000 on the job within the countries themselves. A scholarship program has brought the bright young elite from many countries of Asia and Africa to institutions of higher learning in the Soviet Union.

Military aid has often been the most productive aspect of Soviet aid as far as Soviet political aims are concerned. The Soviets frequently have entered into areas of political and military chaos at critical moments when crumbling local regimes were grasping for aid from any quarter and have offered credits to buy sophisticated costly military equipment that will become obsolete very rapidly. This has tied up exports from recipient countries for years to come and has started them down the road of unended buying of new military equipment and retraining of personnel as military equipment becomes more and more sophisticated each year.

Over the years Soviet aid to less developed countries has not amounted to more than one per cent of total world aid to those countries. While the Soviets have devoted 0.05 per cent of their GNP to aid, Western industrialized countries have devoted an average of 0.3 per cent. Nevertheless, in many cases, Soviet aid has had disproportionate propaganda value because the aid has been concentrated in a few countries on a few large visible construction projects and always in the public sectors of the economies. By contrast, aid from the United States, which has been incomparably more in total value than Soviet aid, has often been diffused into human welfare programs such as food relief, which have no lasting concrete edifices, or has been infused into developing countries through local privately owned concerns.

Another difference between Soviet aid and large shares of the aid from the United States and other Western countries is that the Soviets have given very few grants. Aid is usually extended in the form of credits which are to be paid back, typically over a period of twelve years, often in the form of export products from the developing countries. Interest rates commonly have been about 2.5 per cent, although recently they have been rising. In contrast, much aid from the United States has been outright grants. Strangely enough, the low interest loans from the Soviet Union seem to have impressed many of the less developed countries more than gifts have. Loans seem to convey the impression of aid that allows a country to retain its dignity by paying its own

way rather than accepting charity. Also, in cases where credit has been granted by Western countries, interest rates have typically been much more than the Soviets have charged, which has given the Soviets opportunities to point out that the Western countries are being usurious.

Ultimately, aid costs the Soviets very little, since most of it will eventually be paid back. In fact the payments from developing countries to the Soviet Union on previous loans are already counterbalancing to a great extent new loans being made by the Soviet Union to developing countries. Over the entire period of Soviet aid, repayments have equalled about 40 per cent of deliveries, and this percentage has risen over time. Repayments of principal and interest to the Soviet Union in 1975 approached 300 million dollars while aid deliveries to the developing countries reached 400 million dollars; thus the net aid transfer in 1975 was only about 100 million dollars. Veteran recipients of Soviet aid are already paying more to service debts than they are receiving in new aid. This has been the case with India since 1969, and in 1975 Iran and Iraq approached that point.

The Soviets have frequently helped on projects that Western countries have declined to aid for political reasons. An outstanding example is the Aswan Dam in Egypt, for which the United States and other Western countries withdrew financing after Nasser nationalized the Suez Canal in 1956. The Soviets subsequently stepped in to aid the Egyptians. Another example is the establishment of a national oil industry in India after Western oil companies had told India it had no petroleum resources. The Indians later realized that the Western oil companies had not given them accurate information on Indian oil deposits, because these companies wanted to continue selling oil to India. Still another example is Soviet participation in developing the Indian iron and steel industry, a project Western corporations and governments refused to aid because the Indian government wished to make the industry a public, not private, enterprise.

Between 1954 and 1975 the U.S.S.R. pledged about 11 billion dollars to the Third

World in economic assistance, but only about 6 billion dollars of this aid has been delivered. Deliveries have lagged behind commitments by an average of 7 years. Although Soviet foreign aid was a creation of Khrushchev and received much propaganda during his regime, commitments and deliveries of Soviet aid have been growing quietly throughout the current regime, so that annual deliveries are now nearly three times what they were under Khrushchev. Soviet trade with LDCs, however, has been increasing at a rapid rate, so that the share of aid deliveries in total Soviet exchange with LDCs has decreased from about 50 per cent in 1964 to about 25 per cent in 1974. Those countries which have received the most Soviet

aid — Egypt, India, Iran, and Iraq — have become the largest Soviet trading partners among LDCs. During the first half of the 1970s these four countries accounted for between one-third and one-half of all Soviet-LDC trade.

Soviet aid has emphasized its southern neighbors in Asia and north Africa, in a belt extending from the western Mediterranean to the borders of China. (Table 17-6) Over the entire period, 1954-1975, these countries have received 80 per cent of Soviet aid. The remainder has gone in scattered amounts to 40 other LDCs of varying location and political persuasion. Sub-Saharan Africa has received about 8 per cent of Soviet aid, Latin America a little

Table 17-6   Soviet Economic Credits and Grants Extended to Less Developed Countries, 1954-1975, in Millions of U.S. Dollars

Total	10,859	East Asia	156
Africa	1,435	Burma	16
Algeria	425	Cambodia	25
Cameroon	8	Indonesia	114
Central African Republic	2	Laos	1
Chad	10	Latin America	602
Congo	14	Argentina	245
Equatorial Guinea	1	Bolivia	31
Ethiopia	104	Brazil	30
Ghana	93	Chile	238
Guinea	200	Colombia	10
Guinea Bissau	1	Peru	28
Kenya	48	Uruguay	20
Mali	86	Near East and South Asia	8,666
Mauritania	4	Afghanistan	1,263
Morocco	98	Bangladesh	300
Niger	2	Egypt	1,300
Nigeria	7	Greece	84
Rwanda	1	India	1,943
Senegal	9	Iran	750
Sierra Leone	28	Iraq	549
Somalia	153	Nepal	20
Sudan	64	Pakistan	652
Tanzania	20	Sri Lanka	95
Tunisia	34	Syria	417
Uganda	16	Turkey	1,180
Upper Volta	1	Yemen (Aden)	15
Zambia	6	Yemen (Sana)	98

Source: Cooper, Orah, "Soviet Economic Aid to the Third World," in *Soviet Economy in a New Perspective*, p. 194.

more than 5 per cent. The geographical distribution of aid to the belt of Afro-Asian countries bordering the Soviet Union has shifted somewhat from year to year. Over the entire aid period India has received the most Soviet aid, 18 per cent of total. Egypt has ranked second, with 12 per cent. Both these countries are important regional powers in their corners of the world. Egypt has recently turned more and more toward the West, however, and Turkey has become more neutral, so Soviet aid has turned from Egypt to Turkey. During the years 1973-1975 Turkey received 26 per cent of all Soviet aid to LDCs. (Table 17-7)

Table 17-7   Major Recipients of Soviet Economic Aid, 1954-1975 and 1973-1975, in Per Cents of Total

Country	1954-1975	1973-1975
India	18	14
Afghanistan	12	18
Egypt	12	—
Turkey	11	26
Iran	7	—
Pakistan	6	11
Algeria	4	—
Other	30	31

Source: Cooper, Orah, "Soviet Economic Aid to the Third World," in *Soviet Economy in a New Perspective,* p. 195.

The three political aims underlying Soviet aid to LDCs are: (1) to extend influence among the newly independent countries of Africa and Asia at the expense of the West; (2) to protect Soviet interests in countries bordering the U.S.S.R., presenting to them the Soviet model of economic development; and (3) to maintain a presence in uncommitted countries, playing a waiting game in the hope of alignment eventually on the side of the Soviet Union. The Soviets have often interjected themselves into uncertain political situations at or even before

the independence of LDCs, hoping to exert great influence with little effort in fluid situations. Often as not such actions have backfired on the Soviets, and although they have been fairly successful in establishing ongoing relations with many countries, they have gained only few if any significant conversions to communism. This has been particularly true in Africa where nationalistic young leaders have arisen in newly emerging countries. In the last decade, the Soviets have negotiated with these people on their own terms, even at the detriment of local communist parties in these countries.

Of course, Soviet actions have been more politically motivated in countries nearer to their own borders or in strategic areas of the world where the Soviets are trying to establish a presence. Ancient rivalries with Persian, Turkic, Arabic, and Mongolian Empires still color relations between the Soviet Union and their neighbors to the south, and the desire for port facilities in the Mediterranean has had great influence on Soviet relations with Egypt and other north African countries. Thier present ambition to establish a large naval presence in the Indian Ocean has greatly influenced their activities in countries around the Red Sea, the Persian Gulf, and Southeast Asia. In remote parts of the world, such as Latin America, their activities have been more economically motivated to gain certain much needed commodities such as corn from Argentina and Brazil in recent years. Because of the different motives and different forms of activity in different parts of the world, Soviet relations with the developing countries will be discussed in several groupings.

Southern Neighbors

Arab States and Israel

In 1955 Gamal ab'd el-Nasser, to whom the West refused to sell arms, bought some machine guns from Czechoslovakia. Thus began Soviet military penetration of the Middle East. Since the end of the Second

World War, Moscow's primary aim in the Middle East has been to remove Western influence from the area. Such was the Soviet goal when the United Kingdom had hegemony in the region; such remains its goal now that British influence has waned and American influence has grown.

Until 1970, the year of Nasser's death, Egypt received somewhere between one-third and two-fifths of all Soviet military aid to LDCs. Since then, the amount has declined drastically. Syria, by contrast, received about one-twentieth of all Soviet military aid to LDCs until 1970, since which time it has received about three-tenths of such aid, or about 430 million dollars per year, more than any other country. Iraq, as a recipient of Soviet military aid, is third, behind Egypt and Syria. These three countries together received over half of all Soviet military aid between 1955 and 1974, and more than two-thirds in recent years.

During the twenty years from 1955 to 1974, Egypt received about 3.1 billion dollars worth of Soviet military aid. In the second decade, 1964–1973, she received 2.3 billion dollars worth, or 15 per cent of total Soviet arms exports to all recipients, including the Warsaw Pact countries and North Vietnam. Moscow's policy with respect to Egypt has been heavy handed; not only has it opposed Egyptian national interests, including Sadat's trip to Jerusalem to seek peace with Israel, but it has also upon occasion interfered in domestic Egyptian affairs. The Soviet insistence that her naval facilities at Alexandria be declared off limits to Egyptian personnel is one of the milder infringements on Egyptian sovereignty.

As a result of such tensions between the Soviet Union and post-Nasser Egypt, Sadat ordered all Soviet military advisors out of Egypt in 1972 and then in 1976 abrogated the Treaty of Friendship and Cooperation signed in Cairo in 1971. The latter action particularly disturbed the Soviets in view of their having granted Egypt 1.3 billion dollars in economic loans and credits over the 22-year period, 1954–1975, or 12 per cent of all Soviet foreign aid to LDCs. The most famous of these aid projects was the Aswan High Dam, begun in the late 1950s with Soviet help after the West retaliated against Nasser's nationalization of the Suez Canal by refusing Egypt economic aid.

Soviet-Egyptian trade, however, remains high. As late as 1975 the total turnover between the two countries was the highest among all Soviet trade with the Third World, excluding socialist LDCs such as Cuba. Soviet-Egyptian trade has decreased somewhat since then, but in 1976 Egypt still ranked third in total trade on the Soviet-LDC list, following Iraq and India. Half of all Soviet imports from Egypt are cotton fiber and cotton thread. Other major commodities are leather footwear, perfumes and cosmetic articles, rice, essential oils and natural fragrances, and fresh oranges. These Egyptian exports comprise most of the trade now, as the Soviet Union is collecting for past aid on development projects.

In 1972 there were about 18,000 Soviet military men in Egypt: 4000 advisors, 12,000 members of regular units, and 2000 specialized technicians, including 100 Soviet Mig pilots sent to Egypt in air defense squadrons in 1970. When Sadat ordered them to leave, however, he indicated that Egypt would continue to provide the Soviet navy with refueling and refitting facilities at Egyptian ports and that Soviet civilian advisors engaged in industrial projects and electrification of the countryside would be permitted to remain. The U.S.S.R. had about 100 development projects going on in Egypt at that time.

Thus, despite all the political backing and all the military and economic aid that the Soviets have extended to Egypt, it appears that the Soviet presence in Egypt for the foreseeable future will be minimal. The Soviet Union is playing no significant role at present in negotiations that are going on between Egypt and Israel, both sides now relying on the United States for mediation.

As their presence and influence on Egypt have waned, the Soviets have turned their attention increasingly to Syria. Since 1970 Syria has received about 30 per cent of all Soviet military aid to LDCs, or about 430 million dollars worth per year. Soviet economic aid to Syria between 1954 and 1975 amounted to only 417 million dollars, or 4 per cent of all Soviet aid to the Third World; most of Syria's economic aid has come from Saudi Arabia. However, Syria has consistently ranked fifth or sixth among developing countries trading with the Soviet Union. Soviet imports from Syria consist primarily of cotton, wool, silk, knitted fabrics, and synthetic fabrics.

Although the Soviets in the past have traded with and offered economic and military aid to other Arab countries, including Algeria, Morocco, Tunisia, Libya, Kuwait, Jordan, Saudi Arabia, Sudan, Lebanon, the Peoples' Democratic Republic of Yemen, and the Yemeni Arab Republic, most of this activity has been minimal in recent years. During the civil war in Yemen in the early 1960s, the Soviets attempted without success to establish a presence in the critical southwest corner of the Arabian Peninsula, which controls the southern approach to the Red Sea.

In recent years Morocco has been the main Soviet source of fresh oranges, a commodity that Soviet citizens are eager to buy. Trade with Morocco might expand significantly in the near future as a result of a 30-year agreement signed in 1974 providing for Soviet aid in prospecting and mining phosphate ores in Morocco for shipment to the U.S.S.R. Apparently the Soviets are eager to assure a continuing adequate supply for their phosphate fertilizer industry in the event that Kola apatites become depleted.

Mideast oil is important to the U.S.S.R. for three reasons: (1) the rising costs of exploiting their own domestic preserves, (2) the rapidly rising oil consumption among CMEA states, and (3) the desire to obtain hard currency and technology from the West.

The Soviet approach with respect to oil matters in the Arab states has been politically circumspect, though guided by opportunism. During the oil crises of 1973–1974, for instance, the Soviets encouraged the oil producing countries to impose sanctions on their customers; after this was done, however, the Soviet Union turned around and violated the embargo against the United States and the Netherlands, selling oil directly to those countries. It is estimated that this operation brought the Soviets a windfall profit of about 500 million dollars.

Soviet attitudes toward Israel are affected by both external and internal factors. Internationally Israel is a problem for the Soviets because although most Arab states unequivocally oppose the very existence of Israel, the destruction of that state would vitiate much of Moscow's influence on the Arabs and in the Middle East generally. Domestically, Israel is a problem to the Soviet Union because it offers an alternative to Soviet Jews that entices many of them to apply for emigration permits. Since emigration is viewed by the Soviets as a condemnation of the Soviet system, the more than 100,000 Jews that have emigrated from the Soviet Union to Israel since 1971 is perceived by the Soviets as a national disgrace and attempts by Soviet authorities to deny emigration have aroused world-wide indignation and resulted in such punitive measures against the Soviet Union as the Jackson Amendment attached to the U.S. Trade Act of 1974 which denies "Most Favored Nation" status to any country practicing restrictive emigration policies. The Soviets have not traded with Israel since the June 1967 war in the Middle East.

Turkey

Turkey's relations with the Soviet Union historically have been uneasy and developed over time only in an atmosphere of mutual suspicion. Relations between the two countries since World War II have blown hot and cold having by now seemingly equilibrated to lukewarm. Since Turkey is a member of NATO she has not received any Soviet military aid but she has received an increasing amount of economic aid in recent years. Between 1954 and 1975 Soviet aid to Turkey reached a total of 1.2 billion dollars which is 11 per cent of all Soviet economic aid to developing countries during that period. In the years 1973–1975 however, Turkey has received 26 per cent of all

Soviet economic aid to developing countries. In recent years Turkey has in fact become the biggest recipient of Soviet aid. Nevertheless, the U.S.S.R. has been unable to obtain Turkish permission for the Soviet fleet to pass freely from the Black Sea into the Mediterranean, a goal which the Russians have been after since the occupation of the Turkish Steppes along the Black Sea Coast in the late eighteenth century. This, despite the fact that the Soviet Union is helping Turkey build a bridge over the Bosporus!

Iraq and Iran

The Soviets' interest in the Persian Gulf is long-standing. If Persia had been incorporated into the Russian Empire, the U.S.S.R. could have had an outlet to the warm seas via the Persian Gulf. Today the Soviets are interested in Middle Eastern oil, and they have been bothered by the strong Western presence in Iran — first British and later American. The Soviets' interest in the area has increased in the last few years because they now have the capability to establish a strong naval presence in the Indian Ocean.

During the last decade Soviet opportunities have appeared in both Iran and Iraq, for these countries have assumed independent military stances. In Iraq in particular a 1968 coup replaced a pro-Western government with one that is more tolerant of Soviet cooperation.

Both countries have been major recipients of Soviet military aid in recent years. Over the period 1954–1975 Iran received about 7 per cent of all Soviet aid to developing countries. The Soviets have helped Iran to construct an iron and steel works at Isfahan, a hydropower station, grain elevators, and a trans-Iranian gas pipeline which will facilitate exports to the Transcaucasus region of the Soviet Union. At the present time natural gas comprises about 55 per cent of all Iranian exports to the Soviet Union.

The Soviets signed a treaty of friendship and cooperation with Iraq after the 1968 coup there. That treaty laid the basis for rapidly expanding Soviet aid and trade. In 1976 Iraq shot into first place among the developing countries in trade with the Soviet Union. Almost all Iraqi exports to the Soviet Union are crude oil. After they nationalized their oil industry, the Iraqis were eager to conclude barter deals with the U.S.S.R. and Eastern Europe because of difficulties they encountered in marketing. However, in 1973 they announced that they would not pursue such deals in the future because they wanted to acquire hard currency.

Afghanistan

Although the economic significance of Afghanistan to the Soviet Union is minimal, the U.S.S.R. has made propaganda of its aid to that country as a model of Soviet benevolence to a smaller, less developed neighbor. Afghanistan has received far more Soviet aid per capita than any other country in the world. Between 1954 and 1975 Afghanistan received 12 per cent of all Soviet aid extended to developing countries, and during 1973–1975 this portion increased to 18 per cent. Although Afghanistan has received some aid from other countries, including the United States, its preponderant source has been the Soviet Union. Soviet aid has helped to construct highways and agricultural facilities such as grain elevators.

Trade between the two countries has been moderate, averaging only about 120 million rubles per year. Over half of all Afghanistani exports to the Soviet Union is natural gas, piped into the Tadzhik Republic of the Soviet Union just across the border. Afghanistan also sends cotton, wool, fruits, berries, and raisins to the Soviet Union. In return, she receives machinery, transport equipment, and geological surveying equipment. The Soviet presence in Afghanistan has escalated rapidly since the pro Soviet coup in Afghanistan in May, 1978.

India, Pakistan, Bangladesh

The Indian subcontinent has low per capita income and much human poverty, but the sheer magnitude of its population gives it weight in world affairs. As a result, major powers have taken special notice of it. The Soviets currently hope that the area will remain neutral and not enter any regional alliances that would injure Soviet interests there. The U.S.S.R. has in recent years acted as supplier of aid to the subcontinent and a mediator of political difficulties among the three states of the subcontinent, India, Pakistan, and Bangladesh. In the 1960s in particular, the Soviets successfully arbitrated the Indo-Pakistani border dispute over Kashmir, and during the 1971 war the Soviets abetted the creation of the independent state of Bangladesh (formerly East Pakistan) while the United States tilted with China toward the West Pakistanis, who failed to repress the grass-roots aspirations of their ethnically distinct coreligionists in the East. Soviet mediation negotiations of the military situation on the subcontinent brought about an agreement between India and Pakistan in March, 1972 on the non-use of armed force and withdrawal of troops from occupied areas.

India, by far the most populous of the three countries, has taken the lion's share of Soviet aid and trade with the region. Between 1954 and 1975 India received 18 per cent of all Soviet exports to LDCs, and Pakistan received 6 per cent. In recent years, Soviet aid to India has decreased and that to Pakistan has risen. Between 1973 and 1975, for example, India received 14 per cent of Soviet aid while Pakistan received 11 per cent. On a per capita basis, therefore, Pakistan received considerably more aid than India. During those three years, however, Turkey and Afghanistan received significantly more than either India or Pakistan.

Over the years, Soviet aid to the Indian subcontinent has been far less than American aid has been, but once again the Soviets have generally derived more propaganda mileage from their aid which has concentrated on such things as steel mills, oil prospecting and refining, thermal and hydropower stations, and plants for producing electrical equipment, pharmaceuticals and surgical instruments.

The Soviets have supplied a modest amount of military aid to India, and during the Indian-Chinese border conflicts in 1962 and 1965 the Soviets supported the Indian effort against the Chinese. India has traditionally been the Soviet Union's primary trading partner in the Third World, although she was edged out of first place by Iraq in 1976. Soviet exports to India consist mainly of machinery and equipment for Soviet-aided construction works, oil and oil products, nitrogenous fertilizers, and urea. In return, the Soviets receive tea, cashew nuts, jute, rawhides, tobacco, and cotton goods, as well as a fairly wide variety of other consumer items. Soviet military aid to India has been modest.

In 1965 the Soviets signed an agreement with Pakistan committing them to assist that country in the implementation of thirty major development projects over a five-year period. These projects were primarily in the steel and power industries and for the construction of seaports and airfields. Relations between the two countries were severely strained by the Bangladesh crisis in 1971, but in March, 1972 Pakistan and the Soviet Union agreed to restore and extend economic, scientific, technical, and cultural relations. In March, 1973 Moscow released Pakistan from the obligations to pay debts incurred by East Pakistan before it gained its independence as Bangladesh in 1971. In 1973 the Soviets also signed a three-year trade agreement with Pakistan. Although Soviet economic aid to Pakistan has been rather high during the last few years, trade between the two countries has remained quite low. In return for Soviet equipment for aid projects, Pakistani exports to the Soviet Union are mainly cloth, fabrics, and leather products. Soviet military aid to Pakistan has been minimal.

The Soviet Union has offered aid to Bangladesh from the beginning in 1971 and had, through 1975, committed 300 million dollars to assist in the construction of a thermal power station, a radio broadcasting station, and an electrical equipment plant, and for geological prospecting for oil and gas. Actual trade, however, has remained rather low. The minor exports from Bangladesh to the Soviet Union are mainly jute, leather, and tea.

Subsaharan Africa

During the 1960s the Soviets envisioned great opportunities in Subsaharan Africa as one new country after another emerged from the disintegrating empires of Belgium, France, and Britain. Most of these emerging countries were in stages of political, military, and economic turmoil, and the Soviets tried to manipulate unstable situations to their favor. But in spite of economic and military aid to such countries as Guinea, the Congo, Ghana, Mali, and Ivory Coast, the Soviets' success in influencing their economic and political development has been marginal. More recently the Soviets have turned their attention more to establishing a military presence bordering the Indian Ocean, either in newly independent East African states such as Mozambique or near the Gulf of Aden farther north.

In 1975 Somalia was the only major Soviet aid recipient in Subsaharan Africa. At the time the U.S.S.R. was building a naval base there at Berbera on the Indian Ocean. However, during the Somali-Ethiopian war in 1977, the Soviets began giving military support to Ethiopia, a genuinely fascist country masquerading as a Marxist-Leninist regime. For this the Soviets were kicked out of Somalia. It appears that the Soviets have committed the main error of post-1945 American foreign policy: supporting a dictatorship because of its ideological garb.

In the final analysis Soviet aid to Subsaharan Africa has been minimal. The biggest recipients have been Guinea, Somalia, and Ethiopia, which between 1954 and 1975 received 200, 153, and 104 million dollars respectively. In recent years Ethiopia, Somalia, and Angola have received the most military aid. Most Soviet aid to Guinea was extended during the 1960s, and Ghana and Mali responded to Soviet attention at that time as well. However, during the mid and late 1960s a large number of military coups in Africa surprised and chagrined the Soviets, particularly the ones in Mali, Ghana, and Guinea. Guinean authorities especially hurt the Soviets during the Cuban missile crisis in the fall of 1962 when they denied the Soviets the right to land planes bound for Cuba at the Conakry airport, which the Soviets had reconstructed only a few months before.

In most of their attempts to interject themselves into critical military and political situations in Africa, the Soviets have run head on into competition with the Chinese, who, in East Africa, at least, seem to have had some natural advantages. Since 1970 China has granted almost twice as much aid to Africa as the Soviets have.

Major Soviet trading partners in the region are presently Nigeria, Ghana, Cameroon, Guinea, and the Ivory Coast. Soviet imports typically account for 80 per cent of all such trade with those countries, and cocoa represents between 80 and 100 per cent of all Soviet imports from these countries except for Guinea, where bauxite accounts for about 70 per cent of the imports. The Soviets are helping the Guineans develop bauxite mines and are taking bauxite in payment. It is shipped to a new alumina plant at Nikalayev on the north coast of the Black Sea. The Soviets are also becoming interested in aiding the development in Nigeria of iron, steel, and oil industries, which might supply products to the Soviet Union. But Soviet trade and aid in Subsaharan Africa remains low in comparison with their activities in the Mediterranean and the Middle East.

Latin America

If Subsaharan Africa seems to the Soviets too far away to be of great interest, Latin America is once more removed. Excluding Cuba as a socialist country, Soviet trade and aid in Latin America has been low indeed. From 1954 to 1975 Soviet aid to all countries of Latin America totaled only 5 per cent of Soviet aid to the Third World.

Soviet imports from Brazil and Argentina have increased greatly over the last few years as the Soviets more and more need to import grains and other foodstuffs. Corn and wheat make up more than 70 per cent of Argentina's exports to the U.S.S.R., and wool and frozen meat make up almost all the remainder. Brazil ships corn, raw sugar, coffee, cocoa beans, and cocoa liqueur to the Soviet Union. Much farther down the line in quantitative terms, Guiana ranks third among Latin American exporters to the Soviet Union, sending primarily bauxite. There is also very minor Soviet trade with Uruguay, Ecuador, Bolivia, Jamaica (alumina), Colombia, Mexico, Costa Rica, Venezuela, and El Salvador.

SOVIET INTENTIONS TOWARD THE SEA

During the last fifteen years the Soviets have made a major reorientation from a country that is primarily a land power to one that also aspires to sea power. They have been rapidly building up their navy, their merchant marine, their fishing fleet, and their oceanographic research fleet. Some of the ships they have been building themselves, but many of them they have been purchasing from countries such as East Germany, Poland, Finland, Sweden, West Germany, Japan, England, Denmark, and the Netherlands. As a result their merchant marine probably is now the largest and most modern in the world, their naval power is essentially on a par with that of the United States, although varying in makeup, and their fishing fleet is certainly the largest and most modern in the world, as is their oceanographic research fleet. In general most of their ships are more adaptable to multipurpose uses than are ships of other nations. This is particularly true of their merchant marine, which is primarily made up of general cargo vessels that can handle virtually any type of cargo and operate in areas that lack port facilities and cargo handling equipment. Such ships could easily be converted to military auxiliary vessels when necessary.

Soviet objectives in the use of the seas seem to be both strategically to deny to the U.S. control of such constricted shipping lanes as the Suez Canal, the Straits of Malacca, the Panama Canal, and the Straits of Gibraltar, and to use the sea as a source of food and other materials. To these ends they have expended much energy to secure footholds in the ports of the Arab world along the Mediterranean and the ports of Aden in South Yemen and Singapore in Malaysia, and they have spread their fishing activities all over the world until at present they rank second in the world in total fish catch, after Japan. They look upon fish as a major source of protein which can augment their meat diet at home where they have chronic shortages of meat. They also look upon the sea as a source for future vegetable and mineral products, and are currently carrying on underwater explorations for oil and gas in shelf areas such as those around the Island of Sakhalin and along the Arctic coast.

They also look upon the merchant marine as a source of hard currency, for they are now not only carrying more than 60 per cent of their own foreign commerce in their own bottoms but are also providing services to many other countries of the world. This is a complete reversal of the situation 15 years ago when most of the minimal Soviet trade moved in foreign vessels and therefore represented a drain on the national economy to pay for foreign transport services.

To these ends, the Soviets are engaging in perhaps the most vigorous scientific exploration of the sea of any country in the world. Their modern and well equipped research vessels are everywhere measuring bottom topography, sea currents, marine life, and other valuable information.

CURRENT TRENDS AND PROSPECTS FOR THE FUTURE

During the last decade the world situation seems to have settled down somewhat, with the end of the war in Vietman and the attempts for peace in the Middle East, and the Soviet Union has entered more widely into trade and aid with the developed West and the developing world. Soviet attention in recent years has turned more and more toward domestic problems of decreasing growth rates of their economy and the need to stimulate these by the importation of advanced technology from the West and consumer goods for their people. Thus, Soviet concerns seem to be more economic and less political as time goes on and the Soviet Union gets more and more of a vested interest in material gains and world order.

The world is no longer polarized between the U.S. and the U.S.S.R., although Moscow continues to refuse to recognize that a tripolar or multipolar system is arriving on the world scene. In Europe the U.S.S.R. has been more interested in influencing political changes than in institutionalizing military and strategic security. Her aim of making impossible the political unification of the continent has largely been achieved. Even western Europe, though not as disarrayed as the Soviets might wish, is not without internal divisions. Soviet trade with the West will not decrease, and its economic relationships, coupled with political contracts and treaties, may well assume a momentum of their own, decreasing the probability that any post-Brezhnev regime may reverse them.

The Soviets see in China the only country that not only poses a direct threat to Soviet territory but also threatens Soviet ideological hegemony. However, Sino-Soviet relations seem to be in a more quiescent state now, and India, with its change of government, has become more strictly nonaligned. Thus, it appears that the more populous countries of the world are acting more independently, and their potential adversaries are accepting them as such and not committing them to political alignments. All this seems to augur well for world order in the foreseeable future.

Soviet policy toward the Third World has in the last decade or so been based on support for control by LDCs of their own natural resources and on encouragement of regional integration outside the world capitalist economy. The U.S.S.R. has especially concentrated its attention on its "southern neighbors," a band of countries stretching from North Africa to East Asia. However, it has not increased its influence even within this target area. Although its share of trade with these countries has risen signally, that share remains substan-

tially smaller, in most cases, than that of the West. In the Middle East, Soviet influence remains limited, its policy a series of reactions to events it largely cannot control or even influence. In Africa it has refurbished its image as a partisan of the national liberations movements, but its ability — even its desire — to control the policies of the regimes it helps to establish (with Cuban troops) is questionable.

Reading List

1. Abate, Yohannis, *Foreign Aid, UN Voting Behavior and Alliances: The Case of Africa, the U.S., and the USSR,* PhD Dissertation, Michigan State, 1976.
2. Ackley, Richard Thomas, *Soviet Maritime Power: An Appraisal of the Development, Capabilities, and International Influence of the Soviet Navy, Fishing Fleet, and Merchant Marine,* PhD Dissertation, University of Southern California, 1974.
3. Adomeit, Hannes, "Soviet Policy in the Middle East: Problems of Analysis," *Soviet Studies,* April 1975, pp. 288–305.
4. An, Tai Sung, *The Sino-Soviet Territorial Dispute,* Westminster Press, Philadelphia, 1973, 254 pp.
5. Borisov, O. B., and Koloskov, B. T., *Soviet-Chinese Relations, 1945–1970,* Indiana University Press, Bloomington, 1975, 384 pp.
6. Cline, Ray S., *World Power Assessment, 1977: A Calculus of Strategic Drift,* Westview Press, Boulder, 1977, 200 pp.
7. Cohn, Helen Desfosses, *Soviet Policy Toward Black Africa: The Focus on National Integration,* Praeger, New York, 1972, 336 pp.
8. *Comecon: Progress and Prospects,* NATO Directorate of Economic Affairs, Series No. 6, Brussels, 1977, 281 pp.
9. Czerwinski, E. J., and Piekalkiewicz, Jaroslaw, eds., *The Soviet Invasion of Czechoslovakia: Its Effects on Eastern Europe,* Praeger, New York, 1972, 224 pp.
10. Dean, Robert W., *The Politics of West German Trade with the Communist States,* Praeger, New York, 1974, 220 pp.
11. Dibb, Paul, *Siberia and the Pacific: a Study of Economic Development and Trade Prospects,* Praeger, New York, 1972, 288 pp.

12. Donaldson, Robert H., *Soviet Policy Toward India: Ideology and Strategy,* Russian Research Center Studies, Harvard University Press, 1974, 338 pp.

13. *East-West Foreign Trade Board Report,* U.S. Department of Commerce, Washington, quarterly.

14. Feinstein, J. M. Thatcher, *Fifty Years of U.S.-Soviet Trade,* Symposium Press, New York, 1974, 256 pp.

15. Freedman, Robert O., *Soviet Policy Toward the Middle East Since 1970,* Praeger, New York, 1975, 224 pp.

16. Friesen, Connie M., *The Political Economy of East-West Trade,* Praeger, New York, 1976, 205 pp.

17. Gidwitz, Betsy Rose, *The Political and Economic Implications of the International Routes of Aeroflot,* PhD Dissertation, Washington, Seattle, 1976.

18. Gitelman, Zvi, "The Jewish Question in the USSR Since 1964," in Simmonds, George W., ed., *Nationalism in the USSR and Eastern Europe in the Era of Brezhnev and Kosygin,* University of Detroit Press, Detroit, 1977, pp. 324–334.

19. Glassman, Jon D., *Arms for the Arabs: The Soviet Union and War in the Middle East,* The Johns Hopkins University Press, 1975, 243 pp.

20. Goldman, Marshall I., *Detente and Dollars: Doing Business with the Soviets,* Basic Books, New York, 1975, 337 pp.

21. Gupta, Bhabani Sen, *Soviet-Asian Relations in the 1970s and Beyond, An Interperceptional Study,* Praeger, New York, 1976, 400 pp.

22. Hatzilambrou, Lambros, *Soviet Foreign Policy in the Eastern Mediterranean: A Systematic Approach,* PhD Dissertation, Howard University, 1976.

23. Hensel, Howard Milton, *Soviet Policy in the Persian Gulf: 1968–1975,* PhD Dissertation, Virginia, 1976.

24. Holzman, Franklyn D., *International Trade Under Communism — Politics and Economics,* Basic Books, New York, 1976, 239 pp.

25. Hunter, Brian, *Soviet-Yugoslav Relations, 1948-1972: A Bibliography of Soviet, Western, and Yugoslav Comment and Analysis,* Garland Publishers, New York and London, 1976, 223 pp.

26. Jain, J. P., *Soviet Policy Towards Pakistan and Bangladesh,* Radiant Publishers, New Delhi, 1974, 258 pp.

27. Jelavich, Barbara, *St. Petersburg and Moscow: Tsarist and Soviet Foreign Policy, 1814–1974,* Indiana University Press, Bloomington, 1974, 480 pp.

28. Jukes, Geoffrey, *The Soviet Union in Asia,* University of California Press, Berkeley and Los Angeles, 1973, 304 pp.

29. Kanet, Roger E., ed., *The Soviet Union and the Developing Nations,* Johns Hopkins University Press, Baltimore, 1974, 302 pp.

30. Kanet, Roger E., and Bahry, Donna, eds., *Soviet Economic and Political Relations with the Developing World,* Praeger, New York, 1975, 242 pp.

31. Kass, Ilana, *Soviet Involvement in the Middle East: Policy Formulation, 1966–1973,* Westview, Boulder, 1978, 275 pp.

32. Kim, Young C., *Japanese-Soviet Relations: Interaction of Politics, Economics, and National Security,* Sage Publishers, Beverly Hills, 1974, 88 pp.

33. Kosnik, Joseph T., *Natural Gas Imports From the Soviet Union: Financing the North Star Joint Venture Project,* Praeger, New York, 1975, 236 pp.

34. Krivoruchko, O. N., "Maritime Economic Systems of the USSR," *Soviet Geography: Review and Translation,* March 1976, pp. 153–159.

35. Kulski, Wladyslaw W., *The Soviet Union in World Affairs: A Documented Analysis, 1964–1972,* Syracuse University Press, Syracuse, 1973, 526 pp.

36. Lederer, Ivo J., and Vucinich, Wayne S., eds., *The Soviet Union and the Middle East: The Post-World War II Era,* Hoover Institution Press, Stanford, 1974, 302 pp.

37. Lenz, Allen J., and Kravalis, Hedija H., "An Analysis of Recent and Potential Soviet and East European Exports to Fifteen Industrialized Western Countries," in *East European Economics, Post Helsinki,* Joint Economic Committee, Congress of the United States, Washington, August 25, 1977, pp. 1055–1131.

38. Lowenthal, Richard, *Model or Ally: The Communist Powers and the Developing Countries,* Oxford University Press, London, 1977.

39. Marer, Paul, "Soviet Economic Policy in Eastern Europe," in Hardt, John P., ed., *Reorientation and Commercial Relations of the Economies of Eastern Europe,* Joint Economic Committee, Congress of the United States, Washington, 1974.

40. ———, ed., *US Financing of East-West Trade:*

The Political Economy of Government Credits and the National Interest, Indiana University, Bloomington, 1975, 442 pp.

41. MacGwire, Michael, and McDonnell, John, eds., *Soviet Naval Influence,* Praeger, New York, 1977, 698 pp.

42. McLane, Charles B., *Soviet-African Relations, Soviet-Third World Relations,* Vol. 3., Central Asian Research Centre, London, 1974, 190 pp.

43. ———, *Soviet-Asian Relations,* Vol. 2 of *Soviet-Third World Relations,* Central Asian Research Centre, London, 1973, 150 pp.

44. ———, *Soviet-Middle East Relations,* Central Asian Research Centre, London, 1973, 126 pp.

45. Mitchell, Donald W., *A History of Russian and Soviet Sea Power,* Macmillan, New York, 1974, 657 pp.

46. Nagorski, Zygmunt, Jr., *The Psychology of East-West Trade: Illusions and Opportunities,* Mason and Lipscomb, New York, 1974, 228 pp.

47. Naik, J. A., *India, Russia, China, and Bangla Desh,* S. Chand, Ram Nagar, New Delhi, 1972, 163 pp.

48. Natufe, Omajuwa Igho, *Soviet Policy in Africa 1945-1970: A Study in Political History,* PhD Dissertation, McGill, 1975.

49. Parvin, M., "The Political Economy of Soviet-Iranian Trade: An Overview of Theory and Practice," *Middle East Journal,* Winter 1977, pp. 31–42.

50. Potichnyj, Peter J., and Shapiro, Jane P., eds., *From the Cold War to Detente,* Praeger, New York, 1976, 238 pp.

51. Roi, Yaacov, *From Encroachment to Involvement: A Documentary Study of Soviet Policy in the Middle East, 1945–1973,* Halsted Press, New York, 1974, 616 pp.

52. Rubinstein, Alvin Z., ed., *Soviet and Chinese Influence in the Third World,* Praeger, New York, 1975, 246 pp.

53. Savin, V. A., "The Territorial Structure of Soviet Export Industries," *Soviet Geography: Review and Translation,* January 1974, pp. 29–34.

54. Schaefer, Henry Wilcox, *Comecon and the Politics of Integration,* Praeger, New York, 1972, 200 pp.

55. Schwartz, Morton, "The USSR and Leftist Regimes in Less-Developed Countries," *Survey,* Spring 1973, pp. 209–244.

56. *Selected Trade and Economic Data of the Centrally Planned Economies,* Bureau of East-West Trade, U.S. Department of Commerce, Washington, September 1976, 66 pp.

57. Shanina, V., "The Impact of the Transport Factor on the Location of Export Industries in the Comecon Countries," *Soviet Geography: Review and Translation,* April 1975, pp. 262–270.

58. Shattan, Joseph Jacob, *Soviet Military Aid and the Politics of Leverage: The Soviet-Egyptian Case,* PhD Dissertation, Tufts, 1977.

59. Smith, Glen Alden, *Soviet Foreign Trade: Organization, Operations, and Policy, 1918–1971,* Praeger, New York, 1973, 370 pp.

60. *Soviet and Eastern European Foreign Trade,* quarterly journal published by International Arts and Sciences Press.

61. *Soviet Economy in a New Perspective,* Joint Economic Committee, Congress of the United States, U.S. Government Printing Office, Washington, D.C., October 14, 1976, pp. 67–96.

62. *Soviet Export,* Vneshtorgreklama, Moscow, Published bimonthly in English, Russian, Czech, French, German, Hungarian, Polish, and Spanish.

63. *Soviet Oceans Development,* Committee on Commerce and National Ocean Policy Study, Congress of the United States, U.S. Government Printing Office, Washington, October 1976, 646 pp.

64. *Soviet Sea Power,* Center for Strategic and International Studies, Georgetown University, Washington, Special Report Series No. 10, 1969, 134 pp.

65. Staar, Richard F., ed., *Yearbook on International Communist Affairs, 1976,* Hoover Institution Press, Stanford, 1976, 636 pp.

66. Stevens, Christopher, *The Soviet Union and Black Africa,* Holmes and Meier, New York, 1976, 236 pp.

67. Stowell, Christopher E., *Soviet Industrial Import Priorities: With Marketing Considerations for Exporting to the USSR,* Praeger, New York, 1975, 452 pp.

68. Szporluk, Roman, ed., *The Influence of East Europe and the Soviet West on the USSR,* Praeger, New York, 1976, 260 pp.

69. Turpin, William Nelson, *Soviet Foreign Trade: Purpose and Performance,* PhD Dissertation, George Washington University, 1976, 192 pp.

70. Ulam, Adam B., *Expansion and Coexistence: Soviet Foreign Policy, 1917–1973,* 2nd ed., Praeger, New York, 1974, 797 pp.

71. "The USSR and Africa" (Three Parts): Legum, Colin, "The African Environment," pp. 1–19;

Albright, David E., "Soviet Policy," pp. 20–39; and Yu, George T., "China's Impact," pp. 40–50. *Problems of Communism,* January–February 1978.

72. *U.S. Trade Status with Communist Countries,* Bureau of East-West Trade, U.S. Department of Commerce, Washington. (Published Monthly.)

73. *Vneshnyaya torgovlya SSSR* (Foreign Trade of the U.S.S.R.), Statistika, Moscow. A statistical handbook, published annually, approximately 300 pp.

74. Walters, Robert S., *American and Soviet Aid: A Comparative Analysis,* University of Pittsburgh Press, Pittsburgh, 1970, 299 pp.

75. Weinstein, Warren, ed., *Chinese and Soviet Aid to Africa,* Praeger, New York, 1975, 316 pp.

76. Wright, Arthur W., "The Soviet Union in World Energy Markets," in Erickson, Edward W., and Waverman, Leonard, eds., *The Energy Question: An International Failure of Policy,* University of Toronto Press, Toronto, 1974, pp. 85–99.

Index

The fold map inside the back cover has been printed in the Soviet Union. The transliteration scheme from the Cyrillic to the Latin alphabet is not the same as that used throughout this text. Following are some examples of differences:

Cyrillic	Text	Map
Й	y	j
Ж	zh	ž
Х	kh	ch
Ц	ts	c
Ч	ch	č
Ш	sh	š
Щ	shch	šč
Ь	omit	′
Ю	yu	′u
Я	ya	′a